PREFACE

The Commission has initiated numerous measures aimed at improving the economic and social condition of women in the Member States. These measures centre on three main lines of action: legislation, financial support and information. Legislation has taken the form of three directives of the Council of Ministers concerning, respectively, equal pay, equal treatment as regards access to employment, vocational training and promotion and working conditions and equal treatment as regards social security.

To promote equal treatment of men and women at work, the European Social Fund finances specific vocational training projects for adult women faced with particular difficulties on the job market. The aims of financial support are to reduce the disparities which characterize the position of women in the job hierarchy and to help women to move into traditionally male-dominated areas offering greater opportunities.

These legislative and logistical measures are based on studies and research conducted by various departments of the Commission and, for the most part, made available to the public.

To implement Community measures in favour of women, the Commission has set up a specialist department, the Bureau for questions concerning employment and equal treatment for women.

Recognizing that the measures would not produce the desired results unless the public are informed, the Commission has also set up, within the Directorate-General for Information, a department for relations with the press and womens' organizations.

A recent publication, 'Women and the European Community', gives details not only of Community measures but also of the mechanisms governing these measures and the way they operate.

The Statistical Office has been closely involved in work in this area, on the one hand supplying the basic statistical data necessary for the formulation of the above-mentioned Community initiatives and directives, and on the other hand adapting existing data collection systems in order to compile systematically the different statistics relating to the economic and social condition of women. Thus, at Community level, practically all social statistics are systematically compiled separately for men and women.

However, the diversification of existing sources due to the wide range of areas involved (demography, employment, health, education, earnings, etc.) and the large number of reference publications did not always facilitate access to the data in this field and prevented more extensive use of such data.

To fill this gap the Statistical Office asked the 'Comitato italiano per lo studio dei problemi della popolazione' (CISP) to analyse and study all these sources with a view to formulating the most appropriate statistical tables and indicators to describe the economic and social situation of women in the Community. The aim of this work was not only to meet a specific requirement, but also to provide a reference framework for monitoring trends in this field.

The statistical tables in this volume were drawn up on the basis of statistics compiled by the departments of the Directorate for Demographic and Social Statistics. The Comitato italiano forwarded this study in November 1978. To ensure widespread distribution, the Statistical Office has translated it into English and French and has updated it with the most recent data, available at the beginning of 1980.

This study was prepared, under the coordination of Mme Nora Federici, by the researchers of the Comitato italiano per lo studio dei problemi della popolazione (CISP): C. Bielli, V. Egidi, D. Maffioli, A. Nobile.

CONTENTS

*   *   *

SYMBOLS

*	Eurostat estimate
:	Figure not available
#	Provisional figure or estimate
0,0	Figure less than half of the unit shown
.	Figure not available because the sampling fraction does not permit a breakdown
( )	Figure uncertain or not available because the sample is too small
-	Non-existent
o	Mean value for which the standard error of estimation is between 5 and 10%
.l.	Figure included in another category

5

LIST OF TABLES

Section II – Employment

II.1 – *Structure of employment*

II.1.1. – *Structure of employment in industry*

II.1.2. – *Structure of employment in agriculture*

II.1.3. – *Structure of employment in wholesale and retail distribution, banking and insurance*

II.2 – *Earnings*

II.2.1. – *Earnings in industry*

Section III – Unemployment

Section IV – Geographical and occupational mobility

PART 3: GENERAL AND VOCATIONAL TRAINING

Section I – Ongoing training

Section II – Training completed

Section III – Training and occupation

PRÉFACE

La Commission est à l'origine de nombreuses actions visant à améliorer la condition économique et sociale des femmes dans les États membres. L'ensemble de ces initiatives s'articule autour de trois axes fondamentaux: l'action normative, le soutien financier et l'information.

L'action normative s'est concrétisée par trois directives du Conseil de Ministres, qui concernent respectivement l'égalité de rémunérations, l'égalité de traitement devant l'accès à l'emploi, à la formation et à la promotion professionnelles et les conditions de travail ainsi que la sécurité sociale.

Pour stimuler la mise en œuvre de l'égalité entre hommes et femmes au travail, le fonds social européen intervient d'une manière spécifique pour faire aboutir des projets de formation de femmes adultes confrontées à des difficultés particulières sur le marché du travail. La participation financière vise à réduire les écarts qui caractérisent la place des femmes dans la hiérarchie et à les insérer dans des domaines non traditionnellement féminins, offrant plus de débouchés.

Cette action législative et logistique se fonde sur les travaux d'études et de recherche accomplis par les différents services de la Commission, et mis pour la plupart à la disposition du public.

Pour mettre en œuvre l'action communautaire en faveur des femmes, la Commission a créé le Service spécialisé «Bureau pour les problèmes concernant l'emploi des femmes et l'égalité».

Consciente du fait que les efforts entrepris n'apporteraient pas les résultats voulus sans mettre le public au courant, la Commission a également mis en place, au sein de la Direction générale de l'information, un «Service chargé de l'information de la presse et des organisations féminines».

Une récente publication «Les femmes et la Communauté européenne» présente en détail non seulement l'action communautaire mais également les mécanismes qui régissent cette action ainsi que les aspects opérationnels de sa mise en œuvre.

L'Office statistique a été étroitement associé aux travaux effectués dans ce domaine en fournissant, d'une part, les éléments statistiques de base nécessaires à l'élaboration des initiatives communautaires et des directives déjà citées, et en adaptant, d'autre part, les dispositifs de collecte existants pour rassembler d'une façon systématique les différentes statistiques touchant au problème de la condition économique et sociale de la femme. Ainsi pratiquement toutes les statistiques sociales sont établies au niveau communautaire distinctement pour les hommes et les femmes d'une façon systématique.

Toutefois, la diversification des sources existantes due aux différents domaines intéressés, démographie, emploi, santé, éducation, salaires . . . ainsi que le volume de publications de référence, n'ont pas toujours facilité l'accès à l'information dans ce domaine et n'ont pas permis une plus large utilisation de ces données.

Pour combler cette lacune, l'Office a chargé le «Comitato Italiano per lo Studio dei problemi della Popolazione» (CISP) d'analyser et d'étudier l'ensemble de ces sources, aux fins d'établir les tableaux statistiques et les indicateurs les plus appropriés pour la description de la situation économique et sociale des femmes dans la Communauté. L'objectif de ce travail n'était pas seulement de répondre à une demande ponctuelle mais aussi de fournir un cadre de référence pour suivre les évolutions dans ce domaine.

Les tableaux statistiques repris dans ce volume ont été élaborés à partir des statistiques établies par les services de la Direction «Statistiques démographiques et sociales». Le CISP a transmis cette étude en novembre 1978. Pour faciliter une large diffusion de ce travail, l'Office en a effectué la traduction en Anglais et Français et sa mise à jour avec les données les plus récentes, disponibles au début de l'année 1980.

Cette étude a été préparée sous la coordination de Mme Nora Federici, par les chercheurs du Comitato Italiano per gli Studi dei problemi della Popolazione (CISP): C. Bielli, V. Egidi, D. Maffioli, A. Nobile.

TABLE DES MATIÈRES

*

*   *

EXPLICATION DES SYMBOLES

*	Estimation de l'Eurostat
:	Donnée non disponible
#	Donnée ou estimation provisoire
0,0	Chiffre inférieur à la moitié de l'unité indiquée
.	Donnée non disponible, le taux de sondage ne permettant pas la subdivision
( )	Donnée incertaine et non disponible en raison d'un effectif trop faible de l'échantillon
-	Néant
o	Valeur moyenne pour laquelle l'erreur type d'estimation est comprise entre 5 et 10%
.I.	Donnée comprise dans une autre catégorie

LISTE DES TABLEAUX

Section II – Emploi

17

Section III – Formation et activité

1

Demography
Démographie

Numbers and structure of the female population
Importance et structure de la population féminine

TAB. 1

Female population, numbers and percentage of the total population

Population féminine, importance et pourcentage par rapport au total de la population

1000

	1971	1972	1973	1974	1975	1976	1977
	F	F	F	F	F	F	F
EUR 9	130 182	130 949	131 671	132 244	132 607	132 840	133 094
BR Deutschland	32 038	32 204	32 330	32 385	32 330	32 215	32 156
France	26 197	26 408	26 600	26 762	26 886	26 982	27 077
Italia	27 631	27 821	28 054	28 309	28 525	28 703	28 859
Nederland	6 608	6 679	6 741	6 798	6 862	6 920	6 967
Belgique/België	4 940	4 959	4 975	4 989	5 002	5 011	5 019
Luxembourg	175	177	178	180	181	181	181
United Kingdom	28 613	28 688	28 744	28 736	28 708	28 691	28 670
Ireland	1 482	1 501	1 520	1 540	1 559	1 574	1 593
Danmark	2 498	2 514	2 530	2 544	2 554	2 563	2 572

%

	1971	1972	1973	1974	1975	1976	1977
	$\frac{F}{T}100$	$\frac{F}{T}100$	$\frac{F}{T}100$	$\frac{F}{T}100$	$\frac{F}{T}100$	$\frac{F}{T}100$	$\frac{F}{T}100$
EUR 9	51,4	51,3	51,3	51,3	51,3	51,3	51,3
BR Deutschland	52,3	52,2	52,2	52,2	52,3	52,4	52,4
France	51,1	51,1	51,0	51,0	51,0	51,0	51,0
Italia	51,2	51,2	51,1	51,1	51,1	51,1	51,1
Nederland	50,1	50,1	50,2	50,2	50,2	50,2	50,3
Belgique/België	51,1	51,1	51,1	51,1	51,0	51,0	51,1
Luxembourg	50,7	50,7	50,6	50,4	50,4	50,4	50,4
United Kingdom	51,4	51,3	51,3	51,3	51,3	51,3	51,3
Ireland	49,8	49,8	49,8	49,8	49,9	49,9	49,9
Danmark	50,3	50,4	50,4	50,4	50,5	50,5	50,5

TAB. 2
Female population by broad age groups
Population féminine par grand groupe d'âge

	1971			1975			1977		
	f	$\frac{f}{F}100$	$\frac{f}{m}100$	f	$\frac{f}{F}100$	$\frac{f}{m}100$	f	$\frac{f}{F}100$	$\frac{f}{m}100$
< 15									
EUR 9	29 920	23,0	95,4	29 324*	22,1	95,1	28 412	21,3	95,2
BR Deutschland	6 874	21,4	94,9	6 383*	19,8	95,1	6 077	18,9	95,4
France	6 187	23,6	96,1	6 189*	23,0	95,7	6 025	22,3	95,6
Italia	6 428	23,2	95,9	6 560*	23,0	94,7	6 458	22,4	95,0
Nederland	1 743	26,4	95,5	1 692	24,7	95,5	1 635	23,5	95,4
Belgique/België	1 109	22,5	95,5	1 072*	21,4	95,3	1 025	20,4	95,5
Luxembourg	38	21,7	97,4	35*	19,3	97,2	35	19,1	96.1
United Kingdom	6 527	22,8	94,8	6 359*	22,1	94,7	6 105	21,3	94,6
Ireland	455	30,7	95,6	476*	30,5	95,6	502	30,9	95,9
Danmark	559	22,4	95,1	558	21,8	95,4	550	21,4	95,4
15 – 64									
EUR 9	81 050	62,2	102,1	82 383*	62,1	101,2	83 038	62,4	101,0
BR Deutschland	20 110	62,8	106,7	20 344*	62,9	104,7	20 260	63,0	104,1
France	15 905	60,7	99,0	16 360*	60,9	98,1	16 608	61,3	98,5
Italia	17 757	64,3	102,7	18 037*	63,3	102,7	18 230	63,2	102,4
Nederland	4 102	62,1	98,4	4 322	63,0	98,1	4 441	63,7	97,9
Belgique/België	3 060	61,9	100,7	3 118*	62,4	99,8	3 166	63,1	99,4
Luxembourg	113	64,5	100,9	118*	65,2	95,9	119	65,4	100,1
United Kingdom	17 564	61,4	101,0	17 580	61,2	100,1	17 665	61,6	100,0
Ireland	848	57,2	97,6	894	57,3	98,0	930	57,2	97,2
Danmark	1 591	63,6	99,1	1 610	63,1	98,8	1 619	62,9	98,8
65+									
EUR 9	19 217	14,8	154,0	20 915	15,8	154,1	21 679	16,3	154,5
BR Deutschland	5 053	15,8	160,0	5 602*	17,3	167,5	5 819	16,1	171,1
France	4 106	15,7	161,6	4 337*	16,1	159,7	4 444	16,4	156,5
Italia	3 446	12,5	144,6	3 919*	13,7	138,3	4 171	14,4	139,5
Nederland	763	11,5	129,1	848	12,3	135,2	891	12,8	138,9
Belgique/België	771	15,6	143,0	811*	16,2	147,5	828	16,5	149,5
Luxembourg	26	14,8	144,4	28*	15,5	147,4	28	15,5	146,4
United Kingdom	4 524	15,8	160,4	4 794	16,7	158,0	4 901	17,1	156,9
Ireland	179	12,1	118,5	190*	12,2	119,5	194	11,9	120,5
Danmark	349	14,0	129,3	386	15,2	132,2	403	15,7	133,9

TAB. 3

Indices of the structure of the female population
Indices de structure de la population féminine

A – Index of ageing of female population
Indice de vieillissement de la population féminine $I_v = \dfrac{f_{65+}}{f_{0-15}} 100$

	1971	1972	1973	1974	1975	1976	1977
EUR 9	64,2	65,6	67,3	69,1	71,3*	72,5	
BR Deutschland	73,5	75,8	78,8	82,3	87,8*	88,5	
France	66,4	67,0	67,9	68,9	70,1*	71,2	72,7
Italia	53,6	55,3	57,3	58,7	59,7	61,4	
Nederland	43,8	45,0	46,4	48,2	50,1	51,1	
Belgique/België	69,5	70,8	72,6	74,2	75,7*	77,6	
Luxembourg	68,4	72,2	75,0	77,1	80,0*	–	
United Kingdom	69,3	70,3	71,6	73,3	75,4	77,6	80,2
Ireland	39,3	39,6	39,6	39,7	39,9*	38,8	
Danmark	62,4	63,8	65,4	67,3	69,2	70,1	72,1

B – Index of dependency of female population
Indice de dépendance de la population féminine $I_d = \dfrac{f_{0-15} + f_{65+}}{f_{15-65}} 100$

	1971	1972	1973	1974	1975	1976	1977
EUR 9	60,6	61,0	61,2	61,3	61,0*	61,0	
BR Deutschland	59,3	59,6	59,7	59,7	58,9*	59,4	
France	64,7	64,7	64,7	64,6	64,3*	63,5	63,2
Italia	55,6	56,5	57,5	57,9	58,1	58,3	
Nederland	61,1	60,7	60,3	59,5	58,8	58,4	
Belgique/België	61,4	61,3	61,1	60,7	60,4*	59,7	
Luxembourg	56,6	54,4	54,3	53,0	53,4*	–	
United Kingdom	62,9	63,4	63,6	63,6	63,4	63,2	62,3
Ireland	74,8	74,7	74,6	74,5	74,5*	74,2	
Danmark	57,1	57,5	57,9	58,3	58,6	58,9	58,9

TAB. 4

Female population by age groups and regions (%)

Population féminine par groupe d'âge et par région (%)

1975

	TOTAL	0 – 4	5 – 9	10 – 14	15 – 19	20 – 24	25 – 29	30 – 34	35 – 39	40 – 44	45 – 49	50 – 54	55 – 59	60 – 64	65 – 69	70 +
BR DEUTSCHLAND	100,0	5,0	7,1	7,8	6,9	6,5	6,2	6,1	7,5	5,9	6,0	6,6	4,7	6,2	6,2	11,3
Schleswig-Holstein	100,0	5,0	7,7	8,0	6,5	5,8	5,9	6,5	7,8	5,7	5,5	6,2	4,7	6,3	6,2	12,2
Hamburg	100,0	3,7	5,6	6,2	5,5	5,7	6,2	6,7	7,5	5,9	6,0	6,8	5,2	6,9	7,3	14,8
Niedersachsen	100,0	5,3	7,7	8,2	7,0	6,1	5,8	5,9	7,4	5,8	5,8	6,5	4,6	6,3	6,1	11,5
Hannover	100,0	4,7	6,9	7,3	6,3	6,1	5,9	6,3	7,6	6,0	6,0	6,6	4,8	6,5	6,5	12,5
Hildesheim	100,0	4,7	6,8	7,5	6,9	7,0	5,8	5,5	6,9	5,5	5,9	6,7	4,8	6,6	6,6	12,8
Lüneburg	100,0	5,3	7,8	8,5	7,1	5,7	5,6	6,2	7,6	5,9	5,9	6,5	4,6	6,2	6,0	11,1
Stade	100,0	5,7	8,4	8,7	7,0	5,7	6,0	6,2	7,6	5,7	5,7	6,3	4,5	6,0	5,7	10,8
Osnabrück	100,0	6,5	9,0	9,5	8,1	6,1	5,3	5,3	7,1	5,8	5,9	6,1	4,3	5,5	5,5	9,5
Aurich	100,0	6,4	9,0	9,0	7,7	6,2	6,1	5,4	7,1	5,8	5,9	6,3	4,3	5,6	5,2	10,0
Braunschweig	100,0	4,6	6,7	7,0	6,5	6,1	5,4	5,7	7,1	5,6	6,1	7,0	5,0	6,9	7,0	13,3
Oldenburg	100,0	5,9	8,8	9,3	7,3	6,2	5,9	5,8	7,3	5,5	5,6	6,1	4,3	6,0	5,7	10,3
Bremen	100,0	4,3	6,5	7,1	6,3	6,1	6,2	6,3	7,4	5,8	6,0	6,8	5,1	6,8	6,8	12,5
Nordrhein-Westfalen	100,0	4,9	7,1	7,8	7,1	6,6	6,1	6,1	7,6	6,2	6,4	6,7	4,7	6,1	6,1	10,5
Düsseldorf	100,0	4,5	6,6	7,3	6,8	6,3	6,1	6,3	7,7	6,3	6,5	6,8	4,9	6,3	6,4	11,2
Köln	100,0	4,8	7,1	7,8	6,9	7,0	6,7	6,6	7,8	6,2	6,2	6,6	4,7	5,8	5,8	10,0
Münster	100,0	5,6	8,0	8,7	7,9	7,2	6,0	5,6	7,2	6,1	6,4	6,6	4,4	5,8	5,4	9,1
Detmold	100,0	5,2	7,4	8,1	7,1	6,1	5,5	5,6	7,4	6,0	6,1	6,5	4,7	6,5	6,3	11,5
Arnsberg	100,0	4,9	7,1	7,8	7,1	6,4	5,7	5,8	7,4	6,1	6,5	7,0	4,8	6,3	6,2	10,9
Hessen	100,0	4,8	6,8	7,4	6,6	6,6	6,7	6,4	7,5	5,9	6,1	6,8	4,7	6,2	6,2	11,3
Darmstadt	100,0	4,7	6,7	7,2	6,5	6,7	7,0	6,7	7,7	6,0	6,1	6,7	4,7	6,1	6,1	11,1
Kassel	100,0	5,0	7,3	7,9	7,0	6,5	5,9	5,4	7,1	5,6	6,0	6,8	4,8	6,5	6,4	11,8
Rheinland-Pfalz	100,0	4,8	7,2	8,4	7,5	6,6	5,6	5,4	7,2	5,9	6,2	6,9	4,7	6,2	6,2	11,2
Koblenz	100,0	4,8	7,3	8,3	7,5	6,3	5,5	5,3	7,2	5,8	6,2	7,0	4,9	6,4	6,3	11,2
Trier	100,0	5,2	7,6	9,4	8,1	6,4	4,8	4,8	6,7	5,7	6,3	7,2	4,7	6,4	6,1	10,6
Rheinhessen-Pfalz	100,0	4,8	6,9	8,0	7,5	6,9	5,9	5,7	7,3	6,1	6,3	6,8	4,6	6,0	6,2	11,0
Baden-Württemberg	100,0	5,4	7,4	8,1	7,2	6,9	6,5	6,4	7,7	6,0	5,9	6,3	4,5	5,9	5,8	10,0
Stuttgart	100,0	5,5	7,4	7,9	7,0	6,6	6,6	6,8	7,9	6,2	6,0	6,3	4,5	5,9	5,6	9,8
Karlsruhe	100,0	4,8	6,8	7,7	7,0	7,0	6,7	6,3	7,6	6,0	6,1	6,6	4,6	6,0	6,1	10,7
Freiburg	100,0	5,4	7,7	8,5	7,6	7,2	6,2	6,0	7,4	5,9	5,8	6,2	4,3	5,8	5,8	10,2
Tübingen	100,0	6,0	8,0	8,7	7,7	7,0	6,3	6,0	7,5	5,7	5,7	6,0	4,4	5,8	5,5	9,7
Bayern	100,0	5,1	7,1	7,8	7,0	6,5	6,4	6,2	7,5	5,8	5,9	6,6	4,8	6,2	6,0	11,1
Oberbayern	100,0	4,6	6,5	7,0	6,2	6,8	7,5	7,6	8,1	5,9	5,7	6,5	4,8	6,1	5,9	10,8
Niederbayern	100,0	5,8	8,0	9,0	8,0	6,1	5,7	5,1	6,7	5,7	6,0	6,7	4,8	6,2	5,8	10,4
Oberpfalz	100,0	5,6	7,8	8,8	7,8	6,7	5,8	5,1	7,0	5,9	6,2	6,7	4,6	6,0	5,7	10,3
Oberfranken	100,0	5,0	7,0	7,9	7,2	5,9	5,4	5,0	7,1	6,0	6,3	6,9	4,8	6,6	6,6	12,3
Mittelfranken	100,0	4,7	6,8	7,3	6,8	6,6	6,4	6,1	7,5	6,0	6,0	6,7	4,8	6,3	6,4	11,6
Unterfranken	100,0	5,4	7,5	8,8	7,9	7,0	6,0	5,2	7,2	5,7	6,0	6,6	4,5	5,9	5,8	10,5
Schwaben	100,0	5,5	7,5	8,0	7,2	6,1	6,0	6,0	7,2	5,6	5,8	6,7	4,9	6,4	6,0	11,2
Saarland	100,0	4,4	6,7	8,4	8,0	6,9	5,7	5,5	7,6	6,2	6,4	7,3	4,7	6,1	6,1	10,0
Berlin (West)	100,0	3,8	4,9	5,2	4,3	5,5	6,3	6,8	6,8	5,1	5,0	5,6	5,0	7,6	8,9	19,2
FRANCE	100,0	6,2	7,6	7,8	7,7	7,8	7,9	5,5	5,5	6,0	6,1	6,1	3,9	4,9	5,1	11,9
Île-de-France	100,0	6,1	7,0	6,9	6,8	8,3	9,6	6,6	6,2	6,5	6,5	6,2	4,0	4,3	4,4	10,6
Bassin parisien	100,0	6,7	8,2	8,4	8,2	7,8	7,7	5,1	5,3	5,8	5,7	5,7	3,7	4,7	5,0	12,0
Champagne-Ardenne	100,0	7,0	8,5	8,5	8,4	8,1	8,2	5,0	5,3	5,7	5,7	5,7	3,4	4,5	4,8	11,2
Picardie	100,0	7,2	8,8	8,8	8,5	8,0	8,0	5,1	5,2	5,7	5,7	5,5	3,4	4,3	4,6	11,2
Haute-Normandie	100,0	7,0	8,6	8,6	8,4	8,1	8,2	5,4	5,5	5,9	5,8	5,5	3,7	4,4	4,5	10,4
Centre	100,0	6,4	7,7	7,9	7,6	7,5	7,6	5,2	5,2	5,7	5,7	5,8	3,8	5,1	5,4	13,3
Basse-Normandie	100,0	6,7	8,3	8,7	8,6	7,8	7,5	4,7	5,3	5,9	5,9	5,9	3,8	4,7	4,8	11,3
Bourgogne	100,0	6,1	7,5	7,9	7,9	7,4	7,2	4,9	5,1	5,7	5,8	5,9	3,8	5,1	5,6	14,1
Nord-Pas-de-Calais	100,0	7,2	8,6	8,8	8,7	8,3	7,8	4,6	5,2	5,8	6,2	6,0	3,4	4,6	4,6	10,2

TAB. 4

(continued)

(suite)

1975

	TOTAL	0 – 4	5 – 9	10 – 14	15 – 19	20 – 24	25 – 29	30 – 34	35 – 39	40 – 44	45 – 49	50 – 54	55 – 59	60 – 64	65 – 69	70 +
Est	100,0	6,6	8,4	8,7	8,6	8,3	7,8	5,2	5,5	5,9	6,1	5,9	3,5	4,5	4,7	10,3
Lorraine	100,0	6,7	8,3	8,9	9,0	8,5	7,8	5,0	5,6	5,9	6,2	6,0	3,5	4,3	4,5	9,8
Alsace	100,0	6,3	8,1	8,3	8,2	8,3	7,7	5,5	5,5	6,0	6,1	5,9	3,5	4,7	5,1	10,8
Franche-Comté	100,0	6,9	8,6	8,5	8,3	8,0	7,9	5,4	5,5	5,9	5,7	5,6	3,6	4,6	4,6	10,9
Ouest	100,0	6,6	8,0	8,3	8,3	7,5	7,3	4,7	5,2	5,8	5,9	6,0	3,8	5,2	5,2	12,2
Pays-de-la-Loire	100,0	7,2	8,4	8,6	8,4	7,8	7,6	4,9	5,4	5,7	5,8	5,7	3,5	4,8	4,8	11,4
Bretagne	100,0	6,3	7,8	8,2	8,1	7,3	7,2	4,6	5,1	5,8	6,0	6,3	4,1	5,5	5,6	12,1
Poitou-Charentes	100,0	6,1	7,5	7,9	8,2	7,3	7,0	4,7	5,0	5,8	6,0	6,2	3,9	5,3	5,5	13,6
Sud-Ouest	100,0	5,3	6,7	7,2	7,3	7,2	7,0	5,1	5,1	6,0	6,3	6,6	4,2	5,6	5,9	14,5
Aquitaine	100,0	5,4	6,9	7,4	7,4	7,3	7,2	5,1	5,1	5,9	6,2	6,5	4,2	5,5	5,7	14,2
Midi-Pyrénées	100,0	5,3	6,8	7,2	7,3	7,3	7,0	5,2	5,2	6,1	6,4	6,6	4,1	5,6	5,8	14,1
Limousin	100,0	4,8	6,3	6,6	6,9	6,6	6,4	4,5	4,7	5,9	6,3	6,9	4,1	6,1	6,8	17,1
Centre-Est	100,0	6,3	7,8	7,9	7,6	7,6	7,9	5,9	5,5	6,0	6,2	6,0	3,7	4,8	5,0	11,8
Rhône-Alpes	100,0	6,4	8,0	8,0	7,6	7,7	8,2	6,2	5,6	6,1	6,1	5,9	3,7	4,6	4,7	11,2
Auvergne	100,0	5,8	7,3	7,3	7,6	7,1	7,1	5,0	5,1	5,8	6,3	6,5	3,9	5,3	5,7	14,2
Méditerranée	100,0	5,0	6,7	7,2	7,1	7,0	7,0	5,7	5,3	6,1	6,3	6,5	4,6	5,8	5,7	14,0
Languedoc-Roussillon	100,0	4,9	6,6	7,4	7,3	7,0	6,6	5,1	5,0	5,9	6,3	6,6	4,6	5,9	5,9	14,9
Provence-Alpes-Côte d'Azur	100,0	5,1	6,8	7,2	7,0	7,0	7,3	6,0	5,5	6,1	6,3	6,4	4,5	5,7	5,6	13,5
Corse	100,0	4,1	5,2	5,3	5,5	6,1	6,8	6,0	5,8	6,9	6,8	7,5	5,8	6,6	6,2	15,4
ITALIA	100,0	7,5	7,9	7,4	7,0	6,8	7,0	6,4	6,8	6,6	6,5	6,5	4,2	5,6	4,9	8,9
Nord Ovest	100,0	6,1	6,6	6,3	5,6	5,8	6,8	6,6	7,1	7,0	6,9	7,0	4,6	6,5	5,8	11,3
Piemonte	100,0	6,4	6,8	6,5	5,7	6,1	7,0	6,7	7,3	7,0	6,8	6,7	4,4	6,2	5,6	10,9
Valle d'Aosta	100,0	6,6	7,1	6,9	6,2	6,7	7,1	6,7	7,1	6,9	6,9	7,4	4,4	5,9	5,2	8,9
Liguria	100,0	5,3	6,0	6,0	5,2	5,3	6,2	6,3	6,9	6,9	7,2	7,6	5,3	7,1	6,3	12,4
Lombardia	100,0	7,0	7,6	7,2	6,3	6,5	7,4	7,1	7,4	7,0	6,6	6,6	4,1	5,8	5,0	8,4
Nord Est	100,0	7,2	7,7	7,7	6,8	6,7	6,9	6,7	6,5	6,2	6,4	6,7	4,0	5,9	5,1	9,2
Trentino Alto-Adige	100,0	7,6	8,6	8,4	7,3	7,0	6,8	6,8	6,2	6,0	6,2	6,6	3,4	5,8	4,9	8,4
Veneto	100,0	7,4	8,1	8,0	7,0	6,9	7,0	6,7	6,6	6,3	6,4	6,5	4,0	5,5	4,8	8,8
Friuli-Venezia Giulia	100,0	6,0	6,4	6,4	5,6	5,8	6,5	6,6	6,5	6,1	6,5	7,6	4,5	7,2	6,5	11,8
Emilia-Romagna	100,0	5,9	6,4	6,5	5,9	6,0	6,8	6,5	7,0	6,9	7,1	7,6	4,9	6,7	5,5	10,3
Centro	100,0	6,1	6,5	6,5	6,0	6,1	6,9	6,3	6,9	6,7	7,0	7,5	4,7	6,5	5,6	10,7
Toscana	100,0	6,0	6,4	6,3	5,7	5,8	7,0	6,4	6,9	6,6	6,9	7,5	4,6	6,5	5,9	11,5
Umbria	100,0	6,1	6,5	6,7	6,2	6,3	6,7	6,3	6,9	7,0	7,4	7,8	4,9	6,4	5,2	9,6
Marche	100,0	6,4	6,8	7,0	6,7	6,6	6,6	6,0	7,0	6,8	7,0	7,2	4,7	6,4	5,2	9,6
Lazio	100,0	7,6	8,1	7,9	7,0	6,8	7,3	6,9	7,3	7,0	6,7	6,7	4,1	5,1	4,2	7,2
Campania	100,0	9,4	9,7	9,6	8,4	7,6	7,1	5,7	6,1	6,1	5,9	5,6	3,7	4,5	3,8	6,8
Abruzzi-Molise	100,0	6,9	7,5	7,7	7,4	7,1	6,4	5,3	6,3	6,6	6,8	6,9	4,5	5,8	5,3	9,5
Abruzzi	100,0	6,8	7,5	7,6	7,3	7,1	6,5	5,5	6,3	6,7	6,8	6,9	4,5	5,8	5,1	9,6
Molise	100,0	6,9	7,5	7,7	7,6	7,2	6,2	4,8	6,1	6,6	6,7	6,8	4,4	6,1	5,7	9,7
Sud	100,0	8,9	9,5	9,4	8,6	7,6	6,9	5,6	6,1	6,1	5,8	5,7	3,6	4,7	4,1	7,4
Puglia	100,0	9,3	9,6	9,4	8,4	7,6	7,3	5,9	6,2	6,1	5,8	5,6	3,5	4,5	3,9	6,9
Basilicata	100,0	8,3	8,9	9,3	8,7	7,6	6,3	5,0	6,4	6,6	6,2	5,9	3,6	5,0	4,5	7,7
Calabria	100,0	8,5	9,2	9,7	8,9	7,7	6,4	5,2	5,9	6,1	5,7	5,7	3,8	4,8	4,4	8,0
Sicilia	100,0	8,5	8,6	8,8	8,0	7,3	6,9	5,8	6,2	6,3	6,0	6,0	4,1	5,1	4,4	8,0
Sardegna	100,0	9,0	9,3	9,5	8,8	8,1	7,0	6,4	6,0	5,8	5,5	5,2	3,7	4,2	3,9	7,6

TAB. 4
(continued)
(suite)

1975

	TOTAL	0 – 4	5 – 9	10 – 14	15 – 19	20 – 24	25 – 29	30 – 34	35 – 39	40 – 44	45 – 49	50 – 54	55 – 59	60 – 64	65 – 69	70 +
NEDERLAND	100,0	7,6	8,6	8,8	8,3	8,0	8,4	6,4	5,7	5,6	5,5	5,6	4,7	4,6	4,2	8,0
Noord-Nederland	100,0	8,1	9,0	8,7	8,2	7,8	7,8	6,0	5,4	5,3	5,2	5,6	4,8	4,7	4,4	9,0
Groningen	100,0	7,6	8,2	8,0	7,9	8,6	8,2	6,0	5,3	5,3	5,2	5,7	4,9	5,0	4,7	9,4
Friesland	100,0	8,6	9,5	9,0	8,3	7,3	7,4	5,9	5,3	5,0	5,0	5,2	4,7	4,8	4,4	9,6
Drenthe	100,0	8,4	9,3	9,2	8,4	7,5	7,8	6,3	5,8	5,7	5,5	5,7	4,7	4,3	3,9	7,5
Oost-Nederland	100,0	8,2	9,3	9,2	8,6	8,0	8,1	6,3	5,7	5,6	5,4	5,4	4,4	4,4	3,9	7,5
Overijssel	100,0	8,4	9,5	9,4	8,8	7,6	7,7	6,1	5,6	5,6	5,4	5,4	4,4	4,5	4,0	7,6
Gelderland	100,0	8,1	9,2	9,1	8,7	8,2	8,3	6,4	5,7	5,6	5,3	5,3	4,4	4,3	3,9	7,5
West-Nederland	100,0	7,0	7,9	8,1	7,9	8,1	8,6	6,4	5,6	5,5	5,6	5,8	5,0	5,0	4,5	9,0
Utrecht	100,0	7,5	8,5	8,6	8,4	8,7	8,8	6,4	5,6	5,4	5,3	5,4	4,6	4,5	4,0	8,3
Noord-Holland	100,0	6,7	7,7	8,0	7,8	8,1	8,8	6,5	5,5	5,4	5,6	5,9	5,1	5,0	4,6	9,3
Zuid-Holland	100,0	7,1	7,9	8,1	7,9	7,9	8,5	6,3	5,6	5,5	5,6	5,8	5,0	5,0	4,6	9,2
Zuidwest-Nederland																
Zeeland	100,0	7,7	8,6	8,1	7,7	7,1	7,7	6,0	5,3	5,3	5,3	5,8	5,0	5,2	4,9	10,3
Zuid-Nederland	100,0	7,8	9,3	9,7	9,1	8,3	8,3	6,7	6,1	6,0	5,6	5,3	4,2	4,0	3,5	6,1
Noord-Brabant	100,0	8,2	9,6	9,8	9,0	8,3	8,5	6,8	6,1	5,9	5,4	5,1	4,1	3,9	3,4	5,9
Limburg	100,0	7,1	8,7	9,5	9,2	8,2	7,9	6,6	6,2	6,1	5,9	5,8	4,5	4,3	3,6	6,4
BELGIQUE/BELGIË	100,0	6,3	7,0	7,8	7,5	7,3	7,2	5,7	5,9	6,2	6,4	6,5	4,5	5,4	5,3	11,0
Vlaams Gew./Rég. Flamande	100,0	6,3	7,4	8,3	8,1	7,6	7,1	6,0	6,2	6,5	6,3	6,1	4,2	5,1	5,0	9,8
Région Wallonne/ Waals Gewest	100,0	6,3	6,9	7,4	7,4	7,3	7,3	5,1	5,3	5,9	6,5	6,8	4,6	5,5	5,5	12,2
Rég. Bruxelloise/ Brussels Gew.	100,0	5,8	5,8	6,2	6,0	6,0	7,1	6,0	5,7	6,1	6,6	7,2	5,2	6,2	6,0	14,1
Antwerpen/Anvers	100,0	6,1	7,2	8,1	8,0	7,6	7,1	6,0	6,1	6,4	6,4	6,2	4,4	5,3	5,1	10,0
Brabant	100,0	5,8	6,4	7,0	6,9	6,6	7,1	6,1	6,0	6,5	6,7	6,9	4,8	5,7	5,5	12,0
Hainaut/Henegouwen	100,0	6,5	6,8	7,2	7,3	7,4	7,4	4,9	5,0	5,8	6,6	6,9	4,5	5,5	5,6	12,6
Liège/Luik	100,0	6,0	6,6	7,2	7,2	7,1	7,2	5,2	5,5	6,0	6,7	6,8	4,7	5,6	5,7	12,5
Limburg/Limbourg	100,0	7,3	8,7	10,1	9,9	9,2	7,9	6,2	6,5	6,4	5,9	5,3	3,4	3,8	3,4	6,0
Luxembourg/Luxemburg	100,0	6,7	7,6	8,5	8,2	7,6	6,6	4,6	5,4	5,8	6,4	6,4	4,8	5,6	5,5	11,3
Namur/Namen	100,0	6,5	7,1	7,9	7,8	7,4	7,2	4,8	5,3	5,8	6,3	6,6	4,7	5,4	5,3	11,9
O.-Vlaand/Fland.Or.	100,0	6,4	7,2	7,7	7,6	7,2	7,0	5,8	6,1	6,4	6,2	6,2	4,3	5,5	5,4	11,0
W.-Vlaand/Fland.Oc.	100,0	6,5	7,4	8,2	8,0	7,5	6,9	5,9	6,2	6,4	6,3	6,1	4,1	5,1	5,1	10,3
LUXEMBOURG (GRAND-DUCHÉ)	100,0	5,6	6,8	7,2	7,3	7,6	6,9	6,4	6,5	6,7	6,8	6,4	4,7	5,8	5,4	9,9

TAB. 4
(continued)
(suite)

1975

	TOTAL	0 – 4	5 – 9	10 – 14	15 – 19	20 – 24	25 – 29	30 – 34	35 – 39	40 – 44	45 – 49	50 – 54	55 – 59	60 – 64	65 – 69	70 +
UNITED KINGDOM	100,0	6,7	7,6	7,8	7,0	6,6	7,1	6,0	5,6	5,5	5,8	6,3	5,5	5,9	5,5	11,1
North	100,0	6,6	7,7	8,2	7,4	6,5	6,9	5,8	5,6	5,7	6,0	6,5	5,5	5,8	5,4	10,5
Yorkshire and Humberside	100,0	6,8	7,7	7,9	6,9	6,4	7,0	5,9	5,6	5,4	5,7	6,3	5,5	6,0	5,5	11,4
East Midlands	100,0	7,0	7,8	8,0	7,0	6,6	7,5	6,1	5,7	5,5	5,8	6,2	5,3	5,6	5,2	10,7
East Anglia	100,0	6,9	7,5	7,5	6,7	6,8	7,6	6,1	5,6	5,4	5,5	5,9	5,3	5,9	5,5	11,8
South-East	100,0	6,3	7,2	7,4	6,7	6,8	7,6	6,1	5,7	5,5	5,8	6,3	5,5	5,9	5,5	11,7
South West	100,0	6,2	7,1	7,3	6,6	6,2	6,9	5,6	5,3	5,2	5,7	6,3	5,6	6,4	6,2	13,4
West Midlands	100,0	7,2	8,1	8,1	7,1	6,6	7,5	6,3	5,8	5,6	5,9	6,4	5,4	5,5	4,9	9,6
North-West	100,0	6,7	7,7	8,1	7,1	6,4	6,9	5,8	5,4	5,3	5,7	6,3	5,5	6,1	5,6	11,4
Wales	100,0	6,6	7,5	7,7	7,0	6,4	6,9	5,7	5,4	5,3	5,9	6,5	5,8	6,0	5,7	11,6
Scotland	100,0	6,8	7,8	8,3	7,7	6,8	6,8	5,7	5,6	5,6	5,8	6,1	5,4	5,8	5,4	10,4
Northern Ireland	100,0	8,6	9,5	9,6	8,4	6,8	6,4	6,0	5,4	5,3	5,4	5,5	4,8	5,0	4,5	8,8
IRELAND	100,0	10,7	10,1	9,9	9,0	7,5	6,3	5,4	4,8	4,8	4,9	5,1	4,9	4,5	3,9	8,2
DANMARK	100,0	6,9	7,5	7,5	7,1	7,2	8,0	7,0	5,8	5,4	5,6	6,0	5,5	5,5	5,0	10,0
Storkøbenhavn	100,0	6,3	6,9	6,6	6,2	7,5	8,6	7,5	5,8	5,4	5,6	6,2	5,8	5,8	5,2	10,4
Øst for Storebælt Ekskl. Storkøbenhavn	100,0	6,6	7,6	7,7	7,4	6,3	7,3	6,5	5,6	5,5	5,8	6,3	5,7	5,8	5,3	10,6
Vest for Storebælt	100,0	7,4	8,0	8,0	7,6	7,2	7,8	6,7	5,8	5,5	5,5	5,9	5,2	5,3	4,8	9,3

TAB. 4.1

Female population by age groups (females for 100 males)
Population féminine par groupe d'âge (femmes pour 100 hommes)

1975

	TOTAL	0 – 4	5 – 9	10 – 14	15 – 19	20 – 24	25 – 29	30 – 34	35 – 39	40 – 44	45 – 49	50 – 54	55 – 59	60 – 64	65 – 69	70 +
BR DEUTSCHLAND	109,8	95,4	95,2	95,2	94,8	98,5	94,0	92,4	92,3	93,5	100,7	136,1	144,3	147,6	151,3	179,0
Schleswig-Holstein	108,5	95,3	94,7	94,6	94,2	84,4	86,7	95,0	92,2	95,6	106,2	138,1	148,1	147,6	145,1	171,4
Hamburg	115,4	95,8	95,5	96,1	98,6	102,1	90,9	88,6	92,0	99,1	110,8	142,8	148,8	145,8	153,2	192,5
Niedersachsen	97,4	95,9	95,6	94,8	93,9	91,7	91,5	93,7	92,9	95,2	103,6	136,9	145,2	145,7	144,7	169,9
Hannover	111,1	96,1	95,5	95,2	95,5	99,8	91,9	94,0	92,9	94,7	102,5	137,2	145,1	145,3	147,1	178,5
Hildesheim	111,6	93,9	96,0	95,5	94,3	98,1	88,3	92,0	93,2	96,9	105,5	142,5	150,7	150,5	148,5	176,1
Lüneburg	106,7	96,7	95,7	93,7	92,0	87,6	95,0	96,0	91,9	92,8	98,4	132,0	140,4	141,7	137,7	162,1
Stade	103,9	95,2	94,8	93,1	90,6	82,4	88,8	93,4	88,2	91,6	100,5	131,3	139,6	136,8	135,4	156,4
Osnabrück	108,1	97,1	95,9	95,2	94,1	95,1	94,8	94,4	95,8	96,0	103,0	134,9	149,6	144,7	144,9	162,8
Aurich	107,5	95,1	94,1	92,8	96,5	89,3	97,0	96,7	97,5	98,4	106,8	136,4	145,3	143,4	142,3	156,3
Braunschweig	111,9	97,0	95,9	95,3	94,9	88,4	90,8	91,4	92,7	96,2	106,8	142,1	146,2	148,7	149,1	178,4
Oldenburg	107,0	96,0	95,9	96,1	93,0	84,5	87,3	93,2	93,0	96,5	108,6	137,0	146,3	146,2	145,7	166,9
Bremen	112,7	93,8	93,6	94,7	96,0	99,6	97,5	90,8	93,0	102,3	109,7	141,8	141,9	142,0	149,4	182,7
Nordrhein-Westfalen	109,3	94,9	95,0	95,2	95,0	101,3	96,3	93,6	92,2	92,4	97,9	132,2	139,4	146,3	153,3	181,5
Düsseldorf	111,1	95,2	95,3	94,9	95,3	104,9	101,0	95,1	92,5	91,6	96,9	132,4	138,4	147,9	157,3	187,8
Köln	107,7	94,8	94,9	95,2	95,0	102,0	94,9	92,6	90,4	90,3	96,5	131,3	136,3	141,4	151,9	180,4
Münster	107,6	94,4	95,0	95,8	96,0	98,6	91,9	92,4	94,3	96,6	99,6	130,7	137,0	145,2	149,9	177,2
Detmold	110,7	95,1	93,7	95,0	94,2	98,3	96,3	94,0	94,1	96,1	103,1	135,3	147,8	149,9	151,0	174,8
Arnsberg	109,1	95,1	94,9	95,3	94,2	99,1	94,1	93,2	91,4	91,4	97,3	131,9	142,1	147,5	151,9	179,7
Hessen	108,2	94,8	95,0	94,8	94,3	100,5	93,7	90,5	90,5	91,8	98,0	131,4	139,7	143,3	145,8	171,5
Darmstadt	108,1	95,1	94,9	95,2	94,7	102,7	95,1	90,3	90,0	90,7	96,5	129,6	137,3	142,8	147,1	174,6
Kassel	108,5	93,8	95,1	93,9	93,0	94,3	89,0	91,1	92,4	95,2	103,0	136,8	146,5	144,6	142,1	164,0
Rheinland-Pfalz	109,5	95,6	95,0	95,3	94,8	94,6	93,5	95,7	94,4	93,5	100,3	136,6	145,3	146,6	148,6	170,2
Koblenz	109,2	95,3	95,1	94,9	95,5	92,6	91,6	95,2	94,5	94,5	101,6	137,3	147,1	147,9	142,9	162,9
Trier	110,4	94,2	93,6	96,7	93,5	87,9	95,2	103,5	98,2	98,6	104,0	143,7	153,2	150,0	147,1	164,2
Rheinhessen-Pfalz	109,4	96,2	95,4	95,2	94,8	98,2	94,5	94,6	93,6	91,6	98,4	134,0	142,4	143,6	155,2	177,8
Baden-Württemberg	108,3	95,9	95,5	95,2	95,2	102,9	94,7	91,3	91,2	90,3	98,6	135,5	145,9	148,1	149,7	174,7
Stuttgart	107,3	95,8	95,8	95,3	94,5	106,8	97,0	90,7	89,7	87,3	96,6	132,6	142,0	143,3	146,2	174,8
Karlsruhe	109,2	96,2	95,2	95,3	96,2	101,4	93,0	90,1	91,2	91,8	100,0	134,4	141,1	149,3	155,2	180,4
Freiburg	109,4	95,4	95,8	94,3	95,0	102,7	95,3	94,2	93,9	93,3	99,6	140,0	151,4	153,8	153,2	172,0
Tübingen	107,4	96,4	95,2	96,2	95,3	97,6	91,3	91,6	92,0	91,8	99,8	139,6	151,6	151,5	144,7	168,0
Bayern	109,8	96,0	95,1	95,2	94,9	98,1	93,8	91,7	93,3	95,1	102,0	138,8	146,6	147,5	149,5	176,0
Oberbayern	107,7	96,1	94,9	95,1	95,2	98,6	92,5	89,0	90,1	91,0	97,9	136,3	143,4	142,0	146,6	177,9
Niederbayern	112,5	95,3	95,4	96,1	94,6	95,8	99,3	98,9	100,6	101,4	101,1	148,3	154,3	152,8	149,3	171,0
Oberpfalz	109,3	96,0	95,4	94,7	92,1	90,7	89,3	93,9	97,3	99,0	106,4	139,3	150,6	151,7	151,3	177,2
Oberfranken	113,5	97,3	95,9	95,5	95,1	98,8	95,6	94,4	96,4	99,1	105,3	137,2	149,7	157,9	156,0	181,2
Mittelfranken	111,4	97,2	95,4	95,0	96,4	102,5	94,8	82,1	93,8	95,6	101,1	136,9	142,6	149,0	155,1	181,3
Unterfranken	108,7	95,2	94,6	94,9	94,4	98,0	92,1	93,4	94,9	96,2	101,6	137,2	144,0	145,7	147,8	168,0
Schwaben	110,2	95,4	94,9	95,4	95,1	99,2	95,9	92,2	91,9	94,7	102,9	142,0	151,0	147,1	146,2	171,7
Saarland	110,6	96,6	95,6	96,0	95,0	97,5	93,5	97,2	99,3	97,3	101,9	135,8	138,6	148,3	155,9	171,5
Berlin (West)	126,2	94,8	96,1	95,6	92,9	98,7	94,7	88,0	89,3	96,6	114,2	167,6	175,4	183,1	193,2	244,3
FRANCE	104,3	95,4	93,2	95,7	96,2	97,9	93,9	91,9	94,5	97,3	99,2	104,4	107,0	114,8	123,4	173,0
Île-de-France	105,2	95,9	97,3	95,6	96,7	103,4	95,6	89,0	91,5	96,3	100,8	107,0	110,2	119,8	138,3	192,8
Bassin parisien	102,9	95,2	95,6	96,2	95,8	95,5	93,4	91,1	94,9	97,2	97,4	100,8	105,6	112,1	118,4	166,0
Champagne-Ardenne	101,2	94,4	95,0	94,4	95,6	95,5	92,0	86,0	92,1	92,4	97,2	102,1	104,0	112,3	120,8	163,1
Picardie	101,5	95,6	95,5	95,1	97,7	93,3	92,5	89,0	92,8	96,4	95,9	98,5	103,6	111,4	120,7	162,2
Haute-Normandie	103,5	95,3	96,3	96,8	97,2	96,8	95,5	92,4	95,7	99,6	97,9	99,8	107,4	113,8	122,9	176,4
Centre	102,8	96,6	94,9	96,7	92,8	96,6	93,5	93,1	93,3	97,2	96,7	102,1	105,4	109,7	112,5	156,1
Basse-Normandie	106,0	94,9	96,6	97,8	96,0	95,6	94,6	95,2	103,5	102,3	100,5	102,1	107,1	116,6	123,3	197,7
Bourgogne	103,1	93,5	95,6	95,6	96,6	94,7	92,2	90,7	93,8	95,4	96,9	100,2	105,5	111,5	116,1	159,7
Nord-Pas-de-Calais	104,2	95,1	97,2	95,2	95,9	97,0	92,9	92,6	97,5	98,7	100,0	103,7	107,5	122,7	132,3	179,1

TAB. 4.1
(continued)
(suite)

1975

	TOTAL	0 – 4	5 – 9	10 – 14	15 – 19	20 – 24	25 – 29	30 – 34	35 – 39	40 – 44	45 – 49	50 – 54	55 – 59	60 – 64	65 – 69	70 +
Est	102,0	95,8	97,0	96,0	96,0	96,1	87,2	86,5	90,8	92,6	95,9	109,2	111,0	116,4	126,3	172,6
Lorraine	100,8	96,9	97,0	95,9	95,7	94,6	87,7	91,5	91,6	94,7	104,3	108,7	108,7	111,0	123,5	171,8
Alsace	104,2	96,6	96,7	96,4	97,3	96,8	87,6	85,8	88,5	93,0	98,8	121,3	119,4	127,0	134,6	175,8
Franche-Comté	101,4	95,4	97,3	95,4	95,5	98,0	85,4	86,4	93,0	94,0	95,0	104,2	104,9	112,7	120,4	169,7
Ouest	105,7	95,3	95,8	95,4	96,6	96,7	96,3	97,2	99,5	99,8	100,2	104,0	107,7	114,7	121,6	178,1
Pays-de-la-Loire	106,1	97,0	96,2	95,9	97,0	98,8	97,6	98,2	102,4	100,0	101,7	103,2	107,7	115,8	121,3	182,0
Bretagne	106,3	92,8	94,7	96,0	96,4	96,2	95,3	96,1	97,4	100,1	99,3	105,9	109,8	117,9	128,4	189,7
Poitou-Charentes	103,8	96,2	96,8	93,3	96,1	93,8	95,8	96,8	98,2	98,7	99,2	102,4	104,1	107,6	111,4	158,1
Sud-Ouest	105,8	95,9	95,2	96,0	95,6	96,6	95,8	98,8	99,8	99,8	101,8	103,7	103,3	109,3	114,6	162,2
Aquitaine	106,7	95,0	94,8	97,0	96,7	98,6	97,4	99,0	99,7	100,1	102,0	104,9	105,7	110,8	116,8	168,4
Midi-Pyrénées	104,7	97,5	94,9	94,7	94,3	96,0	95,5	100,5	100,2	99,6	102,2	102,7	101,5	108,0	111,3	157,0
Limousin	105,9	94,8	98,0	96,9	96,3	92,3	91,4	92,4	98,4	100,0	100,0	103,5	100,0	107,9	117,0	158,6
Centre-Est	103,3	94,6	95,8	95,5	96,8	98,3	93,6	91,2	92,4	95,8	96,9	101,4	103,0	113,2	123,8	173,4
Rhône-Alpes	103,1	94,1	95,3	96,1	96,5	99,3	94,1	91,1	92,1	95,6	96,9	101,1	103,3	114,2	126,1	175,0
Auvergne	104,2	96,6	98,0	93,6	97,9	94,2	91,8	91,9	93,3	96,6	96,8	102,5	101,9	110,7	117,3	168,9
Méditerranée	105,3	95,1	94,1	95,7	95,8	97,2	94,0	93,3	93,7	98,8	100,1	106,6	107,7	114,2	118,0	164,2
Languedoc-Roussillon	106,8	95,6	94,7	96,4	96,4	97,0	96,5	97,5	100,7	103,8	102,3	106,1	105,0	112,7	115,7	161,0
Provence-Alpes-Côte d'Azur	105,4	95,1	93,5	95,6	95,8	98,4	95,8	93,5	93,0	98,0	100,1	106,7	109,7	116,6	120,2	165,6
Corse	90,9	91,5	94,7	90,2	86,4	81,0	60,2	67,7	65,9	79,1	85,5	109,9	100,0	93,2	103,2	167,7
ITALIA	104,5	94,6	95,2	95,1	96,0	96,3	98,1	100,9	102,1	102,4	103,8	110,0	112,7	113,4	120,2	152,4
Nord Ovest	105,8	94,5	95,0	95,2	95,1	96,7	96,9	98,4	99,0	100,1	102,8	109,4	113,2	115,5	123,0	156,9
Piemonte	104,8	94,6	95,2	95,4	95,0	97,1	96,7	97,4	97,5	98,8	101,5	108,1	112,6	114,6	122,3	155,7
Valle d'Aosta	99,3	94,9	95,2	95,1	97,2	92,7	88,9	84,4	93,0	92,9	97,5	108,1	100,0	103,1	111,5	151,5
Liguria	108,7	94,5	94,8	94,8	95,3	96,2	97,9	102,0	103,6	104,2	106,3	112,5	115,1	118,0	125,2	159,6
Lombardia	105,8	94,2	95,2	95,1	97,0	99,0	99,3	99,0	98,8	100,2	103,3	111,4	117,7	120,6	131,3	169,9
Nord Est	105,1	94,8	95,4	95,4	96,6	96,4	95,7	97,4	98,7	100,2	103,0	111,5	113,0	116,9	127,4	167,8
Trentino-Alto Adige	103,6	94,9	94,9	95,8	96,1	96,5	93,5	97,1	98,2	99,6	101,5	112,9	119,4	118,1	122,2	152,3
Veneto	104,6	94,7	95,6	95,7	96,8	96,4	96,6	98,0	99,1	100,1	102,4	110,1	111,7	116,1	126,9	167,4
Friuli-Venezia Giulia	108,0	95,6	94,5	94,0	96,0	96,4	93,9	95,7	97,4	100,8	105,8	114,8	113,8	118,8	131,7	177,5
Emilia-Romagna	104,9	94,5	95,5	95,4	96,4	98,0	99,1	99,0	100,7	100,1	101,7	106,7	108,8	110,6	117,7	151,4
Centro	104,9	95,1	95,4	94,8	96,3	96,4	99,0	101,3	103,0	100,9	101,9	105,4	108,2	110,0	117,9	148,6
Toscana	105,5	95,1	95,6	95,0	96,6	96,7	99,9	101,7	102,6	100,8	102,3	105,7	109,0	110,6	118,4	149,7
Umbria	102,6	94,6	94,5	94,7	93,9	95,5	97,5	100,0	103,0	101,1	101,7	104,7	105,3	104,5	112,4	137,6
Marche	104,5	94,7	95,3	94,5	96,9	96,3	97,5	101,0	104,4	101,7	101,0	104,9	107,8	111,6	119,8	151,7
Lazio	104,7	94,7	95,3	95,4	96,5	97,6	102,1	106,0	105,6	104,4	104,1	109,5	110,8	112,1	116,5	151,5
Campania	103,3	94,6	95,1	95,0	95,6	96,1	97,2	101,8	104,9	105,2	105,5	112,5	115,1	113,7	120,2	153,4
Abruzzi-Molise	103,6	95,2	94,6	93,7	95,7	93,2	94,7	99,3	103,2	104,0	104,6	110,3	112,2	111,5	114,2	144,0
Abruzzi	103,5	94,8	94,2	93,6	95,3	93,3	95,2	99,1	102,1	104,1	104,0	109,6	111,3	111,4	114,6	144,6
Molise	104,4	96,6	96,2	92,9	95,5	93,0	92,9	97,6	107,3	103,8	106,7	112,9	117,5	112,1	114,5	142,2
Sud	102,7	94,8	95,0	95,2	95,7	93,9	97,7	103,1	105,9	105,7	106,0	111,4	112,6	109,9	112,3	140,2
Puglia	103,6	95,0	95,5	95,5	96,8	96,4	100,9	105,7	108,2	108,1	107,5	110,7	111,3	108,9	112,0	139,0
Basilicata	100,9	95,5	94,2	94,7	95,7	93,9	97,0	101,3	102,1	102,0	100,5	108,3	112,0	105,5	105,3	129,1
Calabria	101,7	94,2	94,2	94,7	94,0	89,5	91,4	98,3	102,6	102,8	105,0	113,4	115,3	113,2	114,9	146,2
Sicilia	103,0	94,5	95,1	95,0	94,6	94,0	97,2	104,1	107,1	106,8	106,7	113,7	115,5	109,2	110,7	131,6
Sardegna	101,2	94,0	94,8	94,5	95,8	96,0	99,8	106,7	106,4	104,4	103,4	106,7	105,9	101,2	107,0	125,5

TAB. 4.1
(continued)
(suite)

1975

	TOTAL	0 – 4	5 – 9	10 – 14	15 – 19	20 – 24	25 – 29	30 – 34	35 – 39	40 – 44	45 – 49	50 – 54	55 – 59	60 – 64	65 – 69	70 +
NEDERLAND	100,8	95,0	95,4	95,5	95,8	95,9	93,8	91,7	92,7	96,9	102,1	105,9	108,0	113,8	123,0	141,2
Noord-Nederland	99,6	95,4	95,0	95,6	95,2	93,7	91,8	92,8	94,6	95,9	101,6	105,4	106,9	109,7	114,8	126,1
Groningen	100,2	94,9	94,8	95,6	95,1	92,0	89,8	93,6	95,3	96,6	102,2	106,2	107,3	110,7	119,0	131,3
Friesland	100,1	94,4	94,6	95,4	95,5	94,4	92,0	92,7	93,0	95,2	103,0	105,8	110,3	112,8	115,0	128,3
Drenthe	98,2	97,7	95,9	95,3	94,4	95,5	94,5	93,3	95,0	95,8	99,1	102,7	102,2	102,4	108,5	144,4
Oost-Nederland	99,5	95,3	95,6	95,2	96,3	94,1	93,6	91,2	93,0	98,0	100,9	104,8	105,5	112,7	117,6	130,8
Overijssel	99,8	94,9	95,7	96,0	95,9	91,8	91,3	89,7	92,2	96,8	100,4	104,3	104,9	112,4	116,2	130,0
Gelderland	100,0	95,4	95,6	94,8	96,6	95,6	95,0	92,2	93,4	98,7	100,9	105,0	105,9	112,7	118,5	131,3
West-Nederland	103,0	95,7	95,1	95,5	96,1	97,8	95,1	92,5	93,3	97,3	103,1	107,9	110,9	116,7	129,8	153,7
Utrecht	102,9	95,3	94,8	94,4	96,1	98,7	97,7	93,3	93,1	97,9	101,8	107,8	111,2	120,5	132,6	159,0
Noord-Holland	103,1	95,4	95,5	95,1	95,2	96,9	95,3	92,5	93,0	97,8	104,0	108,0	111,0	117,5	130,6	154,4
Zuid-Holland	102,9	95,9	94,9	96,1	96,9	98,1	94,2	92,4	93,6	96,8	102,9	107,8	110,6	115,2	128,2	152,1
Zuidwest-Nederland																
Zeeland	99,8	94,0	95,2	95,0	94,7	95,1	93,3	91,6	94,6	98,9	101,2	104,4	102,5	107,7	114,3	123,7
Zuid-Nederland	98,4	95,5	96,1	96,1	95,3	93,9	90,7	89,6	91,6	95,2	101,1	102,6	105,2	111,7	119,1	135,6
Noord-Brabant	98,1	95,1	96,0	96,2	95,6	93,9	90,8	89,7	91,2	94,9	100,6	102,1	106,3	111,4	119,8	131,7
Limburg	99,0	96,6	96,2	95,8	95,2	94,2	90,5	89,5	92,5	95,7	102,3	103,5	103,1	112,2	118,6	142,1
BELGIQUE/BELGIË	104,2	94,8	95,7	95,7	95,8	94,9	94,2	96,0	98,2	99,8	101,5	103,6	107,1	114,3	126,1	161,7
Vlaams Gewest/Région Flamande	101,6	94,7	95,3	95,2	95,5	95,3	94,2	95,3	97,0	98,3	99,4	101,2	104,2	101,1	119,9	144,7
Région Wallonne/ Waals Gewest	106,1	95,1	95,8	96,0	96,5	94,7	92,7	96,5	100,1	101,3	102,0	103,6	107,5	115,1	131,5	176,6
Région Bruxelloise/ Brussels Gewest	112,8	94,8	97,6	98,6	95,7	92,8	98,0	98,2	99,1	104,3	110,1	114,9	119,8	131,9	140,3	199,5
Antwerpen/Anvers	102,4	94,8	95,1	95,5	96,0	96,0	95,4	95,0	96,0	99,4	99,8	102,5	104,8	110,5	120,5	148,9
Brabant	107,3	94,5	97,0	97,5	95,9	94,4	96,8	97,2	98,1	101,0	103,1	106,9	110,7	121,6	131,2	177,2
Hainaut/Henegouwen	106,2	95,3	96,1	96,6	96,9	95,6	93,0	94,1	99,1	102,3	102,5	102,4	104,4	114,8	132,1	170,0
Liège/Luik	107,0	94,9	94,8	96,2	96,9	94,0	92,9	98,6	101,0	100,3	102,6	104,4	110,1	118,6	134,1	181,9
Limburg/Limbourg	97,1	95,0	96,1	96,0	94,6	94,0	93,3	94,1	92,5	92,3	92,6	94,7	96,7	102,4	117,2	136,7
Luxembourg/Luxemburg	103,5	98,7	101,2	97,9	96,8	94,4	89,2	96,2	103,4	100,0	102,9	110,8	112,5	108,8	124,5	160,8
Namur/Namen	106,0	94,2	94,7	95,2	95,7	93,7	92,3	98,0	100,9	103,6	100,8	105,6	111,9	114,9	130,5	180,5
O.-Vlaand/Fland. Or.	102,5	95,3	95,3	94,4	95,7	94,9	93,6	95,1	98,8	99,8	102,0	103,0	105,1	110,2	119,3	141,0
W.-Vlaand/Fland Oc.	102,1	94,4	94,6	93,1	94,7	95,8	92,8	96,4	99,4	99,1	102,7	103,4	107,8	111,2	120,0	142,3
LUXEMBOURG (GRAND-DUCHÉ)	101,7	94,4	95,3	97,0	95,0	97,1	84,5	87,9	89,3	91,0	94,6	122,3	109,0	116,7	127,3	155,8

TAB. 4.1
(continued)
(suite)

1975

	TOTAL	0 – 4	5 – 9	10 – 14	15 – 19	20 – 24	25 – 29	30 – 34	35 – 39	40 – 44	45 – 49	50 – 54	55 – 59	60 – 64	65 – 69	70 +
UNITED KINGDOM	105,5	94,3	94,8	94,9	95,5	96,6	98,0	97,4	97,2	98,6	101,2	103,9	108,4	113,6	124,3	182,0
North	104,5	94,1	95,2	95,2	95,3	96,2	97,7	97,2	97,7	98,7	98,7	100,9	107,0	112,7	125,6	177,3
Yorkshire and Humberside	105,1	95,4	95,7	95,4	94,7	94,6	97,5	97,6	97,2	91,3	99,1	101,7	107,2	113,0	124,0	182,5
East Midlands	102,7	94,0	95,5	95,4	94,8	97,0	97,0	96,5	95,9	96,6	96,8	98,8	102,8	107,7	117,0	167,2
East Anglia	102,4	94,4	94,8	93,4	94,2	92,6	94,6	94,6	95,2	96,6	99,6	100,8	106,2	111,3	113,4	158,1
South East	106,5	94,2	94,3	94,5	95,4	98,9	100,1	98,4	97,1	98,8	102,7	105,1	108,5	112,5	124,4	188,1
South West	106,9	94,8	94,4	94,9	92,6	95,5	98,4	98,6	98,1	99,3	104,8	108,1	112,1	116,8	120,8	168,2
West Midlands	102,0	95,0	95,1	94,6	95,0	94,7	95,9	93,9	93,6	94,0	96,4	99,1	102,4	107,9	119,6	182,1
North West	106,7	93,5	94,9	95,6	98,4	94,9	96,5	96,8	96,5	97,8	100,6	104,7	110,7	117,7	131,5	198,1
Wales	106,0	94,0	95,9	95,2	97,9	97,3	99,1	96,7	96,8	97,8	100,2	104,5	108,9	114,1	125,9	176,7
Scotland	107,9	94,7	94,5	95,2	96,2	98,8	98,5	100,4	103,6	104,4	106,2	108,2	115,3	120,2	130,4	187,7
Northern Ireland	102,1	93,0	93,7	93,7	93,3	89,9	91,9	95,5	97,9	104,3	107,1	107,0	106,2	116,0	128,6	165,4
IRELAND	99,4	95,3	95,5	96,1	96,2	95,8	96,3	97,3	97,4	98,5	100,9	101,5	100,0	100,3	103,9	128,1
DANMARK	101,8	95,5	95,0	95,6	94,5	95,1	93,9	95,3	97,6	100,3	101,9	103,7	104,5	108,5	117,0	141,4
Storkøbenhavn	106,1	96,0	95,4	96,5	96,4	99,6	94,5	95,0	95,2	98,6	104,3	107,8	112,8	118,7	133,0	176,3
Øst for Storebælt ekskl. Storkøbenhavn	98,6	94,9	93,9	94,4	92,0	89,4	93,6	93,8	97,5	102,6	99,4	101,1	97,0	100,0	109,5	121,6
Vest for Storebælt	99,8	95,0	94,9	95,6	94,0	93,3	93,6	95,9	99,1	100,9	100,8	101,7	100,4	103,9	109,1	127,4

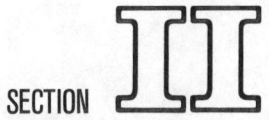

Vital characteristics of the female population

Aspects dynamiques de la population féminine

TAB. 5

Birth rates (‰)

Taux de natalité (‰)

	1960	1970	1976	1977
EUR 9	17,9	15,9	12,4	12,2
BR Deutschland	17,4	13,4	9,8	9,5
France	17,9	16,8	13,6	14,0
Italia	17,9	16,5	13,9	13,2
Nederland	20,8	18,3	12,9	12,5
Belgique/België	17,0	14,8	12,3	12,4
Luxembourg	16,0	13,0	11,0	11,4
United Kingdom	17,5	16,3	12,1	11,8
Ireland	21,5	21,9	21,4	21,4
Danmark	16,6	14,4	12,9	12,2

$$\text{Birth rate} = \frac{\text{live births}}{\text{population}} \times 1\,000$$

$$\text{Taux de natalité} = \frac{\text{naissances vivantes}}{\text{population}} \times 1\,000$$

TAB. 6

Specific fertility rates (‰)

Taux spécifiques de fécondité (‰)

	15 – 19	20 – 24	25 – 29	30 – 34	35 – 39	40 – 44	45 – 49	15 – 49	Total
BR Deutschland									
1960	24,7	126,0	157,1	101,2	50,7	16,9	1,0	68,8	2372,1
1970	36,0	124,9	115,1	76,2	39,1	11,1	0,8	56,9	2016,3
1975	21,1	87,8	99,2	52,2	21,9	6,6	0,5	41,2	1451,3
1976	19,8	88,3	103,5	52,4	20,8	6,0	0,4	41,2	1458,7
France									
1960	22,9	161,0	175,0	108,0	55,0	21,1	1,3	81,7	2727,0
1970	27,0	159,0	158,0	93,0	44,9	13,7	1,2	71,0	2484,0
1975	25,3	127,0	127,0	68,0	29,2	8,2	0,7	59,7	1927,0
1976	23,0	122,0	125,0	65,2	25,1	6,6	0,6	57,4	1838,0
1977*	:	:	:	:	:	:	:	:	:
Italia									
1960	18,2	109,0	155,9	111,6	61,9	22,6	1,9	72,4	2405,5
1970	26,5	130,8	150,6	99,9	53,3	16,2	1,2	68,7	2392,5
1976									
1977									
Nederland									
1960	16,3	120,1	208,0	152,4	88,5	33,1	2,8	89,3	3106,0
1970	22,6	136,8	185,0	108,3	48,8	14,1	1,2	77,3	2584,0
1975	12,6	97,9	137,6	60,5	19,9	4,7	0,4	53,9	1668,0
1976	11,3	94,5	138,0	60,4	18,2	4,4	0,3	52,8	1635,5
Belgique/België									
1960	24,9	150,1	162,3	99,1	50,4	16,8	1,1	74,3	2575,0
1970	31,0	149,4	143,0	78,1	36,4	9,9	0,6	63,0	2200,0
1975	28,0	119,6	119,2	54,9	20,7	5,2	0,3	51,8	1736,0
1976	26,8	118,4	121,6	55,0	19,0	4,6	0,4	52,0	1725,0
Luxembourg									
1960	23,2	142,9	149,5	90,4	37,9	11,9	1,0	66,4	2284,0
1970	27,7	132,1	126,6	64,5	33,1	9,3	0,5	54,5	1969,0
1974	23,9	97,3	105,1	55,9	22,0	5,2	0,3	45,1	1548,5
1977									
United Kingdom									
1960	33,8[1]	166,9	172,5	102,2	47,3	13,9	0,9	74,2	2692,0
1970	49,7	157,0	155,6	80,8	35,0	8,7	0,6	71,9	2437,0
1976	32,8	101,0	120,3	57,8	18,8	4,4	0,3	53,1	1727,0
1977	30,0	105,1	119,1	59,0	18,3	4,1	0,3	51,2	1679,5
Ireland									
1960	8,9	101,6	205,0	217,9	157,8	54,2	4,1	100,0	3747,0
1970	16,3	145,5	228,7	201,9	131,9	45,3	3,7	103,8	3866,5
1975	22,7	141,0	226,7	173,4	104,7	38,1	2,5	100,4	3545,5
1976	22,7	139,6	219,4	170,3	98,4	35,1	3,1	99,8	3444,0
Danmark									
1960	41,8	170,7	157,6	87,7	38,7	11,5	0,7	70,1	2543,0
1970	32,4	130,4	130,8	66,0	24,7	5,4	0,3	61,4	1950,0
1975	26,8	136,6	137,0	61,8	18,1	3,3	0,2	61,3	1919,0
1976	23,1	121,1	126,0	57,8	18,0	3,2	0,1	55,3	1747,0
1977	22,1	115,2	120,6	54,8	16,4	2,8	0,1	52,0	1660,0

$$\text{Specific fertility rates} = \frac{\text{Live births per women aged from (x) to (x+4) years}}{\text{Women aged from (x) to (x+4) years}} \times 1\,000$$

$$\text{Taux spécifiques de fécondité} = \frac{\text{Naissances vivantes par femmes âgées de (x) à (x+4)}}{\text{Femmes âgées de (x) à (x+4)}} \times 1\,000$$

[1] Includes under 15 years.   [1] Y compris moins de 15 ans.

TAB. 7

Gross (¹) and net (²) reproduction rates
Taux brut (¹) et taux net (²) de reproduction

	1960		1970		1976		1977	
	1	2	1	2	1	2	1	2
BR Deutschland	1,152	1,110	0,981	0,947	0,710	0,686		0,659
France	1,326	1,279	1,212	1,180	0,893	0,875	0,912	0,895
Italia	1,154	1,071	1,163	1,105	1,100	1,054(74)		
Nederland	1,520	1,470	1,250	1,230	0,790	0,780		
Belgique/België	1,242	1,193	1,094	1,060	0,840	0,815		
Luxembourg	1,114	—	0,959	0,931	0,755	0,733		
United Kingdom	1,300	1,260	1,180	1,150	0,840	0,820	0,820	0,800
Ireland	1,860	1,803	1,877	1,810	1,672	1,619		
Danmark	1,241	1,201	0,948	0,927	0,844	0,829	0,807	0,794

(¹) *Gross reproduction rate:* Average number of liveborn fermale children per woman during the course of her life, assuming current fertility rates applied thoughout, and in absence of mortality.

(²) *Net reproduction rate:* Average number of liveborn female children per woman during the course of her life, assuming current fertility rates applied thoughout. Allowance is made for deaths of these children before they themselves reach childbearing ages.

(¹) *Taux brut de reproduction:* Nombre moyen d'enfants nés vivants de sexe féminin mis au monde par une femme au cours de sa vie, dans l'hypothèse du maintien des taux de fécondité au même niveau, sans tenir compte de la mortalité.

(²) *Taux net de reproduction:* Nombre moyen d'enfants nés vivants de sexe féminin mis au monde par une femme au cours de sa vie, dans l'hypothèse du maintien des taux de fécondité au même niveau. Il est tenu compte de la possibilité que ces enfants meurent avant d'avoir eux-mêmes atteint l'âge de procéer.

TAB. 8

Live births by parity (%)
Naissances vivantes par rang (%)

	BR Deutschland	France	Italia	Nederland	Belgique België	Luxembourg	United Kingdom	Ireland	Danmark	EUR 9	
First births as % of the total											Premières naissances en % du total
1960	41,9	36,0	37,3	31,1	36,3	41,1	36,4	21,0	33,9	37,2	1960
1970	41,9	42,4	38,6	39,0	42,7	42,9	38,4	27,2	41,9	40,1	1970
1975/76	46,7	48,2	42,9	43,0	49,1	48,5	41,1	30,7	44,6	44,5	1975/76
1977	48,2	48,1	43,5	42,7	49,0	50,8	41,8	29,9(1)	43,9	–	1977
Second births as % of the total											Deuxièmes naissances en % du total
1960	29,9	25,2	27,9	27,1	26,4	31,1	30,4	18,1	30,1	28,1	1960
1970	31,8	27,7	31,2	33,5	28,1	31,2	32,9	21,5	35,9	30,9	1970
1975/76	33,0	31,0	31,8	39,8	30,8	33,4	38,1	24,4	36,1	33,3	1975/76
1977	33,9	33,6	34,4	40,0	32,6	33,2	37,9	25,0(1)	37,7	–	1977
Third or higher order births as % of the total											Troisièmes naissances et suivantes en % du total
1960	28,2	38,8	34,8	41,8	37,3	27,8	33,2	60,9	36,0	34,7	1960
1970	26,3	29,9	30,2	27,5	29,2	25,9	28,6	51,3	22,2	29,0	1970
1975/76	20,3	20,8	25,3	17,2	20,1	18,1	20,8	44,9	19,3	22,2	1975/76
1977	17,9	18,2	22,2	17,3	18,5	16,0	20,3	45,1(1)	18,4	–	1977

(¹) 1976.

TAB. 9

Specific female mortality rates and comparison with the male rates
Taux spécifiques de mortalité féminine et comparaison avec les taux masculins

	BR Deutschland		France		Italia		Nederland		Belgique België		Luxembourg	
	q_f	$\frac{q_f}{q_m}100$	q_f	$\frac{q_f}{q_m}100$	q_f	$\frac{q_f}{q_m}100$	q_f	$\frac{q_f}{q_m}100$	q_f	$\frac{q_f}{q_m}100$	q_f	$\frac{q_f}{q_m}100$
1960												
TOTAL	10,3	82,4	10,9	90,8	8,7	85,3	7,0	78,7	11,3	83,1	10,6	26,6
< 1	30,7	78,3	23,9	75,9	10,1	84,2	14,5	77,5	26,6	74,3	24,1	60,4
1 – 4	1,2	80,8	1,1	84,6			1,0	76,9	1,0	90,9	1,4	60,9
5 – 9	0,4	66,7	0,3	60,0	0,5	71,4	0,4	66,7	0,4	66,7	0,5	71,4
10 – 14	0,3	60,0	0,3	75,0	0,4	66,7	0,2	50,0	0,3	60,0	0,3	50,0
15 – 19	0,5	38,5	0,4	44,4	0,5	45,5	0,3	42,9	0,4	44,4	0,3	30,0
20 – 24	0,6	33,3	0,7	58,3	0,6	46,2	0,5	50,0	0,6	37,5	0,5	26,3
25 – 29	0,9	50,0	0,8	50,0	0,9	64,3	0,6	60,0	0,7	43,8	0,9	64,3
30 – 34	1,1	61,1	1,1	52,4	1,1	68,8	0,7	63,6	1,0	58,8	0,9	50,0
35 – 39	1,7	68,0	1,6	59,3	1,5	68,2	1,0	66,7	1,4	66,7	1,9	111,8
40 – 44	2,3	67,6	2,3	59,0	2,2	62,9	1,8	75,0	2,1	61,8	2,9	80,6
45 – 49	3,7	67,3	3,6	54,5	3,3	60,0	2,7	67,5	3,4	54,8	3,6	52,2
50 – 54	5,3	55,8	5,3	48,2	5,0	54,9	4,2	58,3	5,0	47,2	5,7	49,6
55 – 59	8,3	50,9	7,7	45,6	7,8	52,0	6,9	57,0	8,3	46,6	8,3	53,9
60 – 64	14,0	52,0	12,0	46,9	12,8	58,2	10,8	57,1	14,2	51,4	13,4	54,9
65 – 69	24,8	60,0	19,9	53,2	22,5	62,8	18,9	63,2	23,9	58,4	24,2	63,0
70 – 74	44,7	70,3	34,0	58,7	39,4	75,2	36,5	80,2	43,4	68,2	49,2	72,6
75 – 79	81,6	80,6	60,9	65,8	72,1	85,2	65,7	87,3	76,4	76,5	81,6	84,1
80 – 84	140,7	86,5	108,9	72,9	128,2	90,1	114,7	89,8	127,9	80,4	134,6	81,5
85 +	254,8	92,2	206,3	79,8	240,0	97,0	210,3	92,1	229,2	80,4	223,5	108,1
1970												
TOTAL	11,5	89,8	10,1	90,2	8,9	84,0	7,4	78,7	11,3	85,0	10,8	78,8
< 1	19,8	74,7	13,3	76,4	25,7	79,6	11,0	76,9	18,2	73,7	22,0	78,0
1 – 4	0,9	81,8	0,7	77,8	0,8	80,0	0,7	77,8	0,8	80,0	0,9	100,0
5 – 9	0,4	66,7	0,3	60,0	0,3	60,0	0,3	50,0	0,3	50,0	0,2	25,0
10 – 14	0,3	60,0	0,3	75,0	0,3	60,0	0,3	60,0	0,3	60,0	0,3	60,0
15 – 19	0,6	40,0	0,5	41,7	0,4	40,0	0,5	50,0	0,4	36,4	0,7	46,7
20 – 24	0,6	33,3	0,6	37,5	0,5	41,7	0,5	45,5	0,5	35,7	1,1	57,9
25 – 29	0,7	43,8	0,7	43,8	0,6	54,4	0,5	50,0	0,6	46,2	0,9	42,8
30 – 34	0,9	47,4	0,9	47,4	0,8	61,5	0,7	63,6	0,9	60,0	1,2	52,2
35 – 39	1,4	56,0	1,4	51,9	1,2	60,0	1,0	66,7	1,4	60,9	1,5	71,4
40 – 44	2,2	59,5	2,0	47,6	1,7	51,5	1,6	61,5	2,1	61,8	2,8	57,1
45 – 49	3,6	62,1	3,2	50,8	2,8	50,9	2,8	63,6	3,4	60,7	3,6	64,3
50 – 54	5,4	58,1	4,5	47,4	4,7	52,8	4,2	52,5	4,7	51,1	5,7	43,8
55 – 59	7,8	51,0	6,7	44,4	6,6	49,3	6,3	46,0	8,2	48,0	9,1	44,8
60 – 64	12,8	48,1	9,9	41,6	11,6	49,6	10,3	45,4	13,1	47,1	13,0	48,0
65 – 69	22,6	50,9	16,4	45,2	19,3	51,5	17,6	49,7	22,4	50,9	26,3	61,0
70 – 74	40,4	58,2	28,0	49,6	34,3	58,1	32,1	59,9	38,5	59,5	36,5	51,3
75 – 79	71,6	69,9	51,4	61,9	63,3	72,0	56,8	70,0	67,9	69,6	72,0	74,3
80 – 84	123,6	81,3	90,5	74,4	141,8	85,6	101,1	81,7	115,7	79,5	116,7	75,1
85 +	223,9	89,1	186,3	82,6			195,8	89,4	210,3	84,8	201,1	84,4
	1975		**1972**		**1972**		**1975**		**1974**		**1974**	
TOTAL	11,7	93,2	10,0	89,3	8,8	83,0	7,3	78,5	11,0	85,9	11,1	84,7
< 1	17,1	76,7	11,7	77,5	23,6	78,4	9,0	75,6	14,7	75,4	8,5	46,4
1 – 4	0,6	85,7	0,6	66,7	0,7	77,8	0,6	75,0	0,7	87,5	0,9	56,3
5 – 9	0,3	60,0	0,3	60,0	0,3	60,0	0,3	75,0	0,3	75,0	0,2	22,2
10 – 14	0,3	75,0	0,3	75,0	0,3	60,0	0,2	50,0	0,3	60,0	0,1	50,0
15 – 19	0,6	40,0	0,6	46,2	0,4	36,4	0,3	37,5	0,5	41,7	0,5	33,3
20 – 24	0,6	75,0	0,7	38,9	0,5	41,7	0,3	33,3	0,6	37,5	0,3	14,3
25 – 29	0,6	42,9	0,7	43,8	0,6	54,5	0,4	50,0	0,6	50,0	0,4	28,6
30 – 34	0,9	50,0	0,9	47,4	0,8	61,5	0,7	70,0	0,8	53,3	0,9	33,3
35 – 39	1,3	54,2	1,4	51,9	1,1	55,0	0,9	69,2	1,2	63,2	0,6	13,6
40 – 44	2,0	51,3	2,1	48,8	1,8	46,9	1,6	69,6	1,9	61,3	2,2	37,3
45 – 49	3,2	54,9	3,1	47,0	2,8	50,0	2,5	56,8	3,1	56,4	3,8	64,4
50 – 54	5,0	53,2	4,5	45,9	4,7	52,2	3,9	51,3	5,1	57,3	5,7	54,3
55 – 59	7,2	49,3	6,7	43,2	6,5	48,5	5,7	43,8	7,3	48,0	10,6	53,8
60 – 64	11,6	47,3	9,9	42,7	11,2	48,7	9,3	43,9	11,6	45,1	14,4	52,2
65 – 69	20,1	48,6	16,0	43,8	18,9	49,9	15,5	43,7	19,4	46,5	22,2	53,8
70 – 74	36,5	55,0	27,3	49,5	33,9	56,5	28,2	52,2	34,6	53,6	44,0	60,4
75 – 79	66,7	64,8	49,8	60,4	61,0	67,3	51,0	61,8	64,3	68,5	71,7	71,2
80 – 84	116,7	75,5	87,6	68,7	134,7	82,6	92,2	73,2	109,9	76,6	112,2	75,5
85 +	214,0	85,9	176,6	79,9			185,6	83,8	205,8	86,1	193,7	80,4

TAB. 9

Specific female mortality rates and comparison with the male rates
Taux spécifiques de mortalité féminine et comparaison avec les taux masculins

| United Kingdom | | | | | | Ireland | | Danmark | | |
| England Wales | | Northern Ireland | | Scotland | | | | | | |
q_f	$\frac{q_f}{q_m}100$	q_f	$\frac{q_f}{q_m}100$	q_f	$\frac{q_f}{q_m}100$	q_f	$\frac{q_f}{q_m}100$	q_f	$\frac{q_f}{q_m}100$	
1960										
10,9	89,3	10,2	89,5	11,1	88,1	11,4	86,4	8,9	88,1	TOTAL
19,9	76,8	25,7	81,6	24,2	77,1	26,0	81,3	19,4	79,2	< 1
0,8	88,9	1,1	91,7	0,9	75,0	1,3	92,9	0,7	63,6	1 - 4
0,3	60,0	0,4	66,7	0,5	83,3	0,4	80,0	0,3	60,0	5 - 9
0,3	75,0	0,2	50,0	0,3	60,0	0,4	100,0	0,2	50,0	10 - 14
0,4	44,4	0,3	33,3	0,4	57,1	0,3	50,0	0,3	37,5	15 - 19
0,4	33,3	0,4	36,4	0,5	45,5	0,6	60,0	0,3	30,0	20 - 24
0,6	60,0	0,7	63,6	0,8	61,5	0,9	75,0	0,6	50,0	25 - 29
0,9	75,0	0,9	60,0	1,0	62,5	1,4	87,5	1,0	71,4	30 - 34
1,4	73,7	1,6	88,9	1,8	81,8	2,0	87,0	1,5	88,2	35 - 39
2,2	73,3	2,6	78,8	2,6	70,3	2,4	70,6	2,2	91,7	40 - 44
3,4	65,4	4,5	80,4	4,1	65,1	4,1	75,9	3,2	72,7	45 - 49
5,3	57,0	6,5	85,0	6,5	54,6	6,8	70,8	5,1	69,9	50 - 54
8,1	48,5	2,3	57,1	10,0	49,8	9,5	62,9	8,0	65,0	55 - 59
13,5	49,3	16,9	58,9	16,4	51,4	16,0	64,3	12,9	65,8	60 - 64
22,4	52,3	25,8	65,8	28,3	59,2	26,9	67,3	21,1	66,6	65 - 69
38,1	57,9	48,6	72,3	47,0	64,6	46,2	75,1	39,6	78,7	70 - 74
68,0	66,9	79,8	77,9	77,2	73,2	78,4	80,6	71,6	85,0	75 - 79
113,1	73,0	112,3	82,6	133,1	80,1	138,0	82,3	126,0	92,4	80 - 84
205,4	88,5	266,0	80,9	236,5	101,8	245,8	84,4	228,3	96,2	85 +
1970										
11,2	91,1	9,8	86,0	11,1	88,1	10,4	83,2	8,9	83,2	TOTAL
16,2	76,8	20,9	84,3	17,6	78,6	4,3	84,3	11,1	62,4	< 1
0,6	75,0	0,7	77,8	0,6	75,0			0,5	55,6	1 - 4
0,3	75,0	0,2	40,0	0,3	75,0	0,3	75,0	0,4	80,0	5 - 9
0,2	50,0	0,2	50,0	0,3	60,0	0,3	37,5	0,2	50,0	10 - 14
0,3	33,3	0,4	40,0	0,3	30,0	0,5	62,5	0,5	55,6	15 - 19
0,4	40,0	0,3	23,1	0,3	25,0	0,5	45,5	0,5	50,0	20 - 24
0,5	55,6	0,6	60,0	0,6	54,5	0,6	54,5	0,5	45,5	25 - 29
0,7	63,6	0,6	42,9	0,8	61,5	0,7	53,8	0,9	75,0	30 - 34
1,1	73,3	1,2	57,1	1,5	75,0	1,4	73,7	1,3	72,2	35 - 39
2,1	72,4	2,4	70,6	2,5	65,8	2,6	74,3	2,1	75,0	40 - 44
3,5	67,3	3,5	61,4	4,3	60,6	3,9	66,1	3,3	66,0	45 - 49
5,3	58,2	5,1	53,7	6,6	60,6	6,3	67,7	5,6	71,8	50 - 54
7,9	49,7	9,2	58,6	9,9	54,7	9,3	58,5	7,4	57,8	55 - 59
12,7	47,7	12,6	44,7	15,2	52,8	16,7	63,7	12,1	58,7	60 - 64
21,3	48,4	22,0	50,5	23,6	49,8	24,4	56,6	18,7	55,8	65 - 69
35,9	52,6	40,8	63,4	38,9	54,2	42,3	66,4	32,2	59,4	70 - 74
60,2	58,9	62,9	64,8	65,5	62,3	65,3	71,2	53,4	69,1	75 - 79
101,7	67,6	110,8	72,5	102,5	68,7	117,5	81,8	96,5	80,8	80 - 84
203,3	80,3	226,3	81,3	205,7	83,7	245,3	82,5	183,3	87,0	85 +
1974		**1975**		**1975**		**1973**		**1973**		
11,5	93,5	10,1	88,6	11,5	89,8	10,2	83,6	9,0	81,1	TOTAL
13,9	74,7	4,2	89,4	3,3	80,5	3,7	75,5	10,0	79,4	< 1
0,7	100,0							0,4	57,1	1 - 4
0,2	50,0	0,3	50,0	0,3	60,0	0,2	66,7	0,3	50,0	5 - 9
0,3	100,0	0,2	33,3	0,2	50,0	0,2	66,7	0,3	75,0	10 - 14
0,4	44,4	0,5	38,5	0,4	44,4	0,3	33,3	0,4	40,0	15 - 19
0,4	40,0	0,4	22,2	0,4	33,3	0,5	35,7	0,4	33,3	20 - 24
0,5	55,6	0,4	21,1	0,6	60,0	0,6	50,0	0,5	55,6	25 - 29
0,6	54,5	0,9	42,9	0,8	53,3	0,8	57,1	0,8	66,7	30 - 34
1,1	73,3	1,2	57,1	1,4	65,5	1,4	60,9	1,3	65,0	35 - 39
1,9	67,9	2,1	58,3	2,5	69,4	2,1	60,0	2,5	89,3	40 - 44
3,4	65,4	4,0	62,5	3,8	55,9	4,3	75,4	3,7	74,0	45 - 49
5,2	56,5	4,9	48,0	6,3	58,3	6,4	64,0	4,6	56,1	50 - 54
8,2	53,2	9,4	58,0	9,9	55,3	8,9	57,8	7,4	56,5	55 - 59
12,4	51,8	14,5	52,9	15,0	52,4	15,3	59,5	11,2	53,1	60 - 64
20,0	48,9	22,3	52,1	22,9	49,1	23,6	59,0	17,7	50,7	65 - 69
34,3	51,8	38,0	58,6	36,9	51,8	41,2	64,8	29,1	54,3	70 - 74
58,3	59,6	64,2	64,1	62,0	59,8	70,4	71,4	52,6	65,9	75 - 79
101,6	68,1	115,6	71,2	103,7	64,7	121,8	77,1	90,4	75,0	80 - 84
194,3	80,1	223,4	72,9	194,0	80,3	230,1	87,0	180,0	83,8	85 +

TAB. 10

Average life expectancy at various ages and difference between average female and male life expectancy

Espérance de vie aux différents âges et différence entre l'espérance de vie de la femme et l'espérance de vie de l'homme

EUR 9	1951		1961		1971					
	l_F	$l_F - l_M$	l_F	$l_F - l_M$	l_F	$l_F - l_M$	l_F	$l_F - l_M$	l_F	$l_F - l_M$
0	68,3	4,3	73,7	6,1	75,1	6,5				
1	70,5	3,8	74,1	5,2	75,3	6,1				
10	63,1	3,6	65,6	5,2	66,7	6,1				
50	26,1	3,0	27,5	4,1	28,5	4,9				

BR Deutschland	1949 – 1951		1960 – 1962		1970 – 1972		1973 – 1975		1977	
	l_F	$l_F - l_M$	l_F	$l_F - l_M$	l_F	$l_F - l_M$	l_F	$l_F - l_M$	l_F	$l_F - l_M$
0	68,48	3,92	72,39	5,53	73,83	6,42	74,54	6,50		
1	71,01	3,21	73,46	5,15	74,32	6,12	74,91	6,21		
10	62,84	3,08	64,93	5,05	65,70	6,02	66,25	6,15		
50	25,75	2,00	27,00	3,90	27,65	4,60	28,10	4,80		

France	1950		1960		1970		1975		1977	
	l_F	$l_F - l_M$	l_F	$l_F - l_M$	l_F	$l_F - l_M$	l_F	$l_F - l_M$	l_F	$l_F - l_M$
0	68,5	5,6	73,6	6,7	75,9	7,6	76,9	7,9		
1	71,1	4,9	74,3	6,3	76,1	7,3	76,8	7,7		
10	63,1	4,9	65,7	6,2	67,4	7,2	68,1	7,7		
50	26,5	3,9	27,9	5,0	29,4	5,7	29,9	5,9		

Italia	1950 – 1953		1960 – 1962		1970 – 1972					
	l_F	$l_F - l_M$	l_F	$l_F - l_M$	l_F	$l_F - l_M$	l_F	$l_F - l_M$	l_F	$l_F - l_M$
0	67,24	3,49	72,27	5,03	74,88	5,91				
1	70,41	3,08	74,10	4,66	75,76	5,62				
10	62,87	3,07	65,80	4,61	67,13	5,57				
50	25,79	2,27	27,82	3,53	28,81	4,40				

Nederland	1950 – 1952		1960		1970		1975		1977	
	l_F	$l_F - l_M$	l_F	$l_F - l_M$	l_F	$l_F - l_M$	l_F	$l_F - l_M$	l_F	$l_F - l_M$
0	72,9	2,3	75,3	3,8	76,5	5,8	77,6	6,2		
1	73,5	1,9	75,4	3,6	76,3	5,5	77,4	6,1		
10	65,1	1,7	66,9	3,5	67,7	5,4	68,7	6,1		
50	27,1	1,2	28,4	2,7	29,2	4,5	30,1	5,3		

Belgique/België	1946 – 1949		1959 – 1963		1968 – 1972					
	l_F	$l_F - l_M$	l_F	$l_F - l_M$	l_F	$l_F - l_M$	l_F	$l_F - l_M$	l_F	$l_F - l_M$
0	66,75	5,36	73,04	5,88	74,21	6,42				
1	69,72	4,47	73,90	5,51	74,53	6,09				
10	61,71	4,35	65,32	5,45	65,88	6,02				
50	25,47	2,95	27,20	4,27	27,69	4,90				

Luxembourg	1946 – 1948		1960		1971 – 1973		1972 – 1974		1977	
	l_F	$l_F - l_M$	l_F	$l_F - l_M$	l_F	$l_F - l_M$	l_F	$l_F - l_M$	l_F	$l_F - l_M$
0	65,7	4,0	71,9	5,8	73,9	6,9	74,5	7,2		
1	68,6	3,4	73,6	5,8	73,9	6,5	74,1	6,6		
10	60,8	3,4	64,7	4,9	65,3	6,3	65,5	6,5		
50	24,7	2,5	26,8	3,6	27,4	5,3	27,5	5,1		

United Kingdom	1950 – 1952		1960 – 1962		1970 – 1972		1973 – 1975		1977	
	l_F	$l_F - l_M$	l_F	$l_F - l_M$	l_F	$l_F - l_M$	l_F	$l_F - l_M$	l_F	$l_F - l_M$
0	71,2	5,0	73,7	5,8	75,0	6,3	75,5	6,3		
1	72,1	4,6	74,2	5,5	75,2	6,1	75,6	6,1		
10	63,6	4,5	65,5	5,4	66,5	6,0	66,9	6,1		
50	26,2	4,0	27,3	4,7	28,2	5,3	28,6	5,3		

Ireland	1950 – 1952		1960 – 1962		1965 – 1967		1970 – 1972		1977	
	l_F	$l_F - l_M$	l_F	$l_F - l_M$	l_F	$l_F - l_M$	l_F	$l_F - l_M$	l_F	$l_F - l_M$
0	67,1	2,6	71,9	3,8	72,9	4,3	73,5	4,7		
1	68,8	1,9	72,7	3,4	73,4	3,9	73,8	4,6		
10	60,6	1,8	64,1	3,3	64,8	4,0	65,1	4,5		
50	24,7	1,9	26,3	2,8	26,6	3,2	27,0	3,7		

Danmark	1961 – 1962		1970 – 1971		1972 – 1973		1974 – 1975		1976 – 1977	
	l_F	$l_F - l_M$	l_F	$l_F - l_M$	l_F	$l_F - l_M$	l_F	$l_F - l_M$	l_F	$l_F - l_M$
0	74,4	4,0	75,9	5,2	76,3	5,5	76,8	5,7	77,1	5,9
1	74,8	3,7	75,9	4,9	76,1	5,3	76,6	5,5	76,7	5,6
10	66,1	3,5	67,2	4,8	67,4	5,2	67,8	5,5	67,9	5,5
50	27,9	2,9	29,1	4,1	29,2	4,4	29,5	4,6	29,7	4,7

Life expectancy: Further number of years which a person can expect to live at each year of age.

Espérance de vie: Nombre moyen d'années restant à vivre à une personne à un âge donné.

TAB. 11

Average age of brides at marriage and difference between average age of brides and grooms (first marriage)
Age moyen au moment du mariage des épouses, et différence entre l'âge moyen des épouses et des époux (premier mariage)

	BR Deutschland		France		Italia		Nederland		Belgique/ België		Luxem-bourg [1]		United Kingdom [2]		Ireland		Danmark	
	F	M–F	F	M–F	F	M–F	F	M–F	F	M–F	F	M–F	F	M–F	F	M–F	F	M–F
1960	23,7	2,2	23,5	2,6	24,8	3,8	24,5	2,3	23,4	2,5	:	:	23,3	2,4	26,0	3,7	22,9	3,1
1970	23,0	2,6	22,4	2,0	24,1	3,4	22,9	1,9	22,4	2,2	23,2	3,1	22,4	2,0	24,3	2,5	22,8	2,3
1975	22,7	2,6	22,5	2,1	24,0	3,2	22,7	2,1	22,0	2,3	23,3	2,9	22,7	2,1	23,9	2,2	23,7	2,6
1977	22,9 (3)	2,7	22,6 (3)	2,1	:	:	22,8	2,3	22,0 (3)	2,4	23,6	2,9	22,9	2,2	:	:	24,0	2,7

(1) All marriages.
(1) Ensemble des mariages.
(2) England and Wales only.
(2) Angleterre et pays de Galles seulement.
(3) 1976.

TAB. 12

Divorce rate (per thousand inhabitants)
Taux de divorce (pour 1 000 habitants)

	BR Deutschland	France	Italia	Nederland	Belgique België	Luxembourg	United Kingdom	Ireland	Danmark
1960	0,9	0,6	–	0,5	0,5	0,5	0,5	–	1,5
1970	1,3	0,8	–	0,8	0,7	0,6	1,1	–	1,9
1975	1,7	1,2	0,2	1,5	1,3	0,8	2,3	–	2,6
1977	1,8	1,2	0,2	1,6	1,3	1,2	2,4	–	2,6

TAB. 13

Projections of the female population by broad age groups
Projections de la population féminine par grand groupe d'âge

	1980 f	1980 $\frac{f}{f+m}100$	1985 f	1985 $\frac{f}{f+m}100$	1990 f	1990 $\frac{f}{f+m}100$	1995 f	1995 $\frac{f}{f+m}100$	2000 f	2000 $\frac{f}{f+m}100$
BR Deutschland										
0 – 14	4 963	48,9	4 013	48,9	3 915	48,9	:	:	3 807	48,9
15 – 44	12 114	49,2	12 113	49,1	11 543	49,1	:	:	} 17 831	} 49,8
45 – 64	7 072	55,1	7 762	53,2	7 599	51,3	:	:		
65 +	5 975	64,3	5 565	66,6	5 696	67,5	:	:	5 352	63,4
Total	30 124	52,9	29 453	52,8	28 753	52,5	:	:	26 989	51,9
France										
0 – 14	6 257	48,9	6 336	48,9	6 345	48,9	6 286	48,9	6 274	48,9
15 – 44	10 994	49,0	11 519	49,1	12 160	49,2	12 306	49,3	12 367	49,2
45 – 64	5 671	50,8	6 144	50,5	5 864	50,0	6 182	49,8	6 579	49,8
65 +	4 454	59,8	4 097	59,7	4 367	58,4	4 569	57,2	4 731	56,1
Total	27 376	50,8	28 096	50,7	28 736	50,5	29 343	50,4	29 951	50,3
Italia										
0 – 14	6 313	48,7	6 150	48,8	6 251	48,8	6 268	48,8	6 331	48,8
15 – 44	11 783	49,6	12 024	49,3	12 245	49,1	12 050	49,3	12 212	49,3
45 – 64	6 593	52,1	7 158	52,0	7 011	51,8	6 946	51,5	6 895	51,4
65 +	4 328	58,2	4 189	58,9	4 544	59,0	5 206	59,5	5 500	59,8
Total	29 017	51,1	29 521	50,6	30 051	51,0	30 470	51,2	30 938	51,2
Nederland										
0 – 14	1 508	48,9	1 311	48,9	1 204	48,9	1 199	48,9	1 180	48,9
15 – 44	3 105	48,6	3 296	48,8	3 365	49,0	3 197	49,1	3 036	49,1
45 – 64	1 426	51,2	1 470	50,6	1 513	49,8	1 693	49,3	1 848	49,4
65 +	928	58,4	987	59,1	1 073	59,5	1 121	59,5	1 153	59,1
Total	6 967	50,3	7 064	50,4	7 155	50,5	7 210	50,5	7 217	50,5
Belgique/België										
0 – 14	975	48,8	877	48,6	794	48,6	743	48,6	701	48,6
15 – 44	2 075	48,9	2 165	48,7	2 245	48,6	2 214	48,5	2 137	48,4
45 – 64	1 139	51,3	1 199	51,4	1 138	51,2	1 159	50,8	1 205	50,3
65 +	821	59,8	746	60,4	770	59,9	785	59,5	799	59,3
Total	5 010	50,9	4 987	50,8	4 947	50,7	4 901	50,5	4 842	50,5
Luxembourg										
0 – 14	32	48,6	30	49,3	29	48,5	29	49,4	27	48,3
15 – 44	76	48,1	76	48,1	75	48,7	72	48,9	69	49,3
45 – 64	43	51,3	45	50,3	45	49,3	45	48,8	46	48,9
65 +	29	59,9	28	61,7	28	61,5	29	60,2	30	59,8
Total	180	50,6	179	50,6	177	50,5	175	50,5	172	50,6
United Kingdom										
0 – 14	5 633	48,6	5 220	48,6	5 447	48,6	6 011	48,6	6 145	48,6
15 – 44	11 485	49,1	12 002	49,0	12 136	48,9	11 594	48,8	11 491	48,8
45 – 64	6 392	51,3	6 274	50,9	6 101	50,6	6 418	50,5	6 625	50,4
65 +	5 049	60,9	5 053	61,0	5 160	60,7	5 083	60,4	4 929	60,4
Total	28 559	51,2	28 549	51,1	28 844	51,0	29 106	50,9	29 190	50,7
Ireland										
0 – 14	500	48,7	518	48,7	:	:	:	:	:	:
15 – 44	667	49,1	735	49,0	:	:	:	:	:	:
45 – 64	298	50,7	295	50,6	:	:	:	:	:	:
65 +	198	54,9	206	55,7	:	:	:	:	:	:
Total	1 663	49,9	1 754	49,9	:	:	:	:	:	:
Danmark										
0 – 14	537	48,9	514	48,9	510	48,9	515	48,9	511	48,9
15 – 44	1 078	49,0	1 120	48,9	1 118	49,0	1 082	49,2	1 069	49,2
45 – 64	558	51,1	555	51,0	571	50,5	626	50,1	663	50,0
65 +	423	57,7	449	58,6	470	59,1	469	59,4	458	59,5
Total	2 596	50,6	2 638	50,8	2 669	50,8	2 691	50,8	2 701	50,8

Mortalité groupe de cause

SECTION III

Female mortality by cause
Mortalité féminine par cause

TAB. 14

Mortality by groups of causes
Mortalité par groupe de causes

WHO Nomenclature		BR Deutschland		France		Italia		Nederland		Belgique/België	
		q_F	$\frac{q_F}{q_M}100$	q_F	$\frac{q_F}{q_M}100$	q_F	$\frac{q_F}{q_M}100$	q_F	$\frac{q_F}{q_M}100$	q_F	$\frac{q_F}{q_M}100$
000 – 136 Infective and parasitic diseases	1960	12,9	40,7	19,0	45,2	18,2	48,4	6,1	72,6	11,7	33,9
	1970	9,3	51,4	11,5	67,6	13,1	58,0	6,1	92,4	9,4	59,1
	1975	8,1	60,4	13,1	76,6	10,3	55,1	5,5	98,2	6,8	59,1
	1976	7,5	61,0	13,7	78,7			4,5	97,8		
140 – 239 Neoplasms	1960	213,0	91,7	191,1	86,6	141,3	85,3	158,6	83,7	208,1	85,4
	1970	236,3	92,8	185,8	75,1	158,0	74,1	174,2	76,1	214,4	76,5
	1975	249,5	88,9	190,0	70,9	164,1	73,4	179,9	61,6	211,7	72,4
	1976	248,8	92,1	189,5	68,0			74,1	69,1		
of which: **174** malignant tumour of breast	1960	25,4	–	25,2	–	19,0	–	29,7	–	:	–
	1970	31,7	–	27,4	–	24,6	–	34,7	–	37,1	–
	1975	35,0	–	29,8	–	26,5	–	36,4	–	36,5	–
	1976										
180 – 182 malignant tumour of uterus	1960	19,0	–	19,1	–	:	–	6,1	–	11,5	–
	1970	18,8	–	16,0	–	:	–	6,2	–	8,8	–
	1975	18,0	–	15,6	–	:	–	5,6	–	7,8	–
	1976										
410 – 414 Ischaemic heart disease	1960	66,1	46,9	44,6	61,7	:	:	77,1	56,0	:	:
	1970	137,1	63,8	67,2	70,6	118,3	78,9	131,9	57,1	138,1	60,4
	1975	184,8	74,2	76,2	72,6	121,5	79,8	135,6	59,0	137,1	62,1
	1976	194,8	75,4	79,5	72,7			140,1	59,0		
430 – 438 Cerebrovascular disease	1960	185,4	111,6	147,5	117,5	131,9	98,5	101,0	119,4	78,6	104,1
	1970	194,6	125,1	161,0	122,0	135,7	106,4	105,5	118,8	179,2	118,5
	1975	192,6	133,9	162,0	125,6	135,5	109,6	100,5	118,5	176,3	124,9
	1976	192,3	134,9	157,7	127,7			98,2	120,6		
390 – 458 Other diseases of the circulatory system	1960	192,1	112,5	203,0	113,1	:	:	139,0	115,4	389,5	86,2
	1970	205,2	127,2	176,0	117,7	190,1	122,2	109,0	113,1	336,7	82,2
	1975	197,8	131,1	160,1	116,7	189,5	122,2	102,1	111,5	183,0	107,5
	1976										
460 – 519 Diseases of the respiratory system	1960	83,7	67,9	91,0	93,8	77,1	78,3	43,0	68,8	75,2	68,8
	1970	74,6	61,7	64,4	87,1	79,0	71,6	44,7	59,6	66,5	65,5
	1975	61,9	60,9	62,2	81,4	62,1	64,8	35,5	50,1	53,1	
	1976										
520 – 577 Diseases of the digestive system	1960	56,8	77,2	36,0	50,7	46,0	64,2	25,2	89,7	36,3	78,4
	1970	57,2	75,4	50,2	64,4	40,7	54,3	24,6	94,6	37,8	87,1
	1975	56,9	71,8	50,8	63,8	42,4	53,1	25,1	93,7	39,0	89,2
	1976										
000 – 786 Other diseases	1960	191,3	85,2	307,0	99,4	:	:	89,4	90,4	:	:
	1970	168,4	101,0	222,9	107,9	124,3	99,8	77,7	96,8	202,6	103,5
	1975	159,2	106,3	:	:	119,6	98,3	72,7	103,3	233,1	182,1
	1976										
E800 – E999 External causes of injury	1960	49,1	45,8	43,6	57,8	24,1	34,1	28,6	48,6	45,3	47,7
	1970	65,4	57,5	69,0	58,7	31,1	40,8	45,2	63,4	64,8	60,8
	1975	59,4	61,7	71,1	61,8	34,8	44,7	40,5	69,5	63,1	64,8
	1976										
E800 – E807 E830 – E949 All other accidents	1960	25,4	68,5	35,0	74,3	14,7	47,0	16,1	66,5	:	:
	1970	32,0	95,5	46,4	81,1	16,0	60,6	25,9	107,9	:	:
	1975	29,8	96,4	48,4	94,5	19,6	73,4	23,3	109,4	:	:
	1976										
E950 – E959 Suicide and self-inflicted injuries	1960	13,3	50,6	8,2	34,2	3,7	43,0	5,1	62,2	8,0	37,6
	1970	15,2	53,3	8,6	37,7	3,5	43,2	6,2	62,6	11,3	51,6
	1975	14,6	52,7	8,8	38,8	3,6	43,9	7,0	64,8	10,1	47,4
	1976	14,9	51,2	9,0	39,5			7,0	58,8		
000 – 999 All causes	1960	1050,5	82,7	1082,8	95,6	880,9	84,8	696,9	84,3	1129,9	83,2
	1970	1147,9	89,6	1008,0	90,0	890,5	84,4	743,6	79,3	1131,7	85,0
	1975	1169,8	93,0	990,0	89,2	880,0	83,9	731,7	78,4	1103,6	86,4
	1976	1151,0	93,6	1119,9	113,2			729,7	78,2		

q_F: number of female deaths per 100 000 females.
q_F: nombre de femmes décédées pour 100 000 femmes.

q_M: number of male deaths per 100 000 males.
q_M: nombre d'hommes décédés pour 100 000 hommes.

TAB. 14

Mortality by groups of causes
Mortalité par groupe de causes

Luxembourg qF	Luxembourg qF/qM·100	United Kingdom qF	United Kingdom qF/qM·100	Ireland qF	Ireland qF/qM·100	Danmark qF	Danmark qF/qM·100		Nomenclature OMS
									000 – 136
16,0	61,5	8,1	47,1	17,5	65,8	7,2	71,3	1960	Maladies infectieuses et parasitaires
7,0	87,5	5,9	62,1	12,2	71,3	6,5	90,3	1970	
6,0	120,0	5,4	69,2	7,9	58,5	4,3	78,2	1975	
6,0	100,0	4,8	72,7	8,6	71,7	4,0	67,8	1976	
									140 – 239
191,0	81,3	196,4	82,0	162,2	88,8	213,4	98,1	1960	Néoplasmes
202,0	67,6	214,1	80,4	177,9	86,8	219,7	94,3	1970	
224,0	75,9	233,5	84,8	176,7	84,9	227,6	90,9	1975	
207,0	65,3	231,5	82,2	181,0	81,7	241,7	93,6	1976	
									dont:
									174
:	–	37,6	–	25,4	–	33,8	–	1960	tumeurs malignes du sein
34,6	–	42,2	–	27,6	–	40,5	–	1970	
32,7	–	43,8	–	32,4	–	40,9	–	1975	
								1976	
									180 – 182
:	–	17,2	–	5,1	–	25,3	–	1960	tumeurs malignes de l'utérus
:	–	15,1	–	5,5	–	20,1	–	1970	
:	–	14,4	–	4,2	–	20,1	–	1975	
								1976	
									410 – 414
:	:	276,8	80,8	312,5	80,7	167,5	65,2	1960	Maladies ischémiques du cœur
90,0	50,6	237,9	68,4	202,2	62,4	238,8	66,8	1970	
90,0	48,1	263,2	70,7	218,0	63,4	262,1	68,3	1975	
85,0	47,8	272,3	72,3	219,9	64,9	280,8	69,4	1976	
									430 – 438
84,0	87,5	192,2	134,3	148,8	123,0	125,0	116,6	1960	Maladies cérébrovasculaires
120,0	106,2	196,2	147,7	167,5	116,7	114,3	114,2	1970	
165,0	132,0	195,7	151,1	170,1	120,0	102,0	114,5	1975	
146,0	116,8	188,5	153,6	158,0	126,5	101,6	106,8	1976	
									390 – 458
:	:	139,9	122,2	89,0	94,7	–	–		Autres maladies de l'appareil
:	:	167,0	135,3	155,1	105,2	88,1	110,4	1960	circulatoire
		159,9	137,3	141,6	110,2	88,4	108,7	1970	
								1975	
								1976	
									460 – 519
–	–	94,1	59,7	83,6	72,2	42,5	87,8	1960	Maladies des voies respiratoires
43,0	65,2	145,8	72,7	148,0	74,2	45,7	62,0	1970	
37,0	48,1	141,0	79,5	138,0	79,4	56,3	68,4	1975	
								1976	
									520 – 577
:	:	29,6	84,6	26,5	82,3	42,4	112,2	1960	Maladies de l'appareil digestif
44,0	75,9	27,8	102,2	21,2	81,2	30,7	97,8	1970	
40,0	64,5	31,1	104,7	22,0	77,7	28,6	85,4	1975	
								1976	
									000 – 786
:	:	108,9	98,6	214,9	97,9	246,7	97,5	1960	Autres maladies
:	:	89,9	110,4	118,3	96,9	92,6	94,7	1970	
58,4	121,9	89,7	116,5	110,1	95,8	85,2	90,7	1975	
								1976	
									E800 – E999
31,0	35,6	40,3	65,1	25,0	54,0	49,2	60,9	1960	Accidents et autres causes
58,0	44,6	40,2	72,8	35,8	59,7	55,4	62,5	1970	extérieures
54,0	46,9	38,9	72,8	35,5	52,1	50,0	61,3	1975	
								1976	
									E800 – E807 E830 – E949
16,0	48,5	23,8	91,2	19,1	67,0	27,6	89,6	1960	Autres accidents
17,0	42,5	24,7	102,5	26,2	78,2	21,9	89,4	1970	
29,0	80,6	23,5	104,4	25,3	80,6	17,4	75,3	1975	
								1976	
									E950 – E 959
4,0	23,5	8,2	61,7	1,8	43,9	13,6	50,2	1960	Suicides et blessures causés
7,0	31,8	6,5	68,4	0,5	16,7	15,7	57,3	1970	par soi-même
6,0	42,9	6,3	67,7	1,9	38,0	18,4	61,5	1975	
10,0	43,5	5,9	61,5	3,4	42,0	17,7	58,6	1976	
									000 – 999
1061,0	81,5	1086,4	88,9	1080,1	88,2	894,1	88,3	1960	Toutes causes
1076,0	78,3	1124,8	90,4	1038,1	83,4	891,9	83,4	1970	
1131,0	86,2	1148,2	92,7	1019,9	83,6	904,4	82,1	1975	
994,0	78,3	1181,1	94,2	987,6	84,8	965,8	82,9	1976	

TAB. 15

Deaths from malignant tumour of breast: mortality rates by age

Mortalité due aux tumeurs malignes du sein: taux de mortalité par âge

A – Periods 1965 – 1969 and 1972 – 1973   A – Périodes 1965 – 1969 et 1972 – 1973

	TOTAL		35 – 44		45 – 54		55 – 64		65 – 74		75 +	
	1965–69	1972–73	1965–69	1972–73	1965–69	1972–73	1965–69	1972–73	1965–69	1972–73	1965–69	1972–73
BR Deutschland	30,2	33,6	15,9	16,9	41,3	44,5	61,9	69,2	82,6	87,4	135,1	141,8
France	27,6	28,9	13,2	14,3	37,8	40,4	58,0	64,7	77,4	80,2	133,3	124,5
Italia	22,9	26,6	16,8	17,9	39,4	43,9	54,9	60,4	71,7	79,6	101,3	116,3
Nederland	34,3	37,0	22,8	24,2	60,7	61,4	87,1	92,7	113,9	118,6	208,2	207,5
Belgique/België	34,2	37,0	19,3	21,1	51,8	53,7	68,4	76,0	92,3	102,1	156,5	154,7
Luxembourg	:	29,7	:	33,5	:	43,1	:	67,4	:	56,5	:	108,7
United Kingdom												
England and Wales	40,7	45,2	22,2	25,3	58,3	66,6	87,6	91,3	107,3	121,8	162,3	170,3
Scotland	37,2	42,6	21,9	32,6	57,4	66,1	79,2	90,0	106,4	113,5	161,4	162,8
Ireland	28,9	:	24,1	:	55,5	:	69,5	:	94,7	:	129,9	:
Danmark	36,8	39,2	19,8	23,7	55,0	52,7	83,5	85,1	112,1	123,0	184,6	166,7

B – Period 1920 – 1973   B – Période 1920 – 1973

		35 – 44	45 – 54	55 – 64	65 – 74	75 +
France	1950 – 1954	11,7	28,3	43,7	61,7	109,1
	1965 – 1969	13,2	37,8	58,0	77,4	133,3
	1971	13,9	36,6	62,9	77,2	117,3
	1973	14,3	40,4	64,7	80,2	124,5
Nederland	1950 – 1954	21,0	50,8	76,6	116,1	155,4
	1965 – 1969	22,8	60,7	87,1	113,9	208,2
	1971	22,3	65,1	87,5	117,0	191,8
	1973	24,2	61,4	92,7	118,6	207,5
United Kingdom						
England and Wales	1920 – 1922	19,9	51,0	79,9	101,2	177,9
	1950 – 1954	22,0	51,2	77,0	107,2	164,9
	1965 – 1969	22,2	58,3	87,6	107,3	162,3
	1971	24,0	61,4	94,6	118,3	170,9
	1973	25,3	66,6	91,3	121,8	170,3
Northern Ireland	1950 – 1954	19,5	41,9	59,5	88,8	126,9
	1965 – 1969	28,3	52,5	75,7	90,8	125,7
	1971	20,2	59,7	65,5	111,7	157,0
	1973	33,3	56,9	81,2	83,9	149,3
Scotland	1920 – 1922	16,5	46,6	75,1	88,5	155,4
	1950 – 1954	21,3	50,5	70,9	106,4	155,0
	1965 – 1969	21,9	57,4	79,2	106,4	161,4
	1971	18,9	57,2	83,3	105,5	163,2
	1973	32,6	66,1	90,0	113,5	162,8
Ireland	1925 – 1927	16,9	41,5	51,2	50,5	60,3
	1950 – 1954	21,1	43,7	62,1	76,9	97,2
	1965 – 1969	24,1	55,5	69,5	94,7	129,9
	1971	25,4	67,7	81,5	98,5	134,8
	1973	:	:	:	:	:
Danmark	1920 – 1921	13,2	36,0	49,8	59,0	92,2
	1950 – 1952	20,7	50,6	73,2	122,3	200,0
	1965 – 1969	19,8	55,0	83,5	112,1	184,6
	1971	19,9	55,7	82,9	118,9	203,3
	1973	23,7	52,7	85,1	123,0	166,7

TAB. 16

Deaths from malignant tumour of uterus: standardized rates by age
Mortalité due aux tumeurs malignes de l'utérus: taux standardisés par âge

		TOTAL			35 – 65 years – ans		
		Malignant tumour of uterus Tumeurs malignes de l'utérus	Other causes Autres causes	Total	Malignant tumour of uterus Tumeurs malignes de l'utérus	Other causes Autres causes	Total
BR Deutschland							
Bundesrepublik	1955 – 1959	3,6	9,7	13,3	8,8	19,9	28,7
	1960 – 1964	4,5	8,2	12,7	11,1	16,8	27,9
	1965 – 1969	5,6	7,1	12,7	13,5	13,6	27,1
	1970	5,9	5,9	11,8	13,7	10,5	24,2
	1971	5,9	5,7	11,6	13,6	9,7	23,3
Berlin	1965 – 1969	9,3	7,1	16,4	23,0	14,7	37,7
	1970	10,0	5,2	15,2	24,6	9,8	34,4
France	1950 – 1954	2,2	10,9	13,1	5,0	21,9	26,9
	1955 – 1959	2,9	9,9	12,8	6,6	19,4	26,0
	1960 – 1964	2,9	9,1	12,0	6,8	17,7	24,5
	1965 – 1969	2,8	8,1	10,9	6,6	15,5	22,1
	1970	2,4	7,4	9,8	5,5	13,7	19,2
	1971	2,6	7,2	9,8	5,8	13,1	18,9
Italia	1955 – 1959	1,8	12,1	13,9	4,3	25,8	30,1
	1960 – 1964	1,8	11,8	13,6	4,4	24,6	29,0
	1965 – 1969	1,7	11,2	12,9	4,0	22,9	26,9
	1970	1,6	10,5	12,1	3,6	20,7	24,3
	1971	1,5	10,3	11,8	3,3	20,3	23,6
Nederland	1950 – 1954	5,8	5,4	11,2	12,3	9,6	21,9
	1955 – 1959	6,2	4,6	10,8	13,9	8,0	21,9
	1960 – 1964	6,0	4,4	10,4	14,0	7,0	21,0
	1965 – 1969	5,6	4,7	10,3	13,1	7,2	21,0
	1970	5,4	4,2	9,6	12,4	6,5	18,9
	1971	5,4	4,0	9,4	12,2	5,8	18,0
Luxembourg	1970	3,8	7,3	11,1	10,6	14,0	24,6
	1971	8,0	4,7	12,7	21,4	6,6	28,0
Ireland	1950 – 1954	1,8	6,9	8,7	4,3	14,9	19,2
	1955 – 1959	2,6	6,6	9,2	5,9	13,7	19,6
	1960 – 1964	2,7	5,4	8,1	6,4	10,7	17,1
	1965 – 1969	3,6	4,4	8,0	8,6	8,2	16,8
	1970	4,2	4,3	8,5	9,6	8,7	18,3
	1971	3,5	4,2	7,7	7,0	5,7	12,7

TAB. 17

Deaths from road accidents: mortality rates by age
Mortalité due à des accidents de la circulation: taux de mortalité par âge

	BR Deutschland [1]		France		Italia		Nederland		Belgique/ België	
	q_F	$\frac{q_F}{q_M} 100$	q_F	$\frac{q_F}{q_M} 100$	q_F	$\frac{q_F}{q_M} 100$	q_F	$\frac{q_F}{q_M} 100$	q_F	$\frac{q_F}{q_M} 100$
1974										
0 – 14	0,9	69,2	0,6	60,0	0,4	57,1	0,6	50,0	:	:
15 – 20	2,4	28,2	2,1	31,3	1,0	25,6	1,8	24,0	:	:
21 – 24	1,4	21,9	1,6	23,2	0,4	13,3	0,7	21,2	:	:
25 – 34	0,9	27,3	1,0	25,0	0,2	15,4	0,7	30,4	:	:
35 – 44	0,8	29,6	1,0	25,0	0,7	18,4	0,5	25,0	:	:
45 – 54	0,9	33,3	1,2	31,6	0,7	24,1	0,6	31,6	:	:
55 – 64	1,1	32,4	1,5	31,3	0,8	19,5	1,2	42,9	:	:
65 +	2,5	46,3	1,9	38,0	1,3	26,0	1,7	28,8	:	:
Total	1,3	36,1	1,4*	32,6*	0,8*	25,8*	0,9	32,1	:	:
1976										
0 – 14	0,9	69,2	0,6	66,7	0,4	57,1	0,7	63,6	0,8	66,7
15 – 20	2,2	25,9	2,2	32,3	0,8	26,7	1,5	34,9	2,2	27,8
21 – 24	1,4	22,2	1,7	21,0	0,8	22,9	1,1	26,8	1,0	16,9
25 – 34	0,8	25,8	0,9	23,7	} 0,4	} 16,7	0,6	28,6	1,0	27,0
35 – 44	0,7	25,9	1,0	25,6			0,5	25,0	1,0	29,4
45 – 54	0,8	28,6	1,1	28,2	0,6	22,2	0,8	40,0	1,1	42,3
55 – 64	1,2	35,3	1,4	32,6	0,7	21,2	1,2	41,4	1,4	40,0
65 +	2,6	45,6	1,9	38,0	1,2	29,3	1,9	33,3	2,3	44,2
Total	1,3	36,1	1,2	30,8	0,7	28,0	1,0	38,5	1,4	37,8

[1] 1975.

TAB. 17

Deaths from road accidents: mortality rates by age
Mortalité due à des accidents de la circulation: taux de mortalité par âge

Luxembourg		United Kingdom		Ireland		Danmark		
q_f	$\frac{q_f}{q_m}100$	q_f	$\frac{q_f}{q_m}100$	q_f	$\frac{q_f}{q_m}100$	q_f	$\frac{q_f}{q_m}100$	
				1974				
:	:	:	:	:	:	0,7	70,0	0 – 14
:	:	:	:	:	:	1,2	19,0	15 – 20
:	:	:	:	:	:	0,5	21,7	21 – 24
:	:	:	:	:	:	0,3	18,8	25 – 34
:	:	:	:	:	:	0,4	30,0	35 – 44
:	:	:	:	:	:	0,5	41,7	45 – 54
:	:	:	:	:	:	1,0	40,0	55 – 64
:	:	:	:	:	:	1,9	41,3	65 +
:	:	:	:	:	:	0,8	36,4	Total
				1976				
:	:	0,3	50,0	0,4	66,7	0,8	100,0	0 – 14
:	:	1,0	22,2	1,2	31,6	1,8	29,0	15 – 20
:	:	0,6	19,4	1,1	20,4	0,4	10,8	21 – 24
:	:	0,4	23,5	0,8	27,6	0,4	22,2	25 – 34
:	:	0,4	33,3	0,3	12,0	0,3	27,3	35 – 44
:	:	0,5	41,7	0,8	36,4	0,6	42,9	45 – 54
:	:	0,7	43,7	1,0	38,5	1,4	60,9	55 – 64
:	:	1,6	66,7	2,0	46,5	2,7	61,4	65 +
:	:	0,7	41,2	0,9	37,5	1,1	47,8	Total

Women and work
La femme et le travail

SECTION I

Female population and activity
Population féminine et activité

TAB. 18
Population of the Community by main type of activity (1 000)
Population de la Communauté selon les principaux critères d'activité (1 000)

	BR Deutschland		France		Italia		Nederland		Belgique/België	
	F	M	F	M	F	M	F	M	F	M
1968										
Persons with a main occupation	7 785	15 290	7 432	12 918	5 042	13 913	995	3 276	972	2 454
Unemployed persons	62	128	149	185	179	443	(8)	52	32	59
Total labour force	7 847	15 418	7 581	13 103	5 221	14 356	1 003	3 328	1 004	2 513
Non-active persons	17 024	5 703	2 376	4 525	15 785	4 914	3 526	1 064	2 724	1 037
Persons less than 14 years old	6 127	6 447	5 461	5 653	5 728	5 999	1 478	1 565	1 046	1 104
Total population	30 998	27 568	5 418	23 281	26 734	25 269	6 006	5 957	4 775	4 654
1970										
Persons with a main occupation	7 962	15 560	7 477	12 736	4 881	13 701	:	:	1 003	2 445
Unemployed persons	22	35	146	167	180	337	:	:	15	18
Total labour force	7 984	15 595	7 622	12 902	5 061	14 038	:	:	1 017	2 463
Non-active persons	17 335	6 112	12 338	4 818	16 175	5 499	:	:	2 821	1 142
Persons less than 14 years old	6 184	6 607	5 531	5 642	6 029	6 212	:	:	994	1 041
Total population	31 503	28 314	25 492	23 363	27 265	25 748	:	:	4 832	4 646
1973										
Persons with a main occupation	9 106	16 478	7 554	12 640	4 328	12 691	981	3 325	1 073	2 443
Unemployed persons	69	64	190	185	282	435	17	65	29	30
Total labour force	9 175	16 542	7 744	12 825	4 610	13 126	998	3 390	1 102	2 473
Non-active persons	16 481	5 937	12 577	5 342	17 111	6 738	3 924	1 416	2 745	1 139
Persons less than 14 years old	6 033	6 409	5 350	5 528	5 844	6 022	1 348	1 454	1 020	1 068
Total population	31 709	28 889	25 671	23 695	27 567	25 892	6 270	6 260	4 866	4 680
1975										
Persons with a main occupation	8 997	15 703	7 807	13 056	4 761	13 139	1 076	3 350	1 132	2 428
Unemployed persons	295	455	351	354	248	370	32	116	65	54
Total labour force	9 292	16 158	8 158	13 411	5 008	13 509	1 108	3 466	1 197	2 482
Non-active persons	16 857	6 583	12 380	5 486	17 233	6 980	4 003	1 588	2 704	1 184
Persons less than 14 years old	5 663	5 936	5 251	5 447	5 864	6 055	1 503	1 563	1 002	1 046
Total population	31 813	28 678	25 790	24 343	28 106	26 544	6 613	6 616	4 903	4 713
1977										
Persons with a main occupation	9 012	15 738	8 078	12 917	5 266	13 010	1 155	3 405	1 120	2 437
Unemployed persons	353	386	524	434	394	442	40	115	138	77
Total labour force	9 365	16 125	8 602	13 351	5 660	13 452	1 194	3 520	1 258	2 514
Non-active persons	17 101	7040	12 326	5 698	16 844	7 256	4 139	1 692	2 732	1 261
Persons less than 14 years old	5 253	5 466	5 172	5 375	5 872	6 054	1 434	1 524	908	947
Total population	31 719	28 630	26 100	24 425	28 376	26 762	6 768	6 736	4 898	4 722

Luxembourg		United Kingdom		Ireland		Danmark		EUR 9		
F	M	F	M	F	M	F	M	F	M	
1968										
:	:	:	:	:	:	:	:	:	:	Personnes ayant un emploi principal
:	:	:	:	:	:	:	:	:	:	Personnes en chômage
:	:	:	:	:	:	:	:	:	:	Total des forces de travail
:	:	:	:	:	:	:	:	:	:	Personnes non actives
:	:	:	:	:	:	:	:	:	:	Personnes de moins de 14 ans
:	:	:	:	:	:	:	:	:	:	Population totale
1970										
33	95	:	:	:	:	:	:	:	:	Personnes ayant un emploi principal
.	.	:	:	:	:	:	:	:	:	Personnes en chômage
33	96	:	:	:	:	:	:	:	:	Total des forces de travail
99	35	:	:	:	:	:	:	:	:	Personnes non actives
34	34	:	:	:	:	:	:	:	:	Personnes de moins de 14 ans
166	165	:	:	:	:	:	:	:	:	Population totale
1973										
36	98	8 711	14 972	:	:	:	:	:	:	Personnes ayant un emploi principal
.	.	154	361	:	:	:	:	:	:	Personnes en chômage
36	99	8 865	15 333	:	:	:	:	:	:	Total des forces de travail
108	38	13 298	4 911	:	:	:	:	:	:	Personnes non actives
33	34	5 669	5 942	:	:	:	:	:	:	Personnes de moins de 14 ans
177	170	27 831	26 186	:	:	:	:	:	:	Population totale
1975										
40	101	9 078	14 804	268	739	838	1 292	33 996	64 612	Personnes ayant un emploi principal
.	.	501	646	26	82	59	98	1 577	2 176	Personnes en chômage
40	101	9 579	15 450	293	821	897	1 390	35 572	66 788	Total des forces de travail
110	39	12 505	4 771	779	264	1 107	543	67 679	27 438	Personnes non actives
32	34	5 848	6 143	428	452	493	516	26 085	27 193	Personnes de moins de 14 ans
183	174	27 931	26 364	1 500	1 538	2 496	2 449	129 337	121 419	Population totale
1977										
40	98	9 373	14 847	265	741	879	1 346	35 189	64 540	Personnes ayant un emploi principal
(1)	(1)	427	754	21	80	86	81	1 983	2 371	Personnes en chômage
41	99	9 800	15 601	286	821	965	1 428	37 171	66 911	Total des forces de travail
110	42	12 932	5 364	813	283	1 077	539	68 073	29 175	Personnes non actives
31	31	5 471	5 790	439	460	484	507	25 065	26 115	Personnes de moins de 14 ans
181	172	28 203	26 755	1 537	1 564	2 526	2 474	130 309	122 240	Population totale

TAB. 18.1

Population of the Community by main type of activity (%)
Population de la Communauté selon les principaux critères d'activité (%)

	BR Deutschland		France		Italia		Nederland		Belgique België	
	$\frac{f}{F}100$	$\frac{f}{f+m}100$	$\frac{f}{F}100$	$\frac{f}{f+m}100$	$\frac{f}{F}100$	$\frac{f}{f+m}100$	$\frac{f}{F}100$	$\frac{f}{f+m}100$	$\frac{f}{F}100$	$\frac{f}{f+m}100$
1968										
Persons with a main occupation	25,1	33,7	29,2	36,5	18,9	26,6	16,6	23,3	20,3	28,4
Unemployed persons	0,2	32,6	0,6	44,6	0,6	28,8	(0,1)	(13,3)	0,7	35,2
Total labour force	25,3	33,7	29,8	36,7	19,5	26,7	16,7	23,2	21,0	28,5
Non-active persons	54,9	74,9	48,7	73,2	59,1	76,3	58,7	76,8	57,1	72,4
Persons less than 14 years old	19,8	48,7	21,5	49,1	21,4	48,8	24,6	48,6	21,9	48,7
Total population	100,0	52,9	100,0	52,2	100,0	51,4	100,0	50,2	100,0	50,6
1970										
Persons with a main occupation	25,3	33,8	29,3	37,0	17,9	26,3	:	:	20,8	29,1
Unemployed persons	0,2	38,6	0,6	46,6	0,7	34,8	:	:	0,3	45,5
Total labour force	25,4	33,9	29,9	37,1	18,6	26,5	:	:	21,1	29,2
Non-active persons	55,0	73,9	48,8	71,9	59,3	74,6	:	:	58,4	71,2
Persons less than 14 years old	19,6	48,3	21,7	49,5	22,1	49,3	:	:	20,5	48,8
Total population	100,0	52,7	100,0	52,2	100,0	51,4	:	:	100,0	51,0
1973										
Persons with a main occupation	28,7	35,6	29,4	37,4	15,7	25,4	15,6	22,8	22,1	30,5
Unemployed persons	0,2	51,9	0,7	50,7	1,0	39,3	0,3	20,7	0,6	49,2
Total labour force	28,9	35,7	30,2	37,6	16,7	26,0	15,9	22,7	22,7	30,8
Non-active persons	52	73,5	49	70,2	62,1	71,7	62,6	73,5	56,4	70,7
Persons less than 14 years old	19,1	48,5	20,8	49,2	21,2	49,2	21,5	48,1	20,9	48,9
Total population	100,0	52,3	100,0	52,0	100,0	51,6	100,0	50,0	100,0	51,0
1975										
Persons with a main occupation	28,3	36,4	30,3	37,4	16,9	26,6	16,3	24,3	23,1	31,8
Unemployed persons	0,9	39,3	1,4	49,8	0,9	40,1	0,7	21,6	1,3	54,6
Total labour force	29,2	36,5	31,6	37,8	17,8	27,0	16,8	24,2	24,4	32,5
Non-active persons	53	71,9	48	69,3	61,3	71,2	60,5	71,6	55,2	69,5
Persons less than 14 years old	17,8	48,8	20,4	49,1	20,9	49,2	22,7	49,0	20,4	48,9
Total population	100,0	52,6	100,0	51,4	100,0	51,4	100,0	50,0	100,0	51,0
1977										
Persons with a main occupation	28,4	36,4	31,0	38,5	18,6	28,8	17,1	25,3	22,9	31,5
Unemployed persons	1,1	47,8	2,0	54,7	1,4	47,1	0,6	25,8	2,8	64,2
Total labour force	29,5	36,7	33,0	39,2	19,9	29,6	17,6	25,3	25,7	33,4
Non-active persons	53,9	70,8	47,2	68,4	59,4	69,9	61,2	71,0	55,8	68,4
Persons less than 14 years old	16,6	49,0	19,8	49,0	20,7	49,2	21,2	48,5	18,5	48,9
Total population	100,0	52,6	100,0	51,7	100,0	51,5	100,0	50,1	100,0	50,9

TAB. 18.1

Population of the Community by main type of activity (%)
Population de la Communauté selon les principaux critères d'activité (%)

Luxembourg		United Kingdom		Ireland		Danmark		EUR 9		
$\frac{f}{F}100$	$\frac{f}{f+m}100$	$\frac{f}{F}100$	$\frac{f}{f+m}100$	$\frac{f}{F}100$	$\frac{f}{f+m}100$	$\frac{f}{F}100$	$\frac{f}{f+m}100$	$\frac{f}{F}100$	$\frac{f}{f+m}100$	
1968										
:	:	:	:	:	:	:	:	:	:	Personnes ayant un emploi principal
:	:	:	:	:	:	:	:	:	:	Personnes en chômage
:	:	:	:	:	:	:	:	:	:	Total des forces de travail
:	:	:	:	:	:	:	:	:	:	Personnes non actives
:	:	:	:	:	:	:	:	:	:	Personnes de moins de 14 ans
:	:	:	:	:	:	:	:	:	:	Population totale
1970										
19,7	25,8	:	:	:	:	:	:	:	:	Personnes ayant un emploi principal
.	.	:	:	:	:	:	:	:	:	Personnes en chômage
19,8	25,6	:	:	:	:	:	:	:	:	Total des forces de travail
59,8	73,9	:	:	:	:	:	:	:	:	Personnes non actives
20,4	50,0	:	:	:	:	:	:	:	:	Personnes de moins de 14 ans
100,0	50,2	:	:	:	:	:	:	:	:	Population totale
1973										
20,3	26,9	31,3	24,4	:	:	:	:	:	:	Personnes ayant un emploi principal
.	.	0,6	29,9	:	:	:	:	:	:	Personnes en chômage
20,3	26,7	31,9	36,6	:	:	:	:	:	:	Total des forces de travail
61,0	74,0	47,8	73,0	:	:	:	:	:	:	Personnes non actives
18,7	49,3	20,3	48,8	:	:	:	:	:	:	Personnes de moins de 14 ans
100,0	51,0	100,0	51,5	:	:	:	:	:	:	Population totale
1975										
21,8	28,4	32,5	38,0	17,9	26,6	33,6	39,3	26,3	34,5	Personnes ayant un emploi principal
.	.	1,8	43,7	1,7	24,1	2,3	37,6	1,2	42,0	Personnes en chômage
22,0	28,4	34,3	38,3	19,6	26,3	35,9	39,2	27,5	34,8	Total des forces de travail
60,2	73,3	44,8	72,4	51,9	74,7	44,3	67,1	52,3	71,2	Personnes non actives
17,7	48,5	20,9	48,8	28,5	48,6	19,8	48,9	20,2	49,0	Personnes de moins de 14 ans
100,0	51,3	100,0	51,4	100,0	49,4	100,0	50,5	100,0	51,6	Population totale
1977										
22,1	28,8	33,2	38,7	17,2	26,3	34,8	39,5	27,0	35,3	Personnes ayant un emploi principal
(0,3)	(50,0)	1,5	36,2	1,4	20,8	3,4	51,5	1,5	45,6	Personnes en chômage
22,4	29,3	34,7	38,6	18,6	25,8	38,2	40,3	28,5	35,7	Total des forces de travail
60,7	72,4	45,9	70,7	52,9	74,2	42,6	66,6	52,2	70,0	Personnes non actives
16,9	50,0	19,4	48,6	28,5	48,8	19,2	48,8	19,2	48,9	Personnes de moins de 14 ans
100,0	51,1	100,0	51,3	100,0	49,6	100,0	50,5	100,0	51,6	Population totale

TAB. 19
Population of the Community by main type of activity (1 000)
Population de la Communauté selon les principaux critères d'activité (1 000)

	BR Deutschland		France		Italia		Nederland		Belgique België	
	F	M	F	M	F	M	F	M	F	M
1973										
Persons with a main occupation	9 106	16 478	7 554	12 640	4 328	12 691	981	3 325	1 073	2 443
of which:										
with two or more activities	58	559	:	:	40	421	16	89	10	75
looking for another job	:	:	225	314	184	634	34	103	10	22
Unemployed persons	69	64	190	185	282	435	17	65	29	30
of which:										
looking for a 1st job	14	13	38	26	202	249	(4)	6	7	5
looking for a job after voluntary spell away from work	17	13	25	16	.	.	.	(2)	.	.
Non-active persons	16 481	5 937	12 577	5 342	17 111	6 738	3 924	1 416	2 745	1 139
of which:										
with an occasional occupation	586	145	403	226	565	584	255	60	25	14
looking for a job	:	:	304	64	567	274	48	17	12	5
1975										
Persons with a main occupation	8 997	15 703	7 807	13 056	4 761	13 139	1 076	3 350	1 132	2 248
of which:										
with two or more activities	40	448	:	:	52	436	14	82	11	85
looking for another job	60	100	277	415	192	594	46	115	14	25
Unemployed persons	295	455	351	354	248	370	32	116	65	54
of which:										
looking for a 1st job	48	49	58	42	175	207	6	10	17	9
looking for a job after voluntary spell away from work	49	59	67	21	.	.	.	(3)	.	.
Non-active persons	16 857	6 583	12 380	5 486	17 233	6 980	4 003	1 588	2 074	1 184
of which:										
with an occasional occupation	501	121	308	156	407	410	168	35	20	12
looking for a job	62	77	344	122	392	206	84	27	7	4
1977										
Persons with a main occupation	9 012	15 738	8 078	12 917	5 266	13 010	1 155	3 405	1 120	2 437
of which:										
with two or more activities	47	429	:	:	89	431	17	85	12	77
looking for another job	90	153	350	469	120	299	54	148	26	48
Unemployed persons	353	386	524	434	394	442	40	115	138	77
of which:										
looking for a 1st job	52	53	102	69	297	284	8	13	20	10
looking for a job after a voluntary spell away from work	103	113	81	27	.	(5)	.	(3)	.	.
Non active persons	17 101	7 040	12 326	5 698	16 844	7 256	4 139	1 692	2 732	1 261
of which:										
with an occasional occupation	516	123	344	167	827	911	163	36	8	4
looking for a job	83	88	387	103	492	320	94	57	36	16

TAB. 19

Population of the Community by main type of activity (1 000)

Population de la Communauté selon les principaux critères d'activité (1 000)

Luxembourg		United Kingdom		Ireland		Danmark		EUR 9		
F	M	F	M	F	M	F	M	F	M	

1973

F	M	F	M	F	M	F	M	F	M	
36	98	8 711	14 972	:	:	:	:	:	:	Personnes ayant un emploi principal
										dont:
.	5	127	315	:	:	:	:	:	:	avec deux activités et plus
.	.	256	534	:	:	:	:	:	:	à la recherche d'un autre emploi
.	.	154	361	:	:	:	:	:	:	Personnes en chômage
										dont:
.	.	11	15	:	:	:	:	:	:	à la recherche d'un 1er emploi
										à la recherche d'un emploi après
.	–	42	43	:	:	:	:	:	:	interruption volontaire
108	38	13 298	4 911	:	:	:	:	:	:	Personnes non actives
										dont:
2	.	220	164	:	:	:	:	:	:	avec activité occasionnelle
.	.	278	116	:	:	:	:	:	:	à la recherche d'un emploi

1975

F	M	F	M	F	M	F	M	F	M	
40	101	9 078	14 804	268	739	838	1 292	33 996	64 612	Personnes ayant un emploi principal
										dont:
(1)	5	130	275	(4)	32	:	:	:	:	avec deux activités et plus
.	.	279	487	6	24	26	29	900	1 791	à la recherche d'un autre emploi
.	.	501	646	26	82	59	98	1 577	2 176	Personnes en chômage
										dont:
.	.	24	35	10	12	(4)	5	342	369	à la recherche d'un 1er emploi
										à la recherche d'un emploi après
.	.	158	61	.	.	8	(3)	286	148	interruption volontaire
110	39	12 505	4 771	779	264	1 107	543	67 679	27 438	Personnes non actives
										dont:
(1)	(1)	32	28	28	5	79	41	1 544	808	avec activité occasionnelle
(1)	.	85	64	18	9	21	11	1 014	519	à la recherche d'un emploi

1977

F	M	F	M	F	M	F	M	F	M	
40	98	9 373	14 874	265	741	879	1 346	35 189	64 540	Personnes ayant un emploi principal
										dont:
(1)	4	139	253	(2)	30	:	:	:	:	avec deux activités et plus
.	(1)	405	627	7	25	22	18	1 074	1 788	à la recherche d'un autre emploi
(1)	(1)	427	754	21	80	86	81	1 983	2 371	Personnes en chômage
										dont:
.	.	45	48	6	10	6	6	535	492	à la recherche d'un 1er emploi
										à la recherche d'un emploi après
.	.	72	66	.	.	9	.	273	215	interruption volontaire
110	42	12 932	5 364	813	283	1 077	539	68 073	29 175	Personnes non actives
										dont:
2	(1)	97	63	32	8	66	40	2 053	1 352	avec activité occasionnelle
(1)	.	493	208	26	13	32	26	1 644	831	à la recherche d'un emploi

TAB. 19.1

Population of the Community by main type of activity (%)

Population de la Communauté selon les principaux critères d'activité (%)

	BR Deutschland		France		Italia		Nederland		Belgique Belgïe	
	$\frac{f}{F}100$	$\frac{f}{f+m}100$	$\frac{f}{F}100$	$\frac{f}{f+m}100$	$\frac{f}{F}100$	$\frac{f}{f+m}100$	$\frac{f}{F}100$	$\frac{f}{f+m}100$	$\frac{f}{F}100$	$\frac{f}{f+m}100$
1973										
Persons with a main occupation	100,0	35,6	100,0	37,4	100,0	25,4	100,0	22,8	100,0	30,5
of which:										
with two or more activities	0,6	9,4	:	:	0,9	8,7	1,6	15,2	0,9	11,8
looking for another job	:	:	3,0	41,7	4,3	22,5	3,5	24,8	0,9	31,3
Unemployed persons	100,0	51,9	100,0	50,7	100,0	39,3	100,0	20,7	100,0	49,2
of which:										
looking for a 1st job	20,3	51,9	20,0	59,4	71,6	44,8	(23,5)	(40,0)	24,1	58,3
looking for a job after a voluntary spell away from work	24,6	56,7	13,2	61,0	.	.	.	.	.	.
Non-active persons	100,0	73,5	100,0	70,2	100,0	71,7	100,0	73,5	100,0	70,7
of which:										
with an occasional occupation	3,6	80,2	3,2	64,1	3,3	49,2	6,5	81,0	0,9	64,1
looking for a job	:	:	2,4	82,6	3,3	67,4	1,2	73,8	0,4	70,6
1975										
Persons with a main occupation	100,0	36,4	100,0	37,4	100,0	26,6	100,0	24,3	100,0	31,8
of which:										
with two or more activities	0,4	8,2	:	:	1,1	10,7	1,3	14,6	1,0	11,5
looking for another job	0,7	37,5	3,6	40,0	4,0	24,4	4,3	28,6	1,2	35,9
Unemployed persons	100,0	39,3	100,0	49,8	100,0	40,1	100,0	21,6	100,0	54,6
of which:										
looking for a 1st job	16,3	49,5	16,5	58,0	70,6	45,8	18,8	37,5	26,2	65,4
looking for a job after a voluntary spell away from work	16,6	45,4	19,1	76,1	.	.	.	.	.	.
Non-active persons	100,0	71,9	100,0	69,3	100,0	71,2	100,0	71,6	100,0	69,5
of which:										
with an occasional occupation	3,0	80,5	2,5	66,4	2,4	49,8	4,2	82,8	0,7	62,5
looking for a job	0,4	44,6	2,8	73,8	2,3	65,6	2,1	75,7	0,3	63,6
1977										
Persons with a main occupation	100,0	36,4	100,0	38,5	100,0	28,8	100,0	25,3	100,0	31,5
of which:										
with two or more activities	0,5	9,9	:	:	1,7	17,1	1,5	16,7	1,1	13,5
looking for another job	1,0	37,0	4,3	42,7	2,3	28,6	4,7	26,7	2,3	35,1
Unemployed persons	100,0	47,8	100,0	54,7	100,0	47,1	100,0	25,8	100,0	64,2
of which:										
looking for a 1st job	14,7	49,5	19,5	59,6	75,4	51,1	20,0	38,1	14,5	66,7
looking for a job after a voluntary spell away from work	29,2	47,7	15,5	75,0	.	.	.	.	.	.
Non-active persons	100,0	70,8	100,0	68,4	100,0	69,9	100,0	71,0	100,0	68,4
of which:										
with an occasional occupation	3,0	80,8	2,8	67,3	4,9	47,6	3,9	81,9	0,3	66,7
looking for a job	0,5	48,5	3,1	79,0	2,9	60,6	2,3	62,3	1,3	69,2

TAB. 19.1

Population of the Community by main type of activity (%)
Population de la Communauté selon les principaux critères d'activité (%)

Luxembourg		United Kingdom		Ireland		Danmark		EUR 9		
$\frac{f}{F}100$	$\frac{f}{f+m}100$	$\frac{f}{F}100$	$\frac{f}{f+m}100$	$\frac{f}{F}100$	$\frac{f}{f+m}100$	$\frac{f}{F}100$	$\frac{f}{f+m}100$	$\frac{f}{F}100$	$\frac{f}{f+m}100$	
				1973						
100,0	26,9	100,0	36,8	:	:	:	:	:	:	Personnes ayant un emploi principal *dont:*
.	.	1,5	28,7	:	:	:	:	:	:	avec deux activités et plus
.	.	2,9	32,4	:	:	:	:	:	:	à la recherche d'un autre emploi
.	.	100,0	29,9	:	:	:	:	:	:	Personnes en chômage *dont:*
.	.	7,1	42,3	:	:	:	:	:	:	à la recherche d'un 1er emploi
.	.	27,3	49,4	:	:	:	:	:	:	à la recherche d'un emploi après interruption volontaire
100,0	74,0	100,0	73,0	:	:	:	:	:	:	Personnes non actives *dont:*
1,9	.	1,7	57,3	:	:	:	:	:	:	avec activité occasionnelle
.	.	2,1	70,6	:	:	:	:	:	:	à la recherche d'un emploi
				1975						
100,0	28,4	100,0	38,0	100,0	26,6	100,0	39,3	100,0	34,5	Personnes ayant un emploi principal *dont:*
(2,5)	(16,7)	1,4	32,1	(1,5)	(11,1)	:	:	:	:	avec deux activités et plus
.	.	3,1	36,4	2,2	20,0	3,1	47,3	2,6	33,4	à la recherche d'un autre emploi
.	.	100,0	43,7	100,0	24,1	100,0	37,6	100,0	42,0	Personnes en chômage *dont:*
.	.	4,8	40,7	38,5	45,5	(6,8)	(44,4)	21,7	48,1	à la recherche d'un 1er emploi
.	.	31,5	72,1	.	.	13,6	72,7	18,1	65,9	à la recherche d'un emploi après interruption volontaire
100,0	73,8	100,0	72,4	100,0	74,7	100,0	67,1	100,0	71,2	Personnes non actives *dont:*
(0,9)	(50,0)	0,3	53,3	3,6	84,8	7,1	65,8	2,3	65,6	avec activité occasionnelle
(0,9)	.	0,7	57,0	2,3	66,7	1,9	69,6	1,5	66,1	à la recherche d'un emploi
				1977						
100,0	29,00	100,0	38,7	100,0	26,3	100,0	39,5	100,0	35,3	Personnes ayant un emploi principal *dont:*
2,5	20,0	1,5	35,5	0,8	6,3	:	:	:	:	avec deux activités et plus
.	.	4,3	39,2	2,6	21,9	2,5	55,0	3,1	37,5	à la recherche d'un autre emploi
100,0	50,0	100,0	36,2	100,0	20,8	100,0	51,5	100,0	45,5	Personnes en chômage *dont:*
.	.	10,5	48,4	28,6	37,5	7,0	50,0	27,0	52,1	à la recherche d'un 1er emploi
.	.	16,9	52,2	.	.	10,5		13,8	55,9	à la recherche d'un emploi après interruption volontaire
100,0	72,4	100,0	70,7	100,0	74,2	100,0	66,6	100,0	70,0	Personnes non actives *dont:*
1,8	66,7	0,8	60,6	3,9	80,0	6,1	62,3	3,0	60,3	avec activité occasionnelle
(0,9)	.	3,8	70,3	3,2	66,7	3,0	55,2	2,4	66,4	à la recherche d'un emploi

TAB. 20
Labour force by age groups (1 000)
Forces de travail par groupe d'âge (1 000)

	BR Deutschland		France		Italia		Nederland		Belgique Belgïe	
	F	M	F	M	F	M	F	M	F	M
1973										
14 – 24	2 207	2 471	1 718	1 922	1 210	1 691	459	527	301	351
25 – 34	1 973	3 964	1 823	3 133	1 138	3 112	216	943	301	603
35 – 44	1 887	4 336	1 543	3 114	1 028	3 490	132	764	234	607
45 – 54	1 959	3 238	1 602	2 853	894	3 066	109	654	180	541
55 – 64	912	2 017	831	1 467	288	1 520	72	445	71	334
65 +	238	516	230	336	53	247	10	56	15	37
Total labour force	9 175	16 542	7 744	12 825	4 610	13 126	998	3 390	1 102	2 473
1975										
14 – 24	2 181	2 340	1 748	1 989	1 181	1 674	452	499	305	352
25 – 34	2 003	3 690	2 151	3 673	1 313	3 204	272	1 025	356	626
35 – 44	2 047	4 513	1 616	3 059	1 114	3 578	160	786	256	602
45 – 54	1 953	3 413	1 635	2 973	1 016	3 270	141	675	204	571
55 – 64	904	1 823	787	1 372	321	1 420	72	427	65	298
65 +	204	379	222	344	64	304	10	55	12	33
Total labour force	9 292	16 158	8 158	13 411	5 008	13 509	1 108	3 466	1 197	2 482
1977										
14 – 24	2 144	2 332	1 755	1 892	1 298	1 640	456	474	317	364
25 – 34	2 071	3 558	2 428	3 805	1 565	3 243	321	1 102	419	684
35 – 44	2 177	4 683	1 635	2 912	1 264	3 553	184	809	248	568
45 – 54	1 839	3 488	1 712	2 976	1 042	3 218	153	664	199	571
55 – 64	970	1 755	877	1 469	393	1 491	71	427	64	297
65 +	164	307	195	298	100	309	10	44	12	31
Total labour force	9 365	16 125	8 602	13 351	5 660	13 452	1 194	3 520	1 258	2 514

TAB. 20
Labour force by age groups (1 000)
Forces de travail par groupe d'âge (1 000)

Luxembourg		United Kingdom		Ireland		Danmark		EUR 9		
F	M	F	M	F	M	F	M	F	M	
1973										
13	15	1 856	2 480	:	:	:	:	:	:	14 – 24
8	23	1 601	3 489	:	:	:	:	:	:	25 – 34
6	25	1 803	3 070	:	:	:	:	:	:	35 – 44
6	21	2 105	3 236	:	:	:	:	:	:	45 – 54
3	12	1 250	2 559	:	:	:	:	:	:	55 – 64
1	2	249	497	:	:	:	:	:	:	65 +
36	99	8 865	15 333	:	:	:	:	:	:	Total des forces de travail
1975										
14	15	1 874	2 437	133	178	165	195	8 051	9 681	14 – 24
9	25	1 886	3 640	58	184	262	367	8 310	16 433	25 – 34
7	25	2 012	3 091	30	149	178	279	7 421	16 083	35 – 44
6	23	2 237	3 190	35	145	164	261	7 390	14 521	45 – 54
3	11	1 328	2 558	28	118	109	221	3 616	8 308	55 – 64
1	3	242	534	10	46	19	66	785	1 764	65 +
40	101	9 579	15 450	293	821	897	1 390	35 572	66 788	Total des forces de travail
1977										
14	15	1 988	2 568	120	165	182	214	8 275	9 665	14 – 24
10	24	2 009	3 790	69	205	288	378	9 179	16 789	25 – 34
7	24	2 032	3 085	30	156	208	298	7 783	16 087	35 – 44
6	23	2 161	3 111	32	138	165	256	7 308	14 445	45 – 54
3	10	1370	2544	25	111	104	217	3 879	8 322	55 – 64
(1)	2	240	502	10	45	18	64	748	1 603	65 +
41	99	9 800	15 601	286	821	965	1 428	37 171	66 911	Total des forces de travail

TAB. 20.1
Labour force by age groups (%)
Forces de travail par groupe d'âge (%)

	BR Deutschland		France		Italia		Nederland		Belgique België	
	$\frac{f}{F}100$	$\frac{f}{f+m}100$	$\frac{f}{F}100$	$\frac{f}{f+m}100$	$\frac{f}{F}100$	$\frac{f}{f+m}100$	$\frac{f}{F}100$	$\frac{f}{f+m}100$	$\frac{f}{F}100$	$\frac{f}{f+m}100$
1973										
14 – 24	24,1	47,2	22,2	47,2	26,2	41,7	46,0	46,6	27,3	46,2
25 – 34	21,5	33,2	23,5	36,8	24,7	26,8	21,7	18,6	27,3	33,3
35 – 44	20,5	30,3	19,9	33,1	22,3	22,8	13,2	14,7	21,2	27,8
45 – 54	21,4	37,7	20,7	36,0	19,4	22,6	10,9	14,3	16,3	25,0
55 – 64	9,9	31,1	10,7	36,2	6,2	15,9	7,2	13,9	6,5	17,5
65 +	2,6	31,6	3	40,6	1,2	17,7	1,0	15,2	1,4	28,8
Total labour force	100,0	35,7	100,0	37,6	100,0	26,0	100,0	22,7	100,0	30,8
1975										
14 – 24	23,5	48,2	21,4	46,8	23,6	41,4	40,8	47,5	25,5	46,4
25 – 34	21,6	35,2	26,4	36,9	26,2	29,1	24,6	21,0	29,7	36,3
35 – 44	22,0	31,2	19,8	34,6	22,2	23,7	14,5	16,9	21,4	29,8
45 – 54	21,0	36,4	20,0	35,5	20,3	23,7	12,7	17,3	17,0	26,3
55 – 64	9,7	33,1	9,7	36,5	6,4	18,4	6,5	14,4	5,4	17,9
65 +	2,2	35,0	2,7	39,2	1,3	17,4	0,9	15,4	1,0	26,7
Total labour force	100,0	36,5	100,0	37,8	100,0	27,1	100,0	24,2	100,0	32,5
1977										
14 – 24	22,9	47,9	20,4	48,1	23,0	44,2	38,2	49,0	25,2	46,5
25 – 34	22,1	36,8	28,2	39,0	27,7	32,5	26,9	22,6	33,3	38,0
35 – 44	23,2	31,7	19,0	36,0	22,3	26,2	15,4	18,5	19,7	30,4
45 – 54	19,6	34,5	19,9	36,5	18,4	24,5	12,8	18,7	15,8	25,8
55 – 64	10,4	35,6	10,2	37,4	6,9	20,9	5,9	14,3	5,1	17,7
65 +	1,8	34,8	2,3	39,6	1,8	24,4	0,8	18,5	1,0	27,9
Total labour force	100,0	36,7	100,0	39,2	100,0	29,5	100,0	25,3	100,0	33,4

TAB. 20.1

Labour force by age groups (%)
Forces de travail par groupe d'âge (%)

Luxembourg		United Kingdom		Ireland		Danmark		EUR 9		
$\frac{f}{F}100$	$\frac{f}{f+m}100$	$\frac{f}{F}100$	$\frac{f}{f+m}100$	$\frac{f}{F}100$	$\frac{f}{f+m}100$	$\frac{f}{F}100$	$\frac{f}{f+m}100$	$\frac{f}{F}100$	$\frac{f}{f+m}100$	
1973										
35,1	46,4	20,9	42,8	:	:	:	:	:	:	14 – 24
21,6	25,8	18,1	31,5	:	:	:	:	:	:	25 – 34
16,2	19,4	20,3	37,0	:	:	:	:	:	:	35 – 44
16,2	22,2	23,8	39,4	:	:	:	:	:	:	45 – 54
8,1	20,0	14,1	32,8	:	:	:	:	:	:	55 – 64
2,8	33,3	2,8	33,4	:	:	:	:	:	:	65 +
100,0	25,7	100,0	36,6	:	:	:	:	:	:	Total des forces de travail
1975										
35,0	48,3	19,6	43,5	45,3	42,8	18,4	45,7	22,6	45,4	14 – 24
22,5	26,5	19,7	34,1	19,7	24,0	29,2	41,7	23,4	33,6	25 – 34
17,5	21,9	21,0	39,4	10,2	16,8	19,8	38,9	20,9	31,6	35 – 44
15,0	20,7	23,3	41,2	11,9	19,4	18,3	38,6	20,8	33,7	45 – 54
7,5	21,4	13,9	34,2	9,5	19,2	12,2	33,0	10,2	27,8	55 – 64
2,5	25,0	2,5	31,2	3,4	17,9	2,1	22,4	2,2	30,8	65 +
100,0	28,4	100,0	38,3	100,0	26,3	100,0	39,2	100,0	34,8	Total des forces de travail
1977										
34,1	46,7	20,3	43,7	42,0	42,3	18,9	45,8	22,3	46,1	14 – 24
24,4	29,4	20,5	34,6	24,1	25,2	29,8	43,2	24,7	35,3	25 – 34
17,1	22,6	20,7	39,7	10,5	16,1	21,6	41,1	20,9	32,6	35 – 44
14,6	20,7	22,1	41,0	11,2	18,8	17,1	39,2	19,7	33,6	45 – 54
7,3	23,1	14,0	35,0	8,7	18,4	10,8	32,4	10,4	31,8	55 – 64
(2,4)	(33,3)	2,4	32,3	3,5	18,2	1,9	22,0	2,0	31,8	65 +
100,0	29,3	100,0	38,6	100,0	25,8	100,0	40,3	100,0	35,7	Total des forces de travail

TAB. 21

Ratios of activity by age groups (%)
Taux d'activité par groupe d'âge (%)

	BR Deutschland		France		Italia		Nederland		Belgique België	
	F	M	F	M	F	M	F	M	F	M
1960										
14 – 19	70,6	72,1	43,1	49,8	45,4	65,6	53,7	50,3	37,0	38,4
20 – 24	74,6	90,5	68,3	84,6	48,7	76,8	62,6	85,3	57,0	86,8
25 – 29	51,0	96,1	49,5	97,0	36,9	95,8	25,8	96,0	42,5	94,6
30 – 34	44,0	98,3	46,0	96,3	34,0	97,9	20,1	97,7	34,7	95,5
35 – 39	44,6	97,7	45,2	98,0	34,6	97,4	18,2	98,4	35,1	96,3
40 – 44	43,6	97,1	46,6	97,3	33,4	96,3	19,0	98,5	33,3	95,9
45 – 49	40,3	96,0	52,7	97,1	33,0	95,2	22,1	97,7	33,7	94,1
50 – 54	36,5	94,0	52,2	94,1	30,2	93,1	20,3	96,7	31,5	91,4
55 – 59	31,6	88,5	45,7	85,8	24,2	86,6	17,3	95,6	23,8	83,9
60 – 64	19,9	71,4	38,3	71,0	17,7	61,4	12,8	85,1	13,6	68,7
65 – 69	11,9	31,1	21,3	42,3	11,7	39,7	5,7	39,4	8,4	26,2
70 +	4,9	15,2	9,5	22,6	4,7	20,0	2,7	16,6	7,5	11,4
TOTAL (2)	:	:	:	:	:	:	:	:	:	:
1968										
14 – 19	48,8	50,3	30,4	40,4	30,9	44,5	34,5	33,7	22,4	24,2
20 – 24	67,4	85,6	66,1	84,1	42,9	79,1	65,9	83,3	61,0	73,6
25 – 29	48,5	93,9	52,8	97,2	31,8	95,3	26,7	96,4	46,8	96,2
30 – 34	37,2	98,5	44,3	98,7	28,7	98,4	14,6	98,8	35,7	99,0
35 – 39	37,4	98,7	44,8	98,4	28,9	98,0	15,8	98,9	34,4	98,4
40 – 44	41,0	98,1	46,7	97,7	31,1	97,4	17,5	98,4	33,2	96,5
45 – 49	41,8	96,7	48,6	96,5	29,4	95,4	17,3	98,5	31,0	95,4
50 – 54	42,6	94,6	49,6	93,8	25,7	92,0	20,0	95,7	30,5	92,0
55 – 59	36,1	89,9	46,7	85,0	18,3	82,9	16,6	92,5	23,0	89,3
60 – 64	22,5	75,7	36,8	67,6	12,7	51,9	12,8	83,9	11,9	74,6
65 – 69	12,0	33,2	16,5	32,6	6,2	27,0	4,6	38,4	4,9	22,8
70 +	4,6	13,1	5,4	12,9	1,8	9,2	1,6	13,5	2,4	7,6
TOTAL (2)	:	73,0	:	74,3	:	74,5	:	75,8	:	70,8
1975										
14 – 19	32,9	37,0	19,7	25,3	17,8	23,2	21,7	17,7	17,7	20,2
20 – 24	68,0	76,7	67,0	81,4	42,8	66,8	59,4	72,4	62,4	73,1
25 – 29	55,0	89,0	62,6	95,6	37,4	89,5	31,3	93,6	61,8	95,8
30 – 34	48,5	96,8	56,7	98,0	31,8	96,3	20,9	97,4	51,0	98,2
35 – 39	46,6	98,1	54,1	97,8	28,5	95,4	20,3	97,2	97,6	45,5
40 – 44	47,6	97,9	52,9	97,1	28,5	95,2	21,5	95,8	38,1	96,4
45 – 49	48,0	96,9	52,9	95,8	28,9	93,1	20,1	93,5	35,3	93,4
50 – 54	46,1	94,0	50,4	93,0	24,4	88,1	17,7	89,8	28,2	88,7
55 – 59	37,8	87,0	42,1	82,6	16,3	76,8	14,0	80,9	21,3	82,7
60 – 64	15,8	62,4	28,3	55,3	7,4	42,4	8,4	65,4	7,8	58,3
65 – 69	6,6	17,2	10,7	20,5	3,2	17,6	2,6	17,2	2,5	12,4
70 +	2,0	6,3	2,7	7,2	0,8	5,0	(0,6)	4,0	1,2	2,3
TOTAL (2)	35,5	71,7	39,7	71,0	22,5	65,9	21,7	68,6	30,7	67,7
1977										
14 – 19	28,5	32,3	17,9	22,5	18,8	23,0	16,1	14,2	15,1	18,0
20 – 24	67,8	76,7	68,4	81,1	45,7	65,8	63,5	71,8	65,9	74,3
25 – 29	58,4	87,6	66,3	95,0	43,0	88,5	36,3	92,4	67,2	95,9
30 – 34	50,1	96,2	59,6	98,0	35,9	94,8	22,7	97,2	56,1	98,3
35 – 39	48,3	98,0	57,2	97,7	33,7	95,0	23,6	96,9	47,5	97,7
40 – 44	49,2	98,0	55,2	97,0	31,6	93,0	23,1	95,5	39,4	96,2
45 – 49	47,6	97,0	55,4	95,9	29,7	91,6	22,0	92,0	33,8	93,2
50 – 54	45,4	93,8	50,9	93,0	25,4	86,7	19,1	87,7	28,2	88,9
55 – 59	38,9	86,0	44,9	83,2	18,4	75,4	13,6	80,5	18,9	81,1
60 – 64	13,8	53,2	26,3	48,0	9,0	36,9	7,4	61,6	7,1	48,0
65 – 69	4,7	13,8	9,6	18,2	4,2	16,1	2,3	13,7	2,1	10,3
70 +	1,8	5,4	2,3	5,8	1,8	6,1	(0,7)	3,0	1,2	2,5
TOTAL (2)	35,4	69,6	41,1	70,1	25,2	65,0	22,4	67,5	31,5	66,6

(1) 1969.
(2) As a % of the population aged 14 years and over.
(1) 1969.
(2) En % de la population de 14 ans et plus.

TAB. 21
Ratios of activity by age groups (%)
Taux d'activité par groupe d'âge (%)

Luxembourg		United Kingdom		Ireland		Danmark		EUR 9		
F	M	F	M	F	M	F	M	F	M	
1960										
55,4	58,9	:	:	:	:	:	:	:	:	14 – 19
52,6	92,2	:	:	:	:	:	:	:	:	20 – 24
34,2	98,2	:	:	:	:	:	:	:	:	25 – 29
21,9	99,9	:	:	:	:	:	:	:	:	30 – 34
28,6	95,4	:	:	:	:	:	:	:	:	35 – 39
25,3	97,7	:	:	:	:	:	:	:	:	40 – 44
24,3	91,9	:	:	:	:	:	:	:	:	45 – 49
26,0	94,4	:	:	:	:	:	:	:	:	50 – 54
21,7	88,8	:	:	:	:	:	:	:	:	55 – 59
19,1	50,0	:	:	:	:	:	:	:	:	60 – 64
11,8	31,1	:	:	:	:	:	:	:	:	65 – 69
6,2	13,8	:	:	:	:	:	:	:	:	70 +
:	:	:	:	:	:	:	:	:	:	TOTAL [2]
1968										
(1)	(1)									14 – 19
36,3	32,3	:	:	:	:	:	:	:	:	20 – 24
57,4	79,0	:	:	:	:	:	:	:	:	25 – 29
35,6	96,5	:	:	:	:	:	:	:	:	30 – 34
23,1	97,8	:	:	:	:	:	:	:	:	35 – 39
23,9	98,8	:	:	:	:	:	:	:	:	40 – 44
23,9	97,7	:	:	:	:	:	:	:	:	45 – 49
25,8	97,5	:	:	:	:	:	:	:	:	50 – 54
28,2	91,9	:	:	:	:	:	:	:	:	55 – 59
21,7	85,1	:	:	:	:	:	:	:	:	60 – 64
14,9	56,9	:	:	:	:	:	:	:	:	65 – 69
9,8	23,7	:	:	:	:	:	:	:	:	70 +
6,4	14,0	:	:	:	:	:	:	:	:	TOTAL [2]
:	71,6	:	:	:	:	:	:	:	:	
1975										
36,4	32,6	29,1	33,1	32,2	36,3	21,2	26,7	24,7	28,9	14 – 19
62,5	80,9	65,8	89,6	69,0	91,6	68,5	76,5	61,4	78,4	20 – 24
44,6	95,0	50,0	96,7	38,4	97,4	70,1	88,3	50,9	93,0	25 – 29
30,8	99,0	51,8	97,8	23,7	98,3	65,6	95,0	97,2	45,6	30 – 34
29,4	98,9	62,2	98,1	18,5	97,7	62,0	95,7	45,3	97,3	35 – 39
26,3	98,7	66,9	97,6	22,1	97,1	62,1	95,0	46,1	96,8	40 – 44
24,5	98,1	67,2	97,6	22,6	95,1	59,9	95,9	46,4	95,6	45 – 49
24,7	92,0	64,7	96,3	23,0	94,6	53,4	91,8	43,9	92,5	50 – 54
19,4	81,2	53,4	93,9	21,1	90,3	47,9	87,1	36,2	85,4	55 – 59
(13,3)	50,1	30,4	84,3	18,4	81,0	29,2	77,6	19,1	62,1	60 – 64
(7,9)	19,5	11,1	31,4	10,4	50,3	12,3	49,1	7,5	21,9	65 – 69
.	(7,6)	2,4	8,8	3,9	19,1	(1,4)	6,3	2,0	6,6	70 +
26,8	72,0	43,4	76,4	27,4	75,6	44,8	71,9	34,5	70,9	TOTAL [2]
1977										
31,0	31,1	29,4	33,1	25,1	31,2	21,7	28,4	23,2	26,9	14 – 19
66,1	79,8	67,5	89,2	69,1	88,0	75,0	81,1	63,1	78,2	20 – 24
46,9	94,6	52,7	96,3	41,4	97,1	76,1	89,3	54,8	92,3	25 – 29
35,9	98,6	51,5	97,7	23,6	98,1	72,4	97,1	47,8	96,8	30 – 34
30,7	99,0	62,0	97,3	18,8	98,0	69,4	97,4	47,8	97,1	35 – 39
27,6	99,2	68,3	97,2	20,4	96,6	70,0	97,4	48,3	96,3	40 – 44
23,9	97,2	68,8	96,9	22,4	95,3	63,3	92,0	47,0	95,0	45 – 49
22,4	91,1	63,9	95,5	22,0	93,5	55,3	92,6	43,9	91,8	50 – 54
20,1	73,2	56,9	91,9	20,0	89,6	44,4	88,5	38,0	84,2	55 – 59
(13,5)	46,5	26,7	80,1	17,1	80,2	28,6	76,9	17,8	56,8	60 – 64
(5,3)	(15,9)	10,9	27,2	9,5	49,8	11,6	47,0	6,9	19,2	65 – 69
.	(6,2)	2,1	8,1	(3,4)	17,9	(1,0)	5,4	1,9	6,1	70 +
27,0	70,5	43,1	74,4	26,0	74,4	47,3	72,6	35,3	69,6	TOTAL [2]

[1] 1969.
[2] As a % of the population aged 14 years and over.
[1] 1969.
[2] En % de la population de 14 ans et plus.

TAB. 22

Population aged between 14 and 24 by main type of activity (1 000)

Population de 14 à 24 ans selon les principaux critères d'activité (1 000)

	BR Deutschland		France		Italia		Nederland		Belgique Belgremoveië	
	F	M	F	M	F	M	F	M	F	M
1973										
Persons with a main occupation	2 185	2 450	1 633	1 857	1 024	1 444	448	509	289	343
of which:										
working part time	102	12	62	30	39	29	29	8	8	.
Unemployed persons	22	21	85	65	186	247	11	18	12	8
of which:										
seeking a 1st job	12	10	32	23	159	194	(3)	5	5	4
Total labour force	2 207	2 471	1 718	1 922	1 210	1 691	459	527	301	351
Non-active persons	2 166	1 967	2 465	1 964	2 764	2 216	707	650	494	441
of which:										
students, schoolchildren	1 636	1 869	1 982	1 903	1 710	2 114	515	639	394	434
looking for a job	(5)	(4)	90	26	245	101	19	13	6	(3)
with an occasional occupation	30	17	50	37	61	65	37	32	(2)	.
working part-time	27	15	36	23	27	16	27	25	.	.
Population between 14 and 24 years old	4 375	4 438	4 183	3 886	3 974	3 907	1 166	1 178	795	792
1975										
Persons with a main occupation	2 074	2 208	1 591	1 857	1 017	1 468	435	462	275	331
of which:										
working part-time	95	10	93	51	55	44	32	8	12	(2)
Unemployed persons	107	132	156	133	164	206	17	37	30	21
of which:										
seeking a 1st job	41	42	54	36	136	160	5	8	12	7
Total labour force	2 181	2 340	1 748	1 989	1 181	1 674	452	499	305	352
Non-active persons	2 413	2 162	2 402	1 962	2 969	2 453	746	739	508	464
of which:										
students, schoolchildren	1 921	1 448	1 944	1 858	1 990	2 352	579	727	424	458
looking for a job	17	21	145	80	184	89	30	15	(4)	(3)
with an occasional occupation	28	14	31	28	47	51	18	14	(2)	.
working part-time	26	13	19	15	16	13	17	13	.	.
Population between 14 and 24 years old	4 594	4 502	4 149	3 952	4 150	4 127	1 198	1 238	813	816
1977										
Persons with a main occupation	2 018	2 222	1 499	1 728	1 034	1 376	434	444	265	339
of which:										
working part-time	96	12	103	49	34	16	31	8	17	(3)
Unemployed persons	126	111	256	163	264	264	22	30	52	25
of which:										
seeking a 1st job	45	41	94	61	224	217	8	9	17	8
Total labour force	2 144	2 332	1 755	1 892	1 298	1 640	456	474	317	364
Non-active persons	2 673	2 446	2 471	2 046	2 992	2 524	790	778	521	484
of which:										
students, schoolchildren	2 222	2 338	2 049	1 956	2 051	2 348	652	766	453	478
looking for a job	23	20	141	61	200	141	33	21	22	13
with an occasional occupation	26	16	47	31	98	115	15	15	.	.
working part-time	24	14	25	16	42	38	15	14	.	.
Population between 14 and 24 years old	4 817	4 778	4 226	3 938	4 291	4 164	1 247	1 252	838	849

TAB. 22

Population aged between 14 and 24 by main type of activity (1 000)
Population de 14 à 24 ans selon les principaux critères d'activité (1 000)

Luxembourg		United Kingdom		Ireland		Danmark		EUR 9		
F	M	F	M	F	M	F	M	F	M	
				1973						
13	15	1 807	2 390	:	:	:	:	:	:	Personnes ayant un emploi principal *dont:*
.	.	112	17	:	:	:	:	:	:	travaillant à temps partiel
.	.	49	90	:	:	:	:	:	:	Personnes en chômage *dont:*
.	.	9	13	:	:	:	:	:	:	recherchant un 1er emploi
13	15	1 856	2 480	:	:	:	:	:	:	Total des forces de travail
14	12	2 204	1 676	:	:	:	:	:	:	Personnes non actives *dont:*
10	12	1 500	1 588	:	:	:	:	:	:	étudiants, élèves
		80	53	:	:	:	:	:	:	à la recherche d'un emploi
		51	39	:	:	:	:	:	:	avec activité occasionnelle
		35	18	:	:	:	:	:	:	travaillant à temps partiel
27	28	4 060	4 156	:	:	:	:	:	:	Population de 14 à 24 ans
				1975						
14	15	1 728	2 251	116	149	144	167	7 392	8 907	Personnes ayant un emploi principal *dont:*
.	.	122	17	(2)	(2)	17	(4)	428	139	travaillant à temps partiel
.	.	146	186	17	29	21	28	659	774	Personnes en chômage *dont:*
.	.	21	30	10	11	(4)	(4)	282	298	recherchant un 1er emploi
14	15	1 874	2 437	133	178	165	195	8 051	9 681	Total des forces de travail
16	14	2 280	1 804	150	128	222	205	11 705	9 930	Personnes non actives *dont:*
12	14	1 695	1 747	116	125	131	130	8 812	9 459	étudiants, élèves
.	.	50	51	8	7	8	7	447	273	à la recherche d'un emploi
.	.	26	22	(3)	(3)	22	24	175	158	avec activité occasionnelle
.	.	24	19	(2)	(3)	20	24	126	99	travaillant à temps partiel
30	29	4 154	4 241	283	306	387	400	19 757	19 611	Population de 14 à 24 ans
				1977						
13	15	1 822	2 342	106	138	149	194	7 340	8 798	Personnes ayant un emploi principal *dont:*
(1)	.	146	37	(2)	.	25	9	453	134	travaillant à temps partiel
.	.	167	226	14	27	33	20	935	867	Personnes en chômage *dont:*
.	.	39	44	6	10	5	4	436	394	recherchant un 1er emploi
14	15	1 988	2 568	120	165	182	214	8 275	9 665	Total des forces de travail
16	14	2 395	1 977	163	141	216	198	12 238	10 607	Personnes non actives *dont:*
13	13	1 845	1 924	133	138	199	194	9 615	10 153	étudiants, élèves
.	.	191	146	14	12	24	21	648	435	à la recherche d'un emploi
.	.	38	37	(3)	4	24	27	251	244	avec activité occasionnelle
.	.	31	23	(3)	(3)	24	26	163	134	travaillant à temps partiel
30	29	4 384	4 545	283	306	398	412	20 513	20 272	Population de 14 à 24 ans

TAB. 22.1
Population aged between 14 and 24 by main type of activity (%)
Population de 14 à 24 ans selon les principaux critères d'activité (%)

	BR Deutschland		France		Italia		Nederland		Belgique Belgïe	
	$\frac{f}{F}100$	$\frac{f}{m+f}100$	$\frac{f}{F}100$	$\frac{f}{m+f}100$	$\frac{f}{F}100$	$\frac{f}{m+f}100$	$\frac{f}{F}100$	$\frac{f}{m+f}100$	$\frac{f}{F}100$	$\frac{f}{m+f}100$
1973										
Persons with a main occupation	49,9	47,1	39,1	46,8	25,7	41,5	38,4	46,8	36,4	45,7
of which:										
working part time	4,7	89,5	3,8	67,4	3,8	57,4	6,5	78,4	2,8	.
Unemployed persons	0,5	51,2	2,0	56,7	4,7	43,0	1,0	37,9	1,5	60,0
of which:										
seeking a 1st job	54,5	54,5	37,6	58,2	85,5	45,0	(27,3)	(37,5)	41,7	55,6
Total labour force	50,5	47,2	41,1	47,2	30,4	41,7	39,4	46,6	37,9	46,2
Non-active persons	49,5	52,4	58,9	55,7	69,6	55,5	60,6	52,1	62,1	52,8
of which:										
students, schoolchildren	75,5	46,7	80,4	51,0	61,9	44,7	72,8	44,6	79,8	47,6
looking for a job	(0,2)	(55,6)	3,7	77,6	8,9	70,8	2,7	59,4	1,2	(66,7)
with an occasional occupation	1,4	63,8	2,0	57,5	2,2	48,4	5,2	53,6	(0,4)	.
working part-time	1,2	64,3	1,5	61,0	1,0	62,8	3,8	51,9	.	.
Population between 14 and 24 years old	100,0	49,6	100,0	51,8	100,0	50,4	100,0	49,7	100,0	50,1
1975										
Persons with a main occupation	45,2	48,4	38,3	46,1	24,5	40,9	36,3	48,5	33,8	45,4
of which:										
working part time	4,6	90,5	5,8	64,6	5,4	55,6	7,4	80,0	4,4	(85,7)
Unemployed persons	2,3	44,8	3,8	54,0	4,0	44,3	1,4	31,5	3,7	58,8
of which:										
seeking a 1st job	38,3	49,4	34,6	60,0	82,9	45,9	29,4	38,5	40,0	63,2
Total labour force	47,5	48,2	42,1	46,8	28,5	41,4	37,7	47,5	37,5	46,4
Non active persons	52,5	52,7	57,9	55,0	71,5	54,8	62,3	50,2	62,5	52,3
of which:										
students, schoolchildren	79,6	57,0	80,9	51,1	67,0	45,8	77,6	44,3	83,5	48,1
looking for a job	(0,7)	44,7	6,0	64,4	6,2	67,4	4,0	66,7	(0,8)	(57,1)
with an occasional occupation	1,2	66,7	1,3	52,5	1,6	48,0	2,4	56,3	(0,4)	.
working part-time	1,1	66,7	0,8	55,9	0,5	55,2	2,3	56,7	.	.
Population between 14 and 24 years old	100,0	50,5	100,0	51,2	100,0	50,1	100,0	49,2	100,C	49,9
1977										
Persons with a main occupation	41,9	47,6	35,5	46,5	24,1	42,9	34,8	49,4	31,6	43,9
of which:										
working part-time	4,8	88,9	6,9	67,8	3,3	68,0	7,1	79,5	6,4	(85,0)
Unemployed persons	2,6	53,2	6,1	61,1	6,2	50,0	1,8	42,3	6,2	67,5
of which:										
seeking a 1st job	35,7	52,3	36,7	60,6	84,8	50,8	36,4	47,1	32,7	68,0
Total labour force	44,5	47,9	41,5	48,1	30,2	44,2	36,6	49,0	37,8	46,5
Non-active persons	55,5	52,2	58,5	54,7	69,8	54,2	63,4	50,4	62,2	51,8
of which:										
students, schoolchildren	83,1	48,7	82,9	51,2	68,5	46,6	82,5	46,0	86,9	48,7
looking for a job	0,9	53,5	6,9	69,8	6,7	58,7	4,2	61,1	4,2	62,9
with an occasional occupation	1,0	61,9	2,3	60,3	3,3	46,0	1,9	50,0	.	.
working part-time	0,9	63,2	1,2	61,0	1,4	52,5	1,9	51,7	.	.
Population between 14 and 24 years old	100,0	50,2	100,0	51,8	100,0	50,8	100,0	49,9	100,0	49,7

TAB. 22.1

Population aged between 14 and 24 by main type of activity (%)
Population de 14 à 24 ans selon les principaux critères d'activité (%)

Luxembourg		United Kingdom		Ireland		Danmark		EUR 9		
$\frac{f}{F}100$	$\frac{f}{f+m}100$	$\frac{f}{F}100$	$\frac{f}{f+m}100$	$\frac{f}{F}100$	$\frac{f}{f+m}100$	$\frac{f}{F}100$	$\frac{f}{f+m}100$	$\frac{f}{F}100$	$\frac{f}{f+m}100$	
					1973					
48,1	46,4	44,5	43,1	:	:	:	:	:	:	Personnes ayant un emploi principal *dont:*
.	.	6,2	86,8	:	:	:	:	:	:	travaillant à temps partiel
.	.	1,2	35,3	:	:	:	:	:	:	Personnes en chômage *dont:*
.	.	18,4	40,9	:	:	:	:	:	:	recherchant un 1er emploi
48,1	46,4	45,7	42,8	:	:	:	:	:	:	Total des forces de travail
51,9	53,8	54,3	56,8	:	:	:	:	:	:	Personnes non actives *dont:*
71,4	45,5	68,0	48,6	:	:	:	:	:	:	étudiants, élèves
.	.	3,6	60,2	:	:	:	:	:	:	à la recherche d'un emploi
.	.	2,3	56,7	:	:	:	:	:	:	avec activité occasionnelle
.	.	1,6	66,0	:	:	:	:	:	:	travaillant à temps partiel
100,0	49,1	100,0	49,4	:	:	:	:	:	:	Population de 14 à 24 ans
					1975					
46,7	48,3	41,6	43,4	41,0	43,8	37,2	46,3	37,4	45,4	Personnes ayant un emploi principal *dont:*
.	.	7,1	87,8	(1,7)	(50,0)	11,8	(81,0)	5,8	75,5	travaillant à temps partiel
.	.	3,5	44,0	6,0	37,0	5,4	42,9	3,3	46,0	Personnes en chômage *dont:*
.	.	14,4	41,2	58,8	47,6	(19,0)	(50,0)	42,8	48,6	recherchant un 1er emploi
46,7	48,3	45,1	43,5	47,0	42,8	42,6	45,8	40,8	45,4	Total des forces de travail
53,3	53,3	54,9	55,8	53,0	54,0	57,4	52,0	59,2	54,1	Personnes non actives *dont:*
75,0	46,2	74,3	49,2	77,3	48,1	59,0	50,2	75,3	48,2	étudiants, élèves
.	.	2,2	49,5	5,3	53,3	3,6	53,3	3,8	62,1	à la recherche d'un emploi
.	.	1,1	54,2	(2,0)	(50,0)	9,9	47,8	1,5	52,6	avec activité occasionnelle
.	.	1,1	55,8	(1,3)	(40,0)	9,0	45,5	1,1	56,0	travaillant à temps partiel
100,0	50,8	100,0	49,5	100,0	48,0	100,0	49,2	100,0	50,2	Population de 14 à 24 ans
					1977					
43,3	46,4	41,6	43,8	37,5	43,4	37,4	43,4	35,8	45,5	Personnes ayant un emploi principal *dont:*
(7,7)	.	8,0	79,8	(1,9)	.	16,8	73,5	6,2	77,2	travaillant à temps partiel
.	.	3,8	67,9	4,9	34,1	8,3	62,3	4,6	51,9	Personnes en chômage *dont:*
.	.	23,4	47,0	42,9	37,5	15,2	55,6	46,6	52,5	recherchant un 1er emploi
46,7	48,3	45,3	43,6	42,4	42,1	45,7	46,0	40,3	46,1	Total des forces de travail
53,3	53,3	54,7	54,8	57,6	53,6	54,3	52,2	59,7	53,6	Personnes non actives *dont:*
81,3	50,0	77,0	49,0	81,6	49,1	92,1	50,6	78,6	48,6	étudiants, élèves
.	.	8,0	56,7	8,6	53,8	11,1	53,3	5,3	59,8	à la recherche d'un emploi
.	.	1,6	50,7	1,8	42,0	11,1	47,1	2,1	50,7	avec activité occasionnelle
.	.	1,3	57,4	1,7	47,4	11,0	48,0	1,3	54,9	travaillant à temps partiel
100,0	50,8	100,0	49,1	100,0	48,0	100,0	49,1	100,0	50,3	Population de 14 à 24 ans

TAB. 23
Population aged 60 and over by main type of activity (1 000)

Population âgée de 60 ans et plus selon les principaux critères d'activité (1 000)

	BR Deutschland		France		Italia		Nederland		Belgique België	
	F	M	F	M	F	M	F	M	F	M
1973										
Persons with a main occupation	624	1 611	664	1 067	172	858	36	245	40	183
of which:										
60–64 years old	388	1 095	435	735	119	611	17	189	25	147
Total labour force	627	1 617	675	1 089	172	863	36	249	40	189
Non-active persons	6 867	3 424	4 922	2 902	5 100	3 431	974	610	954	571
with an occasional occupation	129	102	88	126	53	137	15	19	5	9
Total population	7 506	5 041	5 596	3 991	5 257	4 294	1 010	859	994	760
of which:										
60–64 years old	2 159	1 564	1 432	1 234	1 622	1 471	303	275	275	243
1975										
Persons with a main occupation	523	1 247	572	933	180	902	36	231	33	169
of which:										
60–64 years old	319	869	352	590	116	599	26	177	21	137
Total labour force	528	1 272	582	951	180	907	36	238	34	174
Non-active persons	7 133	3 752	5 035	2 977	5 160	3 500	1 017	651	971	591
with an occasional occupation	101	83	48	63	42	83	11	15	(4)	8
Total population	7 661	5 024	5 617	3 928	5 340	4 407	1 053	889	1 005	765
of which:										
60–64 years old	2 039	1 432	1 272	1 097	1 571	1 422	309	279	273	242
1977										
Persons with a main occupation	382	885	450	700	222	749	33	204	27	124
of which:										
60–64 years old	219	578	257	405	123	442	23	161	16	94
Total labour force	389	899	466	724	223	753	33	214	28	129
Non-active persons	7 111	3 833	4 913	3 057	4 923	3 478	1 094	685	980	635
with an occasional occupation	81	73	46	61	88	226	10	14	(2)	(3)
Total population	7 500	4 732	5 378	3 781	5 146	4 231	1 128	898	1 008	764
of which:										
60–64 years old	1 623	1 113	1 028	888	1 366	1 204	315	275	228	205

TAB. 23

Population aged 60 and over by main type of activity (1 000)
Population âgée de 60 ans et plus selon les principaux critères d'activité (1 000)

Luxembourg		United Kingdom		Ireland		Danmark		EUR 9		
F	M	F	M	F	M	F	M	F	M	
					1973					
2	7	726	1 679	:	:	:	:	:	:	Personnes ayant un emploi principal *dont:*
1	5	477	1 193	:	:	:	:	:	:	de 60–64 ans
2	7	733	1 731	:	:	:	:	:	:	Total des forces de travail
34	22	5 593	2 796	:	:	:	:	:	:	Personnes non actives
.	.	25	63	:	:	:	:	:	:	avec activité occasionnelle
36	29	6 326	4527	:	:	:	:	:	:	Population totale *dont:*
10	9	1 698	1 502	:	:	:	:	:	:	de 60–64 ans
					1975					
3	7	725	1 666	22	94	58	153	2 152	5 401	Personnes ayant un emploi principal *dont:*
1	5	488	1 159	12	49	40	91	1 375	3 674	de 60–64 ans
3	7	745	1 756	23	100	60	165	2 189	5 570	Total des forces de travail
36	22	5 416	2 604	212	114	453	257	25 434	14 467	Personnes non actives
.	.	.	(4)	(4)	(2)	10	9	219	167	avec activité occasionnelle
38	29	6 161	4 360	235	214	512	422	27 621	20 037	Population totale *dont:*
10	9	1 651	1 451	65	67	140	127	7 332	6 125	de 60–64 ans
					1977					
2	6	650	1 544	20	88	54	148	1 840	4 448	Personnes ayant un emploi principal *dont:*
(1)	4	413	1 052	11	44	38	89	1 100	2 869	de 60–64 ans
2	6	659	1 610	21	94	58	160	1 877	4 588	Total des forces de travail
36	23	5 737	2 933	217	117	476	270	25 487	15 031	Personnes non actives
.	.	8	14	5	(3)	8	5	248	400	avec activité occasionnelle
38	29	6 396	4 543	238	211	534	430	27 364	19 619	Population totale *dont:*
9	8	1 569	1 384	65	60	140	124	6 343	5 260	de 60–64 ans

TAB. 23.1

Population aged 60 and over by main type of activity (%)

Population âgée de 60 ans et plus selon les principaux critères d'activité (%)

	BR Deutschland		France		Italia		Nederland		Belgique België	
	$\frac{f}{F}100$	$\frac{f}{f+m}100$	$\frac{f}{F}100$	$\frac{f}{f+m}100$	$\frac{f}{F}100$	$\frac{f}{f+m}100$	$\frac{f}{F}100$	$\frac{f}{f+m}100$	$\frac{f}{F}100$	$\frac{f}{f+m}100$
1973										
Persons with a main occupation	8,3	27,9	11,9	38,4	3,3	16,7	3,6	12,8	4,0	17,9
of which:										
60–64 years old	62,2	26,2	65,5	37,2	69,2	16,3	75,0	12,5	62,5	14,5
Total labour force	8,4	27,9	12,1	38,3	3,3	16,6	3,6	12,6	4,0	17,5
Non-active persons	91,6	66,7	87,9	62,9	96,7	59,8	96,4	61,5	96,0	62,6
with an occasional occupation	1,9	55,8	1,8	41,1	1,0	27,9	1,5	44,1	0,5	35,7
Total population	100,0	59,8	100,0	58,4	100,0	55,1	100,0	54,0	100,0	56,7
of which:										
60–64 years old	28,8	58,0	25,6	53,7	30,8	52,4	30,0	52,4	27,7	53,1
1975										
Persons with a main occupation	6,8	29,5	10,2	38,0	3,4	16,6	3,4	13,5	3,3	16,3
of which:										
60–64 years old	61,0	26,9	61,5	37,4	64,4	17,2	72,2	12,8	63,6	13,3
Total labour force	6,9	29,3	10,4	38,0	3,4	16,6	3,4	13,1	3,4	16,3
Non-active persons	93,1	65,5	89,6	62,8	96,6	59,6	96,6	61,0	96,6	62,2
with an occasional occupation	1,4	55,0	1,0	43,2	0,8	33,6	1,1	42,3	(0,4)	(33,3)
Total population	100,0	60,4	100,0	58,8	100,0	54,8	100,0	54,2	100,0	56,8
of which:										
60–64 years old	26,6	58,7	22,7	53,7	29,4	52,5	29,3	52,6	27,2	53,0
1977										
Persons with a main occupation	5,1	30,1	8,4	39,1	4,3	22,9	2,9	13,9	2,7	17,9
of which:										
60–64 years old	57,3	27,5	57,1	38,8	55,4	21,8	69,7	12,5	59,3	14,5
Total labour force	5,2	30,2	8,7	39,2	4,3	22,8	2,9	13,4	2,8	17,8
Non-active persons	94,8	65,0	91,4	61,6	95,7	58,6	97,0	61,5	97,2	60,7
with an occasional occupation	1,1	52,6	0,9	43,0	1,8	28,0	0,9	41,7	(0,2)	(40,0)
Total population	100,0	61,3	100,0	58,7	100,0	54,9	100,0	55,7	100,0	56,9
of which:										
60–64 years old	21,6	59,3	19,1	53,7	26,5	53,2	27,9	53,4	22,6	52,7

TAB. 23.1

Population aged 60 and over by main type of activity (%)
Population âgée de 60 ans et plus selon les principaux critères d'activité (%)

Luxembourg		United Kingdom		Ireland		Danmark		EUR 9		
$\frac{f}{F}100$	$\frac{f}{f+m}100$	$\frac{f}{F}100$	$\frac{f}{f+m}100$	$\frac{f}{F}100$	$\frac{f}{f+m}100$	$\frac{f}{F}100$	$\frac{f}{f+m}100$	$\frac{f}{F}100$	$\frac{f}{f+m}100$	
				1973						
5,6	22,2	11,5	30,2	:	:	:	:	:	:	Personnes ayant un emploi principal *dont:*
50,0	16,7	65,7	28,6	:	:	:	:	:	:	de 60–64 ans
5,6	22,2	11,6	29,7	:	:	:	:	:	:	Total des forces de travail
94,4	60,7	88,4	66,7	:	:	:	:	:	:	Personnes non actives
.	.	0,5	28,4	:	:	:	:	:	:	avec activité occasionnelle
100,0	53,4	100,0	58,3	:	:	:	:	:	:	Population totale *dont:*
27,8	52,6	26,8	53,1	:	:	:	:	:	:	de 60–64 ans
				1975						
7,8	30,0	11,8	30,3	9,4	19,0	11,3	27,5	7,8	28,5	Personnes ayant un emploi principal *dont:*
33,3	16,7	67,3	29,6	54,5	19,7	69,0	30,5	63,9	27,2	de 60–64 ans
7,7	30,0	12,1	29,8	9,8	18,7	11,6	26,7	7,9	28,2	Total des forces de travail
92,3	62,1	87,9	67,5	90,2	65,0	88,4	63,8	92,1	63,7	Personnes non actives
.	.	.	.	(1,9)	(66,7)	2,2	52,6	0,9	45,1	avec activité occasionnelle
100,0	56,7	100,0	58,6	100,0	52,3	100,0	54,8	100,0	58,0	Population totale *dont:*
26,3	52,6	26,8	53,2	27,7	49,2	27,3	52,4	26,5	54,5	de 60–64 ans
				1977						
5,3	25,0	10,2	29,6	8,4	18,5	10,1	26,7	6,7	29,3	Personnes ayant un emploi principal *dont:*
62,3	(23,1)	63,5	28,2	55,0	20,0	70,4	29,9	59,8	27,7	de 60–64 ans
5,3	25,0	10,3	29,0	8,8	18,3	10,9	26,6	6,9	29,0	Total des forces de travail
94,7	61,0	89,7	65,9	91,2	65,0	89,1	63,8	93,1	62,9	Personnes non actives
.	.	0,1	36,4	2,3	(62,5)	1,7	61,5	1,0	38,3	avec activité occasionnelle
100,0	56,7	100,0	58,5	100,0	53,0	100,0	55,4	100,0	58,2	Population totale *dont:*
23,7	52,9	24,5	53,1	27,3	52,0	26,2	53,0	23,2	54,7	de 60–64 ans

TAB. 24
Married women by main type of activity (1 000)

Femmes mariées selon les principaux critères d'activité (1 000)

	BR Deutschland	France	Italia	Nederland	Belgique België
1973					
Persons with a main occupation	5 437	4 734	2 320	402	709
of which:					
age groups					
14 – 24	593	544	119	86	98
25 – 44	2 974	2 521	1 392	221	428
45 – 59	1 600	1 357	714	84	162
60 +	271	311	95	10	20
Unemployed persons	32	78	48	(4)	16
of which:					
looking for a job after a voluntary spell away from work	10	17	.	.	.
Total labour force	5 469	4 812	2 368	405	726
Non-active persons	9 904	7 356	10 987	2 822	1 765
of which:					
housewives	8 849	6 236	9 610	2 741	1 559
with an occasional occupation	485	298	429	218	21
working part time	453	239	242	146	19
looking for a job	12	209	240	30	5
Total married women	15 387	12 168	13 356	3 228	2 491
1975					
Persons with a main occupation	5 476	5 007	2 773	502	790
of which:					
age groups					
14 – 24	567	562	158	101	100
25 – 44	3 065	2 790	1 683	284	490
45 – 59	1 618	1 401	826	104	180
60 +	227	254	107	13	20
Unemployed persons	155	168	45	11	40
of which:					
looking for a job after a voluntary spell away from work	25	48	.	.	.
Total labour force	5 631	5 175	2 818	513	830
Non-active persons	9 884	7 290	11 009	2 791	1 726
of which:					
housewives	8 521	5 770	9 349	2 722	1 488
with an occasional occupation	414	244	304	148	15
working part time	400	197	140	138	14
looking for a job	36	222	166	54	(3)
Total married women	15 515	12 465	13 827	3 304	2 556
1977					
Persons with a main occupation	5 444	5 266	3 295	597	782
of which:					
age groups					
14 – 24	497	532	206	115	95
25 – 44	3 119	2 952	2 033	341	499
45 – 59	1 667	1 583	933	128	173
60 +	161	199	124	12	15
Unemployed persons	192	243	76	9	99
of which:					
looking for a job after a voluntary spell away form work	64	58	(3)	.	.
Total labour force	5 636	5 509	3 371	606	881
Non-active persons	9 664	6 923	10 800	2 793	1 723
of which:					
housewives	8 245	5 683	9 169	2 703	1 449
with an occasional occupation	430	251	610	143	6
working part time	415	203	297	134	6
looking for a job	44	252	242	52	15
Total married women	15 300	12 432	14 171	3 399	2 604

Luxembourg	United Kingdom	Ireland	Danmark	EUR 9	
		1973			
16	5 873	:	:	:	Personnes ayant un emploi principal
					dont:
					groupes d'âge
2	520	:	:	:	14 – 24
9	2 757	:	:	:	25 – 44
4	2 212	:	:	:	45 – 59
(1)	383	:	:	:	60 +
.	83	:	:	:	Personnes en chômage
					dont:
					à la recherche d'un emploi après
.	30	:	:	:	interruption volontaire
16	5 956	:	:	:	Total des forces de travail
73	8 152	:	:	:	Personnes non actives
					dont:
72	6 882	:	:	:	ménagères
2	154	:	:	:	avec activité occasionnelle
2	122	:	:	:	travaillant à temps partiel
.	201	:	:	:	à la recherche d'un emploi
89	14 108	:	:	:	Total des femmes mariées
		1975			
19	6 302	74	544	21 486	Personnes ayant un emploi principal
					dont:
					groupes d'âge
3	513	7	30	2 039	14 – 24
11	3 033	38	318	11 712	25 – 44
5	2 346	23	164	6 667	45 – 59
(1)	410	6	32	1 067	60 +
.	329	(4)	30	780	Personnes en chômage
					dont:
					à la recherche d'un emploi après
.	133	.	7	215	interruption volontaire
19	6 631	79	574	22 267	Total des forces de travail
72	7 343	487	601	41 202	Personnes non actives
					dont:
70	5 369	473	493	34 255	ménagères
(1)	(7)	22	50	1 203	avec activité occasionnelle
(1)	(5)	19	49	963	travaillant à temps partiel
.	33	9	10	533	à la recherche d'un emploi
91	13 974	565	1 175	63 469	Total des femmes mariées
		1977			
19	6 539	81	581	22 604	Personnes ayant un emploi principal
					dont:
					groupes d'âge
3	518	9	27	2 002	14 – 24
11	3 212	46	358	12 571	25 – 44
5	2 428	21	163	7 100	45 – 59
(1)	381	5	33	931	60 +
.	223	(3)	46	892	Personnes en chômage
					dont:
					à la recherche d'un emploi après
.	52	.	7	184	interruption volontaire
19	6 763	84	627	23 496	Total des forces de travail
72	7296	507	562	40 339	Personnes non actives
					dont:
68	5 648	497	441	33 903	ménagères
(1)	54	26	35	1 558	avec activité occasionnelle
(1)	40	25	35	1 156	travaillant à temps partiel
.	302	13	7	927	à la recherche d'un emploi
91	14 058	591	1 190	63 835	Total des femmes mariées

TAB. 24.1

Married women by main type of activity (%)
Femmes mariées selon les principaux critères d'activité (%)

	BR Deutschland	France	Italia	Nederland	Belgique België
1973					
Persons with a main occupation	35,3	38,9	17,4	12,5	28,5
of which:					
age groups					
14 – 24	10,9	11,5	5,1	21,5	13,8
25 – 44	54,7	53,2	60,0	55,1	60,5
45 – 59	29,4	28,7	30,8	20,9	22,9
60 +	5,0	6,6	4,1	2,5	2,8
Unemployed persons	0,2	0,6	0,3	(0,1)	0,6
of which:					
looking for a job after a voluntary spell away from work	31,3	21,8	.	.	.
Total labour force	35,5	39,5	17,7	12,6	29,1
Non-active persons	64,5	60,5	82,3	87,4	70,9
of which:					
housewives	89,4	84,8	87,5	97,1	88,3
with an occasional occupation	4,9	4,1	3,9	7,7	1,2
working part time	4,6	3,2	2,2	5,2	1,1
looking for a job	0,1	2,8	2,2	1,1	0,3
Total married women	100,0	100,0	100,0	100,0	100,0
1975					
Persons with a main occupation	35,3	40,2	20,1	15,2	30,9
of which:					
age groups					
14 – 24	10,4	11,2	5,7	20,1	12,7
25 – 44	56,0	55,7	60,7	56,6	62,0
45 – 59	29,5	28,0	29,8	20,7	22,8
60 +	4,1	5,1	3,8	2,6	2,5
Unemployed persons	1,0	1,3	0,3	0,3	1,6
of which:					
looking for a job after a voluntary spell away from work	16,1	28,6	.	.	.
Total labour force	36,3	41,5	20,4	15,5	32,5
Non-active persons	63,7	58,5	79,6	84,5	67,5
of which:					
housewives	86,2	79,1	84,9	97,5	86,2
with an occasional occupation	4,2	3,3	2,8	5,3	0,9
working part time	4,0	2,7	1,3	4,9	0,8
looking for a job	0,4	3,0	1,5	1,9	(0,2)
Total married women	100,0	100,0	100,0	100,0	100,0
1977					
Persons with a main occupation	35,6	42,4	23,3	17,6	30,0
of which:					
age groups					
14 – 24	9,1	10,1	6,3	19,3	12,1
25 – 44	57,3	56,1	61,7	57,2	63,8
45 – 59	30,6	30,1	28,3	21,5	22,1
60 +	3,0	3,8	3,8	2,0	1,9
Unemployed persons	1,3	2,0	0,5	0,3	3,8
of which:					
looking for a job after a voluntary spell away from work	33,3	23,9	(3,9)	.	.
Total labour force	36,8	44,3	23,8	17,8	33,8
Non-active persons	63,2	55,7	76,2	82,2	66,2
of which:					
housewives	85,3	82,1	84,9	96,8	84,1
with an occasional occupation	4,4	3,6	5,6	5,1	0,3
working part time	4,3	2,9	2,8	4,8	0,3
looking for a job	0,5	3,6	2,2	1,9	0,9
Total married women	100,0	100,0	100,0	100,0	100,0

TAB. 24.1

Married women by main type of activity (%)
Femmes mariées selon les principaux critères d'activité (%)

Luxembourg	United Kingdom	Ireland	Danmark	EUR 9	
		1973			
18,0	41,6	:	:	:	Personnes ayant un emploi principal
					dont:
					groupes d'âge
12,5	8,9	:	:	:	14 – 24
56,2	46,9	:	:	:	25 – 44
25,0	37,7	:	:	:	45 – 59
(6,3)	6,5	:	:	:	60 +
.	0,6	:	:	:	Personnes en chômage
					dont:
					à la recherche d'un emploi après
.	36,1	:	:	:	interruption volontaire
18,0	42,2	:	:	:	Total des forces de travail
82,0	57,8	:	:	:	Personnes non actives
					dont:
98,6	84,4	:	:	:	ménagères
2,7	1,9	:	:	:	avec activité occasionnelle
2,7	1,5	:	:	:	travaillant à temps partiel
.	2,5	:	:	:	à la recherche d'un emploi
100,0	100,0	:	:	:	Total des femmes mariées
		1975			
20,9	45,1	13,1	46,3	33,9	Personnes ayant un emploi principal
					dont:
					groupes d'âge
15,7	8,2	9,4	5,5	9,5	14 – 24
57,8	48,1	51,4	58,5	54,5	25 – 44
26,3	37,2	31,1	30,1	31,1	45 – 59
(5,2)	6,5	8,1	5,9	5,0	60 +
.	2,4	(0,7)	2,6	1,2	Personnes en chômage
					dont:
					à la recherche d'un emploi après
.	40,4	.	23,3	27,6	interruption volontaire
20,9	47,5	13,8	48,9	35,1	Total des forces de travail
79,1	52,5	86,2	51,1	64,9	Personnes non actives
					dont:
97,2	73,1	97,1	82,0	83,1	ménagères
(1,4)	(0,1)	4,5	8,3	2,9	avec activité occasionnelle
(1,4)	(0,1)	3,9	8,1	2,3	travaillant à temps partiel
.	0,4	1,8	1,6	1,3	à la recherche d'un emploi
100,0	100,0	100,0	100,0	100,0	Total des femmes mariées
		1977			
21,2	46,5	13,7	48,8	35,4	Personnes ayant un emploi principal
					dont:
					groupes d'âge
15,0	7,9	11,1	4,6	8,9	14 – 24
58,5	49,1	56,8	61,6	55,6	25 – 44
23,3	37,1	25,9	28,1	31,4	45 – 59
3,1	5,8	6,2	5,7	4,1	60 +
.	1,6	(0,5)	3,9	1,4	Personnes en chômage
					dont:
					à la recherche d'un emploi après
.	23,3	.	15,2	20,6	interruption volontaire
21,2	48,1	14,2	52,7	36,8	Total des forces de travail
78,8	51,9	85,8	47,2	63,2	Personnes non actives
					dont:
94,4	77,4	98,0	78,5	84,0	ménagères
1,9	0,7	5,1	6,2	3,9	avec activité occasionnelle
1,3	0,5	4,9	6,2	2,9	travaillant à temps partiel
.	4,1	2,6	1,2	2,3	à la recherche d'un emploi
100,0	100,0	100,0	100,0	100,0	Total des femmes mariées

TAB. 25
Non-active population aged 14 and over by main categories of activity (1 000)
Population non active de 14 ans et plus selon les principales catégories (1 000)

	BR Deutschland		France		Italia		Nederland		Belgique België	
	F	M	F	M	F	M	F	M	F	M
1973										
Total non-active persons:	16 481	5 937	12 577	5 342	17 111	6 738	3 924	1 416	2 745	1 139
students, schoolchildren	1 692	2 051	2 014	1 961	1 765	2 233	523	668	398	445
housewives	8 942	–	7 173	–	11 691	–	3 150	–	1 722	–
retired, pensioner	5 335	3 690	2 696	2 992	3 119	3 656	234	597	587	598
of which:										
with an occasional occupation:	586	145	403	226	565	584	255	60	25	14
students, schoolchildren	(6)	18	23	32	.	(4)	24	37	.	.
housewives	416	–	252	–	412	–	229	–	18	–
looking for a job:	:	:	304	64	567	274	48	17	12	5
students, schoolchildren	:	:	50	24	74	78	13	16	5	(4)
housewives	:	–	225	–	446	–	35	–	7	–
1975										
Total non-active persons:	16 857	6 583	12 380	5 486	17 233	6 980	4 003	1 588	2 704	1 184
students, schoolchildren	2 000	2 274	1 986	1 922	2 051	2 472	591	762	428	470
housewives	8 618	–	6 698	–	11 236	–	3 161	–	1 622	–
retired, pensioner	5 611	4 041	2 820	3 092	3 232	3 717	205	599	606	603
of which:										
with an occasional occupation:	501	121	308	156	407	410	168	35	20	12
students, schoolchildren	8	12	(6)	(8)	.	(5)	12	16	.	.
housewives	349	–	2 259	–	91	–	153	–	15	–
looking for a job:	62	77	345	122	392	206	84	27	7	(4)
students, schoolchildren	(3)	(6)	96	72	66	77	22	19	(4)	(4)
housewives	42	–	226	–	265	–	61	–	(3)	–
1977										
Total non-active persons:	17 101	7 040	12 326	5 698	16 844	7 256	4 139	1 692	2 732	1 261
students, schoolchildren	2 324	2 608	2 095	2 031	2 127	2 467	669	811	457	489
housewives	8 336	–	6 620	–	10 948	–	3 164	–	1 749	–
retired, pensioner	5 757	4 084	2 875	3 195	3 141	3 502	273	623	448	609
of which:										
with an occasional occupation:	516	123	344	167	827	911	163	36	8	(4)
students, schoolchildren	12	21	11	10	18	31	12	19	.	.
housewives	353	–	250	–	741	–	147	–	6	–
looking for a job:	83	88	387	103	492	320	94	57	36	16
students, schoolchildren	.	(6)	85	52	99	113	25	25	19	14
housewives	50	–	277	–	368	–	65	–	16	–

TAB. 25

Non-active population aged 14 and over by main categories of activity (1 000)

Population non active de 14 ans et plus selon les principales catégories (1 000)

Luxembourg		United Kingdom		Ireland		Danmark		EUR 9		
F	M	F	M	F	M	F	M	F	M	
1973										
108	38	13 298	4 911	:	:	:	:	:	:	Total des personnes non actives:
10	13	1 533	1 634	:	:	:	:	:	:	étudiants, élèves
76	–	7 901	–	:	:	:	:	:	:	ménagères
22	25	3 662	2 887	:	:	:	:	:	:	pensionnés, retraités
										dont:
2	.	220	164	:	:	:	:	:	:	ayant une activité occasionnelle:
–	.	23	20	:	:	:	:	:	:	étudiants, élèves
2	–	142	–	:	:	:	:	:	:	ménagères
.		278	116	:	:	:	:	:	:	à la recherche d'un emploi:
.		49	53	:	:	:	:	:	:	étudiants, élèves
.	–	205	–	:	:	:	:	:	:	ménagères
1975										
110	39	12 505	4 771	779	264	1 107	543	67 679	27 438	Total des personnes non actives:
12	14	1 734	1 812	117	126	148	159	9 067	10 011	étudiants, élèves
73	–	5 820	–	582	–	519	–	38 327	–	ménagères
25	25	4 785	2 795	68	112	367	309	17 718	15 293	pensionnés, retraités
										dont:
(1)	(1)	32	28	28	5	79	41	1 544	808	ayant une activité occasionnelle:
.	.	26	24	(2)	(3)	23	30	79	98	étudiants, élèves
(1)	–	(5)	–	25	–	48	–	913	–	ménagères
(1)	.	85	64	18	9	21	11	1 014	519	à la recherche d'un emploi:
.	.	51	56	6	7	9	9	258	249	étudiants, élèves
.	–	26	–	11	–	11	–	644	–	ménagères
1977										
110	42	12 392	5 364	813	283	1 077	539	68 073	29 175	Total des personnes non actives:
13	14	1 895	1 986	134	139	215	216	9 929	10 762	étudiants, élèves
70	–	6 625	–	621	–	463	–	38 596	–	ménagères
26	27	3 971	2 711	41	105	336	258	16 866	15 144	pensionnés, retraités
										dont:
(2)	(1)	97	63	32	8	66	40	2 053	1 352	ayant une activité occasionnelle:
.	.	33	32	(2)	(4)	27	31	115	148	étudiants, élèves
(1)	–	47	–	29	–	33	–	1 607	–	ménagères
(1)	.	493	208	26	13	32	26	1 644	831	à la recherche d'un emploi:
.	.	149	144	12	12	24	25	416	395	étudiants, élèves
(1)	–	313	–	14	–	6	–	1 110	–	ménagères

TAB. 25.1

Non-active population aged 14 and over by main categories of activity (%)

Population non active de 14 ans et plus selon les principales catégories (%)

	BR Deutschland		France		Italia		Nederland		Belgique België	
	$\frac{f}{F}100$	$\frac{f}{f+m}100$	$\frac{f}{F}100$	$\frac{f}{f+m}100$	$\frac{f}{F}100$	$\frac{f}{f+m}100$	$\frac{f}{F}100$	$\frac{f}{f+m}100$	$\frac{f}{F}100$	$\frac{f}{f+m}100$
1973										
Total non-active persons:	100,0	73,5	100,0	70,2	100,0	71,7	100,0	73,5	100,0	70,7
students, schoolchildren	10,3	45,2	16,0	50,7	10,3	44,1	13,3	43,9	14,5	47,3
housewives	54,3	100,0	57,0	100,0	68,3	100,0	80,3	100,0	62,7	100,0
retired, pensioner	32,3	59,1	21,4	47,4	18,2	46,0	6,0	28,2	21,4	49,5
of which:										
with an occasional occupation:	3,6	80,2	3,2	64,1	3,3	49,2	6,5	81,0	0,9	64,1
students, schoolchildren	(1,0)	(25,0)	5,7	41,8	.	.	9,4	39,3	.	.
housewives	71,0	100,0	62,5	100,0	72,9	100,0	89,8	100,0	72,0	100,0
looking for a job:	:	:	2,4	82,6	3,3	67,4	1,2	73,8	0,4	70,6
students, schoolchildren	:	:	16,4	67,6	13,1	48,7	27,1	44,8	41,7	(55,6)
housewives	:	:	74,0	100,0	78,6	100,0	72,9	100,0	58,3	100,0
1975										
Total non-active persons:	100,0	71,9	100,0	69,3	100,0	71,2	100,0	71,6	100,0	69,5
students, schoolchildren	11,9	46,8	16,0	50,8	11,9	45,3	14,8	43,7	15,8	47,7
housewives	51,1	100,0	54,1	100,0	65,2	100,0	79,0	100,0	60,0	100,0
retired, pensioner	33,3	58,1	22,8	47,7	18,8	46,5	5,1	25,5	22,4	50,1
of which:										
with an occasional occupation:	3,0	80,6	2,5	66,4	2,4	49,8	4,2	82,8	0,7	62,5
students, schoolchildren	1,6	40,0	(1,9)	(42,9)	.	.	7,1	42,9	.	.
housewives	69,7	100,0		100,0	22,4	100,0	91,1	100,0	75,0	100,0
looking for a job:	0,4	44,6	2,8	73,9	2,3	65,6	2,1	75,7	0,3	(63,6)
students, schoolchildren	(4,8)	(33,3)	27,8	57,1	16,8	46,2	26,2	53,7	(57,1)	(50,0)
housewives	67,7	100,0	65,5	100,0	67,6	100,0	72,6	100,0	(42,9)	100,0
1977										
Total non-active persons:	100,0	70,8	100,0	68,4	100,0	69,9	100,0	71,0	100,0	68,4
students, schoolchildren	13,6	47,1	17,0	50,8	12,6	46,3	16,2	45,2	16,7	48,3
housewives	48,7	100,0	53,7	100,0	65,0	100,0	76,4	100,0	64,0	100,0
retired, pensioner	33,7	58,5	23,3	47,4	18,6	47,3	6,6	30,5	16,4	42,4
of which:										
with an occasional occupation:	3,0	80,8	2,8	67,3	4,9	47,6	3,9	81,9	0,3	66,7
students, schoolchildren	2,3	36,4	3,2	52,4	2,2	36,7	7,4	38,7	.	.
housewives	68,4	100,0	72,7	100,0	89,6	100,0	90,2	100,0	75,0	100,0
looking for a job:	0,5	48,5	3,1	79,0	2,9	60,6	2,3	62,3	1,3	69,2
students, schoolchildren	.	.	22,0	62,0	20,1	46,7	26,6	50,0	52,8	57,6
housewives	60,2	100,0	71,6	100,0	74,8	100,0	69,1	100,0	44,4	100,0

TAB. 25.1

Non-active population aged 14 and over by main cotegories of activity (%)
Population non active de 14 ans et plus selon les principales catégories (%)

Luxembourg		United Kingdom		Ireland		Danmark		EUR 9		
$\frac{f}{F}100$	$\frac{f}{f+m}100$	$\frac{f}{F}100$	$\frac{f}{f+m}100$	$\frac{f}{F}100$	$\frac{f}{f+m}100$	$\frac{f}{F}100$	$\frac{f}{f+m}100$	$\frac{f}{F}100$	$\frac{f}{f+m}100$	
				1973						
100,0	74,0	100,0	73,0	:	:	:	:	:	:	Total des personnes non actives:
9,3	43,5	11,5	48,4	:	:	:	:	:	:	étudiants, élèves
70,4	100,0	59,4	100,0	:	:	:	:	:	:	ménagères
20,4	47,8	27,5	55,9	:	:	:	:	:	:	pensionnés, retraités
										dont:
1,9	.	1,7	57,3	:	:	:	:	:	:	ayant une activité occasionnelle:
–	–	10,5	53,5	:	:	:	:	:	:	étudiants, élèves
100,0	100,0	64,5	100,0	:	:	:	:	:	:	ménagères
.	.	2,1	70,6	:	:	:	:	:	:	à la recherche d'un emploi:
.	.	17,6	48,0	:	:	:	:	:	:	étudiants, élèves
.	.	73,7	100,0	:	:	:	:	:	:	ménagères
				1975						
100,0	73,8	100,0	72,4	100,0	74,7	100,0	67,1	100,0	71,2	Total des personnes non actives:
10,9	46,2	13,9	48,9	15,0	48,1	13,4	48,2	13,4	47,5	étudiants, élèves
66,4	100,0	46,5	100,0	74,7	100,0	46,9	100,0	56,6	100,0	ménagères
22,7	50,0	38,3	63,1	8,7	37,8	33,2	54,3	26,2	53,7	pensionnés, retraités
										dont:
(0,9)	(50,0)	0,3	53,3	3,6	84,8	7,1	65,8	2,3	65,6	ayant une activité occasionnelle:
.	.	81,3.	52,0	(7,1)	(40,0)	29,1	43,4	5,1	44,6	étudiants, élèves
(100,0)	100,0	(15,6)	100,0	89,3	100,0	60,8	100,0	59,1	100,0	ménagères
(0,9)	.	0,7	57,0	2,3	66,7	1,9	65,6	1,5	66,1	à la recherche d'un emploi:
.	.	60,0	47,7	33,3	46,2	42,9	50,0	25,4	50,9	étudiants, élèves
.	.	30,6	100,0	61,1	100,0	52,4	100,0	63,5	100,0	ménagères
				1977						
100,0	72,4	100,0	69,8	100,0	74,2	100,0	66,6	100,0	70,0	Total des personnes non actives:
11,8	48,1	15,3	48,8	16,5	49,1	20,0	49,9	14,6	48,0	étudiants, élèves
63,6	100,0	53,5	100,0	76,4	100,0	43,0	100,0	56,7	100,0	ménagères
23,6	49,1	32,0	59,4	5,0	28,1	31,2	56,6	24,8	52,7	pensionnés, retraités
										dont:
(1,8)	66,7	0,8	60,6	3,9	80,0	6,1	62,3	3,0	60,3	ayant une activité occasionnelle:
.	.	34,0	50,8	(6,3)	(33,3)	40,9	46,6	5,6	43,7	étudiants, élèves
(50,0)	100,0	48,5	100,0	90,6	100,0	50,0	100,0	78,3	100,0	ménagères
(1,0)	.	4,0	70,3	3,2	66,7	3,0	55,2	2,4	66,4	à la recherche d'un emploi:
.	.	30,2	50,9	46,2	50,0	75,0	49,0	25,3	51,3	étudiants, élèves
(72,7)	100,0	63,5	100,0	53,8	100,0	18,8	100,0	67,5	100,0	ménagères

TAB. 26

Non-active population by age groups (%)

Population non active par groupe d'âge (%)

	BR Deutschland		France		Italia		Nederland		Belgique België	
	F	M	F	M	F	M	F	M	F	M
1973										
TOTAL (1 000)	22 515	12 346	17 927	10 871	22 955	12 760	5 272	2 870	3 764	2 207
0 – 13	26,8	51,9	29,8	50,9	25,2	47,2	25,6	50,7	27,1	48,3
14 – 24	9,6	15,9	13,8	18,1	12,0	17,4	13,4	22,6	13,1	19,9
25 – 34	9,0	1,7	8,0	0,9	11,2	1,9	13,6	1,4	8,0	0,8
35 – 44	9,9	0,5	8,9	0,5	12,2	1,4	12,1	0,7	10,3	1,0
45 – 54	9,9	1,2	9,0	1,4	12,0	2,8	11,7	1,6	11,2	2,2
55 – 64	12,1	4,8	8,6	5,9	11,5	9,1	10,4	4,5	11,7	5,9
65 +	22,7	24,0	21,9	22,3	15,7	20,2	13,2	18,4	18,7	21,7
1975										
TOTAL (1 000)	22 521	12 520	17 631	10 932	23 098	13 035	5 506	3 150	3 706	2 231
0 – 13	25,1	47,4	29,8	49,8	25,4	46,5	27,3	49,6	27,0	46,9
14 – 24	10,7	17,3	13,6	17,9	12,9	18,8	13,5	23,5	13,7	20,8
25 – 34	8,2	2,2	8,1	1,2	10,6	1,8	13,5	1,6	7,2	0,9
35 – 44	10,2	0,7	8,0	0,7	12,1	1,4	11,0	0,9	9,7	0,9
45 – 54	9,8	1,3	8,7	1,6	12,1	2,6	11,0	1,9	11,8	2,5
55 – 64	11,9	5,4	8,5	6,0	10,8	8,3	10,3	4,9	11,1	6,1
65 +	24,1	25,7	23,4	22,7	16,0	20,6	13,3	17,6	19,4	22,0
1977										
TOTAL (1 000)	22 354	12 506	17 498	11 073	22 716	13 310	5 573	3 216	3 640	2 208
0 – 13	23,5	43,7	29,6	48,5	25,8	45,5	25,7	47,4	24,9	42,9
14 – 24	12,0	19,6	14,1	18,5	13,2	19,0	14,2	24,2	14,3	21,9
25 – 34	7,8	2,5	8,1	1,2	10,6	2,2	13,6	1,9	7,1	0,9
35 – 44	10,3	0,7	7,3	0,7	11,5	1,7	10,8	1,0	8,9	0,8
45 – 54	9,5	1,3	8,6	1,6	12,0	2,9	10,6	2,3	12,2	2,5
55 – 64	11,5	5,7	8,6	6,1	10,7	8,3	10,6	5,2	11,5	6,9
65 +	25,5	26,5	23,7	23,4	16,2	20,4	14,4	18,0	21,1	24,0

TAB. 26

Non-active population by age groups (%)
Population non-active par groupe d'âge (%)

Luxembourg		United Kingdom		Ireland		Danmark		EUR 9		
F	M	F	M	F	M	F	M	F	M	
1973										
140	72	18 966	10 853	:	:	:	:	:	:	TOTAL (1 000)
23,6	47,2	29,9	54,8	:	:	:	:	:	:	0 – 13
10,0	18,1	11,6	15,4	:	:	:	:	:	:	14 – 24
10,7	1,4#	10,5	1,1	:	:	:	:	:	:	25 – 34
12,9	0,0#	0,7	0,7	:	:	:	:	:	:	35 – 44
13,6	1,4#	7,3	1,2	:	:	:	:	:	:	45 – 54
11,4	8,3	10,6	3,5	:	:	:	:	:	:	55 – 64
18,6	25,0	23,1	23,3	:	:	:	:	:	:	65 +
1975										
143	73	18 353	10 914	1 207	717	1 600	1 059	93 764	54 631	TOTAL (1 000)
22,4	46,6	31,9	56,3	35,5	63,2	30,8	48,7	:	:	0 – 13
11,2	19,2	12,4	16,5	12,4	17,9	13,9	19,4	:	:	14 – 24
10,5	1,4#	9,0	1,0	10,4	0,6	7,8	3,2	:	:	25 – 34
12,6	0,0#	6,0	0,6	9,7	0,6	6,8	1,3	:	:	35 – 44
13,3	1,4#	6,3	0,9	9,7	1,1	7,9	1,6	:	:	45 – 54
11,2	8,2	10,2	2,9	9,2	2,8	10,8	4,4	:	:	55 – 64
18,9	24,7	23,2	21,8	13,2	14,1	22,1	21,5	:	:	65 +
1977										
141	73	18 403	11 154	1 252	743	1 561	1 046	93 138	55 330	TOTAL (1 000)
22,0	42,5	29,7	51,9	35,1	61,9	31,0	48,5	26,9	47,3	0 – 13
11,3	18,6	13,0	17,7	13,0	19,0	13,8	18,9	13,1	19,2	14 – 24
10,1	(1,2)	10,0	1,1	11,2	0,7	6,5	2,5	9,3	1,8	25 – 34
11,8	.	5,9	0,8	10,0	0,6	5,8	0,8	9,0	1,0	35 – 44
13,7	(1,9)	6,2	1,1	9,0	1,1	7,3	2,0	9,5	1,8	45 – 54
11,7	9,0	10,2	3,6	8,7	2,6	11,5	4,3	10,4	5,9	55 – 64
19,5	25,9	24,9	23,8	13,0	14,1	24,1	23,1	21,8	23,1	65 +

TAB. 27

Ratios of activity by broad age groups and regions (%)

Taux d'activité par grand groupe d'âge et par région (%)

1975

	14 – 24		25 – 34		35 – 44		45 – 54		55 – 64		65 +		TOTAL	
	F	M	F	M	F	M	F	M	F	M	F	M	F	M
BR DEUTSCHLAND	47,5	52,0	52,0	93,0	47,0	98,0	47,0	95,6	25,3	72,9	3,6	10,6	35,5	71,1
Schleswig-Holstein	43,9	56,9	52,3	94,3	49,0	97,7	50,1	95,0	25,0	76,6	2,8#	8,8	35,2	71,2
Hamburg	40,2	50,4	58,8	85,8	59,7	97,2	57,3	95,9	33,0	78,9	3,2#	14,2	37,9	69,4
Niedersachsen	48,5	55,5	48,7	94,6	45,0	98,2	50,5	96,5	26,0	75,3	3,3	11,3	35,0	71,2
Hannover	47,6	51,1	56,3	91,9	50,6	98,7	54,2	97,2	26,3	78,1	3,1#	10,3	36,5	70,0
Hildesheim	46,8	59,4	45,5	92,4	46,8	98,0	57,6	92,8	25,9	72,8	2,7#	11,4#	34,4	69,5
Lüneburg	55,0	58,0	50,3	96,7	46,7	98,1	53,3	96,8	29,7	79,0	2,4#	10,4#	38,9	72,3
Stade	51,1	54,7	48,6	94,8	42,1	97,9	44,4	97,4	21,1	74,1	4,6#	10,9#	33,9	70,3
Osnabrück	50,7	52,4	42,2	96,3	31,3	97,4	45,5	93,7	28,0	75,1	4,9#	17,0#	33,9	72,5
Aurich	56,1	64,3	30,7	97,9	34,0	97,8	31,8	99,1	22,4	72,0	4,8#	14,3#	28,8	74,4
Braunschweig	49,3	56,7	47,9	95,5	52,6	98,7	49,4	98,0	21,0	70,9	2,4#	9,1#	34,1	70,2
Oldenburg	37,2	54,4	45,3	96,5	40,7	97,7	53,7	97,1	31,3	74,4	3,7#	12,7#	33,8	73,2
Bremen	40,3	42,2	47,0	94,3	47,2	97,0	44,3	95,7	23,2	73,7	2,2#	7,3#	31,9	68,3
Nordrhein-Westfalen	45,2	49,4	44,3	92,1	36,3	97,7	38,3	94,8	19,8	68,5	2,5	8,7	30,5	70,6
Düsseldorf	44,8	51,8	45,0	94,0	37,5	97,7	39,8	95,8	21,6	71,1	1,6	7,5	30,6	71,9
Köln	43,0	44,3	45,2	89,0	36,7	98,2	37,4	95,6	20,0	71,3	2,5	10,3	31,2	71,0
Münster	44,8	46,5	42,9	89,0	30,4	96,9	34,6	93,1	18,4	61,9	3,5#	9,9	29,3	67,7
Detmold	51,6	54,1	47,5	93,5	46,1	98,0	47,9	95,5	24,0	72,2	3,9#	10,1	35,8	70,7
Arnsberg	44,8	50,8	41,7	93,9	33,6	97,8	34,5	93,4	16,2	63,2	2,4	7,5	28,1	70,0
Hessen	45,7	49,4	51,6	93,6	44,9	98,3	46,2	97,6	22,2	75,2	2,8	7,7	33,6	70,2
Darmstadt	46,1	47,1	53,3	93,7	46,4	98,6	47,5	97,7	22,8	75,5	2,5	7,5	34,6	70,1
Kassel	44,5	55,5	45,5	93,6	40,0	97,5	42,3	97,3	20,7	74,1	3,5#	8,2	30,5	70,5
Rheinland-Pfalz	51,4	57,5	45,9	95,0	43,0	98,6	38,3	94,8	19,6	66,8	3,5	10,1	32,2	70,3
Koblenz	51,6	60,1	39,7	96,9	41,2	98,5	35,1	95,3	17,5	63,9	4,8#	11,4	30,6	71,5
Trier	52,9	56,3	40,9	98,1	32,7	98,2	36,3	94,2	22,7	64,2	4,2#	16,0#	30,4	68,8
Rheinhessen-Pfalz	51,0	55,8	51,3	92,8	46,5	98,8	41,4	94,5	20,1	69,8	2,4#	7,4	33,9	69,9
Baden-Württemberg	48,1	50,9	57,0	93,9	53,7	98,3	54,0	96,0	30,3	77,7	5,0	13,8	40,4	72,9
Stuttgart	46,7	48,4	55,4	94,8	53,8	98,6	54,6	96,6	29,5	77,8	4,4	12,2	40,3	74,0
Karlsruhe	49,9	52,3	59,9	90,2	51,9	97,6	51,5	95,2	27,0	76,0	4,6	11,7	39,5	71,6
Freiburg	49,0	50,0	54,1	94,9	51,4	98,1	51,9	96,5	29,4	78,3	5,9	15,9	39,6	72,0
Tübingen	46,6	54,8	60,5	95,8	59,8	98,8	59,4	95,3	38,3	79,8	5,7#	17,9	43,3	73,4
Bayern	51,6	54,1	61,4	93,7	58,9	98,2	55,5	95,9	31,0	74,2	6,3	13,2	42,7	72,7
Oberbayern	52,4	53,0	63,9	93,4	59,9	98,1	54,6	96,4	32,7	75,7	5,3	10,9	43,4	73,4
Niederbayern	52,9	57,9	59,6	99,6	61,3	96,5	55,2	94,3	32,9	76,7	8,8	12,7	43,4	72,1
Oberpfalz	52,6	57,6	52,8	94,9	52,5	98,4	50,4	96,9	28,5	68,0	5,3#	16,0	39,0	71,7
Oberfranken	49,6	56,1	60,1	96,9	61,3	97,7	59,0	91,8	33,8	71,2	7,9	13,3	43,1	72,6
Mittelfranken	58,0	50,5	65,1	87,2	63,2	98,6	62,1	97,5	26,2	74,9	6,2	13,7	45,7	71,3
Unterfranken	47,3	54,3	55,4	91,4	49,0	99,1	48,1	96,3	26,8	75,4	4,3#	12,4	37,7	71,9
Schwaben	47,1	53,2	62,7	97,1	60,5	98,3	57,6	96,3	32,9	73,3	8,0	17,5	43,3	74,0
Saarland	45,2	54,1	35,2	94,5	27,1	97,8	28,0	92,9	13,1	56,6	1,0#	3,8#	25,2	68,6
Berlin (West)	48,8	47,8	67,6	85,5	67,1	96,4	58,0	93,8	32,5	75,1	2,3	8,1	37,3	64,9
FRANCE	42,1	50,4	60,2	96,6	53,5	97,5	51,7	94,4	34,4	67,8	5,1	12,2	39,7	71,0
Île-de-France	44,0	47,0	71,1	94,9	66,0	97,4	62,6	96,5	48,8	76,4	8,0	14,3	50,2	75,2
Bassin parisien	43,1	53,1	60,0	97,4	52,7	97,8	52,7	95,8	32,3	69,9	5,0	12,0	39,2	70,9
Champagne-Ardennes	43,2	51,8	61,6	97,9	44,5	96,4	51,3	96,0	28,4	65,5	3,4#	12,7	37,5	70,2
Picardie	41,4	54,7	55,5	96,1	47,3	96,4	48,7	94,5	28,3	67,3	2,7#	10,8	37,4	71,6
Haute-Normandie	42,6	58,8	61,8	99,4	55,3	97,4	49,6	96,5	35,4	73,2	6,6#	14,3	40,6	75,5
Centre	45,9	47,1	65,3	97,0	60,1	99,1	52,8	95,8	33,8	70,2	4,8	12,4	41,1	67,8
Basse-Normandie	42,4	54,1	56,7	97,3	56,0	98,9	60,5	95,5	34,9	69,5	7,1#	10,3#	41,1	71,6
Bourgogne	43,0	52,9	57,4	97,2	50,7	99,0	53,2	96,7	31,5	70,8	5,6	11,5	37,3	69,7
Nord-Pas-de-Calais	41,9	49,9	48,7	97,6	37,9	97,0	39,2	87,9	25,1	54,8	3,5	6,7	31,8	68,1
Est	47,2	55,7	53,1	98,6	43,1	98,5	45,7	94,6	30,7	59,8	3,2	10,8	37,6	73,2
Lorraine	39,1	52,9	48,4	99,0	39,0	98,1	40,8	94,1	28,4	57,8	1,4#	9,0	33,9	73,7
Alsace	55,7	60,0	56,0	97,9	48,3	99,3	46,2	94,4	26,5	56,8	4,9#	12,0	40,3	73,2
Franche-Comté	51,9	55,0	61,4	98,6	46,6	98,1	54,6	96,0	40,4	66,5	4,0#	12,5#	42,0	72,1

TAB. 27
(continued)
(suite)

1975

	14 – 24		25 – 34		35 – 44		45 – 54		55 – 64		65 +		TOTAL	
	F	M	F	M	F	M	F	M	F	M	F	M	F	M
Ouest	44,2	57,1	60,8	97,5	56,6	96,8	53,1	94,5	34,4	66,5	4,1	10,9	39,8	70,4
Pays de la Loire	49,5	60,6	61,8	98,1	57,9	97,3	56,4	97,2	38,9	65,4	5,5	11,9	43,7	72,4
Bretagne	42,3	54,5	60,6	97,3	57,4	96,2	52,6	92,2	32,2	65,1	3,9	11,0	39,0	69,6
Poitou-Charentes	36,2	54,4	58,7	96,6	52,7	97,1	48,2	93,3	29,9	70,6	2,2#	9,1	34,2	68,2
Sud-Ouest	38,7	44,8	57,3	95,8	50,6	96,9	51,4	94,6	33,3	67,0	5,1	14,3	36,6	67,6
Aquitaine	40,3	45,1	57,7	93,8	49,4	96,6	49,1	95,1	33,6	63,7	4,4	12,7	36,6	66,1
Midi-Pyrénées	36,7	43,8	57,9	97,4	51,7	97,3	48,8	93,9	31,2	67,9	5,1	16,7	36,8	69,7
Limousin	40,0	47,3	52,1	97,6	51,0	96,5	65,6	95,5	37,5	73,5	6,9#	13,4	36,3	66,0
Centre-Est	38,8	47,2	59,1	97,8	54,5	97,6	52,5	94,7	36,1	70,3	6,3	14,8	39,7	71,8
Rhône-Alpes	38,3	45,6	59,4	97,6	54,5	97,6	53,8	95,1	36,8	72,5	6,7	15,4	40,9	72,7
Auvergne	40,4	53,8	58,1	98,5	54,6	97,7	47,6	93,1	33,6	63,7	5,2	13,5	35,7	68,7
Méditerranée	34,5	46,8	53,1	94,8	47,1	97,4	40,9	91,8	24,3	64,3	3,8	10,5	31,3	66,4
Languedoc-Roussillon	31,3	43,6	51,4	94,9	44,6	97,1	36,9	92,0	21,9	64,2	2,5#	11,9	28,4	65,4
Provence-Alpes- Côte d'Azur-Corse	35,9	48,1	53,8	94,7	48,1	97,5	42,6	91,7	25,3	64,3	4,3	9,9	32,5	66,9
ITALIA	28,4	40,6	34,8	92,8	28,5	95,3	26,7	90,7	11,3	57,7	1,7	10,2	22,5	65,9
Nord-Ovest	37,9	45,8	43,5	95,2	35,4	97,2	30,1	93,7	9,6	57,6	2,3	10,5	25,8	67,7
Piemonte	38,9	49,5	46,2	95,5	37,8	97,4	33,3	93,6	9,0	57,1	2,0#	11,1	27,4	69,0
Valle d' Aosta	37,6#	52,1#	31,5#	95,2	33,9#	96,7	34,5#	83,3	12,0#	46,4#	2,8#	12,0#	25,8	67,5
Liguria	35,2	36,2	37,7	94,3	29,2	96,7	23,0	94,4	10,7	59,4	2,9	9,2	21,9	64,7
Lombardia	44,7	49,2	43,1	95,8	30,4	96,5	28,2	93,1	9,5	53,5	1,7	9,6	27,1	70,2
Nord-Est	44,3	44,2	35,4	95,1	24,4	97,5	24,0	91,1	11,2	57,3	1,0#	10,3	23,8	67,8
Trentino-Alto-Adige	41,5	47,4	34,3	94,6	21,8	97,0	21,0	92,2	13,6#	60,5	2,0#	16,1#	23,6	69,6
Friuli Venezia Giulia	35,1	39,5	40,0	96,0	27,2	97,3	26,7	91,5	11,0	49,7	0,4#	7,4#	22,8	64,6
Veneto	47,3	44,8	34,4	95,0	24,0	97,6	23,7	90,8	10,8	59,5	1,0#	10,1	24,2	68,3
Emilia Romagna	37,0	42,6	51,8	93,4	42,9	96,1	37,5	90,8	14,8	63,1	2,2#	14,7	30,7	68,5
Centro	33,8	38,1	43,2	93,9	33,2	95,8	26,2	92,1	12,2	58,4	2,4	12,4	25,1	66,0
Marche	37,2	39,7	52,2	94,4	39,8	95,0	33,4	91,0	13,2	59,4	4,4#	15,2	30,6	66,8
Toscana	33,0	37,6	39,4	94,1	31,3	96,3	24,2	93,0	11,3	58,3	1,7#	12,0	23,2	66,3
Umbria	31,2	37,3	46,1	91,5	30,2	94,8	23,6	90,8	14,6#	57,5	2,8#	10,2#	24,1	63,6
Lazio	20,6	28,7	28,0	89,5	19,9	96,2	19,1	92,1	9,5	62,1	1,2#	10,1	18,1	66,3
Campania	16,6	35,6	23,3	89,5	24,2	92,8	28,6	88,6	12,8	56,6	1,1#	7,7	18,2	61,6
Abruzzi e Molise	22,0	32,4	36,9	92,3	35,0	94,3	35,7	86,9	18,0	59,6	2,7#	11,9	24,4	61,6
Abruzzi	23,6	32,4	36,6	91,9	33,9	93,8	32,6	87,6	15,8	60,8	2,3#	11,6	23,6	62,0
Molise	15,5	32,3	37,9	93,9	39,1	96,1	47,0	84,3	26,8#	54,5	3,9#	12,9#	27,4	60,2
Sud	16,9	39,5	25,3	90,5	28,2	91,8	27,0	85,2	14,6	58,2	1,2#	7,4	19,2	62,0
Puglia	19,4	41,8	24,9	92,3	27,9	91,1	25,4	85,1	12,6	57,1	1,1#	7,1	19,2	62,5
Basilicata	13,8	31,8	29,8	88,6	35,8	93,2	37,7	90,7	16,0#	61,0	0,5#	8,9	22,6	61,5
Calabria	13,5	37,8	24,8	87,7	26,3	92,7	26,5	83,6	17,4	58,9	1,6#	7,6	18,0	61,2
Sicilia	8,5	40,7	18,9	89,7	15,3	91,9	17,9	88,3	9,1	58,1	1,1#	7,8	11,9	62,8
Sardegna	17,1	36,7	24,0	89,5	18,7	93,9	15,0	84,9	7,3#	49,2	2,1#	11,9	14,9	60,9
NEDERLAND	37,7	40,3	26,7	95,3	20,9	96,5	18,9	91,7	11,3	73,5	1,4	9,0	21,7	68,6
Noord-Nederland	33,6	39,8	20,2	95,0	14,6	95,8	14,1	91,5	8,7	74,0	0,6#	6,6	17,0	66,0
Groningen	32,5	37,8	24,0	91,1	16,2	95,2	17,6	91,6	10,8#	74,0	0,9#	7,1#	18,5	64,7
Friesland	33,5	39,0	17,1	96,8	10,8#	96,2	11,3#	91,3	7,9#	74,5	0,4#	5,9#	15,1	65,8
Drenthe	35,5	43,6	19,5	97,9	17,3	96,1	12,8#	91,8	6,7#	73,6	0,6#	7,1#	17,6	68,2
Oost Nederland	37,0	39,8	23,5	95,9	16,9	97,0	15,3	91,6	8,9	72,3	1,5#	9,8	19,8	68,5
Overijssel	36,2	39,6	22,6	97,3	16,2	96,7	15,5	89,4	8,5#	70,1	1,4#	9,4#	19,3	68,0
Gelderland	37,5	39,9	24,1	95,0	17,2	97,2	15,1	93,0	9,3	73,6	1,6#	10,0	20,2	68,7
West Nederland	38,8	40,2	31,0	94,2	26,4	96,8	23,2	93,4	14,3	77,4	1,6	10,8	24,2	69,2
Utrecht	33,3	37,5	29,1	92,7	22,4	97,2	24,7	92,4	15,1	81,7	1,3#	9,1#	23,0	68,1

TAB. 27
(continued)
(suite)

1975

	14 – 24		25 – 34		35 – 44		45 – 54		55 – 64		65 +		TOTAL	
	F	M	F	M	F	M	F	M	F	M	F	M	F	M
Noord Holland	39,1	39,6	33,2	93,2	28,7	96,2	23,4	92,9	13,4	73,7	1,9#	12,0	24,9	68,9
Zuid Nederland	40,4	41,6	29,8	95,4	25,8	97,1	22,6	94,0	14,7	79,1	1,5#	10,4	23,9	69,8
Noord-Brabant	39,5	41,6	23,0	96,6	17,1	96,5	15,2	90,6	7,2	72,2	1,3#	6,5	20,7	70,3
Limburg	36,1	39,5	25,6	97,0	16,3	93,6	14,4	84,0	8,0#	48,2	0,7#	3,9#	20,1	65,2
Zuidwest Nederland	35,9	42,2	23,4	97,4	16,4#	99,5	20,8#	92,9	11,7#	82,9	0,3#	7,4#	18,7	69,1
BELGIQUE/BELGIË	37,5	43,1	57,0	96,8	41,7	97,0	31,8	91,9	13,6	68,8	1,7	6,3	30,7	67,7
Vlaams Gewest/Région Flamande	40,1	43,0	56,4	97,6	39,2	97,5	28,5	93,8	11,3	71,9	1,6	5,5	30,9	68,8
Région wallonne/Waals Gewest	33,3	45,1	52,9	96,1	40,9	95,4	30,6	85,9	13,6	60,2	1,8	5,6	28,0	65,1
Région bruxelloise/ Brussels G.	35,2	35,9	70,7	94,8	56,9	98,7	49,1	93,7	22,8	79,4	1,4#	11,9	37,8	69,9
Antwerpen/Anvers	39,0	44,1	51,1	98,5	36,4	98,2	28,4	96,1	10,1	77,2	1,7#	5,8	28,7	70,4
Brabant	35,4	36,8	65,5	95,5	49,0	98,3	37,8	93,8	18,0	75,3	1,3#	8,8	34,0	68,3
W.Vlaand/Fland. occ.	41,7	44,6	57,4	98,3	40,3	98,0	29,4	95,6	12,2	71,3	2,1#	5,5	31,7	69,7
O.Vlaand/Fland. or.	43,0	45,8	61,5	97,0	42,9	98,5	33,8	96,2	11,7	73,9	1,6#	5,5	33,0	69,1
Hainaut/Henegouwen	34,7	46,7	52,6	96,9	42,9	93,3	30,1	80,5	13,5	53,7	1,4#	4,8	27,9	63,1
Liège/Luik	33,2	46,4	54,3	94,8	39,7	96,3	32,4	88,9	14,3	63,1	2,6#	6,1	28,9	67,1
Limburg/Limbourg	38,8	40,7	49,3	97,6	32,7	93,0	20,4	80,5	9,6	53,2	0,8#	5,0	29,7	65,3
Luxembourg/Luxemburg	28,9	44,1	47,4	93,8	38,9	98,1	28,7	94,0	15,2	66,9	1,6#	3,8	25,6	65,1
Namur/Namen	34,5	44,0	54,0	97,8	37,5	96,5	30,2	87,7	12,7	65,1	1,8#	7,2	27,6	66,00
LUXEMBOURG (GR.-DUCHÉ)	47,5	52,8	37,7	97,0	27,8	98,8	24,5	95,6	16,2	64,7	4,0#	12,5	26,8	72,0
UNITED KINGDOM	45,1	57,5	50,8	97,2	64,5	97,8	65,9	96,9	41,5	89,0	5,5	18,3	43,4	76,4
North	47,3	58,5	48,6	97,4	62,6	97,9	60,2	96,0	33,2	84,8	2,2#	11,6	40,9	75,3
Yorkshire and Humberside	45,4	58,8	52,1	98,0	65,8	97,5	66,5	95,6	39,3	87,8	5,2	15,7	43,5	76,0
North West	45,1	57,5	55,0	97,2	69,8	97,4	69,8	97,4	44,6	87,4	5,0	16,8	45,5	76,3
East Midlands	43,3	57,0	50,6	96,9	64,0	98,5	66,7	97,9	42,9	91,6	5,7	18,1	43,8	77,2
West Midlands	45,4	61,5	51,4	98,1	65,0	98,3	65,5	97,0	44,2	91,1	5,4	17,3	45,1	79,3
East Anglia	47,2	61,2	47,2	99,0	64,5	99,0	70,6	97,9	37,0	89,0	5,5	14,6	42,7	76,2
South East	45,8	55,1	52,1	96,4	65,2	98,3	68,9	97,7	45,6	92,0	6,9	22,9	45,1	77,2
South West	43,9	59,7	45,1	97,9	64,1	98,3	61,6	97,2	36,0	87,9	3,9	15,3	38,9	74,2
Wales	40,3	59,6	45,8	97,7	57,1	95,4	58,8	95,5	32,3	78,4	3,1#	15,2	37,4	74,0
Scotland	45,3	56,3	49,5	96,5	63,4	97,3	63,6	96,1	41,5	89,5	4,8	18,5	42,6	75,1
Northern Ireland	44,5	55,3	50,3	97,0	50,7	96,2	51,3	94,0	32,8	82,4	5,5#	20,1	39,2	74,3
IRELAND	47,1	58,2	31,7	97,8	20,3	97,4	22,8	94,9	19,8	85,8	6,1	31,4	27,4	75,6
DANMARK	42,7	48,9	67,9	91,6	62,1	95,4	56,5	93,9	38,6	82,6	5,0	22,5	44,8	71,9
EUR 9	40,8	49,4	48,5	95,0	45,7	97,1	45,1	94,1	26,9	72,9	3,9	12,7	34,5	70,9

TAB. 27

(continued)

(suite)

1977

	14 – 24		25 – 34		35 – 44		45 – 54		55 – 64		65 +		TOTAL	
	F	M	F	M	F	M	F	M	F	M	F	M	F	M
BR DEUTSCHLAND	44,5	48,8	54,4	91,8	48,7	98,0	46,4	95,5	27,4	71,1	2,7	8,4	35,3	69,6
Schleswig-Holstein	42,4	47,3	55,1	93,0	49,4	98,6	47,6	97,6	26,0	77,8	(2,2)	6,5	34,3	68,7
Hamburg	43,6	38,8	61,2	86,5	60,4	98,0	60,9	95,8	30,8	80,0	(2,7)	8,8	38,6	67,6
Niedersachsen	42,1	49,6	51,6	93,6	47,1	97,9	47,7	95,9	26,7	72,7	2,3	8,6	33,5	68,8
Hannover	42,4	46,3	54,5	89,4	50,7	98,8	52,6	95,4	30,8	72,3	(2,2)	7,0	36,4	68,6
Hildesheim	41,8	51,3	53,0	91,1	49,4	95,6	46,3	96,1	22,6	67,9	(1,7)	(8,3)	31,7	66,8
Lüneburg	45,2	47,9	62,7	95,3	48,0	98,3	47,4	98,2	22,3	76,7	(1,9)	(9,2)	34,4	69,0
Stade	49,2	52,0	50,4	95,9	46,2	99,0	48,7	95,0	26,5	77,0	(2,6)	(6,8)	35,2	71,1
Osnabrück	40,2	49,2	47,5	97,0	31,0	99,2	45,8	94,0	29,1	73,7	(2,2)	(15,4)	31,1	70,3
Aurich	35,1	48,1	(25,4)	96,0	31,1	94,5	33,0	93,3	19,9	69,7	(3,3)	(14,8)	23,6	67,7
Braunschweig	47,5	56,3	55,7	93,3	35,8	97,6	48,7	97,5	28,2	70,9	(2,6)	(6,2)	34,9	67,7
Oldenburg	32,3	48,8	42,2	97,7	51,5	97,9	46,5	95,6	28,0	73,0	(2,8)	(7,4)	32,0	69,1
Bremen	48,3	47,9	62,0	88,5	58,7	98,9	43,4	95,7	27,2	79,3	(0,7)	(8,1)	37,0	69,3
Nordrhein-Westfalen	42,6	47,3	47,9	92,8	39,2	98,1	38,6	95,0	21,4	67,9	1,7	6,4	30,8	69,6
Düsseldorf	43,1	47,2	49,3	94,6	41,9	98,4	39,2	96,5	23,3	69,2	1,8	6,8	31,8	71,2
Köln	41,4	45,9	46,6	90,4	37,7	97,9	39,9	95,7	21,5	69,0	(1,9)	6,1	30,8	70,1
Münster	40,6	46,0	42,6	92,4	32,9	98,2	31,8	93,0	16,6	60,0	(1,3)	6,2	27,6	67,4
Detmold	43,0	45,5	51,3	90,9	43,7	97,4	50,2	96,6	25,9	74,9	(2,9)	8,5	33,7	68,2
Arnsberg	44,4	50,3	49,3	94,3	38,5	97,9	35,2	92,9	19,0	65,8	(0,9)	5,4	30,1	69,1
Hessen	41,4	45,9	49,9	92,2	48,2	97,4	43,7	96,1	25,8	70,7	2,0	7,0	32,7	68,1
Darmstadt	40,9	44,6	51,4	91,5	48,7	97,2	44,3	96,1	25,5	73,3	1,7	6,2	33,3	68,4
Kassel	42,7	49,7	44,6	94,5	46,6	98,4	41,8	95,9	26,7	63,3	(1,8)	9,1	31,1	67,1
Rheinland-Pfalz	47,1	53,7	49,9	94,6	45,8	98,1	38,4	94,7	23,0	65,3	2,9	9,1	32,7	69,5
Koblenz	45,0	53,4	46,9	96,0	42,1	98,9	34,9	94,4	21,3	69,7	(2,2)	9,3	30,4	70,0
Trier	46,1	59,6	51,6	93,0	49,4	95,0	37,9	94,0	26,2	70,4	(4,6)	(12,2)	33,2	70,0
Rheinhessen-Pfalz	48,9	52,1	51,7	93,7	47,5	98,5	41,2	95,1	23,3	60,2	(3,0)	8,1	34,2	68,9
Baden-Württemberg	45,0	47,4	58,7	90,2	52,5	98,6	52,4	96,0	31,2	73,9	3,6	10,2	39,4	70,9
Stuttgart	45,0	48,8	59,0	91,4	54,3	98,7	54,4	95,2	29,3	74,9	2,8	8,6	40,3	72,4
Karlsruhe	44,7	47,4	57,4	87,2	51,2	97,6	46,9	96,3	28,5	72,5	(2,3)	9,9	36,6	69,3
Freiburg	43,5	47,1	58,5	90,7	52,2	99,1	52,0	96,7	32,5	73,0	(4,0)	8,5	39,3	70,3
Tübingen	47,2	44,2	60,1	91,5	50,7	99,1	56,9	96,8	38,4	75,1	7,3	15,7	42,3	71,0
Bayern	50,2	53,5	62,1	92,0	58,0	97,8	54,9	96,1	34,4	74,3	4,6	11,7	42,1	71,2
Oberbayern	50,3	49,0	63,8	90,1	61,1	98,0	57,1	97,4	35,1	76,4	5,7	11,3	43,7	71,9
Niederbayern	54,0	55,7	59,8	94,5	58,1	96,8	56,5	95,3	31,2	77,4	(7,4)	17,7	42,6	70,9
Oberpfalz	46,0	54,7	58,5	91,8	51,2	97,5	46,9	92,8	32,9	68,7	(3,3)	(9,4)	39,7	71,3
Oberfranken	52,9	55,8	63,6	96,0	62,2	98,5	59,8	94,1	41,0	75,1	(2,8)	10,9	44,1	70,7
Mittelfranken	49,5	52,9	63,2	88,3	63,3	97,9	58,0	95,6	33,7	67,1	(4,3)	10,0	42,8	69,7
Unterfranken	47,9	55,1	58,3	95,3	48,8	98,0	48,8	95,8	26,9	75,0	(1,9)	(8,5)	36,8	70,2
Schwaben	51,5	58,1	61,9	95,5	53,9	97,6	52,1	97,3	38,2	76,0	(4,9)	14,0	41,7	72,5
Saarland	43,8	50,2	44,0	92,1	29,6	98,9	26,3	91,3	20,4	54,1	(1,3)	(2,5)	26,0	65,6
Berlin (West)	39,7	42,2	69,2	83,4	71,9	95,9	63,8	91,9	36,7	65,5	3,6	8,3	40,2	65,6
FRANCE	41,5	48,0	63,2	96,6	56,1	97,3	53,1	94,4	36,8	68,6	4,4	10,3	41,1	70,0
Région Parisienne	42,1	42,7	71,7	95,0	66,6	97,3	64,1	96,3	48,9	79,9	6,5	13,0	50,0	74,4
Bassin Parisien	44,2	53,3	63,2	97,5	57,0	97,6	55,7	95,7	39,3	69,6	4,3	10,1	42,4	70,9
Champagne-Ardennes	40,3	50,4	60,4	97,7	52,5	98,3	46,9	97,8	34,2	66,9	(2,6)	(7,1)	39,4	71,9
Picardie	39,6	53,4	58,8	95,4	52,7	96,9	44,1	93,5	29,7	63,4	(2,3)	(8,5)	38,4	70,4
Haute-Normandie	43,9	57,5	55,7	98,1	58,3	98,8	55,5	94,0	43,1	73,9	7,1	13,4	42,6	74,9
Centre	50,3	53,0	71,3	98,1	63,2	97,3	63,1	95,9	42,3	70,5	(4,0)	8,2	46,4	69,0
Basse-Normandie	45,1	55,5	70,0	97,5	55,4	97,0	62,2	97,1	44,9	73,5	(5,7)	13,5	45,0	72,3
Bourgogne	45,6	49,9	64,3	98,1	57,9	97,6	58,0	96,0	39,7	69,2	(4,4)	11,4	41,7	68,5
Nord-Pas-de-Calais	42,7	47,8	53,4	97,5	39,3	96,6	37,8	87,3	24,7	53,4	2,7	7,3	33,6	67,6
Est	43,3	50,3	58,9	97,5	48,6	98,0	45,0	93,9	29,0	65,5	2,3	9,1	38,1	71,1
Lorraine	38,2	49,3	53,5	98,0	44,0	98,1	39,0	94,4	27,4	65,7	(1,4)	8,7	34,9	71,8
Alsace	52,3	55,7	66,4	97,0	53,2	97,7	47,3	93,9	28,7	60,3	(3,5)	9,2	41,0	70,9
Franche-Comté	43,2	46,4	60,6	97,2	53,4	98,1	54,1	93,0	32,4	69,6	(1,9)	9,9	40,8	69,7

TAB. 27
(continued)
(suite)

1977

	14 – 24		25 – 34		35 – 44		45 – 54		55 – 64		65 +		TOTAL	
	F	M	F	M	F	M	F	M	F	M	F	M	F	M
Ouest	43,7	51,5	64,9	97,4	57,2	97,0	57,1	94,7	38,0	66,0	4,3	8,3	41,9	68,5
Pays de la Loire	46,8	54,9	66,6	97,6	54,6	96,7	59,3	97,2	39,6	68,5	4,7	7,7	44,3	70,8
Bretagne	43,1	48,1	64,2	97,0	60,0	96,8	56,9	91,4	38,0	60,0	4,7	8,4	40,7	66,3
Poitou-Charentes	38,2	49,0	62,5	97,7	57,9	97,9	53,5	94,6	35,2	69,9	(2,9)	8,9	39,4	67,4
Sud-Ouest	41,7	46,9	63,8	96,1	54,7	97,1	51,8	94,3	34,8	67,1	4,2	10,8	38,5	66,9
Aquitaine	40,2	47,7	61,6	96,3	55,0	97,4	49,2	94,7	34,3	67,3	4,1	8,6	37,4	67,0
Midi-Pyrénées	40,0	45,8	65,0	95,6	54,7	96,7	52,6	94,3	33,6	67,8	4,3	13,2	39,7	67,5
Limousin	53,7	46,9	68,3	97,0	53,9	97,6	57,7	93,2	39,7	64,3	(4,2)	10,7	38,9	64,9
Centre-Est	39,3	46,3	59,9	97,6	56,4	98,0	53,2	95,1	37,2	70,6	5,7	12,0	40,7	71,4
Rhône-Alpes	38,9	45,2	59,1	97,7	55,0	98,1	52,9	96,1	39,1	74,7	6,4	12,4	41,5	72,9
Auvergne	41,3	51,2	62,9	97,1	59,8	97,5	54,2	91,3	31,3	57,6	(4,0)	11,1	38,1	65,8
Méditerranée	30,8	44,5	55,6	95,5	49,4	96,3	43,2	93,4	29,8	63,6	3,4	9,8	32,1	64,8
Languedoc-Roussillon	25,7	44,6	53,7	94,3	48,4	96,8	38,8	93,3	23,0	64,6	2,7	10,0	28,5	63,6
Provence-Alpes-														
Côte d'Azur-Corse	33,0	44,5	56,7	95,9	50,0	96,1	45,0	93,5	32,9	63,4	3,8	9,8	33,6	65,4
ITALIA	30,2	39,3	39,4	91,6	32,6	94,0	27,5	89,1	13,8	57,5	2,6	10,1	25,1	64,9
Nord-Ovest	30,5	42,4	49,6	94,5	39,8	95,7	31,0	91,2	14,4	55,8	2,9	10,7	28,7	66,6
Piemonte	35,8	45,6	52,9	95,7	42,2	96,9	33,7	92,6	13,8	56,9	2,8	11,4	30,5	68,2
Valle d' Aosta	(35,7)	(49,0)	(48,6)	92,2	(36,2)	92,7	(34,2)	88,5	(22,7)	(42,6)	(3,5)	(11,1)	29,6	65,9
Liguria	33,1	34,0	40,9	91,3	33,7	93,0	24,6	88,2	15,4	54,0	(3,0)	8,9	24,4	62,6
Lombardia	45,7	47,2	51,7	95,1	36,9	97,0	28,8	93,3	11,9	56,6	1,8	8,9	30,3	69,9
Nord-Est	45,7	43,6	40,6	93,9	30,8	96,3	24,5	90,1	12,4	56,2	2,8	10,6	26,8	67,2
Trentino Alto Adige	40,1	45,9	39,1	90,9	27,0	94,9	21,8	89,4	(12,2)	59,8	(3,3)	(12,6)	24,5	66,5
Friuli Venezia Giulia	48,7	44,4	40,2	94,2	28,9	96,7	24,8	89,9	12,2	54,2	2,9	11,3	27,5	68,0
Veneto	39,0	38,7	43,5	94,4	39,1	95,8	25,2	91,6	13,3	60,3	2,3	(7,5)	26,1	65,0
Emilia Romagna	38,6	40,2	56,3	93,1	48,0	96,1	38,3	90,0	17,4	60,0	2,6	12,2	33,0	66,1
Centro	36,9	40,1	46,7	94,5	39,3	95,4	33,2	91,5	18,4	63,0	3,1	14,8	29,3	67,3
Marche	40,8	37,1	51,4	93,0	49,7	96,7	40,3	91,4	23,1	65,0	(6,0)	16,2	35,5	67,4
Toscana	35,7	42,5	44,0	95,3	35,7	95,4	30,9	91,8	16,5	63,6	(1,8)	14,8	26,8	67,8
Umbria	34,9	36,3	51,1	93,7	37,8	92,7	30,6	90,3	19,4	61,1	(4,2)	(12,5)	29,4	64,5
Lazio	27,4	32,4	33,9	90,8	26,5	94,5	23,2	90,3	11,9	62,4	3,0	9,5	23,0	64,8
Campania	17,1	35,1	26,2	87,2	22,4	90,1	28,3	86,3	14,6	57,1	3,8	8,5	19,4	61,5
Abruzzi e Molise	23,4	29,5	41,8	89,0	36,1	90,5	32,4	86,7	16,0	55,8	(2,2)	11,6	24,9	58,9
Abruzzi	24,6	28,7	42,2	88,5	34,0	90,3	30,5	88,5	13,5	57,2	(1,4)	11,3	24,3	59,9
Molise	23,2	32,1	40,3	91,4	44,8	91,1	39,6	80,0	(25,3)	50,5	(4,5)	(12,3)	27,4	55,3
Sud	17,9	35,0	27,8	87,4	27,3	87,4	23,0	82,8	12,7	51,5	2,8	6,9	19,2	59,3
Puglia	19,6	40,0	27,2	89,0	27,9	88,4	22,6	82,2	12,6	55,0	(2,5)	6,0	20,0	62,4
Basilicata	14,2	27,2	30,4	88,3	30,0	91,3	35,2	84,5	(17,9)	54,4	(3,8)	(8,7)	21,7	58,0
Calabria	15,4	28,0	28,1	83,3	25,5	84,6	19,9	83,2	11,4	44,9	(2,8)	7,6	17,1	54,2
Sicilia	12,2	39,1	19,3	85,9	21,0	89,1	17,1	82,1	11,3	55,3	(1,3)	7,3	13,9	59,6
Sardegna	20,8	39,2	29,2	90,6	20,8	94,8	14,8	85,4	(9,0)	56,4	(1,6)	10,8	17,0	62,2
NEDERLAND	36,6	37,8	29,6	94,7	23,3	96,1	20,5	89,9	10,6	71,7	1,2	7,0	22,3	67,5
Noord-Nederland	32,9	37,0	25,3	93,8	20,2	96,0	14,4	90,4	8,4	70,7	(0,7)	(5,1)	18,6	64,3
Groningen	31,7	32,6	29,8	89,2	23,2	96,3	(14,3)	88,9	(7,7)	67,5	(1,0)	(5,5)	19,4	61,7
Friesland	33,1	39,0	20,1	96,7	15,6	96,5	(13,1)	91,6	(8,7)	71,8	(0,6)	(4,0)	16,8	64,6
Drenthe	34,2	40,2	25,7	96,7	21,8	94,9	(16,4)	90,7	(8,9)	73,5	(0,5)	(6,4)	19,9	67,5
Oost Nederland	36,6	37,6	20,4	96,1	19,3	96,4	16,9	89,9	8,0	72,2	(0,9)	7,2	20,2	67,7
Overijssel	36,2	36,6	23,2	97,2	18,3	95,7	16,2	89,8	7,4	69,3	(0,8)	(6,3)	19,2	66,7
Gelderland	36,9	38,3	25,1	95,4	19,8	96,8	17,3	89,9	8,4	73,9	(1,0)	7,7	20,7	68,3
West Nederland	37,4	38,9	33,6	93,5	27,5	96,7	25,5	91,5	12,7	75,8	1,5	8,4	24,5	68,4
Utrecht	37,9	37,8	29,6	91,3	26,7	95,9	22,9	89,4	12,2	75,3	(1,6)	(8,1)	24,1	67,4

TAB. 27
(continued)
(suite)

	1977													
	14 – 24		25 – 34		35 – 44		45 – 54		55 – 64		65 +		TOTAL	
	F	M	F	M	F	M	F	M	F	M	F	M	F	M
Noord-Holland	38,3	38,8	38,2	92,2	30,0	96,6	29,1	90,3	13,7	73,7	(1,3)	8,7	26,5	67,8
Zuid-Holland	36,7	39,3	31,1	95,1	25,8	97,0	23,6	92,9	12,0	77,6	(1,6)	8,3	23,0	69,1
Zuid-Nederland	36,6	36,7	28,4	96,0	20,0	95,0	16,7	85,6	9,1	61,5	(0,9)	4,5	21,9	67,0
Noord-Brabant	36,5	38,3	27,2	96,1	21,1	94,9	17,7	88,8	10,0	69,8	(1,0)	(5,1)	22,2	68,9
Limburg	36,8	33,6	30,8	95,7	18,1	95,0	14,9	79,7	7,6	48,2	(0,6)	(3,5)	21,4	63,4
Zuidwest Nederland (Zeeland)	34,5	35,2	22,8	99,0	24,6	97,7	(14,4)	96,7	(12,2)	78,1	(0,6)	(6,8)	18,9	67,7
BELGIQUE/BELGIË	37,8	42,9	61,9	97,0	43,2	96,9	30,9	91,0	13,3	65,9	1,4	5,4	31,5	66,5
Vlaams Gewest/Région Flamande	40,6	44,6	61,5	97,5	39,7	97,5	27,2	92,9	11,1	67,4	1,0	4,5	31,5	67,9
Région wallonne/Waals Gewest	34,2	42,6	59,6	97,0	44,3	95,6	31,1	87,4	13,0	59,7	1,7	5,1	29,5	64,0
Région bruxelloise/ Brussels G.	31,0	32,0	70,9	93,9	58,9	97,2	48,1	92,9	23,3	77,7	(2,4)	11,2	37,5	67,3
Antwerpen/Anvers	39,3	46,0	57,5	97,6	39,8	97,9	27,3	94,9	12,1	69,7	(1,0)	4,8	30,6	68,9
Brabant	34,7	37,9	68,2	95,5	51,9	97,6	38,5	94,2	18,6	74,5	(1,8)	8,1	35,3	68,1
W.Vlaand/Fland. occ.	42,3	45,1	61,4	97,5	37,5	97,8	27,4	94,2	9,7	70,7	(1,0)	(3,9)	30,6	67,8
O. Vlaand/Fland. or.	42,2	44,4	63,0	97,5	42,2	98,0	29,6	93,8	11,2	67,5	(1,1)	(4,3)	31,4	66,7
Hainaut/Henegouwen	33,4	43,9	59,4	97,1	44,2	93,9	31,0	81,3	12,4	53,7	(1,8)	(4,6)	28,7	61,7
Liège/Luik	36,1	43,8	63,7	97,3	46,0	97,7	34,7	91,5	14,9	63,5	(1,8)	(6,0)	31,6	66,1
Limburg/Limbourg	41,2	45,0	58,8	98,2	31,3	94,4	19,7	80,6	(8,8)	50,8	(1,4)	(3,6)	32,5	67,0
Luxembourg/Luxemburg	32,0	39,8	55,9	96,6	39,7	95,5	(22,5)	93,6	(4,7)	62,4	(1,1)	(6,0)	25,3	64,0
Namur/Namen	34,6	36,7	51,8	96,8	39,9	93,2	25,4	89,7	(12,2)	58,6	(1,1)	(3,6)	26,8	62,3
LUXEMBOURG (GR.-DUCHÉ)	46,3	53,2	41,4	96,5	29,1	99,1	23,1	94,3	17,0	59,6	2,6	10,1	26,9	70,5
UNITED KINGDOM	45,3	56,5	52,1	96,9	65,1	97,2	65,3	96,2	42,2	86,3	4,9	15,8	43,1	74,4
North	45,6	59,2	48,5	97,9	65,6	97,3	65,7	94,5	35,2	83,3	4,3	11,8	42,1	74,4
Yorkshire and Humberside	46,3	56,5	54,4	97,5	67,0	97,4	66,0	95,0	41,0	85,6	4,2	14,6	43,6	74,1
North West	43,8	56,5	48,4	97,9	59,2	96,8	62,1	97,2	38,2	89,4	3,3	14,4	40,5	75,1
East Midlands	48,4	57,3	46,2	97,3	61,3	97,2	63,9	97,5	40,3	87,4	5,2	17,6	41,3	74,3
West Midlands	46,0	55,5	53,3	96,7	65,9	97,6	67,2	97,4	45,0	89,5	5,8	18,2	44,3	75,3
East Anglia	41,8	52,2	50,8	97,4	65,6	98,5	62,6	96,7	38,7	84,7	3,8	13,6	39,5	70,7
South East	46,5	59,2	52,9	97,3	66,1	97,1	67,5	96,2	44,6	86,8	4,7	15,8	45,4	76,6
South West	45,5	57,4	56,8	96,9	68,6	96,9	67,0	95,7	44,3	83,9	4,6	14,9	44,6	74,3
Wales	40,2	55,7	47,9	95,7	60,3	96,4	57,7	93,7	36,4	79,7	6,3	12,6	38,7	71,8
Scotland	46,9	57,6	49,4	96,3	66,0	96,8	66,8	95,6	45,4	84,5	4,9	17,2	43,9	74,0
Northern Ireland	42,7	54,2	49,7	95,7	52,4	93,4	50,3	91,5	34,7	81,4	(4,7)	16,5	38,6	71,7
IRELAND	42,4	53,8	33,0	97,5	19,5	97,3	22,1	94,3	18,5	85,2	5,5	30,1	26,0	74,3
DANMARK	45,7	51,9	74,1	93,4	69,6	97,3	59,1	92,3	36,6	83,0	4,4	21,0	47,2	72,5
EUR 9	40,3	47,7	51,5	94,5	43,8	96,7	45,4	93,5	28,6	71,8	3,6	11,2	35,3	69,6

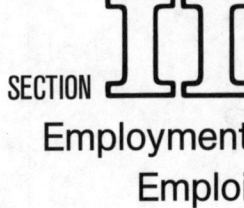

SECTION II

Employment

Emploi

TAB. 28

Persons with a main occupation by sector of economic activity and age (1 000)

Personnes ayant un emploi principal par secteur d'activité économique et par âge (1 000)

	BR Deutschland F	BR Deutschland M	France F	France M	Italia F	Italia M	Nederland F	Nederland M	Belgique België F	Belgique België M
1973										
Agriculture										
14 – 24	56	90	51	144	61	161	(4)	34	(4)	12
25 – 59	661	541	593	1 047	532	1 459	9	182	43	95
60 +	168	225	106	251	56	313	(2)	35	(3)	19
Industry										
14 – 24	729	1 351	573	1 006	567	952	97	254	116	199
25 – 59	2 150	7 009	1 255	4 558	907	4 885	85	1 157	183	931
60 +	115	696	134	369	12	222	(4)	93	(4)	75
Services										
14 – 24	1 383	992	1 009	707	396	331	338	210	168	133
25 – 59	3 443	4 823	3 408	4 112	1 692	4 046	390	1 191	520	890
60 +	337	684	425	447	104	323	30	110	33	90
Total										
14 – 24	2 185	2 450	1 633	1 857	1 023	1 444	448	509	290	343
25 – 59	6 297	12 417	5 257	9 716	3 132	10 389	498	2 571	742	1 916
60 +	624	1 611	664	1 067	172	858	35	245	41	183
1975										
Agriculture										
14 – 24	46	80	42	145	64	140	(4)	29	(3)	14
25 – 59	606	507	548	1 052	568	1 343	13	178	37	84
60 +	132	179	94	242	57	326	(2)	32	(4)	15
Industry										
14 – 24	626	1 178	518	1 001	531	993	86	228	104	186
25 – 59	2 048	6 790	1 344	4 716	1 064	5 187	94	1 162	197	916
60 +	90	480	95	296	17	224	(4)	85	(3)	68
Services										
14 – 24	1 385	930	1 031	710	422	335	344	203	168	131
25 – 59	3 701	4 868	3 752	4 499	1 932	4 239	495	1 310	591	928
60 +	298	582	383	395	106	352	30	114	27	86
Total										
14 – 24	2 074	2 208	1 591	1 857	1 017	1 468	435	462	275	331
25 – 59	6 400	12 248	5 644	10 267	3 564	10 769	605	2 657	824	1 928
60 +	523	1 247	572	932	180	902	36	231	33	169
1977										
Agriculture										
14 – 24	44	80	48	137	63	133	(2)	27	(3)	11
25 – 59	543	493	577	1 032	564	1 255	17	174	24	79
60 +	95	136	69	183	70	278	.	29	(2)	12
Industry										
14 – 24	555	1 229	462	899	496	722	73	208	84	176
25 – 59	2 040	6 798	1 438	4 839	1 122	4 703	95	1 190	174	887
60 +	64	310	73	189	23	154	(3)	74	(2)	37
Services										
14 – 24	1 391	883	989	692	475	522	358	209	174	148
25 – 59	3 948	5 199	4 113	4 619	2 324	4 926	574	1 386	614	986
60 +	217	431	309	327	129	317	29	101	23	72
Total										
14 – 24	2 018	2 222	1 499	1 728	1 034	1 376	434	444	265	339
25 – 59	6 612	12 631	6 128	10 490	4 010	10 884	687	2 757	828	1 974
60 +	382	885	450	700	222	749	33	204	27	124

TAB. 28

Persons with a main occupation by sector of economic activity and age (1 000)
Personnes ayant un emploi principal par secteur d'activité économique et par âge (1 000)

Luxembourg		United Kingdom		Ireland		Danmark		EUR 9		
F	M	F	M	F	M	F	M	F	M	
				1973						
										Agriculture
.	(1)	12	78	:	:	:	:	:	:	14 – 24
3	5	83	367	:	:	:	:	:	:	25 – 59
(1)	2	11	85	:	:	:	:	:	:	60 +
										Industrie
2	8	583	1 264	:	:	:	:	:	:	14 – 24
3	42	1 708	5 630	:	:	:	:	:	:	25 – 59
(1)	2	162	757	:	:	:	:	:	:	60 +
										Services
11	6	1 168	989	:	:	:	:	:	:	14 – 24
16	30	4 240	4 645	:	:	:	:	:	:	25 – 59
(1)	3	533	800	:	:	:	:	:	:	60 +
										Total
13	15	1 808	2 390	:	:	:	:	:	:	14 – 24
21	76	6 177	10 903	:	:	:	:	:	:	25 – 59
3	7	726	1 679	:	:	:	:	:	:	60 +
				1975						
										Agriculture
.	(1)	11	74	.	24	.	14	172	519	14 – 24
3	4	68	329	14	133	30	104	1 886	3 734	25 – 59
(1)	2	11	86	6	52	(3)	36	308	968	60 +
										Industrie
2	8	538	1 198	41	64	24	76	2 469	4 932	14 – 24
3	43	1 570	5 261	26	177	114	406	6 459	24 655	25 – 59
.	2	149	771	(2)	16	7	61	368	2 005	60 +
										Services
11	7	1 153	944	74	61	118	76	4 705	3 397	14 – 24
18	31	4 216	4 312	90	186	486	458	15 280	20 831	25 – 59
2	3	555	787	14	26	47	55	1 461	2 399	60 +
										Total
14	15	1 728	2 251	116	149	144	167	7 392	8 907	14 – 24
24	79	6625	10 887	130	496	636	972	24 452	50 304	25 – 59
2	7	725	1 666	22	94	58	153	2 152	5 407	60 +
				1977						
										Agriculture
.	(1)	9	93	.	23	.	15	172	518	14 – 24
2	4	102	396	12	127	29	96	1869	3 659	25 – 59
.	2	13	92	5	49	4	31	259	810	60 +
										Industrie
2	8	550	1 238	35	60	31	93	2 288	4 632	14 – 24
3	41	1 734	5 656	28	185	120	418	6 756	24 720	25 – 59
.	2	116	693		16	8	58	289	1 532	60 +
										Services
11	7	1 250	994	69	55	115	85	4 831	3 593	14 – 24
19	32	5 016	4 837	99	201	521	481	17 230	22 669	25 – 59
2	2	514	748	13	23	41	58	1 277	2 080	60 +
										Total
13	15	1 822	2 342	106	138	149	194	7 340	8 798	14 – 24
25	77	6 901	10 961	139	515	676	1 004	26 009	51 294	25 – 59
2	6	650	1 544	20	88	54	148	1 840	4 448	60 +

TAB. 28.1

Persons with a main occupation by sector of economic activity and age (%)

Personnes ayant un emploi principal par secteur d'activité économique et par âge (%)

	BR Deutschland		France		Italia		Nederland		Belgique Belgïe	
	$\frac{f}{F}100$	$\frac{f}{f+m}100$	$\frac{f}{F}100$	$\frac{f}{f+m}100$	$\frac{f}{F}100$	$\frac{f}{f+m}100$	$\frac{f}{F}100$	$\frac{f}{f+m}100$	$\frac{f}{F}100$	$\frac{f}{f+m}100$
1973										
Agriculture										
14 – 24	6,3	38,4	6,8	26,2	9,4	27,6	(26,7)	(10,5)	(8,0)	25,0
25 – 59	74,7	55,0	79,1	36,2	82,0	26,7	60,0	4,7	86,0	31,2
60 +	19,0	42,7	14,1	29,7	8,6	15,2	(13,3)	(5,4)	(6,0)	13,6
Industry										
14 – 24	24,3	35,0	29,2	36,3	38,2	37,3	52,2	27,6	38,3	36,8
25 – 59	71,8	23,5	64,0	21,6	61,0	15,7	45,7	6,8	60,4	16,4
60 +	3,8	14,2	6,8	26,6	0,8	5,1	(2,1)	(4,1)	(1,3)	5,1
Services										
14 – 24	26,8	58,2	20,8	58,8	18,1	54,5	44,6	61,7	23,3	55,8
25 – 59	66,7	41,7	70,4	45,3	77,2	29,5	51,5	24,7	72,1	36,9
60 +	6,5	33,0	8,8	48,7	4,7	24,4	4,0	21,4	4,6	26,8
Total										
14 – 24	24,0	47,1	21,6	46,8	23,6	41,5	45,7	46,8	27,0	45,8
25 – 59	69,2	33,6	69,6	35,1	72,4	23,2	50,8	16,2	69,2	27,9
60 +	6,9	27,9	8,8	38,4	4,0	16,7	3,6	12,5	3,8	18,3
1975										
Agriculture										
14 – 24	5,9	36,5	6,1	22,5	9,3	31,4	(21,1)	12,1	(6,4)	17,6
25 – 59	77,3	54,4	80,1	34,2	82,4	29,7	68,4	6,8	84,1	30,3
60 +	16,8	42,4	13,7	28,0	8,3	14,9	(10,5)	5,9	(9,1)	(21,1)
Industry										
14 – 24	22,6	34,7	26,5	34,1	32,9	34,8	46,7	27,4	34,2	35,9
25 – 59	74,1	23,2	68,7	22,2	66,0	17,0	51,1	7,5	64,8	17,7
60 +	3,3	15,8	4,9	24,3	1,1	7,1	(2,2)	(4,5)	(1,0)	4,2
Services										
14 – 24	25,7	59,8	20,0	59,2	17,2	55,7	39,6	62,9	21,4	56,2
25 – 59	68,8	43,2	72,6	45,5	78,5	31,3	57,0	27,4	75,2	38,9
60 +	5,5	33,9	7,4	49,2	4,3	23,1	3,5	20,8	3,4	23,9
Total										
14 – 24	23,1	48,4	20,4	46,1	21,4	40,9	40,4	48,5	24,3	45,4
25 – 59	71,1	34,3	72,3	35,5	74,9	24,9	56,2	18,5	72,8	29,9
60 +	5,8	29,5	7,3	38,0	3,8	16,6	3,3	13,5	2,9	16,3
1977										
Agriculture										
14 – 24	6,5	35,5	6,9	25,9	9,0	32,1	(10,7)	6,9	10,3	21,4
25 – 59	79,6	52,4	83,1	35,9	80,9	31,0	85,2	8,9	82,8	23,3
60 +	13,9	41,1	9,9	27,4	10,0	20,1	.	.	6,9	14,3
Industry										
14 – 24	20,9	31,1	23,4	33,9	30,2	40,7	42,7	26,0	32,3	32,3
25 – 59	76,7	23,1	72,9	22,9	68,4	19,3	55,6	7,4	66,9	16,4
60 +	2,4	17,1	3,7	27,9	1,4	13,0	1,8	3,9	0,8	5,1
Services										
14 – 24	25,0	61,2	18,3	58,8	16,2	47,6	37,3	63,1	21,5	54,0
25 – 59	71,1	43,2	76,0	47,1	79,4	32,1	59,7	29,3	75,7	38,4
60 +	3,9	33,5	5,7	48,6	4,4	28,9	3,0	22,3	2,8	24,2
Total										
14 – 24	22,4	47,6	18,6	46,5	19,6	42,9	37,6	49,4	23,7	43,8
25 – 59	73,4	34,4	75,9	36,9	76,1	26,9	59,5	20,0	73,9	29,4
60 +	4,2	30,1	5,6	39,1	4,2	22,9	2,9	13,9	2,4	18,2

TAB. 28.1

Persons with a main occupation by sector of economic activity and age (%)
Personnes ayant un emploi principal par secteur d'activité économique et par âge (%)

Luxembourg		United Kingdom		Ireland		Danmark		EUR 9		
$\frac{f}{F}100$	$\frac{f}{f+m}100$	$\frac{f}{F}100$	$\frac{f}{f+m}100$	$\frac{f}{F}100$	$\frac{f}{f+m}100$	$\frac{f}{F}100$	$\frac{f}{f+m}100$	$\frac{f}{F}100$	$\frac{f}{f+m}100$	
				**1973**						
										Agriculture
.	.	11,3	15,0	:	:	:	:	:	:	14 – 24
75,0	37,5	78,3	18,4	:	:	:	:	:	:	25 – 59
(25,0)	.	10,4	11,4	:	:	:	:	:	:	60 +
										Industrie
33,3	20,0	23,8	31,6	:	:	:	:	:	:	14 – 24
50,0	6,7	69,6	23,3	:	:	:	:	:	:	25 – 59
(16,6)	(33,3)	6,6	17,6	:	:	:	:	:	:	60 +
										Services
39,3	64,7	19,7	54,2	:	:	:	:	:	:	14 – 24
57,1	34,8	71,4	47,7	:	:	:	:	:	:	25 – 59
(5,4)	(25,0)	9,0	40,0	:	:	:	:	:	:	60 +
										Total
35,1	46,4	20,8	43,1	:	:	:	:	:	:	14 – 24
56,8	21,6	70,9	36,2	:	:	:	:	:	:	25 – 59
8,1	30,0	8,3	30,2	:	:	:	:	:	:	60 +
				1975						
										Agriculture
.	.	12,2	12,9	.	.	.	.	7,3	24,9	14 – 24
73,9	37,1	75,6	17,1	65,8	9,5	89,6	22,4	79,7	33,6	25 – 59
(17,4)	(23,1)	12,2	11,3	28,4	10,3	(8,6)	7,7	13,0	24,1	60 +
										Industrie
42,3	23,0	23,8	30,1	59,4	39,0	16,6	24,0	26,6	33,4	14 – 24
54,0	6,3	69,6	23,0	37,7	12,8	78,6	21,9	69,5	20,8	25 – 59
.	.	6,6	16,2	(2,9)	11,1	4,8	10,3	3,8	15,5	60 +
										Services
35,5	62,5	19,5	55,0	41,6	54,8	18,1	60,8	21,4	58,1	14 –24
58,1	37,3	71,2	49,4	50,6	32,6	74,7	51,5	71,9	42,3	25 – 59
6,4	36,4	9,4	41,4	7,9	35,0	7,2	46,1	4,0	37,8	60 +
										Total
34,1	47,4	19,0	43,4	43,3	43,8	17,2	46,3	21,7	45,3	14 – 24
59,7	23,3	73,0	37,8	48,5	20,8	75,9	39,6	71,9	32,7	25 – 59
6,2	26,3	8,0	30,3	8,2	19,0	6,9	37,9	6,3	28,5	60 +
				1977						
										Agriculture
.	.	7,3	8,8	.	.	.	.	7,5	24,9	14 – 24
73,4	26,6	82,3	20,5	65,6	8,6	82,4	22,9	81,3	33,8	25 – 59
.	.	10,5	12,4	26,8	9,1	12,7	12,3	11,2	24,2	60 +
										Industrie
36,2	20,8	22,9	30,8	54,8	37,0	19,5	25,0	24,5	33,1	14 – 24
60,8	7,5	72,3	23,5	42,4	12,9	75,5	22,3	72,4	21,5	25 – 59
.	.	4,8	14,3	.	.	5,0	12,1	3,1	15,9	60 +
										Services
34,4	62,1	18,4	55,7	38,1	55,6	17,0	57,5	20,7	57,3	14 – 24
60,9	33,3	74,0	50,9	54,7	33,0	77,0	52,0	73,8	43,2	25 – 59
4,7	38,6	7,6	40,7	7,2	36,1	6,0	41,4	5,5	38,0	60 +
										Total
33,4	46,4	19,4	43,8	40,0	43,5	17,0	43,5	20,9	45,5	14 – 24
61,6	24,5	73,6	38,6	53,6	21,6	77,0	40,2	73,9	33,6	25 – 59
5,0	25,3	6,9	29,6	7,5	18,5	6,0	26,0	5,2	29,3	60 +

TAB. 29

Persons with a main occupation by occupational status (%)

Personnes ayant un emploi principal par statut professionnel (%)

	BR Deutschland		France		Italia		Nederland		Belgique België	
	$\frac{f}{F}$ 100	$\frac{m}{M}$ 100	$\frac{f}{F}$ 100	$\frac{m}{M}$ 100	$\frac{f}{F}$ 100	$\frac{m}{M}$ 100	$\frac{f}{F}$ 100	$\frac{m}{M}$ 100	$\frac{f}{F}$ 100	$\frac{m}{M}$ 100
1960										
Total	100,0	100,0	100,0	100,0	100,0	100,0	100,0	100,0	100,0	100,0
Employers and self-employed	(8,6)	(15,8)	10,5	24,8	17,9	29,2	5,5	18,7	19,0	21,7
Employees	74,4	(77,9)	61,9	70,4	53,1	61,1	78,5	77,9	59,3	74,4
Family workers	(22,0)	(3,6)	27,6	5,9	29,0	9,6	16,0	3,4	21,5	3,8
1968										
Total	100,0	100,0	100,0	100,0	100,0	100,0	100,0	100,0	100,0	100,0
Employers and self-employed	6,4	14,2	8,9	20,2	16,4	28,0	4,5	17,1	15,8	19,8
Employees	76,0	84,3	75,3	77,3	62,3	66,8	85,7	81,5	69,3	78,4
Family workers	17,7	1,5	15,9	2,5	21,2	5,1	11,4	1,3	14,8	1,8
1970										
Total	100,0	100,0	100,0	100,0	100,0	100,0	100,0	100,0	100,0	100,0
Employers and self-employed	6,1	13,6	7,7	19,2	15,5	26,2	(4,2)	:	14,9	19,1
Employees	78,4	85,3	78,8	78,6	67,2	69,9	:	:	73,6	79,1
Family workers	15,5	1,1	14,4	2,2	17,3	4,2	(10,8)	:	11,6	1,8
1973										
Total	100,0	100,0	100,0	100,0	100,0	100,0	100,0	100,0	100,0	100,0
Employers and self-employed	5,2	11,8	6,9	17,9	14,9	24,6	3,8	14,1	11,7	17,2
Employees	83,4	87,2	80,3	80,5	71,6	72,4	89,7	84,4	77,4	81,5
Family workers	11,4	1,0	12,8	1,6	13,4	3,0	6,4	1,1	10,9	1,4
1975										
Total	100,0	100,0	100,0	100,0	100,0	100,0	100,0	100,0	100,0	100,0
Employers and self-employed	5,2	11,9	6,8	16,9	13,5	24,0	3,6	12,8	10,9	16,7
Employees	84,7	87,2	82,1	81,6	72,5	73,1	90,3	86,5	78,4	81,9
Family workers	10,1	1,0	11,1	1,5	14,0	2,8	6,0	0,6	10,7	1,4
1977										
Total	100,0	100,0	100,0	100,0	100,0	100,0	100,0	100,0	100,0	100,0
Employers and self-employed	5,0	11,6	6,6	16,7	14,3	25,1	4,4	11,9	11,1	15,4
Employees	86,3	87,6	82,4	81,9	73,2	72,3	90,8	87,7	82,8	83,8
Family workers	8,7	0,7	11,0	1,4	12,4	2,6	4,8	0,4	6,1	0,8

TAB. 29

Persons with a main occupation by occupational status (%)
Personnes ayant un emploi principal par statut professionnel (%)

Luxembourg		United Kingdom		Ireland		Danmark		EUR 9		
$\frac{f}{F}100$	$\frac{m}{M}100$	$\frac{f}{F}100$	$\frac{m}{M}100$	$\frac{f}{F}100$	$\frac{m}{M}100$	$\frac{f}{F}100$	$\frac{m}{M}100$	$\frac{f}{F}100$	$\frac{m}{M}100$	
1960										
100,0	100,0	100,0	100,0	100,0	100,0	100,0	100,0	100,0	100,0	Total
13,3	19,1	:	:	:	:	:	:	:	:	Employeurs et indépendants
53,3	76,4	:	:	:	:	:	:	:	:	Salariés
33,3	4,5	:	:	:	:	:	:	:	:	Aides familiaux
1968										
100,0	100,0	100,0	100,0	100,0	100,0	100,0	100,0	100,0	100,0	Total
(12,9)	15,4	:	:	:	:	:	:	:	:	Employeurs et indépendants
(64,5)	80,2	:	:	:	:	:	:	:	:	Salariés
(25,8)	3,3	:	:	:	:	:	:	:	:	Aides familiaux
1970										
100,0	100,0	100,0	100,0	100,0	100,0	100,0	100,0	100,0	100,0	Total
9,1	16,7	:	:	:	:	:	:	:	:	Employeurs et indépendants
66,7	81,1	:	:	:	:	:	:	:	:	Salariés
24,2	2,2	:	:	:	:	:	:	:	:	Aides familiaux
1973										
100,0	100,0	100,0	100,0	100,0	100,0	100,0	100,0	100,0	100,0	Total
11,1	14,3	4,1	11,2	:	:	:	:	:	:	Employeurs et indépendants
75,9	83,7	95,9	88,8	:	:	:	:	:	:	Salariés
13,9	2,0	:	:	:	:	:	:	:	:	Aides familiaux
1975										
100,0	100,0	100,0	100,0	100,0	100,0	100,0	100,0	100,0	100,0	Total
10,0	12,9	4,2	11,4	9,7	30,2	3,5	21,5	6,6	15,9	Employeurs et indépendants
77,5	85,1	95,8	88,6	84,7	66,2	87,9	78,5	85,2	82,8	Salariés
12,5	2,0	:	:	5,6	3,5	8,6	0,0	8,2	1,3	Aides familiaux
1977										
100,0	100,0	100,0	100,0	100,0	100,0	100,0	100,0	100,0	100,0	Total
9,8	12,2	4,3	11,1	9,1	29,8	3,9	19,2	6,8	15,8	Employeurs et indépendants
80,4	86,7	95,7	88,9	86,0	66,9	88,7	80,8	86,0	83,2	Salariés
9,8	1,0	:	:	4,9	3,2	7,4	.	7,2	1,1	Aides familiaux

TAB. 30

Persons with a main occupation by sector of economic activity and occupational status (1 000)

Personnes ayant un emploi principal par secteur d'activité économique et statut professionnel (1 000)

	BR Deutschland		France		Italia		Nederland		Belgique België	
	F	M	F	M	F	M	F	M	F	M
1973										
Total	9 106	16 478	7 554	12 640	4 328	12 691	981	3 325	1 073	2 443
Agriculture	885	856	750	1 442	649	1 933	14	251	50	125
Industry	2 995	9 055	1 962	5 933	1 486	6 058	185	1 504	303	1 205
Services	5 163	6 498	4 842	5 266	2 192	4 700	758	1 512	721	1 113
Employers and self-employed	471	1 948	520	2 262	646	3 117	37	463	126	419
Agriculture	103	542	104	942	165	1 063	(2)	158	12	98
Industry	43	476	41	497	122	839	(2)	81	7	101
Service	323	924	375	823	359	1 215	32	221	107	221
Employees	7 594	14 369	6 069	10 176	3 101	9 190	866	2 794	831	1 990
Agriculture	67	181	59	339	184	682	(5)	72	(2)	13
Industry	2 876	8 570	1 837	5 426	1 323	5 155	175	1 416	286	1 098
Services	4 592	5 555	4 173	4 411	1 594	3 354	677	1 278	543	879
Family workers	1 041	162	965	203	581	383	62	37	117	34
Agriculture	715	133	587	161	300	188	7	22	36	14
Industry	76	9	84	10	41	64	7	5	9	6
Services	248	19	294	32	240	131	48	11	72	13
1975										
Total	8 997	15 703	7 807	13 056	4 761	13 139	1 076	3 350	1 132	2 428
Agriculture	784	765	683	1 438	689	1 808	18	238	43	112
Industry	2 763	8 447	1 957	6 014	1 612	6 404	184	1 475	304	1 170
Services	5 383	6 380	5 167	5 604	2 460	4 926	869	1 626	785	1 146
Employers and self-employed	467	1 865	528	2 205	642	3 159	39	429	123	405
Agriculture	102	494	109	918	154	1 012	(3)	150	11	84
Industry	47	444	44	477	124	910	.	70	6	97
Services	316	918	374	809	364	1 237	35	208	107	224
Employees	7 619	13 688	6 410	10 649	3 450	9 608	969	2 897	887	1 989
Agriculture	64	155	62	360	204	633	5	77	.	13
Industry	2 651	7 995	1 834	5 526	1 430	5 422	175	1 402	290	1 067
Services	4 841	5 437	4 514	4 763	1 816	3 553	787	1 411	596	908
Family workers	910	150	869	202	668	371	65	20	121	34
Agriculture	618	117	512	160	331	163	11	11	31	15
Industry	65	8	79	10	58	72	7	(3)	8	6
Services	225	25	278	33	279	136	47	6	82	13
1977										
Total	9 012	15 738	8 078	12 917	5 266	13 010	1 155	3 405	1 120	2 437
Agriculture	682	709	694	1 352	697	1 666	20	230	29	102
Industry	2 659	8 337	1 973	5 927	1 641	5 579	171	1 472	260	1 100
Services	5 556	6 513	5 411	5 638	2 928	5 765	961	1 696	811	1 206
Employers and self-employed	454	1 828	534	2 158	755	3 264	51	404	124	376
Agriculture	80	447	118	899	217	984	5	139	12	83
Industry	46	450	36	464	99	737	(3)	65	5	81
Services	319	915	380	795	439	1 543	43	200	107	210
Employees	7 778	13 794	6 659	10 573	3 857	9 407	1 048	2 986	928	2 042
Agriculture	66	168	65	308	182	543	5	83	.	10
Industry	2 555	7 883	1 844	5 454	1 493	4 791	162	1 406	249	1 016
Services	5 057	5 580	4 750	4 810	2 182	4 074	878	1 491	658	988
Family workers	780	117	886	187	654	339	55	13	68	19
Agriculture	535	93	511	144	298	139	10	8	16	9
Industry	58	(5)	94	9	50	51	6	.	6	(3)
Services	180	18	281	33	307	149	39	4	46	7

TAB. 30

Persons with a main occupation by sector of economic activity and occupational status (1 000)
Personnes ayant un emploi principal par secteur d'activité économique et statut professionnel (1 000)

Luxembourg		United Kingdom		Ireland		Danmark		EUR 9		
F	M	F	M	F	M	F	M	F	M	
						1973				
36	98	8 711	14 972	:	:	:	:	:	:	Total
4	8	104	530	:	:	:	:	:	:	Agriculture
5	52	2 453	7 651	:	:	:	:	:	:	Industrie
27	38	5 942	6 434	:	:	:	:	:	:	Services
4	14	347	1 634	:	:	:	:	:	:	Employeurs et indépendants
.	6	28	249	:	:	:	:	:	:	Agriculture
.	3	29	543	:	:	:	:	:	:	Industrie
3	6	283	812	:	:	:	:	:	:	Services
27	82	8 082	12 924	:	:	:	:	:	:	Salariés
.	(1)	72	226	:	:	:	:	:	:	Agriculture
4	49	2 368	6 960	:	:	:	:	:	:	Industrie
22	33	5 502	5 466	:	:	:	:	:	:	Services
5	2	:	:	:	:	:	:	:	:	Aides familiaux
3	2	:	:	:	:	:	:	:	:	Agriculture
:	:	:	:	:	:	:	:	:	:	Industrie
2	:	:	:	:	:	:	:	:	:	Services
						1975				
40	101	9 078	14 804	268	739	838	1 292	33 996	64 612	Total
3	7	90	489	21	208	34	154	2 366	5 221	Agriculture
5	53	2 257	7 230	69	257	145	543	9 296	31 592	Industrie
31	40	5 924	6 043	177	273	651	589	21 446	26 627	Services
4	13	348	1 576	26	223	29	278	2 207	10 153	Employeurs et indépendants
(1)	5	28	234	9	158	.	110	417	3 165	Agriculture
.	2	27	503	.	22	(3)	60	255	2 585	Industrie
3	6	289	828	16	43	24	109	1 529	4 381	Services
31	86	8 011	12 296	227	489	737	1 014	28 341	52 716	Salariés
:	(1)	62	255	.	27	5	44	405	1 565	Agriculture
5	51	2 230	6 727	67	234	129	483	8 811	28 907	Industrie
26	34	5 635	5 216	157	227	594	480	18 967	22 030	Services
5	2	:	:	15	26	72	.	2 726	807	Aides familiaux
3	2	:	:	11	24	27	.	1 544	491	Agriculture
.	.	:	:	.	.	13	.	230	100	Industrie
2	.	:	:	4	.	32	.	950	216	Services
						1977				
40	98	9 373	14 847	265	741	879	1 346	35 189	64 540	Total
2	6	124	581	18	199	34	142	2 300	4 987	Agriculture
6	51	2 400	7 587	64	261	159	569	9 333	30 884	Industrie
32	41	6 780	6 579	181	279	677	624	23 338	28 342	Services
4	12	404	1 641	24	221	34	258	2 382	10 160	Employeurs et indépendants
.	4	46	290	9	152	(3)	101	491	3 099	Agriculture
.	2	30	472	.	22	(3)	55	223	2 347	Industrie
3	6	320	853	14	46	28	102	1 653	4 670	Services
33	85	8 913	13 157	228	496	777	1 083	30 221	53 624	Salariés
.	(1)	78	288	.	25	5	41	404	1 469	Agriculture
5	49	2 357	7 105	63	238	144	514	8 872	28 457	Industrie
28	35	6 437	5 712	163	232	623	522	20 776	23 445	Services
4	(1)	:	:	13	24	65	.	2 524	699	Aides familiaux
2	(1)	:	:	8	22	26	.	1 405	417	Agriculture
.	.	:	:	.	.	12	.	226	70	Industrie
2	.	:	:	4	.	26	.	885	213	Services

TAB. 30.1 A

Persons with a main occupation by sector of economic activity and occupational status (%)

Personnes ayant un emploi principal par secteur d'activité économique et statut professionnel (%)

	BR Deutschland $\frac{f}{F}100$	BR Deutschland $\frac{f}{f+m}100$	France $\frac{f}{F}100$	France $\frac{f}{f+m}100$	Italia $\frac{f}{F}100$	Italia $\frac{f}{f+m}100$	Nederland $\frac{f}{F}100$	Nederland $\frac{f}{f+m}100$	Belgique België $\frac{f}{F}100$	Belgique België $\frac{f}{f+m}100$
					1973					
Total	100,0	35,6	100,0	37,4	100,0	25,4	100,0	22,8	100,0	30,5
Employers and self-employed	5,2	19,5	6,9	18,7	14,9	17,2	3,8	7,4	11,7	23,1
Employees	83,4	34,6	80,3	37,4	71,7	25,2	89,6	23,7	77,4	29,5
Family workers	11,4	86,5	12,8	82,6	13,4	60,3	6,6	62,6	10,9	77,5
Agriculture	9,8	50,8	9,9	34,2	15,0	25,1	1,5	5,3	4,7	28,6
Employers and self-employed	11,6	16,0	13,9	9,9	25,4	13,4	(14,3)	(1,3)	24,0	10,9
Employees	7,6	27,0	7,9	14,8	28,4	21,2	(35,7)	(6,5)	(4,0)	(13,3)
Family workers	80,8	84,3	78,2	78,5	46,2	61,5	50,0	24,1	72,0	72,0
Industry	33,1	24,9	26,0	24,9	34,3	19,7	19,3	11,0	28,2	20,1
Employers and self-employed	1,4	8,3	2,1	7,6	8,2	12,7	(1,1)	(2,4)	2,3	6,5
Employees	96,0	25,1	93,6	25,3	89,0	20,4	95,1	11,0	94,7	20,7
Family workers	2,5	89,4	4,3	89,4	2,8	39,0	3,8	58,3	3,0	60,0
Service	57,1	44,3	64,1	47,9	50,7	31,8	79,2	33,4	67,1	39,3
Employers and self-employed	6,3	25,9	7,7	31,3	16,4	22,8	4,2	12,6	14,8	32,6
Employees	88,9	45,3	86,2	48,6	72,7	32,2	89,4	34,6	75,2	38,2
Family workers	4,8	92,9	6,1	90,2	10,9	64,7	6,4	81,4	10,0	84,7
					1975					
Total	100,0	36,4	100,0	37,4	100,0	26,6	100,0	24,3	100,0	31,8
Employers and self-employed	5,2	20,0	6,8	19,3	13,5	16,8	3,6	8,3	11,0	23,3
Employees	84,7	35,8	82,1	37,6	72,5	26,4	90,3	25,1	78,3	30,8
Family workers	10,1	85,8	11,1	81,1	14,0	64,3	6,1	76,5	10,7	78,1
Agriculture	8,8	50,6	8,7	32,2	14,5	27,6	1,7	7,0	3,8	27,7
Employers and self-employed	13,0	17,1	16,0	10,6	22,4	13,2	(15,8)	(2,0)	25,6	11,6
Employees	8,2	29,2	9,1	14,7	29,6	24,4	26,3	6,1	.	.
Family workers	78,8	84,1	74,9	76,2	48,0	67,0	57,9	50,0	72,1	67,4
Industry	30,9	24,6	25,1	24,6	33,9	20,1	17,2	11,1	26,9	20,6
Employers and self-employed	1,7	9,6	2,3	8,4	7,7	12,0	.	.	2,0	5,8
Employees	95,9	24,9	93,7	24,9	88,7	20,9	95,1	11,1	95,4	21,4
Family workers	2,4	89,0	4,0	88,8	3,6	44,6	3,9	(70,0)	2,6	57,1
Service	60,3	45,8	66,2	48,0	51,7	33,3	81,1	34,8	69,3	40,7
Employers and self-employed	5,9	25,6	7,2	31,6	14,8	22,7	4,0	14,4	13,6	32,3
Employees	89,9	47,1	87,4	48,7	73,8	33,8	90,6	35,8	75,9	39,6
Family workers	4,2	90,0	5,4	89,4	11,4	67,2	5,4	88,7	10,5	86,3
					1977					
Total	100,0	36,4	100,0	38,5	100,0	28,8	100,0	25,3	100,0	31,5
Employers and self-employed	5,0	19,9	6,6	19,8	14,3	18,8	4,4	11,2	11,1	24,8
Employees	86,3	36,1	82,4	38,6	73,2	29,1	90,7	26,0	82,8	31,2
Family workers	8,7	87,0	11,0	82,6	12,4	65,9	4,8	80,9	6,1	78,4
Agriculture	7,7	49,0	8,6	33,9	13,2	29,5	1,7	8,0	2,6	22,2
Employers and self-employed	11,7	15,2	17,0	11,6	31,1	18,1	25,0	3,5	4,6	12,8
Employees	9,7	28,2	9,4	17,4	26,1	25,1	25,0	5,7	.	.
Family workers	78,6	85,2	73,6	78,0	42,8	68,2	50,0	55,6	54,0	63,8
Industry	29,9	24,2	24,4	25,0	31,2	22,7	14,8	10,4	23,6	19,1
Employers and self-employed	1,7	9,3	1,8	7,2	6,0	11,8	(1,8)	(4,4)	1,8	5,6
Employees	96,1	25,5	93,4	25,3	90,9	23,8	94,7	10,3	95,8	19,7
Family workers	2,2	92,1	4,8	91,3	3,0	49,5	3,5	(80,3)	2,3	(67,0)
Service	62,5	46,0	67,0	49,0	55,6	33,7	83,4	36,2	73,7	40,2
Employers and self-employed	5,7	25,9	7,0	32,3	15,0	22,1	4,5	17,7	13,2	33,6
Employees	91,0	47,5	87,8	49,7	74,5	34,9	91,5	37,1	81,1	40,0
Family workers	3,2	90,9	5,2	89,5	10,5	67,3	4,0	90,7	5,7	87,1

TAB. 30.1 A

Persons with a main occupation by sector of economic activity and occupational status (%)

Personnes ayant un emploi principal par secteur d'activité économique et statut professionnel (%)

Luxembourg		United Kingdom		Ireland		Danmark		EUR 9		
$\frac{f}{F}100$	$\frac{f}{f+m}100$	$\frac{f}{F}100$	$\frac{f}{f+m}100$	$\frac{f}{F}100$	$\frac{f}{f+m}100$	$\frac{f}{F}100$	$\frac{f}{f+m}100$	$\frac{f}{F}100$	$\frac{f}{f+m}100$	
				1973						
100,0	26,9	100,0	36,8	:	:			:	:	Total
11,1	22,2	4,0	17,5	:	:			:	:	Employeurs et indépendants
75,0	24,8	93,5	38,5	:	:			:	:	Salariés
13,9	71,4	:	:	:	:			:	:	Aides familiaux
11,1	33,3	1,2	16,4	:	:			:	:	Agriculture
		28,0	10,1	:	:			:	:	Employeurs et indépendants
		72,0	21,3	:	:			:	:	Salariés
75,0	60,0	:	:	:	:			:	:	Aides familiaux
13,9	8,8	28,9	24,3	:	:			:	:	Industrie
		1,2	5,1	:	:			:	:	Employeurs et indépendants
80,0	7,5	98,8	25,4	:	:			:	:	Salariés
				:	:			:	:	Aides familiaux
75,0	41,5	69,9	48,0	:	:			:	:	Services
11,1	33,3	4,9	25,8	:	:			:	:	Employeurs et indépendants
81,5	40,0	95,1	50,2	:	:			:	:	Salariés
7,4	100,0	:	:	:	:			:	:	Aides familiaux
				1975						
100,0	28,4	100,0	38,0	100,0	26,6	100,0	39,3	100,0	34,5	Total
10,0	23,5	4,2	18,1	9,4	10,4	3,3	9,4	6,7	17,9	Employeurs et indépendants
77,5	26,5	95,8	39,4	83,9	31,7	87,7	42,1	85,1	35,0	Salariés
12,5	71,4	:	:	5,6	36,6	8,7	98,6	8,7	77,2	Aides familiaux
7,7	30,0	1,1	15,5	7,9	9,2	7,9	18,1	7,1	31,2	Agriculture
(33,3)	(16,7)	31,1	10,7	45,0	5,4			17,6	11,6	Employeurs et indépendants
	:	68,9	19,6			15,6	10,2	17,1	20,6	Salariés
66,7	60,0	:	:	55,0	31,4	84,4		65,3	75,9	Aides familiaux
12,8	8,6	27,3	23,8	25,8	21,2	25,8	21,1	28,1	22,7	Industrie
		1,2	5,1			(2,1)	(4,8)	2,7	9,0	Employeurs et indépendants
100,0	8,9	98,8	24,9	97,1	22,3	88,9	21,1	94,8	23,4	Salariés
		:	:			9,0	100,0	2,5	69,7	Aides familiaux
79,5	43,7	71,6	49,5	66,3	39,3	62,3	52,5	64,8	44,6	Services
9,7	33,3	4,9	25,9	9,0	27,1	3,7	18,0	7,1	25,9	Employeurs et indépendants
83,9	43,3	95,1	51,9	88,7	40,9	91,4	55,3	88,5	46,3	Salariés
6,4	100,0	:	:	2,3	66,7	4,9	97,0	4,4	81,5	Aides familiaux
				1977						
100,0	28,9	100,0	38,7	100,0	26,3	100,0	39,5	100,0	35,3	Total
8,9	22,7	4,3	19,8	8,9	9,6	3,8	11,6	6,8	19,0	Employeurs et indépendants
82,2	27,9	95,7	40,4	86,3	31,5	88,7	41,8	86,0	36,0	Salariés
8,9	(74,1)	:	:	4,8	34,7	7,4	99,7	7,2	78,3	Aides familiaux
5,3	25,2	1,3	17,6	6,9	8,4	4,0	19,5	6,6	31,6	Agriculture
		37,1	13,7	48,9	5,5	9,0	3,0	21,3	13,7	Employeurs et indépendants
		62,9	21,3			14,5	10,8	17,6	21,6	Salariés
76,8	60,7	:	:	44,5	27,0	76,5	100,0	61,1	77,1	Aides familiaux
13,9	9,8	25,7	24,0	24,4	19,8	18,2	21,8	26,7	23,2	Industrie
		1,3	6,0			1,7	4,7	2,4	8,7	Employeurs et indépendants
90,0	9,3	98,7	24,9	98,3	21,0	90,5	21,8	95,2	23,8	Salariés
		:	:			7,8	100,0	2,4	76,4	Aides familiaux
80,8	44,1	73,0	50,8	68,7	39,3	77,8	52,0	66,7	45,2	Services
9,2	34,5	4,7	27,3	7,6	23,0	4,1	21,6	7,1	26,1	Employeurs et indépendants
86,1	44,2	95,3	53,0	90,0	41,2	92,0	54,4	89,1	47,0	Salariés
4,7	91,3	:	:	2,4	74,6	3,8	99,2	3,8	80,6	Aides familiaux

TAB. 30.1 B

Persons with a main occupation by sector of economic activity and occupational status (%)

Personnes ayant un emploi principal par secteur d'activité économique et statut professionnel (%)

	BR Deutschland		France		Italia		Nederland		Belgique Belgïe	
	$\frac{f}{F}100$	$\frac{f}{f+m}100$	$\frac{f}{F}100$	$\frac{f}{f+m}100$	$\frac{f}{F}100$	$\frac{f}{f+m}100$	$\frac{f}{F}100$	$\frac{f}{f+m}100$	$\frac{f}{F}100$	$\frac{f}{f+m}100$
1973										
Total	100,0	35,6	100,0	37,4	100,0	25,4	100,0	22,8	100,0	30,5
Agriculture	9,8	50,8	9,9	34,2	15,0	25,1	1,5	5,3	4,7	28,6
Industry	33,1	14,0	26,0	24,9	34,3	19,7	19,3	11,0	28,2	20,1
Services	57,1	44,3	64,1	47,9	50,7	31,8	79,2	33,4	67,1	39,3
Employers and self-employed	100,0	19,5	100,0	18,7	100,0	17,2	100,0	7,4	100,0	23,1
Agriculture	21,9	16,0	20,0	9,9	25,5	13,4	(5,6)	(1,3)	9,5	10,9
Industry	9,2	8,3	7,9	7,6	18,9	12,7	(5,6)	(2,4)	5,6	6,5
Services	68,9	25,9	72,1	31,3	55,6	22,8	88,9	12,6	84,9	32,6
Employees	100,0	34,6	100,0	37,4	100,0	25,2	100,0	23,7	100,0	29,5
Agriculture	0,9	27,0	1,0	14,8	5,9	21,2	(0,6)	(6,5)	(2,6)	(13,3)
Industry	38,2	25,1	30,3	25,3	42,7	20,4	20,4	11,0	51,2	20,7
Services	60,9	45,3	68,8	48,6	51,4	32,2	79,0	34,6	46,2	38,2
Family workers	100,0	86,5	100,0	82,6	100,0	60,3	100,0	62,6	100,0	77,5
Agriculture	68,8	84,3	60,8	78,5	51,6	61,5	11,3	24,1	30,8	72,0
Industry	7,3	89,4	8,7	89,4	7,1	39,0	11,3	58,3	7,7	60,0
Services	23,9	92,9	30,5	90,2	41,3	64,7	77,4	81,4	61,5	84,7
1975										
Total	100,0	36,4	100,0	37,4	100,0	26,6	100,0	24,3	100,0	31,8
Agriculture	8,8	50,6	8,7	32,2	14,5	27,6	1,7	7,0	3,8	27,7
Industry	30,9	24,6	25,1	24,6	33,9	20,1	17,2	11,1	26,9	20,6
Services	60,3	45,8	66,2	48,0	51,7	33,3	81,1	34,8	69,3	40,7
Employers and self-employed	100,0	20,0	100,0	19,3	100,0	16,9	100,0	8,3	100,0	23,3
Agriculture	21,9	17,1	20,7	10,6	24,0	13,2	(7,9)	(2,0)	8,9	11,6
Industry	10,1	9,6	8,3	8,4	19,3	12,0	.	.	4,8	5,8
Services	68,0	25,6	71,0	31,6	56,7	22,7	92,1	14,4	86,3	32,3
Employees	100,0	35,8	100,0	37,6	100,0	26,4	100,0	25,1	100,0	30,8
Agriculture	0,8	29,2	1,0	14,7	5,9	24,4	0,5	6,1	2,7	.
Industry	35,1	24,9	28,6	24,9	41,4	20,9	18,1	11,1	48,5	21,4
Services	64,1	47,1	70,4	48,7	52,6	33,8	81,4	35,8	48,8	39,6
Family workers	100,0	85,8	100,0	81,1	100,0	64,3	100,0	76,5	100,0	78,1
Agriculture	68,1	84,1	58,9	76,2	49,6	67,0	16,9	50,0	25,6	67,4
Industry	7,1	89,0	9,1	88,8	8,7	44,6	10,8	(70,0)	6,6	57,1
Services	24,8	90,0	32,0	89,4	41,8	67,2	72,3	88,7	67,8	86,3
1977										
Total	100,0	36,4	100,0	38,5	100,0	28,8	100,0	25,3	100,0	31,5
Agriculture	7,7	49,0	86,0	33,9	13,2	29,5	1,7	8,0	2,6	22,2
Industry	29,9	24,2	24,4	25,0	31,2	22,7	14,8	10,4	23,6	19,1
Services	62,5	46,0	67,0	49,0	55,6	33,7	83,4	36,2	73,7	40,2
Employers and self-employed	100,0	19,9	100,0	19,8	100,0	18,8	100,0	11,2	100,0	24,8
Agriculture	18,0	15,2	22,1	11,6	28,7	18,1	9,8	3,5	9,7	12,8
Industry	10,3	9,3	6,7	7,2	13,1	11,8	(5,9)	(4,4)	4,0	5,6
Services	71,7	25,9	71,2	32,3	58,1	22,1	84,3	17,7	86,3	33,6
Employees	100,0	36,1	100,0	38,6	100,0	29,1	100,0	26,0	100,0	31,2
Agriculture	0,8	28,2	1,0	17,4	4,7	25,1	0,5	5,7	.	.
Industry	33,3	24,5	27,7	25,3	38,7	23,8	15,5	10,3	16,1	19,7
Services	65,9	47,5	71,3	49,7	56,6	34,4	84,0	37,1	70,9	40,0
Family workers	100,0	87,0	100,0	82,6	100,0	65,9	100,0	80,9	100,0	78,4
Agriculture	69,2	85,2	57,7	78,0	45,5	68,2	18,2	55,6	23,5	63,8
Industry	7,5	92,1	10,6	91,3	7,6	49,5	10,9	80,3	8,8	67,0
Services	23,3	90,9	31,7	89,5	46,9	67,3	70,9	90,7	67,6	87,1

TAB. 30.1 B

Persons with a main occupation by sector of economic activity and occupational status (%)
Personnes ayant un emploi principal par secteur d'activité économique et statut professionnel (%)

Luxembourg		United Kingdom		Ireland		Danmark		EUR 9		
$\frac{f}{F}100$	$\frac{f}{f+m}100$	$\frac{f}{F}100$	$\frac{f}{f+m}100$	$\frac{f}{F}100$	$\frac{f}{f+m}100$	$\frac{f}{F}100$	$\frac{f}{f+m}100$	$\frac{f}{F}100$	$\frac{f}{f+m}100$	
				1973						
100,0	26,9	100,0	36,8	:	:	:	:	:	:	Total
11,1	33,3	1,2	16,4	:	:	:	:	:	:	Agriculture
13,9	8,8	28,9	24,3	:	:	:	:	:	:	Industrie
75,0	41,5	69,9	48,0	:	:	:	:	:	:	Services
100,0	22,2	100,0	17,5	:	:	:	:	:	:	Employeurs et indépendants
.	.	8,3	10,1	:	:	:	:	:	:	Agriculture
.	.	8,5	5,1	:	:	:	:	:	:	Industrie
100,0	33,3	83,2	25,8	:	:	:	:	:	:	Services
100,0	24,8	100,0	38,5	:	:	:	:	:	:	Salariés
.	.	0,9	21,3	:	:	:	:	:	:	Agriculture
15,4	7,5	29,8	25,4	:	:	:	:	:	:	Industrie
84,6	40,0	69,3	50,2	:	:	:	:	:	:	Services
100,0	71,4	:	:	:	:	:	:	:	:	Aides familiaux
60,0	60,0	:	:	:	:	:	:	:	:	Agriculture
.	.	:	:	:	:	:	:	:	:	Industrie
40,0	.	:	:	:	:	:	:	:	:	Services
				1975						
100,0	28,4	100,0	38,0	100,0	26,6	100,0	39,3	100,0	34,5	Total
7,7	30,0	1,1	15,5	7,9	9,2	7,9	18,1	7,1	31,2	Agriculture
12,8	8,6	27,3	23,8	25,8	21,2	25,8	21,1	28,1	22,7	Industrie
79,5	43,7	71,6	49,5	66,3	39,3	62,3	52,5	64,8	44,6	Services
100,0	23,5	100,0	18,1	100,0	10,4	100,0	9,4	100,0	17,9	Employeurs et indépendants
(25,0)	(16,7)	8,1	10,7	36,0	5,4	.	.	18,9	11,6	Agriculture
.	.	7,9	5,1	.	.	(11,1)	(4,8)	11,6	9,0	Industrie
75,0	33,3	84,0	25,9	64,0	27,1	88,9	18,0	69,5	25,9	Services
100,0	26,5	100,0	39,4	100,0	31,7	100,0	42,1	100,0	35,0	Salariés
:	:	0,8	19,6	.	.	.	10,2	1,4	20,6	Agriculture
16,1	8,9	28,1	24,9	29,9	22,3	29,9	21,1	31,3	23,4	Industrie
83,9	43,3	71,1	51,9	70,1	40,9	70,1	55,3	67,3	46,3	Services
100,0	71,4	100,0	:	100,0	36,6	100,0	.	100,0	77,2	Aides familiaux
60,0	60,0	:	:	73,3	31,4	73,3	.	56,7	75,9	Agriculture
.	.	.	.	.	.	.	.	8,4	69,7	Industrie
40,0	.	:	.	26,7	.	26,7	.	34,9	81,5	Services
				1977						
100,0	28,9	100,0	38,7	100,0	26,3	100,0	39,5	100,0	35,3	Total
5,3	25,2	1,3	17,6	6,9	8,4	4,0	19,5	6,16	31,6	Agriculture
13,9	9,8	25,8	24,0	24,4	19,8	18,2	21,8	26,7	23,2	Industrie
80,8	44,1	72,9	50,8	68,7	39,3	77,8	52,0	66,7	45,2	Services
100,0	22,7	100,0	19,8	100,0	9,7	100,0	11,6	100,0	19,0	Employeurs et indépendants
.	.	11,6	13,7	37,7	5,5	(9,2)	(3,0)	20,7	13,7	Agriculture
.	.	7,6	6,0	.	.	(8,0)	(4,7)	9,4	8,7	Industrie
83,1	34,5	80,8	27,3	58,1	23,0	82,8	21,6	69,8	26,1	Services
100,0	27,9	100,0	40,4	100,0	31,5	100,0	41,8	100,0	36,0	Salariés
.	.	0,9	21,3	.	.	0,6	10,8	1,3	21,6	Agriculture
15,2	9,9	26,6	24,9	27,8	21,0	18,6	21,8	29,5	23,8	Industrie
84,6	44,2	72,6	53,0	71,6	41,2	80,8	54,4	69,1	47,0	Services
100,0	74,1	:	:	100,0	34,7	100,0	99,7	100,0	78,3	Aides familiaux
46,3	60,7	:	:	64,3	27,0	40,7	100,0	55,8	77,1	Agriculture
.	.	:	:	.	.	19,0	100,0	9,0	76,4	Industrie
42,9	91,3	:	:	34,9	74,6	40,2	99,2	35,2	80,6	Services

TAB. 31

Young persons, old persons and married women with a main occupation by sector of activity (1 000)
Jeunes, personnes âgées et femmes mariées ayant un emploi principal, selon le secteur d'activité (1 000)

	BR Deutschland		France		Italia		Nederland		Belgique België	
	F	M	F	M	F	M	F	M	F	M
1973										
Young persons (14 to 24 years old)	2 185	2 450	1 633	1 857	1 023	1 444	448	509	290	343
Agriculture	56	90	51	144	61	161	(4)	34	(4)	12
Industry	729	1 351	573	1 006	567	952	97	254	116	199
Services	1 383	992	1 009	707	396	331	338	210	168	133
Elderly persons (60 years and over)	624	1 611	664	1 067	172	858	35	245	41	183
Agriculture	168	225	106	251	56	313	2	35	3	19
Industry	115	696	134	369	12	222	4	93	4	75
Services	337	684	425	447	104	323	30	110	33	90
Married women	5 437		4 734		2 320		402		709	
Agriculture	727		607		507		7		40	
Industry	1 870		1 181		642		75		195	
Services	2 812		2 946		1 171		307		474	
1975										
Young persons (14 to 24 years old)	2 074	2 208	1 591	1 857	1 017	1 468	435	462	275	331
Agriculture	46	80	42	145	64	140	(4)	29	(3)	14
Industry	626	1 177	518	1 001	531	993	86	228	104	186
Services	1 385	930	1 031	710	422	335	344	203	168	131
Elderly persons (60 years and over)	523	1 247	572	932	180	902	36	231	33	169
Agriculture	132	179	94	242	57	326	(2)	32	(4)	15
Industry	90	480	95	296	17	224	(4)	85	(3)	68
Services	298	582	383	395	106	352	30	114	27	86
Married women	5 476		5 007		2 773		502		790	
Agriculture	641		546		551		13		36	
Industry	1 753		1 244		811		84		206	
Services	3 042		3 217		1 411		404		548	
1977										
Young persons (14 to 24 years old)	2 018	2 222	1 499	1 728	1 034	1 376	434	444	265	339
Agriculture	44	80	48	137	63	133	(2)	27	(3)	11
Industry	555	1 229	462	899	496	722	73	208	84	176
Services	1 391	883	989	692	475	522	358	209	174	148
Elderly persons (60 years and over)	382	885	450	700	222	749	33	204	27	124
Agriculture	95	136	69	183	70	278	.	29	(2)	12
Industry	64	310	73	189	23	154	(3)	74	(2)	37
Services	217	431	309	327	129	317	29	101	23	72
Married women	5 444		5 266		3 295		597		782	
Agriculture	557		562		549		15		23	
Industry	1 685		1 293		944		87		182	
Services	3 140		3 412		1 801		494		563	

TAB. 31

Young persons, old persons and married women with a main occupation by sector of activity (1 000)
Jeunes, personnes âgées et femmes mariées ayant un emploi principal, selon le secteur d'activité (1 000)

Luxembourg		United Kingdom		Ireland		Danmark		EUR 9		
F	M	F	M	F	M	F	M	F	M	
1973										
13	15	1 808	2 390	:	:	:	:	:	:	Jeunes (14 – 24 ans)
.	(1)	12	78	:	:	:	:	:	:	Agriculture
2	8	583	1 264	:	:	:	:	:	:	Industrie
11	6	1 168	989	:	:	:	:	:	:	Services
3	7	726	1 679	:	:	:	:	:	:	Personnes âgées (60 ans et plus)
(1)	2	11	85	:	:	:	:	:	:	Agriculture
(1)	2	162	757	:	:	:	:	:	:	Industrie
(1)	3	533	800	:	:	:	:	:	:	Services
16		5 873		:	:	:	:	:	:	Femmes mariées
3		75		:	:	:	:	:	:	Agriculture
2		1 646		:	:	:	:	:	:	Industrie
11		4 011		:	:	:	:	:	:	Services
1975										
14	15	1 728	2 251	116	149	144	167	7 392	8 907	Jeunes (14 – 24 ans)
.	(1)	11	74	.	24	.	14	172	519	Agriculture
2	8	538	1 198	41	64	24	76	2 469	4 932	Industrie
11	7	1 153	944	74	61	118	76	4 705	3 397	Services
2	7	725	1 666	22	94	58	153	2 152	5 401	Personnes âgées (60 ans et plus)
(1)	2	11	86	6	52	(3)	36	308	968	Agriculture
.	2	149	771	(2)	16	7	61	368	2 005	Industrie
2	3	555	787	14	26	47	55	1 461	2 399	Services
19		6 302		74		544		21 486		Femmes mariées
3		70		9		31		1 899		Agriculture
2		1 663		13		98		5 875		Industrie
14		4 481		52		409		13 577		Services
1977										
13	15	1 822	2 342	106	138	149	194	7 340	8 798	Jeunes (14 – 24 ans)
.	(1)	9	93	.	23	.	15	172	518	Agriculture
2	8	550	1 238	35	60	31	93	2 288	4 632	Industrie
11	7	1 250	994	69	55	115	85	4 831	3 593	Services
2	6	650	1 544	20	88	54	148	1 840	4 448	Personnes âgées (60 ans et plus)
.	2	13	92	5	49	4	31	259	810	Agriculture
.	2	116	693	.	16	8	58	289	1 532	Industrie
2	2	514	748	13	23	41	58	1 277	2 080	Services
19		6 539		81		581		22 604		Femmes mariées
2		97		7		30		1 841		Agriculture
3		1 636		15		105		5 949		Industrie
15		4 763		59		439		14 686		Services

TAB. 31.1

Young persons, old persons and married women with a main occupation by sector of activity (%)

Jeunes, personnes âgées et femmes mariées ayant un emploi principal selon le secteur d'activité (%)

	BR Deutschland		France		Italia		Nederland		Belgique België	
	$\frac{f}{F}100$	$\frac{f}{f+m}100$	$\frac{f}{F}100$	$\frac{f}{f+m}100$	$\frac{f}{F}100$	$\frac{f}{f+m}100$	$\frac{f}{F}100$	$\frac{f}{f+m}100$	$\frac{f}{F}100$	$\frac{f}{f+m}100$
1973										
Young persons (14 to 24 years old)	100,0	47,1	100,0	46,8	100,0	41,5	100,0	46,8	100,0	45,8
Agriculture	2,6	38,4	3,1	26,2	5,9	27,5	0,9	10,5	1,4	25,0
Industry	33,6	35,0	35,1	36,3	55,4	37,3	22,1	27,6	40,3	36,8
Services	63,8	58,2	61,8	58,8	38,7	54,5	77,0	61,7	58,3	55,8
Elderly persons (60 years and over)	100,0	27,9	100,0	38,4	100,0	16,7	100,0	12,5	100,0	18,3
Agriculture	27,1	42,7	15,9	29,7	32,6	15,2	5,6	5,4	7,5	13,6
Industry	18,5	14,2	20,2	26,6	7,0	5,1	11,1	4,1	10,0	5,1
Services	54,4	33,0	63,9	48,7	60,4	24,4	83,3	21,4	82,5	26,8
Married women	100,0		100,0		100,0		100,0		100,0	
Agriculture	13,4		12,8		21,8		1,8		5,6	
Industry	34,6		25,0		27,7		19,3		27,5	
Services	52,0		62,2		50,5		78,9		66,9	
1975										
Young persons (14 to 24 years old)	100,0	48,4	100,0	46,1	100,0	40,9	100,0	48,5	100,0	45,4
Agriculture	2,2	36,5	2,6	22,5	6,3	31,4	(0,9)	(12,1)	(1,1)	(17,6)
Industry	30,4	34,7	32,6	34,1	52,2	34,8	19,8	27,4	37,8	35,9
Services	67,4	59,8	64,8	59,2	41,5	55,7	79,3	62,9	61,1	56,2
Elderly persons (60 years and over)	100,0	29,5	100,0	38,0	100,0	16,6	100,0	13,5	100,0	16,8
Agriculture	25,4	42,4	16,4	28,0	31,7	14,9	(5,6)	(5,9)	(11,8)	(21,1)
Industry	17,3	15,8	16,6	24,3	9,4	7,1	(11,1)	(4,5)	8,8	(4,2)
Services	57,3	33,9	67,0	49,2	58,9	23,1	83,3	20,8	79,4	23,9
Married women	100,0		100,0		100,0		100,0		100,0	
Agriculture	11,8		10,9		19,9		2,6		4,5	
Industry	32,3		24,9		29,2		16,8		26,1	
Services	55,9		64,2		50,9		80,6		69,4	
1977										
Young persons (14 to 24 years old)	100,0	47,5	100,0	46,5	100,0	42,9	100,0	49,4	100,0	43,8
Agriculture	2,2	35,5	3,2	25,9	6,1	32,1	(0,5)	(7,3)	(1,1)	20,7
Industry	27,9	31,1	30,8	33,9	48,0	40,7	16,9	26,0	32,3	32,2
Services	69,9	61,2	66,0	58,8	45,9	47,7	82,6	63,1	66,6	54,0
Elderly persons (60 years and over)	100,0	30,1	100,0	39,1	100,0	22,9	100,0	13,9	100,0	17,9
Agriculture	25,3	41,1	15,3	27,4	31,5	20,1	.	.	(5,6)	(11,5)
Industry	17,0	17,1	16,2	27,9	10,4	13,0	(7,9)	3,4	(8,9)	(6,1)
Services	57,7	33,5	68,5	48,6	58,1	28,9	87,9	22,1	85,4	24,2
Married women	100,0		100,0		100,0		100,0		100,0	
Agriculture	10,3		10,7		16,7		2,5		3,0	
Industry	31,3		24,5		28,7		14,6		23,7	
Services	58,3		64,8		54,7		82,9		73,3	

TAB. 31.1

Young persons, old persons and married women with a main occupation by sector of activity (%)
Jeunes, personnes âgées et femmes mariées ayant un emploi principal selon le secteur d'activité (%)

Luxembourg		United Kingdom		Ireland		Danmark		EUR 9		
$\frac{f}{F}100$	$\frac{f}{f+m}100$	$\frac{f}{F}100$	$\frac{f}{f+m}100$	$\frac{f}{F}100$	$\frac{f}{f+m}100$	$\frac{f}{F}100$	$\frac{f}{f+m}100$	$\frac{f}{F}100$	$\frac{f}{f+m}100$	
						1973				
100,0	46,4	100,0	43,1	:	:	:	:	:	:	Jeunes (14 – 24 ans)
0,0	(0,0)	0,7	13,3	:	:	:	:	:	:	Agriculture
15,4	20,0	33,1	31,6	:	:	:	:	:	:	Industrie
84,6	64,7	66,2	54,1	:	:	:	:	:	:	Services
100,0	30,0	100,0	30,2	:	:	:	:	:	:	Personnes âgées (60 ans et plus)
(33,4)	33,3	1,5	11,5	:	:	:	:	:	:	Agriculture
(33,3)	33,3	23,0	17,6	:	:	:	:	:	:	Industrie
(33,3)	25,0	75,5	40,0	:	:	:	:	:	:	Services
100,0		100,0		:	:	:	:	:	:	Femmes mariées
18,8		1,3		:	:	:	:	:	:	Agriculture
12,5		28,7		:	:	:	:	:	:	Industrie
68,7		70,0		:	:	:	:	:	:	Services
						1975				
100,0	48,3	100,0	43,4	100,0	43,8	100,0	46,3	100,0	45,4	Jeunes (14 – 24 ans)
		0,7	12,9	.	.	.	.	2,3	24,9	Agriculture
15,4	20,0	31,6	31,0	35,7	39,0	16,9	24,0	33,6	33,4	Industrie
84,6	61,1	67,7	55,0	64,3	54,8	83,1	60,8	64,1	58,2	Services
100,0	22,2	100,0	30,3	100,0	19,0	100,0	27,5	100,0	28,5	Personnes âgées (60 ans et plus)
(33,3)	(33,3)	1,6	11,3	(27,3)	10,3	(5,3)	(7,7)	14,4	24,1	Agriculture
.	.	20,8	16,2	9,1	11,1	12,3	10,3	17,2	15,5	Industrie
66,7	40,0	77,6	41,4	63,6	35,0	82,4	46,1	68,4	37,8	Services
100,0		100,0		100,0		100,0		100,0		Femmes mariées
15,8		1,1		12,1		5,8		8,9		Agriculture
10,5		26,8		17,6		18,2		27,5		Industrie
73,7		72,1		70,3		76,0		63,6		Services
						1977				
100,0	47,0	100,0	43,8	100,0	43,4	100,0	43,4	100,0	45,5	Jeunes (14 – 24 ans)
		0,5	8,8	.	.	.	.	2,4	24,9	Agriculture
15,0	20,8	30,4	29,6	33,3	36,8	20,9	25,0	31,4	33,5	Industrie
83,3	62,1	69,1	55,7	65,7	55,6	77,7	57,5	66,3	57,3	Services
100,0	25,3	100,0	29,6	100,0	18,5	100,0	26,7	100,0	29,3	Personnes âgées (60 ans et plus)
.	.	2,0	12,4	24,6	9,3	7,5	11,1	14,2	24,2	Agriculture
.	.	18,0	14,4	.	.	15,1	12,3	15,8	15,9	Industrie
74,3	38,5	80,0	40,7	66,3	36,1	77,4	41,4	70,0	38,1	Services
100,0		100,0		100,0		100,0		100,0		Femmes mariées
7,8		1,5		8,7		5,2		8,2		Agriculture
14,2		25,2		18,0		18,3		26,5		Industrie
78,0		73,3		73,4		76,5		65,3		Services

TAB. 32

Employees by branch of economic activity (1 000)

Salariés par branche d'activité économique (1 000)

NACE Nomenclature	BR Deutschland		France		Italia		Nederland		Belgique België	
	F	M	F	M	F	M	F	M	F	M
1973										
0. Agriculture, forestry and fishing, hunting	67	181	59	339	184	682	(5)	72	(2)	13
1. Energy and water	44	514	36	247	11	190	5	73	(3)	76
2. Extraction and processing of non-energy-producing minerals and derived products; chemical industry	344	1 249	215	814	49	273	15	146	29	226
3. Metal manufacture; mechanical, electrical and instrument engineering	1 037	3 272	508	1 764	278	1 444	35	369	62	287
4. Other manufacturing industries	1 326	1 650	1 002	1 186	967	1 897	106	386	186	295
5. Building and civil engineering	125	1 886	77	1 415	19	1 351	14	442	7	216
6. Distributive trades, hotels, catering, repairs	1 701	1 534	1 602	1 446	299	694	177	368	135	194
7. Transport and communication	272	1 213	259	856	67	755	24	232	21	209
8. Banking and finance, insurance, business services, renting	552	533	493	508	54	239	81	176	57	94
9.1 Public administration, national defence and compulsory social security	583	1 516	574	833	189	838	41	211	53	204
9. Other services (9.1 not included)	1 484	759	1 785	768	984	828	354	292	278	178
Total	7 594	14 369	6 069	10 176	3 101	9 190	866	2 794	831	1 990
1975										
0. Agriculture, forestry and fishing, hunting	64	155	62	360	204	633	5	77	13	14
1. Energy and water	46	470	43	229	13	239	7	63	(3)	66
2. Extraction and processing of non-energy-producing minerals and derived products; chemical industry	322	1 203	194	754	53	287	16	158	32	219
3. Metal manufacture; mechanical, electrical and instrument engineering	974	3 171	561	1 897	251	1 515	36	388	66	287
4. Other manufacturing industries	1 183	1 536	952	1 192	1 096	1 952	101	374	180	288
5. Building and civil engineering	126	1 614	84	1 455	17	1 429	16	419	9	207
6. Distributive trades, hotels, catering, repairs	1 642	1 434	1 058	1 400	336	647	197	382	146	194
7. Transport and communication	274	1 131	264	877	76	814	33	259	25	219
8. Banking and finance, insurance, business services, renting	594	555	571	619	59	262	88	198	64	104
9.1 Public administration, national defence and compulsory social security	658	1 491	584	924	169	828	48	234	79	223
9. Other services (9.1 not included)	1 673	827	2 037	943	1 177	1 001	419	339	282	169
Total	7 619	13 688	6 410	10 649	3 450	9 608	969	2 897	887	1 989
1977										
0. Agriculture, forestry and fishing, hunting	66	168	65	308	182	543	5	83	.	10
1. Energy and water	57	559	39	228	12	170	4	59	4	67
2. Extraction and processing of non-energy-producing minerals and derived products; chemical industry	331	1 139	203	781	93	479	15	164	26	213
3. Metal manufacture; mechanical, electrical and instrument engineering	929	3 082	561	1 819	211	1 176	34	367	56	265
4. Other manufacturing industries	1 108	1 513	944	1 212	1 183	1 590	91	379	154	250
5. Building and civil engineering	130	1 589	96	1 414	39	1 377	18	437	8	222
6. Distributive trades, hotels, catering, repairs	1 666	1 433	1 065	1 461	429	1 071	205	404	156	222
7. Transport and communication	256	1 127	275	907	97	859	30	259	27	229
8. Banking and finance, insurance, business services, renting	589	571	603	606	93	290	101	209	68	105
9.1 Public administration, national defence and compulsory social security	695	1 552	623	830	247	888	58	252	82	241
9. Other services (9.1 not included)	1 851	897	2 183	1 006	1 317	965	485	366	325	191
Total	7 778	13 794	6 659	10 573	3 857	9 407	1 048	2 986	928	2 042

TAB. 32

Employees by branch of economic activity (1 000)

Salariés par branche d'activité économique (1 000)

1973

Luxembourg		United Kingdom		Ireland		Danmark		EUR 9		Nomenclature NACE
F	M	F	M	F	M	F	M	F	M	
.	(1)	72	264	:	:	:	:	:	:	0. Agriculture, sylviculture et pêche, chasse
.	(1)	76	632	:	:	::	:	:	:	1. Energie et eau
(1)	25	235	882	:	:	:	:	:	:	2. Extraction et transformation de minéraux non énergétiques et produits dérivés; industrie chimique
.	4	762	2 578	:	:	:	:	:	:	3. Industries transformatrices des métaux, mécanique de précision
2	8	1 201	1 608	:	:	:	:	:	:	4. Autres industries manufacturières
.	10	90	1 257	:	:	:	:	:	:	5. Bâtiment et génie civil
8	8	1 762	1 520	:	:	:	:	:	:	6. Commerce, restauration et hébergement, réparat.
.	6	270	1 143	:	:	:	:	:	:	7. Transports et communications
3	4	568	655	:	:	:	:	:	:	8. Institutions de crédit, assurances, services fournis aux entreprises, location
3	9	780	1 195	:	:	:	:	:	:	9.1 Administration générale, défense nationale et sécurité sociale
8	5	2 118	950	:	:	:	:	:	:	9. Autres services (9.1 non compris)
27	82	8 082	12 924	:	:	:	:	:	:	Total

1975

Luxembourg		United Kingdom		Ireland		Danmark		EUR 9		Nomenclature NACE
F	M	F	M	F	M	F	M	F	M	
.	(1)	62	255	.	27	5	44	405	1 565	0. Agriculture, sylviculture et pêche, chasse
.	(1)	92	650	.	14	.	14	206	1 746	1. Energie et eau
(1)	25	236	905	5	25	10	39	869	3 614	2. Extraction et transformation de minéraux non énergétiques et produits dérivés; industrie chimique
.	6	732	2 499	9	37	27	155	2 657	9 955	3. Industries transformatrices des métaux, mécanique de précision
2	7	1 075	1 476	49	90	85	144	4 723	7 060	4. Autres industries manufacturières
(1)	11	95	1 196	.	69	6	131	355	6 531	5. Bâtiment et génie civil
9	10	1 715	1 420	47	77	129	150	5 280	5 713	6. Commerce, restauration et hébergement, réparat.
(1)	6	246	1 071	11	50	29	104	958	4 531	7. Transports et communications
4	4	589	655	18	21	57	52	2 045	2 471	8. Institutions de crédit, assurances, services fournis aux entreprises, location
3	9	454	844	14	40	43	70	2 052	4 663	9.1 Administration générale, défense nationale et sécurité sociale
9	5	2 631	1 225	68	39	337	103	8 633	4 652	9. Autres services (9.1 non compris)
31	86	8 011	12 296	227	489	737	1 014	28 341	52 716	Total

1977

Luxembourg		United Kingdom		Ireland		Danmark		EUR 9		Nomenclature NACE
F	M	F	M	F	M	F	M	F	M	
.	(1)	78	288	.	25	5	41	404	1 469	0. Agriculture, sylviculture et pêche, chasse
.	(1)	95	633	.	11	.	12	215	1 740	1. Energie et eau
(1)	22	279	938	5	27	13	39	966	3 802	2. Extraction et transformation de minéraux non énergétiques et produits dérivés; industrie chimique
(1)	6	718	2 565	8	39	30	171	2 548	9 492	3. Industries transformatrices des métaux, mécanique de précision
2	8	1 166	1 635	46	92	90	147	4 740	6 826	4. Autres industries manufacturières
(1)	11	100	1 354	(2)	69	9	145	403	6 598	5. Bâtiment et génie civil
9	9	1 984	1 640	47	78	126	160	5 687	6 477	6. Commerce, restauration et hébergement, réparat.
(1)	6	271	1 185	12	48	29	106	997	4 728	7. Transports et communications
4	4	681	708	19	24	61	65	2 219	2 582	8. Institutions de crédit, assurances, services fournis aux entreprises, location
4	10	465	842	15	38	43	74	2 231	4 728	9.1 Administration générale, défense nationale et sécurité sociale
10	5	3 036	1 337	71	44	364	118	9 642	4 930	9. Autres services (9.1 non compris)
33	85	8 913	13 157	228	496	777	1 083	30 221	53 624	Total

TAB. 33

Persons with an occasional occupation by sector of economic activity and occupational status (1 000)
Personnes ayant une activité occasionnelle par secteur d'activité économique et statut professionnel (1 00(

	BR Deutschland		France		Italia		Nederland		Belgique België	
	F	M	F	M	F	M	F	M	F	M
1973										
Total	581	142	410	235	568	584	255	60	25	14
Agriculture	158	63	109	93	367	297	44	7	5	(2)
Industry	115	28	65	36	75	198	35	14	(3)	(3)
Services	308	51	236	106	126	93	171	37	17	8
Employers and self-employed	36	40	30	53	108	164	6	5	(2)	(3)
Agriculture	(7)	15	(8)	26	64	92	.	.	.	.
Industry	(6)	9	(6)	8	33	35	.	.	.	.
Services	23	16	16	19	11	37	5	.	.	.
Employees	320	43	211	117	300	389	157	49	10	9
Agriculture	8	.	11	18	185	182	(2)	(3)	.	.
Industry	83	15	33	24	34	158	25	14	.	(3)
Services	229	28	167	75	81	49	126	32	8	6
Family workers	225	58	172	63	158	36	89	6	13	.
Agriculture	143	46	92	48	117	24	41	(3)	5	.
Industry	26	(5)	26	(4)	8	5	9	.	.	.
Services	56	7	54	11	33	8	39	(3)	7	.
1975										
Total	501	121	313	164	407	410	169	37	20	12
Agriculture	121	43	89	53	260	185	27	6	(3)	.
Industry	97	25	47	27	50	151	17	7	(2)	(4)
Services	278	51	177	84	97	74	119	21	14	8
Employers and self-employed	32	35	14	35	68	112	8	5	(2)	(3)
Agriculture	(5)	10	.	10	38	52	.	(2)	.	.
Industry	(6)	(6)	.	(5)	22	30	.	.	.	.
Services	20	18	14	20	8	30	6	(3)	.	(2)
Employees	277	46	149	88	236	274	106	27	7	7
Agriculture	9	.	12	17	154	122	(2)	(2)	.	.
Industry	67	16	24	18	21	118	12	7	.	(3)
Services	198	27	113	53	61	34	90	18	6	5
Family workers	193	40	146	38	102	25	49	(3)	11	(2)
Agriculture	107	30	75	27	68	11	23	(2)	(3)	.
Industry	25	(4)	21	.	(6)	(4)	4	.	.	.
Services	60	(7)	50	11	28	10	22	.	7	.
1977										
Total	516	123	352	178	852	952	163	39	8	4
Agriculture	108	39	92	51	454	407	27	5	.	.
Industry	99	27	58	39	118	297	15	7	.	.
Services	295	51	202	87	279	249	121	27	6	(3)
Employers and self-employed	36	33	27	42	180	331	11	6	.	.
Agriculture	(4)	8	(6)	9	97	156	4	(2)	.	.
Industry	(4)	(6)	.	13	37	73	.	.	.	.
Services	27	19	19	21	46	102	8	4	.	.
Employees	306	52	176	97	484	1 039	108	30	(3)	(2)
Agriculture	10	(2)	20	21	245	466	(3)	.	.	.
Industry	68	19	31	24	71	283	11	.	.	.
Services	217	27	125	52	168	290	94	22	(3)	.
Family workers	174	38	150	38	187	254	43	.	4	.
Agriculture	95	29	66	22	112	142	20	.	.	.
Industry	26	.	26	.	11	21	4	.	.	.
Services	50	(6)	58	14	65	90	20	.	(3)	.

TAB. 33

Persons with an occasional occupation by sector of economic activity and occupational status (1 000)

Personnes ayant une activité occasionnelle par secteur d'activité économique et statut professionnel (1 000)

Luxembourg		United Kingdom		Ireland		Danmark		EUR 9		
F	M	F	M	F	M	F	M	F	M	
										1973
2	.	220	164	:	:	:	:	:	:	Total
(1)	.		4	:	:	:	:	:	:	Agriculture
	.	43	67	:	:	:	:	:	:	Industrie
(1)	.	157	87	:	:	:	:	:	:	Services
.		9	12	:	:	:	:	:	:	Employeurs et indépendants
.		.		:	:	:	:	:	:	Agriculture
.			(5)	:	:	:	:	:	:	Industrie
.		(6)	(4)	:	:	:	:	:	:	Services
(1)		197	151	:	:	:	:	:	:	Salariés
.		.		:	:	:	:	:	:	Agriculture
.		41	62	:	:	:	:	:	:	Industrie
(1)		151	83	:	:	:	:	:	:	Services
(1)	.	:	:	:	:	:	:	:	:	Aides familiaux
(1)	.	:	:	:	:	:	:	:	:	Agriculture
.	.	:	:	:	:	:	:	:	:	Industrie
.	.	:	:	:	:	:	:	:	:	Services
										1975
(1)	(1)	44	45	29	9	79	41	1 563	839	Total
.	.		.	13	4	9	5	523	298	Agriculture
.	.	4	14	(2)	.	11	8	230	237	Industrie
(1)	.	35	24	14	(4)	56	26	790	293	Services
.	.	.	.	(3)	.	.	(4)	133	196	Employeurs et indépendants
.	.	.	.	.	.	.	(2)	48	78	Agriculture
.	.	.	.	.	.	.	.	31	43	Industrie
.	.	.	.	.	.	.	.	52	75	Services
(1)	.	39	40	10	4	64	37	888	524	Salariés
.	.	.	.	.	.	.	(3)	178	147	Agriculture
.	.	4	14	.	.	9	7	139	183	Industrie
(1)	.	34	24	9	(3)	52	25	564	189	Services
.	.	.	.	16	(3)	14	.	531	113	Aides familiaux
.	.	.	.	12	(3)	8	.	297	73	Agriculture
.	.	.	.	.	.	(2)	.	60	11	Industrie
.	.	.	.	(3)	.	(4)	.	174	29	Services
										1977
(2)	(1)	122	89	33	11	66	40	2 113	1 437	Total
(1)	.		(3)	19	6	.	(3)	706	515	Agriculture
.	.	16	30	.	.	9	8	318	409	Industrie
(1)	.	101	50	12	(4)	55	27	1 071	499	Services
.	.	4	8	(2)	.	.	.	262	426	Employeurs et indépendants
.	.	.	.	.	.	.	.	113	177	Agriculture
.	.	.	(3)	.	.	.	.	45	97	Industrie
.	.	(4)	5	.	.	.	.	106	153	Services
(1)	.	115	75	9	5	60	37	1 262	854	Salariés
.	.	.	(3)	.	.	.	(2)	282	252	Agriculture
.	.	16	26	.	.	8	8	206	297	Industrie
(1)	.	96	45	8	(3)	51	27	762	299	Services
(1)	.	:	:	22	4	5	.	585	149	Aides familiaux
(1)	.	:	:	18	(4)	.	.	312	86	Agriculture
.	.	:	:	.	.	.	.	67	15	Industrie
.	.	:	:	(3)	.	(3)	.	203	46	Services

TAB. 34

Female manual workers by qualifications and nature of duties (%)
Ouvrières selon la qualification et la mixité des fonctions (%)

1972

Work done by:	BR Deutschland	Italia	Nederland	Belgique/België	Luxembourg	Travaux exécutés par:
A – Women only	49,50	60,20	51,45	61,58	72,93	A – Femmes seulement
B – Mainly women	23,65	18,81	14,13	18,22	8,27	B – Femmes pour la plupart
C – Men and women	21,84	18,61	25,36	18,81	18,80	C – Hommes et femmes
D – Mainly men	5,01	2,38	9,06	1,39	–	D – Hommes pour la plupart
E – Total	100,00	100,00	100,00	100,00	100,00	E – Total
A – Women only						A – Femmes seulement
1) Apprentices	31,99	73,68	59,86	58,52	68,04	1) Apprenties ouvrières
2) Semi-skilled workers	51,82	2,30	23,94	14,15	20,62	2) Spécialisées
3) Skilled, highly-skilled workers	10,93	16,78	16,20	21,86	11,34	3) Qualifiées, hautement qualifiées
4) Others	5,26	7,24	–	5,47	–	4) Autres
B – Mainly women						B – Femmes pour la plupart
1) Apprentices	27,97	76,84	56,41	48,91	54,55	1) Apprenties ouvrières
2) Semi-skilled workers	55,93	6,32	23,08	23,91	45,45	2) Spécialisées
3) Skilled, highly-skilled workers	15,25	12,63	20,51	22,83	–	3) Qualifiées, hautement qualifiées
4) Others	0,85	4,21	–	4,35	–	4) Autres
C – Men and women						C – Hommes et femmes
1) Apprentices	33,95	74,47	62,86	43,16	36,00	1) Apprenties ouvrières
2) Semi-skilled workers	45,87	6,38	25,71	15,79	24,00	2) Spécialisées
3) Skilled, highly-skilled workers	20,18	14,89	11,43	24,21	40,00	3) Qualifiées, hautement qualifiées
4) Others	–	4,26	–	16,84	–	4) Autres
D – Mainly men						D – Hommes pour la plupart
1) Apprentices	28,00	66,67	52,00	42,86	–	1) Apprenties ouvrières
2) Semi-skilled workers	56,00	–	36,00	28,57	–	2) Spécialisées
3) Skilled, highly-skilled workers	16,00	25,00	12,00	28,57	–	3) Qualifiées, hautement qualifiées
4) Others	–	8,33	–	–	–	4) Autres
E – Total						E – Total
1) Apprentices	31,26	74,26	59,42	53,66	60,90	1) Apprenties ouvrières
2) Semi-skilled workers	51,70	3,76	25,36	16,44	23,31	2) Spécialisées
3) Skilled, highly-skilled workers	14,23	15,84	15,22	22,57	15,79	3) Qualifiées, hautement qualifiées
4) Others	2,81	6,14	–	7,33	–	4) Autres

TAB. 35

Female non-manual workers by qualifications and nature of duties (%)

Employées selon la qualification et la mixité des fonctions (%)

1972

	BR Deutschland	Italia	Nederland	Belgique België	Luxembourg
Work done by:					
A – Women only	32,77	43,09	40,62	40,72	55,87
B – Mainly women	24,61	17,04	16,85	20,46	5,16
C – Men and women	36,57	35,37	32,30	32,28	36,15
D – Mainly men	6,05	4,50	10,23	6,54	2,82
E – Total	100,00	100,00	100,00	100,00	100,00
A – Women only					
1) Unskilled workers	28,20	20,15	32,02	15,03	38,66
2) Skilled workers	39,91	40,30	55,38	62,69	45,38
3) Highly-skilled workers	10,73	23,88	1,57	8,29	9,24
4) Executives	1,29	5,22	2,62	3,63	0,84
5) Managers	6,87	0,75	8,41	5,18	5,88
6) Others	3,00	9,70	–	5,18	–
B – Mainly women					
1) Unskilled workers	23,43	5,66	29,75	20,62	45,46
2) Skilled workers	51,43	41,51	60,76	59,79	36,36
3) Highly-skilled workers	8,57	45,28	1,90	9,28	9,09
4) Executives	2,86	5,66	5,06	6,19	–
5) Managers	10,28	–	2,53	3,09	9,09
6) Others	3,43	1,89	–	1,03	–
C – Men and women					
1) Unskilled workers	30,39	11,82	32,34	14,38	16,88
2) Skilled workers	51,15	45,45	54,46	58,82	63,64
3) Highly-skilled workers	8,46	33,64	3,30	9,15	9,09
4) Executives	3,85	3,64	4,95	8,50	2,60
5) Managers	4,23	–	4,95	3,92	7,79
6) Others	1,92	5,45	–	5,23	–
D – Mainly men					
1) Unskilled workers	23,25	7,14	39,59	12,90	33,33
2) Skilled workers	53,49	35,71	51,04	38,71	33,33
3) Highly-skilled workers	13,95	35,72	5,21	16,13	16,67
4) Executives	2,33	14,29	2,08	16,13	16,67
5) Managers	4,65	–	2,08	9,68	–
6) Others	2,33	7,14	–	6,45	–
E – Total					
1) Unskilled workers	30,80	14,15	32,52	15,83	30,99
2) Skilled workers	47,68	42,12	55,54	59,28	51,17
3) Highly-skilled workers	9,57	31,51	2,56	9,28	9,39
4) Executives	2,67	5,15	3,73	6,54	1,88
5) Managers	6,61	0,32	5,65	4,64	6,57
6) Others	2,67	6,75	–	4,43	–

Travaux exécutés par:

A – Femmes seulement
B – Femmes pour la plupart
C – Hommes et femmes
D – Hommes pour la plupart
E – Total

A – Femmes seulement
  1) Non qualifiées
  2) Qualifiées
  3) Hautement qualifiées
  4) Cadres
  5) Dirigeantes
  6) Autres

B – Femmes pour la plupart
  1) Non qualifiées
  2) Qualifiées
  3) Hautement qualifiées
  4) Cadres
  5) Dirigeantes
  6) Autres

C – Hommes et femmes
  1) Non qualifiées
  2) Qualifiées
  3) Hautement qualifiées
  4) Cadres
  5) Dirigeantes
  6) Autres

D – Hommes pour la plupart
  1) Non qualifiées
  2) Qualifiées
  3) Hautement qualifiées
  4) Cadres
  5) Dirigeantes
  6) Autres

E – Total
  1) Non qualifiées
  2) Qualifiées
  3) Hautement qualifiées
  4) Cadres
  5) Dirigeantes
  6) Autres

TAB. 36

Women with a main occupation by sector of economic activity and region (%)

Femmes ayant un emploi principal par secteur d'activité économique et par région (%)

1975

	Agriculture		Industry/Industrie		Services		Total	
	f/F 100	f/f+m 100	f/F 100	f/f+m 100	f/F 100	f/f+m 100	f/F 100	f/f+m 100
BR DEUTSCHLAND	8,8	50,6	30,9	24,9	60,3	45,8	100,0	36,4
Schleswig-Holstein	6,4	37,8	20,4	22,1	73,2	44,4	100,0	36,5
Hamburg	0,3	17,6 #	23,1	27,4	76,6	47,6	100,0	40,5
Niedersachsen	11,4	47,7	24,9	21,8	63,7	45,0	100,0	35,7
Bremen	.	57,1 #	20,2	19,5	79,8	44,5	100,0	35,4
Nordrhein-Westfalen	4,0	41,6	29,8	19,7	66,2	46,7	100,0	33,1
Hessen	6,3	51,2	30,8	24,3	62,9	42,8	100,0	35,0
Rheinland-Pfalz	10,6	49,8	27,9	21,8	61,5	43,4	100,0	34,3
Baden-Württemberg	9,4	54,2	41,4	29,4	49,2	46,6	100,0	37,9
Bayern	16,9	55,3	33,2	30,3	49,9	45,9	100,0	40,2
Saarland	2,6	44,8 #	23,5	15,2	73,9	42,5	100,0	29,9
Berlin (West)	0,6	32,8 #	26,7	31,5	72,7	50,7	100,0	43,5
FRANCE	8,7	32,2	25,1	24,6	66,2	48,0	100,0	37,4
Région parisienne – Île-de-France	0,5	24,3	24,6	28,3	74,9	50,4	100,0	42,1
Bassin parisien	10,7	31,5	29,5	25,8	59,8	47,8	100,0	36,6
Nord-Pas-de-Calais	7,4	33,6	28,8	21,2	63,8	46,6	100,0	33,9
Est	8,2	37,1	31,6	24,0	60,2	45,9	100,0	35,1
Ouest	20,0	36,1	23,1	26,2	56,9	47,4	100,0	37,9
Sud-Ouest	16,6	34,4	17,3	19,8	66,1	47,7	100,0	36,4
Centre-Est	9,6	33,3	29,8	25,6	60,6	48,3	100,0	37,0
Méditerranée	4,0	13,7	13,3	15,4	82,7	44,9	100,0	33,3
ITALIA	14,5	27,6	33,8	20,1	51,7	33,3	100,0	26,6
Nord Ovest	10,1	30,5	37,3	21,1	52,6	39,2	100,0	29,1
Lombardia	1,3	9,3	54,3	26,1	44,4	37,9	100,0	29,5
Nord Est	7,0	16,3	36,2	21,7	56,8	37,1	100,0	27,6
Emilia Romagna	14,1	28,3	35,9	25,2	50,0	39,2	100,0	31,3
Centro	11,2	24,0	39,2	24,2	49,6	35,8	100,0	28,8
Lazio	11,0	29,8	18,2	12,5	70,8	26,4	100,0	22,2
Campania	38,2	44,7	17,2	11,3	44,6	23,9	100,0	23,6
Abruzzi e Molise	38,7	37,6	16,2	15,4	45,1	34,9	100,0	29,7
Sud	40,6	36,2	13,7	10,1	45,7	28,4	100,0	24,5
Sicilia	22,5	15,0	14,0	6,7	63,5	23,9	100,0	16,0
Sardegna	2,6	2,9 #	11,9	6,4	85,5	35,4	100,0	19,7
NEDERLAND	1,7	7,2	17,2	11,1	81,1	34,8	100,0	24,3
Noord	2,2	3,5 #	18,7	9,5	79,1	33,2	100,0	20,7
Oost	3,2	8,5	19,4	10,6	72,4	34,5	100,0	22,6
West	1,1	7,0	13,5	11,4	85,4	35,1	100,0	26,5
Zuid	2,3	8,9	24,1	11,9	73,6	35,2	100,0	22,8
Zuidwest	4,3	6,4 #	17,4	8,9	78,3	34,2	100,0	21,0
BELGIQUE/BELGIË	3,8	27,9	29,6	20,6	69,3	40,7	100,0	31,8
Région de langue néerlandaise	4,8	28,1	32,2	22,4	63,0	39,0	100,0	31,0
Région de langue française	3,9	27,3	20,7	15,8	75,4	42,2	100,0	30,9
Bruxelles capitale	.	25,0 #	18,6	24,5	81,4	43,2	100,0	37,8
LUXEMBOURG	7,7	32,4	12,8	9,3	79,5	43,6	100,0	28,4
UNITED KINGDOM	1,1	15,5	27,3	23,8	71,6	49,5	100,0	38,0
North	0,5	6,2 #	26,7	19,7	72,8	55,3	100,0	39,6
Yorkshire and Humberside	1,2	18,0	31,8	24,0	67,0	51,6	100,0	37,5
North-West	0,6	19,5 #	30,6	25,6	68,8	52,6	100,0	39,8
East Midlands	0,9	13,0 #	34,6	25,5	64,5	50,6	100,0	37,1
West Midlands	1,0	17,9	36,6	24,5	62,4	53,1	100,0	36,9
East Anglia	3,5	14,4	25,4	24,1	71,1	48,3	100,0	37,0
South-East	1,0	25,7	22,9	24,7	76,1	46,4	100,0	39,0
South-West	1,4	12,0	21,4	21,6	77,2	46,8	100,0	36,6
Wales	2,0	19,0 #	23,4	18,0	74,6	50,0	100,0	35,3
Scotland	1,1	10,4	25,1	22,4	73,8	52,5	100,0	38,6
Northern Ireland	1,0	5,0 #	30,1	26,0	68,9	47,6	100,0	35,4
IRELAND	7,9	9,1	25,8	21,1	66,3	39,4	100,0	26,6
DANMARK	4,1	17,9	17,5	21,1	78,4	52,5	100,0	39,3
EUR 9	7,1	31,1	28,1	22,8	64,8	44,8	100,0	34,5

TAB. 36

Women with a main occupation by sector of economic activity and region (%)
Femmes ayant un emploi principal par secteur d'activité économique et par région (%)
1977

	Agriculture		Industry / Industrie		Services		Total	
	$\frac{f}{F}100$	$\frac{f}{f+m}100$	$\frac{f}{F}100$	$\frac{f}{f+m}100$	$\frac{f}{F}100$	$\frac{f}{f+m}100$	$\frac{f}{F}100$	$\frac{f}{f+m}100$
BR DEUTSCHLAND	7,7	49,0	29,9	24,2	62,4	46,0	100,0	36,4
Schleswig-Holstein	7,2	34,7	20,8	22,0	71,9	46,5	100,0	37,1
Hamburg	(1,4)	(34,8)	20,0	25,7	78,7	46,5	100,0	39,9
Niedersachsen	9,5	44,3	25,2	21,5	65,3	44,4	100,0	35,0
Bremen	.	.	17,3	18,7	82,3	50,4	100,0	38,9
Nordrhein-Westfalen	3,1	39,9	28,8	19,3	68,1	46,7	100,0	33,2
Hessen	6,6	46,9	31,1	24,1	62,3	43,0	100,0	34,8
Rheinland-Pfalz	9,9	47,6	24,6	20,5	65,5	43,0	100,0	34,1
Baden-Württemberg	8,6	54,5	39,0	29,5	52,4	46,6	100,0	38,4
Bayern	13,9	55,2	32,7	29,2	53,4	46,1	100,0	39,5
Saarland	(4,6)	(59,1)	23,1	14,7	72,3	46,7	100,0	31,2
Berlin (West)	(1,0)	(35,5)	24,6	32,3	74,4	52,8	100,0	45,5
FRANCE	8,6	33,9	24,4	25,0	67,0	49,0	100,0	38,5
Région parisienne – Île-de-France	0,5	25,2	23,6	28,5	75,8	50,6	100,0	42,6
Bassin parisien	11,4	35,0	27,9	26,4	60,6	50,0	100,0	38,5
Nord-Pas-de-Calais	7,0	41,4	28,3	19,9	64,7	48,4	100,0	34,2
Est	8,1	37,0	32,4	25,5	59,5	47,7	100,0	36,5
Ouest	18,7	38,4	23,2	27,0	58,1	58,8	100,0	39,6
Sud-Ouest	16,6	33,2	18,2	21,6	65,2	48,7	100,0	37,3
Centre-Est	8,2	33,2	28,1	24,8	63,6	48,8	100,0	37,2
Méditerranée	3,9	16,1	12,6	16,5	83,5	45,1	100,0	35,1
ITALIA	13,2	29,5	31,2	22,7	55,6	33,7	100,0	28,8
Nord Ovest	9,9	34,7	34,5	22,9	55,6	39,3	100,0	31,2
Lombardia	2,0	15,6	49,0	28,3	49,1	38,5	100,0	31,9
Nord Est	7,8	22,1	33,1	23,1	59,1	38,0	100,0	29,9
Emilia Romagna	13,6	30,8	34,2	29,6	52,2	40,0	100,0	34,5
Centro	12,2	29,2	37,7	27,6	50,1	35,8	100,0	31,4
Lazio	9,8	31,3	13,7	13,8	76,5	30,3	100,0	26,1
Campania	34,5	43,7	14,8	13,9	50,6	23,7	100,0	25,0
Abruzzi e Molise	27,4	32,7	16,6	18,9	56,1	34,9	100,0	30,2
Sud	35,7	35,2	12,2	10,8	52,0	26,4	100,0	24,3
Sicilia	21,4	17,9	9,8	6,9	68,8	24,2	100,0	18,3
Sardegna	(4,5)	5,8	12,9	9,4	82,5	31,0	100,0	20,8
NEDERLAND	1,7	7,9	14,9	10,4	83,4	36,2	100,0	25,3
Noord	2,9	6,9	13,4	8,0	83,7	49,8	100,0	22,8
Oost	2,4	7,8	18,3	10,6	79,3	34,8	100,0	23,2
West	1,0	7,2	12,1	10,8	86,9	77,3	100,0	27,2
Zuid	.	.	(12,1)	(6,7)	84,6	46,4	100,0	21,7
Zuidwest	2,3	10,1	19,9	11,2	77,8	37,7	100,0	24,6
BELGIQUE/BELGIË	2,6	22,2	23,6	19,1	73,7	40,2	100,0	31,5
Région de langue néerlandaise	2,8	20,4	28,9	20,6	68,3	38,7	100,0	30,3
Région de langue française	3,4	25,1	17,8	14,9	78,7	42,0	100,0	31,3
Bruxelles capitale	.	.	14,8	23,8	84,9	42,0	100,0	38,0
LUXEMBOURG	5,3	25,2	13,9	9,8	80,8	44,1	100,0	28,9
UNITED KINGDOM	1,3	17,6	25,8	24,0	72,9	50,8	100,0	38,7
North	(1,4)	18,8	23,9	19,9	74,8	54,3	100,0	37,8
Yorkshire and Humberside	1,1	16,5	30,2	25,1	68,7	52,6	100,0	38,9
North-West	3,7	19,9	26,1	21,9	70,1	50,5	100,0	36,1
East Midlands	4,6	24,0	22,4	21,6	73,0	48,6	100,0	36,7
West Midlands	0,6	20,1	22,1	24,2	77,3	47,9	100,0	39,1
East Anglia	2,1	17,6	19,1	21,4	78,8	49,5	100,0	38,4
South-East	1,4	25,2	36,4	26,2	62,1	53,4	100,0	38,3
South-West	(0,5)	19,9	32,9	26,8	66,6	53,7	100,0	40,1
Wales	2,4	14,3	17,8	18,2	79,8	52,2	100,0	37,4
Scotland	1,3	11,9	24,7	24,4	74,0	54,2	100,0	40,2
Northern Ireland	(1,3)	6,5	26,8	25,6	71,9	48,8	100,0	36,7
IRELAND	6,9	8,4	24,4	19,8	68,7	39,3	100,0	26,3
DANMARK	4,0	19,5	18,2	21,8	77,8	52,0	100,0	39,5
EUR 9	6,6	31,6	26,7	23,2	66,7	45,2	100,0	35,3

TAB. 37
Female employees in industry by NACE classes (%)
Salariées de l'industrie par classe de la NACE (%)

			BR Deutschland		France		Italia		Nederland		Belgique Belgié	
			$\frac{f}{F}100$	$\frac{f}{f+m}100$	$\frac{f}{F}100$	$\frac{f}{f+m}100$	$\frac{f}{F}100$	$\frac{f}{f+m}100$	$\frac{f}{F}100$	$\frac{f}{f+m}100$	$\frac{f}{F}100$	$\frac{f}{f+m}100$
Extraction and briquetting of solid fuels, coke ovens	11/12	1974	0,1	2,3	0,1	2,7	.	3,4	0,1	4,8	0,1	0,9
		1975	0,2	2,3	0,1	2,5	.	3,0	0,2	5,9	0,1	0,7
		1976	0,2	2,7	0,1	3,1			.		0,1	0,6
		1977	0,2	2,6	0,1	3,4			0,1	14,3	0,1	0,6
		1978	0,2	2,6	0,2	3,7			0,1	14,3	0,1	0,6
									:	:	0,1	0,5
of which:												
Coke ovens	12	1974	:	:	:	:	.	5,9	:	:	.	1,1
		1975	:	:	:	4,4	.	5,3			.	1,1
		1976	:	:	:	4,1					.	1,1
		1977	:	:	:	4,4			:	:	.	1,1
		1978	:	:	:	4,4					.	1,1
Extraction of petroleum and natural gas	13	1974	:	14,9	0,1	15,0	.	1,8	0,1	9,7	:	:
		1975	:	15,4	0,1	20,0	.	0,7	0,2	12,1	:	:
		1976	:	12,7	0,1	19,8			0,2	10,3	:	:
		1977	:	11,9	0,1	20,8			0,2	8,3	:	:
		1978	:	11,9	0,1	20,2			0,2	9,1	:	:
Mineral oil refining	14	1974	0,2	14,4	0,3	14,0	.	1,9	0,3	6,5	0,2	7,9
		1975	0,2	14,2	0,3	16,5	.	0,8	0,3	6,4	0,1	7,1
		1976	0,2	14,7	0,3	16,7	:		0,4	6,7	0,1	6,7
		1977	0,2	14,6	0,3	16,6			0,4	6,7	0,2	7,2
		1978	0,2	12,9	0,3	16,5			0,4	7,0	0,2	7,4
Nuclear fuels industry	15	1974	:	:	:	:	:	:	:	:	.	8,3
		1975	:	:	:	10,8	:	:	:	:	.	16,4
		1976	:	:	:	10,8	:	:	:	:	.	15,1
		1977	:	16,7	:	10,7	:	:	:	:	.	15,1
		1978	:	16,4	:	11,2	:	:	:	:		
Production and distrib. of electricity, gas, steam, etc.	16/17	1974	1,1	14,3	1,5	17,4	0,1	0,8	1,5	7,5	0,6	5,8
		1975	1,2	14,4	1,6	17,4	0,1	0,7	1,6	7,6	0,7	5,9
		1976	1,2	14,3	1,7	17,8			1,8	7,8	0,7	6,0
		1977	1,3	14,5	1,7	17,8			1,9	7,9	0,8	6,3
		1978	1,2	14,4	1,8	17,8			1,9	7,8	0,9	6,7
of which:												
Water supply: collection, purification and distrib. of water	17	1974	:	:	0,2	17,4	:	:	0,4	9,4	0,2	7,1
		1975	:	:	0,2	14,9	:	:	0,4	9,5	0,2	7,6
		1976	:	:	0,2	15,5	:	:	0,4	9,6	0,2	8,0
		1977	0,1	14,4	0,2	14,7	:	:	0,4	9,6	0,3	8,0
		1978	0,1	14,4	0,2	14,8			0,4	9,6	0,3	8,4
Energy and water		1974	1,4	9,3	2,1	12,4	0,1	1,0	2,1	7,2	0,9	3,8
		1975	1,6	9,1	2,2	13,1	0,1	0,8	2,2	7,5	0,9	3,7
		1976	1,7	9,1	2,3	13,6			2,4	7,8	1,0	3,8
		1977	1,7	9,1	2,3	13,9			2,5	7,8	1,1	4,2
		1978	1,7	9,0	2,4	14,2			2,5	7,7	1,2	4,3
Extraction and preparation of metalliferous ores	21	1974	.	3,0	:	4,8	.	3,2	:	:	:	:
		1975	.	3,0	:	3,9	.	3,1	:	:	:	:
		1976	.	2,5	:	4,1			:	:	:	:
		1977	.	3,5	:	4,6			:	:	:	:
		1978	.	3,8	:	4,6			:	:	:	:
Production and preliminary processing of metals	22	1974	1,7	10,9	1,6	10,2	0,5	3,2	1,2	6,9	1,3	3,8
		1975	1,8	10,6	1,5	10,1	0,5	3,1	1,4	6,9	1,4	3,8
		1976	1,7	10,4	1,5	10,1			1,3	6,3	1,4	3,8
		1977	1,7	10,5	1,5	10,3			1,3	6,4	1,4	3,7
		1978	1,6	10,3	1,5	10,5			1,3	6,5	1,4	3,7
Extraction of minerals other than metalliferous and energy-producing minerals	23/24	1974	3,1	19,3	2,7	16,1	3,3	14,8	1,7	7,6	2,8	11,4
		1975	3,0	19,5	2,7	16,3	3,4	14,7	1,7	7,6	2,8	11,3
		1976	3,0	19,1	2,7	16,5			1,6	7,1	2,6	10,3
		1977	2,9	19,2	2,7	16,7			1,7	7,5	2,7	10,1
		1978	2,9	19,4	2,7	16,9			1,7	7,2	2,6	9,8

TAB. 37

Female employees in industry by NACE classes (%)

Salariées de l'industrie par classe de la NACE (%)

Luxembourg		United Kingdom		Ireland		Danmark		EUR 9				
$\frac{f}{F}100$	$\frac{f}{f+m}100$	$\frac{f}{F}100$	$\frac{f}{f+m}100$	$\frac{f}{F}100$	$\frac{f}{f+m}100$	$\frac{f}{F}100$	$\frac{f}{f+m}100$	$\frac{f}{F}100$	$\frac{f}{f+m}100$			
:	:	0,4	3,4	:	:	:	:	:	:	1974	11/12	Extract. et agglomération
:	:	0,4	3,3			:	:	:	:	1975		de combustibles solides,
:	:	0,5	3,4			:	:	:	:	1976		cokeries
:	:	0,4	3,3					:	:	1977		
:	:	0,4	3,4					:	:	1978		
												dont:
:	:	.	4,4	:	:	:	:	:	:	1974	12	Cokeries
:	:	.	4,9	:	:	:	:			1975		
:	:	.	4,2	:	:	:	:			1976		
:	:	.	3,6	:	:	:	:			1977		
:	:	.	3,7	:	:	:	:	:	:	1978		
:	:	.	15,9	:	:	:	:	.	12,5	1974	13	Extract. de pétrole et de
:	:	.	15,1	:	:	:	:	.	13,7	1975		gaz naturel
:	:	.	14,5			:	:	.	12,6	1976		
:	:	.	14,1			:	:			1977		
:	:	.	15,3			:	:			1978		
:	:	0,1	13,7	:	:	0,1	10,0	:	:	1974	14	Raffinage de pétrole
:	:	0,2	13,7	:	:	0,1	5,9	:	:	1975		
:	:	0,2	13,8	:	:	0,1	5,6	:	:	1976		
:	:	0,2	13,6	:	:	0,1	5,6	:	:	1977		
:	:	0,2	13,7					:	:	1978		
:	:	:	:	:	:	:	:	:	:	1974	15	Industrie des combustibles
:	:	:	:	:	:	:	:	:	:	1975		nucléaires
:	:	:	:	:	:	:	:	:	:	1976		
:	:	:	:	:	:	:	:	:	:	1977		
:	:	:	:	:	:	:	:	:	:	1978		
1,4	5,3	2,5	18,5	2,4	10,5	:	:	:	:	1974	16/17	Product. et distribution
1,6	5,9	2,7	19,2			:	:	:	:	1975		d'énergie, etc.
1,6	5,9	3,0	19,1			:	:	:	:	1976		
1,6	5,9	3,0	19,6			:	:	:	:	1977		
		2,9	19,7			:	:	:	:	1978		
												dont:
:	:	0,2	10,6	0,1	5,6	:	:	:	:	1974	17	Captage, épuration et
0,2	6,5	0,3	11,2			:	:	:	:	1975		distribution d'eau
0,2	6,6	0,3	11,2			:	:	:	:	1976		
0,2	6,7	0,4	13,4			:	:	:	:	1977		
		0,3	12,3							1978		
1,4	5,3	3,1	11,5	2,4	10,1	0,1	10,0	1,8	9,6	1974		Énergie et eau
1,6	5,9	3,3	11,8			0,1	5,9	1,9	9,8	1975		
1,6	5,9	3,6	11,9			0,1	5,6	2,0	9,8	1976		
1,6	5,9	3,6	12,1			0,1	5,6	:	10,4	1977		
		3,6	12,2					:	10,5	1978		
0,2	:	.	6,3	0,1	5,9	:	:	:	:	1974	21	Extract. et préparation
0,2	:	.	5,0			:	:	:	:	1975		de minerais métalliques
0,2	:	.	5,3			:	:	:	:	1976		
0,1	:	.	5,1			:	:	:	:	1977		
		.	5,1							1978		
8,7	1,8	2,3	12,8	0,4	7,3	0,3	9,3	1,6	9,4	1974	22	Production et première
9,2	1,9	2,4	12,7			0,4	9,3	1,6	9,2	1975		transformation des métaux
9,0	1,9	2,4	12,5			0,5	11,1	1,5	8,7	1976		
8,9	1,9	2,3	12,3			0,5	10,5	:	9,0	1977		
		2,3	12,6					:	9,0	1978		
10,3	20,4	2,7	20,5	3,6	10,8	3,1	14,7	2,9	17,1	1974	23/24	Extract. de minéraux autres
11,7	21,5	2,8	21,7			2,9	14,7	3,0	17,3	1975		que métalliques et énerg.
11,7	21,5	2,8	21,1			3,1	15,4	2,7	16,1	1976		tourbières, etc.
11,4	21,7	2,8	21,4			3,2	15,4	:	17,2	1977		
		2,8	21,8					:	17,3	1978		

TAB. 37
(continued)
(suite)

			BR Deutschland		France		Italia		Nederland		Belgique België	
			$\frac{f}{F}100$	$\frac{f}{f+m}100$	$\frac{f}{F}100$	$\frac{f}{f+m}100$	$\frac{f}{F}100$	$\frac{f}{f+m}100$	$\frac{f}{F}100$	$\frac{f}{f+m}100$	$\frac{f}{F}100$	$\frac{f}{f+m}100$
of which:												
Manufacture of	24	1974	:	:	2,5	18,3	2,8	14,8	1,6	7,7	2,7	12,2
non-metalliferous		1975	:	:	2,4	18,8	3,0	14,7	1,6	7,7	2,7	12,0
mineral products		1976	:	:	2,5	18,9			1,5	7,1	2,4	10,9
		1977	2,7	20,4	2,5	19,0			1,6	7,4	2,5	10,7
		1978	2,8	20,6	2,5	19,3			1,6	7,4	2,4	10,2
Chemical industry,	25/26	1974	5,9	28,6	5,9	31,9	4,5	25,3	6,0	14,1	5,3	21,3
man-made		1975	6,2	28,2	5,9	31,6	3,9	22,1	6,4	13,8	5,5	20,8
fibres industry		1976	6,2	27,8	6,1	31,7			6,4	13,4	5,9	20,7
		1977	6,0	27,6	5,9	31,5			6,1	12,8	6,0	20,0
		1978	6,0	27,3	6,1	31,6			6,1	12,8	6,1	19,6
of which:												
Man-made fibres industry	26	1974	0,2	18,3	0,4	24,2	0,5	25,3	:	:	0,2	19,2
		1975	0,3	18,2	0,3	21,7	0,4	22,1	:	:	0,2	19,3
		1976	0,2	17,7	0,3	21,6			:	:	0,2	19,8
		1977	0,2	16,9	0,2	21,7			:	:	0,2	19,8
		1978	0,2	16,3	0,2	21,7			:	:	0,2	17,8
Extraction and processing	2	1974	10,7	20,4	10,2	19,7	8,2	14,8	8,9	10,8	9,5	11,3
of non-energy-producing		1975	11,0	20,2	10,1	20,0	7,8	13,6	9,4	10,7	9,8	11,0
minerals, etc.		1976	10,9	20,0	10,3	20,2			9,3	10,3	9,9	10,9
		1977	10,6	20,0	10,2	20,2			9,2	10,0	10,1	10,7
		1978	10,5	20,0	10,3	20,6			9,0	10,0	10,1	10,6
Manufacture of metal	31	1974	7,6	22,6	5,9	17,6	5,8	24,3	4,4	8,4	5,3	14,5
articles (except for		1975	7,3	21,9	6,8	18,1	6,0	24,4	4,4	8,1	5,2	14,6
mechanical engineering)		1976	7,3	21,5	6,6	18,0			4,7	8,6	5,2	14,5
		1977	7,3	21,6	6,7	18,4			4,3	8,0	5,3	14,5
		1978	7,3	21,6	6,7	18,6			4,4	8,2	5,3	14,3
Mechanical engineering	32	1974	6,2	16,9	3,4	15,5	1,8	8,2	2,5	6,3	2,0	9,1
		1975	6,3	16,4	3,3	15,3	1,8	8,0	2,6	6,1	2,2	9,1
		1976	6,2	16,0	3,3	15,4			2,3	5,2	2,2	9,1
		1977	6,0	16,2	3,3	15,9			2,7	6,2	2,2	9,2
		1978	5,9	15,9	3,4	16,2			2,7	6,2	2,3	9,3
Manufacture of office	33	1974	1,1	34,0	0,5	26,6	1,0	33,1	0,6	13,8	0,2	38,7
machinery and data-		1975	1,1	32,8	0,6	25,6	1,0	32,1	0,6	14,0	0,2	35,5
processing machinery		1976	1,0	31,9	0,6	25,0			0,6	12,5	0,2	33,6
		1977	0,9	32,2	0,6	24,8			0,6	13,4	0,2	33,6
		1978	0,9	31,3	0,6	23,7			0,5	11,1	0,1	26,1
Electrical engineering	34	1974	14,2	41,1	10,1	40,2	10,2	45,1	10,1	17,9	12,1	36,5
		1975	13,7	39,5	11,3	40,7	10,9	48,5	10,6	17,8	12,0	36,1
		1976	13,2	38,6	11,2	40,1			10,3	17,1	12,1	35,1
		1977	14,7	37,9	11,4	40,4			10,2	16,4	11,7	34,1
		1978	14,4	37,5	11,2	40,0			9,9	16,2	11,9	33,2
Manufacture of motor	35	1974	3,6	16,8	3,9	18,3	0,9	5,9	0,6	6,1	1,9	11,2
vehicles, accessories		1975	3,5	16,4	4,4	18,2	0,9	6,0	0,7	6,4	1,9	11,8
		1976	3,5	15,6	4,7	18,1			0,6	5,6	2,1	11,3
		1977	3,5	15,3	4,9	18,1			0,7	5,8	2,3	11,1
		1978	3,7	15,1	4,9	17,8			0,7	5,7	2,4	10,3
Manufacture of other	36	1974	0,7	12,9	1,8	12,5	0,6	8,0	1,1	3,8	0,5	6,6
means of transport		1975	0,7	12,5	1,9	12,9	0,5	6,8	1,3	4,0	0,5	6,4
		1976	0,7	12,2	1,9	12,6			1,3	4,1	0,5	6,0
		1977	0,7	12,3	1,9	12,9			1,3	4,1	0,6	6,0
		1978	0,7	12,5	1,9	13,1			1,3	4,2	0,6	6,4
Instrument engineering	37	1974	3,0	43,9	2,3	40,3	0,7	33,1	1,0	17,4	0,5	30,8
		1975	3,0	42,6	1,8	41,8	0,6	31,9	1,1	18,0	0,7	34,8
		1976	3,1	42,6	1,8	41,3			1,1	18,2	0,6	32,9
		1977	3,2	42,9	1,8	41,8			1,3	20,3	0,7	32,8
		1978	3,3	42,5	1,9	41,8			1,2	19,2	0,7	33,8

TAB. 37
(continued)
(suite)

Luxembourg		United Kingdom		Ireland		Danmark		EUR 9				
$\frac{f}{F}100$	$\frac{f}{f+m}100$	$\frac{f}{F}100$	$\frac{f}{f+m}100$	$\frac{f}{F}100$	$\frac{f}{f+m}100$	$\frac{f}{F}100$	$\frac{f}{f+m}100$	$\frac{f}{F}100$	$\frac{f}{f+m}100$			
												dont:
10,1	22,7	2,6	22,1	3,0	14,7	3,0	15,1	:	:	1974	24	Industrie des produits
11,3	24,1	2,7	23,4			2,7	15,1	:	:	1975		minéraux non métalliques
11,2	24,1	2,6	22,9			2,9	15,2	:	:	1976		
11,0	24,1	2,6	23,2			2,9	15,4	:	18,6	1977		
		2,7	23,6						18,8	1978		
7,9	21,4	5,2	27,8	4,0	26,7	5,0	35,6	5,4	27,6	1974	25/26	Industrie chimique,
7,7	21,1	5,4	27,8			5,4	35,8	5,5	26,8	1975		production de fibres
7,8	21,1	5,4	26,7			5,0	35,3	5,5	26,0	1976		artific. et synthétiques
8,0	21,6	5,4	26,5			5,1	35,1	:	25,9	1977		
		5,5	27,1					:	26,0	1978		
												dont:
6,3	25,2	0,2	13,1	:	:	:	:	:	:	1974	26	Production de fibres
6,2	24,5	0,2	12,5	:	:	:	:	:	:	1975		artific. et synthétiques
6,6	24,5	0,2	13,0	:	:	:	:	:	:	1976		
6,7	24,5	0,2	13,0	:	:	:	:	:	:	1977		
		0,2	12,1							1978		
27,0	4,6	10,2	20,4	8,2	14,4	8,4	21,7	9,9	18,4	1974	2	Extract. et transformation
28,8	4,8	10,7	20,7			8,7	22,2	10,1	18,2	1975		de minéraux non énerg.
28,6	4,9	10,5	20,1			8,6	22,4	9,8	18,0	1976		industrie chimique
28,5	5,0	10,5	20,0			8,8	22,3	.	18,0	1977		
		10,6	20,5					.	18,1	1978		
2,9	5,4	6,6	23,7	2,2	12,9	4,8	18,2	6,5	21,1	1974	31	Fabrication d'ouvrages en
2,7	5,7	6,5	22,9			4,8	18,4	6,6	20,7	1975		métaux (machines et mat.
2,8	5,7	6,4	22,1			4,7	18,5	6,1	18,9	1976		de transport exclus)
2,8	5,7	6,5	22,6			4,7	18,4	.	19,0	1977		
		6,5	22,4					.	19,0	1978		
4,9	7,1	5,5	16,5	1,3	16,1	6,9	15,0	4,5	15,0	1974	32	Construction de machines
4,9	6,9	5,7	16,3			7,5	15,1	4,5	14,6	1975		et de matériel mécanique
4,9	6,9	5,7	15,9			7,1	15,4	4,4	14,2	1976		
4,9	6,9	5,6	15,9			7,4	15,5	:	15,0	1977		
		5,7	15,9					:	14,9	1978		
:	:	0,8	27,9	0,7	41,7	:	:	:	:	1974	33	Construct. de machines de
:	:	0,8	26,9			:	:	:	:	1975		bureau etc.
:	:	0,8	27,9			:	:	:	:	1976		
:	:	0,8	27,7			:	:	:	:	1977		
		0,8	28,0					:	:	1978		
1,7	11,7	12,7	41,4	7,8	46,4	11,0	39,0	12,1	40,4	1974	34	Construction électrique
1,5	12,3	12,2	39,6			10,7	38,9	12,1	39,9	1975		et électronique
1,8	12,3	11,4	37,3			10,0	38,9	11,7	38,0	1976		
2,3	12,3	11,4	37,6			10,3	39,3	:	38,0	1977		
		11,4	37,8					.	38,0	1978		
2,2	19,0	2,4	12,4	0,6	5,3	0,3	8,3	2,7	14,1	1974	35	Construction d'auto-
2,8	19,6	2,4	12,3			0,3	10,0	2,7	14,1	1975		mobiles et pièces
3,3	19,5	2,3	12,0			0,2	7,7	2,8	14,1	1976		détachées
3,3	19,6	2,4	11,9			0,3	9,3		14,3	1977		
		2,5	12,1						14,2	1978		
:	:	1,8	10,1	0,4	4,8	0,8	4,3	:	:	1974	36	Construction d'autre
:	:	2,0	10,7			0,9	4,4	:	:	1975		matériel de transport
:	:	2,0	10,4			0,6	3,3	:	:	1976		
:	:	2,0	10,4			0,5	3,1	:	:	1977		
		2,0	10,6					:	:	1978		
:	:	2,3	37,3	1,5	37,0	0,8	34,4	2,1	39,7	1974	37	Fabrication d'instruments
:	:	2,4	37,3			0,7	32,1	2,0	39,3	1975		de précision, d'optique et
:	:	2,3	35,8			0,8	32,3	2,1	39,0	1976		similaires
:	:	2,3	35,8			0,8	32,4		39,3	1977		
		2,3	35,6						39,1	1978		

TAB. 37
(continued)
(suite)

			BR Deutschland		France		Italia		Nederland		Belgique Belgïe	
			$\frac{f}{F}100$	$\frac{f}{f+m}100$	$\frac{f}{F}100$	$\frac{f}{f+m}100$	$\frac{f}{F}100$	$\frac{f}{f+m}100$	$\frac{f}{F}100$	$\frac{f}{f+m}100$	$\frac{f}{F}100$	$\frac{f}{f+m}100$
Metal manufacture: mechan. electrical and instrument engineering	3	1974	36,5	25,7	27,9	22,5	20,8	21,8	20,3	10,2	22,5	19,1
		1975	35,6	24,7	30,0	22,8	21,6	22,3	21,2	10,2	22,7	19,0
		1976	35,0	24,1	30,2	22,5			21,0	9,8	23,0	18,4
		1977	36,3	24,4	30,6	22,9			21,1	9,8	23,0	18,0
		1978	36,2	24,1	30,6	22,8			20,7	9,8	23,3	17,5
Food, drink and tobacco industry	41/42	1974	10,4	41,1	8,6	33,6	8,0	37,6	19,1	22,4	10,6	28,6
		1975	10,8	40,8	8,9	32,4	7,7	34,8	19,5	22,3	10,6	28,4
		1976	11,3	41,0	9,1	32,4			19,6	21,6	10,7	27,6
		1977	11,2	41,3	9,1	32,5			19,9	21,8	11,1	27,5
		1978	11,5	41,6	9,5	33,0			20,2	22,3	11,7	28,1
Textile industry	43	1974	7,8	54,3	11,2	55,8	23,9	72,5	7,7	28,1	15,3	44,2
		1975	7,7	53,8	11,1	55,9	23,4	70,4	7,1	26,7	14,7	44,1
		1976	7,5	53,7	10,7	55,4			5,8	24,1	15,1	44,5
		1977	7,2	53,9	10,3	55,6			5,6	23,9	14,8	44,4
		1978	7,1	53,9	9,9	55,4			5,0	23,7	14,4	45,2
Leather and leather goods industry (exc. footwear and clothing)	44	1974	1,0	61,3	1,2	52,1	2,8	71,1	0,9	35,1	0,8	42,7
		1975	1,1	61,1	1,2	51,1	2,8	70,4	0,8	34,7	0,8	40,9
		1976	1,1	60,9	1,2	51,8			0,8	34,9	0,8	41,8
		1977	1,1	61,4	1,2	53,0			0,9	37,2	0,7	40,9
		1978	1,0	61,1	1,2	53,2			0,7	32,5	0,7	42,0
Footwear and clothing industry	45	1974	11,1	80,1	17,4	80,7	21,5	71,2	15,7	66,3	25,7	85,1
		1975	11,4	80,2	15,7	78,4	21,9	70,4	13,2	64,6	25,6	85,5
		1976	11,5	80,0	15,3	78,2			12,9	62,9	24,4	85,4
		1977	11,1	80,0	15,1	78,6			11,8	62,3	23,3	85,6
		1978	10,9	80,2	14,7	78,4			11,2	63,1	22,1	85,6
Timber and wooden furnit. industries	46	1974	3,4	21,2	3,0	24,1	4,7	23,2	2,4	9,8	2,7	15,2
		1975	3,3	20,8	3,1	24,1	4,7	22,8	2,4	9,4	2,7	15,3
		1976	3,4	20,3	3,1	24,2			2,3	9,5	2,7	15,0
		1977	3,4	20,3	3,1	24,7			2,3	9,1	2,8	15,0
		1978	3,5	20,1	3,2	24,9			2,4	9,7	2,7	14,6
Manufacture of paper of paper products: printing and publishing	47	1974	7,3	39,2	7,6	37,9	3,6	25,8	8,3	17,6	6,0	26,8
		1975	7,3	38,6	6,3	33,5	3,6	24,8	8,8	18,2	5,9	26,5
		1976	7,3	38,2	6,3	33,6			9,2	18,3	5,9	26,2
		1977	7,0	38,3	6,3	33,8			8,9	17,5	5,8	26,2
		1978	7,2	38,1	6,4	34,1			9,4	18,3	6,0	26,3
Processing of rubber and plastics	48	1974	4,2	35,6	3,6	32,6	4,0	33,8	1,8	13,7	2,3	27,6
		1975	4,0	34,7	3,8	32,1	4,1	33,4	1,7	12,5	2,2	27,0
		1976	4,1	34,1	3,8	31,7			1,7	11,9	2,2	26,1
		1977	4,1	34,1	3,9	31,9			1,7	11,7	2,3	25,0
		1978	4,1	33,7	3,9	31,8			1,7	12,0	2,3	24,9
Other manufacturing industries	49	1974	1,3	56,3	2,6	47,0	1,8	49,0	5,9	19,9	1,6	26,2
		1975	1,2	55,1	2,6	49,3	1,9	49,1	6,6	20,4	1,6	27,7
		1976	1,3	54,7	2,6	48,4			7,5	19,9	1,6	28,1
		1977	1,3	55,5	2,7	48,4			8,1	20,2	1,8	29,3
		1978	1,3	55,1	2,7	48,1			8,8	20,1	2,1	31,0
Other manufacturing industries	4	1974	46,4	44,8	55,4	46,5	70,3	50,8	61,9	24,4	64,9	41,0
		1975	46,9	44,4	52,8	44,5	70,1	49,5	60,1	23,4	64,1	41,0
		1976	47,4	44,0	52,1	44,1			59,7	22,6	63,4	40,2
		1977	46,3	44,0	51,7	44,2			59,3	22,2	62,7	39,4
		1978	46,6	43,6	51,4	44,0			59,4	22,4	62,1	39,1
Building and civil engineering	5	1974	5,0	7,5	4,5	5,1	0,6	0,6	6,8	3,7	2,3	2,9
		1975	5,0	8,0	4,8	5,5	0,3	0,4	7,1	3,9	2,6	3,0
		1976	5,1	7,8	5,0	5,7			7,5	3,9	2,8	3,1
		1977	5,1	8,0	5,2	5,9			8,0	3,9	3,1	3,1
		1978	5,1	8,0	5,3	6,1			8,4	4,1	3,4	3,3
TOTAL	1–5	1974	100,0	26,3	100,0	25,1	100,0	25,6	100,0	13,4	100,0	21,7
		1975	100,0	26,1	100,0	24,6	100,0	25,2	100,0	13,1	100,0	21,1
		1976	100,0	25,6	100,0	24,4			100,0	12,6	100,0	20,4
		1977	100,0	25,7	100,0	24,6			100,0	12,4	100,0	19,7
		1978	100,0	25,6	100,0	24,7			100,0	12,4	100,0	19,4

TAB. 37
(continued)
(suite)

Luxembourg		United Kingdom		Ireland		Danmark		EUR 9				
$\frac{f}{F}100$	$\frac{f}{f+m}100$	$\frac{f}{F}100$	$\frac{f}{f+m}100$	$\frac{f}{F}100$	$\frac{f}{f+m}100$	$\frac{f}{F}100$	$\frac{f}{f+m}100$	$\frac{f}{F}100$	$\frac{f}{f+m}100$			
11,9	8,0	32,1	23,3	14,7	21,3	24,5	19,8	29,9	23,1	1974	3	Industries transformatrices
12,3	8,4	32,0	22,6			24,9	19,1	30,1	22,7	1975		des métaux, mécanique
13,1	8,6	31,0	21,6			23,4	19,4	29,1	21,6	1976		de précision
13,5	8,6	31,0	21,7			24,0	19,6	.	21,9	1977		
		31,2	21,7					.	21,8	1978		
21,6	30,2	12,2	41,0	23,7	27,6	22,2	35,3	10,6	37,1	1974	41/42	Industrie des produits
21,3	29,4	12,0	40,4			23,0	35,3	10,6	36,3	1975		alimentaires, des boissons
21,5	29,7	12,2	39,6			22,3	35,3	10,8	36,1	1976		et du tabac
21,8	29,7	12,3	40,0			22,4	35,3	.	36,1	1977		
		12,1	39,9					.	36,4	1978		
:	:	9,6	46,6	13,0	43,1	7,3	57,3	11,9	56,0	1974	43	Industrie textile
:	:	9,1	46,2			6,5	57,2	11,7	55,6	1975		
:	:	9,1	45,6			6,7	57,1	11,0	53,2	1976		
:	:	9,1	45,7			6,3	56,8	.	50,0	1977		
:	:	8,9	46,1					.	50,0	1978		
:	:	0,7	43,7	0,7	23,8	0,8	50,0	:	:	1974	44	Industrie du cuir
:	:	0,7	44,0			0,9	52,4	:	:	1975		
:	:	0,7	42,5			0,8	52,6	:	:	1976		
:	:	0,7	42,7			0,8	52,6	:	:	1977		
:	:	0,7	43,3					:	:	1978		
16,1	82,7	13,9	74,1	23,4	72,9	12,5	79,1	15,4	76,3	1973	45	Industrie des chaussures
15,2	82,1	13,8	74,4			11,7	78,8	15,3	75,6	1975		et de l'habillement
14,2	82,1	13,9	74,1			12,8	79,2	16,6	77,8	1976		
12,8	82,1	13,9	74,3			12,5	78,9	.	76,9	1977		
		13,7	74,3					.	76,9	1978		
1,3	10,7	1,9	18,3	1,5	11,8	3,4	18,1	3,1	20,8	1974	46	Industrie du bois et du
1,0	9,4	1,9	18,3			3,2	18,1	3,1	20,6	1975		meuble en bois
1,1	9,4	2,0	17,9			3,7	18,9	3,3	20,7	1976		
1,1	9,4	2,0	18,2			3,7	18,8	.	21,4	1977		
		2,0	18,3					.	21,4	1978		
6,0	25,5	7,6	33,1	7,5	30,3	8,7	26,8	6,8	33,7	1974	47	Industrie du papier et
4,2	19,7	7,7	32,9			9,1	26,6	6,6	32,4	1975		fabrication d'art. en papier:
4,5	19,7	7,5	31,8			8,6	27,0	6,5	31,6	1976		imprimerie et édition
5,1	19,7	7,4	31,8			8,5	26,9	.	31,8	1977		
		7,5	32,4					.	32,0	1978		
6,1	8,1	3,1	31,7	2,1	20,9	4,2	35,3	3,6	32,8	1974	48	Industrie du caoutchouc
5,8	7,5	3,0	30,7			3,7	35,1	3,7	32,0	1975		transformation des
6,0	7,5	3,0	30,0			4,2	35,9	3,6	31,0	1976		matières plastiques
6,2	7,5	3,1	30,0			4,2	35,9	.	30,8	1977		
		3,0	29,9					.	30,7	1978		
0,6	:	2,0	51,8	1,2	40,0	2,0	43,9	1,9	44,7	1974	49	Autres industries manu-
0,6	:	2,0	51,5			2,1	43,5	2,0	45,0	1975		facturières
0,6	:	2,0	49,9			2,0	44,3	2,1	44,4	1976		
0,6	:	2,1	50,4			2,0	43,3	.	43,8	1977		
		2,0	49,8					.	43,1	1978		
51,8	25,3	50,9	43,3	73,2	36,2	61,0	38,0	54,7	44,5	1974	4	Autres industries
48,2	23,8	50,1	42,9			60,2	37,5	54,1	43,8	1975		manufacturières
47,9	23,3	50,4	42,1			61,1	38,2	55,1	43,4	1976		
47,6	22,6	50,5	42,3			60,3	37,8	.	40,8	1977		
		50,1	42,3					.	40,7	1978		
7,9	2,3	3,7	7,2	1,5	1,4	6,0	5,3	3,8	5,0	1974	5	Bâtiment et génie civil
9,1	2,7	4,0	7,6			6,1	5,3	3,8	5,2	1975		
8,8	2,7	4,5	7,8			6,9	5,6	4,0	5,2	1976		
8,8	2,7	4,4	8,2			6,8	5,5	.	6,0	1977		
		4,4	8,3					.	6,1	1978		
100,0	7,6	100,0	26,0	100,0	21,7	100,0	22,9	100,0	25,1	1974	1–5	TOTAL
100,0	7,6	100,0	25,7			100,0	22,4	100,0	24,7	1975		
100,0	7,7	100,0	24,8			100,0	22,6	100,0	24,0	1976		
100,0	7,7	100,0	25,1			100,0	22,5	.	23,5	1977		
		100,0	25,2					.	23,5	1978		

TAB. 38

Female manual and non-manual workers in the various branches of industry (%)

Les femmes dans la main-d'œuvre ouvrière et parmi les employés dans les différentes branches industrielles (%)

1972

NACE Nomenclature		BR Deutschland		France		Italia	
		A	B	A	B	A	B
Extraction and briquetting of solid fuels	11	0,8	9,3	0,1	6,2	–	–
Extraction of solid fuels- Underground	111 A	–	–	–	–	–	–
Extraction of solid fuels- Surface	111 B	2,4	14,2	0,3	9,4	–	–
Coke ovens	12	–	–	.	.	1,1	11,7
Extraction of petroleum and natural gas	13	5,4	24,1	8,5	23,9	–	6,0
Mineral oil refining	14	4,7	20,5	3,4	25,0	0,6	8,6
Nuclear fuels industry	15	–	–	–	27,6	–	–
Electricity, gas, steam and hot water	16	7,6	22,7	0,5	17,7	0,4	15,3
Water supply	17	6,6	25,1	3,8	32,0	0,3	9,4
Extraction and preparation of metalliferous ores	21	0,5	10,9	0,8	9,2	0,9	7,7
Extraction of metalliferous ores - Underground	211 A	–	–	0,1	0,3	–	–
Extraction of metalliferous ores – Surface	211 B	2,8	24,1	2,5	15,2	0,9	4,9
Production of metals	22	5,9	24,8	4,7	22,5	2,4	13,5
Ferrous metals	22 A	4,7	23,1	3,4	20,8	1,4	11,7
Non-ferrous metals	224	10,9	29,9	11,1	28,5	8,3	21,5
Minerals other than metalliferous; peat extraction	23	3,0	28,2	2,1	22,8	0,5	15,5
Building materials and refractory clays	231	2,5	32,6	1,5	27,6	0,4	24,3
Other mineral u.e.c.; peat cutting	23 A	4,3	17,4	3,5	14,5	0,8	5,3
Manufacture of non-metallic mineral products	24	17,8	32,3	14,4	27,9	13,7	23,5
Manufacture of cement	242.1	3,7	22,8	2,2	18,2	0,7	9,9
Manufacture of glass and glassware	247	20,6	33,9	15,7	28,8	11,3	19,6
Manufacture of ceramic products	248	39,6	32,6	36,2	32,0	33,2	29,4
Chemical industry	25	26,9	33,9	29,8	38,2	20,6	25,4
Manufacture of basic industrial chemicals	25 A	23,8	31,7	5,3	19,4	4,0	11,9
Production of man-made fibres	26	16,9	24,1	17,2	31,3	24,9	20,2
Manufacture of metal articles	31	21,9	33,4	15,3	27,3	14,3	25,9
Foundry	311	9,3	30,0	10,7	24,0	5,7	20,6
Manufacture of structural metal products	314	4,1	23,9	3,3	21,3	3,5	21,3
Manufacture of tools and finished metal goods	316	31,8	37,0	34,3	36,3	28,6	31,6
Mechanical engineering	32	9,7	29,5	7,5	25,3	6,1	22,2
Manufacture of agricultural machinery and tractors	321	5,0	24,9	2,8	24,8	1,1	21,8
Manufacture of machine-tools	322	11,7	30,5	7,4	26,0	4,4	22,2
Manufacture of office machinery	33	41,3	24,5	47,5	21,4	23,9	26,1
Electrical engineering	34	44,2	31,3	44,0	30,7	39,0	25,3
Manufacture of motor vehicles parts and accessories	35	13,7	24,4	13,2	19,8	8,0	21,8
Manufacture and assembly of motor vehicles	351	10,4	22,7	9,0	17,7	5,6	21,4
Manufacture of other means of transport	36	8,6	23,0	8,3	17,0	3,6	18,4
Shipbuilding and marine engineering	361	2,7	17,6	2,0	17,0	0,8	15,5
Aerospace equipment manufacturing	364	12,8	25,1	5,9	15,5	1,1	18,0
Instrument engineering	37	47,7	36,9	44,4	34,2	38,5	30,3

A Female manual workers.
   Ouvrières.

B Female non-manual workers.
   Employées.

TAB. 38

Female manual and non-manual workers in the various branches of industry (%)
Les femmes dans la main-d'œuvre ouvrière et parmi les employés dans les différentes branches industrielles (%)
1972

Nederland		Belgique Belgïe		Luxembourg		Nomenclature NACE		
A	B	A	B	A	B			
–	–	0,6	2,3	–	–	11	Extraction et agglomération de combustibles solides
–	–	0,2	–	–	–	111 A	Extraction de combustibles solides – mines de fond
–	–	1,8	3,8	–	–	111 B	Extraction de combustibles solides – mines à ciel ouvert
–	–	0,4	3,8	–	–	12	Cokeries
.	.	–	–	–	–	13	Extraction de pétrole et de gaz naturel
1,9	13,5	1,5	8,0	–	–	14	Raffinage de pétrole
–	.	–	–	–	–	15	Industrie des combustibles nucléaires
2,3	10,9	1,6	9,1	2,7	5,2	16	Énergie électrique, gaz, vapeur et eau chaude
2,4	13,6	1,2	14,6	.	.	17	Captage, épuration et distribution d'eau
–	–	–	–	–	4,5	21	Extraction et préparation de minerais métalliques
–	–	–	–	–	–	211 A	Extraction de minerais métalliques – mines de fond
–	–	–	–	–	4,5	211 B	Extraction de minerais métalliques – mines à ciel ouvert
2,7	13,3	2,2	11,8	0,5	7,0	22	Production et première transformation des métaux
.	.	2,0	12,2	0,5	6,8	22 A	Métaux ferreux
.	.	3,5	10,1	–	.	224	Métaux non ferreux
0,4	18,2	1,8	18,4	0.9	27,7	23	Minéraux autres que métalliques et énergétiques; tourbières
.	.	1,4	18,4	0,9	27,7	231	Extraction de métaux de construction et terre à feu
–	.	6,4	17,6	–	–	23 A	Extraction d'autres minéraux n.d.a.; tourbières
3,8	17,0	9,2	22,3	23,7	21,7	24	Industrie des produits minéraux non métalliques
–	–	0,8	20,7	.	.	242.1	Fabrication de ciment
3,7	17,7	14,5	21,7	–	–	247	Industrie du verre
15,4	17,4	19,6	28,2	.	.	248	Fabrication de produits céramiques
13,4	20,1	18,8	20,9	13,4	33,9	25	Industrie chimique
2,5	14,8	2,1	12,0	–	.	25 A	Fabrication de produits chimiques de base
.	.	19,3	6,8	.	.	26	Production de fibres artificielles et synthétiques
4,4	17,1	11,1	23,8	2,9	22,5	31	Fabrication d'ouvrages en métaux
1,2	15,7	4,4	16,9	3,3	19,1	311	Fonderies
1,3	13,6	1,6	17,6	0,4	26,6	314	Construction métallique
7,5	18,1	15,6	31,1	14,8	.	316	Fabrication d'outillage et d'articles finis en métal
1,5	15,0	3,2	19,7	3,2	19,7	32	Construction de machines et de matériel mécanique
2,6	11,4	1,5	14,6	–	–	321	Construction de machines et tracteurs agricoles
3,1	15,9	4,3	21,1	–	–	322	Construction de machines-outils
14,2	12,5	51,7	36,1	–	–	33	Construction de machines de bureau
22,4	8,0	37,0	21,0	6,5	25,0	34	Construction électrique et électronique
1,2	13,1	5,5	15,9	.	.	35	Construction d'automobiles et pièces détachées
0,6	7,3	5,4	15,1	–	–	351	Construction et assemblage de véhicules automobiles
1,1	11,1	3,3	14,3	–	–	36	Construction d'autre matériel de transport
0,6	10,5	1,5	10,9	–	–	361	Construction navale, réparation et entretien des navires
.	.	.	.	–	–	364	Construction et réparation d'aéronefs
13,0	21,8	39,5	30,8	–	–	37	Fabrication d'instruments de précision

A   female manual workers.
    Ouvrières.
B   Female non-manual workers.
    Employées.

TAB. 38
(continued)
(suite)

1972

NACE Nomenclature		BR Deutschland		France		Italia	
		A	B	A	B	A	B
Food, drink and tobacco industry	41/42	36,5	37,9	34,4	38,4	37,1	30,2
Food industry, except sugar	41 A	43,9	41,7	39,0	40,4	37,3	31,4
Slaughtering, preparing and preserving of meat	412	34,7	40,7	37,1	39,8	29,1	35,2
Manufacture of dairy products	413	27,5	37,2	20,6	40,1	19,8	24,2
Confectionery of bread and sugared products	41 B	54,4	54,7	53,5	51,4	50,0	40,9
Drink industry	42 A	14,1	29,2	17,4	34,8	23,9	32,7
Tobacco industry	429	62,5	35,2	.	.	73,1	23,8
Textile industry	43	57,6	40,0	60,1	42,1	62,6	36,8
Wool industry	431	49,6	29,9	44,7	29,9	48,3	26,8
Cotton industry	432	50,1	32,3	56,8	37,7	67,1	27,8
Knitting mills	436	79,5	51,6	80,0	55,0	83,2	56,5
Manufacture of leather and of leather goods	44	54,6	46,6	47,8	38,8	42,2	37,9
Tanning and dressing of leather	441	27,1	39,6	22,2	29,1	32,1	29,7
Manufacture of leather goods	442	71,0	50,8	67,9	46,5	60,1	53,7
Manufacture of clothing and footwear	45	85,0	53,9	77,6	54,3	75,6	53,0
Manufacture of footwear	45 A	65,2	40,0	64,7	43,2	52,1	44,2
Manufacture of clothing	45 B	90,1	56,4	90,4	64,7	86,6	55,3
Timber and wooden furniture industries	46	17,9	34,6	22,2	35,5	23,5	37,7
Wood industry (without wooden furniture)	46 A	13,4	32,6	17,7	31,1	25,8	32,2
Manufacture of furniture other than metal furniture	467	19,3	35,3	23,8	39,0	20,4	40,4
Manufacture of paper and paper products; printing, publishing	47	32,6	40,7	28,3	42,0	23,8	32,7
Manufacture of pulp, paper and board	47 A	35,0	35,8	31,1	39,2	27,6	25,4
Printing and publishing	47 B	30,7	43,5	25,7	43,2	19,2	37,1
Processing of rubber and plastics	48	34,1	34,8	30,5	32,1	28,1	32,0
Manufacture of rubber products	481	24,7	29,2	24,2	28,1	19,6	27,3
Processing of plastics	483	40,9	37,6	37,9	37,3	38,6	38,2
Other manufacturing industries	49	52,4	44,7	54,8	48,5	49,6	37,5
Building and civil engineering	50	0,8	30,9	0,8	22,9	0,2	20,1
Building and civil engineering (without installation)	50 A	0,7	26,4	0,7	20,9	0,1	19,3
Installation	503	1,6	42,9	1,4	26,9	0,6	22,7
Mining and quarrying	A	1,4	15,8	0,8	14,1	0,6	11,9
Total manufacturing industries	B	30,3	33,0	30,5	31,9	29,7	27,1
All industries	C	24,3	32,4	23,5	30,3	25,8	26,5

A Female manual workers.
Ouvrières.
B Female non-manual workers.
Employées.

TAB. 38
(continued)
(suite)

1972

Nederland		Belgique België		Luxembourg			Nomenclature NACE
A	B	A	B	A	B		
17,9	22,8	26,7	29,5	20,5	29,1	41/42	Industrie des produits alimentaires, des boissons et du tabac
17,3	23,4	29,6	33,7	24,1	33,3	41 A	Industries de produits alimentaires, sauf le sucre
13,8	21,8	15,5	30,7	32,6	35,8	412	Abattage de bétail, préparation et mise en conserve de viande
4,4	22,2	11,5	28,1	14,0	32,4	413	Industrie du lait
31,7	31,4	44,3	52,7	.	–	41 B	Industrie du pain et des produits sucrés
4,4	21,6	5,5	21,4	7,6	24,7	42 A	Industrie des boissons
42,0	21,2	71,8	30,0	.	.	429	Industrie du tabac
26,4	26,2	45,3	35,2	–	–	43	Industrie textile
21,4	30,8	46,9	25,4	–	–	431	Industrie lainière
16,3	26,5	36,4	37,7	–	–	432	Industrie cotonnière
65,5	29,9	81,5	50,5	–	–	436	Bonneterie
26,9	28,1	36,5	31,1	–	–	44	Industrie du cuir
5,0	17,7	11,4	17,5	–	–	441	Tannerie-mégisserie et industries connexes
39,9	34,1	60,6	44,8	–	–	442	Fabrication d'articles en cuir et similaires
69,2	35,9	90,7	51,4	90,9	56,3	45	Industrie des chaussures et de l'habillement
23,5	21,4	65,2	38,8	–	–	45 A	Industrie des chaussures
78,2	39,3	94,4	53,1	90,9	56,3	45 B	Industrie de l'habillement (à l'exclusion des fourrures)
5,0	20,7	11,9	28,6	23,1	50,0	46	Industrie du bois et du meuble en bois
3,3	17,8	8,1	29,8	.	.	46 A	Industrie du bois
7,2	25,3	13,7	26,3	.	.	467	Industrie du meuble en bois
10,9	26,6	25,3	33,1	12,0	32,8	47	Industrie du papier et produits en papier, imprimerie et édition
9,9	21,7	30,5	27,6	.	.	47 A	Fabrication de la pâte, du papier et du carton
11,6	28,0	18,5	37,2	10,7	32,6	47 B	Imprimerie et édition
7,4	16,3	22,9	28,2	3,0	15,9	48	Industrie du caoutchouc – transformation des matières plastiques
5,1	16,0	15,9	27,5	–	.	481	Industrie du caoutchouc
9,1	16,2	32,3	30,6	6,1	13,7	483	Transformation des matières plastiques
18,7	32,7	20,3	47,0	.	.	49	Autres industries manufacturières
0,8	12,7	0,1	22,7	0,4	22,5	50	Bâtiment et génie civil
0,9	10,7	0,1	19,8	0,3	17,9	50 A	Bâtiment et génie civil, à l'exclusion de l'installation
0,6	17,1	0,3	27,9	0,9	34,3	503	Installation
1,3	7,6	0,8	7,4	0,2	12,6	A	Ensemble des industries extractives
15,0	17,8	25,5	24,3	5,3	14,7	B	Ensemble des industries manufacturières
11,3	16,9	20,4	23,8	4,3	15,5	C	Ensemble

A Female manual workers.
   Ouvrières.
B Female non-manual workers.
   Employées.

TAB. 39

Manual workers by size group of establishment and qualifications (unit)
Ouvriers par classe de taille de l'entreprise et par qualification (unité)

1972

	BR Deutschland F	BR Deutschland M	France F	France M	Italia F	Italia M	Nederland F	Nederland M	Belgique/België F	Belgique/België M	
10 – 19											**10 – 19**
Total	57 809	284 990	38 740	196 560	32 445	136 752	5 080	49 533	9 707	47 553	Total
1 Qualified	6 532	192 083	5 191	111 843	8 176	50 735	838	30 710	1 670	24 252	1 Qualifiés
2 Semi-qualified	25 783	52 438	16 891	45 405	12 978	49 641	2 649	14 909	3 853	13 077	2 Semi-qualifiés
3 Unqualified	25 494	40 469	16 658	39 312	11 291	36 376	1 595	3 914	4 184	10 224	3 Non qualifiés
20 – 49											**20 – 49**
Total	179 686	636 570	119 609	472 980	116 289	347 119	13 696	127 911	27 677	93 158	Total
1 Qualified	13 656	396 583	19 496	255 409	25 351	132 599	1 493	66 386	4 594	41 455	1 Qualifiés
2 Semi-qualified	86 429	142 592	50 236	118 245	51 051	115 591	7 081	45 536	10 019	28 506	2 Semi-qualifiés
3 Unqualified	79 601	97 395	49 877	99 326	39 887	98 929	5 122	15 989	13 064	23 197	3 Non qualifiés
(10 – 49)											**(10 – 49)**
Total	237 495	921 560	158 350	669 540	148 735	483 871	18 776	177 444	37 384	140 711	Total
1 Qualified	20 187	587 955	24 703	366 908	33 614	183 387	2 328	97 062	6 243	65 712	1 Qualifiés
2 Semi-qualified	112 098	194 449	67 140	164 037	63 956	165 000	9 726	60 508	13 869	41 651	2 Semi-qualifiés
3 Unqualified	105 210	139 156	66 507	138 595	51 165	135 484	6 722	19 874	17 272	33 348	3 Non qualifiés
50 – 99											**50 – 99**
Total	210 014	595 963	142 181	419 562	114 558	291 739	18 667	120 911	28 442	76 478	Total
1 Qualified	16 381	350 426	21 327	234 116	26 119	116 112	2 371	58 521	4 323	29 520	1 Qualifiés
2 Semi-qualified	98 077	158 526	66 541	109 086	45 823	98 316	9 558	45 583	11 178	27 150	2 Semi-qualifiés
3 Unqualified	95 556	87 011	54 313	76 360	42 616	77 311	6 738	16 807	12 941	19 808	3 Non qualifiés
100 – 199											**100 – 199**
Total	270 758	648 650	173 210	454 817	130 701	287 951	18 748	113 628	35 964	110 062	Total
1 Qualified	17 870	365 190	23 903	252 423	24 049	116 044	2 081	52 610	4 208	43 034	1 Qualifiés
2 Semi-qualified	125 361	179 676	82 621	124 620	57 901	99 919	9 974	43 179	14 493	40 063	2 Semi-qualifiés
3 Unqualified	127 527	103 784	66 686	77 774	48 751	71 988	6 693	17 840	17 263	26 965	3 Non qualifiés
200 – 499											**200 – 499**
Total	340 054	870 207	267 104	578 946	165 890	343 447	16 777	141 777	42 934	122 437	Total
1 Qualified	14 622	465 561	33 121	312 631	30 524	144 248	1 510	61 815	7 642	46 648	1 Qualifiés
2 Semi-qualified	141 803	269 764	141 832	172 526	72 162	122 267	8 724	56 711	18 161	44 323	2 Semi-qualifiés
3 Unqualified	183 629	134 882	92 151	93 789	63 204	76 932	6 543	23 251	17 131	31 466	3 Non qualifiés
500 – 999											**500 – 999**
Total	213 348	575 795	156 660	446 382	91 272	209 702	10 583	92 756	23 300	96 143	Total
1 Qualified	8 534	297 110	18 486	242 832	12 413	83 881	476	40 998	2 330	36 823	1 Qualifiés
2 Semi-qualified	87 259	194 043	85 693	140 164	38 608	78 638	6 604	37 010	9 320	34 420	2 Semi-qualifiés
3 Unqualified	117 555	84 642	52 481	63 386	40 251	47 183	3 503	14 748	11 650	24 900	3 Non qualifiés
≥ 1 000											**≥ 1 000**
Total	437 178	1 721 679	146 824	837 762	105 571	557 367	20 106	162 731	26 562	213 266	Total
1 Qualified	14 864	924 542	16 591	429 772	10 768	212 357	3 016	73 066	558	86 159	1 Qualifiés
2 Semi-Qualified	161 756	604 309	84 571	321 701	38 428	221 275	12 627	73 229	5 339	81 042	2 Semi-qualifiés
3 Unqualified	260 558	192 828	45 662	86 289	56 375	123 735	4 463	16 436	20 665	46 065	3 Non qualifiés
TOTAL											**TOTAL**
Total	1 708 847	5 333 854	1 044 328	3 407 010	756 728	2 174 077	103 848	812 105	194 587	759 097	Total
1 Qualified	92 278	2 992 292	137 851	1 839 785	136 968	856 586	11 735	385 750	25 296	307 434	1 Qualifiés
2 Semi-qualified	726 260	1 600 156	528 430	1 032 324	317 069	784 842	57 324	316 721	72 386	268 721	2 Semi-qualifiés
3 Unqualified	890 309	741 406	378 047	534 901	302 691	532 649	34 789	109 634	96 905	182 942	3 Non qualifiés

TAB. 39.1

Manual workers by size group of establishment and qualifications (%)
Ouvriers par classe de taille de l'entreprise et par qualification (%)

1972

	BR Deutschland		France		Italia		Nederland		Belgique/België	
	$\frac{f}{F}$ 100	$\frac{f}{f+m}$ 100	$\frac{f}{F}$ 100	$\frac{f}{f+m}$ 100	$\frac{f}{F}$ 100	$\frac{f}{f+m}$ 100	$\frac{f}{F}$ 100	$\frac{f}{f+m}$ 100	$\frac{f}{F}$ 100	$\frac{f}{f+m}$ 100
10 – 19										
Total	3,4	16,9	3,6	16,5	4,2	19,2	4,9	9,3	5,0	17,0
1 Qualified	11,3	3,3	13,4	4,4	25,2	13,9	16,5	2,7	17,2	6,4
2 Semi-qualified	44,6	33,0	43,6	27,1	40,0	20,7	52,1	15,1	39,7	22,8
3 Unqualified	44,1	38,6	43,0	29,8	34,8	23,7	31,4	29,0	43,1	29,0
20 – 49										
Total	10,5	22,0	11,5	20,2	15,4	25,1	13,2	9,7	14,2	22,9
1 Qualified	7,6	3,3	16,3	7,1	21,8	16,1	10,9	2,2	16,6	10,0
2 Semi-qualified	48,1	37,7	42,0	29,8	43,9	30,6	51,7	13,5	36,2	26,0
3 Unqualified	44,3	45,0	41,7	33,4	34,3	28,7	37,4	24,3	47,2	36,0
(10 – 49)										
Total	13,9	20,5	15,1	19,1	19,6	23,5	18,1	9,6	19,2	21,0
1 Qualified	8,5	3,3	15,6	6,3	22,6	15,5	12,4	2,3	16,7	8,7
2 Semi-qualified	47,2	36,6	42,4	29,0	43,0	27,9	51,8	13,8	37,1	25,0
3 Unqualified	44,3	43,1	42,0	32,4	34,4	27,4	35,8	25,3	46,2	34,1
50 – 99										
Total	12,3	26,1	13,6	25,3	15,1	28,2	18,0	13,4	14,6	27,1
1 Qualified	7,8	4,5	15,0	8,3	22,8	18,4	12,7	3,9	15,2	12,8
2 Semi-qualified	46,7	38,2	46,8	37,9	40,0	31,8	51,2	17,3	39,3	29,2
3 Unqualified	45,5	52,3	38,2	41,6	37,2	35,5	36,0	28,6	45,5	39,5
100 – 199										
Total	15,8	29,4	16,6	27,6	17,3	31,2	18,1	14,2	18,5	24,6
1 Qualified	6,6	4,7	13,8	8,7	18,4	17,2	11,1	3,8	11,7	8,9
2 Semi-qualified	46,3	41,1	47,7	39,9	44,3	36,7	53,2	18,8	40,3	26,6
3 Unqualified	47,1	55,1	38,5	46,2	37,3	40,4	35,7	27,3	48,0	39,0
200 – 499										
Total	19,9	28,1	25,6	31,6	21,9	32,6	16,2	10,6	22,1	26,0
1 Qualified	4,3	3,0	12,4	9,6	18,4	17,5	9,0	2,4	17,8	14,1
2 Semi-qualified	41,7	34,5	53,1	45,1	43,5	37,1	52,0	13,3	42,3	29,1
3 Unqualified	54,0	57,7	34,5	49,6	38,1	45,1	39,0	22,0	39,9	35,3
500 – 999										
Total	12,5	27,0	15,0	26,0	12,1	30,3	10,2	10,2	12,0	19,5
1 Qualified	4,0	2,8	11,8	7,1	13,6	12,9	4,5	1,2	10,0	6,0
2 Semi-qualified	40,9	31,0	54,7	37,9	42,3	32,9	62,4	15,1	40,0	21,3
3 Unqualified	55,1	58,1	33,5	45,3	44,1	46,0	33,1	19,2	50,0	31,9
≥ 1 000										
Total	25,6	20,3	14,1	14,9	14,0	15,9	19,4	11,0	13,6	11,1
1 Qualified	3,4	1,6	11,3	3,7	10,2	4,8	15,0	4,0	2,1	0,6
2 Semi-Qualified	37,0	21,1	57,6	20,8	36,4	14,8	62,8	14,7	20,1	6,2
3 Unqualified	59,6	57,5	31,1	34,6	53,4	31,3	22,2	21,4	77,8	31,0
TOTAL										
Total	100,0	24,3	100,0	23,5	100,0	25,8	100,0	11,3	100,0	20,4
1 Qualified	5,4	3,0	13,2	7,0	18,1	13,8	11,3	3,0	13,0	7,6
2 Semi-qualified	42,5	31,2	50,6	33,9	41,9	28,8	55,2	15,3	37,2	21,2
3 Unqualified	52,1	54,6	36,2	41,4	40,0	36,2	33,5	24,1	49,8	20,4

125

TAB. 40

Manual workers by age and qualifications (unit)
Ouvriers par âge et par qualification (unité)

1972

	BR Deutschland F	BR Deutschland M	France F	France M	Italia F	Italia M	Nederland F	Nederland M	Belgique/België F	Belgique/België M
<18										
Total	69 329	62 080	52 589	61 038	33 885	19 527	14 368	23 159	22 521	30 248
1 Qualified / Qualifiés	2 149	6 332	1 525	7 874	5 117	1 386	819	5 118	1 194	1 543
2 Semi-qualified / Semi-qualifiés	24 612	14 651	19 668	17 579	13 723	3 984	8 046	9 588	7 364	7 169
3 Unqualified / Non qualifiés	42 568	41 097	31 396	35 585	15 045	14 157	5 503	8 453	13 963	21 536
18 – 20										
Total	138 101	216 432	164 606	266 957	93 487	71 750	21 756	50 645	30 877	46 634
1 Qualified / Qualifiés	9 667	110 164	12 839	92 901	16 454	9 973	2 350	15 852	3 922	7 182
2 Semi-qualified / Semi-qualifiés	61 731	60 168	81 151	98 240	42 630	29 561	12 488	22 790	11 486	18 887
3 Unqualified / Non qualifiés	66 703	46 100	70 616	75 816	34 403	32 216	6 918	12 003	15 469	20 565
<21										
Total	207 431	278 513	217 194	327 994	127 371	91 278	36 123	73 804	53 398	76 881
1 Qualified / Qualifiés	11 824	116 418	14 552	101 022	21 653	11 227	3 179	20 960	5 127	8 687
2 Semi-qualified / Semi-qualifiés	86 291	74 920	100 778	115 782	56 298	33 590	20 518	32 400	18 849	26 063
3 Unqualified / Non qualifiés	109 316	87 175	101 864	111 190	49 420	46 461	12 426	20 444	29 422	42 131
21 – 29										
Total	360 053	1 053 102	298 394	889 562	260 477	502 058	32 983	213 080	63 890	181 835
1 Qualified / Qualifiés	21 963	619 224	43 267	491 038	49 491	172 206	4 849	108 245	9 072	72 370
2 Semi-qualified / Semi-qualifiés	160 944	295 922	160 238	273 985	114 089	208 856	19 229	80 331	25 300	71 825
3 Unqualified / Non qualifiés	177 146	137 956	94 889	124 539	96 897	120 996	8 905	24 504	29 518	37 640
30 – 44										
Total	615 490	2 444 275	251 882	1 243 062	248 768	919 916	20 643	282 660	51 906	266 049
1 Qualified / Qualifiés	34 467	1 439 678	40 805	739 622	44 032	404 763	2 333	146 418	7 474	124 773
2 Semi-qualified / Semi-qualifiés	267 123	718 617	131 986	355 516	101 746	325 650	10 920	104 584	19 673	92 319
3 Unqualified / Non qualifiés	313 900	285 980	79 091	147 924	102 990	189 503	7 390	31 658	24 759	48 953
45 – 54										
Total	363 670	932 675	165 291	620 788	111 561	482 227	10 031	145 213	21 377	149 419
1 Qualified / Qualifiés	17 456	511 716	23 967	348 883	20 750	202 053	993	69 702	2 929	67 089
2 Semi-qualified / Semi-qualifiés	152 014	294 652	83 307	186 857	41 947	160 582	4 855	59 392	7 418	50 504
3 Unqualified / Non qualifiés	194 200	117 307	58 017	85 048	48 864	119 592	4 183	16 119	11 030	31 826
≥ 55										
Total	162 203	634 289	107 322	312 025	8 550	178 601	4 068	97 347	4 016	84 913
1 Qualified / Qualifiés	6 650	303 824	15 669	153 204	1 539	65 368	492	40 691	699	38 814
2 Semi-qualified / Semi-qualifiés	59 691	216 927	50 012	97 040	2 676	57 688	1 745	40 594	1 124	27 852
3 Unqualified / Non qualifiés	95 862	113 538	41 641	61 781	4 335	55 545	1 831	16 062	2 193	22 247
≥21										
Total	1 501 418	5 055 341	822 889	3 065 437	629 356	2 082 800	67 725	738 301	141 189	682 216
1 Qualified / Qualifiés	81 077	2 876 489	124 256	1 731 972	115 802	845 617	8 601	364 721	20 190	298 811
2 Semi-qualified / Semi-qualifiés	639 604	1 526 713	425 434	913 500	260 553	751 891	36 775	284 984	53 511	242 869
3 Unqualified / Non qualifiés	780 737	652 139	273 199	419 965	253 001	485 292	22 349	88 596	67 488	140 536
TOTAL										
Total	1 708 847	5 333 854	1 044 328	3 407 010	756 728	2 174 077	103 848	812 105	194 587	759 097
1 Qualified / Qualifiés	92 278	2 992 292	137 851	1 839 785	136 968	856 586	11 735	385 750	25 296	307 434
2 Semi-qualified / Semi-qualifiés	726 260	1 600 156	528 430	1 032 324	317 069	784 842	57 324	316 721	72 387	268 727
3 Unqualified / Non qualifiés	890 309	741 406	378 047	534 901	302 691	532 649	34 789	109 634	96 904	182 942

TAB. 40.1

Manual workers by age and qualifications (%)
Ouvriers par âge et par qualification (%)

1972

	BR Deutschland		France		Italia		Nederland		Belgique/België	
	$\frac{f}{F}\cdot100$	$\frac{f}{f+m}\cdot100$	$\frac{f}{F}\cdot100$	$\frac{f}{f+m}\cdot100$	$\frac{f}{F}\cdot100$	$\frac{f}{f+m}\cdot100$	$\frac{f}{F}\cdot100$	$\frac{f}{f+m}\cdot100$	$\frac{f}{F}\cdot100$	$\frac{f}{f+m}\cdot100$
<18										
Total	4,0	52,8	5,1	46,3	4,5	63,4	13,8	38,3	11,5	42,7
1 Qualified	3,1	25,3	2,9	16,2	15,1	78,7	5,7	13,8	5,3	43,6
2 Semi-qualified	35,5	62,7	37,4	52,8	40,5	77,5	56,0	45,6	32,7	50,7
3 Unqualified	61,4	50,9	59,7	46,9	44,4	51,5	38,3	39,4	62,0	39,3
18 – 20										
Total	8,1	39,0	15,9	38,1	12,4	56,6	20,9	30,0	15,9	39,8
1 Qualified	7,0	8,1	7,8	12,1	17,6	62,3	10,8	12,9	12,7	35,3
2 Semi-qualified	44,7	50,6	49,3	45,2	45,6	59,1	57,4	35,4	37,2	37,8
3 Unqualified	48,3	59,1	42,9	48,2	36,8	51,6	31,8	36,6	50,1	42,9
<21										
Total	12,1	42,7	21,0	39,8	16,9	58,3	34,7	32,9	27,4	41,0
1 Qualified	5,7	9,2	6,7	12,6	17,0	65,9	8,8	13,2	9,6	37,1
2 Semi-qualified	41,6	53,5	46,4	46,5	44,2	62,6	56,8	38,8	35,3	42,0
3 Unqualified	52,7	55,6	46,9	47,8	38,8	51,5	34,4	37,8	55,1	41,1
21 – 29										
Total	21,1	25,5	28,6	25,1	34,4	34,2	31,8	13,4	32,8	26,0
1 Qualified	6,1	3,4	14,5	8,1	19,0	22,3	14,7	4,3	14,2	11,1
2 Semi-qualified	44,7	35,2	53,7	36,9	43,8	35,3	58,3	19,3	39,6	26,0
3 Unqualified	49,2	56,2	31,8	43,2	37,2	44,5	27,0	26,7	46,2	44,0
30 – 44										
Total	36,0	20,1	24,1	16,8	32,9	21,3	19,9	6,8	26,7	16,3
1 Qualified	5,6	2,3	16,2	5,2	17,7	9,8	11,3	1,6	14,4	5,7
2 Semi-qualified	43,4	27,1	52,4	27,1	40,9	23,8	52,9	9,5	37,9	17,6
3 Unqualified	51,0	52,3	31,4	34,8	41,4	35,2	35,8	18,9	47,7	33,6
45 – 54										
Total	21,3	28,3	15,9	21,0	14,7	18,8	9,7	6,5	11,0	12,5
1 Qualified	4,8	3,3	14,5	6,4	18,6	9,3	9,9	1,4	13,7	4,2
2 Semi-qualified	41,8	34,0	50,4	30,8	37,6	20,7	48,4	7,6	34,7	12,8
3 Unqualified	53,4	62,3	35,1	40,6	43,8	29,0	41,7	20,6	51,6	25,7
≥55										
Total	9,5	20,4	10,4	25,6	1,1	4,6	3,9	4,0	2,1	4,5
1 Qualified	4,1	2,1	14,6	9,3	18,0	2,3	12,1	1,2	17,4	1,8
2 Semi-qualified	36,8	21,6	46,6	34,0	31,3	4,4	42,9	4,1	28,0	3,9
3 Unqualified	59,1	45,8	38,8	40,3	50,7	7,2	45,0	10,2	54,6	9,0
≥21										
Total	87,9	22,9	79,0	21,2	83,1	23,2	65,3	8,4	72,6	17,1
1 Qualified	5,4	2,7	15,1	6,7	18,4	12,0	12,7	2,3	14,3	6,3
2 Semi-qualified	42,6	29,5	51,7	31,8	41,4	25,7	54,3	11,4	37,9	18,1
3 Unqualified	52,0	54,5	33,2	39,4	40,2	34,3	33,0	20,1	47,8	32,4
TOTAL										
Total	100,0	24,3	100,0	23,5	100,0	25,8	100,0	11,3	100,0	20,4
1 Qualified	5,4	3,0	13,2	6,5	18,1	13,8	11,3	3,0	13,0	7,6
2 Semi-qualified	42,5	31,2	50,6	33,9	41,9	28,8	55,2	15,3	37,2	21,2
3 Unqualified	52,1	54,6	36,2	41,4	40,0	36,2	33,5	24,1	49,8	34,6

Right-hand (French) row labels:

<18 — Total / 1 Qualifiés / 2 Semi-qualifiés / 3 Non qualifiés
18 – 20 — Total / 1 Qualifiés / 2 Semi-qualifiés / 3 Non qualifiés
<21 — Total / 1 Qualifiés / 2 Semi-qualifiés / 3 Non qualifiés
21 – 29 — Total / 1 Qualifiés / 2 Semi-qualifiés / 3 Non qualifiés
30 – 44 — Total / 1 Qualifiés / 2 Semi-qualifiés / 3 Non qualifiés
45 – 54 — Total / 1 Qualifiés / 2 Semi-qualifiés / 3 Non qualifiés
≥55 — Total / 1 Qualifiés / 2 Semi-qualifiés / 3 Non qualifiés
≥21 — Total / 1 Qualifiés / 2 Semi-qualifiés / 3 Non qualifiés
TOTAL — Total / 1 Qualifiés / 2 Semi-qualifiés / 3 Non qualifiés

TAB. 41

Manual workers by length of service and qualifications (unit)
Ouvriers par ancienneté dans l'entreprise et par qualification (unité)

1972

	BR Deutschland		France		Italia		Nederland		Belgique/België	
	F	M	F	M	F	M	F	M	F	M
< 2										
Total	531 732	1 357 203	337 302	991 507	140 526	474 406	42 860	217 777	62 405	193 095
1 Qualified / Qualifiés	22 333	576 811	22 262	406 518	18 690	110 062	3 600	82 973	4 618	54 260
2 Semi-qualified / Semi-qualifiés	199 931	451 949	139 980	313 316	49 184	155 605	21 816	85 369	20 843	64 494
3 Unqualified / Non qualifiés	309 468	328 443	175 060	271 673	72 652	208 739	17 444	49 435	36 944	74 341
2 – 4										
Total	515 878	1 208 325	286 026	765 068	272 460	611 654	36 899	194 580	58 643	178 604
1 Qualified / Qualifiés	26 310	623 496	34 037	390 185	45 773	195 118	4 059	86 199	7 623	65 905
2 Semi-qualified / Semi-qualifiés	223 891	409 622	154 740	257 828	114 161	248 943	21 770	81 724	22 402	68 584
3 Unqualified / Non qualifiés	265 677	175 207	97 249	117 055	112 526	167 593	11 070	26 657	28 618	44 115
5 – 9										
Total	315 149	900 347	204 211	619 089	168 535	456 060	16 322	149 376	38 791	147 343
1 Qualified / Qualifiés	20 170	557 315	36 554	368 977	34 213	204 315	2 399	76 182	6 478	66 599
2 Semi-qualified / Semi-qualifiés	144 338	253 898	112 520	185 108	79 043	175 583	9 614	59 601	15 284	53 928
3 Unqualified / Non qualifiés	150 641	89 134	55 137	65 004	55 279	76 162	4 309	13 593	17 029	26 816
10 – 19										
Total	274 748	1 229 928	137 016	587 618	117 079	425 353	6 193	154 236	26 147	145 067
1 Qualified / Qualifiés	17 859	805 603	29 732	381 952	25 289	233 944	1 226	85 138	4 759	72 533
2 Semi-qualified / Semi-qualifiés	125 010	327 161	75 633	162 770	50 110	143 769	3 332	56 296	10 119	49 904
3 Unqualified / Non qualifiés	131 879	97 164	31 651	42 896	41 680	47 640	1 635	12 802	11 269	22 630
≥ 20										
Total	71 341	638 051	67 056	377 045	49 052	168 133	1 572	96 137	8 600	94 990
1 Qualified / Qualifiés	5 779	51 682	15 490	256 391	12 459	104 915	497	55 183	1 909	48 540
2 Semi-qualified / Semi-qualifiés	33 316	297 970	38 557	96 146	21 436	50 104	770	34 032	3 664	31 537
3 Unqualified / Non qualifiés	32 246	288 399	13 009	24 508	15 157	13 114	305	6 922	3 027	14 913
TOTAL										
Total	1 708 847	5 333 854	1 044 328	3 407 010	756 728	2 174 077	103 848	812 105	194 586	759 097
1 Qualified / Qualifiés	92 278	2 992 292	137 851	1 839 785	136 968	856 586	11 735	385 750	25 296	307 434
2 Semi-qualified / Semi-qualifiés	726 260	1 600 156	528 430	1 032 324	317 069	784 842	57 324	316 721	72 386	268 720
3 Unqualified / Non qualifiés	890 309	741 406	378 047	534 901	302 691	532 649	34 789	109 634	96 904	182 943

TAB. 41.1

Manual workers by length of service and qualifications (%)
Ouvriers par ancienneté dans l'entreprise et par qualification (%)

1972

	BR Deutschland		France		Italia		Nederland		Belgique/België	
	$\frac{f}{F}\cdot100$	$\frac{f}{f+m}\cdot100$	$\frac{f}{F}\cdot100$	$\frac{f}{f+m}\cdot100$	$\frac{f}{F}\cdot100$	$\frac{f}{f+m}\cdot100$	$\frac{f}{F}\cdot100$	$\frac{f}{f+m}\cdot100$	$\frac{f}{F}\cdot100$	$\frac{f}{f+m}\cdot100$
< 2 / < 2										
Total / Total	31,1	28,1	32,7	25,4	18,8	22,9	41,3	16,4	32,1	24,4
1 Qualified / 1 Qualifiés	4,2	3,7	6,6	5,2	13,3	14,5	8,4	4,2	7,4	7,8
2 Semi-qualified / 2 Semi-qualifiés	37,6	30,7	41,5	30,9	35,0	24,0	50,9	20,4	33,4	24,4
3 Unqualified / 3 Non qualifiés	58,2	48,5	51,9	39,2	51,7	25,8	40,7	26,1	59,2	33,2
2 – 4 / 2 – 4										
Total / Total	30,2	29,9	27,7	27,2	36,4	30,8	35,5	15,9	30,1	24,7
1 Qualified / 1 Qualifiés	5,1	4,0	11,9	8,0	16,8	19,0	11,0	4,5	13,0	10,4
2 Semi-qualified / 2 Semi-qualifiés	43,4	35,3	54,1	37,5	41,9	31,4	59,0	21,0	38,2	24,6
3 Unqualified / 3 Non qualifiés	51,5	60,3	34,0	45,4	41,3	40,2	30,0	29,3	48,8	39,3
5 – 9 / 5 – 9										
Total / Total	18,4	25,9	19,8	24,8	22,5	27,0	15,7	9,9	19,9	20,8
1 Qualified / 1 Qualifiés	6,4	3,5	17,9	9,0	20,3	14,3	14,7	3,1	16,7	8,9
2 Semi-qualified / 2 Semi-qualifiés	45,8	36,2	55,1	37,8	46,9	31,0	58,9	13,9	39,4	22,1
3 Unqualified / 3 Non qualifiés	47,8	62,8	27,0	45,9	32,8	42,1	26,4	24,1	43,9	38,8
10 – 19 / 10 – 19										
Total / Total	16,1	18,3	13,3	18,9	15,7	21,6	6,0	3,9	13,4	15,3
1 Qualified / 1 Qualifiés	6,5	2,2	21,7	7,2	21,6	9,8	19,8	1,4	18,2	6,2
2 Semi-qualified / 2 Semi-qualifiés	45,5	27,6	55,2	31,7	42,8	25,8	53,8	5,6	38,7	16,9
3 Unqualified / 3 Non qualifiés	48,0	57,6	23,1	42,5	35,6	46,7	26,4	11,3	43,1	33,2
≥ 20 / ≥ 20										
Total / Total	4,2	10,1	6,5	15,1	6,6	22,6	1,5	1,6	4,5	8,3
1 Qualified / 1 Qualifiés	8,1	10,1	23,1	5,7	25,4	10,6	31,6	0,9	22,2	3,8
2 Semi-qualified / 2 Semi-qualifiés	46,7	10,1	57,5	28,6	43,7	30,0	49,0	2,2	42,6	10,4
3 Unqualified / 3 Non qualifiés	45,2	10,1	19,4	34,7	30,9	53,6	19,4	4,2	35,2	16,9
TOTAL / TOTAL										
Total / Total	100,0	24,3	100,0	23,5	100,0	25,8	100,0	11,3	100,0	20,4
1 Qualified / 1 Qualifiés	5,4	3,0	13,2	7,0	18,1	13,8	11,3	3,0	13,0	7,6
2 Semi-qualified / 2 Semi-qualifiés	42,5	31,2	50,6	33,9	41,9	28,8	55,2	15,3	37,2	21,2
3 Unqualified / 3 Non qualifiés	52,1	54,6	36,2	41,1	40,0	36,2	33,0	24,1	49,8	34,6

TAB. 42

Non-manual workers by size group of establishment and qualifications (unit)

Employés par classe de taille de l'entreprise et par qualification (unité)

1972

	BR Deutschland		France		Italia	
	F	M	F	M	F	M
10 – 19						
Total	39 285	36569	30 937	47 647	7 152	9 658
1A Earning more than (^{1}) monthly	–	293	31	524	7	10
1B Earning not more than (^{1}) monthly	236	1 609	712	6 718	57	309
2 Very highly qualified	2 593	8 703	1 856	14 151	257	1 449
3 Less highly qualified	15 321	13 604	1 207	8 005	1 495	3 409
4 Executives	20 978	3 328	26 605	10 530	5 178	3 303
5 Supervisors	157	9 032	526	7 719	157	1 178
of which:						
5A With higher proficiency and responsibilities	–	(8 447)	–	(5 670)	–	(599)
5B With lower proficiency and responsibilities	–	(585)	–	(2 049)	–	(579)
20 – 49						
Total	80 953	121 044	69 809	117 926	22 996	37 981
1A Earning more than (^{1}) monthly	.	1 089	70	1 769	–	114
1B Earning not more than (^{1}) monthly	405	5 689	977	13 561	69	1 557
2 Very highly qualified	5 586	31 714	4 817	30 987	2 208	7 140
3 Less highly qualified	33 919	45 392	2 723	22 288	4 484	12 800
4 Executives	40 719	10 894	59 616	25 472	15 430	10 711
5 Supervisors	324	26 266	1 606	23 939	805	5 659
of which:						
5A With higher proficiency and responsibilities	–	25 419	–	(15 684)	–	(3 266)
5B With lower proficiency and responsibilities	–	848	–	(8 355)	–	(2 393)
(10 – 49)						
Total	120 236	157 613	100 745	165 573	30 148	47 639
1A Earning more than (^{1}) monthly	.	1 419	101	2 484	.	143
1B Earning not more than (^{1}) monthly	721	7 250	1 813	20 200	121	1 858
2 Very highly qualified	8 176	40 507	6 649	45 036	2 472	8 575
3 Less highly qualified	49 177	58 947	3 929	30 300	5 969	16 245
4 Executives	61 681	14 185	86 238	35 929	20 621	14 006
5 Supervisors	481	35 305	2 015	31 624	965	6 812
of which:						
5A With higher proficiency and responsibilities	–	33 887	–	(21 359)	–	(3 859)
5B With lower proficiency and responsibilities	–	1 418	–	(10 265)	–	(2 953)
50 – 99						
Total	74 556	137 344	63 078	113 855	21 000	48 651
1A Earning more than (^{1}) monthly	.	1 099	126	1 822	–	97
1B Earning not more than (^{1}) monthly	447	7 142	631	8 653	147	2 092
2 Very highly qualified	4 473	34 748	3 785	27 553	1 071	9 925
3 Less highly qualified	32 432	52 328	3 595	24 365	5 061	16 736
4 Executives	36 831	13 597	52 607	26 414	13 839	12 309
5 Supervisors	373	28 430	2 334	25 048	882	7 492
of which:						
5A With higher proficiency and responsibilities	–	27 194	–	(15 143)	–	(3 941)
5B With lower proficiency and responsibilities	–	1 236	–	(9 905)	–	(3 551)
100 – 199						
Total	93 092	172 690	69 641	141 017	24 478	62 059
1A Earning more than (^{1}) monthly	.	2 072	.	1 692	–	248
1B Earning not more than (^{1}) monthly	186	7 944	279	6 346	98	3 351
2 Very highly qualified	4 003	42 309	3 343	32 716	1 444	13 653
3 Less highly qualified	37 423	66 659	3 830	31 870	6 071	19 549
4 Executives	50 921	17 614	58 777	32 575	15 666	12 722
5 Supervisors	559	36 092	3 412	35 818	1 199	12 536
of which:						
5A With higher proficiency and responsibilities	–	34 538	–	(21 998)	–	(6 206)
5B With lower proficiency and responsibilities	–	1 554	–	(13 820)	–	(6 330)

(^{1}) DM 4 500 – FF 10 000 – LIT 1 000 000 – HFL 6 000 – BFR 65 000.

TAB. 42

Non-manual workers by size group of establishment and qualifications (unit)

Employés par classe de taille de l'entreprise et par qualification (unité)

1972

Nederland		Belgique/België		
F	M	F	M	
				10 – 19
3 087	9 367	2 937	4 381	Total
–	65	–	5	1A Cadres dont la rémunération mensuelle est supérieure à (^{1})
15	1 902	129	1 021	1B Cadres dont la rémunération mensuelle est inférieure ou égale à (^{1})
77	1 246	226	793	2 Personnel ayant une qualification très élevée
284	1 976	1 142	1 441	3 Personne ayant une qualification moyenne
2 634	2 960	1 348	845	4 Personnel d'exécution
77	1 218	92	276	5 Personnel de maîtrise (contremaîtres, chefs d'équipe)
				dont:
–	(984)	–	(149)	5A Agents ayant une compétence et une responsabilité élevées
–	(234)	–	(127)	5B Agents ayant une compétence et une responsabilité moyennes
				20 – 49
7 221	28 348	6 754	13 960	Total
7	85	–	140	1A Cadres dont la rémunération mensuelle est supérieure à (^{1})
72	3 685	378	2 708	1B Cadres dont la rémunération mensuelle est inférieure ou égale à (^{1})
130	4 394	588	2 597	2 Personnel ayant une qualification très élevée
477	6 577	2 384	4 663	3 Personne ayant une qualification moyenne
6 354	9 043	3 127	2 569	4 Personnel d'exécution
181	4 564	277	1 283	5 Personnel de maîtrise (contremaîtres, chefs d'équipe)
				dont:
–	(3 543)	–	(893)	5A Agents ayant une compétence et une responsabilité élevées
–	(1 021)	–	(390)	5B Agents ayant une compétence et une responsabilité moyennes
				(10 – 49)
10 309	37 715	9 691	18 342	Total
21	151	–	146	1A Cadres dont la rémunération mensuelle est supérieure à (^{1})
82	5 582	543	3 723	1B Cadres dont la rémunération mensuelle est inférieure ou égale à (^{1})
206	5 619	785	3 393	2 Personnel ayant une qualification très élevée
753	8 561	3 527	6 108	3 Personne ayant une qualification moyenne
8 989	12 031	4 477	3 412	4 Personnel d'exécution
258	5 771	359	1 560	5 Personnel de maîtrise (contremaîtres, chefs d'équipe)
				dont:
–	(4 526)	–	(1 045)	5A Agents ayant une compétence et une responsabilité élevées
–	(1 245)	–	(515)	5B Agents ayant une compétence et une responsabilité moyennes
				50 – 99
8 810	33 516	6 963	14 482	Total
–	168	7	159	1A Cadres dont la rémunération mensuelle est supérieure à (^{1})
18	1 743	254	2 143	1B Cadres dont la rémunération mensuelle est inférieure ou égale à (^{1})
88	4 256	509	2 694	2 Personnel ayant une qualification très élevée
626	7 943	2 081	4 982	3 Personne ayant une qualification moyenne
7 964	12 937	3 648	3 244	4 Personnel d'exécution
114	6 469	194	1 260	5 Personnel de maîtrise (contremaîtres, chefs d'équipe)
				dont:
–	(4 625)	–	(738)	5A Agents ayant une compétence et une responsabilité élevées
–	(1 844)	–	(522)	5B Agents ayant une compétence et une responsabilité moyennes
				100 – 199
10 001	37 186	9 585	24 149	Total
–	149	.	290	1A Cadres dont la rémunération mensuelle est supérieure à (^{1})
	892	212	2 391	1B Cadres dont la rémunération mensuelle est inférieure ou égale à (^{1})
90	4 351	498	4 081	2 Personnel ayant une qualification très élevée
780	9 259	2 492	7 341	3 Personne ayant une qualification moyenne
8 951	16 436	5 923	6 303	4 Personnel d'exécution
180	6 099	460	3 743	5 Personnel de maîtrise (contremaîtres, chefs d'équipe)
				dont:
–	(4 314)	–	(2 198)	5A Agents ayant une compétence et une responsabilité élevées
–	(1 785)	–	(1 545)	5B Agents ayant une compétence et une responsabilité moyennes

(^{1}) DM 4 500 – FF 10 000 – LIT 1 000 000 – HFL 6 000 – BFR 65 000.

TAB. 42
(continued)

1972

	BR Deutschland		France		Italia	
	F	M	F	M	F	M
200 – 499						
Total	137 976	277 474	102 528	210 692	30 196	85 336
1A Earning more than (¹) monthly	.	3 330	.	2 528	.	597
1B Earning not more than (¹) monthly	276	11 931	308	5 899	91	4 523
2 Very highly qualified	5 381	70 201	3 896	48 459	1 751	20 481
3 Less highly qualified	52 017	109 880	8 715	49 934	7 156	31 233
4 Executives	79 612	29 967	84 278	49 513	19 537	15 616
5 Supervisors	690	52 165	5 331	54 359	1 661	12 886
of which:						
5A With higher proficiency and responsibilities	–	49 668	–	(31 815)	–	(6 827)
5B With lower proficiency and responsibilities	–	2 497	–	(22 544)	–	(6 059)
500 – 999						
Total	98 972	211 430	73 107	169 992	17 527	59 239
1A Earning more than (¹) monthly	.	3 171	73	1 530	–	355
1B Earning not more than (¹) monthly	198	10 149	146	3 910	53	3 021
2 Very highly qualified	3 266	56 029	3 509	35 358	841	14 751
3 Less highly qualified	36 323	88 801	5 702	47 768	4 680	23 163
4 Executives	58 789	21 777	60 972	40 628	11 287	9 715
5 Supervisors	396	31 503	2 705	40 798	666	8 234
of which:						
5A With higher proficiency and responsibilities	–	30 233	–	(22 949)	–	(4 443)
5B With lower proficiency and responsibilities	–	1 480	–	(17 849)	–	(3 791)
≥1000						
Total	233 659	626 803	92 653	350 709	37 828	143 920
1A Earning more than (¹) monthly	.	8 775	.	1 052	38	576
1B Earning not more than (¹) monthly	935	37 608	185	5 962	113	9 643
2 Very highly qualified	9 814	196 816	3 150	64 180	1 967	38 858
3 Less highly qualified	92 061	258 243	10 933	136 075	11 500	59 151
4 Executives	130 148	48 891	75 791	66 284	23 340	18 134
5 Supervisors	701	76 470	2 594	77 156	870	17 558
of which:						
5A With higher proficiency and responsibilities	–	13 336	–	(43 839)	–	(9 642)
5B With lower proficiency and responsibilities	–	3 134	–	(33 317)	–	(7 916)
TOTAL						
Total	758 491	1 583 354	501 755	1 151 835	161 176	446 844
1A Earning more than (¹) monthly	.	20 584	502	11 518	.	1 787
1B Earning not more than (¹) monthly	3 034	82 334	3 011	50 681	645	24 130
2 Very highly qualified	34 891	440 172	24 084	253 404	9 509	106 349
3 Less highly qualified	299 604	634 925	36 628	320 210	40 455	166 226
4 Executives	417 928	145 669	418 463	251 100	104 281	82 666
5 Supervisors	3 034	259 670	19 067	264 922	6 286	65 686
of which:						
5A With higher proficiency and responsibilities	–	248 587	–	(156 650)	–	(34 854)
5B With lower proficiency and responsibilities	–	11 083	–	(108 272)	–	(30 832)

(¹) DM 4 500 – FF 10 000 – LIT 1 000 000 – HFL 6 000 – BFR 65 000.

TAB. 42
(continued)
(suite)

1972

Nederland		Belgique/België		
F	M	F	M	
				200 – 499
11 476	50 343	9 832	29 565	Total
–	201	10	473	1A Cadres dont la rémunération mensuelle est supérieure à ([1])
–	856	79	1 892	1B Cadres dont la rémunération mensuelle est inférieure ou égale à ([1])
80	5 991	393	4 908	2 Personnel ayant une qualification très élevée
654	12 032	2 271	9 283	3 Personne ayant une qualification moyenne
10 581	22 302	6 686	8 219	4 Personnel d'exécution
161	8 961	393	4 790	5 Personnel de maîtrise (contremaîtres, chefs d'équipe)
				dont:
–	(5 789)	–	(2 660)	5A Agents ayant une compétence et une responsabilité élevées
–	(3 172)	–	(2 130)	5B Agents ayant une compétence et une responsabilité moyennes
				500 – 999
7 748	40 454	7 271	26 253	Total
–	243	.	473	1A Cadres dont la rémunération mensuelle est supérieure à ([1])
16	485	22	7 000	1B Cadres dont la rémunération mensuelle est inférieure ou égale à ([1])
46	4 935	124	4 042	2 Personnel ayant une qualification très élevée
434	10 518	1 534	8 662	3 Personne ayant une qualification moyenne
7 066	18 407	5 337	7 640	4 Personnel d'exécution
186	5 866	254	4 436	5 Personnel de maîtrise (contremaîtres, chefs d'équipe)
				dont:
–	(3 641)	–	(2 374)	5A Agents ayant une compétence et une responsabilité élevées
–	(2 225)	–	(1 892)	5B Agents ayant une compétence et une responsabilité moyennes
				≥ 1000
12 539	99 645	8 692	54 221	Total
–	498	9	1 355	1A Cadres dont la rémunération mensuelle est supérieure à ([1])
26	1 196	18	922	1B Cadres dont la rémunération mensuelle est inférieure ou égale à ([1])
238	22 221	170	8 351	2 Personnel ayant une qualification très élevée
965	24 214	1 452	15 941	3 Personne ayant une qualification moyenne
11 084	38 463	6 892	16 537	4 Personnel d'exécution
226	13 053	151	11 115	5 Personnel de maîtrise (contremaîtres, chefs d'équipe)
				dont:
–	(6 477)	–	(5 097)	5A Agents ayant une compétence et une responsabilité élevées
–	(6 576)	–	(6 018)	5B Agents ayant une compétence et une responsabilité moyennes
				TOTAL
61 212	300 062	52 035	167 011	Total
.	1 800	.	3 006	1A Cadres dont la rémunération mensuelle est supérieure à ([1])
123	10 802	1 093	12 025	1B Cadres dont la rémunération mensuelle est inférieure ou égale à ([1])
134	47 410	2 498	27 390	2 Personnel ayant une qualification très élevée
4 285	72 915	13 373	52 274	3 Personne ayant une qualification moyenne
54 907	120 925	33 250	45 427	4 Personnel d'exécution
1 163	46 210	1 821	26 889	5 Personnel de maîtrise (contremaîtres, chefs d'équipe)
				dont:
–	(29 406)	–	(14 196)	5A Agents ayant une compétence et une responsabilité élevées
–	(16 804)	–	(12 693)	5B Agents ayant une compétence et une responsabilité moyennes

([1]) DM 4 500 – FF 10 000 – LIT 1 000 000 – HFL 6 000 – BFR 65 000.

TAB. 42.1

Non-manual workers by size group of establishment and qualifications (%)

Employés par classe de taille de l'entreprise et par qualification (%)

1972

	BR Deutschland		France		Italia	
	$\frac{f}{F}100$	$\frac{f}{f+m}100$	$\frac{f}{F}100$	$\frac{f}{f+m}100$	$\frac{f}{F}100$	$\frac{f}{f+m}100$
10 – 19						
Total	5,2	51,8	6,2	39,4	4,4	42,5
1A Earning more than ([1]) monthly	–	–	0,1	5,6	0,1	41,2
1B Earning not more than ([1]) monthly	0,6	12,8	2,3	9,6	0,8	15,6
2 Very highly qualified	6,6	23,0	6,0	11,6	3,6	15,1
3 Less highly qualified	39,0	53,0	3,9	13,1	20,9	30,5
4 Executives	53,4	86,3	86,0	71,6	72,4	61,1
5 Supervisors	0,4	1,7	1,7	6,4	2,2	11,8
of which:						
5A With higher proficiency and responsibilities	–	–	–	–	–	–
5B With lower proficiency and responsibilities	–	–	–	–	–	–
20 – 49						
Total	10,7	40,1	13,9	37,2	14,3	37,7
1A Earning more than ([1]) monthly	.	.	0,1	3,8	–	–
1B Earning not more than ([1]) monthly	0,5	6,6	1,4	6,7	0,3	4,2
2 Very highly qualified	6,9	15,0	6,9	13,5	9,6	23,6
3 Less highly qualified	41,9	42,8	3,9	10,9	19,5	25,9
4 Executives	50,3	78,9	85,4	70,1	67,1	59,0
5 Supervisors	0,4	1,2	2,3	6,3	3,5	12,5
of which:						
5A With higher proficiency and responsibilities	–	–	–	–	–	–
5B With lower proficiency and responsibilities	–	–	–	–	–	–
(10 – 49)						
Total	15,9	43,3	20,1	37,8	18,7	38,8
1A Earning more than ([1]) monthly	.	.	0,1	3,9	.	.
1B Earning not more than ([1]) monthly	0,6	9,0	1,8	8,2	0,4	6,1
2 Very highly qualified	6,8	16,8	6,6	12,9	8,2	22,4
3 Less highly qualified	40,9	45,5	3,9	11,5	19,8	26,9
4 Executives	51,3	81,3	85,6	70,6	68,4	59,6
5 Supervisors	0,4	1,3	2,0	6,0	3,2	12,4
of which:						
5A With higher proficiency and responsibilities	–	–	–	–	–	–
5B With lower proficiency and responsibilities	–	–	–	–	–	–
50 – 99						
Total	9,8	35,2	12,6	35,7	13,0	30,2
1A Earning more than ([1]) monthly	.	.	0,2	6,5	–	–
1B Earning not more than ([1]) monthly	0,6	5,9	1,0	6,8	0,7	6,6
2 Very highly qualified	6,0	11,4	6,0	12,1	5,1	9,7
3 Less highly qualified	43,5	38,3	5,7	12,9	24,1	23,2
4 Executives	49,4	73,0	83,4	66,6	65,9	52,9
5 Supervisors	0,5	1,3	3,7	8,5	4,2	10,5
of which:						
5A With higher proficiency and responsibilities	–	–	–	–	–	–
5B With lower proficiency and responsibilities	–	–	–	–	–	–
100 – 199						
Total	12,3	35,0	13,9	33,1	15,2	28,3
1A Earning more than ([1]) monthly	.	.	.	.	–	–
1B Earning not more than ([1]) monthly	0,2	2,3	0,4	4,2	0,4	2,8
2 Very highly qualified	4,3	8,6	4,8	9,3	5,9	9,6
3 Less highly qualified	40,2	36,0	5,5	10,7	24,8	23,7
4 Executives	54,7	74,3	84,4	64,3	64,0	55,2
5 Supervisors	0,6	1,5	4,9	8,7	4,9	8,7
of which:						
5A With higher proficiency and responsibilities	–	–	–	–	–	–
5B With lower proficiency and responsibilities	–	–	–	–	–	–

([1]) DM 4 500 – FF 10 000 – LIT 1 000 000 – HFL 6 000 – BFR 65 000.

TAB. 42.1

Non-manual workers by size group of establishment and qualifications (%)
Employés par classe de taille de l'entreprise et par qualification (%)

1972

Nederland		Belgique/België		
$\frac{f}{F}100$	$\frac{f}{f+m}100$	$\frac{f}{F}100$	$\frac{f}{f+m}100$	
				10 – 19
5,0	24,8	5,6	40,1	Total
–	–	–	–	1A Cadres dont la rémunération mensuelle est supérieure à ([1])
0,5	0,8	5,4	11,2	1B Cadres dont la rémunération mensuelle est inférieure ou égale à ([1])
2,5	5,8	6,9	22,2	2 Personnel ayant une qualification très élevée
9,2	12,6	38,9	44,2	3 Personne ayant une qualification moyenne
85,3	47,1	45,9	61,5	4 Personnel d'exécution
2,5	5,9	2,9	25,0	5 Personnel de maîtrise (contremaîtres, chefs d'équipe)
				dont:
–	–	–	–	5A Agents ayant une compétence et une responsabilité élevées
–	–	–	–	5B Agents ayant une compétence et une responsabilité moyennes
				20 – 49
11,9	20,3	13,0	32,6	Total
0,1	7,6	–	–	1A Cadres dont la rémunération mensuelle est supérieure à ([1])
1,0	1,9	5,6	12,2	1B Cadres dont la rémunération mensuelle est inférieure ou égale à ([1])
1,8	2,9	8,7	18,5	2 Personnel ayant une qualification très élevée
6,6	6,8	35,3	33,8	3 Personne ayant une qualification moyenne
88,0	41,3	46.3	54,9	4 Personnel d'exécution
2,5	3,8	4,1	17,8	5 Personnel de maîtrise (contremaîtres, chefs d'équipe)
				dont:
–	–	–	–	5A Agents ayant une compétence et une responsabilité élevées
–	–	–	–	5B Agents ayant une compétence et une responsabilité moyennes
				(10 – 49)
16,9	21,5	18,6	34,6	Total
0,2	12,2	–	–	1A Cadres dont la rémunération mensuelle est supérieure à ([1])
0,8	1,4	5,6	18,7	1B Cadres dont la rémunération mensuelle est inférieure ou égale à ([1])
2,0	3,5	8,1	18,8	2 Personnel ayant une qualification très élevée
7,3	8,1	36,4	36,6	3 Personne ayant une qualification moyenne
87,2	42,8	46,2	56,7	4 Personnel d'exécution
2,5	4,3	3,7	18,7	5 Personnel de maîtrise (contremaîtres, chefs d'équipe)
				dont:
–	–	–	–	5A Agents ayant une compétence et une responsabilité élevées
–	–	–	–	5B Agents ayant une compétence et une responsabilité moyennes
				50 – 99
14,5	20,8	12,9	32,5	Total
–	–	0,1	4,2	1A Cadres dont la rémunération mensuelle est supérieure à ([1])
0,2	1,0	3,8	10,6	1B Cadres dont la rémunération mensuelle est inférieure ou égale à ([1])
1,0	2,0	7,6	15,9	2 Personnel ayant une qualification très élevée
7,1	7,3	31,1	29,5	3 Personne ayant une qualification moyenne
90,4	38,1	54,5	52,9	4 Personnel d'exécution
1,3	1,7	2,9	13,3	5 Personnel de maîtrise (contremaîtres, chefs d'équipe)
				dont:
–	–	–	–	5A Agents ayant une compétence et une responsabilité élevées
–	–	–	–	5B Agents ayant une compétence et une responsabilité moyennes
				100 – 199
16,4	21,2	18,4	28,4	Total
–	–	.	.	1A Cadres dont la rémunération mensuelle est supérieure à ([1])
.	.	2,2	8,1	1B Cadres dont la rémunération mensuelle est inférieure ou égale à ([1])
0,9	2,0	5,2	10,9	2 Personnel ayant une qualification très élevée
7,8	7,8	26,0	25,3	3 Personne ayant une qualification moyenne
89,5	35,3	61,8	49,4	4 Personnel d'exécution
1,8	2,9	4,8	10,9	5 Personnel de maîtrise (contremaîtres, chefs d'équipe)
				dont:
–	–	–	–	5A Agents ayant une compétence et une responsabilité élevées
–	–	–	–	5B Agents ayant une compétence et une responsabilité moyennes

([1]) DM 4 500 – FF 10 000 – LIT 1 000 000 – HFL 6 000 – BFR 65 000.

TAB. 42.1
(continued)
(suite)

1972

	BR Deutschland		France		Italia	
	$\frac{f}{F}100$	$\frac{f}{f+m}100$	$\frac{f}{F}100$	$\frac{f}{f+m}100$	$\frac{f}{F}100$	$\frac{f}{f+m}100$
200 – 499						
Total	18,2	33,2	20,4	32,7	18,7	26,1
1A Earning more than (¹) monthly	.	.	.	.	.	.
1B Earning not more than (¹) monthly	0,2	2,3	0,2	5,0	0,3	2,0
2 Very highly qualified	3,9	7,1	3,8	7,4	5,8	7,9
3 Less highly qualified	37,7	32,1	8,5	14,9	23,7	18,6
4 Executives	57,7	78,7	52,2	63,0	64,7	55,6
5 Supervisors	0,5	1,3	5,2	8,9	5,5	11,4
of which:						
5A With higher proficiency and responsibilities	–	–	–	–	–	–
5B With lower proficiency and responsibilities	–	–	–	–	–	–
500 – 999						
Total	13,0	31,9	14,6	30,1	10,9	22,8
1A Earning more than (¹) monthly	.	.	0,1	4,6	–	–
1B Earning not more than (¹) monthly	0,2	1,9	0,2	3,6	0,3	1,7
2 Very highly qualified	3,3	5,5	4,8	9,0	4,8	5,4
3 Less highly qualified	36,7	29,0	7,8	10,7	26,7	16,8
4 Executives	59,4	73,0	83,4	60,0	64,4	53,7
5 Supervisors	0,4	1,2	3,7	6,2	3,8	7,5
of which:						
5A With higher proficiency and responsibilities	–	–	–	–	–	–
5B With lower proficiency and responsibilities	–	–	–	–	–	–
⩾ 1000						
Total	30,8	27,2	18,5	20,9	23,5	20,8
1A Earning more than (¹) monthly	.	.	.	.	0,1	6,2
1B Earning not more than (¹) monthly	0,4	2,4	0,2	3,0	0,3	1,2
2 Very highly qualified	4,2	4,7	3,4	4,7	5,2	4,8
3 Less highly qualified	39,4	26,3	11,8	7,4	30,4	16,3
4 Executives	55,7	72,7	81,8	53,3	61,7	56,3
5 Supervisors	0,3	0,9	2,8	3,3	2,3	4,7
of which:						
5A With higher proficiency and responsibilities	–	–	–	–	–	–
5B With lower proficiency and responsibilities	–	–	–	–	–	–
TOTAL						
Total	100,0	32,4	100,0	30,3	100,0	26,5
1A Earning more than (¹) monthly	.	.	0,1	4,2	.	.
1B Earning not more than (¹) monthly	0,4	3,6	0,6	5,6	0,4	2,6
2 Very highly qualified	4,6	7,3	4,8	8,7	5,9	8,2
3 Less highly qualified	39,5	32,1	7,3	10,3	25,1	19,6
4 Executives	55,1	74,2	83,4	62,5	64,7	55,8
5 Supervisors	0,4	1,2	3,8	6,7	3,9	8,7
of which:						
5A With higher proficiency and responsibilities	–	–	–	–	–	–
5B With lower proficiency and responsibilities	–	–	–	–	–	–

(¹) DM 4 500 – FF 10 000 – LIT 1 000 000 – HFL 6 000 – BFR 65 000.

TAB. 42.1
(continued)
(suite)

1972

Nederland		Belgique/België		
$\frac{f}{F}100$	$\frac{f}{f+m}100$	$\frac{f}{F}100$	$\frac{f}{f+m}100$	
				200 – 499
18,8	18,6	18,9	25,0	Total
–	–	0,1	2,1	1A Cadres dont la rémunération mensuelle est supérieure à ([1])
–	–	0,8	4,0	1B Cadres dont la rémunération mensuelle est inférieure ou égale à ([1])
0,7	1,3	4,0	7,4	2 Personnel ayant une qualification très élevée
5,7	5,2	23,1	19,7	3 Personne ayant une qualification moyenne
92,2	32,2	68,0	44,9	4 Personnel d'exécution
1,4	1,8	4,0	7,6	5 Personnel de maîtrise (contremaîtres, chefs d'équipe)
				dont:
–	–	–	–	5A Agents ayant une compétence et une responsabilité élevées
–	–	–	–	5B Agents ayant une compétence et une responsabilité moyennes
				500 – 999
12,8	16,1	14,0	21,7	Total
–	–	.	.	1A Cadres dont la rémunération mensuelle est supérieure à ([1])
0,2	3,2	0,3	0,3	1B Cadres dont la rémunération mensuelle est inférieure ou égale à ([1])
0,6	0,9	1,7	3,0	2 Personnel ayant une qualification très élevée
5,6	4,0	21,1	15,0	3 Personne ayant une qualification moyenne
91,2	27,7	73,4	41,1	4 Personnel d'exécution
2,4	3,1	3,5	5,4	5 Personnel de maîtrise (contremaîtres, chefs d'équipe)
				dont:
–	–	–	–	5A Agents ayant une compétence et une responsabilité élevées
–	–	–	–	5B Agents ayant une compétence et une responsabilité moyennes
				≥1000
20,6	11,2	17,2	13,8	Total
–	–	0,1	0,7	1A Cadres dont la rémunération mensuelle est supérieure à ([1])
0,1	2,1	0,2	1,9	1B Cadres dont la rémunération mensuelle est inférieure ou égale à ([1])
1,9	1,1	1,9	2,0	2 Personnel ayant une qualification très élevée
7,7	3,8	16,2	8,3	3 Personne ayant une qualification moyenne
88,4	22,4	79,9	29,4	4 Personnel d'exécution
1,8	1,7	1,7	1,3	5 Personnel de maîtrise (contremaîtres, chefs d'équipe)
				dont:
–	–	–	–	5A Agents ayant une compétence et une responsabilité élevées
–	–	–	–	5B Agents ayant une compétence et une responsabilité moyennes
				TOTAL
100,0	16,9	100,0	23,8	Total
.	.	.	.	1A Cadres dont la rémunération mensuelle est supérieure à ([1])
0,2	1,1	2,1	8,3	1B Cadres dont la rémunération mensuelle est inférieure ou égale à ([1])
1,2	0,3	4,8	8,4	2 Personnel ayant une qualification très élevée
7,0	5,6	25,7	20,4	3 Personne ayant une qualification moyenne
89,7	31,2	63,9	42,3	4 Personnel d'exécution
1,9	2,5	3,5	6,3	5 Personnel de maîtrise (contremaîtres, chefs d'équipe)
				dont:
–	–	–	–	5A Agents ayant une compétence et une responsabilité élevées
–	–	–	–	5B Agents ayant une compétence et une responsabilité moyennes

([1]) DM 4 500 – FF 10 000 – LIT 1 000 000 – HFL 6 000 – BFR 65 000.

TAB. 43

Non-manual workers by age and qualifications (unit)

Employés par âge et par qualification (unité)

1972

	BR Deutschland		France		Italia	
	F	M	F	M	F	M
< 21						
Total	99 502	18 785	53 437	15 757	21 097	3 850
1A Earning more than (¹) monthly	–	.	–	–	–	
1B Earning not more than (¹) monthly	–	.	.	16	21	23
2 Very highly qualified	299	244	107	32	295	150
3 Less highly qualified	13 134	4 189	588	2 379	612	412
4 Executives	86 069	14 314	52 582	13 015	19 958	3 142
5 Supervisors	.	38	160	315	211	123
of which:						
5A With higher proficiency and responsibilities	–	(19)	–	(157)	–	(11)
5B With lower proficiency and responsibilities	–	(19)	–	(158)	–	(112)
21 – 24						
Total	134 910	70 174	92 313	75 345	41 712	31 792
1A Earning more than (¹) monthly	–	.	–	–	–	
1B Earning not more than (¹) monthly	.	140	.	151	83	63
2 Very highly qualified	1 484	4 070	739	3 391	584	668
3 Less highly qualified	49 647	42 947	3 600	28 706	5 506	11 223
4 Executives	83 644	21 754	86 774	37 748	35 080	18 694
5 Supervisors	135	1 263	1 200	5 349	459	1 144
of which:						
5A With higher proficiency and responsibilities	–	(982)	–	(1 959)	–	(381)
5B With lower proficiency and responsibilities	–	(281)	–	(3 390)	–	(763)
25 – 29						
Total	113 766	184 183	83 345	148 999	36 128	76 731
1A Earning more than (¹) monthly	–	184	–	.	–	.
1B Earning not more than (¹) monthly	114	2 394	167	1 340	181	307
2 Very highly qualified	3 982	43 283	2 833	26 373	1 120	9 515
3 Less highly qualified	55 062	110 326	5 751	60 643	9 646	40 821
4 Executives	54 380	16 945	72 427	40 677	24 133	21 331
5 Supervisors	228	11 051	2 167	19 966	1 048	4 757
of which:						
5A With higher proficiency and responsibilities	–	(10 314)	–	(9 089)	–	(2 072)
5B With lower proficiency and responsibilities	–	(737)	–	(10 877)	–	(2 685)
(21 – 29)						
Total	248 676	254 358	175 658	224 344	77 839	108 522
1A Earning more than (¹) monthly	–	254	–	.	–	.
1B Earning not more than (¹) monthly	249	2 544	176	1 346	234	325
2 Very highly qualified	5 471	47 311	3 513	29 838	1 712	10 201
3 Less highly qualified	104 692	153 378	9 310	89 289	15 179	51 982
4 Executives	138 015	38 662	159 146	78 520	59 235	40 045
5 Supervisors	249	12 209	3 513	25 351	1 479	5 969
of which:						
5A With higher proficiency and responsibilities	–	(11 192)	–	(11 217)	–	(2 496)
5B With lower proficiency and responsibilities	–	(1 017)	–	(14 134)	–	(3 473)
30 – 44						
Total	232 790	763 689	151 303	489 627	42 927	203 889
1A Earning more than (¹) monthly	.	8 401	151	2 938	–	408
1B Earning not more than (¹) monthly	1 164	45 058	908	19 096	215	11 418
2 Very highly qualified	14 666	245 144	10 591	122 896	4 636	59 536
3 Less highly qualified	107 316	294 784	15 736	143 950	16 269	78 828
4 Executives	108 247	41 239	116 352	74 423	18 888	24 874
5 Supervisors	1 397	129 063	7 565	126 324	2 919	32 826
of which:						
5A With higher proficiency and responsibilities	–	(123 717)	–	(72 955)	–	(13 331)
5B With lower proficiency and responsibilities	–	(5 346)	–	(53 369)	–	(15 495)

(¹) DM 4 500 – FF 10 000 – LIT 1 000 000 – HFL 6 000 – BFR 65 000.

Nederland		Belgique/België		
F	M	F	M	
				< 21
19 898	6 621	6 684	1 574	Total
–	–	–	–	1A Cadres dont la rémunération mensuelle est supérieure à (^{1})
–	–	53	13	1B Cadres dont la rémunération mensuelle est inférieure ou égale à (^{1})
20	7	200	28	2 Personnel ayant une qualification très élevée
199	166	936	356	3 Personne ayant une qualification moyenne
19 599	6 369	5 320	1 111	4 Personnel d'exécution
80	79	175	66	5 Personnel de maîtrise (contremaîtres, chefs d'équipe)
				dont:
–	(53)	–	(16)	5A Agents ayant une compétence et une responsabilité élevées
–	(26)	–	(50)	5B Agents ayant une compétence et une responsabilité moyennes
				21 – 24
16 523	20 219	11 360	10 357	Total
–	–	.	–	1A Cadres dont la rémunération mensuelle est supérieure à (^{1})
–	40	91	175	1B Cadres dont la rémunération mensuelle est inférieure ou égale à (^{1})
16	303	341	702	2 Personnel ayant une qualification très élevée
761	2 124	2 351	3 692	3 Personne ayant une qualification moyenne
15 614	16 802	8 270	5 621	4 Personnel d'exécution
132	950	307	767	5 Personnel de maîtrise (contremaîtres, chefs d'équipe)
				dont:
–	(425)	–	(362)	5A Agents ayant une compétence et une responsabilité élevées
–	(525)	–	(405)	5B Agents ayant une compétence et une responsabilité moyennes
				25 – 29
10 168	46 351	10 829	26 050	Total
–	.	–	52	1A Cadres dont la rémunération mensuelle est supérieure à (^{1})
10	511	130	990	1B Cadres dont la rémunération mensuelle est inférieure ou égale à (^{1})
92	3 615	411	4 246	2 Personnel ayant une qualification très élevée
905	12 190	2 967	9 717	3 Personne ayant une qualification moyenne
8 968	26 837	6 920	8 440	4 Personnel d'exécution
193	3 198	401	2 605	5 Personnel de maîtrise (contremaîtres, chefs d'équipe)
				dont:
–	(1 900)	–	(1 433)	5A Agents ayant une compétence et une responsabilité élevées
–	(1 298)	–	(1 172)	5B Agents ayant une compétence et une responsabilité moyennes
				(21 – 29)
26 691	66 570	22 189	37 007	Total
–	.	.	37	1A Cadres dont la rémunération mensuelle est supérieure à (^{1})
.	533	222	1 184	1B Cadres dont la rémunération mensuelle est inférieure ou égale à (^{1})
133	3 928	754	4 959	2 Personnel ayant une qualification très élevée
1 655	14 312	5 303	13 396	3 Personne ayant une qualification moyenne
24 583	43 670	15 200	14 063	4 Personnel d'exécution
320	4 127	710	3 368	5 Personnel de maîtrise (contremaîtres, chefs d'équipe)
				dont:
–	(2 330)	–	(1 776)	5A Agents ayant une compétence et une responsabilité élevées
–	(1 797)	–	(1 592)	5B Agents ayant une compétence et une responsabilité moyennes
				30 – 44
8 689	125 669	14 839	67 890	Total
–	259	15	950	1A Cadres dont la rémunération mensuelle est supérieure à (^{1})
35	4 650	475	5 771	1B Cadres dont la rémunération mensuelle est inférieure ou égale à (^{1})
261	25 133	905	12 763	2 Personnel ayant une qualification très élevée
1 268	35 313	4 481	20 978	3 Personne ayant une qualification moyenne
6 734	40 968	8 369	15 683	4 Personnel d'exécution
382	19 353	594	11 745	5 Personnel de maîtrise (contremaîtres, chefs d'équipe)
				dont:
–	(12 944)	–	(6 178)	5A Agents ayant une compétence et une responsabilité élevées
–	(6 409)	–	(5 567)	5B Agents ayant une compétence et une responsabilité moyennes

(^{1}) DM 4 500 – FF 10 000 – LIT 1 000 000 – HFL 6 000 – BFR 65 000.

TAB. 43
(continued)
(suite)

	BR Deutschland		France		Italia	
	F	M	F	M	F	M
45 – 54						
Total	131 839	341 698	77 035	281 045	17 484	97 391
1A Earning more than ([1]) monthly	132	7 517	154	4 778	·	974
1B Earning not more than ([1]) monthly	923	22 210	1 156	18 549	140	9 552
2 Very highly qualified	10 547	96 017	6 394	69 137	2 465	27 074
3 Less highly qualified	56 163	113 786	7 472	59 862	7 623	29 315
4 Executives	63 019	26 994	57 237	50 026	5 787	10 129
5 Supervisors	1 055	75 174	4 622	78 693	1 469	20 647
of which:						
5A With higher proficiency and responsibilities	–	(72 099)	–	(50 588)	–	(11 784)
5B With lower proficiency and responsibilities	–	(3 075)	–	(28 105)	–	(8 863)
≥ 55						
Total	45 688	204 823	42 646	137 223	1 829	33 190
1A Earning more than ([1]) monthly	46	4 096	171	3 293	27	564
1B Earning not more than ([1]) monthly	503	12 289	1 066	11 390	68	3 518
2 Very highly qualified	4 112	51 820	3 582	31 011	419	9 293
3 Less highly qualified	18 092	69 026	3 582	23 740	772	9 526
4 Executives	22 478	24 374	31 686	34 580	417	4 348
5 Supervisors	457	43 218	2 559	33 208	126	5 941
of which:						
5A With higher proficiency and responsibilities	–	(41 170)	–	(21 544)	–	(3 219)
5B With lower proficiency and responsibilities	–	(2 048)	–	(11 664)	–	(2 722)
≥ 21						
Total	658 988	1 564 569	446 642	1 132 239	140 078	442 992
1A Earning more than ([1]) monthly	·	21 904	447	11 322	·	2 215
1B Earning not more than ([1]) monthly	2 636	81 358	3 126	49 819	700	24 364
2 Very highly qualified	34 926	439 644	24 119	252 489	9 245	105 875
3 Less highly qualified	286 660	630 521	36 178	317 027	39 782	165 679
4 Executives	332 130	131 424	364 460	237 770	84 328	79 296
5 Supervisors	2 636	259 718	18 312	263 812	6 023	65 563
of which:						
5A With higher proficiency and responsibilities	–	(248 766)	–	156 249	–	(34 997)
5B With lower proficiency and responsibilities	–	(10 952)	–	107 563	–	(30 556)
TOTAL						
Total	758 491	1 583 354	501 754	1 151 835	161 176	446 843
1A Earning more than ([1]) monthly	·	20 584	1 004	11 518	·	1 787
1B Earning not more than ([1]) monthly	3 034	82 334	3 010	50 681	645	24 129
2 Very highly qualified	34 891	440 172	24 084	253 404	9 509	106 349
3 Less highly qualified	299 604	634 925	36 628	320 210	40 455	166 226
4 Executives	417 928	145 669	418 463	251 100	104 281	82 666
5 Supervisors	3 034	259 670	18 565	264 922	6 286	65 686
of which:						
5A With higher proficiency and responsibilities	–	(248 587)	–	(156 650)	–	(34 854)
5B With lower proficiency and responsibilities	–	(11 083)	–	(108 272)	–	(30 832)

([1]) DM 4 500 – FF 10 000 – LIT 1 000 000 – HFL 6 000 – BFR 65 000.

TAB. 43

(continued)

(suite)

1972

Nederland		Belgique/België		
F	M	F	M	
				45 – 54
4 159	68 815	6 531	39 489	Total
4	688	13	1 066	1A Cadres dont la rémunération mensuelle est supérieure à ([1])
50	3 647	183	3 317	1B Cadres dont la rémunération mensuelle est inférieure ou égale à ([1])
225	14 176	496	6 318	2 Personnel ayant une qualification très élevée
798	16 516	2 064	11 689	3 Personne ayant une qualification moyenne
2 845	19 062	3 481	9 043	4 Personnel d'exécution
237	14 726	294	8 056	5 Personnel de maîtrise (contremaîtres, chefs d'équipe)
				dont:
–	(9 152)	–	(4 225)	5A Agents ayant une compétence et une responsabilité élevées
–	(5 574)	–	(3 831)	5B Agents ayant une compétence et une responsabilité moyennes
				⩾ 55
1 775	32 387	1 791	21 052	Total
3	454	2	758	1A Cadres dont la rémunération mensuelle est supérieure à ([1])
46	2 073	156	1 789	1B Cadres dont la rémunération mensuelle est inférieure ou égale à ([1])
126	4 210	140	3 389	2 Personnel ayant une qualification très élevée
329	6 542	562	5 895	3 Personne ayant une qualification moyenne
1 154	11 044	874	5 516	4 Personnel d'exécution
117	8 064	57	3 705	5 Personnel de maîtrise (contremaîtres, chefs d'équipe)
				dont:
–	(5 020)	–	(2 021)	5A Agents ayant une compétence et une responsabilité élevées
–	(3 044)	–	(1 684)	5B Agents ayant une compétence et une responsabilité moyennes
				⩾ 21
41 314	293 441	45 350	165 438	Total
·	1 174	91	2 812	1A Cadres dont la rémunération mensuelle est supérieure à ([1])
124	10 857	1 043	12 077	1B Cadres dont la rémunération mensuelle est inférieure ou égale à ([1])
744	47 537	2 267	27 463	2 Personnel ayant une qualification très élevée
4 049	72 774	12 426	51 948	3 Personne ayant une qualification moyenne
35 323	114 735	27 890	44 337	4 Personnel d'exécution
1 074	46 364	1 633	26 801	5 Personnel de maîtrise (contremaîtres, chefs d'équipe)
				dont:
–	(29 638)	–	(14 228)	5A Agents ayant une compétence et une responsabilité élevées
–	(16 726)	–	(12 573)	5B Agents ayant une compétence et une responsabilité moyennes
				TOTAL
61 212	300 062	52 034	167 011	Total
·	1 801	·	3 006	1A Cadres dont la rémunération mensuelle est supérieure à ([1])
122	10 802	1 092	12 025	1B Cadres dont la rémunération mensuelle est inférieure ou égale à ([1])
734	47 410	2 498	27 390	2 Personnel ayant une qualification très élevée
4 286	72 915	13 373	52 274	3 Personne ayant une qualification moyenne
54 907	120 925	33 250	45 427	4 Personnel d'exécution
1 163	46 209	1 821	26 889	5 Personnel de maîtrise (contremaîtres, chefs d'équipe)
				dont:
–	(29 406)	–	(14 196)	5A Agents ayant une compétence et une responsabilité élevées
–	(16 803)	–	(12 693)	5B Agents ayant une compétence et une responsabilité moyennes

([1]) DM 4500 – FF 10000 – LIT 1000000 – HFL 6000 – BFR 65000.

TAB. 43.1

Non-manual workers by age and qualifications (%)
Employés par âge et par qualification (%)

1972

	BR Deutschland		France		Italia	
	$\frac{f}{F}100$	$\frac{f}{f+m}100$	$\frac{f}{F}100$	$\frac{f}{f+m}100$	$\frac{f}{F}100$	$\frac{f}{f+m}100$
< 21						
Total	13,1	84,1	10,8	77,2	13,1	84,6
1A Earning more than ([1]) monthly	−	−	−	−	−	−
1B Earning not more than ([1]) monthly	−	−	.	.	0,1	47,7
2 Very highly qualified	0,3	55,1	0,2	77,0	1,4	66,3
3 Less highly qualified	13,2	75,8	1,1	19,8	2,9	59,8
4 Executives	86,5	85,7	98,4	80,2	94,6	86,4
5 Supervisors	.	.	0,3	33,7	1,0	63,2
of which:						
5A With higher proficiency and responsibilities	−	−	−	−	−	−
5B With lower proficiency and responsibilities	−	−	−	−	−	−
21 – 24						
Total	17,8	65,8	18,4	55,1	25,9	56,7
1A Earning more than ([1]) monthly	−	−	−	−	−	−
1B Earning not more than ([1]) monthly	.	.	.	.	0,2	56,8
2 Very highly qualified	1,1	26,7	0,8	17,9	1,4	46,6
3 Less highly qualified	36,8	53,6	3,9	11,1	13,2	32,9
4 Executives	62,0	79,4	94,0	69,7	84,1	65,2
5 Supervisors	0,1	9,7	1,3	18,3	1,1	28,6
of which:						
5A With higher proficiency and responsibilities	−	−	−	−	−	−
5B With lower proficiency and responsibilities	−	−	−	−	−	−
25 – 29						
Total	15,0	38,2	16,7	35,9	22,4	32,0
1A Earning more than ([1]) monthly	−	−	−	−	−	−
1B Earning not more than ([1]) monthly	0,1	4,5	0,2	11,1	0,5	37,1
2 Very highly qualified	3,5	8,4	3,4	9,7	3,1	10,5
3 Less highly qualified	48,4	33,3	6,9	8,7	26,7	19,1
4 Executives	47,8	76,2	86,9	64,0	66,8	53,1
5 Supervisors	0,2	2,0	2,6	9,8	2,9	18,1
of which:						
5A With higher proficiency and responsibilities	−	−	−	−	−	−
5B With lower proficiency and responsibilities	−	−	−	−	−	−
(21 – 29)						
Total	32,8	49,4	35,1	43,9	48,3	41,8
1A Earning more than ([1]) monthly	−	−	−	−	−	−
1B Earning not more than ([1]) monthly	0,1	8,9	0,1	11,6	0,3	41,9
2 Very highly qualified	2,2	10,4	2,0	10,5	2,2	14,4
3 Less highly qualified	42,1	40,6	5,3	9,4	19,5	22,6
4 Executives	55,5	78,1	90,6	67,0	76,1	59,7
5 Supervisors	0,1	2,0	2,0	12,2	1,9	19,9
of which:						
5A With higher proficiency and responsibilities	−	−	−	−	−	−
5B With lower proficiency and responsibilities	−	−	−	−	−	−
30 – 44						
Total	30,7	23,4	30,2	23,6	26,6	17,4
1A Earning more than ([1]) monthly	−	.	0,1	4,9	−	−
1B Earning not more than ([1]) monthly	0,5	2,5	0,6	4,5	0,5	1,8
2 Very highly qualified	6,3	5,6	7,0	7,9	10,8	7,2
3 Less highly qualified	46,1	26,7	10,4	9,9	37,9	17,1
4 Executives	46,5	72,4	76,9	61,0	44,0	43,2
5 Supervisors	0,6	1,1	5,0	5,7	6,8	8,2
of which:						
5A With higher proficiency and responsibilities	−	−	−	−	−	−
5B With lower proficiency and responsibilities	−	−	−	−	−	−

([1]) DM 4 500 – FF 10 000 – LIT 1 000 000 – HFL 6 000 – BFR 65 000.

TAB. 43.1

Non-manual workers by age and qualifications (%)

Employés par âge et par qualification (%)

1972

Nederland		Belgique/België		
$\frac{f}{F}100$	$\frac{f}{f+m}100$	$\frac{f}{F}100$	$\frac{f}{f+m}100$	
				< 21
32,5	75,0	12,8	80,9	Total
–	–	–	–	1A Cadres dont la rémunération mensuelle est supérieure à ([1])
–	–	0,8	80,3	1B Cadres dont la rémunération mensuelle est inférieure ou égale à ([1])
0,1	74,1	3,0	87,7	2 Personnel ayant une qualification très élevée
1,0	54,5	14,0	72,4	3 Personne ayant une qualification moyenne
98,5	75,5	79,6	82,7	4 Personnel d'exécution
0,4	50,3	2,6	72,6	5 Personnel de maîtrise (contremaîtres, chefs d'équipe)
				dont:
–	–	–	–	5A Agents ayant une compétence et une responsabilité élevées
–	–	–	–	5B Agents ayant une compétence et une responsabilité moyennes
				21 – 24
27,0	45,0	21,8	50,9	Total
–	–	.	.	1A Cadres dont la rémunération mensuelle est supérieure à ([1])
–	–	0,8	34,2	1B Cadres dont la rémunération mensuelle est inférieure ou égale à ([1])
0,1	5,0	3,0	32,7	2 Personnel ayant une qualification très élevée
4,6	26,4	20,7	38,9	3 Personne ayant une qualification moyenne
94,5	48,2	72,8	59,5	4 Personnel d'exécution
0,8	12,2	2,7	28,6	5 Personnel de maîtrise (contremaîtres, chefs d'équipe)
				dont:
–	–	–	–	5A Agents ayant une compétence et une responsabilité élevées
–	–	–	–	5B Agents ayant une compétence et une responsabilité moyennes
				25 – 29
16,6	18,0	20,8	29,4	Total
–	–	–	–	1A Cadres dont la rémunération mensuelle est supérieure à ([1])
0,1	1,9	1,2	11,6	1B Cadres dont la rémunération mensuelle est inférieure ou égale à ([1])
0,9	2,5	3,8	8,8	2 Personnel ayant une qualification très élevée
8,9	6,9	27,4	23,4	3 Personne ayant une qualification moyenne
88,2	25,0	63,9	45,1	4 Personnel d'exécution
1,9	5,7	3,7	13,3	5 Personnel de maîtrise (contremaîtres, chefs d'équipe)
				dont:
–	–	–	–	5A Agents ayant une compétence et une responsabilité élevées
–	–	–	–	5B Agents ayant une compétence et une responsabilité moyennes
				(21 – 29)
43,6	28,6	42,6	37,5	Total
–	–	.	.	1A Cadres dont la rémunération mensuelle est supérieure à ([1])
.	.	1,0	15,8	1B Cadres dont la rémunération mensuelle est inférieure ou égale à ([1])
0,5	3,3	3,4	13,2	2 Personnel ayant une qualification très élevée
6,2	10,4	23,9	28,4	3 Personne ayant une qualification moyenne
92,1	36,0	68,5	51,9	4 Personnel d'exécution
1,2	7,2	3,2	17,4	5 Personnel de maîtrise (contremaîtres, chefs d'équipe)
				dont:
–	–	–	–	5A Agents ayant une compétence et une responsabilité élevées
–	–	–	–	5B Agents ayant une compétence et une responsabilité moyennes
				30 – 44
14,2	6,5	28,5	17,9	Total
–	–	0,1	1,6	1A Cadres dont la rémunération mensuelle est supérieure à ([1])
0,4	0,7	3,2	7,6	1B Cadres dont la rémunération mensuelle est inférieure ou égale à ([1])
3,0	1,0	6,1	6,6	2 Personnel ayant une qualification très élevée
14,6	3,5	30,2	17,6	3 Personne ayant une qualification moyenne
77,6	14,1	56,4	34,8	4 Personnel d'exécution
4,4	1,9	4,0	4,8	5 Personnel de maîtrise (contremaîtres, chefs d'équipe)
				dont:
–	–	–	–	5A Agents ayant une compétence et une responsabilité élevées
–	–	–	–	5B Agents ayant une compétence et une responsabilité moyennes

([1]) DM 4 500 – FF 10 000 – LIT 1 000 000 – HFL 6 000 – BFR 65 000.

TAB. 43.1

(continued)

(suite)

	1972					
	BR Deutschland		France		Italia	
	$\frac{f}{F}100$	$\frac{f}{f+m}100$	$\frac{f}{F}100$	$\frac{f}{f+m}100$	$\frac{f}{F}100$	$\frac{f}{f+m}100$
45 – 54						
Total	17,4	27,8	15,4	21,5	10,9	15,2
1A Earning more than ([1]) monthly	0,1	1,7	0,2	3,1	.	
1B Earning not more than ([1]) monthly	0,7	4,0	1,5	5,9	0,8	1,4
2 Very highly qualified	8,0	9,9	8,3	8,5	14,1	8,3
3 Less highly qualified	42,6	33,0	9,7	11,1	43,6	20,6
4 Executives	47,8	70,0	74,3	53,4	33,1	36,4
5 Supervisors	0,8	1,4	6,0	5,5	8,4	6,6
of which:						
5A With higher proficiency and responsibilities	–	–	–	–	–	–
5B With lower proficiency and responsibilities	–	–	–	–	–	–
≥ 55						
Total	6,0	18,2	8,5	23,7	1,1	5,2
1A Earning more than ([1]) monthly	0,1	1,1	0,4	4,9	1,5	4,6
1B Earning not more than ([1]) monthly	1,1	3,9	2,5	8,6	3,7	1,9
2 Very highly qualified	9,0	7,4	8,4	10,4	22,9	4,3
3 Less highly qualified	39,6	20,8	8,4	13,1	42,2	7,5
4 Executives	49,2	48,0	74,3	47,8	22,8	8,8
5 Supervisors	1,0	1,0	6,0	7,2	6,9	2,1
of which:						
5A With higher proficiency and responsibilities	–	–	–	–	–	–
5B With lower proficiency and responsibilities	–	–	–	–	–	–
≥ 21						
Total	86,9	29,6	89,2	28,3	86,9	24,0
1A Earning more than ([1]) monthly	.	.	0,1	3,8	.	
1B Earning not more than ([1]) monthly	0,4	3,1	0,7	5,9	0,5	2,8
2 Very highly qualified	5,3	7,4	5,4	8,7	6,6	8,0
3 Less highly qualified	43,5	31,3	8,1	10,2	28,4	19,4
4 Executives	50,4	71,6	81,6	60,5	60,2	51,5
5 Supervisors	0,4	1,0	4,1	6,5	4,3	8,4
of which:						
5A With higher proficiency and responsibilities	–	–	–	–	–	–
5B With lower proficiency and responsibilities	–	–	–	–	–	–
TOTAL						
Total	100,0	32,4	100,0	30,3	100,0	26,5
1A Earning more than ([1]) monthly	.	.	0,2	0,8	.	
1B Earning not more than ([1]) monthly	0,4	3,6	0,6	5,6	0,4	2,6
2 Very highly qualified	4,6	7,3	4,8	8,7	5,9	8,2
3 Less highly qualified	39,5	32,1	7,3	10,3	25,1	19,6
4 Executives	55,1	74,2	83,4	62,5	64,7	55,8
5 Supervisors	0,4	1,2	3,7	6,5	3,9	8,7
of which:						
5A With higher proficiency and responsibilities	–	–	–	–	–	–
5B With lower proficiency and responsibilities	–	–	–	–	–	–

([1]) DM 4 500 – FF 10 000 – LIT 1 000 000 – HFL 6 000 – BFR 65 000.

TAB. 43.1
(continued)
(suite)

1972

$\frac{f}{F}100$ (Nederland)	$\frac{f}{f+m}100$ (Nederland)	$\frac{f}{F}100$ (Belgique/België)	$\frac{f}{f+m}100$ (Belgique/België)	
				45 – 54
6,8	5,7	12,6	14,2	Total
0,1	0,6	0,2	1,2	1A Cadres dont la rémunération mensuelle est supérieure à ([1])
1,2	1,4	2,8	5,2	1B Cadres dont la rémunération mensuelle est inférieure ou égale à ([1])
5,4	1,6	7,6	7,3	2 Personnel ayant une qualification très élevée
19,2	4,6	31,6	15,0	3 Personne ayant une qualification moyenne
68,4	13,0	53,3	27,8	4 Personnel d'exécution
5,7	1,6	4,5	3,5	5 Personnel de maîtrise (contremaîtres, chefs d'équipe)
				dont:
–	–	–	–	5A Agents ayant une compétence et une responsabilité élevées
–	–	–	–	5B Agents ayant une compétence et une responsabilité moyennes
				≥ 55
2,9	5,2	3,5	7,8	Total
0,2	0,7	0,1	0,3	1A Cadres dont la rémunération mensuelle est supérieure à ([1])
2,6	2,2	8,7	8,0	1B Cadres dont la rémunération mensuelle est inférieure ou égale à ([1])
7,1	2,9	7,8	4,0	2 Personnel ayant une qualification très élevée
18,5	4,8	31,4	8,7	3 Personne ayant une qualification moyenne
65,0	9,5	48,8	13,7	4 Personnel d'exécution
6,6	1,4	3,2	1,5	5 Personnel de maîtrise (contremaîtres, chefs d'équipe)
				dont:
–	–	–	–	5A Agents ayant une compétence et une responsabilité élevées
–	–	–	–	5B Agents ayant une compétence et une responsabilité moyennes
				≥ 21
67,5	12,3	87,2	2,1	Total
.	.	0,2	3,1	1A Cadres dont la rémunération mensuelle est supérieure à ([1])
0,3	1,1	2,3	7,9	1B Cadres dont la rémunération mensuelle est inférieure ou égale à ([1])
1,8	1,5	5,0	7,6	2 Personnel ayant une qualification très élevée
9,8	5,3	27,4	19,3	3 Personne ayant une qualification moyenne
85,5	23,5	61,5	38,6	4 Personnel d'exécution
2,6	2,3	3,6	5,7	5 Personnel de maîtrise (contremaîtres, chefs d'équipe)
				dont:
–	–	–	–	5A Agents ayant une compétence et une responsabilité élevées
–	–	–	–	5B Agents ayant une compétence et une responsabilité moyennes
				TOTAL
100,0	16,9	100,0	23,8	Total
.	.	.	.	1A Cadres dont la rémunération mensuelle est supérieure à ([1])
0,2	1,1	2,1	8,3	1B Cadres dont la rémunération mensuelle est inférieure ou égale à ([1])
1,2	1,5	4,8	8,4	2 Personnel ayant une qualification très élevée
7,0	5,6	25,7	20,4	3 Personne ayant une qualification moyenne
89,7	31,2	63,9	42,3	4 Personnel d'exécution
1,9	2,5	3,5	6,3	5 Personnel de maîtrise (contremaîtres, chefs d'équipe)
				dont:
–	–	–	–	5A Agents ayant une compétence et une responsabilité élevées
–	–	–	–	5B Agents ayant une compétence et une responsabilité moyennes

([1]) DM 4 500 – FF 10 000 – LIT 1 000 000 – HFL 6 000 – BFR 65 000.

TAB. 44

Non-manual workers by length of service and qualifications (unit)

Employés par ancienneté dans l'entreprise et par qualification (unité)

1972

	BR Deutschland		France		Italia	
	F	M	F	M	F	M
< 2						
Total	206 170	247 960	122 004	154 375	27 782	68 442
1A Earning more than (^{1}) monthly	·	1 240	·	617	–	205
1B Earning not more than (^{1}) monthly		7 439	244	3 705	56	2 669
2 Very highly qualified	4 330	55 047	3 660	32 419	1 111	11 225
3 Less highly qualified	65 974	126 708	4 270	42 762	3 695	22 175
4 Executives	135 660	35 954	112 488	56 810	22 198	25 666
5 Supervisors	206	31 572	1 342	18 062	722	6 502
of which:						
5A With higher proficiency and responsibilities	–	(80 581)	–	(10 652)	–	(2 327)
5B With lower proficiency and responsibilities	–	(92)	–	(7 410)	–	(4 175)
2 – 4						
Total	227 128	301 103	126 431	196 050	48 994	109 166
1A Earning more than (^{1}) monthly	·	1 807	·	980	–	328
1B Earning not more than (^{1}) monthly	454	12 947	632	5 685	147	4 148
2 Very highly qualified	6 132	80 696	4 425	45 680	1 813	19 977
3 Less highly qualified	77 451	138 206	6 322	59 403	8 329	47 924
4 Executives	142 864	37 638	112 650	57 443	37 431	24 672
5 Supervisors	227	29 809	2 402	26 859	1 274	12 117
of which:						
5A With higher proficiency and responsibilities	–	(28 605)	–	(14 900)	–	(5 895)
5B With lower proficiency and responsibilities	–	(1 204)	–	(11 959)	–	(6 222)
5 – 9						
Total	147 470	276 658	99 690	218 337	37 626	94 317
1A Earning more than (^{1}) monthly	·	3 320	·	1 092	–	377
1B Earning not more than (^{1}) monthly	442	15 769	698	7 860	188	5 188
2 Very highly qualified	6 784	84 381	4 187	51 964	1 768	22 730
3 Less highly qualified	65 477	115 090	7 377	63 973	9 294	36 784
4 Executives	74 325	24 069	83 640	48 471	24 871	14 902
5 Supervisors	442	34 029	3 788	44 977	1 505	14 336
of which:						
5A With higher proficiency and responsibilities	–	(32 369)	–	(23 798)	–	(7 640)
5B With lower proficiency and responsibilities	–	(1 660)	–	(21 179)	–	(6 696)
10 – 19						
Total	122 000	431 674	90 844	302 896	31 210	116 232
1A Earning more than (^{1}) monthly	·	8 202	91	2 725	31	814
1B Earning not more than (^{1}) monthly	854	25 900	727	14 534	187	8 020
2 Very highly qualified	10 004	129 502	6 631	65 101	2 746	34 172
3 Less highly qualified	61 366	156 266	10 447	86 903	12 141	40 333
4 Executives	48 556	28 059	66 589	50 567	14 388	11 623
5 Supervisors	1 220	83 745	6 359	82 966	1 717	21 270
of which:						
5A With higher proficiency and responsibilities	–	(79 860)	–	(47 842)	–	(12 088)
5B With lower proficiency and responsibilities	–	(3 885)	–	(35 124)	–	(9 182)

(^{1}) DM 4 500 – FF 10 000 – LIT 1 000 000 – HFL 6 000 – BFR 65 000.

TAB. 44

Non-manual workers by length of service and qualifications (unit)

Employés par ancienneté dans l'entreprise et par qualification (unité)

1972

Nederland		Belgique/België		
F	M	F	M	
				< 2
23 263	37 741	12 658	22 671	Total
–	75	.	91	1A Cadres dont la rémunération mensuelle est supérieure à (^{1})
46	793	152	1 088	1B Cadres dont la rémunération mensuelle est inférieure ou égale à (^{1})
70	4 265	468	3 650	2 Personnel ayant une qualification très élevée
861	7 699	2 696	8 207	3 Personne ayant une qualification moyenne
22 146	21 663	8 874	7 685	4 Personnel d'exécution
140	3 246	468	1 950	5 Personnel de maîtrise (contremaîtres, chefs d'équipe)
				dont:
–	(2 113)	–	(1 043)	5A Agents ayant une compétence et une responsabilité élevées
–	(1 133)	–	(907)	5B Agents ayant une compétence et une responsabilité moyennes
				2 – 4
20 861	60 560	13 737	31 802	Total
–	121	.	127	1A Cadres dont la rémunération mensuelle est supérieure à (^{1})
42	1 514	220	2 099	1B Cadres dont la rémunération mensuelle est inférieure ou égale à (^{1})
167	8 236	536	5 438	2 Personnel ayant une qualification très élevée
1 064	14 161	3 228	10 749	3 Personne ayant une qualification moyenne
19 399	31 370	9 396	9 700	4 Personnel d'exécution
188	5 148	357	3 689	5 Personnel de maîtrise (contremaîtres, chefs d'équipe)
				dont:
–	(3 392)	–	(2 099)	5A Agents ayant une compétence et une responsabilité élevées
–	(1 756)	–	(1 590)	5B Agents ayant une compétence et une responsabilité moyennes
				5 – 9
9 913	56 822	11 601	33 018	Total
–	222	.	396	1A Cadres dont la rémunération mensuelle est supérieure à (^{1})
40	2 159	197	2 542	1B Cadres dont la rémunération mensuelle est inférieure ou égale à (^{1})
109	8 751	453	5 448	2 Personnel ayant une qualification très élevée
862	14 887	3 190	10 533	3 Personne ayant une qualification moyenne
8 555	22 956	7 355	8 948	4 Personnel d'exécution
347	7 841	406	5 151	5 Personnel de maîtrise (contremaîtres, chefs d'équipe)
				dont:
–	(5 170)	–	(2 939)	5A Agents ayant une compétence et une responsabilité élevées
–	(2 671)	–	(2 212)	5B Agents ayant une compétence et une responsabilité moyennes
				10 – 19
4 907	78 923	9 299	40 096	Total
5	316	.	883	1A Cadres dont la rémunération mensuelle est supérieure à (^{1})
20	3 157	316	3 368	1B Cadres dont la rémunération mensuelle est inférieure ou égale à (^{1})
201	14 521	539	6 856	2 Personnel ayant une qualification très élevée
815	20 362	2 818	11 788	3 Personne ayant une qualification moyenne
3 577	27 071	5 273	10 184	4 Personnel d'exécution
289	13 496	353	7 017	5 Personnel de maîtrise (contremaîtres, chefs d'équipe)
				dont:
–	(8 524)	–	(3 609)	5A Agents ayant une compétence et une responsabilité élevées
–	(4 972)	–	(3 408)	5B Agents ayant une compétence et une responsabilité moyennes

(^{1}) DM 4 500 – FF 10 000 – LIT 1 000 000 – HFL 6 000 – BFR 65 000.

TAB. 44

(continued)

(suite)

	1972					
	BR Deutschland		France		Italia	
	F	M	F	M	F	M
≥ 20						
Total	55 722	325 959	53 275	260 720	13 589	53 863
1A Earning more than (^{1}) monthly	56	5 215	53	4 693	14	646
1B Earning not more than (^{1}) monthly	780	20 209	853	17 208	81	4 201
2 Very highly qualified	8 135	90 942	4 848	52 926	2 093	17 506
3 Less highly qualified	29 421	98 766	7 618	63 094	6 849	17 021
4 Executives	16 494	20 210	35 428	34 154	3 642	3 609
5 Supervisors	836	90 617	4 475	88 645	910	10 880
of which:						
5A With higher proficiency and responsibilities	–	(87 357)	–	(57 880)	–	(6 679)
5B With lower proficiency and responsibilities	–	(3 260)	–	(30 765)	–	(4 201)
TOTAL						
Total	758 490	1 583 354	501 754	1 151 835	161 176	446 843
1A Earning more than (^{1}) monthly	.	20 584	1 003	11 518	.	1 787
1B Earning not more than (^{1}) monthly	3 034	82 334	3 011	50 681	645	34 129
2 Very highly qualified	34 890	440 172	24 084	253 404	9 509	106 349
3 Less highly qualified	299 604	634 925	36 628	320 210	40 455	166 226
4 Executives	417 928	145 669	418 463	251 100	104 281	82 666
5 Supervisors	3 034	259 670	18 560	264 299	6 286	65 686
of which:						
5A With higher proficiency and responsibilities	–	(248 587)	–	(156 650)	–	(34 854)
5B With lower proficiency and responsibilities	–	(11 083)	–	(108 272)	–	(30 832)

(^{1}) DM 4 500 – FF 10 000 – LIT 1 000 000 – HFL 6 000 – BFR 65 000.

TAB. 44

(continued)

(suite)

1972

Nederland		Belgique/België		
F	M	F	M	
				≥ 20
2 268	66 016	4 739	39 424	Total
4	660	10	1 263	1A Cadres dont la rémunération mensuelle est supérieure à (^{1})
34	3 235	247	2 996	1B Cadres dont la rémunération mensuelle est inférieure ou égale à (^{1})
166	11 685	483	6 071	2 Personnel ayant une qualification très élevée
651	15 910	1 431	11 078	3 Personne ayant une qualification moyenne
1 236	17 956	2 336	8 870	4 Personnel d'exécution
177	16 570	232	9 146	5 Personnel de maîtrise (contremaîtres, chefs d'équipe)
				dont:
–	(10 232)	–	(4 573)	5A Agents ayant une compétence et une responsabilité élevées
–	(6 338)	–	(4 573)	5B Agents ayant une compétence et une responsabilité moyennes
				TOTAL
61 212	300 062	52 035	167 011	Total
.	1 800	.	3 006	1A Cadres dont la rémunération mensuelle est supérieure à (^{1})
122	10 802	1 093	12 025	1B Cadres dont la rémunération mensuelle est inférieure ou égale à (^{1})
735	47 410	2 498	27 390	2 Personnel ayant une qualification très élevée
4 285	72 915	13 373	52 274	3 Personne ayant une qualification moyenne
54 907	120 926	33 250	45 427	4 Personnel d'exécution
1 163	46 209	1 821	26 889	5 Personnel de maîtrise (contremaîtres, chefs d'équipe)
				dont:
–	(29 406)	–	(14 196)	5A Agents ayant une compétence et une responsabilité élevées
–	(16 803)	–	(12 693)	5B Agents ayant une compétence et une responsabilité moyennes

(^{1}) DM 4 500 – FF 10 000 – LIT 1 000 000 – HFL 6 000 – BFR 65 000.

TAB. 44.1

Non-manual workers by length of service and qualifications (%)
Employés par ancienneté dans l'entreprise et par qualification (%)

1972

	BR Deutschland		France		Italia	
	$\frac{f}{F}100$	$\frac{f}{f+m}100$	$\frac{f}{F}100$	$\frac{f}{f+m}100$	$\frac{f}{F}100$	$\frac{f}{f+m}100$
< 2						
Total	27,2	45,4	24,8	44,1	17,5	28,9
1A Earning more than ([1]) monthly	.	.	.	.	–	–
1B Earning not more than ([1]) monthly	.	.	0,2	6,2	0,2	2,1
2 Very highly qualified	2,1	7,3	3,0	10,1	4,0	9,0
3 Less highly qualified	32,0	34,2	3,5	9,1	13,3	14,3
4 Executives	65,8	79,0	92,2	66,4	79,9	46,4
5 Supervisors	0,1	0,9	1,1	6,9	2,6	10,0
of which:						
5A With higher proficiency and responsibilities	–	–	–	–	–	–
5B With lower proficiency and responsibilities	–	–	–	–	–	–
2 – 4						
Total	29,9	43,0	25,7	39,2	30,8	31,0
1A Earning more than ([1]) monthly	.	.	.	.	–	–
1B Earning not more than ([1]) monthly	0,2	3,4	0,5	10,0	0,3	3,4
2 Very highly qualified	2,7	7,1	3,5	8,8	3,7	8,3
3 Less highly qualified	34,1	35,9	5,0	9,6	17,0	14,8
4 Executives	62,9	79,1	89,1	66,2	76,4	60,3
5 Supervisors	0,1	0,8	1,9	8,2	2,6	9,5
of which:						
5A With higher proficiency and responsibilities	–	–	–	–	–	–
5B With lower proficiency and responsibilities	–	–	–	–	–	–
5 – 9						
Total	19,4	34,8	20,3	31,3	23,6	28,5
1A Earning more than ([1]) monthly	.	.	.	.	–	–
1B Earning not more than ([1]) monthly	0,3	2,7	0,7	8,2	0,5	3,5
2 Very highly qualified	4,6	7,4	4,2	7,5	4,7	7,2
3 Less highly qualified	44,4	36,3	7,4	10,3	24,7	20,2
4 Executives	50,4	75,5	83,9	63,3	66,1	62,5
5 Supervisors	0,3	1,3	3,8	7,8	4,0	9,5
of which:						
5A With higher proficiency and responsibilities	–	–	–	–	–	–
5B With lower proficiency and responsibilities	–	–	–	–	–	–
10 – 19						
Total	16,1	22,0	18,5	23,1	19,6	21,2
1A Earning more than ([1]) monthly	.	.	0,1	3,2	0,1	3,7
1B Earning not more than ([1]) monthly	0,7	3,2	0,8	4,8	0,6	2,3
2 Very highly qualified	8,2	7,2	7,3	9,2	8,8	7,4
3 Less highly qualified	50,3	28,2	11,5	10,7	38,9	23,1
4 Executives	39,8	63,4	73,3	56,8	46,1	55,3
5 Supervisors	1,0	1,4	7,0	7,1	5,5	7,5
of which:						
5A With higher proficiency and responsibilities	–	–	–	–	–	–
5B With lower proficiency and responsibilities	–	–	–	–	–	–

([1]) DM 4 500 – FF 10 000 – LIT 1 000 000 – HFL 6 000 – BFR 65 000.

TAB. 44.1

Non-manual workers by length of service and qualifications (%)

Employés par ancienneté dans l'entreprise et par qualification (%)

1972

Nederland		Belgique/België		
$\frac{f}{F}100$	$\frac{f}{f+m}100$	$\frac{f}{F}100$	$\frac{f}{f+m}100$	
				< 2
38,0	38,1	24,3	35,8	Total
–	–	.	.	1A Cadres dont la rémunération mensuelle est supérieure à ([1])
0,2	5,5	1,2	12,3	1B Cadres dont la rémunération mensuelle est inférieure ou égale à ([1])
0,3	1,6	3,7	11,4	2 Personnel ayant une qualification très élevée
3,7	10,1	21,3	24,7	3 Personne ayant une qualification moyenne
95,2	50,6	70,1	53,6	4 Personnel d'exécution
0,6	4,1	3,7	19,4	5 Personnel de maîtrise (contremaîtres, chefs d'équipe)
				dont:
–	–	–	–	5A Agents ayant une compétence et une responsabilité élevées
–	–	–	–	5B Agents ayant une compétence et une responsabilité moyennes
				2 – 4
34,1	25,6	26,4	30,2	Total
–	–	.	.	1A Cadres dont la rémunération mensuelle est supérieure à ([1])
0,2	2,7	1,6	9,5	1B Cadres dont la rémunération mensuelle est inférieure ou égale à ([1])
0,8	2,0	3,9	9,0	2 Personnel ayant une qualification très élevée
5,1	7,0	23,5	23,1	3 Personne ayant une qualification moyenne
93,0	38,2	68,4	49,2	4 Personnel d'exécution
0,9	3,5	2,6	8,8	5 Personnel de maîtrise (contremaîtres, chefs d'équipe)
				dont:
–	–	–	–	5A Agents ayant une compétence et une responsabilité élevées
–	–	–	–	5B Agents ayant une compétence et une responsabilité moyennes
				5 – 9
16,2	14,9	22,3	26,0	Total
–	–	.	.	1A Cadres dont la rémunération mensuelle est supérieure à ([1])
0,4	1,8	1,7	7,2	1B Cadres dont la rémunération mensuelle est inférieure ou égale à ([1])
1,1	1,2	3,9	7,7	2 Personnel ayant une qualification très élevée
8,7	5,5	27,5	23,2	3 Personne ayant une qualification moyenne
86,3	27,1	63,4	45,1	4 Personnel d'exécution
3,5	4,2	3,5	7,3	5 Personnel de maîtrise (contremaîtres, chefs d'équipe)
				dont:
–	–	–	–	5A Agents ayant une compétence et une responsabilité élevées
–	–	–	–	5B Agents ayant une compétence et une responsabilité moyennes
				10 – 19
8,0	5,9	17,9	18,8	Total
0,1	1,6	.	.	1A Cadres dont la rémunération mensuelle est supérieure à ([1])
0,4	0,6	3,4	8,6	1B Cadres dont la rémunération mensuelle est inférieure ou égale à ([1])
4,1	1,4	5,8	7,3	2 Personnel ayant une qualification très élevée
16,6	3,8	30,3	19,3	3 Personne ayant une qualification moyenne
72,9	11,7	56,7	34,1	4 Personnel d'exécution
5,9	2,1	3,8	4,8	5 Personnel de maîtrise (contremaîtres, chefs d'équipe)
				dont:
–	–	–	–	5A Agents ayant une compétence et une responsabilité élevées
–	–	–	–	5B Agents ayant une compétence et une responsabilité moyennes

([1]) DM 4 500 – FF 10 000 – LIT 1 000 000 – HFL 6 000 – BFR 65 000.

TAB. 44.1
(continued)
(suite)

	BR Deutschland		France		Italia	
1972	$\frac{f}{F}100$	$\frac{f}{f+m}100$	$\frac{f}{F}100$	$\frac{f}{f+m}100$	$\frac{f}{F}100$	$\frac{f}{f+m}100$
≥ 20						
Total	7,4	14,6	10,7	17,0	8,5	20,1
1A Earning more than (^{1}) monthly	0,1	1,1	0,1	1,1	0,1	2,1
1B Earning not more than (^{1}) monthly	1,4	3,7	1,6	4,7	0,6	1,9
2 Very highly qualified	14,6	8,2	9,1	8,4	15,4	10,7
3 Less highly qualified	52,8	23,0	14,3	10,8	50,4	28,7
4 Executives	29,6	44,9	66,5	50,9	26,8	50,2
5 Supervisors	1,5	0,9	8,4	4,8	6,7	7,7
of which:						
5A With higher proficiency and responsibilities	–	–	–	–	–	–
5B With lower proficiency and responsibilities	–	–	–	–	–	–
TOTAL						
Total	100,0	32,4	100,0	30,3	100,0	26,5
1A Earning more than (^{1}) monthly	.	.	0,2	8,0	.	.
1B Earning not more than (^{1}) monthly	0,4	3,6	0,6	5,6	0,4	2,6
2 Very highly qualified	4,6	7,3	4,8	8,7	5,9	8,2
3 Less highly qualified	39,5	32,1	7,3	10,3	25,1	19,6
4 Executives	55,1	74,2	83,4	62,5	64,7	55,8
5 Supervisors	0,4	1,2	3,7	6,5	3,9	8,7
of which:						
5A With higher proficiency and responsibilities	–	–	–	–	–	–
5B With lower proficiency and responsibilities	–	–	–	–	–	–

(^{1}) DM 4 500 – FF 10 000 – LIT 1 000 000 – HFL 6 000 – BFR 65 000.

TAB. 44.1
(continued)
(suite)

1972

Nederland		Belgique/België		
$\frac{f}{F}100$	$\frac{f}{f+m}100$	$\frac{f}{F}100$	$\frac{f}{f+m}100$	
				≥ 20
				Total
3,7	3,3	9,1	10,7	1A Cadres dont la rémunération mensuelle est supérieure à ([1])
0,2	0,6	0,2	0,8	1B Cadres dont la rémunération mensuelle est inférieure ou égale à ([1])
1,5	1,0	5,2	7,6	2 Personnel ayant une qualification très élevée
7,3	1,4	10,2	7,4	3 Personne ayant une qualification moyenne
28,7	3,9	30,2	11,4	4 Personnel d'exécution
54,5	6,4	49,3	20,8	5 Personnel de maîtrise (contremaîtres, chefs d'équipe)
7,8	1,1	4,9	2,5	dont:
–	–	–	–	5A Agents ayant une compétence et une responsabilité élevées
–	–	–	–	5B Agents ayant une compétence et une responsabilité moyennes
				TOTAL
				Total
100,0	16,9	100,0	27,8	1A Cadres dont la rémunération mensuelle est supérieure à ([1])
·	·	·	·	1B Cadres dont la rémunération mensuelle est inférieure ou égale à ([1])
0,2	1,1	2,1	8,3	2 Personnel ayant une qualification très élevée
1,2	1,5	4,8	8,4	3 Personne ayant une qualification moyenne
7,0	5,6	25,7	20,4	4 Personnel d'exécution
89,7	31,2	63,9	42,3	5 Personnel de maîtrise (contremaîtres, chefs d'équipe)
1,9	2,5	3,5	6,3	dont:
–	–	–	–	5A Agents ayant une compétence et une responsabilité élevées
–	–	–	–	5B Agents ayant une compétence et une responsabilité moyennes

([1]) DM 4 500 – FF 10 000 – LIT 1 000 000 – HFL 6 000 – BFR 65 000.

TAB. 45

Permanent female agricultural workers by type of activity performed on the holding and qualifications (%)

Ouvrières agricoles permanentes selon le type d'activité exercée dans l'exploitation et la qualification (%)

1975

	BR Deutschland		France		Italia		Nederland		Belgique België	
	$\frac{f}{F}$ 100	$\frac{f}{f+m}$ 100	$\frac{f}{F}$ 100	$\frac{f}{f+m}$ 100	$\frac{f}{F}$ 100	$\frac{f}{f+m}$ 100	$\frac{f}{F}$ 100	$\frac{f}{f+m}$ 100	$\frac{f}{F}$ 100	$\frac{f}{f+m}$ 100
General agriculture										
Skilled workers	5,3	1,9	2,7	0,8	20,9	3,1	–	–	:	:
Unskilled workers	26,0	19,3	33,0	6,7	18,9	11,3	–	–	17,7	6,9
Livestock production										
Skilled workers	2,4	8,8	3,8	5,7	23,9	5,5	–	–	:	:
Unskilled workers	9,4	35,6	5,8	13,1	6,5	31,3	–	–	13,4	7,4
Specialized production										
Skilled workers	16,2	9,9	7,7	5,6	9,8	7,6	66,7	3,5	13,0	3,2
Unskilled workers	40,7	33,5	47,0	16,1	20,0	51,1	33,3	19,6	50,9	10,7
Total	100,0	13,3	100,0	7,2	100,0	6,8	100,0	3,5	100,0	6,2
Skilled workers	28,3	5,1	14,1	2,6	54,6	4,4	66,7	2,5	18,1	2,6
Unskilled workers	76,2	26,9	85,9	10,4	45,4	20,0	33,3	16,8	81,9	9,0

TAB. 46

Permanent female agricultural workers by size of holding and qualifications (%)

Ouvrières agricoles permanentes selon la taille de l'exploitation et la qualification (%)

1975

	BR Deutschland		France		Italia		Nederland		Belgique België	
	$\frac{f}{F}$ 100	$\frac{f}{f+m}$ 100	$\frac{f}{F}$ 100	$\frac{f}{f+m}$ 100	$\frac{f}{F}$ 100	$\frac{f}{f+m}$ 100	$\frac{f}{F}$ 100	$\frac{f}{f+m}$ 100	$\frac{f}{F}$ 100	$\frac{f}{f+m}$ 100
Holdings with 1 or 2 workers										
Skilled workers	4,6	2,3	3,3	1,4	12,0	2,9	:	:	:	:
Unskilled workers	18,3	15.6	18,6	3,9	8,5	9,2	:	:	30,7	6,0
Holdings with 3 to 9 workers										
Skilled workers	12,3	7,0	3,1	1,5	17,1	3,5	:	:	:	:
Unskilled workers	28,8	34,2	29,0	13,1	9,3	13,7	:	:	35,4	13,9
Holdings with 10 or more workers										
Skilled workers	7,0	7,8	7,7	7,0	27,6	7,4	29,5	5,4	:	:
Unskilled workers	29,1	35,5	38,3	30,3	27,6	41,5	:	:	15,9	10,9
Total	100,0	13,3	100,0	7,2	100,0	6,8	100,0	3,5	100,0	6,2
Skilled workers	28,3	5,1	14,1	2,6	54,6	4,4	29,5	1,1	18,1	2,6
Unskilled workers	76,2	26,9	85,9	10,4	45,4	20,0	70,5	29,9	81,9	9,0

TAB. 47

Permanent female agricultural workers by payment or not of benefits in kind and qualifications (%)

Ouvrières agricoles permanentes selon l'octroi ou non d'avantages en nature et la qualification (%)

1975

	BR Deutschland		France		Italia		Nederland		Belgique België	
	$\frac{f}{F}$ 100	$\frac{f}{f+m}$ 100	$\frac{f}{F}$ 100	$\frac{f}{f+m}$ 100	$\frac{f}{F}$ 100	$\frac{f}{f+m}$ 100	$\frac{f}{F}$ 100	$\frac{f}{f+m}$ 100	$\frac{f}{F}$ 100	$\frac{f}{f+m}$ 100
Accommodation and meals										
Skilled workers	1,7	3,6	1,2	2,4	2,7	5,2	1,7	:	:	:
Unskilled workers	10,5	16,1	8,2	4,8	3	13,1	–	–	:	:
Accommodation only										
Skilled workers	1,3	2,1	2,0	1,1	18,2	2,8	–	–	:	:
Unskilled workers	6,7	24,3	10,5	4,4	7,2	9,8	–	–	:	:
Meals only										
Skilled workers	0,4	2,8	0,2	0,6	0,9	7,1	–	–	:	:
Unskilled workers	1,6	16,8	2,6	4,2	0,2	4,8	–	–	:	:
Neither accom. nor meals										
Skilled workers	20,4	5,9	10,8	3,7	32,8	0,6	65,0	10	:	:
Unskilled workers	57,4	31,7	64,5	18,3	35	21,7	33,3	18,8	72,2	10,5
Total	100,0	13,3	100,0	7,2	100,0	6,8	100,0	3,5	100,0	6,2

TAB. 45

Permanent female agricultural workers by type of activity performed on the holding and qualifications (%)
Ouvrières agricoles permanentes selon le type d'activité exercée dans l'exploitation et la qualification (%)
1975

Luxembourg		United Kingdom		Ireland		Danmark		EUR 9		
$\frac{f}{F}100$	$\frac{f}{f+m}100$	$\frac{f}{F}100$	$\frac{f}{f+m}100$	$\frac{f}{F}100$	$\frac{f}{f+m}100$	$\frac{f}{F}100$	$\frac{f}{f+m}100$	$\frac{f}{F}100$	$\frac{f}{f+m}100$	
										Agriculture générale
–	–	–	–	:	:	4,3	0,8	:	:	Ouvriers qualifiés
61,1	4,9	25,2	2,9	25,6	1,3	3,6	1,6	25,2	5,6	Ouvriers non qualifiés
										Élevage
–	–	4,9	2,2	8,2	0,8	4,3	2,3	:	:	Ouvriers qualifiés
:	:	46,9	21,3	26,8	2,9	3,8	10,7	:	:	Ouvriers non qualifiés
										Cultures spécifiques
–	–	–	–	14,7	7,2	58,4	18,3	10,6	6,9	Ouvriers qualifiés
:	:	23,0	19,5	23,7	10,1	25,6	26,9	:	:	Ouvriers non qualifiés
100,0	5,5	100,0	5,2	100,0	2,2	100,0	7,2	100,0	6,7	**Total**
–	–	4,9	0,7	23,9	1,7	67,0	6,5	25,4	3,2	Ouvriers qualifiés
100,0	6,2	95,1	7,9	76,1	2,4	33,0	9,2	74,6	9,3	Ouvriers non qualifiés

TAB. 46

Permanent female agricultural workers by size of holding and qualifications (%)
Ouvrières agricoles permanentes selon la taille de l'exploitation et la qualification (%)
1975

Luxembourg		United Kingdom		Ireland		Danmark		EUR 9		
$\frac{f}{F}100$	$\frac{f}{f+m}100$	$\frac{f}{F}100$	$\frac{f}{f+m}100$	$\frac{f}{F}100$	$\frac{f}{f+m}100$	$\frac{f}{F}100$	$\frac{f}{f+m}100$	$\frac{f}{F}100$	$\frac{f}{f+m}100$	
										Exploitations ayant 1 ou 2 salariés
–	–	–	–	:	:	14,9	2,9	:	:	Ouvriers qualifiés
:	:	14,5	3,5	:	:	6,4	3,2	:	:	Ouvriers non qualifiés
										Exploitations ayant 3 à 9 salariés
–	–	–	:	:	:	32,6	8,5	:	:	Ouvriers qualifiés
:	:	34,0	6,8	:	:	17,5	15,1	:	:	Ouvriers non qualifiés
										Exploitations ayant 10 salariés et plus
–	–	:	:	:	:	19,5	13,4	:	:	Ouvriers qualifiés
:	:	46,6	15,9	:	:	9,1	23,4	:	:	Ouvriers non qualifiés
100,0	5,5	100,0	5,2	100,0	2,2	100,0	7,2	100,0	6,7	**Total**
–	–	4,9	0,7	:	:	67,0	6,5	:	:	Ouvriers qualifiés
100,0	:	95,1	7,9	:	:	33,0	9,2	:	:	Ouvriers non qualifiés

TAB. 47

Permanent female agricultural workers by payment or not of benefits in kind and qualifications (%)
Ouvrières agricoles permanentes selon l'octroi ou non d'avantages en nature et la qualification (%)
1975

Luxembourg		United Kingdom		Ireland		Danmark		EUR 9		
$\frac{f}{F}100$	$\frac{f}{f+m}100$	$\frac{f}{F}100$	$\frac{f}{f+m}100$	$\frac{f}{F}100$	$\frac{f}{f+m}100$	$\frac{f}{F}100$	$\frac{f}{f+m}100$	$\frac{f}{F}100$	$\frac{f}{f+m}100$	
										Logés et nourris
–	–	–	–	:	:	:	:	:	:	Ouvriers qualifiés
:	:	–	–	:	:	:	:	:	:	Ouvriers non qualifiés
										Logés
–	–	–	–	:	:	:	:	:	:	Ouvriers qualifiés
–	–	3	0,7	:	:	:	:	:	:	Ouvriers non qualifiés
										Nourris
–	–	–	–	–	–	:	:	:	:	Ouvriers qualifiés
–	–	–	–	–	–	:	:	:	:	Ouvriers non qualifiés
										Ni logés ni nourris
–	–	–	–	:	:	59,5	13,1	:	:	Ouvriers qualifiés
:	:	85,3	11,5	57,2	2,6	:	:	59,6	1,8	Ouvriers non qualifiés
100,0	5,5	100,0	5,2	100,0	2,2	100,0	7,2	100,0	6,7	**Total**

TAB. 48

Female agricultural workers by region and qualifications (%)
Salariées agricoles dans les régions selon la qualification (%)

1975

	Skilled workers Ouvriers qualifiés		Unskilled workers Ouvriers non qualifiés		Total	
	$\frac{f}{F}100$	$\frac{f}{f+m}100$	$\frac{f}{F}100$	$\frac{f}{f+m}100$	$\frac{f}{F}100$	$\frac{f}{f+m}100$
DEUTSCHLAND (BR)						
Schleswig-Holstein	14,5	1,7	85,5	17,6	100,0	7,5
Niedersachsen	22,1	2,7	77,9	16,6	100,0	7,7
Nordrhein-Westfalen	37,8	4,6	62,2	14,2	100,0	8,0
Hessen	36,4	5,8	63,6	20,1	100,0	10,6
Rheinland-Pfalz	11,3	2,7	88,7	41,1	100,0	15,7
Baden-Württemberg	29,5	11,2	70,5	33,0	100,0	21,0
Bayern	18,6	7,4	81,4	7,4	100,0	24,2
Übrige Länder	30,6	16,6	69,4	36,4	100,0	26,7
Total	23,8	5,1	76,2	26,9	100,0	13,3
FRANCE						
Région parisienne	17,6	3,6	82,4	27,4	100,0	12,6
Bassin parisien	19,4	2,3	80,6	10,0	100,0	6,1
Nord	13,6	1,6	86,4	8,5	100,0	5,4
Est	18,0	4,6	82,0	13,2	100,0	9,9
Ouest	12,0	4,5	88,0	17,0	100,0	12,8
Sud-Ouest	5,7	1,5	94,3	9,5	100,0	7,3
Centre-Est	21,6	2,4	78,4	4,2	100,0	3,7
Méditerranée	10,3	1,2	89,7	4,7	100,0	3,7
Total	14,1	2,6	85,9	10,4	100,0	7,2
ITALIA						
Piemonte-Val d'Aosta-Liguria	46,3	5,3	53,7	22,5	100,0	9,0
Lombardia	57,3	1,9	42,7	15,1	100,0	3,0
Trentino-Alto Adige-Veneto-Friuli-Venezia Giulia	26,1	5,0	73,9	35,3	100,0	13,7
Emilia-Romagna	91,6	9,0	8,4	14,0	100,0	9,3
Toscana-Marche-Umbria	58,7	4,6	41,3	21,2	100,0	6,8
Lazio	66,8	6,0	33,2	22,0	100,0	7,9
Abruzzi-Molise	28,7	3,1	71,3	19,3	100,0	7,6
Campania	48,8	2,3	51,2	5,6	100,0	3,3
Puglia-Basilicata-Calabria	89,6	1,9	10,4	1,1	100,0	1,8
Sicilia	29,3	1,2	70,7	5,6	100,0	2,7
Sardegna	56,0	2,0	44,0	7,5	100,0	2,9
Total	54,6	4,4	45,4	20,0	100,0	6,8
NEDERLAND						
Noord	–	–	–	–	–	–
Oost	:	:	:	:	:	:
West	:	:	:	:	:	:
Zuid	50,7	2,9	49,3	21,0	100,0	5,0
Total	66,7	2,5	33,3	16,8	100,0	3,5
BELGIQUE/BELGIË						
Région bruxelloise	–	–	–	–	–	–
Région flamande	16,0	2,6	84,0	11,1	100,0	7,3
Région wallonne	27,5	2,5	72,5	4,6	100,0	3,7
Total	18,1	2,6	81,9	8,8	100,0	6,2
UNITED KINGDOM						
North	–	–	:	:	:	2,2
Yorkshire-Humberside	–	–	100,0	6,1	100,0	8,5
East Midlands	–	–	:	:	:	1,2
East Anglia	–	–	100,0	9,7	100,0	6,2
South East	–	–	100,0	22,7	100,0	10,7
South West	19,9	1,3	80,1	3,3	100,0	2,1
West Midlands	:	:	:	:	:	4,7
North West	–	–	100,0	6,0	100,0	4,9
Wales	–	–	–	:	:	–
Scotland	–	–	100,0	24,7	100,0	3,5
Northern Ireland	–	–	–	–	–	–
Total	4,9	0,7	95,1	7,9	100,0	5,2

TAB. 49

Female employees by branch of activity, qualifications and type of work (%)

Femmes parmi les salariés selon les branches d'activité, la qualification et le régime de travail (%)

1974

	BR Deutschland	France	Italia	Nederland	Belgique België
	$\frac{f}{f+m}100$	$\frac{f}{f+m}100$	$\frac{f}{f+m}100$	$\frac{f}{f+m}100$	$\frac{f}{f+m}100$
	Full time / Temps complet				
61 Wholesale distribution					
1 A Top management personnel	9,3	6,4	5,6	3,0	4,3
1 B Management personnel and senior executives	6,7	10,1	7,0	5,8	7,4
2 Executives and management staff	8,8	11,7	12,9	9,0	14,1
3 Highly-skilled junior personnel	21,7	29,3	24,9	14,0	31,2
4 Skilled junior personnel	34,7	35,8	35,5	22,1	35,9
5 Unskilled junior personnel	38,1	38,6	34,2	11,5	28,4
64/653/656 Retail distribution					
1 A Top management personnel	15,4	15,0	6,7	10,3	0,0
1 B Management personnel and senior executives	11,8	27,0	8,8	15,7	23,1
2 Executives and management staff	24,4	35,1	15,7	22,3	31,0
3 Highly-skilled junior personnel	39,6	53,7	35,9	34,6	58,3
4 Skilled junior personnel	74,7	59,0	57,0	57,2	59,7
5 Unskilled junior personnel	64,6	68,6	40,3	–	51,0
812/813 Credit institutions					
1 Directors, top management	–	2,6	3,1	.	–
2 Senior executives	2,6	14,1	1,0	5,0	.
3 Executives (junior management)	14,8	43,6	9,2	6,7	7,8
4 Highly-qualified clerical staff	48,1	53,8	19,8	10,8	27,0
5 Qualified clerical staff	68,3	57,9	35,8	37,5	44,6
6 Other employees	70,2	57,0	4,0	51,6	39,7
82 Insurance					
I Managers and senior management executives	.	.	.	.	.
II Middle management executives	4,8	16,7	4,2	0,0	7,1
III Junior executives and personnel with equivalent qualification	16,8	42,2	5,9	18,2	17,9
IV Highly-skilled employees	53,7	66,8	31,7	13,4	28,6
V Skilled employees	68,7	76,2	64,4	25,0	48,4
VI Other employees	73,8	58,8	8,3	49,3	61,6

TAB. 49.A

Female employees by branch of activity, qualifications and type of work (%)

Femmes parmi les salariés selon les branches d'activité la qualification et le régime de travail (%)

1974

	BR Deutschland	France	Italia	Nederland	Belgique/ België
	$\frac{f}{f+m}100$	$\frac{f}{f+m}100$	$\frac{f}{f+m}100$	$\frac{f}{f+m}100$	$\frac{f}{f+m}100$
	Part time / Temps partiel				
61 Wholesale distribution					
1 A Top management personnel	–	12,5			
1 B Management personnel and senior executives	–	16,7		75,0	.
2 Executives and management staff	76,2	18,8	50,0	85,7	100,0
3 Highly-skilled junior personnel	88,7	64,7	85,7	87,5	81,8
4 Skilled junior personnel	90,8	60,0	64,7	81,9	66,7
5 Unskilled junior personnel	86,3	71,7	82,2	73,1	68,4
64/653/656 Retail distribution					
1 A Top management personnel	–	33,3	.	.	–
1 B Management personnel and senior executives	–	40,0	.	75,0	0,0
2 Executives and management staff	85,7	72,2	0,0	88,9	100,0
3 Highly-skilled junior personnel	92,5	83,0	100,0	85,1	96,9
4 Skilled junior personnel	97,9	84,0	92,2	75,8	96,0
5 Unskilled junior personnel	90,1	80,7	81,6	–	82,1
812/813 Credit institutions					
1 Directors, top management	–	.	.	.	.
2 Senior executives	.	.	100,0	.	.
3 Executives (junior management)	80,0	50,0	.	.	–
4 Highly-qualified clerical staff	96,3	50,0	0,0	100,0	100,0
5 Qualified clerical staff	96,8	72,7	.	94,1	100,0
6 Other employees	94,8	84,3	83,3	87,2	90,9
82 Insurance					
I Managers and senior management executives	–	–	.	.	–
II Middle management executives	.	.	.	.	.
III Junior executives and personnel with equivalent qualification	66,7	.	.	100,0	.
IV Highly-skilled employees	100,0	.	.	100,0	.
V Skilled employees	95,2	50,0	100,0	90,9	100,0
VI Other employees	92,3	87,5	100,0	88,9	100,0

TAB. 49

Female employees by branch of activity, qualifications and type of work (%)
Femmes parmi les salariés selon les branches d'activité, la qualification et le régime de travail (%)
1974

Full-time / Temps complet — $\frac{f}{f+m}\,100$

Luxembourg	United Kingdom	Ireland	Danmark	Description
				61 Commerce de gros
0,0	–	.	.	1 A Personnel supérieur de direction
0,0	.	.	.	1 B Personnel de direction et cadres supérieurs
16,7	6,7	5,0	5,2	2 Personnel d'exécution et d'encadrement
26,7	12,5	8,3	12,2	3 Personnel subalterne très qualifié
33,3	33,2	32,5	24,7	4 Personnel subalterne qualifié
25,0	31,2	15,1	17,3	5 Personnel subalterne non qualifié
				64/653-656 Commerce de détail
.	.	.	.	1 A Personnel supérieur de direction
0,0	.	.	25,0	1 B Cadres supérieurs
50,0	21,9	17,6	12,9	2 Personnel de conception (cadres inférieurs)
71,4	35,4	23,7	38,8	3 Personnel d'exécution très qualifié
76,9	63,2	63,4	56,7	4 Personnel d'exécution qualifié
75,0	56,3	43,8	41,8	5 Autres agents
				812/813 Institutions de
–	–	–	–	1 Personnel supérieur de direction
				2 Cadres supérieurs
25,0	5,3	4,5	9,8	3 Personnel de conception (cadres inférieurs)
33,3	36,7	60,6	27,1	4 Personnel d'exécution très qualifié
54,5	68,1	70,7	57,1	5 Personnel d'exécution qualifié
54,5	67,8	25,0	69,2	6 Autres agents
				82 Assurances
–	–	–	–	I Dirigeants et cadres supérieurs de direction
.	–	–		II Cadres intermédiaires
.		.	20,0	III Agents d'encadrement et assimilés
0,0	13,0	53,3	68,4	IV Travailleurs très qualifiés
100,0	60,3	65,4	82,1	V Travailleurs qualifiés
0,0	65,5	.	60,0	VI Autres travailleurs

TAB. 49.A

Female employees by branch of activity, qualifications and type of work (%)
Femmes parmi les salariés selon les branches d'activité, la qualification et le régime de travail (%)
1974

Part-time / Temps partiel — $\frac{f}{f+m}\,100$

Luxembourg	United Kingdom	Ireland	Danmark	Description
				61 Commerce de gros
.	–	–	–	1 A Personnel supérieur de direction
.	–	–	.	1 B Personnel de direction et cadres supérieurs
.	.	–	.	2 Personnel d'exécution et d'encadrement
0,0	69,2	–	92,3	3 Personnel subalterne très qualifié
100,0	86,5	50,0	93,1	4 Personnel subalterne qualifié
100,0	70,1	66,7	88,0	5 Personnel subalterne non qualifié
				64/653-656 Commerce de détail
–	.	–		1 A Personnel supérieur de direction
.		–	85,7	1 B Cadres supérieurs
	65,5			2 Personnel de conception (cadres inférieurs)
100,0	73,6		95,2	3 Personnel d'exécution très qualifié
100,0	94,3	100,0	96,1	4 Personnel d'exécution qualifié
100,0	84,8	50,0	79,1	5 Autres agents
				812/813 Institutions de crédit
–	–	–	–	1 Personnel supérieur de direction
–	–	–	–	2 Cadres supérieurs
–	–	–	–	3 Personnel de conception (cadres inférieurs)
0,0	.	–	100,0	4 Personnel d'exécution très qualifié
0,0	93,3	–	95,7	5 Personnel d'exécution qualifié
100,0	86,8	–	87,7	6 Autres agents
				82 Assurances
–	–	–	–	I Dirigeants et cadres supérieurs de direction
–	–	–	–	II Cadres intermédiaires
–	–	–	100,0	III Agents d'encadrement et assimilés
.		–	100,0	IV Travailleurs très qualifiés
.	87,2	–	100,0	V Travailleurs qualifiés
.	97,0	–	83,3	VI Autres travailleurs

TAB. 50

Full-time employees by branch of activity and size of undertaking (%)

Salariés à temps complet selon la branche d'activité et la taille de l'entreprise (%)

1974

	BR Deutschland		France		Italia		Nederland		Belgique België	
	$\frac{f}{F}100$	$\frac{m}{M}100$	$\frac{f}{F}100$	$\frac{m}{M}100$	$\frac{f}{F}100$	$\frac{m}{M}100$	$\frac{f}{F}100$	$\frac{m}{M}100$	$\frac{f}{F}100$	$\frac{m}{M}100$
61 Wholesale distribution	100,0	100,0	100,0	100,0	100,0	100,0	100,0	100,0	100,0	100,0
10 - 49	33,2	37,4	37,1	41,1	58,1	58,1	42,7	43,6	48,3	46,8
50 - 99	18,1	18,6	18,2	16,9	17,9	16,8	20,3	18,8	18,3	18,4
100 - 199	16,9	15,2	13,4	11,9	11,1	11,2	15,3	14,3	13,4	13,1
200 - 499	16,0	14,3	14,6	13,2	6,8	7,8	13,0	13,2	12,0	10,4
500 - 999	7,7	6,2	5,5	5,5	4,1	4,2	.	.	6,3	8,9
≥ 1000	8,1	8,3	11,3	11,4	2,0	2,0	.	.	1,7	2,4
64/653-656 Retail distribution	100,0	100,0	100,0	100,0	100,0	100,0	100,0	100,0	100,0	100,0
10 - 49	31,7	32,6	26,0	29,9	38,7	56,5	38,7	36,5	25,9	25,4
50 - 99	7,1	7,9	9,5	9,9	7,0	7,5	9,6	10,3	6,6	8,5
100 - 199	7,9	7,2	7,4	5,8	6,4	6,7	7,3	7,3	3,5	4,8
200 - 499	8,2	8,6	11,6	8,9	5,3	6,1	7,0	9,2	7,7	6,9
500 - 999	6,1	7,0	6,8	6,3	2,1	1,7	4,9	3,7	3,2	5,2
≥ 1000	39,0	36,8	38,7	39,2	40,5	21,4	32,5	33,1	53,1	49,1
812/813 Credit institutions	100,0	100,0	100,0	100,0	100,0	100,0	100,0	100,0	100,0	100,0
10 - 49	8,1	11,0	2,2	2,5	9,3	9,8	18,9	11,1	4,5	2,9
50 - 99	8,5	8,2	2,1	2,8	5,6	4,7	6,6	4,3	5,2	3,1
100 - 199	10,5	10,1	3,0	3,5	5,9	5,2	2,5	2,8	7,7	4,5
200 - 499	17,7	16,0	9,8	11,6	11,8	12,2	5,9	6,6	9,8	7,0
500 - 999	10,1	9,6	15,1	19,8	7,6	6,7	3,4	3,0	7,4	10,8
≥ 1000	45,1	45,1	67,8	59,9	59,7	61,3	62,7	72,2	65,4	71,6
82 Insurance	100,0	100,0	100,0	100,0	100,0	100,0	100,0	100,0	100,0	100,0
10 - 49	1,3	1,1	3,2	2,1	30,7	16,3	6,5	5,2	8,9	4,3
50 - 99	2,1	1,8	5,5	4,2	6,1	5,5	6,4	5,6	8,4	7,1
100 - 199	3,8	3,7	5,1	6,8	7,9	7,7	14,1	11,9	16,1	12,5
200 - 499	11,8	9,9	12,0	13,0	23,7	25,3	19,8	18,7	24,6	21,8
500 - 999	11,6	11,6	18,6	20,3	4,8	6,1	.	.	24,0	27,1
≥ 1000	69,4	72,0	55,7	53,6	26,7	39,1	.	.	18,0	27,3

TAB. 51

Full-time employees by branch of activity and age (%)

Salariés à temps complet selon la branche d'activité et l'âge (%)

1974

	BR Deutschland		France		Italia		Nederland		Belgique België	
	$\frac{f}{F}100$	$\frac{m}{M}100$	$\frac{f}{F}100$	$\frac{m}{M}100$	$\frac{f}{F}100$	$\frac{m}{M}100$	$\frac{f}{F}100$	$\frac{m}{M}100$	$\frac{f}{F}100$	$\frac{m}{M}100$
61 Wholesale distribution	100,0	100,0	100,0	100,0	100,0	100,0	100,0	100,0	100,0	100,0
< 21	17,4	3,8	15,6	5,4	17,0	4,4	36,4	6,5	18,4	6,6
21 - 29	34,7	23,3	37,0	27,9	43,3	25,4	42,6	28,2	38,9	26,8
30 - 44	24,9	43,8	25,2	35,3	26,5	41,6	11,8	38,8	27,4	36,5
45 - 54	16,0	18,2	14,1	20,1	11,3	21,4	6,0	16,7	12,2	20,8
≥ 55	7,0	10,8	7,0	10,1	1,8	7,2	3,2	9,7	3,2	9,4
64/653-656 Retail distribution	100,0	100,0	100,0	100,0	100,0	100,0	100,0	100,0	100,0	100,0
< 21	21,6	7,0	16,0	8,7	13,6	5,4	47,0	15,8	17,7	8,2
21 - 29	27,8	26,8	31,2	30,8	51,7	28,8	31,0	33,2	28,6	25,2
30 - 44	23,1	38,8	26,7	31,6	27,2	41,6	11,1	30,1	31,0	32,3
45 - 54	17,4	15,9	17,5	18,3	6,7	18,5	7,2	12,0	18,9	22,2
≥ 55	10,1	11,3	7,9	9,8	0,9	5,8	3,4	8,7	3,8	12,0
812/813 Credit institutions	100,0	100,0	100,0	100,0	100,0	100,0	100,0	100,0	100,0	100,0
< 21	19,3	3,3	11,2	4,6	6,9	1,1	44,7	9,8	11,0	2,9
21 - 29	42,3	27,0	47,4	43,1	46,7	29,9	41,8	33,6	56,2	36,9
30 - 44	23,1	39,9	23,9	29,2	32,5	45,9	7,3	29,4	24,2	36,6
45 - 54	12,0	19,5	13,5	14,4	12,8	18,5	4,3	16,4	6,8	16,8
≥ 55	3,3	10,2	3,6	8,0	1,2	4,7	1,9	10,8	1,9	6,8
82 Insurance	100,0	100,0	100,0	100,0	100,0	100,0	100,0	100,0	100,0	100,0
< 21	13,3	3,1	14,0	6,9	8,3	1,3	37,3	6,8	16,8	4,8
21 - 29	35,5	19,6	39,9	32,8	48,7	26,3	35,4	27,3	44,2	24,3
30 - 44	28,5	43,1	23,3	27,9	32,8	49,4	12,9	28,8	26,7	39,5
45 - 54	17,1	20,4	15,4	16,9	9,3	17,1	9,7	22,5	9,7	21,9
≥ 55	5,7	13,8	7,2	15,3	0,9	5,9	4,7	14,5	2,6	9,5

TAB. 50

Full-time employees by branch of activity and size of undertaking (%)

Salariés à temps complet selon la branche d'activité et la taille de l'entreprise (%)

1974

Luxembourg		United Kingdom		Ireland		Danmark		
$\frac{f}{F}100$	$\frac{m}{M}100$	$\frac{f}{F}100$	$\frac{m}{M}100$	$\frac{f}{F}100$	$\frac{m}{M}100$	$\frac{f}{F}100$	$\frac{m}{M}100$	
100,0	100,0	100,0	100,0	100,0	100,0	100,0	100,0	**61 Commerce de gros**
46,1	50,1	26,5	31,4	28,5	26,7	38,4	37,3	10 – 49
22,0	27,2	15,3	15,2	17,4	18,9	14,4	15,1	50 – 99
21,0	17,2	12,7	13,1	22,0	22,2	15,0	14,0	100 – 199
10,9	5,5	14,9	12,6	16,8	18,6	16,1	13,0	200 – 499
–	–	11,4	8,1	7,9	10,1	5,4	8,8	500 – 999
–	–	19,2	19,7	7,3	3,4	10,7	11,7	⩾ 1000
100,0	100,0	100,0	100,0	100,0	100,0	100,0	100,0	**64/653-656 Commerce de détail**
51,7	66,9	10,8	17,5	3,2	4,4	41,8	40,9	10 – 49
15,2	12,9	4,1	4,9	5,4	4,1	10,8	10,2	50 – 99
19,8	15,0	4,0	4,7	8,2	6,9	5,5	7,4	100 – 199
13,3	5,2	8,0	8,2	7,7	8,3	2,8	6,1	200 – 499
–	–	6,9	7,7	4,8	4,6	6,9	6,4	500 – 999
–	–	66,3	57,1	70,7	71,7	32,1	29,0	⩾ 1000
100,0	100,0	100,0	100,0	100,0	100,0	100,0	100,0	**812/813 Institutions de crédit**
12,8	10,3	2,0	2,8	3,2	4,4	5,4	5,2	10 – 49
9,0	7,0	1,7	2,4	5,4	4,1	3,4	4,5	50 – 99
14,9	10,6	3,4	5,1	8,2	6,9	6,6	4,7	100 – 199
4,3	4,0	5,3	6,3	7,7	8,3	10,7	10,3	200 – 499
58,9	68,1	5,6	6,8	4,8	4,6	14,9	14,8	500 – 999
–	–	82,0	76,7	70,7	71,7	59,0	60,5	⩾ 1000
100,0	100,0	100,0	100,0	100,0	100,0	100,0	100,0	**82 Assurances**
28,3	28,8	2,6	2,9	3,3	2,2	6,9	7,3	10 – 49
–	–	.	.	5,8	5,4	12,8	6,5	50 – 99
71,7	71,2	2,9	2,0	15,1	12,4	5,1	2,9	100 – 199
–	–	6,2	6,5	39,6	36,4	4,1	6,3	200 – 499
–	–	9,4	11,6	25,6	33,9	16,5	22,7	500 – 999
–	–	77,6	76,0	10,7	9,7	54,5	54,4	⩾ 1000

TAB. 51

Full-time employees by branch of activity and age (%)

Salariés à temps complet selon la branche d'activité et l'âge (%)

1974

Luxembourg		United Kingdom		Ireland		Danmark		
$\frac{f}{F}100$	$\frac{m}{M}100$	$\frac{f}{F}100$	$\frac{m}{M}100$	$\frac{f}{F}100$	$\frac{m}{M}100$	$\frac{f}{F}100$	$\frac{m}{M}100$	
100,0	100,0	100,0	100,0	100,0	100,0	100,0	100,0	**61 Commerce de gros**
40,3	13,0	22,8	10,7	31,4	10,5	8,6	2,3	< 21
32,7	26,0	25,4	22,6	41,8	26,5	42,2	23,4	21 – 29
16,1	35,2	22,6	30,6	13,9	33,0	25,2	37,4	30 – 44
8,3	16,6	19,9	20,1	7,2	17,6	15,6	20,4	45 – 54
2,7	9,3	9,2	16,0	4,9	12,0	8,3	16,6	⩾ 55
100,0	100,0	100,0	100,0	100,0	100,0	100,0	100,0	**64/653-656 Commerce de détail**
38,1	19,0	26,8	14,3	33,1	15,2	13,8	5,6	< 21
29,2	25,7	20,3	24,4	33,3	25,7	42,6	32,3	21 – 29
19,1	30,3	21,2	26,1	14,2	29,7	19,3	32,3	30 – 44
8,6	15,1	21,3	17,6	9,4	16,4	12,6	15,3	45 – 54
4,9	9,9	10,5	17,6	8,5	11,6	11,7	14,6	⩾ 55
100,0	100,0	100,0	100,0	100,0	100,0	100,0	100,0	**812/813 Institutions de crédit**
37,9	10,7	38,4	13,9	32,4	12,8	4,1	2,6	< 21
49,4	41,0	38,1	28,9	51,7	34,7	59,1	43,5	21 – 29
9,3	32,2	12,7	30,5	9,7	31,5	25,2	29,9	30 – 44
2,5	11,4	8,7	16,6	4,2	11,0	7,8	12,4	45 – 54
0,8	4,7	2,1	10,1	2,0	10,0	3,8	11,5	⩾ 55
100,0	100,0	100,0	100,0	100,0	100,0	100,0	100,0	**82 Assurances**
38,2	5,8	31,6	7,8	31,7	15,6	6,7	.	< 21
44,0	31,9	33,2	24,5	41,8	28,6	39,7	20,3	21 – 29
10,5	40,7	14,1	33,8	14,2	35,4	25,2	36,0	30 – 44
6,8	10,6	15,7	18,9	9,4	11,8	16,4	23,2	45 – 54
.	11,1	5,3	15,0	2,8	8,6	12,1	19,0	⩾ 55

TAB. 52

Average age of full-time employees by branch of activity and qualifications

Âge moyen des salariés à temps complet selon la branche d'activité et la qualification

1974

	BR Deutschland		France		Italia		Nederland		Belgique België	
	F	M	F	M	F	M	F	M	F	M
61 Wholesale distribution										
1 A Top management personnel	47,0	43,2	50,8	45,7	45,1	45,2	40,8	43,2	39,0°	43,4
1 B Management personnel and senior executives	39,4	41,0	41,0	39,4	43,1	43,2	31,2	38,6	37,3	38,4
2 Executives and management staff	36,8	38,4	38,6	36,9	37,9	38,2	28,5	36,2	34,1	36,5
3 Highly-skilled junior personnel	31,0	35,5	32,8	34,8	33,2	36,0	24,9	34,2	30,1	35,5
4 Skilled junior personnel	28,7	34,9	28,8	34,2	26,7	34,6	21,9	32,5	26,9	34,3
5 Unskilled junior personnel	33,2	35,6	30,0	32,7	27,4	34,5	24,2	31,6	27,2	32,5
64/653-656 Retail distribution										
1 A Top management personnel	40,2	42,2	46,9	44,9	45,8	44,5	40,3	40,3	44,3	43,4
1 B Management personnel and senior executives	39,4	39,3	41,6	39,3	43,2	43,2	35,2	37,0	39,4	41,2
2 Executives and management staff	39,0	37,1	37,6	36,2	38,0	37,4	31,5	36,1	36,5	38,1
3 Highly-skilled junior personnel	34,6	35,0	36,1	34,9	33,4	35,5	–		31,1	35,7
4 Skilled junior personnel	30,0	32,2	31,6	32,5	26,5	33,5	27,2	32,1	31,3	35,8
5 Unskilled junior personnel	33,2	35,9	29,1	30,8	24,7	32,3	21,5	27,6	29,1	32,7
812/813 Credit institutions										
1 Directors, top management	–	43,3	42,7	45,5	40,9	47,1	.	44,5	–	48,8
2 Senior executives	46,5°	42,3	40,5	38,8	45,5	43,9	29,5°	38,7	.	42,2
3 Executives (junior management)	35,3	35,9	36,2	33,3	39,3	37,7	26,8°	39,9	33,9	38,1
4 Highly-qualified clerical staff	29,3	33,4	31,5	30,8	28,0	28,7	30,4	37,1	30,0	33,0
5 Qualified clerical staff	25,9	34,1	25,8	27,5	24,8	34,4	23,8	32,9	24,5	29,0
6 Other employees	26,4	43,8	23,1	28,4	32,2	34,3	20,3	28,7	28,6	33,2
82 Insurance										
I Managers and senior management executives	.	44,7	.	47,9	.	45,0	.	48,2	.	44,7
II Middle management executives	42,6	41,9	43,0	42,7	41,2	43,8	43,5	44,6	41,5°	41,8
III Junior executives and personnel with equivalent qualification	38,0	38,3	40,3	37,8	38,6	38,0	26,6	42,0	34,6	40,8
IV Highly-skilled employees	32,1	35,0	31,2	29,8	31,0	31,4	36,7	39,0	36,7	37,0
V Skilled employees	29,0	39,3	28,4	29,7	26,3	31,8	26,9	33,9	29,2	33,1
VI Other employees	29,0	42,7	28,5	35,7	23,4°	36,8	21,3	30,6	24,2	30,7

TAB. 52A

Average age of full-time employees by branch of activity and qualifications: coefficient of variation

Âge moyen des salariés à temps complet selon la branche d'activité et la qualification: coefficient de variation

1974

	BR Deutschland		France		Italia		Nederland		Belgique België	
	F	M	F	M	F	M	F	M	F	M
61 Wholesale distribution										
1 A Top management personnel	17,8	24,0	22,7	23,4	13,9	18,0	29,8	23,4	29,7°	21,5
1 B Management personnel and senior executives	27,0	23,1	27,0	26,1	16,2	18,8	38,4	26,1	31,7	24,7
2 Executives and management staff	31,2	26,7	29,0	29,7	24,1	24,3	41,3	27,9	31,4	29,0
3 Highly-skilled junior personnel	37,7	31,9	34,5	32,3	31,1	28,4	40,8	32,9	35,5	32,5
4 Skilled junior personnel	44,2	36,3	41,0	37,0	33,0	30,7	42,4	40,0	39,4	37,0
5 Unskilled junior personnel	44,4	40,5	46,8	44,2	41,8	36,1	45,8	44,6	45,3	43,1
64/653-656 Retail distribution										
1 A Top management personnel	27,0	26,5	27,1	24,6	20,8	15,9	26,0	27,0	17,6	20,6
1 B Management personnel and senior executives	26,3	23,4	25,2	26,2	17,8	16,5	34,9	29,0	29,7	24,2
2 Executives and management staff	28,5	29,4	30,1	30,6	24,3	23,5	37,9	29,4	26,7	28,7
3 Highly-skilled junior personnel	37,0	34,3	33,7	33,7	28,3	26,9	45,0	36,1	36,0	34,5
4 Skilled junior personnel	47,3	42,2	40,9	39,5	30,0	31,4	46,4	47,2	39,6	36,8
5 Unskilled junior personnel	45,4	43,0	46,0	48,9	38,4	37,6	–	–	45,8	45,5
812/813 Credit institutions										
1 Directors, top management	–	21,1	19,9	19,1	15,0	18,0	.	20,8	–	22,0
2 Senior executives	21,2°	21,2	24,5	23,9	15,6	16,2	24,4°	26,7	.	22,1
3 Executives (junior management)	30,1	28,1	28,4	30,1	21,6	21,8	40,7°	27,2	24,5	25,3
4 Highly-qualified clerical staff	37,2	35,7	33,5	36,9	30,5	27,2	40,7	30,0	28,7	30,6
5 Qualified clerical staff	40,1	39,6	35,5	41,7	29,1	30,9	42,6	37,0	31,6	36,7
6 Other employees	47,8	27,8	40,9	51,2	40,3	32,2	34,8	47,0	39,2	40,6
82 Insurance										
I Managers and senior management executives	.	20,0	.	20,8	.	18,3	.	16,2	.	19,7
II Middle management executives	18,4	24,2	25,1	24,9	17,3	18,1	22,7	20,7	24,2°	21,2
III Junior executives and personnel with equivalent qualification	27,7	27,6	27,5	30,9	23,4	22,5	47,3	26,6	30,9	24,4
IV Highly-skilled employees	37,0	33,9	37,8	37,6	29,9	26,8	33,1	29,2	27,0	27,2
V Skilled employees	41,6	35,6	42,9	47,0	29,1	33,7	45,9	39,0	32,9	34,0
VI Other employees	43,3	32,4	48,6	48,3	46,7°	33,5	40,1	48,2	36,2	44,4

TAB. 52

Average age of full-time employees by branch of activity and qualifications
Âge moyen des salariés à temps complet selon la branche d'activité et la qualification
1974

Luxembourg		United Kingdom		Ireland		Danmark			
F	M	F	M	F	M	F	M		
								61	**Commerce de gros**
44,3	44,4	–	47,2	.	42,5	.	47,8	1 A	Personnel supérieur de direction
42,5	41,0	.	40,6	.	–	.	42,9	1 B	Personnel de direction et cadres supérieurs
27,5	37,3	37,9°	38,5	41,8°	39,0	43,4	39,9	2	Personnel d'exécution et d'encadrement
27,3	34,1	35,8	39,1	36,5	36,5	34,7	37,9	3	Personnel subalterne très qualifié
22,1	31,3	29,8	34,8	23,9	33,1	30,5	35,1	4	Personnel subalterne qualifié
23,6	30,1	39,4	34,5	28,6	32,9	31,4	39,7	5	Personnel subalterne non qualifié
								64/653-656	**Commerce de détail**
.	41,5	.	46,7	.	41,6	.	44,7	1 A	Personnel supérieur de direction
43,5	36,2	.	41,0	–	–	38,4	40,2	1 B	Cadres supérieurs
35,4	35,4	38,5	38,0	40,6	38,0	45,6	39,8	2	Personnel de conception (cadres inférieurs)
29,6	33,7	35,9	37,1	35,9	36,5	28,5	34,1	3	Personnel d'exécution très qualifié
24,6	29,4	31,5	33,6	25,5	31,4	31,1	32,2	4	Personnel d'exécution qualifié
21,1	27,9	33,7	33,0	33,9	31,4	30,8	35,8	5	Autres agents
								812/813	**Institutions de crédit**
–	40,6	–	49,9°	–	42,5	–	50,5	1	Personnel supérieur de direction
.	36,8	–	42,3	.	43,2	.	43,5	2	Cadres supérieurs
30,8	36,3	30,0°	37,5	36,5	35,6	40,0	41,3	3	Personnel de conception (cadres inférieurs)
25,5	28,3	30,7	32,3	28,3	26,0	32,2	30,9	4	Personnel d'exécution très qualifié
21,0	27,4	23,3	28,5	19,2	20,0	24,8	23,1	5	Personnel d'exécution qualifié
20,0	27,4	22,7	32,8	45,8	45,5	29,5	33,8	6	Autres agents
								82	**Assurances**
–	41,9	–	47,6°	–	41,3°	–	48,3	I	Dirigeants et cadres supérieurs de direction
.	38,7	–	43,8	–	42,6	.	45,2	II	Cadres intermédiaires
.	35,0	.	40,2	.	35,7	48,4	39,4	III	Agents d'encadrement et assimilés
30,3	31,5	38,1°	36,6	34,3	36,2	36,1	34,0	IV	Travailleurs très qualifiés
22,0	24,2	28,4	31,3	20,7	20,9	30,8	36,9	V	Travailleurs qualifiés
17,6	30,4	25,3	36,1	.	45,0°	26,8	42,5	VI	Autres travailleurs

TAB. 52A

Average age of full-time employees by branch of activity and qualifications: coefficient of variation
Âge moyen des salariés à temps complet selon la branche d'activité et la qualification: coefficient de variation

1974

Luxembourg		United Kingdom		Ireland		Danmark			
F	M	F	M	F	M	F	M		
								61	**Commerce de gros**
24,3	22,6	–	23,1	.	27,8	.	22,3	1 A	Personnel supérieur de direction
15,3	24,9	.	22,8	–	–	.	25,2	1 B	Personnel de direction et cadres supérieurs
42,8	31,2	29,2°	31,1	29,0°	28,9	24,5	26,2	2	Personnel d'exécution et d'encadrement
43,9	34,8	30,3	33,5	36,1	32,4	36,7	30,2	3	Personnel subalterne très qualifié
43,5	40,5	46,6	40,5	43,3	40,2	38,5	36,2	4	Personnel subalterne qualifié
49,1	47,3	36,4	48,1	50,3	45,5	43,6	36,2	5	Personnel subalterne non qualifié
								64/653-656	**Commerce de détail**
.	23,0	.	27,7	.	29,3	.	24,7	1 A	Personnel supérieur de direction
24,2	29,9	.	28,6	–	–	30,5	24,4	1 B	Cadres supérieurs
41,7	33,6	34,2	35,5	31,5	30,2	26,0	26,0	2	Personnel de conception (cadres inférieurs)
42,3	38,7	37,5	36,8	36,4	35,4	40,1	34,7	3	Personnel d'exécution très qualifié
47,5	45,4	47,1	45,4	49,8	44,5	45,1	43,3	4	Personnel d'exécution qualifié
50,8	57,6	45,3	50,3	50,6	50,6	47,4	45,4	5	Autres agents
								812/813	**Institutions de crédit**
.	22,4	–	22,7°	–	21,7	–	17,5	1	Personnel supérieur de direction
.	23,8	–	23,2	.	23,8	.	24,5	2	Cadres supérieurs
26,5	26,1	34,5°	25,3	23,1	27,1	26,4	25,6	3	Personnel de conception (cadres inférieurs)
29,3	28,1	31,5	33,6	27,9	22,8	30,9	30,2	4	Personnel d'exécution très qualifié
31,1	42,0	42,0	47,1	19,2	30,9	28,1	28,9	5	Personnel d'exécution qualifié
33,5	47,4	52,1	50,9	27,1	29,1	37,9	42,2	6	Autres agents
								82	**Assurances**
–	25,9	–	21,3°	–	22,7°	–	15,8	I	Dirigeants et cadres supérieurs de direction
.	27,9	–	20,7	–	24,5	.	20,5	II	Cadres intermédiaires
.	23,8	.	28,3	.	28,2	17,8	27,0	III	Agents d'encadrement et assimilés
35,1	40,6	35,4°	29,4	32,2	29,6	33,0	42,7	IV	Travailleurs très qualifiés
33,8	37,9	44,1	43,7	32,5	30,8	39,9	42,3	V	Travailleurs qualifiés
19,7	39,4	51,5	46,0	.	34,8°	44,9	43,9	VI	Autres travailleurs

TAB. 53

Full-time employees by branch of activity and length of service (%)

Salariés à temps complet selon la branche d'activité et l'ancienneté de service dans l'entreprise (%)

1974

	BR Deutschland		France		Italia		Nederland		Belgique België	
	$\frac{f}{F}$ 100	$\frac{m}{M}$ 100	$\frac{f}{F}$ 100	$\frac{m}{M}$ 100	$\frac{f}{F}$ 100	$\frac{m}{M}$ 100	$\frac{f}{F}$ 100	$\frac{m}{M}$ 100	$\frac{f}{F}$ 100	$\frac{m}{M}$ 100
61 Wholesale distribution										
< 2 years	34,9	26,7	32,7	28,0	35,6	27,1	51,4	28,6	37,0	30,4
2 – 4 years	30,5	23,9	27,9	24,1	28,2	25,1	29,3	24,2	27,5	24,2
5 – 9 years	19,1	20,2	18,2	20,2	19,6	20,6	11,7	19,6	18,5	19,2
10 – 19 years	11,3	19,8	12,7	17,3	13,1	20,2	4,8	17,1	11,7	16,9
⩾ 20 years	4,2	9,4	5,4	7,8	3,5	7,0	2,3	9,9	5,3	9,3
64/653-656 Retail distribution										
< 2 years	31,2	29,5	32,0	31,8	26,3	24,8	48,0	34,1	26,3	26,9
2 – 4 years	30,4	26,9	26,1	22,8	29,0	27,8	30,2	24,6	25,1	21,5
5 – 9 years	20,7	19,9	18,4	17,9	25,2	20,9	13,3	17,9	19,4	18,9
10 – 19 years	13,0	16,4	14,8	16,5	17,0	20,2	5,5	14,0	18,8	20,0
⩾ years	4,8	7,3	5,9	7,9	2,5	6,3	2,3	8,4	10,4	12,6
812/813 Credit institutions										
< 2 years	20,0	10,5	19,4	15,9	27,0	17,6	39,1	22,2	19,5	12,5
2 – 4 years	36,1	22,4	25,5	26,1	21,5	17,3	37,0	24,2	26,9	20,1
5 – 9 years	26,2	27,7	23,0	21,5	16,9	15,0	16,1	20,1	26,9	24,3
10 – 19 years	12,5	24,0	18,4	21,1	23,4	32,4	5,2	17,3	20,5	23,8
⩾ 20 years	5,2	15,4	12,7	14,5	11,2	17,6	2,6	16,1	6,2	19,4
82 Insurance										
< 2 years	22,7	16,3	25,2	21,0	20,0	15,6	39,0	19,1	21,5	14,1
2 – 4 years	31,7	22,1	23,3	20,6	25,5	25,7	30,4	20,4	28,2	17,8
5 – 9 years	23,5	22,7	21,5	21,8	26,5	26,0	14,6	20,5	22,9	18,7
10 – 19 years	15,7	22,5	18,5	20,8	21,5	22,5	8,9	21,6	17,7	27,0
⩾ 20 years	6,4	16,3	11,2	15,5	6,5	10,2	7,2	18,5	9,7	22,5

TAB. 54

Average length of service of full-time employees by branch of activity and qualifications

Ancienneté moyenne de service dans l'entreprise des travailleurs à temps complet selon la branche d'activité et la qualification

1974

	BR Deutschland		France		Italia		Nederland		Belgique België	
	F	M	F	M	F	M	F	M	F	M
61 Wholesale distribution										
1 A Top management personnel	15,0°	14,1	14,6	15,3	.	10,3	.	13,3	.	12,6
1 B Management personnel and senior executives	12,7°	11,9	12,5	9,7	11,8°	9,7	6,7°	9,9	.	9,4
2 Executives and management staff	10,1	10,2	10,8	8,1	10,6	9,4	4,7	8,6	8,1	8,2
3 Highly-skilled junior personnel	6,1	7,8	7,0	6,9	8,7	8,0	3,5	7,3	6,1	7,3
4 Skilled junior personnel	3,9	5,6	4,9	5,6	5,3	6,8	2,3	5,6	4,6	6,1
5 Unskilled junior personnel	3,5	4,2	3,4	3,8	3,0	5,3	2,1°	4,2	3,0°	4,2
64/653-656 Retail distribution										
1 A Top management personnel	.	15,0°	13,0	14,3	.	11,9	.	11,4	.	14,3°
1 B Management personnel and senior executives	.	11,5	13,9	11,0	8,6°	8,5	9,9°	9,9	13,8°	11,8
2 Executives and management staff	11,9	9,3	9,4	8,0	10,2	10,5	7,4	10,1	11,8	11,5
3 Highly-skilled junior personnel	7,6	6,7	8,4	7,3	9,5	8,3	4,8	6,2	7,2	8,3
4 Skilled junior personnel	4,5	4,6	5,6	5,3	6,1	6,9	2,4	4,6	8,1	7,8
5 Unskilled junior personnel	3,4	3,3	3,5	3,5	2,2	4,5	–	–	3,6	4,4
812/813 Credit institutions										
1 Directors, top management	–	18,3°	17,4°	18,4	.	16,4	.	15,6	–	21,5°
2 Senior executives	.	16,2	18,1	16,3	21,2	19,7	.	11,7	.	16,9
3 Executives (junior management)	11,3	12,6	15,9	12,1	18,2	14,9	.	12,9	11,9°	15,6
4 Highly-qualified clerical staff	7,7	9,9	10,2	7,3	6,7	6,0	8,5°	12,8	9,7	10,9
5 Qualified clerical staff	4,4	5,9	4,9	4,2	3,7	9,7	4,9	9,2	5,5	7,2
6 Other employees	2,8	6,1	2,1	2,2	5,4°	6,9	2,7	5,1	5,3°	6,9
82 Insurance										
I Managers and senior management executives	.	18,2	.	17,5	.	9,4°	.	16,7	.	17,2°
II Middle management executives	.	16,1	19,1	15,5	.	12,2	.	15,9	.	16,8
III Junior executives and personnel with equivalent qualification	12,2	12,1	17,9	13,3	14,8	11,6	7,5°	16,0	12,7°	16,3
IV Highly-skilled employees	7,3	8,7	8,9	7,4	9,1	6,5	11,3	12,7	13,7	13,2
V Skilled employees	4,5	5,9	5,5	5,1	5,9	7,0	5,9	8,8	8,2	9,6
VI Other employees	3,2°	.	3,2	4,1	.	6,0	2,6	4,3	4,8	6,2

TAB. 53

Full-time employees by branch of activity and length of service (%)

Salariés à temps complet selon la branche d'activité et l'ancienneté de service dans l'entreprise (%)

1974

Luxembourg		United Kingdom		Ireland		Danmark		
$\frac{f}{F}$ 100	$\frac{m}{M}$ 100	$\frac{f}{F}$ 100	$\frac{m}{M}$ 100	$\frac{f}{F}$ 100	$\frac{m}{M}$ 100	$\frac{f}{F}$ 100	$\frac{m}{M}$ 100	
								61 Commerce de gros
48,5	33,6	38,3	30,6	26,3	13,0	32,0	20,0	< 2 années
28,1	24,3	29,4	23,7	36,1	24,8	32,3	25,1	2 – 4 années
13,9	16,0	17,1	17,5	19,9	22,5	17,9	20,9	5 – 9 années
6,5	17,2	9,1	15,6	10,6	21,3	10,1	18,5	10 – 19 années
3,0	8,9	4,7	12,1	7,0	18,3	5,5	13,0	≥ 20 années
								64/653-656 Commerce de détail
40,6	40,8	57,6	31,2	27,3	16,0	35,2	28,7	< 2 années
32,6	27,7	27,7	22,7	31,2	19,8	33,1	26,3	2 – 4 années
15,1	15,4	18,2	16,6	21,6	21,1	18,4	17,7	5 – 9 années
8,9	10,7	10,5	14,8	11,4	20,8	8,2	16,3	10 – 19 années
2,8	5,4	4,7	13,9	7,1	20,9	3,9	8,9	≥ 20 années
								812/813 Institutions de crédit
35,6	22,9	36,2	20,9	31,0	15,6	14,3	6,7	< 2 années
37,2	28,9	28,3	18,2	37,0	22,0	36,6	20,4	2 – 4 années
19,9	20,8	23,1	20,7	20,9	19,8	30,8	25,9	5 – 9 années
5,9	14,9	8,9	22,0	7,2	22,2	14,2	24,2	10 – 19 années
1,5	12,4	3,2	18,2	3,9	20,4	3,8	22,8	≥ 20 années
								82 Assurances
25,1	16,8	35,3	18,6	28,9	17,3	17,7	9,6	< 2 années
35,6	24,3	29,3	20,1	31,7	23,1	31,7	18,7	2 – 4 années
22,5	20,8	15,7	18,3	17,4	13,3	19,4	17,8	5 – 9 années
12,0	22,6	10,4	20,1	8,7	22,5	16,7	24,0	10 – 19 années
.	15,5	8,4	21,9	13,2	23,8	13,6	29,4	≥ 20 années

TAB. 54

Average length of service of full-time employees by branch of activity and qualifications

Ancienneté moyenne de service dans l'entreprise des travailleurs à temps complet selon la branche d'activité et la qualification

1974

Luxembourg		United Kingdom		Ireland		Danmark		
F	M	F	M	F	M	F	M	
								61 Commerce de gros
15,2	17,2	.	.	.	17,0	.	19,0	1 A Personnel supérieur de direction
15,8	13,8	.	.	–	–	.	15,4	1 B Personnel de direction et cadres supérieurs
6,5	10,2	.	.	.	14,8	.	12,6	2 Personnel d'exécution et d'encadrement
5,0	7,8	.	.	12,3°	11,5	8,8	9,8	3 Personnel subalterne très qualifié
9,3	4,6	.	.	5,1	9,1	4,6	6,5	4 Personnel subalterne qualifié
2,0	3,0	.	.	5,3°	9,0	3,6	6,5	5 Personnel subalterne non qualifié
								64/653-656 Commerce de détail
.	11,6	.	.	.	16,9°	.	15,4	1 A Personnel supérieur de direction
12,0	7,1	.	.	–	–	.	14,1	1 B Cadres supérieurs
11,1	6,8	.	.	.	14,2	.	10,8	2 Personnel de conception (cadres inférieurs)
5,6	5,4	.	.	12,5°	13,0	4,8	7,3	3 Personnel d'exécution très qualifié
3,2	3,2	.	.	5,5	9,6	4,1	4,0	4 Personnel d'exécution qualifié
1,7	2,0	.	.	5,2°	9,0°	2,5	.	5 Autres agents
								812/813 Institutions de crédit
–	10,8	.	.	–	.	–	20,5	1 Personnel supérieur de direction
.	11,5	.	.	.	22,9	.	22,4	2 Cadres supérieurs
9,2	13,7	.	.	.	16,2	20,0	21,1	3 Personnel de conception (cadres inférieurs)
4,8	6,9	.	.	10,4	9,0	12,2	11,9	4 Personnel d'exécution très qualifié
3,4	6,3	.	.	2,0	2,4	5,7	5,3	5 Personnel d'exécution qualifié
2,8	3,9	.	.	.	11,1°	4,3	7,6	6 Autres agents
								82 Assurances
–	17,8	.	.	–	.	–	22,4	I Dirigeants et cadres supérieurs de direction
.	14,7	.	.	–	20,6°	.	20,8	II Cadres intermédiaires
.	12,3	.	.	.	15,2°	24,2	16,5	III Agents d'encadrement et assimilés
8,9	6,8	.	.	15,5	16,6	11,6	.	IV Travailleurs très qualifiés
4,8	5,0	.	.	3,2°	.	5,8	.	V Travailleurs qualifiés
2,9	5,9	.	.	.	.	.	.	VI Autres travailleurs

TAB. 54A

Average length of service of full-time employees by branch of activity and qualifications: coefficient of variation

Ancienneté moyenne de service dans l'entreprise des travailleurs à temps complet selon la branche d'activité et la qualification: coefficient de variation

1974

	BR Deutschland		France		Italia		Nederland		Belgique België	
	F	M	F	M	F	M	F	M	F	M
61 Wholesale distribution										
1 A Top management personnel	64,0°	75,2	.	93,4°	.	87,1	.	83,0	.	79,5
1 B Management personnel and senior executives	88,7°	83,0	.	98,7°	72,3°	91,8	127,8°	96,9	.	95,2
2 Executives and management staff	97,4	93,1	.	113,3°	84,7	90,7	140,8	104,5	106,1	102,2
3 Highly-skilled junior personnel	113,7	103,0	123,8°	.	92,4	100,4	159,6	112,8	118,8	110,8
4 Skilled junior personnel	122,9	121,0	121,9	152,9°	103,4	101,1	151,6	127,9	131,0	123,0
5 Unskilled junior personnel	123,9	142,8	139,5	152,9	140,8	117,1	168,9°	148,8	196,3°	151,9
64/653-656 Retail distribution										
1 A Top management personnel	.	70,9°	.	98,2°	.	72,7	.	98,5	.	75,1°
1 B Management personnel and senior executives	.	73,1	.	.	91,4°	89,8	103,7°	94,6	95,0°	83,2
2 Executives and management staff	83,8	92,2	109,7	115,1°	81,0	82,9	114,5	96,5	79,1	87,6
3 Highly-skilled junior personnel	103,4	109,5	126,6	138,3°	79,6	90,9	129,2	123,5	106,7	110,7
4 Skilled junior personnel	115,1	131,4	143,0	194,7°	84,1	94,8	157,3	156,0	104,4	110,3
5 Unskilled junior personnel	124,3	158,2	179,2	211,3°	157,1	125,2	–	–	141,7	142,9
812/813 Credit institutions										
1 Directors, top management	–	63,9°	68,5°	65,6	.	68,0	.	65,6	.	57,3°
2 Senior executives	.	66,9	60,8	65,6	43,7	43,6	.	89,7	.	66,2
3 Executives (junior management)	77,5	76,4	60,6	72,7	50,0	53,1	.	90,3	69,8°	65,4
4 Highly-qualified clerical staff	87,8	88,5	74,8	79,2	108,6	110,4	119,3°	88,7	71,0	82,8
5 Qualified clerical staff	94,0	97,3	91,9	96,5	125,5	87,8	127,3	102,5	105,7	122,3
6 Other employees	129,0	97,6	160,9	156,5	125,5°	106,6	130,5	137,7	106,0°	99,9
82 Insurance										
I Managers and senior management executives	.	62,4	.	66,5	.	113,4°	.	60,4	.	60,2°
II Middle management executives	.	72,8	59,5	74,5	.	90,9	.	73,9	.	59,7
III Junior executives and personnel with equivalent qualification	78,4	84,3	60,3	82,9	73,6	80,2	126,8°	72,9	84,0°	66,2
IV Highly-skilled employees	96,2	104,6	92,8	102,9	92,5	103,3	92,7	83,9	66,3	75,8
V Skilled employees	109,4	110,8	123,0	133,3	93,0	95,7	124,8	105,6	90,9	96,7
VI Other employees	142,1°	.	143,7	145,7	.	106,5	148,1	137,1	111,7	120,8

TAB. 55

Full-time employees by branch of activity and type of remuneration (%)

Salariés à temps complet selon la branche d'activité et le type de rémunération (%)

1974

	BR Deutschland		France		Italia		Nederland		Belgique België	
	$\frac{f}{F}100$	$\frac{m}{M}100$	$\frac{f}{F}100$	$\frac{m}{M}100$	$\frac{f}{F}100$	$\frac{m}{M}100$	$\frac{f}{F}100$	$\frac{m}{M}100$	$\frac{f}{F}100$	$\frac{m}{M}100$
61 Wholesale distribution	100,0	100,0	100,0	100,0	100,0	100,0	100,0	100,0	100,0	100,0
Paid on commission	1,4	9,3	1,9	11,9	1,5	5,3	–	–	5,4	11,8
Not paid on commission	98,5	90,6	97,9	87,8	98,5	94,7	100,0	100,0	94,6	88,2
64 Retail distribution	100,0	100,0	100,0	100,0	100,0	100,0	100,0	100,0	100,0	100,0
Paid on commission	1,0	4,1	6,9	13,4	0,4	2,1	–	–	5,9	6,7
Not paid on commission	98,9	95,8	92,2	85,6	99,6	97,9	100,0	100,0	94,1	93,3
812/813 Credit institutions	100,0	100,0	100,0	100,0	100,0	100,0	100,0	100,0	100,0	100,0
Paid on commission	0,3	0,9	1,7	2,4	0,2	0,2	–	–	1,6	4,9
Not paid on commission	99,6	99,0	98,3	97,5	99,8	99,8	100,0	100,0	98,4	95,1
82 Insurance	100,0	100,0	100,0	100,0	100,0	100,0	100,0	100,0	100,0	100,0
Paid on commission	–	–	–	–	–	–	–	–	–	–
Not paid on commission	99,1	98,9	99,7	99,6	100,0	100,0	100,0	100,0	100,0	100,0

Average length of service of full-time employees by branch of activity and qualifications: coefficient of variation

Ancienneté moyenne de service dans l'entreprise des travailleurs à temps complet selon la branche d'activité et la qualification: coefficient de variation
1974

Luxembourg		United Kingdom		Ireland		Danmark			
F	M	F	M	F	M	F	M		
90,4	65,2	.	.	.	73,3	.	63,7	**61**	**Commerce de gros**
								1 A	Personnel supérieur de direction
55,4	73,1	.	.	–	–	.	80,0	1 B	Personnel de direction et cadres supérieurs
130,3	91,5	.	.	.	80,0	.	84,2	2	Personnel d'exécution et d'encadrement
126,3	105,8	.	.	86,7°	86,1	108,1	96,7	3	Personnel subalterne très qualifié
155,4	126,8	.	.	127,6	103,6	130,2	120,3	4	Personnel subalterne qualifié
190,9	165,0	.	.	130,9°	109,3	140,5	120,3	5	Personnel subalterne non qualifié
	81,2	.	.	.	74,3°	.	69,7	**64/653-656**	**Commerce de détail**
								1 A	Personnel supérieur de direction
99,3	90,3	.	.	–	–	.	72,1	1 B	Cadres supérieurs
108,1	119,0	.	.	.	82,7	.	89,2	2	Personnel de conception (cadres inférieurs)
110,4	135,5	.	.	89,8°	81,8	128,1	112,5	3	Personnel d'exécution très qualifié
122,5	146,2	.	.	135,1	106,5	134,1	139,7	4	Personnel d'exécution qualifié
130,2	220,7	.	.	133,0°	122,4°	130,4	.	5	Autres agents
–	101,0	.	.	–	.	–	58,8	**812/813**	**Institutions de crédit**
								1	Personnel supérieur de direction
.	89,5	.	.	.	58,1	.	61,4	2	Cadres supérieurs
92,3	72,6	.	.	.	64,6	60,7	57,3	3	Personnel de conception (cadres inférieurs)
109,6	98,8	.	.	65,3	59,4	71,6	77,5	4	Personnel d'exécution très qualifié
110,0	125,9	.	.	69,7	69,6	76,0	69,7	5	Personnel d'exécution qualifié
105,1	115,5	.	.	.	98,0°	97,0	95,8	6	Autres agents
–	69,5	.	.	–	.	–	47,8	**82**	**Assurances**
								I	Dirigeants et cadres supérieurs de direction
.	77,3	.	.	–	57,9°	.	66,1	II	Cadres intermédiaires
.	69,7	.	.	.	72,5°	40,5	72,0	III	Agents d'encadrement et assimilés
102,4	132,8	.	.	65,4	60,9	92,1	.	IV	Travailleurs très qualifiés
91,9	97,6	.	.	156,9°	.	122,6	.	V	Travailleurs qualifiés
101,4	141,7	.	.	.	.	.	.	VI	Autres travailleurs

TAB. 55

Full-time employees by branch of activity and type of remuneration (%)

Salariés à temps complet selon la branche d'activité et le type de rémunération (%)
1974

Luxembourg		United Kingdom		Ireland		Danmark		
$\frac{f}{F}\cdot100$	$\frac{m}{M}\cdot100$	$\frac{f}{F}\cdot100$	$\frac{m}{M}\cdot100$	$\frac{f}{F}\cdot100$	$\frac{m}{M}\cdot100$	$\frac{f}{F}\cdot100$	$\frac{m}{M}\cdot100$	
100,0	100,0	100,0	100,0	100,0	100,0	100,0	100,0	**61 Commerce de gros**
17,7	22,9	.	6,0	3,1	9,9	.	6,9	Rémunéré à la commission
82,3	77,1	98,9	94,0	96,9	90,1	99,5	92,2	Non rémunéré à la commission
100,0	100,0	100,0	100,0	100,0	100,0	100,0	100,0	**64/653-656 Commerce de détail**
16,9	13,8	1,0	2,6	24,2	25,8	3,3	8,3	Rémunéré à la commission
83,1	86,2	99,0	97,4	78,8	74,2	96,0	90,1	Non rémunéré à la commission
100,0	100,0	100,0	100,0	100,0	100,0	100,0	100,0	**812/813 Institutions de crédit**
2,9	2,7	.	.	–	–	.	.	Rémunéré à la commission
97,1	97,3	99,9	99,6	100,0	100,0	99,8	99,9	Non rémunéré à la commission
100,0	100,0	100,0	100,0	100,0	100,0	100,0	100,0	**82 Assurances**
–	–	–	–	–	–	–	–	Rémunéré à la commission
100,0	100,0	100,0	100,0	100,0	100,0	99,4	99,6	Non rémunéré à la commission

TAB. 56

Average weekly hours of work of full-time employees by branch of activity and qualifications

Horaire de travail hebdomadaire moyen des travailleurs à temps complet selon la branche d'activité et la qualification 1974

	BR Deutschland		France		Italia		Nederland		Belgique België	
	F	M	F	M	F	M	F	M	F	M
61 Wholesale distribution										
1 A Top management personnel	40,1	40,4	43,2	43,3	40,2	39,9	40,6	40,9	40,2	40,1
1 B Management personnel and senior executives	40,3	40,3	41,7	42,3	40,0	40,0	40,2	40,5	40,2	40,0
2 Executives and management staff	40,4	40,4	41,5	42,8	40,0	40,0	40,4	40,6	40,1	40,0
3 Highly-skilled junior personnel	40,2	40,5	41,4	44,0	40,0	40,0	40,4	40,9	40,3	40,4
4 Skilled junior personnel	40,3	40,7	41,8	44,6	40,1	40,2	40,6	41,2	40,3	40,5
5 Unskilled junior personnel	40,4	40,7	42,1	44,3	40,6	40,3	41,1	41,1	40,6	40,7
64/653-656 Retail distribution										
1 A Top management personnel	41,1	41,1	42,6	43,4	39,7	40,0	41,1	41,9	40,5	40,1
1 B Management personnel and senior executives	40,2	40,5	41,3	42,6	40,0	40,0	40,9	40,9	40,7	40,6
2 Executives and management staff	40,3	40,3	41,9	43,7	40,1	40,0	40,6	41,1	40,2	40,2
3 Highly-skilled junior personnel	40,2	40,6	41,3	43,6	40,1	40,3	41,1	41,3	40,8	40,5
4 Skilled junior personnel	40,2	40,6	41,4	44,3	40,1	40,3	41,2	41,3	40,3	40,4
5 Unskilled junior personnel	40,3	40,4	41,4	42,8	40,4	40,5	–	–	40,4	40,4
812/813 Credit institutions										
1 Directors, top management	–	40,0	40,5	40,1	39,4	38,3	.	39,9	–	39,4
2 Senior executives	40,0	40,0	40,1	40,0	38,4	38,8	38,9	39,8	.	39,3
3 Executives (junior management)	40,0	40,0	40,0	40,0	38,5	38,5	39,7	40,0	38,8	39,1
4 Highly-qualified clerical staff	40,0	40,0	40,0	40,0	38,5	38,5	39,6	40,0	38,9	38,9
5 Qualified clerical staff	40,0	40,1	40,0	40,1	38,7	38,6	40,4	40,3	39,2	39,0
6 Other employees	40,0	40,1	40,0	40,0	39,3	39,1	40,0	40,0	38,8	38,8
82 Insurance										
I Managers and senior management executives	.	40,0	.	40,1	.	38,5	.	39,6	.	39,6
II Middle management executives	39,1	40,0	40,1	40,1	39,0	38,5	39,9	39,8	39,1	39,4
III Junior executives and personnel with equivalent qualification	40,0	40,0	40,1	40,1	38,2	38,1	39,9	39,9	39,3	39,4
IV Highly-skilled employees	40,0	40,0	40,1	40,1	38,2	38,1	39,8	39,7	39,3	39,4
V Skilled employees	40,0	40,0	40,2	40,1	38,3	38,3	39,7	39,7	39,2	39,3
VI Other employees	40,0	40,0	40,3	40,1	39,0	39,4	39,5	39,7	39,4	39,4

TAB. 56A

Average weekly hours of work of full-time employees by branch of activity and qualifications: coefficient of variation

Horaire de travail hebdomadaire moyen des travailleurs à temps complet selon la branche d'activité et la qualification: coefficient de variation 1974

	BR Deutschland		France		Italia		Nederland		Belgique België	
	F	M	F	M	F	M	F	M	F	M
61 Wholesale distribution										
1 A Top management personnel	9,7	4,9	8,4	8,3	3,6	3,0	3,0	4,6	1,0	2,8
1 B Management personnel and senior executives	5,0	2,6	6,4	7,2	1,1	2,5	3,4	3,4	2,6	2,7
2 Executives and management staff	2,9	3,0	5,5	7,3	2,0	3,1	3,1	3,2	2,8	3,1
3 Highly-skilled junior personnel	2,2	3,4	5,0	7,8	2,7	3,2	3,2	3,7	2,8	2,1
4 Skilled junior personnel	2,4	4,0	5,2	7,6	3,5	3,6	2,9	3,4	2,8	2,3
5 Unskilled junior personnel	2,9	3,6	6,0	7,4	5,4	3,8	3,5	3,1	2,7	2,2
64/653/656 Retail distribution										
1 A Top management personnel	7,8	5,6	8,2	9,4	2,9	2,2	4,6	5,4	1,5	1,5
1 B Management personnel and senior executives	11,6	4,2	6,3	7,9	3,6	2,3	3,1	3,7	5,7	5,4
2 Executives and management staff	2,9	3,1	7,2	9,1	2,5	2,2	2,8	3,0	1,6	1,9
3 Highly-skilled junior personnel	2,5	3,8	5,9	8,1	2,9	3,8	3,1	2,8	4,9	2,5
4 Skilled junior personnel	2,4	3,8	6,0	8,9	2,3	3,2	3,2	2,9	1,7	1,7
5 Unskilled junior personnel	2,7	3,4	5,9	7,7	3,6	4,4	–	–	1,9	1,5
812/813 Credit institutions										
1 Directors, top management	–	1,4	4,0	2,2	2,0	2,1	.	1,9	–	3,0
2 Senior executives	0,0	0,5	1,2	1,1	3,8	4,7	3,9	2,0	.	2,6
3 Executives (junior management)	0,2	0,8	0,6	1,1	0,7	0,5	1,8	1,1	2,9	2,8
4 Highly-qualified clerical staff	0,6	1,3	0,8	1,0	0,9	0,7	2,8	1,4	2,9	3,1
5 Qualified clerical staff	0,9	1,3	0,9	1,4	1,8	1,1	2,1	1,7	2,9	3,1
6 Other employees	0,7	2,1	1,2	1,5	3,0	3,7	1,3	0,9	4,0	3,8
82 Insurance										
I Managers and senior management executives	.	0,2	.	1,2	.	3,4	.	3,7	.	3,2
II Middle management executives	6,1	0,5	1,4	2,1	2,7	3,1	1,5	1,6	3,6	2,7
III Junior executives and personnel with equivalent qualification	0,2	0,2	1,8	1,5	2,8	1,8	1,3	1,1	2,5	2,2
IV Highly-skilled employees	0,5	0,3	1,3	1,5	2,5	2,2	1,3	1,5	2,9	2,3
V Skilled employees	0,3	0,3	1,8	1,9	2,5	2,6	1,5	1,7	3,1	2,3
VI Other employees	1,1	0,5	2,4	1,4	3,2	4,0	2,2	1,5	2,4	2,3

TAB. 56

Average weekly hours of work of full-time employees by branch of activity and qualifications

Horaire de travail hebdomadaire moyen des travailleurs à temps complet selon la branche d'activité et la qualification

1974

Luxembourg		United Kingdom		Ireland		Danmark			
F	M	F	M	F	M	F	M		
40,5	41,3	–	39,5	.	39,5	.	40,7	**61**	**Commerce de gros**
40,0	40,1	.	38,0	–	–	.	40,1	1 A	Personnel supérieur de direction
40,1	40,3	37,2	38,4	38,6	39,1	39,6	39,9	1 B	Personnel de direction et cadres supérieurs
40,3	41,2	36,9	38,9	38,4	39,1	39,4	40,1	2	Personnel d'exécution et d'encadrement
40,2	42,1	37,0	39,9	38,3	40,2	39,7	40,7	3	Personnel subalterne très qualifié
41,5	42,5	38,1	40,0	39,8	40,5	40,2	41,3	4	Personnel subalterne qualifié
								5	Personnel subalterne non qualifié
.	40,9	.	40,4	.	41,1	.	43,6	**64/653-656**	**Commerce de détail**
40,7	40,7	.	38,7	–	–	40,0	40,9	1 A	Personnel supérieur de direction
40,5	41,0	38,6	39,7	38,9	40,2	40,3	41,2	1 B	Cadres supérieurs
40,4	41,5	38,4	39,6	39,2	39,8	40,4	41,5	2	Personnel de conception (cadres inférieurs)
40,6	43,2	38,3	39,8	39,1	40,2	41,0	41,5	3	Personnel d'exécution très qualifié
41,2	42,7	38,7	39,6	39,2	40,0	40,8	41,3	4	Personnel d'exécution qualifié
								5	Autres agents
–	40,0	–	.	–	36,7	–	37,7	**812/813**	**Institutions de crédit**
.	40,0	–	35,2	.	36,0	.	39,3	1	Personnel supérieur de direction
40,0	40,0	35,8	35,4	35,8	36,1	38,6	38,9	2	Cadres supérieurs
40,0	40,0	35,2	35,3	36,0	36,3	39,1	39,3	3	Personnel de conception (cadres inférieurs)
40,0	40,1	35,3	35,3	36,0	36,1	39,3	39,3	4	Personnel d'exécution très qualifié
40,0	40,0	35,5	36,1	39,2	39,7	38,8	39,0	5	Personnel d'exécution qualifié
								6	Autres agents
–	40,0	–	35,8	–	35,6	–	37,9	**82**	**Assurances**
.	40,0	–	35,0	–	35,6	.	37,4	I	Dirigeants et cadres supérieurs de direction
.	40,0	.	34,8	.	34,9	37,7	37,6	II	Cadres intermédiaires
40,0	40,0	34,7	35,0	34,6	34,4	37,4	37,5	III	Agents d'encadrement et assimilés
40,0	40,0	34,9	35,1	34,7	35,9	37,6	38,3	IV	Travailleurs très qualifiés
39,9	40,0	35,2	35,9	.	37,4	37,5	38,5	V	Travailleurs qualifiés
								VI	Autres travailleurs

Average weekly hours of work of full-time employees by branch of activity and qualifications: coefficient of variation

Horaire de travail hebdomadaire moyen des travailleurs à temps complet selon la branche d'activité et la qualification: coefficient de variation

1974

Luxembourg		United Kingdom		Ireland		Danmark			
F	M	F	M	F	M	F	M		
3,6	12,3	–	14,1	.	10,5	.	5,8	**61**	**Commerce de gros**
0,0	2,7	.	7,7	–	–	.	5,6	1 A	Personnel supérieur de direction
2,8	3,0	5,7	6,8	5,6	8,3	2,7	4,8	1 B	Personnel de direction et cadres supérieurs
2,9	5,3	5,7	8,5	4,5	8,2	4,7	4,1	2	Personnel d'exécution et d'encadrement
2,1	6,4	6,1	6,3	5,8	7,7	4,2	4,3	3	Personnel subalterne très qualifié
4,6	5,2	6,8	6,6	5,8	7,9	4,7	3,5	4	Personnel subalterne qualifié
								5	Personnel subalterne non qualifié
.	6,0	.	14,0	.	11,9	.	12,0	**64/653-656**	**Commerce de détail**
5,0	4,5	.	6,5	–	–	0,0	5,3	1 A	Personnel supérieur de direction
3,9	5,0	5,1	6,3	5,8	11,1	5,5	4,8	1 B	Cadres supérieurs
3,1	5,5	5,5	5,3	5,9	6,8	4,4	5,1	2	Personnel de conception (cadres inférieurs)
3,7	9,7	5,8	5,1	5,8	7,6	3,6	4,4	3	Personnel d'exécution très qualifié
4,7	9,6	6,8	4,3	5,6	5,8	3,4	4,1	4	Personnel d'exécution qualifié
								5	Autres agents
–	0,3	–	.	–	8,4	–	8,1	**812/813**	**Institutions de crédit**
.	0,0	–	2,5	.	4,3	.	3,8	1	Personnel supérieur de direction
0,0	0,2	4,6	3,5	2,7	2,7	4,9	4,6	2	Cadres supérieurs
0,2	0,2	2,3	3,0	2,0	2,9	5,0	3,8	3	Personnel de conception (cadres inférieurs)
0,5	3,4	2,4	3,3	3,0	2,6	4,3	4,1	4	Personnel d'exécution très qualifié
0,2	1,0	2,9	4,2	5,2	4,5	4,7	4,2	5	Personnel d'exécution qualifié
								6	Autres agents
–	0,0	–	7,4	–	6,7	–	4,1	**82**	**Assurances**
.	0,0	–	3,3	–	6,6	.	4,3	I	Dirigeants et cadres supérieurs de direction
.	0,5	.	3,1	.	5,2	3,2	3,0	II	Cadres intermédiaires
0,0	0,6	2,7	3,2	3,8	3,7	2,8	2,9	III	Agents d'encadrement et assimilés
0,4	0,0	2,7	3,8	4,6	7,1	4,0	4,5	IV	Travailleurs très qualifiés
0,9	0,0	4,0	6,8	.	7,6	7,3	4,6	V	Travailleurs qualifiés
								VI	Autres travailleurs

TAB. 57
Full-time female employees by branch of activity, qualifications and region (%)

Salariées à temps complet selon la branche d'activité, la qualification et par région (%)

1974

	1A/1/I		1B/2/II		2/3/III		3/4/IV		4/5/V		5/6/VI		TOTAL	
	$\frac{f}{F}$ 100	$\frac{f}{f+m}$ 100	$\frac{f}{F}$ 100	$\frac{f}{f+m}$ 100	$\frac{f}{F}$ 100	$\frac{f}{f+m}$ 100	$\frac{f}{F}$ 100	$\frac{f}{f+m}$ 100	$\frac{f}{F}$ 100	$\frac{f}{f+m}$ 100	$\frac{f}{F}$ 100	$\frac{f}{f+m}$ 100	$\frac{f}{F}$ 100	$\frac{f}{f+m}$ 100
BR DEUTSCHLAND														
Schleswig-Holstein														
Wholesale distribution	·	·	·	·	4,5	8,0	47,7	24,4	31,8	29,8	15,9	24,1	100,0	22,8
Retail distribution	·	·	·	·	3,0	21,4	34,3	41,0	52,5	73,2	10,1	66,7	100,0	52,9
Credit institutions	–	–	–	–	7,7	18,8	38,5	46,9	41,0	66,7	12,8	50,0	100,0	46,4
Insurance	–	–	·	·	·	·	20,0	33,3	40,0	66,7	20,0	100,0	100,0	55,6
Hamburg														
Wholesale distribution	0,9	10,0	·	·	6,3	12,3	43,8	31,0	32,1	39,1	16,1	31,0	100,0	28,9
Retail distribution	·	·	·	·	7,3	23,5	30,3	36,3	42,2	64,8	19,3	61,8	100,0	46,6
Credit institutions	–	–	–	–	8,2	17,2	60,6	60,7	19,7	60,0	11,5	58,3	100,0	46,9
Insurance	·	–	·	–	9,4	23,3	53,8	52,3	24,5	68,4	12,3	81,3	100,0	48,6
Berlin (West)														
Wholesale distribution	·	·	·	·	2,9	11,1	35,3	20,7	47,6	39,0	11,8	57,1	100,0	28,8
Retail distribution	·	·	·	·	2,7	28,6	17,8	31,7	65,1	69,3	15,1	66,7	100,0	54,3
Credit institutions	–	–	–	–	·	·	63,0	56,9	34,8	72,7	·	·	100,0	52,3
Insurance	–	–	–	–	·	·	66,7	60,0	22,2	66,7	·	·	100,0	56,3
Bremen														
Wholesale distribution	·	·	·	·	7,1	11,8	39,3	28,9	35,7	27,8	14,3	18,2	100,0	23,7
Retail distribution	·	·	·	·	3,8	14,3	34,6	42,9	53,8	70,0	3,8	33,3	100,0	49,1
Credit institutions	–	–	–	–	5,3	12,5	57,9	64,7	21,1	66,7	10,5	66,7	100,0	54,3
Insurance	–	·	–	–	–	–	100,0	100,0	0,0	0,0	·	·	100,0	33,3
Niedersachsen														
Wholesale distribution	–	–	·	·	1,8	5,3	24,6	14,6	53,5	23,5	20,2	31,1	100,0	20,0
Retail distribution	–	–	·	·	2,8	23,1	18,7	34,8	70,1	70,4	8,4	66,7	100,0	55,7
Credit institutions	–	·	·	·	3,6	11,1	28,3	36,4	44,9	68,9	23,2	69,6	100,0	47,1
Insurance	·	·	–	–	5,0	13,3	52,5	53,8	32,5	68,4	10,0	80,0	100,0	49,4
Nordrhein-Westfalen														
Wholesale distribution	0,2	6,3	0,9	10,3	4,8	8,8	34,8	21,0	37,1	34,5	21,9	36,7	100,0	25,0
Retail distribution	·	·	0,3	16,7	3,8	28,0	21,2	41,5	61,6	76,6	13,1	63,9	100,0	59,6
Credit institutions	–	·	–	–	4,4	13,4	49,0	51,5	38,5	70,2	7,9	77,1	100,0	50,6
Insurance	·	·	–	–	4,8	13,3	53,3	51,2	33,3	71,4	7,3	70,6	100,0	48,0

TAB. 57 (continued) (suite)

1974

	1A/1/I $\frac{f}{F}\cdot100$	1A/1/I $\frac{f}{f+m}\cdot100$	1B/2/II $\frac{f}{F}\cdot100$	1B/2/II $\frac{f}{f+m}\cdot100$	2/3/III $\frac{f}{F}\cdot100$	2/3/III $\frac{f}{f+m}\cdot100$	3/4/IV $\frac{f}{F}\cdot100$	3/4/IV $\frac{f}{f+m}\cdot100$	4/5/V $\frac{f}{F}\cdot100$	4/5/V $\frac{f}{f+m}\cdot100$	5/6/VI $\frac{f}{F}\cdot100$	5/6/VI $\frac{f}{f+m}\cdot100$	TOTAL $\frac{f}{F}\cdot100$	TOTAL $\frac{f}{f+m}\cdot100$
Hessen														
Commerce de gros / Wholesale distribution	·		0,6	5,6	4,7	8,6	45,0	25,7	33,3	35,5	15,8	37,0	100,0	26,2
Commerce de détail / Retail distribution	·		0,3	20,0	3,7	21,3	25,3	45,6	59,5	72,1	11,5	63,5	100,0	57,1
Institutions de crédit / Credit institutions	—	—	·	·	7,6	16,4	46,8	49,3	25,5	63,9	19,6	62,1	100,0	45,3
Assurances / Insurance	—	—	·	·	6,3	23,5	61,9	66,1	23,8	65,2	7,9	71,4	100,0	55,3
Rheinland-Pfalz														
Commerce de gros / Wholesale distribution	·		·	·	4,7	10,0	25,9	19,3	42,3	37,1	24,7	50,0	100,0	28,3
Commerce de détail / Retail distribution	·		·	·	3,9	30,8	28,4	43,9	57,8	81,9	9,8	71,4	100,0	60,7
Institutions de crédit / Credit institutions	—	—	—	—	3,8	13,0	24,4	35,8	47,4	72,5	23,1	85,7	100,0	52,0
Assurances / Insurance	—	—	·	·	·	·	58,3	63,6	25,0	60,0	8,3	100,0	100,0	63,2
Baden-Württemberg														
Commerce de gros / Wholesale distribution	·		·	·	2,7	6,7	37,3	21,5	45,0	41,6	15,0	48,5	100,0	27,6
Commerce de détail / Retail distribution	·		·	·	3,2	21,1	26,5	39,0	56,8	80,2	13,2	64,5	100,0	56,2
Institutions de crédit / Credit institutions	—	—	—	—	5,0	13,4	34,4	44,7	37,1	70,7	23,5	77,6	100,0	50,3
Assurances / Insurance	—	—	·	·	1,6	6,3	43,5	50,9	41,9	76,5	12,9	72,7	100,0	52,5
Bayern														
Commerce de gros / Wholesale distribution	—	—	·	·	2,7	9,1	30,7	19,3	47,1	37,8	19,1	47,1	100,0	27,8
Commerce de détail / Retail distribution	—	—	·	·	2,4	20,8	26,6	36,5	60,5	74,0	10,5	68,8	100,0	54,9
Institutions de crédit / Credit institutions	—	—	·	·	4,8	14,6	30,4	44,4	36,0	66,7	28,8	74,2	100,0	50,3
Assurances / Insurance	—	—	·	·	8,2	19,6	47,0	51,2	33,6	63,4	10,4	73,7	100,0	47,5
Saarland														
Commerce de gros / Wholesale distribution	—	—	·	·	5,0	9,1	35,0	18,9	45,0	34,6	10,0	25,0	100,0	23,5
Commerce de détail / Retail distribution	—	—	·	·	2,8	25,0	22,2	36,4	69,4	78,1	5,6	66,7	100,0	58,1
Institutions de crédit / Credit institutions	—	—	·	·	7,4	15,4	29,6	57,1	29,6	80,0	37,0	83,3	100,0	52,9
Assurances / Insurance	—	—	—	—	·	·	50,0	50,0	25,0	50,0	25,0	100,0	100,0	40,0

TAB. 57
(continued)
(suite)

1974

FRANCE

	1A/1/I $\frac{f}{F}100$	1A/1/I $\frac{f}{f+m}100$	1B/2/II $\frac{f}{F}100$	1B/2/II $\frac{f}{f+m}100$	2/3/III $\frac{f}{F}100$	2/3/III $\frac{f}{f+m}100$	3/4/IV $\frac{f}{F}100$	3/4/IV $\frac{f}{f+m}100$	4/5/V $\frac{f}{F}100$	4/5/V $\frac{f}{f+m}100$	5/6/VI $\frac{f}{F}100$	5/6/VI $\frac{f}{f+m}100$	TOTAL $\frac{f}{F}100$	TOTAL $\frac{f}{f+m}100$
Île-de-France / Commerce de gros (Wholesale distribution)	0,0	5,1	4,4	11,6	8,0	13,5	21,1	40,9	46,2	43,7	19,8	41,2	100,0	32,1
Commerce de détail (Retail distribution)	0,3	12,0	3,8	34,7	10,2	43,6	19,2	68,6	39,9	65,7	26,4	67,3	100,0	60,6
Institutions de crédit (Credit institutions)	0,2	3,5	3,2	16,8	31,1	48,4	15,5	64,4	31,1	64,1	19,0	61,2	100,0	52,0
Assurances (Insurance)	·		2,5	19,6	12,1	44,3	33,5	70,0	39,4	75,3	12,7	55,6	100,0	60,7
Bassin parisien / Commerce de gros (Wholesale distribution)	1,0	8,3	1,4	7,7	4,3	11,3	11,1	18,9	51,7	32,7	30,4	34,8	100,0	26,8
Commerce de détail (Retail distribution)	0,7	15,4	1,4	15,4	6,0	27,9	9,2	44,8	50,7	56,7	31,7	66,7	100,0	51,8
Institutions de crédit (Credit institutions)	·		1,1	5,9	9,7	26,5	19,4	41,9	45,2	56,8	23,7	55,0	100,0	44,1
Assurances (Insurance)	−	−	2,9	12,5	8,8	33,3	20,6	63,6	50,0	81,0	17,6	66,7	100,0	57,6
Nord / Commerce de gros (Wholesale distribution)	1,2	10,0	2,5	11,1	3,7	8,8	13,6	21,2	45,7	28,0	34,6	34,6	100,0	24,8
Commerce de détail (Retail distribution)	0,5	16,7	1,1	20,0	10,8	38,5	9,1	43,6	38,2	54,6	40,3	67,6	100,0	53,4
Institutions de crédit (Credit institutions)	−	−	3,2	12,5	25,8	40,0	14,5	47,4	40,3	49,0	16,1	43,5	100,0	40,8
Assurances (Insurance)	−	−					20,0	50,0	50,0	83,3	30,0	60,0	100,0	50,0
Est / Commerce de gros (Wholesale distribution)	1,0	7,1	1,9	7,7	2,9	7,7	14,3	25,0	49,5	33,3	30,5	40,5	100,0	28,2
Commerce de détail (Retail distribution)	0,4	11,1	1,2	18,8	6,0	27,3	8,9	39,3	40,3	55,9	42,7	73,6	100,0	53,9
Institutions de crédit (Credit institutions)	·		1,5	6,7	15,4	29,4	10,8	36,8	36,9	52,2	33,8	57,9	100,0	41,7
Assurances (Insurance)	−	−			9,1	50,0	18,2	66,7	36,4	80,0	36,4	80,0	100,0	61,1
Ouest / Commerce de gros (Wholesale distribution)	0,6	5,6	1,3	8,3	3,8	10,3	10,8	20,2	47,8	29,2	35,7	37,6	100,0	26,6
Commerce de détail (Retail distribution)	0,4	12,5	1,3	21,4	7,1	32,0	9,3	41,2	44,7	62,3	37,2	69,4	100,0	55,7
Institutions de crédit (Credit institutions)	−	−	1,6	8,3	9,8	20,7	18,0	34,4	44,3	43,5	26,2	48,5	100,0	35,7
Assurances (Insurance)	−	−			10,7	40,0	32,1	56,3	42,9	77,4	12,5	53,8	100,0	55,4
Sud-Ouest / Commerce de gros (Wholesale distribution)	1,6	12,5	1,6	9,1	4,7	12,8	11,6	24,6	48,1	36,5	32,6	42,4	100,0	31,1
Commerce de détail (Retail distribution)	0,8	16,7	1,5	25,0	5,3	26,9	12,8	43,6	43,6	52,7	36,1	67,6	100,0	51,2
Institutions de crédit (Credit institutions)	·		·		9,5	20,0	21,4	37,5	35,7	39,5	33,3	51,9	100,0	35,3
Assurances (Insurance)	·		·		·		·		66,7	100,0	33,3	100,0	100,0	60,0

TAB. 57
(continued)
(suite)

1974

	1A/1/I		1B/2/II		2/3/III		3/4/IV		4/5/V		5/6/VI		TOTAL	
	$\frac{f}{F}$·100	$\frac{f}{f+m}$·100	$\frac{f}{F}$·100	$\frac{f}{f+m}$·100	$\frac{f}{F}$·100	$\frac{f}{f+m}$·100	$\frac{f}{F}$·100	$\frac{f}{f+m}$·100	$\frac{f}{F}$·100	$\frac{f}{f+m}$·100	$\frac{f}{F}$·100	$\frac{f}{f+m}$·100	$\frac{f}{F}$·100	$\frac{f}{f+m}$·100
Centre-Est / **Centre-Est**														
Wholesale distribution — Commerce de gros	0,8	7,1	1,7	6,1	4,2	8,1	16,7	24,1	48,3	34,1	28,3	32,7	100,0	25,8
Retail distribution — Commerce de détail	0,5	14,3	1,4	15,0	8,8	26,8	11,1	36,9	43,5	52,8	34,7	64,1	100,0	47,2
Credit institutions — Institutions de crédit	·	·	1,4	8,3	14,3	27,8	21,4	46,9	40,0	54,9	22,9	47,1	100,0	41,9
Insurance — Assurances	-	-	9,1	33,3	9,1	33,3	18,2	66,7	27,3	60,0	36,4	80,0	100,0	61,1
Méditerranée / **Méditerranée**														
Wholesale distribution — Commerce de gros	1,0	6,3	1,9	9,5	4,8	10,4	11,5	22,2	45,2	30,9	35,6	43,0	100,0	27,6
Retail distribution — Commerce de détail	0,7	14,3	2,0	33,3	4,7	28,0	10,7	57,1	38,3	52,8	43,0	73,6	100,0	60,6
Credit institutions — Institutions de crédit	·	·	·	·	14,6	25,0	22,0	32,1	39,0	39,0	24,4	38,5	100,0	31,8
Insurance — Assurances	-	-	·	·	·	·	25,0	50,0	50,0	66,7	·	·	100,0	44,4
ITALIA / **ITALIA**														
Nord-Ovest / **Nord-Ovest**														
Wholesale distribution — Commerce de gros	·	·	0,6	11,1	2,8	17,9	7,8	28,6	46,7	44,0	42,2	43,9	100,0	39,6
Retail distribution — Commerce de détail	·	·	·	·	0,7	12,5	5,0	41,2	72,3	68,4	21,3	46,2	100,0	58,0
Credit institutions — Institutions de crédit	·	·	1,2	1,9	12,8	9,6	61,6	22,7	22,1	44,2	2,3	4,4	100,0	17,4
Insurance — Assurances	-	-	·	·	·	·	30,6	34,4	69,4	75,8	·	·	100,0	40,0
Lombardia / **Lombardia**														
Wholesale distribution — Commerce de gros	0,2	5,3	0,7	8,3	3,1	14,9	14,3	5,1	49,5	39,7	32,1	33,1	100,0	33,0
Retail distribution — Commerce de détail	·	·	0,3	6,7	2,0	16,7	8,6	37,1	68,1	58,1	20,7	42,0	100,0	48,2
Credit institutions — Institutions de crédit	·	·	·	·	18,1	10,5	57,1	21,9	20,0	37,5	3,8	5,5	100,0	15,9
Insurance — Assurance	·	·	·	·	4,1	9,7	31,1	33,3	64,9	63,2	1,4	11,1	100,0	37,4
Nord-Est / **Nord-Est**														
Wholesale distribution — Commerce de gros	·	·	0,7	16,7	1,4	11,1	0,7	18,5	43,7	31,5	47,2	38,1	100,0	31,3
Retail distribution — Commerce de détail	·	·	·	·	0,8	11,1	6,5	32,0	65,0	55,2	26,0	47,1	100,0	49,0
Credit institutions — Institutions de crédit	·	·	·	·	14,7	6,9	55,9	14,7	26,5	30,0	2,9	3,7	100,0	11,6
Insurance — Assurances	-	-	-	-	5,6	10,0	38,9	35,0	61,1	68,7	5,6	50,0	100,0	35,3
Emilia-Romagna / **Emilia-Romagna**														
Wholesale distribution — Commerce de gros	·	·	·	·	0,8	8,3	5,4	21,2	35,4	34,8	57,7	54,3	100,0	40,4
Retail distribution — Commerce de détail	·	·	·	·	1,8	16,7	5,4	27,3	75,0	54,5	17,9	30,3	100,0	47,1
Credit institutions — Institutions de crédit	·	·	·	·	18,7	7,0	59,4	17,0	21,9	35,0	·	·	100,0	12,2
Insurance — Assurances	-	-	·	·	·	·	50,0	50,0	41,7	71,4	·	·	100,0	38,7

TAB. 57
(continued)
(suite)

1974

	1A/1/I f/F·100	1A/1/I f/(f+m)·100	1B/2/II f/F·100	1B/2/II f/(f+m)·100	2/3/III f/F·100	2/3/III f/(f+m)·100	3/4/IV f/F·100	3/4/IV f/(f+m)·100	4/5/V f/F·100	4/5/V f/(f+m)·100	5/6/VI f/F·100	5/6/VI f/(f+m)·100	TOTAL f/F·100	TOTAL f/(f+m)·100
Centro														
Commerce de gros / Wholesale distribution	—	·	·	·	1,0	12,5	5,2	15,2	33,3	28,3	60,4	38,4	100,0	31,1
Commerce de détail / Retail distribution	·	·	·	·	1,1	16,7	5,7	33,3	70,5	54,9	22,7	21,7	100,0	48,1
Institutions de crédit / Credit institutions	·	·	·	·	15,4	6,5	60,0	16,7	21,5	36,8	1,6	2,9	100,0	12,8
Assurances / Insurance	—	—	—	—	·	·	33,3	18,2	66,7	57,1	·	·	100,0	24,0
Lazio														
Commerce de gros / Wholesale distribution	·	·	·	·	3,5	13,3	10,5	18,2	47,4	29,7	38,6	25,9	100,0	24,4
Commerce de détail / Retail distribution	·	·	·	1,1	0,8	16,7	5,9	36,8	69,5	59,0	22,9	39,7	100,0	50,2
Institutions de crédit / Credit institutions	—	—	0,8	1,1	19,8	13,2	58,0	25,9	19,8	48,1	1,5	2,9	100,0	18,3
Assurances / Insurance	·	·	·	·	5,4	8,3	43,2	34,0	51,4	55,9	·	·	100,0	31,4
Campania														
Commerce de gros / Wholesale distribution	·	·	·	—	·	·	5,3	16,7	52,6	29,4	42,1	26,2	100,0	26,0
Commerce de détail / Retail distribution	—	—	—	—	·	·	6,5	23,1	67,4	51,7	26,1	42,9	100,0	44,7
Institutions de crédit / Credit institutions	—	—	—	—	21,1	8,9	47,4	17,3	26,3	31,2	5,3	5,6	100,0	12,3
Assurances / Insurance	·	·	·	·	·	·	50,0	20,0	50,0	33,3	—	—	100,0	16,7
Abruzzi-Molise														
Commerce de gros / Wholesale distribution	—	—	—	—	·	·	12,0	33,3	28,0	25,0	60,0	25,4	100,0	24,3
Commerce de détail / Retail distribution	—	—	—	—	·	·	6,9	40,0	72,4	43,7	20,7	33,3	100,0	39,7
Institutions de crédit / Credit institutions	—	—	·	·	28,6	11,1	57,1	16,7	14,3	25,0	·	·	100,0	12,3
Assurances / Insurance	—	—	—	—	—	—	·	·	·	·	—	—	·	·
Sud														
Commerce de gros / Wholesale distribution	—	—	—	—	·	·	9,5	12,5	52,4	28,9	38,1	12,1	100,0	16,4
Commerce de détail / Retail distribution	·	·	·	·	·	·	4,2	25,0	77,1	58,7	20,8	20,8	100,0	37,5
Institutions de crédit / Credit institutions	—	—	—	—	14,3	5,0	64,3	13,2	14,3	18,2	·	·	100,0	9,1
Assurances / Insurance	—	—	—	—	·	·	·	·	100,0	50,0	—	—	100,0	12,5
Sicilia														
Commerce de gros / Wholesale distribution	·	·	·	·	·	·	8,0	22,2	48,0	20,7	44,0	16,4	100,0	17,2
Commerce de détail / Retail distribution	·	·	·	·	·	·	4,5	28,6	60,2	54,6	35,2	36,5	100,0	43,6
Institutions de crédit / Credit institutions	—	—	15,8	6,8	15,8	6,8	68,4	14,3	15,8	12,5	5,3	6,2	100,0	9,7
Assurances / Insurance	·	·	·	·	·	·	—	—	100,0	50,0	—	—	100,0	14,3
Sardegna														
Commerce de gros / Wholesale distribution	·	·	·	·	·	·	13,2	38,5	57,9	43,1	23,7	15,3	100,0	29,5
Commerce de détail / Retail distribution	·	·	·	·	·	·	8,7	77,8	53,7	51,2	36,2	40,3	100,0	46,2
Institutions de crédit / Credit institutions	—	—	·	·	·	·	50,0	9,1	50,0	50,0	·	·	100,0	8,3
Assurances / Insurance	—	—	—	—	—	—	·	·	·	·	—	—	·	·

TAB. 57
(continued)
(suite)

1974

	1A/1/I		1B/2/II		2/3/III		3/4/IV		4/5/V		5/6/VI		TOTAL	
	$\frac{f}{F}100$	$\frac{f}{f+m}100$	$\frac{f}{F}100$	$\frac{f}{f+m}100$	$\frac{f}{F}100$	$\frac{f}{f+m}100$	$\frac{f}{F}100$	$\frac{f}{f+m}100$	$\frac{f}{F}100$	$\frac{f}{f+m}100$	$\frac{f}{F}100$	$\frac{f}{f+m}100$	$\frac{f}{F}100$	$\frac{f}{f+m}100$
NEDERLAND														
Noord														
Wholesale distribution	·	·	·	·	14,3	13,6	23,8	10,0	52,4	14,9	4,8	12,5	100,0	12,5
Retail distribution	·	·	·	·	3,5	20,0	17,5	32,3	78,9	58,4	–	–	100,0	46,0
Credit institutions	–	–	·	·	·	·	5,0	12,5	35,0	36,8	55,0	50,0	100,0	37,7
Insurance	–	–	–	–	·	·	·	·	14,3	12,5	71,4	50,0	100,0	29,2
Oost														
Wholesale distribution	·	·	2,5	5,3	7,5	7,9	30,0	13,2	52,5	22,1	5,0	8,7	100,0	14,5
Retail distribution	·	·	1,1	20,0	4,3	21,1	21,3	33,3	72,3	57,6	–	–	100,0	45,2
Credit institutions	–	–	·	·	1,9	25,0	1,9	5,9	40,7	42,3	57,4	64,6	100,0	42,9
Insurance	–	–	–	–	–	–	·	·	16,7	20,0	66,7	40,0	100,0	28,6
Zuidwest														
Wholesale distribution	0,5	2,6	3,0	5,8	10,1	9,0	32,3	15,0	49,0	24,0	5,1	13,2	100,0	15,6
Retail distribution	0,3	7,1	1,6	14,7	5,5	24,6	24,0	34,3	68,2	55,3	–	–	100,0	43,2
Credit institutions	·	·	·	·	0,7	5,0	6,5	12,2	25,5	30,2	68,0	45,6	100,0	32,2
Insurance	·	·	·	·	4,2	11,1	14,6	12,7	35,4	26,2	43,7	48,8	100,0	25,0
West														
Wholesale distribution	0,7	16,7	3,9	8,7	9,8	9,6	29,4	13,8	54,9	19,7	3,9	8,3	100,0	14,0
Retail distribution	·	·	0,7	12,5	2,8	18,2	22,4	38,1	73,4	60,7	–	–	100,0	48,6
Credit institutions	–	–	·	·	·	·	3,3	9,1	37,7	56,1	59,0	67,9	100,0	47,7
Insurance	–	–	·	·	14,3	50,0	14,3	16,7	28,6	40,0	28,6	50,0	100,0	38,9
UNITED KINGDOM														
South-East														
Wholesale distribution	–	–	·	·	·	·	6,8	10,2	72,9	33,3	17,8	36,3	100,0	24,0
Retail distribution	·	·	·	·	4,3	13,9	11,5	35,3	33,0	57,9	11,0	55,2	100,0	46,0
Credit institutions	–	–	–	–	2,1	8,3	16,4	39,0	54,3	63,2	27,2	63,5	100,0	49,1
Insurance	–	–	–	–	·	·	6,9	15,4	59,9	56,7	41,6	62,2	100,0	41,9
East Anglia														
Wholesale distribution	–	–	–	–	–	–	·	·	79,4	23,5	·	·	100,0	17,0
Retail distribution	–	–	–	–	·	·	·	·	74,1	63,6	11,4	51,4	100,0	50,3
Credit institutions	–	–	–	–	–	–	·	·	48,8	65,6	39,5	89,5	100,0	60,6
Insurance	–	–	–	–	–	–	·	·	40,6	41,9	53,1	70,8	100,0	40,5

Region labels also given in French: Commerce de gros, Commerce de détail, Institutions de crédit, Assurances.

TAB. 57 (continued) (suite)

1974

	1A/1/I $\frac{f}{F}\cdot100$	1A/1/I $\frac{f}{f+m}\cdot100$	1B/2/II $\frac{f}{F}\cdot100$	1B/2/II $\frac{f}{f+m}\cdot100$	2/3/III $\frac{f}{F}\cdot100$	2/3/III $\frac{f}{f+m}\cdot100$	3/4/IV $\frac{f}{F}\cdot100$	3/4/IV $\frac{f}{f+m}\cdot100$	4/5/V $\frac{f}{F}\cdot100$	4/5/V $\frac{f}{f+m}\cdot100$	5/6/VI $\frac{f}{F}\cdot100$	5/6/VI $\frac{f}{f+m}\cdot100$	TOTAL $\frac{f}{F}\cdot100$	TOTAL $\frac{f}{f+m}\cdot100$
South-West														
Wholesale distribution	—	—	—	—	·	·	·	·	77,7	28,7	·	·	100,0	22,8
Retail distribution	—	—	—	—	·	·	8,3	78,7	63,6	8,6	58,7	100,0	100,0	48,5
Credit institutions	—	—	—	—	—	—	·	·	64,0	76,3	27,9	71,7	100,0	56,9
Insurance	—	—	—	—	—	—	·	·	54,8	48,6	38,7	52,2	100,0	36,5
West Midlands														
Wholesale distribution	—	—	—	—	5,8	24,2	·	·	78,0	35,1	16,5	34,0	100,0	25,9
Retail distribution	—	—	—	—	—	—	9,6	44,9	72,9	63,4	11,7	52,7	100,0	53,8
Credit institutions	—	—	—	—	—	—	14,6	41,2	56,9	81,2	27,8	61,5	100,0	56,9
Insurance	—	—	—	—	—	—	—	—	48,9	71,9	51,1	77,4	100,0	51,6
East Midlands														
Wholesale distribution	·	—	·	—	5,1	24,2	·	·	53,7	24,2	33,3	47,4	100,0	21,5
Retail distribution	·	—	·	—	—	—	10,8	33,3	74,8	58,3	8,3	46,4	100,0	48,6
Credit institutions	·	—	·	—	—	—	·	·	54,1	65,6	29,7	75,9	100,0	50,3
Insurance	·	—	·	—	—	—	·	·	·	·	·	·	100,0	38,1
Yorks/Humberside														
Wholesale distribution	—	—	—	—	4,6	19,8	·	·	65,6	27,5	17,2	27,6	100,0	22,7
Retail distribution	—	—	—	—	—	—	7,1	28,2	78,6	66,6	8,9	43,5	100,0	52,1
Credit institutions	—	—	—	—	—	—	·	·	61,5	78,6	33,6	80,0	100,0	57,7
Insurance	—	—	—	—	—	—	·	·	63,6	66,7	29,5	76,5	100,0	51,8
North-West														
Wholesale distribution	—	—	—	—	4,5	25,3	·	·	68,4	34,8	22,4	27,9	100,0	25,1
Retail distribution	—	·	—	—	—	—	6,6	31,2	77,4	67,3	10,8	59,9	100,0	56,4
Credit institutions	—	—	—	—	—	—	9,8	30,0	52,1	69,1	38,1	62,6	100,0	53,8
Insurance	—	—	—	—	—	—	·	·	66,3	71,4	30,6	73,2	100,0	49,0
North														
Wholesale distribution	—	—	—	—	6,0	33,3	·	·	68,6	41,0	·	·	100,0	32,7
Retail distribution	—	·	—	—	—	—	6,5	39,4	74,1	71,2	12,6	71,4	100,0	62,2
Credit institutions	—	—	—	—	—	—	22,0	45,0	47,6	75,0	30,4	92,6	100,0	62,6
Insurance	—	—	—	—	—	—	·	·	57,1	57,1	37,1	72,2	100,0	58,3
Wales														
Wholesale distribution	—	—	—	—	7,4	38,1	·	·	85,0	30,9	·	·	100,0	22,7
Retail distribution	—	—	—	—	—	—	12,0	60,5	63,0	70,1	·	·	100,0	63,7
Credit institutions	—	—	—	—	—	—	·	·	57,5	59,0	17,6	84,4	100,0	42,6
Insurance	—	—	—	—	—	—	·	·	59,1	68,4	32,5	81,3	100,0	51,2

Region labels (French): South-West — Commerce de gros, Commerce de détail, Institutions de crédit, Assurances; West Midlands; East Midlands; Yorks/Humberside; North-West; North; Wales.

TAB. 57
(continued)
(suite)

1974

	1A/1/I f/F·100	1A/1/I f/(f+m)·100	1B/2/II f/F·100	1B/2/II f/(f+m)·100	2/3/III f/F·100	2/3/III f/(f+m)·100	3/4/IV f/F·100	3/4/IV f/(f+m)·100	4/5/V f/F·100	4/5/V f/(f+m)·100	5/6/VI f/F·100	5/6/VI f/(f+m)·100	TOTAL f/F·100	TOTAL f/(f+m)·100
Scotland														
Wholesale distribution — Commerce de gros	—	—	—	—	.	.	9,1	21,6	71,0	43,4	18,2	42,7	100,0	33,7
Retail distribution — Commerce de détail	—	—	—	—	6,4	36,4	9,8	44,3	74,8	65,9	9,0	61,6	100,0	58,6
Credit institutions — Institutions de crédit	—	—	—	—	.	.	13,4	44,6	58,8	70,5	27,3	78,5	100,0	58,1
Insurance — Assurances	—	—	—	—	—	—	.	.	66,2	64,5	29,7	62,9	100,0	48,1
Northern Ireland														
Wholesale distribution — Commerce de gros	—	—	—	—	.	.	.	.	77,1	32,9	.	.	100,0	23,3
Retail distribution — Commerce de détail	—	—	—	—	.	.	.	.	77,1	55,1	.	.	100,0	47,0
Credit institutions — Institutions de crédit	—	—	—	—	.	.	.	.	50,0	63,3	.	.	100,0	53,5
Insurance — Assurances	—	—	—	—	—	—	—	—	.	.	.	.	100,0	.
BELGIQUE/BELGIË														
Vlaams gebied														
Wholesale distribution — Commerce de gros	.	.	1,3	9,5	5,1	12,7	2,1	28,2	41,6	33,9	19,9	26,3	100,0	26,9
Retail distribution — Commerce de détail	.	.	0,9	28,6	2,8	25,0	4,9	58,1	46,5	56,8	14,9	54,2	100,0	54,0
Credit institutions — Institutions de crédit	.	—	.	.	1,5	0,5	19,7	6,0	71,2	21,8	7,6	2,3	100,0	30,6
Insurance — Assurances	.	—	.	.	.	.	13,0	27,3	30,4	58,3	56,5	76,5	100,0	46,0
Région wallonne														
Wholesale distribution — Commerce de gros	.	.	.	.	6,0	12,0	34,0	31,5	38,0	30,2	20,0	26,3	100,0	26,6
Retail distribution — Commerce de détail	.	.	0,5	20,0	3,3	31,6	33,5	59,8	50,5	62,6	11,5	51,2	100,0	57,8
Credit institutions — Institutions de crédit	—	—	—	—	.	.	35,7	10,0	53,6	15,0	7,1	2,0	100,0	28,0
Insurance — Assurances	—	—	.	.	.	.	20,0	50,0	30,0	60,0	40,0	57,1	100,0	47,6
Bruxelles														
Wholesale distribution — Commerce de gros	.	.	1,8	7,1	10,0	16,2	37,3	36,6	35,5	43,8	15,4	35,4	100,0	30,8
Retail distribution — Commerce de détail	.	.	1,8	21,4	5,4	33,3	28,1	56,6	52,7	60,7	12,0	47,6	100,0	52,0
Credit institutions — Institutions de crédit	—	—	.	.	6,1	1,9	30,3	9,4	46,4	14,3	17,2	5,3	100,0	30,9
Insurance — Assurances	—	—	1,7	0,7	6,9	2,7	8,6	3,4	34,5	13,5	48,3	19,6	100,0	39,9
DANMARK														
Øerne øst for Storebælt														
Wholesale distribution — Commerce de gros	.	.	1,2	14,3	3,7	6,2	16,5	14,9	52,3	28,9	27,5	21,6	100,0	19,6
Retail distribution — Commerce de détail	.	.	.	.	3,6	15,8	21,4	37,5	57,1	55,2	16,7	40,0	100,0	42,0
Credit institutions — Institutions de crédit	.	—	.	.	2,8	9,1	12,5	27,3	38,9	56,0	44,4	64,0	98,6	44,2
Insurance — Assurances	—	—	.	.	7,9	23,1	31,6	66,7	52,6	83,3	7,9	75,0	100,0	55,2

TAB. 57
(continued)
(suite)

1974

Jylland og Fyn	1A/1/I		1B/2/II		2/3/III		3/4/IV		4/5/V		5/6/VI		TOTAL	
	$\frac{f}{F}\,100$	$\frac{f}{f+m}\,100$	$\frac{f}{F}\,100$	$\frac{f}{f+m}\,100$	$\frac{f}{F}\,100$	$\frac{f}{f+m}\,100$	$\frac{f}{F}\,100$	$\frac{f}{f+m}\,100$	$\frac{f}{F}\,100$	$\frac{f}{f+m}\,100$	$\frac{f}{F}\,100$	$\frac{f}{f+m}\,100$	$\frac{f}{F}\,100$	$\frac{f}{f+m}\,100$
Commerce de gros / Wholesale distribution	·	·	2,9	25,0	·	·	13,3	8,0	53,3	18,3	33,4	13,2	100,0	12,1
Commerce de détail / Retail distribution	·	·	·	·	·	·	21,7	41,7	59,4	58,6	13,0	45,0	97,0	46,0
Institutions de crédit / Credit institutions	–	–	·	·	1,5	5,0	10,4	26,9	41,8	58,3	44,8	73,2	98,5	46,5
Assurances / Insurance	–	–	·	·	·	·	·	·	60,0	100,0	·	·	60,0	71,4

Commerce de gros et de détail / Wholesale and retail distribution

1A	Personnel supérieur de direction	Top management personnel
1B	Personnel de direction et cadres supérieurs	Management personnel and senior executives
2	Personnel d'exécution et d'encadrement	Executives and management staff
3	Personnel subalterne très qualifié	Highly-skilled junior personnel
4	Personnel subalterne qualifié	Skilled junior personnel
5	Personnel subalterne non qualifié	Unskilled junior personnel

Banques / Banking

1	Personnel supérieur de direction	Directors, top management
2	Cadres supérieurs	Senior executives
3	Personnel de conception (cadres inférieurs)	Executives (junior management)
4	Personnel d'exécution très qualifié	Highly-qualified clerical staff
5	Personnel d'exécution qualifié	Qualified clerical staff
6	Autres agents	Other employees

Assurances / Insurance

I	Dirigeants et cadres supérieurs de direction	Managers and senior management executives
II	Cadres intermédiaires	Middle management executives
III	Agents d'encadrement et assimilés	Junior executives and personnel with equivalent qualification
IV	Travailleurs très qualifiés	Highly-skilled employees
V	Travailleurs qualifiés	Skilled employees
VI	Autres travailleurs	Other employees

TAB. 58

Female workers by earnings and nature of duties: Employees in industry and services (%)
Travailleuses selon le salaire et la mixité des fonctions: Salariées dans l'industrie et dans les services (%)

	BR Deutschland	France	Italia	Nederland	Belgique Belgïe	Luxembourg	
Women only	100,0	100,0	100,0	100,0	100,0	100,0	**Femmes seulement**
1st class	1,4	18,3	21,1	9,7	7,0	8,0	1e classe
2nd class	12,0	25,9	57,2	20,1	46,3	52,4	2e classe
3rd class	42,0	17,0	19,1	42,1	34,9	26,4	3^e classe
4th class	23,3	14,0	2,0	18,3	9,3	9,4	4^e classe
5th class	17,6	9,1	0,4	8,0	1,9	1,9	5^e classe
6th class	3,7	5,2	0,2	1,8	0,6	1,9	6^e classe
7th class	–	10,5	–	–	–	–	7^e classe
Mainly women	100,0	100,0	100,0	100,0	100,0	100,0	**Femmes pour la plupart**
1st class	–	8,1	13,0	2,6	3,2	9,1	1^e classe
2nd class	7,9	28,0	45,6	19,1	47,1	27,3	2^e classe
3rd class	37,4	22,9	30,7	45,5	38,1	36,3	3^e classe
4th class	33,1	13,5	9,8	18,0	10,0	18,2	4^e classe
5th class	19,3	9,3	0,9	7,9	1,1	9,1	5^e classe
6th class	2,3	7,6	–	6,9	0,5	–	6^e classe
7th class	–	10,6	–	–	–	–	7^e classe
Men and women	100,0	100,0	100,0	100,0	100,0	100,0	**Hommes et femmes**
1st class	1,5	7,9	11,0	3,2	1,7	3,1	1^e classe
2nd class	10,3	16,3	39,6	17,1	30,1	17,7	2^e classe
3rd class	28,5	21,0	34,8	49,7	46,6	32,3	3^e classe
4th class	28,1	14,7	11,9	17,9	15,3	31,3	4^e classe
5th class	25,5	13,5	2,1	7,4	4,2	13,5	5^e classe
6th class	6,1	10,7	0,6	4,7	2,1	2,1	6^e classe
7th class	–	15,8	–	–	–	–	7^e classe
Mainly men	100,0	100,0	100,0	100,0	100,0	100,0	**Hommes pour la plupart**
1st class	2,9	7,1	6,7	1,9	2,9	–	1^e classe
2nd class	15,7	10,7	46,7	21,1	11,8	16,7	2^e classe
3rd class	18,6	17,9	30,0	54,1	55,9	33,2	3^e classe
4th class	27,1	19,7	13,3	15,6	17,6	16,7	4^e classe
5th class	28,6	12,5	3,3	6,4	5,9	16,7	5^e classe
6th class	7,1	12,5	–	0,9	5,9	16,7	6^e classe
7th class	–	19,6	–	–	–	–	7^e classe
Total	100,0	100,0	100,0	100,0	100,0	100,0	**Total**
1st class	1,2	13,6	16,1	5,8	4,8	6,5	1^e classe
2nd class	10,7	23,6	49,4	19,1	41,2	40,2	2^e classe
3rd class	35,3	18,9	26,3	46,1	39,2	28,9	3^e classe
4th class	27,4	14,3	6,8	17,9	11,2	16,4	4^e classe
5th class	21,1	10,3	1,1	7,6	2,4	5,9	5^e classe
6th class	4,3	7,2	0,3	3,5	1,2	2,1	6^e classe
7th class	–	12,1	–	–	–	–	7e classe

1st class: lower earnings.
1e classe: salaires les plus bas.

TAB. 59

Earnings in industry: gross hourly average earnings of female industrial workers in relation to those of male workers (male earnings = 100)

Salaires dans l'industrie: gain horaire moyen brut des ouvrières dans l'industrie par rapport à celui des ouvriers (gain masculin = 100)

	BR Deutschland $\frac{f}{m}100$	France $\frac{f}{m}100$	Italia $\frac{f}{m}100$	Nederland $\frac{f}{m}100$	Belgique Belgïe $\frac{f}{m}100$	Luxembourg $\frac{f}{m}100$	United Kingdom $\frac{f}{m}100$	Ireland $\frac{f}{m}100$	Danmark $\frac{f}{m}100$	
1964 April	67,5	76,6	69,5	54,3	64,8	46,1	:	:	:	**1964** Avril
October	67,5	70,4	71,4	54,3	64,6	47,2	:	:	:	Octobre
1969 April	69,4	78,7	73,4	59,2	67,9	55,5	:	:	:	**1969** Avril
October	69,3	78,0	74,4	59,1	67,8	54,9	:	:	:	Octobre
1970 April	70,0	78,6	71,3	59,4	67,8	54,5	:	:	:	**1970** Avril
October	68,8	77,9	74,2	59,2	66,7	57,0	:	:	:	Octobre
1971 April	69,8	79,1	77,1	59,8	67,3	59,0	:	:	:	**1971** Avril
October	69,9	78,1	76,9	58,8	67,5	59,5	:	:	:	Octobre
1972 April	70,2	78,6	77,9	60,4	68,6	60,7	:	:	:	**1972** Avril
October	69,7	78,7	76,3	64,6	68,5	62,9	59,5	:	:	Octobre
1973 April	70,1	81,9	76,3	66,2	68,7	59,3	60,2	:	:	**1973** Avril
October	70,7	78,9	78,3	66,9	68,8	58,1	62,1	:	:	Octobre
1974 April	71,4	77,9	79,2	68,3	69,5	60,4	63,1	:	:	**1974** Avril
October	71,6	78,3	78,6	70,2	69,5	60,5	66,5	:	:	Octobre
1975 April	72,8	78,0	81,2	71,8	70,9	64,5	67,1	:	:	**1975** Avril
October	72,5	78,5	–	72,4	71,3	63,3	67,6	:	:	Octobre
1976 April	72,8	77,6	80,2	73,8	71,6	66,8	69,4	:	:	**1976** Avril
October	72,5	77,1	83,0	73,6	71,6	66,7	70,9	:	:	Octobre
1977 April	73,1	77,3	84,2	74,1	70,7	64,1	71,2	:	:	**1977** Avril
October	72,8	77,4	84,6	74,2	71,0	65,0	71,4	:	:	Octobre
1978 April	73,4	77,4	:	73,7	70,9	62,4	71,0	:	:	**1978** Avril
October	:	:	:	:	:	:	:	:	:	Octobre

TAB. 60

Earnings in industry: gross hourly average earnings of female workers in relation to those of male workers (male earnings = 100) and CV of female earnings by size group of establishment and qualifications

Salaires dans l'industrie: gain horaire moyen brut des ouvrières par rapport à celui des ouvriers (gain masculin = 100) et CV des gains des ouvrières selon la classe de taille de l'entreprise et la qualification

1972

	BR Deutschland $\frac{f}{m}100$	CV	France $\frac{f}{m}100$	CV	Italia $\frac{f}{m}100$	CV	Nederland $\frac{f}{m}100$	CV	Belgique/België $\frac{f}{m}100$	CV	Luxembourg $\frac{f}{m}100$	CV
10 – 19												
Total	61,5	23,6	78,6	27,1	72,4	29,1	64,4	36,3	68,5	19,2	61,7	24,9
1 Qualified	69,3	24,8	90,6	28,3	69,2	28,0	62,3	34,3	66,1	15,8		
2 Semi-qualified	66,3	22,1	87,2	23,9	73,2	30,0	64,2	33,9	71,1	17,7	82,0	10,6
3 Unqualified	68,7	22,1	88,8	22,1	78,8	28,7	83,7	39,7	80,2	21,5	67,6	22,9
20 – 49												
Total	63,3	24,7	76,3	26,0	79,1	26,1	62,3	37,3	69,8	20,5	58,3	26,3
1 Qualifiés	67,1	24,1	80,7	27,3	73,5	31,5	64,6	28,7	68,4	17,0	68,5	18,0
2 Semi-qualifiés	69,7	21,5	84,8	21,9	80,3	23,4	62,7	34,3	72,3	16,6	59,9	25,3
3 Non qualifiés	72,9	27,3	88,6	24,8	88,7	25,3	76,9	42,7	78,5	23,7	69,1	26,0
(10 – 49)												
Total	63,1	24,5	77,0	26,3	77,6	27,0	62,4	37,1	69,4	20,2	59,1	26,1
1 Qualified	67,9	24,3	83,1	27,7	72,5	31,0	63,8	30,8	67,8	16,8	70,2	15,2
2 Semi-qualified	68,9	21,7	85,5	22,4	78,5	24,9	63,0	34,3	72,0	17,0	62,0	25,7
3 Unqualified	71,9	26,3	88,7	24,2	86,4	26,3	78,1	42,0	79,0	23,1	68,7	25,2
50 – 99												
Total	64,5	21,5	76,8	23,9	76,7	22,0	63,6	31,7	70,4	19,9	63,2	20,2
1 Qualifiés	67,2	22,5	81,5	25,7	71,4	22,8	62,9	32,1	69,0	17,0	61,8	14,2
2 Semi-qualifiés	71,6	21,0	87,1	20,5	78,4	19,4	65,1	29,1	71,6	19,6	61,6	22,5
3 Non qualifiés	73,3	20,5	89,6	21,6	87,0	23,6	74,8	34,5	77,9	20,5	75,6	19,7
100 – 199												
Total	67,0	20,6	77,4	25,1	77,3	22,9	63,6	30,6	69,0	20,1	66,6	73,0
1 Qualified	68,7	22,1	79,2	29,6	71,9	22,5	61,0	29,7	66,5	18,5		
2 Semi-qualified	73,3	20,1	87,7	24,2	79,8	21,5	64,3	28,0	70,2	17,6		
3 Unqualified	76,9	20,0	89,6	20,4	87,9	24,5	75,5	33,7	78,5	22,3		
200 – 499												
Total	70,3	21,1	78,0	27,1	78,1	20,3	68,7	36,6	71,6	19,3	84,4	26,4
1 Qualifiés	74,0	21,9	79,3	27,6	72,5	19,8	67,1	28,2	66,4	17,4		
2 Semi-qualifiés	76,8	18,8	87,0	27,5	81,0	18,6	69,8	32,2	71,7	19,5	99,5	4,5
3 Non qualifiés	79,4	22,3	89,6	23,2	89,3	22,1	78,0	42,8	80,8	19,9	80,5	22,9
500 – 999												
Total	71,4	18,6	77,7	24,4	79,2	22,6	66,7	25,7	72,9	16,9	70,8	54,4
1 Qualified	75,0	22,8	80,2	29,2	73,0	21,3	68,2	21,7	65,8	20,3		
2 Semi-qualified	77,4	17,7	87,2	20,8	81,4	22,1	69,2	26,2	75,2	16,2	71,2	58,6
3 Unqualified	80,3	18,1	91,9	24,3	90,8	23,4	75,5	25,1	80,6	16,6		
≥1000												
Total	73,0	18,7	79,2	24,5	82,9	21,9	70,0	29,7	71,6	18,3	83,0	24,1
1 Qualifiés	84,1	25,6	88,9	25,3	78,7	27,2	76,3	18,7	79,5	25,2		
2 Semi-qualifiés	79,8	16,7	86,5	20,7	84,1	19,3	72,4	30,2	75,5	18,9	102,7	7,2
3 Non qualifiés	81,3	17,8	88,8	23,6	90,9	22,4	71,3	31,4	76,1	17,4	66,1	14,9
TOTAL												
Total	68,8	21,4	76,8	26,6	77,5	25,9	65,7	33,3	68,5	21,8	60,3	50,8
1 Qualified	72,0	25,1	80,5	28,9	70,6	26,8	66,9	29,0	63,9	19,5	74,6°	74,0°
2 Semi-qualified	74,3	20,3	85,0	24,7	78,5	24,1	67,5	31,6	68,8	20,6	73,2	54,7
3 Unqualified	78,4	21,2	89,8	23,9	89,5	27,0	75,1	37,0	77,5	23,3	57,0	24,7

CV: coefficient of variation.
CV: coefficient de variation.

TAB. 61

Earnings in industry: gross hourly average earnings of female workers in relation to those of male workers (male earnings = 100) and CV of female earnings by age group and qualifications

Salaires dans l'industrie: gain horaire moyen brut des ouvrières par rapport à celui des ouvriers (gain masculin = 100) et CV des gains des ouvrières selon la classe d'âge et la qualification

1972

	BR Deutschland		France		Italia		Nederland		Belgique/België		Luxembourg	
	$\frac{f}{m}$ 100	CV	$\frac{f}{m}$ 100	CV	$\frac{f}{m}$ 100	CV	$\frac{f}{m}$ 100	CV	$\frac{f}{m}$ 100	CV	$\frac{f}{m}$ 100	CV
< 18												
Total	83,1	22,3	91,2	16,5	93,6	23,9	95,7	28,0	85,4	24,3	79,2	53,3
1 Qualified	71,1	23,0	82,2	17,5	85,8	35,3	91,8	27,0	76,5	20,7		
2 Semi-qualified	81,6	20,4	90,6	15,0	93,6	19,0	93,3	26,3	81,4	22,6	85,3	23,5
3 Unqualified	86,7	23,0	94,4	16,6	92,2	22,8	98,9	30,4	87,2	25,3	75,5	23,6
18 – 20												
Total	75,0	19,8	85,8	20,1	84,5	24,6	84,3	26,8	76,9	19,2	67,5	78,2
1 Qualifiés	76,2	21,4	85,2	32,2	78,3	26,1	85,6	26,6	70,3	13,0		
2 Semi-qualifiés	77,7	19,6	88,1	17,7	84,2	22,3	83,0	27,8	73,0	18,6	81,0°	95,8°
3 Non qualifiés	81,1	19,3	92,5	18,0	87,1	26,3	88,4	24,8	83,2	20,5	62,5	19,7
< 21												
Total	74,3	23,9	85,9	20,2	85,6	24,9	84,7	31,2	79,0	24,6	66,1	78,4
1 Qualified	73,9	23,3	84,5	31,6	78,7	28,4	86,4	31,1	70,4	16,7		
2 Semi-qualified	76,7	22,7	88,0	17,9	84,1	21,9	82,9	31,1	87,6	22,7	78,6	95,7
3 Unqualified	85,2	24,3	93,3	18,5	88,4	26,5	90,9	31,1	85,8	26,9	64,6	25,9
21 – 29												
Total	70,9	20,8	78,0	22,1	79,3	26,0	72,6	19,2	71,2	18,9	61,3	34,0
1 Qualifiés	74,2	23,7	79,3	22,9	72,5	26,4	72,4	18,9	65,1	17,7	68,2°	33,0°
2 Semi-qualifiés	75,9	20,0	84,2	21,7	79,7	24,1	73,9	18,5	71,1	17,7	71,5	35,9
3 Non qualifiés	78,1	20,6	89,2	19,7	87,5	27,5	78,6	20,4	78,1	19,7	56,5	16,3
30 – 44												
Total	68,4	20,6	76,5	26,9	78,9	24,0	72,9	20,9	69,5	17,3	66,7	45,5
1 Qualified	73,2	25,9	81,9	27,7	74,4	24,3	73,8	21,2	65,5	18,7	65,2	52,3
2 Semi-qualified	74,3	19,4	84,9	22,7	80,0	23,1	75,6	16,4	70,8	17,2	82,6	46,1
3 Unqualified	76,4	20,0	89,3	28,1	90,1	24,7	79,6	25,9	75,6	16,9	58,6	18,8
45 – 54												
Total	69,2	18,8	78,1	31,1	81,5	24,0	74,4	40,2	70,5	16,0	62,3	28,0
1 Qualifiés	72,5	22,4	87,9	29,9	74,6	23,1	75,7	26,4	69,0	16,2		
2 Semi-qualifiés	75,1	18,2	87,7	31,6	82,0	23,2	77,0	36,4	70,7	16,2	70,1	31,0
3 Non qualifiés	77,9	18,3	89,3	25,2	96,4	24,8	81,0	46,9	76,6	15,7	65,1	24,2
≥ 55												
Total	71,2	20,6	81,2	29,8	84,4	31,3	74,7	19,4	74,9	17,2	62,7	20,9
1 Qualified	73,0	22,2	83,5	33,4	71,7	28,2	76,5	21,3	73,8	18,5		
2 Semi-qualified	76,4	19,2	90,0	27,3	80,4	32,4	75,7	15,6	75,3	16,5		
3 Unqualified	80,0	21,0	92,5	27,0	102,1	30,7	80,5	21,3	80,9	16,7	68,7	17,9
≥ 21												
Total	69,3	20,3	77,3	26,9	79,0	25,2	72,2	24,7	70,5	17,9	63,1	39,3
1 Qualifiés	73,1	24,5	81,1	28,1	72,4	25,5	72,0	21,5	65,6	18,4	64,0	43,2
2 Semi-qualifiés	75,1	19,4	85,5	25,1	79,7	23,8	74,1	21,9	70,9	17,4	75,0	42,7
3 Non qualifiés	77,7	19,9	89,6	24,8	90,9	26,1	93,8	29,6	77,4	18,0	59,4	20,6
TOTAL												
Total	68,7	21,4	76,8	26,6	77,5	25,9	65,7	33,3	68,5	21,8	60,3	50,8
1 Qualified	72,0	25,1	80,5	28,9	70,6	26,8	66,9	29,0	63,9	19,5	74,6	74,0°
2 Semi-qualified	74,3	20,3	85,0	24,7	78,5	24,1	67,5	31,6	68,8	20,6	73,2	54,7
3 Unqualified	78,4	21,2	89,8	23,9	89,5	27,0	75,1	37,0	77,5	23,3	57,0	24,7

CV: coefficient of variation.
CV: coefficient de variation.

TAB. 62

Earnings in industry: gross hourly average earnings of female workers in relation to those of male workers (male earnings = 100) and CV of female earnings by length of service and qualifications

Salaires dans l'industrie: gain horaire moyen brut des ouvrières par rapport à celui des ouvriers (gain masculin = 100) et CV des gains des ouvrières selon l'ancienneté dans l'entreprise et la qualification

1972

	BR Deutschland		France		Italia		Nederland		Belgique/België		Luxembourg	
	$\frac{f}{m}$ 100	CV	$\frac{f}{m}$ 100	CV	$\frac{f}{m}$ 100	CV	$\frac{f}{m}$ 100	CV	$\frac{f}{m}$ 100	CV	$\frac{f}{m}$ 100	CV
< 2												
Total	67,4	22,5	78,7	21,0	76,6	27,2	64,6	35,1	68,7	25,4	66,7	53,9
1 Qualified	68,5	24,8	79,2	31,7	65,6	30,0	63,7	34,1	61,3	19,8	120,9	90,2
2 Semi-qualified	71,4	21,4	84,5	19,4	74,6	26,2	65,0	33,0	67,1	24,2	79,8	59,4
3 Unqualified	76,2	22,6	90,0	18,2	84,0	26,9	74,0	37,0	77,4	26,6	67,3	27,1
2 – 4												
Total	70,3	20,7	78,1	26,2	78,8	25,5	68,2	32,9	70,4	19,2	63,4	58,9
1 Qualifiés	72,0	25,3	79,0	25,0	70,0	26,9	66,8	28,3	62,9	14,4		
2 Semi-qualifiés	74,7	19,9	83,8	25,8	78,5	22,9	69,3	28,8	69,9	18,9	72,4	70,1
3 Non qualifiés	78,6	20,3	89,7	25,7	88,1	27,0	77,3	40,3	79,1	20,1	57,9	18,9
5 – 9												
Total	69,8	20,1	77,5	26,4	78,0	23,9	70,5	21,6	70,3	18,3	74,1	36,2
1 Qualified	73,6	23,8	80,5	27,4	72,3	22,9	68,6	21,4	64,8	19,3	58,7	14,7
2 Semi-qualified	75,3	19,1	84,6	23,2	79,6	23,3	72,2	20,2	70,8	16,7	88,5	32,2
3 Unqualified	78,1	19,7	89,0	28,7	89,6	24,9	78,9	24,1	78,1	18,8	58,8	21,1
10 – 19												
Total	69,8	19,3	76,2	26,1	78,0	22,4	76,0	33,0	70,3	17,0	58,3	23,4
1 Qualifiés	74,5	25,6	79,5	27,1	75,4	22,5	77,5	18,6	67,6	19,7	68,0°	33,2°
2 Semi-qualifiés	75,9	18,0	85,1	24,6	80,0	21,9	78,8	40,8	71,6	16,6	60,7	25,0
3 Non qualifiés	78,5	18,4	87,4	23,0	89,7	22,5	81,2	21,3	75,1	16,2	59,5	14,8
≥ 20												
Total	71,5	18,5	79,5	29,7	78,5	22,1	78,7	19,0	70,2	15,4	59,6	20,1
1 Qualified	75,8	21,1	84,6	29,8	75,1	20,3	82,9	17,0	68,6	16,4		
2 Semi-qualified	78,4	17,6	89,3	27,0	79,1	20,5	79,6	16,2	70,9	15,0	68,5	23,1
3 Unqualified	80,5	17,8	87,0	29,8	94,2	22,8	82,5	22,1	76,6	15,1		
TOTAL												
Total	68,8	21,4	76,8	26,6	77,5	25,9	65,7	33,3	68,5	21,8	60,3	50,8
1 Qualifiés	72,0	25,1	80,5	28,9	70,6	26,8	66,9	29,0	63,9	19,5	74,6	74,0°
2 Semi-qualifiés	74,3	20,3	85,0	24,7	78,5	24,1	67,5	31,6	68,8	20,6	73,2	54,7
3 Non qualifiés	78,4	21,2	89,8	23,9	89,5	27,0	75,1	37,0	77,5	23,3	57,0	24,7

CV: coefficient of variation.
CV: coefficient de variation.

TAB. 63

Earnings in industry: average gross monthly remuneration of female non-manual workers in relation to that of male non-manual workers (male remuneration = 100) and CV of female remuneration by size group of establishment and qualifications

Salaires dans l'industrie: gain mensuel moyen brut des employées par rapport à celui des employés (gain masculin = 100) et CV des gains des employées selon la classe de taille de l'entreprise et la qualification　　　　1972

	BR Deutschland		France		Italia	
	$\frac{f}{m}$ 100	CV	$\frac{f}{m}$ 100	CV	$\frac{f}{m}$ 100	CV
10 – 19						
Total	61,3	34,5	55,5	50,7	69,5	43,5
1 B Earnings not more than (1) monthly	°77,8	°35,0	°83,2	°49,9	.	.
2　Very highly qualified	79,9	26,9	83,4	36,4	°78,2	°36,2
3　Less highly qualified	75,1	23,1	87,2	24,6	88,7	39,7
4　Executives	74,9	26,5	79,2	34,4	87,7	35.7
5　Supervisors	76,3	19,9	73,9	24,4	67,7	°32,8
20 – 49						
Total	62,2	32,5	55,5	50,1	68,3	42,7
1 B Earnings not more than (1) monthly	84,0	27,9	90,9	42,8	.	.
2　Very highly qualified	80,1	24,4	78,9	39,7	71,2	43,9
3　Less highly qualified	78,2	22,0	89,6	30,3	87,4	27,9
4　Executives	76,4	25,3	79,1	32,1	88,7	41,3
5　Supervisors	66,4	22,9	70,4	34,8	78,0	22,9
(10 – 49)						
Total	65,5	33,2	55,5	50,3	68,4	43,0
1 B Earnings not more than (1) monthly	81,7	30,6	87,3	46,2	.	.
2　Very highly qualified	79,5	25,4	80,3	38,9	72,1	43,1
3　Less highly qualified	77,3	22,5	88,6	29,1	87,6	31,0
4　Executives	75,7	25,9	79,1	32,8	88,4	40,4
5　Supervisors	69,4	22,3	71,2	32,5	76,1	25,4
50 – 99						
Total	63,1	32,3	56,9	45,8	66,9	36,8
1 B Earnings not more than (1) monthly	79,3	28,3	°73,8	°49,8	.	.
2　Very highly qualified	84,1	26,6	81,3	35,9	82,0	39,2
3　Less highly qualified	77,2	21,4	87,8	26,7	88,1	25,2
4　Executives	76,8	23,4	78,9	30,5	84,6	26,9
5　Supervisors	64,3	19,1	75,0	28,5	71,5	27,2
100 – 199						
Total	61,8	30,8	57,3	42,2	65,4	38,3
1 B Earnings not more than (1) monthly	92,2	24,9	78,0	34,3	°84,3	43,9
2　Very highly qualified	81,2	21,8	82,5	33,1	81,6	32,3
3　Less highly qualified	78,0	21,4	91,3	25,0	86,6	25,2
4　Executives	75,2	23,2	77,2	28,6	84,5	24,5
5　Supervisors	67,6	18,9	72,5	25,5	87,5	26,2
200 – 499						
Total	61,9	29,1	57,7	42,0	62,0	38,0
1 B Earnings not more than (1) monthly	91,4	22,1	°87,6	°33,8	.	.
2　Very highly qualified	80,3	20,5	80,1	32,9	83,5	30,6
3　Less highly qualified	78,7	19,5	91,2	35,0	85,7	25,4
4　Executives	78,8	21,7	80,3	28,0	80,1	25,3
5　Supervisors	68,6	18,6	75,2	28,2	75,3	23,9
500 – 999						
Total	61,5	29,1	59,3	41,0	62,2	36,5
1 B Earnings not more than (1) monthly	94,4	18,5	°111,5	°25,2	56,2	°64,4
2　Very highly qualified	84,1	18,9	75,9	31,1	86,2	21,0
3　Less highly qualified	80,0	19,4	89,5	24,2	86,5	26,8
4　Executives	77,5	20,7	81,0	27,7	81,8	25,3
5　Supervisors	70,3	18,7	75,7	23,3	78,3	24,7
≥ 1 000						
Total	61,9	29,5	61,1	37,1	62,9	34,4
1 B Earnings not more than (1) monthly	93,6	19,0	.	.	°65,5	°54,1
2　Very highly qualified	86,4	20,7	78,5	29,4	87,7	27,2
3　Less highly qualified	81,1	19,0	88,6	26,3	89,8	22,2
4　Executives	76,5	20,0	83,4	25,9	85,5	21,4
5　Supervisors	73,0	21,6	73,9	31,7	75,2	22,7
TOTAL						
Total	61,8	30,4	58,0	43,2	61,9	39,2
1 B Earnings not more than (1) monthly	85,7	26,7	80,5	44,8	53,7	65,3
2　Very highly qualified	82,3	22,9	77,5	34,8	77,9	36,8
3　Less highly qualified	79,1	20,4	89,6	28,8	86,0	27,1
4　Executives	76,8	22,0	79,8	29,1	83,7	28,8
5　Supervisors	69,2	21,1	72,9	28,7	75,4	26,9

CV: coefficient of variation.
(1) DM 4 500　　FF 10 000　　LIT 1 000 000　　HFL 6 000　　BFR 65 000　　LFR 65 000.

TAB. 63

Earnings in industry: average gross monthly remuneration of female non-manual workers in relation to that of male non-manual workers (male remuneration = 100) and CV of female remuneration by size group of establishment and qualifications

Salaires dans l'industrie: gain mensuel moyen brut des employées par rapport à celui des employés (gain masculin = 100) et CV des gains des employées selon la classe de taille de l'entreprise et la qualification

1972

Nederland		Belgique/België		Luxembourg		
$\frac{f}{m}$ 100	CV	$\frac{f}{m}$ 100	CV	$\frac{f}{m}$ 100	CV	
						10 – 19
48,9	42,4	60,0	33,7	51,6	31,5	Total
·	·	°63,9	°46,9	·	·	1 B Cadres dont la rémunération mensuelle est inférieure ou égale à (1)
·	·	°60,2	°31,5	·	·	2 Personnel ayant une qualification très élevée
°70,7	°34,2	71,1	28,2	62,7	33,3	3 Personnel ayant une qualification moyenne
61,5	39,0	69,1	28,8	66,4	26,4	4 Personnel d'exécution
·	·	·	·	–		5 Personnel de maîtrise (contremaîtres, chef d'équipe)
						20 – 49
48,1	45,7	61,9	33,0	49,9	39,3	Total
86,4	16,1	64,7	39,9	51,9	48,9	1 B Cadres dont la rémunération mensuelle est inférieure ou égale à (1)
°75,4	°31,2	63,6	38,1	·	·	2 Personnel ayant une qualification très élevée
72,8	28,4	71,0	27,5	56,1	37,6	3 Personnel ayant une qualification moyenne
58,1	38,3	69,4	25,9	58,3	29,9	4 Personnel d'exécution
°63,5	°31,5	°68,6	°39,2	·	·	5 Personnel de maîtrise (contremaîtres, chef d'équipe)
						(10 – 49)
48,3	44,8	61,1	33,6	50,1	37,4	Total
°82,6	°25,9	64,3	42,1	49,2	49,8	1 B Cadres dont la rémunération mensuelle est inférieure ou égale à (1)
°71,0	°40,6	62,4	37,3	·	·	2 Personnel ayant une qualification très élevée
71,6	30,7	70,5	28,0	57,4	36,7	3 Personnel ayant une qualification moyenne
59,0	38,5	68,9	27,2	60,1	28,8	4 Personnel d'exécution
65,0	29,1	°66,4	°38,5	·	·	5 Personnel de maîtrise (contremaîtres, chef d'équipe)
						50 – 99
50,6	38,8	60,4	36,7	52,1	35,9	Total
·	·	°63,0	°58,9	·	·	1 B Cadres dont la rémunération mensuelle est inférieure ou égale à (1)
°90,1	°28,3	64,2	42,2	·	·	2 Personnel ayant une qualification très élevée
70,3	28,5	73,5	26,8	68,4	24,6	3 Personnel ayant une qualification moyenne
60,6	33,2	70,0	27,5	62,2	29,1	4 Personnel d'exécution
70,4	23,8	65,1	34,3	49,1	30,4	5 Personnel de maîtrise (contremaîtres, chef d'équipe)
						100 – 199
51,5	43,3	60,6	34,3	52,1	39,5	Total
·	·	63,4	39,8	·	·	1 B Cadres dont la rémunération mensuelle est inférieure ou égale à (1)
°98,3	27,9	70,7	43,8	·	·	2 Personnel ayant une qualification très élevée
70,7	33,2	70,6	29,7	75,1	35,4	3 Personnel ayant une qualification moyenne
60,4	36,4	69,4	25,9	68,6	24,3	4 Personnel d'exécution
72,5	20,6	63,4	24,6	44,7	13,5	5 Personnel de maîtrise (contremaîtres, chef d'équipe)
						200 – 499
51,4	41,4	61,3	32,5	52,6	34,3	Total
·	–	°70,8	°34,5	·	·	1 B Cadres dont la rémunération mensuelle est inférieure ou égale à (1)
°78,5	°30,3	66,0	38,3	49,6	32,2	2 Personnel ayant une qualification très élevée
75,4	28,9	75,3	28,0	75,5	26,5	3 Personnel ayant une qualification moyenne
63,3	36,5	59,0	25,9	64,0	28,6	4 Personnel d'exécution
71,7	23,6	°67,0	26,3	·	·	5 Personnel de maîtrise (contremaîtres, chef d'équipe)
						500 – 999
52,7	40,6	61,3	31,7	53,9	32,3	Total
·	·	·	·	–	–	1 B Cadres dont la rémunération mensuelle est inférieure ou égale à (1)
79,7	17,4	67,1	30,6	–	–	2 Personnel ayant une qualification très élevée
81,2	28,2	77,1	24,3	·	·	3 Personnel ayant une qualification moyenne
63,7	33,9	75,3	28,7	71,7	31,0	4 Personnel d'exécution
64,8	21,3	57,5	22,1	–	–	5 Personnel de maîtrise (contremaîtres, chef d'équipe)
						≥ 1 000
54,2	42,5	65,0	28,5	62,1	30,0	Total
·	·	·	·	–	–	1 B Cadres dont la rémunération mensuelle est inférieure ou égale à (1)
80,7	29,9	87,3	28,7	·	·	2 Personnel ayant une qualification très élevée
89,3	25,0	79,8	25,8	80,0	24,5	3 Personnel ayant une qualification moyenne
67,7	34,0	78,4	21,8	64,5	21,9	4 Personnel d'exécution
74,5	23,5	70,2	22,7	60,4	18,3	5 Personnel de maîtrise (contremaîtres, chef d'équipe)
						TOTAL
51,1	42,8	60,5	33,5	54,0	36,8	Total
74,1	30,5	59,3	49,8	49,3	55,3	1 B Cadres dont la rémunération mensuelle est inférieure ou égale à (1)
77,4	35,7	60,5	45,1	50,4	32,6	2 Personnel ayant une qualification très élevée
76,7	31,7	70,4	30,1	66,3	36,7	3 Personnel ayant une qualification moyenne
62,5	36,0	72,0	27,6	59,5	29,2	4 Personnel d'exécution
69,2	25,1	59,7	30,4	56,1	23,1	5 Personnel de maîtrise (contremaîtres, chef d'équipe)

CV: coefficient de variation.
(1) DM 4 500 – FF 10 000 – LIT 1 000 000 – HFL 6 000 – BFR 65 000 – LFR – 65 000.

TAB. 64

Earnings in industry: average gross monthly remuneration of female non-manual workers in relation to that of male non-manual workers (male remuneration = 100) and CV of female remuneration by age group and qualifications

Salaires dans l'industrie: gain mensuel moyen brut des employées par rapport à celui des employés (gain masculin = 100) et CV des gains des employées selon la classe d'âge et la qualification

1972

	BR Deutschland		France		Italia	
	$\frac{f}{m}$ 100	CV	$\frac{f}{m}$ 100	CV	$\frac{f}{m}$ 100	CV
< 21						
Total	89,9	22,6	87,1	19,8	87,4	31,8
1 B Earnings not more than (1) monthly	–	–	.	.	.	.
2 Very highly qualified	°60,2	°36,5	.	.	.	.
3 Less highly qualified	93,3	18,3	91,6	24,1	91,8	32,8
4 Executives	90,2	21,8	90,4	19,6	94,3	30,9
5 Supervisors	.	.	79,4	14,1	66,8	26,8
21 – 24						
Total	81,5	20,3	76,5	23,6	84,7	27,0
1 B Earnings not more than (1) monthly	.	.	.	.	.	.
2 Very highly qualified	81,3	22,5	89,0	27,8	80,3	°68,8
3 Less highly qualified	87,5	17,2	94,7	22,1	86,9	24,9
4 Executives	88,5	17,9	83,3	21,8	91,7	23,9
5 Supervisors	74,1	9,7	73,0	19,5	79,0	19,2
25 – 29						
Total	72,7	22,5	68,7	30,9	77,4	28,1
1 B Earnings not more than (1) monthly	79,2	13,3	.	.	°41,7	°20,5
2 Very highly qualified	86,3	24,3	87,5	31,0	80,4	34,2
3 Less highly qualified	82,6	17,0	91,1	23,6	86,5	21,5
4 Executives	81,8	17,9	80,1	23,7	92,3	25,4
5 Supervisors	71,2	18,1	78,4	26,3	76,7	24,0
(21 – 29)						
Total	71,4	22,7	68,4	29,4	76,5	28,6
1 B Earnings not more than (1) monthly	75,0	18,2	.	.	42,3	22,3
2 Very highly qualified	82,5	25,8	86,3	31,9	77,3	44,8
3 Less highly qualified	81,5	18,2	91,2	24,2	85,0	23,4
4 Executives	84,6	18,4	80,7	23,9	91,0	25,0
5 Supervisors	70,2	16,6	74,8	26,9	75,7	23,9
30 – 44						
Total	65,5	27,4	61,9	38,9	69,6	32,0
1 B Earnings not more than (1) monthly	86,4	23,5	80,2	42,8	°57,0	°58,5
2 Very highly qualified	81,9	21,2	77,6	31,8	77,8	32,6
3 Less highly qualified	80,1	18,5	88,7	25,3	86,9	22,5
4 Executives	74,7	19,2	80,3	26,8	89,2	23,3
5 Supervisors	67,1	19,8	72,3	25,4	78,5	21,7
45 – 54						
Total	66,5	29,8	61,2	45,8	73,7	34,1
1 B Earnings not more than (1) monthly	84,5	29,0	81,1	41,1	75,7	41,2
2 Very highly qualified	83,7	22,2	76,1	34,9	85,5	27,5
3 Less highly qualified	82,6	19,2	88,4	30,1	91,9	22,7
4 Executives	77,0	18,6	84,5	28,4	91,2	26,6
5 Supervisors	72,3	22,7	75,8	30,9	81,9	26,3
≥ 55						
Total	69,8	30,8	63,5	49,7	80,8	40,6
1 B Earnings not more than (1) monthly	86,6	26,6	78,7	48,0	°88,7	°30,2
2 Very highly qualified	85,5	19,4	77,0	39,3	89,4	23,7
3 Less highly qualified	84,5	49,2	88,7	28,2	93,4	22,8
4 Executives	83,5	19,2	90,9	29,1	90,8	30,7
5 Supervisors	69,8	18,0	75,1	29,3	82,0	°21,1
≥ 21						
Total	64,8	27,7	59,9	41,9	64,7	37,2
1 B Earnings not more than (1) monthly	85,7	26,7	80,4	44,7	54,5	64,5
2 Very highly qualified	82,5	22,5	77,6	34,6	79,3	35,0
3 Less highly qualified	79,9	19,5	89,9	28,3	86,5	26,5
4 Executives	78,9	18,8	81,3	27,6	86,6	26,5
5 Supervisors	86,4	27,7	73,0	28,6	76,4	25,7
TOTAL						
Total	61,8	30,4	58,0	43,2	61,9	39,2
1 B Earnings not more than (1) monthly	85,7	26,7	80,5	44,8	53,7	65,3
2 Very highly qualified	82,2	22,9	77,5	34,8	77,9	36,8
3 Less highly qualified	79,0	20,4	89,6	28,8	86,0	27,1
4 Executives	76,8	22,0	79,8	29,1	83,7	28,8
5 Supervisors	69,1	21,1	72,9	28,7	75,4	26,9

CV: coefficient of variation.
(1) DM 4 500   FF 10 000   LIT 1 000 000   HFL 6 000   BFR 65 000   LFR 65 000.

TAB. 64

Earnings in industry: average gross monthly remuneration of female, non-manual workers in relation to that of male non-manual workers (male remuneration = 100) and CV of female remuneration by age group and qualifications

Salaires dans l'industrie: gain mensuel moyen brut des employées par rapport à celui des employés (gain masculin = 100) et CV des gains des employées selon la classe d'âge et la qualification

1972

Nederland		Belgique/België		Luxembourg		
$\frac{f}{m}$ 100	CV	$\frac{f}{m}$ 100	CV	$\frac{f}{m}$ 100	CV	
						< 21
93,9	25,4	85,2	19,6	82,2	25,9	Total
–	–	.	°20,8	.	.	1 B Cadres dont la rémunération mensuelle est inférieure ou égale à ([1])
.	.	.	20,8	.	.	2 Personnel ayant une qualification très élevée
°90,9	25,5	81,9	19,4	74,8	26,4	3 Personnel ayant une qualification moyenne
94,8	25,3	88,8	19,6	81,6	24,9	4 Personnel d'exécution
.	°24,4	°65,8	13,1	.	18,9	5 Personnel de maîtrise (contremaîtres, chefs d'équipe)
						21 – 24
84,5	18,1	79,8	20,6	77,1	20,1	Total
–	–	°59,9	°29,3	.	.	1 B Cadres dont la rémunération mensuelle est inférieure ou égale à ([1])
.	.	71,9	26,9	.	.	2 Personnel ayant une qualification très élevée
81,8	16,1	81,6	22,2	80,0	21,2	3 Personnel ayant une qualification moyenne
87,1	17,8	84,0	19,2	76,5	20,8	4 Personnel d'exécution
80,0	18,3	69,8	21,2	79,6	13,3	5 Personnel de maîtrise (contremaîtres, chefs d'équipe)
						25 – 29
77,1	21,9	72,2	23,9	71,5	18,7	Total
.	.	°63,8	°50,5	.	.	1 B Cadres dont la rémunération mensuelle est inférieure ou égale à ([1])
93,9	23,0	71,4	35,9	65,4	23,2	2 Personnel ayant une qualification très élevée
87,3	18,7	78,0	22,9	76,8	19,4	3 Personnel ayant une qualification moyenne
82,6	18,9	79,8	20,8	75,5	15,9	4 Personnel d'exécution
75,1	18,2	67,3	20,0	73,1	9,9	5 Personnel de maîtrise (contremaîtres, chefs d'équipe)
						(21 – 29)
73,4	22,5	71,6	23,9	69,1	21,2	Total
.	.	°57,3	°51,5	.	.	1 B Cadres dont la rémunération mensuelle est inférieure ou égale à ([1])
91,1	27,4	65,6	36,1	61,2	26,3	2 Personnel ayant une qualification très élevée
80,0	22,5	76,8	24,0	74,1	22,5	3 Personnel ayant une qualification moyenne
79,9	20,3	99,6	21,1	73,1	20,1	4 Personnel d'exécution
73,7	19,8	65,7	21,8	69,3	13,7	5 Personnel de maîtrise (contremaîtres, chefs d'équipe)
						30 – 44
70,5	29,2	65,9	28,6	65,2	29,2	Total
78,8	11,2	63,9	39,5	.	.	1 B Cadres dont la rémunération mensuelle est inférieure ou égale à ([1])
85,0	30,2	65,3	38,3	.	.	2 Personnel ayant une qualification très élevée
83,9	24,8	75,2	24,7	79,3	21,6	3 Personnel ayant une qualification moyenne
81,5	21,8	78,0	22,5	69,2	20,9	4 Personnel d'exécution
71,4	19,6	66,2	27,7	57,4	29,1	5 Personnel de maîtrise (contremaîtres, chefs d'équipe)
						45 – 54
72,5	33,0	67,4	30,0	72,4	35,2	Total
°73,1	°33,2	°59,1	°41,3	.	.	1 B Cadres dont la rémunération mensuelle est inférieure ou égale à ([1])
75,6	35,0	65,3	40,6	.	.	2 Personnel ayant une qualification très élevée
86,7	21,5	75,8	25,5	84,1	27,1	3 Personnel ayant une qualification moyenne
84,7	25,1	78,6	22,6	67,7	25,4	4 Personnel d'exécution
77,4	21,5	65,1	26,6	.	.	5 Personnel de maîtrise (contremaîtres, chefs d'équipe)
						≥ 55
73,9	34,4	73,5	38,6	76,9	26,6	Total
.	.	°75,7	°49,2	.	.	1 B Cadres dont la rémunération mensuelle est inférieure ou égale à ([1])
°61,9	°40,4	°71,6	°35,3	.	.	2 Personnel ayant une qualification très élevée
83,6	26,1	75,7	32,7	77,7	24,8	3 Personnel ayant une qualification moyenne
83,1	24,6	85,8	28,7	.	.	4 Personnel d'exécution
75,7	19,6	69,5	26,6	.	.	5 Personnel de maîtrise (contremaîtres, chefs d'équipe)
						≥ 21
60,7	33,5	63,2	31,1	60,3	31,6	Total
74,1	30,5	60,9	48,1	57,0	47,7	1 B Cadres dont la rémunération mensuelle est inférieure ou égale à ([1])
78,2	34,6	57,2	42,2	52,4	30,8	2 Personnel ayant une qualification très élevée
78,8	29,1	72,3	28,1	70,8	31,8	3 Personnel ayant une qualification moyenne
73,2	25,5	75,3	24,7	66,4	22,7	4 Personnel d'exécution
71,4	21,9	62,0	27,7	58,6	22,9	5 Personnel de maîtrise (contremaîtres, chefs d'équipe)
						TOTAL
51,1	42,8	60,5	33,5	54,0	36,8	Total
74,1	30,5	59,3	49,8	49,3	55,3	1 B Cadres dont la rémunération mensuelle est inférieure ou égale à ([1])
77,4	35,7	60,5	45,1	50,4	32,6	2 Personnel ayant une qualification très élevée
76,6	31,7	70,4	30,1	66,3	36,7	3 Personnel ayant une qualification moyenne
62,5	36,0	72,0	27,6	59,5	29,2	4 Personnel d'exécution
69,2	25,1	59,6	30,4	56,1	23,1	5 Personnel de maîtrise (contremaîtres, chefs d'équipe)

CV: coefficient de variation.
([1]) DM 4 500 – FF 10 000 – LIT 1 000 000 – HFL 6 000 – BFR 65 000 – LFR – 65 000.

TAB. 65

Earnings in industry: average gross monthly remuneration of female non-manual workers in relation to that of male non-manual workers (male remuneration = 100) and CV of female remuneration by length of service and qualifications

Salaires dans l'industrie: gain moyen mensuel brut des employées par rapport à celui des employés (gain masculin = 100) et CV des gains des employées selon l'ancienneté dans l'entreprise et la qualificatio

1972

	BR Deutschland		France		Italia	
	$\frac{f}{m}$ 100	CV	$\frac{f}{m}$ 100	CV	$\frac{f}{m}$ 100	CV
< 2						
Total	60,8	29,2	59,1	38,0	60,0	41,2
1 B Earnings not more than (¹) monthly	°79,6	°33,1	°100,2	°43,4	.	.
2 Very highly qualified	77,6	26,1	80,3	37,1	60,2	°59,2
3 Less highly qualified	78,9	20,0	90,8	26,8	78,8	28,6
4 Executives	76,0	24,2	80,5	27,9	79,8	34,0
5 Supervisors	67,0	22,3	71,6	29,1	64,3	26,6
2 – 4						
Total	59,8	29,1	58,3	38,2	61,2	31,3
1 B Earnings not more than (¹) monthly	86,3	25,7	°90,0	°47,9	.	.
2 Very highly qualified	80,3	25,8	76,8	30,3	70,3	43,6
3 Less highly qualified	76,5	21,2	87,9	24,9	81,3	26,5
4 Executives	81,2	21,6	78,4	26,8	83,1	23,6
5 Supervisors	72,6	15,2	75,6	27,9	73,1	26,4
5 – 9						
Total	63,1	26,8	59,9	39,2	61,8	31,8
1 B Earnings not more than (¹) monthly	86,9	26,1	83,9	43,1	.	.
2 Very highly qualified	79,9	23,2	78,9	35,4	77,4	32,1
3 Less highly qualified	78,2	20,3	88,8	27,9	81,5	24,2
4 Executives	80,7	18,4	81,4	25,3	84,3	24,4
5 Supervisors	68,7	18,6	73,4	26,2	76,6	23,4
10 – 19						
Total	67,3	27,6	63,4	40,9	65,9	29,7
1 B Earnings not more than (¹) monthly	84,0	28,5	°73,6	°46,6	°60,1	°53,0
2 Very highly qualified	83,3	21,4	76,2	34,3	81,0	23,8
3 Less highly qualified	81,2	18,7	88,6	30,7	81,7	20,7
4 Executives	78,3	17,6	83,0	26,2	84,9	20,5
5 Supervisors	67,4	22,2	72,7	27,3	78,5	18,8
> 20						
Total	73,2	27,6	65,9	41,8	75,0	28,3
1 B Earnings not more than (¹) monthly	86,5	24,2	78,3	43,7	78,5	29,4
2 Very highly qualified	85,8	19,6	76,8	33,1	83,5	26,2
3 Less highly qualified	84,5	17,5	89,9	23,7	90,0	19,4
4 Executives	78,1	17,1	86,2	27,0	88,4	17,8
5 Supervisors	71,2	21,6	75,6	29,2	81,1	25,2
TOTAL						
Total	61,8	30,4	58,0	43,2	61,9	39,2
1 B Earnings not more than (¹) monthly	85,7	26,7	80,5	44,8	53,7	65,3
2 Very highly qualified	82,2	22,9	77,5	34,8	77,9	36,8
3 Less highly qualified	79,0	20,4	89,6	28,8	86,0	27,1
4 Executives	76,8	22,0	79,8	29,1	83,7	28,8
5 Supervisors	69,2	21,1	72,9	28,7	75,4	26,9

CV: coefficient of variation.
(¹) DM 4 500   FF 10 000   LIT 1 000 000   HFL 6 000   BFR 65 000   LFR 65 000.

TAB. 65

Earnings in industry: average gross monthly remuneration of female non-manual workers in relation to that of male non-manual workers (male remuneration = 100) and CV of female remuneration by length of service and qualifications

Salaires dans l'industrie: gain moyen mensuel brut des employées par rapport à celui des employés gain masculin = 100) et CV des gains des employées selon l'ancienneté dans l'entreprise et la qualification

1972

Nederland		Belgique/België		Luxembourg		
$\frac{f}{m}$ 100	CV	$\frac{f}{m}$ 100	CV	$\frac{f}{m}$ 100	CV	
						< 2
49,6	40,2	60,6	31,8	53,0	31,4	Total
.	.	°50,8	61,3	.	.	1 B Cadres dont la rémunération mensuelle est inférieure ou égale à (¹)
°74,9	°41,8	54,3	46,3	.	.	2 Personnel ayant une qualification très élevée
66,0	34,8	70,4	30,1	57,5	35,5	3 Personnel ayant une qualification moyenne
62,9	36,5	73,1	26,9	59,2	29,7	4 Personnel d'exécution
°58,6	°30,5	59,9	29,9	59,2	19,3	5 Personnel de maîtrise (contremaîtres, chefs d'équipe)
						2 – 4
63,6	34,2	61,7	28,4	55,2	25,6	Total
.	.	°53,0	47,1	.	.	1 B Cadres dont la rémunération mensuelle est inférieure ou égale à (¹)
°67,7	°44,9	58,2	42,2	49,5	24,0	2 Personnel ayant une qualification très élevée
74,3	33,2	71,8	27,4	60,2	26,2	3 Personnel ayant une qualification moyenne
66,4	29,0	73,4	24,2	59,5	23,1	4 Personnel d'exécution
64,9	21,4	58,0	28,6	61,1	14,5	5 Personnel de maîtrise (contremaîtres, chefs d'équipe)
						5 – 9
61,4	29,3	61,7	29,3	61,2	25,4	Total
.	.	°59,8	°52,5	.	.	1 B Cadres dont la rémunération mensuelle est inférieure ou égale à (¹)
85,9	24,3	62,4	45,2	.	.	2 Personnel ayant une qualification très élevée
77,9	25,3	68,2	27,3	67,6	25,5	3 Personnel ayant une qualification moyenne
74,1	23,4	74,2	29,2	73,7	21,3	4 Personnel d'exécution
69,3	23,7	60,9	29,7	56,0	25,4	5 Personnel de maîtrise (contremaîtres, chefs d'équipe)
						10 – 19
70,5	30,0	65,9	28,9	68,0	25,7	Total
.	.	°62,3	°44,7	.	.	1 B Cadres dont la rémunération mensuelle est inférieure ou égale à (¹)
79,1	35,8	59,7	44,0	.	.	2 Personnel ayant une qualification très élevée
81,6	26,1	73,9	25,2	79,1	19,0	3 Personnel ayant une qualification moyenne
83,3	22,1	79,4	22,2	67,6	16,7	4 Personnel d'exécution
74,4	20,3	66,7	20,8	.	.	5 Personnel de maîtrise (contremaîtres, chefs d'équipe)
						> 20
78,3	30,4	71,6	28,4	82,9	25,1	Total
.	.	66,2	40,6	.	.	1 B Cadres dont la rémunération mensuelle est inférieure ou égale à (¹)
°79,8	°28,6	69,3	32,0	.	.	2 Personnel ayant une qualification très élevée
89,9	19,6	76,5	25,6	85,4	21,2	3 Personnel ayant une qualification moyenne
86,3	22,2	82,5	19,9	.	.	4 Personnel d'exécution
76,7	17,4	69,6	23,9	.	.	5 Personnel de maîtrise (contremaîtres, chefs d'équipe)
						TOTAL
51,1	42,8	60,5	33,5	54,0	36,8	Total
74,1	30,5	59,3	49,8	49,3	55,3	1 B Cadres dont la rémunération mensuelle est inférieure ou égale à (¹)
77,4	35,7	60,4	45,1	50,4	32,6	2 Personnel ayant une qualification très élevée
76,7	31,7	70,4	30,1	66,3	36,7	3 Personnel ayant une qualification moyenne
62,5	36,0	72,0	27,6	59,5	29,2	4 Personnel d'exécution
69,2	25,1	59,7	30,4	56,1	23,1	5 Personnel de maîtrise (contremaîtres, chefs d'équipe)

CV: coefficient de variation.
(¹) DM 4 500 – FF 10 000 – LIT 1 000 000 – HFL 6 000 – BFR 65 000 – LFR 65 000.

TAB. 66

Earnings in industry: gross hourly average earnings of female manual workers in relation to those of male workers (male earnings = 100) and CV of female earnings by region

Salaires dans l'industrie: gain horaire moyen brut des ouvrières par rapport à celui des ouvriers (gain masculin = 100) et CV des gains des ouvrières par région

1972

BR Deutschland	$\frac{f}{m}$ 100	France	$\frac{f}{m}$ 100	Italia	$\frac{f}{m}$ 100	Nederland	$\frac{f}{m}$ 100	Belgique/België	$\frac{f}{m}$ 100	Luxembourg $\frac{f}{m}$ 100
Schleswig-Holstein	65,8	Région Parisienne	76,7	Piemonte, Val d'Aosta	–	Noord	65,9	Vlaams Gebied	69,5	60,3
Hamburg	65,2	Bassin Parisien	77,7	Liguria	75,5	Oost	66,0	Région Wallonne	66,7	
Berlin	66,3	Nord	77,8	Lombardia	77,6	Zuid	66,1	Bruxelles	69,9	
Bremen	66,2	Est	75,2	Trentino A. Adige	78,8	West	67,0			
Niedersachsen	69,0	Ouest	80,1	Veneto Friuli V. Giulia	81,4					
Nordrhein-Westfalen	67,9	Sud-Ouest	78,8	Emilia Romagna	76,1					
Hessen	69,1	Centre-Est	78,6	Marche Toscana Umbria	79,5					
Rheinland-Pfalz	67,6	Méditerranée	74,8	Lazio	73,2					
Baden-Württemberg	72,2			Abruzzi Molise	78,0					
Bayern	69,8			Campania						
Saarland	65,4			Puglia, Basilicata						
				Calabria	71,4					
				Sicilia	77,9					
				Sardegna	82,6					

CV: coefficient of variation.
CV: coefficient de variation.

TAB. 67

Earnings in agriculture: average hourly earnings of female workers in relation to those of male workers (male earnings = 100) and CV of female earnings by qualifications and type of activity performed on the holding

Salaires dans l'agriculture: gain horaire moyen des travailleuses par rapport à celui des travailleurs (gain masculin = 100) et CV des gains des travailleuses selon la qualification et le type d'activité exercée dans l'exploitation

1975

	BR Deutschland		France		Italia		Nederland		Belgique Belgïe		Luxembourg		United Kingdom		Danmark		Ireland	
	f/m 100	CV	f/m 100	CV	f/m 100	CV	f/m 100	CV	f/m 100	CV	f/m 100	CV	f/m 100	CV	f/m 100	CV	f/m 100	CV
Skilled workers / Ouvriers qualifiés																		
General agriculture / Agriculture générale	91,2	32,1	105,4	31,4	95,9	30,2	–	–	:	:	–	–	–	–	61,0	53,5	:	
Livestock production / Élevage	71,3	25,9	91,3	20,6	99,8	23,1	–	–	:	:	–	–	96,0	6,3	73,6	40,1	94,7	16,4
Specialized production / Cultures spécifiques	80,3	25,0	102,2	22,0	96,9	16,6	77,1		92,6	8,3	–	–	–	–	92,9	13,8	80,7	21,6
Unskilled workers / Ouvriers non qualifiés																		
General agriculture / Agriculture générale	89,0	34,7	103,7	21,7	98,1	28,1	–	–	85,7	24,6	81,9	41,9	83,9	20,5	69,8	56,4	80,0	37,1
Livestock production / Élevage	80,3	25,7	108,1	16,8	108,6	22,4	–	–	95,0	31,9	:	:	95,5	10,6	49,9	44,4	85,9	21,7
Specialized production / Cultures spécifiques	82,8	22,3	99,1	13,5	89,7	13,3	99,4	13,0	93,5	19,6	:	:	84,4	19,7	100,7	21,6	90,8	21,3
Total	78,5	30,1	95,3	22,2	91,8	25,6	77,8	:	88,2	24,1	82,7	36,2	87,0	17,5	106,3	32,4	87,7	28,1

CV: coefficient of variation.
CV: coefficient de variation.

TAB. 68

Average monthly number of hours of pay of female workers in relation to that of male workers (male average = 100) by qualifications and type of activity performed on the holding

Nombre moyen d'heures payées mensuellement aux travailleuses par rapport aux heures payées aux travailleurs (nombre moyen d'heures payées mensuellement aux travailleurs = 100), selon la qualification et le type d'activité exercée dans l'exploitation

1975

	BR Deutschland	France	Italia	Nederland	Belgique Belgïe	Luxembourg	United Kingdom	Ireland	Danmark
	f/m 100	f/m 100	f/m 100	f/m 100	f/m 100	f/m 100	f/m 100	f/m 100	f/m 100
Skilled workers / Ouvriers qualifiés									
General agriculture / Agriculture générale	92,3	91,7	90,2	–	:	–	–	97,3	:
Livestock production / Élevage	96,2	98,5	90,9	–	:	–	93,2	89,4	99,4
Specialized production / Cultures spécifiques	95,4	101,5	91,2	–	102,2	–	–	90,9	95,4
Unskilled workers / Ouvriers non qualifiés									
General agriculture / Agriculture générale	97,0	98,9	88,9	–	80,6	91,1	86,6	92,0	96,6
Livestock production / Élevage	99,5	97,4	84,3	–	89,2	:	88,2	98,4	92,2
Specialized production / Cultures spécifiques	96,0	100,0	95,9	95,0	91,8	:	90,6	93,7	83,7
Total	94,6	97,4	89,8	94,6	89,8	98,6	89,2	88,5	91,6

TAB. 69

Earnings in agriculture: gross hourly average earnings of female workers in relation to those of male workers (male earnings = 100) by qualifications and size of holding

Salaires dans l'agriculture: gain horaire moyen brut des travailleuses par rapport au gain des travailleurs (gain masculin = 100) selon la qualification et la taille de l'exploitation

	BR Deutschland	France	Italia	Nederland	Belgique/België	Luxembourg	United Kingdom	Ireland	Danmark
	$\frac{f}{m}$ 100	$\frac{f}{m}$ 100	$\frac{f}{m}$ 100	$\frac{f}{m}$ 100	$\frac{f}{m}$ 100	$\frac{f}{m}$ 100	$\frac{f}{m}$ 100	$\frac{f}{m}$ 100	$\frac{f}{m}$ 100
1972									
Skilled workers / Ouvriers qualifiés									
Holdings with 1 or 2 workers — Exploitations ayant 1 ou 2 salariés	84,3	99,0	95,2	·	·	·	·	95,8	·
Holdings with 3 to 9 workers — Exploitations ayant 3 à 9 salariés	71,6	97,1	102,1	·	·	·	·	99,2	·
Holdings with 10 or more workers — Exploitations ayant 10 salariés et plus	84,8	95,0	93,6	·	·	·	·	·	·
TOTAL	87,3	101,9	98,6	·	·	·	·	118,9	·
Unskilled workers / Ouvriers non qualifiés									
Holdings with 1 or 2 workers — Exploitations ayant 1 ou 2 salariés	96,0	95,9	101,0	·	·	·	·	·	·
Holdings with 3 to 9 workers — Exploitations ayant 3 à 9 salariés	84,6	97,6	92,8	·	92,4	·	80,1	·	·
Holdings with 10 or more workers — Exploitations ayant 10 salariés et plus	78,7	97,7	91,5	·	91,9	·	94,7	·	·
TOTAL	90,0	103,8	99,7	·	93,2	·	90,9	·	87,4
1976									
Skilled workers / Ouvriers qualifiés									
Holdings with 1 or 2 workers — Exploitations ayant 1 ou 2 salariés	87,1	91,2	90,3	85,1	89,5	·	90,8	·	99,3
Holdings with 3 to 9 workers — Exploitations ayant 3 à 9 salariés	81,5	88,4	98,1	69,2	91,2	·	96,4	71,9	97,8
Holdings with 10 or more workers — Exploitations ayant 10 salariés et plus	85,2	90,4	90,9	86,1	·	·	105,3	94,5	94,0
TOTAL	87,7	96,0	95,1	79,5	90,0	·	102,7	83,5	105,4
Unskilled workers / Ouvriers non qualifiés									
Holdings with 1 or 2 workers — Exploitations ayant 1 ou 2 salariés	92,1	95,4	97,8	77,8	96,1	·	88,4	75,9	110,0
Holdings with 3 to 9 workers — Exploitations ayant 3 à 9 salariés	82,6	94,8	94,1	74,6	87,6	·	93,9	74,2	110,5
Holdings with 10 or more workers — Exploitations ayant 10 salariés et plus	81,7	95,3	92,7	78,4	88,5	·	91,9	81,6	113,0
TOTAL	91,3	101,9	99,9	74,5	92,0	·	92,8	86,7	121,2

TAB. 70

Average monthly number of hours of pay of female workers in relation to that of male workers (male average = 100) by qualifications and size of holding

Nombre moyen d'heures payées mensuellement aux travailleuses par rapport aux heures payées aux travailleurs (nombre moyen mensuel d'heures des travailleurs = 100) selon la qualification et la taille de l'exploitation

1975

	BR Deutschland	France	Italia	Nederland	Belgique/Belgïe	Luxembourg	United Kingdom	Ireland	Danmark
	f/m·100	f/m·100	f/m·100	f/m·100	f/m·100	f/m·100	f/m·100	f/m·100	f/m·100
Skilled workers									
Holdings with 1 or 2 workers	94,7	97,0	95,6	.		.	.	90,0	.
Holdings with 3 to 9 workers	90,9	96,5	94,1	.	...	.	...	86,5	.
Holdings with 10 or more workers	94,8	96,1	88,7	.	...	.	...		
TOTAL	92,6	97,4	91,1	.	...	.	...	88,2	.
Unskilled workers									
Holdings with 1 or 2 workers	98,6	98,0	80,4	.	91,9	.		92,8	.
Holdings with 3 to 9 workers	95,1	97,3	91,3	.	83,7	.	87,7	91,5	.
Holdings with 10 or more workers	95,7	97,4	93,4	.		.	85,4		
Total	96,8	99,4	89,8	.	88,6	.	89,1	89,4	90,3

TAB. 71

Earnings in agriculture: gross hourly average earnings of female workers in relation to those of male workers (male earnings = 100) by qualifications and the payment or not benefits in kind

Salaires dans l'agriculture: gain horaire moyen brut des travailleuses par rapport au gain des travailleurs (gain masculin = 100) selon la qualification et l'octroi ou non d'avantages en nature

1975

	BR Deutschland	France	Italia	Nederland	Belgique/Belgïe	Luxembourg	United Kingdom	Ireland	Danmark
	f/m·100	f/m·100	f/m·100	f/m·100	f/m·100	f/m·100	f/m·100	f/m·100	f/m·100
Skilled workers									
Total	93,7	101,9	98,6	77,4	92,8	–	98,4	88,1	105,4
Accommodation and meals	87,5	93,7	78,7	:	–	–	–	...	59,4
Accommodation only	82,7	113,6	97,9	–	–	–	–	...	74,9
Meals only	:	115,3	109,5	–	–	–	–	...	...
Neither accommod. nor meals	84,3	98,4	99,2	76,5	67,6	–	99,3	83,0	97,2
Unskilled workers									
Total	86,9	103,8	99,7	98,0	93,2	72,0	90,9	87,4	118,9
Accommodation and meals	89,7	96,6	78,0	–	...	...	–	...	60,0
Accommodation only	79,1	100,0	109,3	–	...	...	75,8	...	...
Meals only	89,1	105,4	77,2	–	...	...	–	...	...
Neither accommod. nor meals	82,6	97,7	94,0	97,8	90,3	:	94,0	85,8	111,0

Ouvriers qualifiés — Exploitations ayant 1 ou 2 salariés; Exploitations ayant 3 à 9 salariés; Exploitations ayant 10 salariés et plus; Total.
Ouvriers non qualifiés — Exploitations ayant 1 ou 2 salariés; Exploitations ayant 3 à 9 salariés; Exploitations ayant 10 salariés et plus; Total.

Ouvriers qualifiés — Total; Logés et nourris; Logés; Nourris; Ni logés ni nourris.
Ouvriers non qualifiés — Total; Logés et nourris; Logés; Nourris; Ni logés ni nourris.

TAB. 72

Average monthly number of hours of pay of female workers in relation to that of male workers (male average = 100) by qualifications and the payment or not of benefits in kind

Nombre moyen d'heures payées mensuellement aux travailleuses agricoles par rapport aux heures payées aux travailleurs (nombre moyen mensuel d'heures des travailleurs = 100) selon la qualification et l'octroi ou non d'avantages en nature

1975

	BR Deutschland $\frac{f}{m}$ 100	France $\frac{f}{m}$ 100	Italia $\frac{f}{m}$ 100	Nederland $\frac{f}{m}$ 100	Belgique België $\frac{f}{m}$ 100	Luxembourg $\frac{f}{m}$ 100	United Kingdom $\frac{f}{m}$ 100	Ireland $\frac{f}{m}$ 100	Danmark $\frac{f}{m}$ 100		
Skilled workers											**Ouvriers qualifiés**
Total	92,6	97,0	91,1	95,0	102,9	—	93,6	94,6	87,6		Total
Accommodation and meals	97,4	92,1	93,8	:	—	—	—	...	99,4		Logés et nourris
Accommodation only	91,3	94,0	89,4	—	—	—	—	...	87,0		Logés
Meals only	94,1	87,0	78,4	—	—	—	—	...	:		Nourris
Neither accommod. nor meals	92,8	97,4	90,8	95,6	102,8	—	93,2	88,4	90,0		Ni logés ni nourris
Unskilled workers											**Ouvriers non qualifiés**
Total	96,8	99,4	89,8	95,1	88,6	94,0	89,1	90,3	89,4		Total
Accommodation and meals	99,4	101,3	80,2	—	:	...	—	...	94,7		Logés et nourris
Accommodation only	96,5	100,5	88,6	—	...	...	83,6	...	...		Logés
Meals only	96,6	99,1	76,5	—	...	...	—	...	...		Nourris
Neither accommod. nor meals	95,8	97,9	93,6	95,6	89,0	:	91,0	86,9	91,9		Ni logés ni nourris

TAB. 73

Earnings in agriculture: gross hourly average earnings and average monthly number of hours of pay of female agricultural workers by qualifications (male earnings = 100, male average hours = 100)

Salaires dans l'agriculture: gain horaire moyen brut et nombre moyen d'heures payées mensuellement aux travailleuses agricoles selon la qualification (gain masculin = 100, nombre moyen d'heures des travailleurs = 100)

1975

	BR Deutschland	France	Italia	Nederland	Belgique België	Luxembourg	United Kingdom	Ireland	Danmark		
Skilled workers											**Ouvriers qualifiés**
Retribution	93,7	101,9	98,6	77,4	92,8	—	98,4	88,1	105,4		Rétribution
Hours worked	92,6	97,0	91,1	95,0	102,9	—	93,6	94,6	87,6		Heures prestées
Unskilled workers											**Ouvriers non qualifiés**
Retribution	86,9	103,8	99,7	98,0	93,2	72,0	90,9	87,4	118,9		Rétribution
Hours worked	96,8	99,4	89,8	95,1	88,6	94,0	89,1	90,3	89,4		Heures prestées

TAB. 74

Earnings in wholesale and retail distribution, banking and insurance: corrected gross monthly average pay of full-time female workers in relation to those of male workers (male pay = 100) and CV of female pay by branch of activity and qualifications

Salaires dans le commerce, les institutions de crédit et les assurances: rémunération mensuelle moyenne brute corrigée des salariées à temps complet par rapport à celle des salariés (rémunération masculine = 100) et CV des rémunérations des salariées selon la branche d'activité et la qualification

1974

	BR Deutschland		France		Italia		Nederland		Belgique België	
	$\frac{f}{m}$ 100	CV	$\frac{f}{m}$ 100	CV	$\frac{f}{m}$ 100	CV	$\frac{f}{m}$ 100	CV	$\frac{f}{m}$ 100	CV
61 Wholesale distribution										
1 A Top management personnel	81,7	34,2	82,1	54,4	87,7°	37,3°	74,0°	49,5°	–	27,6°
1 B Management personnel and senior executives	86,9	36,2	78,9	37,0	91,6	33,7	60,4	44,5	98,9	29,1
2 Executives and management staff	79,4	28,7	86,0	35,2	90,5	27,2	66,5	36,4	86,4°	30,6
3 Highly-skilled junior personnel	82,4	25,7	91,9	42,1	88,6	23,8	71,7	32,2	72,6	31,9
4 Skilled junior personnel	76,7	26,8	86,3	24,1	86,8	23,0	69,3	29,4	87,7	30,5
5 Unskilled junior personnel	72,1	23,8	86,3	19,8	86,3	20,9	74,9	29,2	90,7	29,8
64/653-656 Retail distribution										
1 A Top management personnel	86,1	23,3	79,7	49,8	91,4°	42,2°	65,6	51,9°	60,2°	22,9
1 B Management personnel and senior executives	84,5	32,8	81,2	28,6	87,7	34,9	68,7	36,7	90,7	25,9
2 Executives and management staff	86,1	26,4	79,8	50,0	90,4	27,7	73,0	34,1	83,2	37,3
3 Highly-skilled junior personnel	79,9	27,9	80,6	30,2	93,0	26,8	74,5	33,0	72,8	37,7
4 Skilled junior personnel	74,7	25,1	79,6	23,4	91,5	24,3	73,1	34,1	81,8	54,0
5 Unskilled junior personnel	76,3	25,3	86,9	18,3	92,7	22,2	–	–	78,9	29,4
812/813 Credit institutions										
1 Directors, top management	–	–	73,9	26,0	91,6°	23,8	.			
2 Senior executives	90,1	23,6	88,0	22,3	94,4	25,1	60,6°		–	–
3 Executives (junior management)	82,8	17,5	90,4	22,6	96,1	20,2	48,8°	54,8	84,7	21,6
4 Highly-qualified clerical staff	84,6	18,6	94,4	19,4	99,2	23,9	70,6	38,2	87,2	21,3
5 Qualified clerical staff	88,9	14,8	97,0	19,5	85,9	18,5	70,9	29,9	84,2	24,5
6 Other employees	80,4	19,7	94,9	21,5	87,1	22,2	75,2	39,9	85,4	29,8
82 Insurance										
I Managers and senior management executives	.	.	.	.	.	.	.	.	.	.
II Middle management executives	90,2	17,5	83,1	30,5	87,6	25,2	.	.	88,7	21,5
III Junior executives and personnel with equivalent qualification	88,8	20,4	92,5	28,2	92,4	26,0	51,7	64,8	79,2	29,3
IV Highly-skilled employees	84,9	16,6	94,0	26,7	97,0	21,3	83,4	29,4	91,4	18,7
V Skilled employees	87,8	14,6	95,0	36,4	94,0	19,7	76,5	30,5	88,2	23,7
VI Other employees	87,1	16,7	89,7	19,5	77,0	19,2	75,2	33,5	88,8	22,6

CV: coefficient of variation.

TAB. 74

Earnings in wholesale and retail distribution, banking and insurance: corrected gross monthly average pay of full-time female workers in relation to those of male workers (male pay = 100) and CV of female pay by branch of activity and qualifications

Salaires dans le commerce, les institutions de crédit et les assurances: rémunération mensuelle moyenne brute corrigée des salariées à temps complet par rapport à celle des salariés (rémunération masculine = 100) et CV des rémunérations des salariées selon la branche d'activité et la qualification

1974

Luxembourg		United Kingdom		Ireland		Danmark			
$\frac{f}{m}$ 100	CV	$\frac{f}{m}$ 100	CV	$\frac{f}{m}$ 100	CV	$\frac{f}{m}$ 100	CV		
								61	**Commerce de gros**
.	.	–	–	.	.	.	.	1 A	Personnel supérieur de direction
72,9	29,3	.	.	–	–	.	.	1 B	Personnel de direction et cadres supérieurs
62,0	42,4	54,3°	32,5°	79,7°	32,9°	76,0	27,8	2	Personnel d'exécution et d'encadrement
65,9	36,0	66,0	19,7	64,9	25,5	78,6	18,5	3	Personnel subalterne très qualifié
61,1	33,6	64,7	28,5	63,9	35,9	82,2	17,7	4	Personnel subalterne qualifié
57,8	31,0	63,3	22,4	62,8	27,5	79,9	21,1	5	Personnel subalterne non qualifié
								64/653 – 656	**Commerce de détail**
.	.	.	.	.	.	.	.	1 A	Personnel supérieur de direction
97,5	29,2	.	.	–	–	89,6	22,4	1 B	Cadres supérieurs
71,4	32,7	67,5	37,3	87,9°	70,3°	81,4	28,8	2	Personnel de conception (cadres inférieurs)
65,6	28,0	75,2	35,1	72,0	30,1	80,1	13,7	3	Personnel d'exécution très qualifié
60,3	25,9	62,5	27,3	65,4	32,2	83,1	14,8	4	Personnel d'exécution qualifié
71,5	37,5	67,8	22,7	65,2	37,4	83,6	25,9	5	Autres agents
								812/813	**Institutions de crédit**
–	–	–	–	–	–	–	–	1	Personnel supérieur de direction
–	–	–	–	.	.	.	.	2	Cadres supérieurs
80,9	25,1	78,3°	36,3°	99,5°	37,8°	91,5	16,1	3	Personnel de conception (cadres inférieurs)
83,6	22,0	78,5	27,7	94,0	29,3	93,7	18,8	4	Personnel d'exécution très qualifié
74,5	29,3	77,5	29,0	91,4	19,2	100,0	13,7	5	Personnel d'exécution qualifié
79,7	33,0	72,4	33,2	58,6°	31,3	87,4	15,6	6	Autres agents
								82	**Assurances**
–	–	–	–	–	–	–	–	I	Dirigeants et cadres supérieurs de direction
.	.	–	–	–	–	.	.	II	Cadres intermédiaires
.	.	.	.	.	.	85,4	13,7	III	Agents d'encadrement et assimilés
96,5	32,6	81,4°	31,3°	70,4	25,2	92,8	11,3	IV	Travailleurs très qualifiés
85,1	27,6	69,0	30,5	86,0	27,5	89,3	15,8	V	Travailleurs qualifiés
65,3	28,3	69,9	31,4	–	–	93,3	24,6	VI	Autres travailleurs

CV: coefficient de variation.

TAB. 75

Earnings in wholesale and retail distribution, banking and insurance: corrected gross monthly average pay of part-time female workers in relation to those of male workers (male pay = 100) and CV of female pay by branch of activity and qualifications

Salaires dans le commerce, les institutions de crédit et les assurances: rémunération mensuelle moyenne brute corrigée des salariées à temps partiel par rapport à celle des salariés (rémunération masculine = 100) et CV des rémunérations des salariées selon la branche d'activité et la qualification

1974

	BR Deutschland		France		Italia		Nederland		Belgique België	
	$\frac{f}{m}$ 100	CV	$\frac{f}{m}$ 100	CV	$\frac{f}{m}$ 100	CV	$\frac{f}{m}$ 100	CV	$\frac{f}{m}$ 100	CV
61 Wholesale distribution										
1 A Top management personnel	–	–	.	.	–	–	–	–	.	
1 B Management personnel and senior executives	–	–	75,2°	48,1°	.	.	–	–	.	
2 Executives and management staff	86,9°	41,0	89,2°	59,7°	68,0°	23,3°	–	–	119,0°	30,9°
3 Highly-skilled junior personnel	105,0	37,1	71,3	45,0	80,6	22,8	–	–	96,0	37,2
4 Skilled junior personnel	106,3	35,4	118,6	41,7	90,6	21,7	–	–	100,6	39,5
5 Unskilled junior personnel	90,1	40,5	92,2	57,7	90,7	18,4	–	–	105,0	36,3
64/653-656 Retail distribution										
1 A Top management personnel	–	–	85,7	59,9	.	.	–	–	–	
1 B Management personnel and senior executives	–	–	83,9	42,4	.	.	–	–	159,4°	39,3°
2 Executives and management staff	97,1	46,5	53,8	77,2	.	.	–	–	132,9°	32,6°
3 Highly-skilled junior personnel	97,6	36,7	72,5	55,6	91,3	33,5	–	–	108,1	31,7
4 Skilled junior personnel	101,2	34,5	121,2	45,6	86,3	26,3	–	–	169,1	23,7
5 Unskilled junior personnel	103,1	39,4	111,0	50,8	92,3	22,6	–	–	123,4	40,4
812/813 Credit institutions										
1 Directors, top management	–	–	.	.	.	.	–	–		
2 Senior executives	–	–	.	.	82,2	13,7	–	–		
3 Executives (junior management)	111,9	28,1	.	.	.	.	–	–	.	.
4 Highly-qualified clerical staff	123,4	26,7	.	.	102,7	13,2	–	–	421,1°	27,2°
5 Qualified clerical staff	104,5	30,7	176,1°	62,3°	.	.	–	–	325,8°	28,7°
6 Other employees	100,4	47,4	58,7	109,7	102,0	43,1	–	–	83,4°	62,5°
82 Insurance										
I Managers and senior management executives	–	–	.	.	–		–	–	.	
II Middle management executives	–	–	.	.	–		–	–	–	–
III Junior executives and personnel with equivalent qualification	89,3	10,2	.	.	.	.	–	–	.	.
IV Highly-skilled employees	90,6	25,7	.	.	.	.	–	–	.	.
V Skilled employees	163,2	24,1	100,4	34,4	85,5	10,9	–	–	171,3	11,8
VI Other employees	133,7	47,3	105,9	62,8	.	25,4	–	–	146,3	35,0

CV: coefficient of variation.

TAB. 75

Earnings in wholesale and retail distribution, banking and insurance: corrected gross monthly average pay of part-time female workers in relation to those of male workers (male pay = 100) and CV of female pay by branch of activity and qualifications

Salaires dans le commerce, les institutions de crédit et les assurances: rémunération mensuelle moyenne brute corrigée des salariées à temps partiel par rapport à celle des salariés (rémunération masculine = 100) et CV des rémunérations des salariées selon la branche d'activité et la qualification

1974

$\frac{f}{m}$ 100	CV	$\frac{f}{m}$ 100	CV	$\frac{f}{m}$ 100	CV	$\frac{f}{m}$ 100	CV		
Luxembourg		United Kingdom		Ireland		Danmark			
.	.	.	.	–	–	–	–	**61**	**Commerce de gros**
								1 A	Personnel supérieur de direction
.	.	–	–	–	–	.	.	1 B	Personnel de direction et cadres supérieurs
.	.	.	.	–	–	.	.	2	Personnel d'exécution et d'encadrement
117,2	52,7	.	.	–	–	90,0	33,2	3	Personnel subalterne très qualifié
115,5	39,5	113,0	35,1	–	–	101,2	29,7	4	Personnel subalterne qualifié
99,6	44,0	107,5	37,0	–	–	101,1	41,8	5	Personnel subalterne non qualifié
								64/653 – 656	**Commerce de détail**
–	–	.	.	–	–	.	.	1 A	Personnel supérieur de direction
				–	–	124,9	45,7	1 B	Cadres supérieurs
.	.	.	.	–	–	.	.	2	Personnel de conception (cadres inférieurs)
101,5	39,6	91,7°	43,6°	–	–	86,8	32,2	3	Personnel d'exécution très qualifié
108,4	33,0	117,5	34,2	–	–	105,8	34,1	4	Personnel d'exécution qualifié
107,9	43,0	106,1	34,3	–	–	179,7	47,3	5	Autres agents
								812/813	**Institutions de crédit**
–	–	–	–	–	–	–	–	1	Personnel supérieur de direction
–	–	–	–	–	–	–	–	2	Cadres supérieurs
–	–	–	–	–	–	–	–	3	Personnel de conception (cadres inférieurs)
0,0	22,0	.	.	–	–	58,4	32,3	4	Personnel d'exécution très qualifié
86,1	37,4	137,7	35,8	–	–	79,1	24,3	5	Personnel d'exécution qualifié
60,6	46,8	128,0	43,4	–	–	118,4	51,8	6	Autres agents
								82	**Assurances**
		–	–	–	–	–	–	I	Dirigeants et cadres supérieurs de direction
		–	–	–	–	–	–	II	Cadres intermédiaires
		–	–	–	–	0,0	34,4	III	Agents d'encadrement et assimilés
		–	–	–	–	0,0	27,9	IV	Travailleurs très qualifiés
		65,5	27,4	–	–	236,9	24,8	V	Travailleurs qualifiés
		97,1	39,4	–	–	156,9	64,7	VI	Autres travailleurs

CV: coefficient de variation.

TAB. 76

Earnings in wholesale and retail distribution, banking and insurance: corrected gross monthly average pay of full-time female workers in relation to those of male workers (male pay = 100) and CV of female pay by branch of activity and length of service

Salaires dans le commerce, les institutions de crédit et les assurances: rémunération mensuelle moyenne brute corrigée des salariées à temps complet par rapport à celle des salariés (rémunération masculine = 100) et CV des rémunération des salariées selon la branche d'activité et l'ancienneté de service dans l'entreprise

1974

	BR Deutschland		France		Italia		Nederland		Belgique België	
	$\frac{f}{m}$ 100	CV	$\frac{f}{m}$ 100	CV	$\frac{f}{m}$ 100	CV	$\frac{f}{m}$ 100	CV	$\frac{f}{m}$ 100	CV
61 Wholesale distribution										
< 2	70,9	34,8	71,9	49,6	79,8	27,9	65,7	37,3	66,6	36,5
2 – 4	69,3	32,2	69,2	44,9	81,2	27,8	64,0	32,9	66,8	33,0
5 – 9	72,3	32,4	67,4	42,7	82,1	28,5	70,5	38,7	64,9	32,1
10 – 19	75,6	34,0	67,8	45,7	84,8	30,8	76,3	37,3	68,6	33,0
⩾ 20	83,7	37,6	66,1	57,8	88,3	34,8	82,5	35,7	77,7	34,2
64/653-656 Retail distribution										
< 2	67,1	31,7	73,0	39,5	89,2	27,8	66,6	42,4	63,7	40,2
2 – 4	64,5	32,2	67,5	41,8	88,6	27,5	63,9	32,0	68,8	34,2
5 – 9	66,5	30,5	64,4	39,9	84,5	26,1	70,3	32,0	72,2	71,8
10 – 19	70,0	33,2	63,9	46,2	87,0	27,5	72,6	32,7	75,2	28,9
⩾ 20	77,1	31,0	64,0	51,2	96,2	31,5	77,1	33,5	80,9	32,5
812/813 Credit institutions										
< 2	71,9	23,4	79,7	26,7	94,2	16,3	65,7	33,8	80,0	25,2
2 – 4	76,0	20,6	80,5	26,8	91,8	15,8	65,3	35,2	81,2	22,2
5 – 9	80,5	17,7	76,4	25,4	87,7	18,3	65,6	20,8	79,1	23,2
10 – 19	77,3	16,7	71,5	27,3	84,9	25,0	73,9	42,4	77,3	21,4
⩾ 20	74,4	20,6	63,4	27,6	75,6	26,9	74,3	22,5	74,4	19,7
82 Insurance										
< 2	74,1	19,6	81,2	50,0	69,9	22,9	69,5	38,7	77,7	25,3
2 – 4	74,9	19,0	74,6	28,0	76,9	24,9	67,3	29,8	77,2	23,4
5 – 9	75,4	17,7	69,1	28,5	71,9	25,6	74,0	32,1	75,5	22,1
10 – 19	76,3	22,7	65,1	31,7	72,0	22,6	73,0	26,2	73,0	21,0
⩾ 20	76,1	20,5	67,4	33,7	71,0	27,5	78,6	34,7	78,0	23,1

CV: coefficient of variation.

TAB. 76

Earnings in wholesale and retail distribution, banking and insurance: corrected gross monthly average pay of full-time female workers in relation to those of male workers (male pay = 100) and CV of female pay by branch of activity and length of service

Salariés dans le commerce, les institutions de crédit et les assurances: rémunération mensuelle moyenne brute corrigée des salariées à temps complet par rapport à celle des salariés (rémunération masculine = 100) et CV des rémunérations des salariées selon la branche d'activité et l'ancienneté de service dans l'entreprise

1974

Luxembourg		United Kingdom		Ireland		Danmark		
$\frac{f}{m}100$	CV	$\frac{f}{m}100$	CV	$\frac{f}{m}100$	CV	$\frac{f}{m}100$	CV	
								61 Commerce de gros
61,7	37,2	58,4	29,3	58,9	32,8	77,0	23,2	< 2
62,1	33,7	58,0	24,1	61,0	30,7	72,2	21,6	2 – 4
63,6	30,4	51,8	27,1	62,7	34,5	74,2	19,3	5 – 9
70,5	37,4	50,2	33,9	60,7	30,5	72,0	28,4	10 – 19
81,3	40,6	51,0°	36,0°	66,7	42,3	72,1	25,8	⩾ 20
								64/653 – 656 Commerce de détail
60,3	36,8	61,1	30,0	67,1	37,1	79,7	21,2	< 2
56,4	30,0	60,3	31,7	62,9	35,2	76,9	18,0	2 – 4
53,3	24,8	55,5	32,9	62,4	31,0	71,4	26,1	5 – 9
58,8	28,0	50,6	33,4	60,1	35,3	68,4	31,0	10 – 19
66,4	32,6	58,5	47,5	67,9	59,8	80,1	43,4	⩾ 20
								812/813 Institutions de crédit
68,8	37,3	61,6	29,0	72,1	28,8	70,2	21,3	< 2
70,4	27,5	60,3	28,1	76,1	19,0	83,0	13,8	2 – 4
69,6	25,2	69,4	27,2	79,1	19,5	85,6	16,1	5 – 9
72,8	25,0	71,7	30,9	86,5	25,3	82,4	20,0	10 – 19
86,4	18,4	57,8	23,9	77,3	24,1	76,0	21,5	⩾ 20
								82 Assurances
62,6	37,4	59,9	28,0	78,3	20,6	72,9	15,5	< 2
54,2	39,2	56,4	32,6	73,0	17,5	73,6	12,8	2 – 4
59,5	21,6	56,4	26,2	65,5	17,5	71,1	11,9	5 – 9
66,8	15,6	57,3	28,1	69,7	18,3	61,9	12,6	10 – 19
.	.	51,3	34,7	60,9	21,6	68,6	18,5	⩾ 20

CV: coefficient de variation.

TAB. 77

Earnings in wholesale and retail distribution, banking and insurance: gross monthly average pay of full-time female workers in relation to those of male workers (male pay = 100) according to branch of activity and qualifications, by regions

Salaires dans le commerce, les instituts de crédit et les assurances: rémunération mensuelle brute des salariées à temps complet par rapport à celle des salariés (rémunération masculine = 100) selon la branche d'activité et la qualification par région

1974

		61. Wholesale distribution/Commerce de gros							64. Retail distribution/Commerce de détail						
		Total	1A	1B	2	3	4	5	Total	1A	1B	2	3	4	5
BR DEUTSCHLAND															
Schleswig-Holstein	f/m · 100	66,9	.	.	70,3	72,1	68,2	74,4	59,8	.	.	72,7	69,0	63,2	73,5
	CV	34,3	.	.	29,4	24,7	24,5	19,5	32,7	.	.	23,3	29,2	26,2	23,7
Hamburg	f/m · 100	73,4	88,2°	.	81,7	83,2	82,3	70,5	70,5	.	.	81,7	78,3	77,1	86,5
	CV	36,0	25,6°	.	33,3	24,6	23,4	27,3	32,7	.	.	25,5	28,5	25,2	19,2
Niedersachsen	f/m · 100	70,3	—	.	73,8	80,4	76,8	75,2	63,7	—	.	96,3	79,3	69,3	69,7
	CV	29,7	—	.	20,0	23,6	22,7	21,4	36,7	—	.	29,8	25,0	25,1	26,8
Bremen	f/m · 100	71,6			74,5	75,5	75,5	78,3	65,0			83,6	75,0	69,1	71,6
	CV	30,3			24,0	23,5	22,2	19,0	37,9			21,9	25,4	26,2	31,7
Nordrhein-Westfalen	f/m · 100	68,6		87,4°	74,3	80,9	77,2	70,3	66,9		80,5°	88,7	81,2	74,8	75,2
	CV	37,8		43,7°	28,5	26,2	30,4	25,1	35,9		34,5°	24,9	27,8	25,4	26,0
Hessen	f/m · 100	71,9		86,7°	87,5	84,4	76,0	72,3	68,1		.	84,7	81,4	77,6	74,2
	CV	38,0		30,5°	27,3	26,6	26,8	22,6	33,1		.	28,3	25,5	25,6	21,6
Rheinland-Pfalz	f/m · 100	64,7	.	.	74,5	78,4	70,3	73,8	61,3	—	.	81,0	73,1	67,2	73,1
	CV	36,9	.	.	22,9	27,2	25,9	25,9	33,9	—	.	29,2	26,7	23,7	33,6
Baden-Württemberg	f/m · 100	68,7	.	.	81,3	84,3	77,9	70,5	64,1	—	.	80,3	79,1	73,4	77,3
	CV	30,7	.	.	24,1	21,2	22,2	21,6	33,7	—	.	22,8	29,6	23,1	23,6
Bayern	f/m · 100	69,8	—	.	84,8	83,2	76,0	77,2	67,1	—	.	86,4	81,4	75,5	75,8
	CV	33,1	—	.	22,3	24,6	23,2	21,0	33,8	—	.	26,9	27,4	23,3	22,6
Saarland	f/m · 100	65,3	—	.	92,3	76,5	67,4	68,0	59,5	—	.	79,7	72,4	68,0	74,4
	CV	37,8	—	.	29,2	26,1	24,4	21,0	33,2	—	.	23,5	20,4	23,3	26,8
Berlin (West)	f/m · 100	78,6	.	.	99,4	90,9	89,6	82,1	76,5	.	.	91,2	91,6	92,7	91,7
	CV	33,3	.	.	17,7	17,0	15,6	17,1	30,5	.	.	17,3	17,2	18,3	22,3
FRANCE															
Région parisienne	f/m · 100	64,0	87,7°	76,4	87,4	89,9	87,2	85,0	65,6	82,1°	79,9	79,8	78,5	79,1	86,0
	CV	47,2	52,0°	36,1	32,0	20,9	23,5	21,5	49,0	58,0°	27,4	55,5	28,3	25,0	19,1
Bassin parisien	f/m · 100	66,9	72,7°	76,7	83,1	87,3	82,8	88,1	62,9	80,7°	80,6	73,0	76,2	77,5	87,2
	CV	41,8	37,5°	36,0	38,3	25,2	20,5	18,7	42,2	42,0°	40,6	37,4	25,2	22,3	19,1
Nord	f/m · 100	65,5	64,4°	77,3°	80,8	84,6	81,3	84,9	67,5	74,4°	75,8	79,9	86,2	81,7	88,0
	cV	41,4	25,3°	34,1°	42,3	24,0	20,5	13,8	38,0	39,7°	27,3	29,4	21,0	19,7	18,0
Est	f/m · 100	66,9	97,8°	80,9	84,0	92,1°	80,7	86,8	63,1	79,5°	83,0	80,4	75,3	76,3	88,7
	CV	81,1	44,6°	29,4	39,4	138,9°	19,4	17,7	38,8	37,4°	27,7	34,3	28,7	19,6	15,5
Ouest	f/m · 100	65,0	62,2°	71,2	70,6	84,7	81,5	86,8	66,8	79,0	87,5	77,1	79,6	80,6	87,8
	CV	33,7	34,9°	25,8	26,8	20,1	18,8	15,3	38,1	28,7	29,3	47,1	31,4	20,9	16,7

TAB. 77
(continued)
(suite)

1974

		61. Wholesale distribution/Commerce de gros							64. Retail distribution/Commerce de détail						
		Total	1A	1B	2	3	4	5	Total	1A	1B	2	3	4	5
Sud-Ouest	f/m · 100	69,4	84,1°	77,5	87,0	90,8	88,1	87,7	69,1	85,4°	86,9	73,1	79,8	81,1	83,7
	CV	45,9	42,3	31,3	31,2	22,3	17,9	15,0	40,0	45,1°	25,6	37,9	23,2	18,3	17,9
Centre-Est	f/m · 100	65,6	.	90,8°	78,5	85,4	85,0	84,2	64,2	.	80,8	71,0	79,7	79,6	89,0
	CV	47,4	.	36,6°	37,1	26,3	19,1	17,1	40,8	.	25,7	43,3	46,8	22,6	17,0
Méditerranée	f/m · 100	67,9	.	84,7°	88,6	86,3	82,2	85,1	65,7	74,4°	87,7	88,5	82,0	76,7	88,4
	CV	58,5	.	48,0°	36,0	23,9	19,8	16,0	44,0	49,9°	20,2	43,0	30,9	22,8	17,8
ITALIA															
Nord Ovest	f/m · 100	75,8	.	103,4°	87,9	85,0	83,1	85,1	80,9	.	.	81,8	92,3	85,5	88,2
	CV	34,0	.	38,4°	26,7	22,8	21,6	20,2	26,8	.	.	25,6	19,3	21,6	19,5
Lombardia	f/m · 100	78,4	81,8°	90,3	91,4	89,5	87,0	86,1	81,4	77,2°	87,6	93,0	93,2	89,9	89,6
	CV	30,9	29,7°	29,4	23,4	20,2	20,4	18,1	29,1	34,8°	29,1	22,8	20,9	21,8	20,3
Nord Est	f/m · 100	78,4	.	68,9°	93,5	89,8	84,5	86,4	85,1	.	67,5°	81,0	82,4	93,0	92,1
	CV	27,7	.	31,8°	29,2	20,8	19,7	16,9	25,0	.	35,1°	29,6	32,4	21,2	17,3
Emilia-Romagna	f/m · 100	77,0	.	.	83,9	88,7	86,2	86,9	81,3	.	77,7	79,1	84,2	90,5	86,6
	CV	26,8	.	.	22,8	20,5	21,1	21,8	25,6	.	20,6	21,8	25,0	21,2	17,1
Centro	f/m · 100	75,0	—	—	81,0°	81,4	85,7	81,7	84,6	.	67,3	99,9	90,6	90,0	86,9
	CV	26,4	—	—	20,4°	20,6	17,7	20,8	28,4	.	10,1	25,4	31,0	22,3	17,9
Lazio	f/m · 100	75,3	—	—	78,3°	89,7	83,6	78,1	85,3	.	68,1°	77,9	94,9	87,7	89,1
	CV	36,3	—	—	32,1°	27,0	25,2	24,3	31,0	.	41,6	35,1	26,2	24,0	23,3
Campania	f/m · 100	77,8	—	—	.	96,4	83,9	79,7	95,1	—	—	.	105,3	105,3	86,9
	CV	27,8	—	—	.	20,8	20,0	15,2	34,9	—	—	.	21,8	32,9	25,4
Abruzzi-Molise	f/m · 100	79,3	—	—	.	74,6	89,6	82,6	92,3	—	—	.	99,9	92,3	96,7
	CV	23,7	—	—	.	27,8	22,4	17,2	25,1	—	—	.	18,0	23,3	18,2
Sud	f/m · 100	79,6	—	—	.	77,8	78,1	93,6	97,7	—	—	.	127,3	94,1	108,0
	CV	32,1	—	—	.	34,4	28,2	26,9	28,2	—	—	.	16,5	26,2	21,3
Sicilia	f/m · 100	81,6	.	.	.	73,5	86,8	89,7	95,6	.	.	103,3	120,1	97,7	98,9
	CV	26,1	.	.	.	28,4	26,9	18,2	32,3	.	.	22,6	26,5	26,1	26,3
Sardegna	f/m · 100	91,1	.	.	.	79,6	86,5	92,1	88,1	.	.	.	74,6	89,1	93,0
	CV	27,6	.	.	.	17,0	13,7	11,6	26,6	.	.	.	20,2	23,5	15,4

TAB. 77 (continued) (suite)

1974

		61. Wholesale distribution/Commerce de gros							64. Retail distribution/Commerce de détail						
		Total	1A	1B	2	3	4	5	Total	1A	1B	2	3	4	5
NEDERLAND															
Noord	f/m · 100	64,1	.	.	65,9	72,4	68,5	.	62,0	.	.	73,0	76,3	72,8	–
	CV	39,5	.	.	28,4	28,1	28,0	.	39,9	.	.	20,7	28,4	34,0	
Oost	f/m · 100	60,4	.	66,9°	73,8	65,6	69,8	86,8	61,8	.	71,1	70,9	74,4	76,0	–
	CV	40,3	.	36,9	35,6	28,8	26,7	35,7	40,5	.	30,7	32,1	39,9	30,8	–
Zuid	f/m · 100	61,5	.	60,7	67,6	73,7	70,0	75,2	61,2	74,8°	65,9	74,0	74,5	72,9	–
	CV	40,5	.	43,1	36,6	31,3	28,7	25,9	44,1	45,4°	38,0	35,2	31,5	35,9	–
West	f/m · 100	56,5	.	53,3°	57,3	64,7	64,1	64,9	61,5	.	66,9°	67,8	74,4	72,0	–
	CV	37,7	.	52,9°	29,8	25,6	30,1	30,3	38,1	.	29,2°	30,0	33,2	31,5	–
BELGIQUE/BELGIË															
Vlaams Gebied	f/m · 100	68,4	.	68,4	75,0	72,1	72,6	73,3	71,3	.	87,5	80,9	71,8	78,7	77,2
	CV	36,0	.	25,6	27,4	31,3	30,3	28,9	40,3	.	23,9	31,4	37,1	34,4	27,4
Région Wallonne	f/m · 100	65,5	.	.	78,0	70,8	69,3	79,3	71,9	.	104,0	80,4	68,6	78,8	80,1
	CV	37,6	.	.	33,6	31,1	33,0	25,5	69,4	.	23,1	32,3	38,4	86,2	36,0
Bruxelles	f/m · 100	64,0	.	76,0	77,5	80,3	82,0	70,4	71,7	.	88,8	85,7	80,4	87,9	81,1
	CV	39,1	.	29,0	31,0	29,5	28,3	33,9	36,4	.	28,5	40,1	32,3	23,4	24,8
UNITED KINGDOM															
South-East	f/m · 100	53,6	–	.	.	67,6	72,2	57,9	54,6	.	.	67,5	82,8	62,6	63,4
	CV	31,0	–	.	.	17,7	30,4	20,8	37,5	.	.	28,2	37,5	30,4	26,3
East Anglia	f/m · 100	48,0	–	–	–	.	55,5°	.	53,7°	–	–	.	.	67,0	10,4
	CV	26,6	–	–	–	.	26,6°	.	34,4	–	–	.	.	23,4	
South-West	f/m · 100	57,6	–	–	.	.	65,9	.	52,3°	–	–	.	74,1°	62,5°	65,4°
	CV	28,1	–	–	.	.	21,4	.	27,2	–	–	.	30,9°	22,1	15,8
West Midlands	f/m · 100	52,3	–	–	.	.	65,3	.	51,5	–	–	.	68,7°	55,7°	63,7
	CV	29,2	–	–	.	.	27,3	.	31,0	–	–	.	26,6°	26,8	16,4
East Midlands	f/m · 100	49,8°	–	–	.	.	56,4	.	58,3	–	–	.	72,5	61,4	63,2
	CV	36,3°	–	–	.	.	18,8	.	40,5	–	–	.	18,5	24,6	17,0
Yorkshire and Humberside	f/m · 100	51,4°	–	.	.	.	64,9°	.	59,9	–	–	.	75,5	62,6	70,7°
	CV	31,5	–	.	.	.	33,5°	.	38,2	–	–	.	20,7	24,8	15,7
North-West	f/m · 100	51,5	–	–	.	.	63,3	71,1	56,5	.	.	68,3°	72,8	65,5	75,5°
	CV	22,1	–	–	.	.	18,3	19,3	31,7	.	.	31,6°	23,1	24,9	25,7

TAB. 77
(continued)
(suite)

1974

Region		61. Wholesale distribution / Commerce de gros							64. Retail distribution / Commerce de détail						
		Total	1 A	1 B	2	3	4	5	Total	1 A	1 B	2	3	4	5
North	f/m · 100	49,8°	—	·	·	·	56,5	·	58,5°	—	·	·	64,6°	68,8	75,5°
	CV	28,1	—	·	·	·	21,0	·	31,9	—	·	20,3°	30,0°	31,5	15,4
Wales	f/m · 100	58,5°	—	—	·	·	57,9	·	56,9°	—	—	·	·	67,7°	·
	CV	43,3°	—	—	·	·	24,6°	·	36,3	—	—	·	·	19,9	16,4
Scotland	f/m · 100	49,2	—	—	·	64,0	60,3	68,9°	60,1	—	—	72,2°	65,7	64,5	86,9
	CV	20,5	—	—	·	11,5	17,5	28,3°	29,1	—	—	35,1°	28,6	21,0	16,4
Northern Ireland	f/m · 100	52,5°	—	—	·	·	56,7	·	·	—	—	·	·	66,5°	·
	CV	27,8°	—	—	·	·	28,3°	·	23,1	—	—	·	·	24,6	·
IRELAND	f/m · 100	56,4	·	—	79,7°	64,9	63,9	62,8	58,5	·	—	87,9°	72,0	65,4	65,2
	CV	38,3	·	—	32,9°	25,5	35,9	27,5	42,9	·	—	70,3°	30,1	32,2	37,4
DANMARK															
Øerne øst for Storebælt	f/m · 100	69,5	·	·	74,9	77,1	81,5	78,7	71,3	·	81,4	79,4	77,7	81,8	85,3
	CV	25,7	·	·	27,9	18,3	18,3	22,5	26,7	·	25,2	30,9	13,4	16,5	23,2
Jylland og Fyn	f/m · 100	71,7	·	—	·	79,1	80,2	81,4	74,7	—	99,0	·	84,1	85,2	81,1
	CV	22,1	·	—	·	18,1	12,3	17,7	28,7	—	20,8	·	14,1	12,2	29,2

Top management personnel	1A	Personnel supérieur de direction
Management personnel and senior executives	1B	Personnel de direction et cadres supérieurs
Executives and management staff	2	Personnel d'exécution et d'encadrement
Highly-skilled junior personnel	3	Personnel subalterne très qualifié
Skilled junior personnel	4	Personnel subalterne qualifié
Unskilled junior personnel	5	Personnel subalterne non qualifié

TAB. 77
(continued) (suite)

1974

		812/813. Credit institutions / Institutions de crédit								82. Insurance / Assurances					
		Total	1	2	3	4	5	6	Total	I	II	III	IV	V	VI
BR DEUTSCHLAND															
Schleswig-Holstein	f/m · 100	72,4	—	—	79,3	85,1	88,4	82,8	65,8	—	·	·	88,2	78,1	77,4
	CV	20,7	—	—	19,9	16,1	13,1	10,5	38,2	—	·	·	14,4	14,4	14,1
Hamburg	f/m · 100	69,9	—	—	87,8	82,3	82,8	80,2	72,7	·	·	95,0	84,0	85,5	97,8
	CV	22,1	—	—	17,0	17,1	14,0	10,7	24,7	·	·	17,0	15,2	13,0	11,2
Niedersachsen	f/m · 100	72,9	—	·	87,7	84,0	88,5	82,8	71,2	·	—	95,0	84,6	87,5	97,9
	CV	23,1	—	·	21,7	17,2	15,9	20,4	20,8	·	—	15,8	15,3	11,3	12,5
Bremen	f/m · 100	69,2	—	·	82,6	81,3	82,0	83,3	71,2	·	—	—	85,1	96,6	·
	CV	20,6	—	·	17,1	17,0	13,9	15,4	17,0	·	—	—	14,8	8,6	·
Nordrhein-Westfalen	f/m · 100	72,1	—	·	82,5	86,0	87,4	84,9	70,6	·	—	83,1	84,6	85,7	83,0
	CV	23,9	—	·	18,9	20,1	13,5	17,9	21,7	·	—	16,8	16,5	14,5	13,9
Hessen	f/m · 100	69,1	—	—	78,8	81,4	87,3	80,7	76,2	·	—	84,8	89,8	88,8	86,7
	CV	24,9	—	—	15,3	20,1	16,9	20,3	21,3	·	—	13,4	16,2	13,6	15,8
Rheinland-Pfalz	f/m · 100	69,9	—	—	82,4	85,3	91,7	80,8	75,8	·	—	·	91,3	93,4	109,5
	CV	22,7	—	—	17,8	15,9	13,3	18,6	17,1	·	—	·	11,6	8,6	8,6
Baden-Württemberg	f/m · 100	72,6	—	—	89,0	85,1	93,9	82,8	71,7	·	—	78,6°	89,8	88,8	91,1
	CV	23,3	—	—	18,9	16,9	14,9	19,3	20,1	·	—	22,1°	15,6	14,8	13,1
Bayern	f/m · 100	72,3	—	—	83,9	87,1	90,4	80,0	71,6	·	—	89,9	82,4	90,5	79,2
	CV	22,2	—	—	15,0	15,3	13,1	19,7	25,5	·	—	25,4	19,4	16,0	24,2
Saarland	f/m · 100	65,5	—	·	91,6	89,1	89,0	74,7	68,5	·	—	·	88,8	94,4	94,0
	CV	24,3	—	·	7,9	16,4	12,2	16,4	17,4	·	—	·	8,0	7,6	5,7
Berlin (West)	f/m · 100	72,6	—	·	·	92,2	97,7	·	71,7	·	·	·	89,7	99,3	·
	CV	19,3	—	·	·	12,9	12,7	·	21,3	·	·	·	13,1	11,1	·
FRANCE															
Région parisienne	f/m · 100	69,8	72,6	86,9	90,5	97,3	98,0	94,7	68,2	·	79,6	92,1	93,8	94,1	88,2
	CV	34,6	26,4	22,2	22,4	19,7	19,3	22,2	43,4	·	29,3	27,9	27,7	41,3	20,0
Bassin parisien	f/m · 100	71,6	·	92,3	95,8	94,7	95,9	95,4	61,6	·	93,2	101,1	92,1	97,8	94,0
	CV	32,9	·	18,0	23,3	17,1	16,9	19,6	37,8	·	32,9	26,0	17,3	15,8	16,6
Nord	f/m · 100	74,1	—	86,7	94,6	92,3	99,2	95,8	62,2	—	·	·	87,8	101,7	102,6
	CV	32,3	—	16,0	18,7	15,3	20,3	17,2	35,7	—	·	·	16,5	12,9	11,5
Est	f/m · 100	70,8	·	95,6°	92,6	98,3	94,7	93,7	54,1	—	·	90,2	95,5	94,8	99,9
	CV	34,8	·	27,7°	21,9	17,3	16,9	18,9	29,0	—	·	16,8	18,8	19,2	17,9
Ouest	f/m · 100	71,7	—	91,5°	81,5	92,7	92,0	93,2	71,5	—	·	85,2	96,2	100,5	91,3
	CV	31,2	—	18,5°	24,0	18,6	19,9	20,4	30,5	—	·	28,2	24,4	18,1	20,8

TAB. 77
(continued) (suite)

1974

		812/813. Credit institutions / Institutions de crédit							82. Insurance / Assurances						
		Total	1	2	3	4	5	6	Total	I	II	III	IV	V	VI
Sud-Ouest	f/m · 100	73,9	.	.	90,7	93,4	96,9	96,7	58,1°	–	.	.	.	82,9	77,9
	CV	32,0	.	.	20,5	16,7	23,0	14,8	48,5°	–	.	.	.	15,9	7,8
Centre-Est	f/m · 100	74,8	.	100,6°	88,4	93,4	99,1	97,6	60,2	–	77,4°	86,0	90,1	90,8	96,0
	CV	33,0	.	28,8°	27,3	20,0	21,0	21,2	36,3	–	26,1°	20,9	17,7	23,5	17,0
Méditerranée	f/m · 100	73,9	.	.	90,8	85,8	89,5	92,1	66,4	–	.	.	89,1	95,4	.
	CV	34,7	.	.	29,0	20,6	21,5	26,8	30,3	–	.	.	22,2	22,0	.
ITALIA															
Nord Ovest	f/m · 100	79,2	.	101,5°	96,5	99,3	79,8	77,4	70,4	–	.	102,1°	99,0	89,8	.
	CV	26,8	.	32,3°	19,2	21,1	14,2	19,4	23,7	–	.	29,7	20,0	16,5	.
Lombardia	f/m · 100	77,9	.	98,8°	94,3	96,2	82,5	83,6	69,1	.	.	94,2	93,9	96,5	80,3°
	CV	30,8	.	28,4°	17,0	19,9	16,1	18,2	30,0	.	.	27,5	20,3	20,9	20,8°
Nord-Est	f/m · 100	79,9	.	102,5°	100,1	97,3	85,8	88,4	68,4	–	–	87,5	99,0	84,1	66,4°
	CV	30,8	.	29,0°	13,8	21,1	18,5	26,0	27,2	–	–	21,7	22,0	18,2	24,2°
Emilia-Romagna	f/m · 100	81,6	.	.	99,7	99,5	85,2	100,6°	64,8	–	–	80,2	91,6	95,5	.
	CV	29,3	.	.	20,2	22,0	15,2	28,5°	31,2	–	–	16,9	13,7	14,8	.
Centro	f/m · 100	79,4	.	.	96,0	96,9	85,9	95,5	79,7	–	–	.	109,6	104,0	.
	CV	28,6	.	.	13,9	19,9	18,0	19,1	26,2	–	–	.	19,8	23,7	.
Lazio	f/m · 100	78,1	–	84,0	92,7	104,5	87,7	97,3	74,1	.	.	91,6	99,8	92,8	.
	CV	31,5	–	20,9	23,7	29,5	21,9	19,1	30,9	.	.	23,2	22,5	20,1	.
Campania	f/m · 100	78,6	–	104,5	99,7	104,5	91,3	91,8	78,2	–	–	,	98,6	97,1	–
	CV	32,8	–	12,9	13,8	30,9	12,4	15,9	21,9	–	–	,	14,9	20,7	–
Abruzzi-Molise	f/m · 100	80,8	–	.	96,2	97,4	87,7	91,5	75,4	–	–	–	.	94,6	–
	CV	23,0	–	.	9,0	13,4	13,6	13,5	27,8	–	–	–	.	28,9	–
Sud	f/m · 100	83,8	.	.	106,7	101,1	89,1	93,4	77,3	–	–	–	105,9	94,6	–
	CV	30,6	.	.	34,4	18,4	12,4	16,3	21,6	–	–	–	12,3	20,6	–
Sicilia	f/m · 100	80,9	.	.	88,8	94,2	87,5	82,3	73,1	–	–	–	95,0	96,6	–
	CV	28,5	.	.	23,3	24,1	23,3	21,3	15,7	–	–	–	14,4	14,7	–
Sardegna	f/m · 100	77,7	–	.	97,9	100,2	88,7	.	76,7	–	–	–	.	91,6	–
	CV	23,5	–	.	12,7	18,1	18,7	.	16,9	–	–	–	.	14,9	–

TAB. 77
**(continued)
(suite)**

1974

		812/813. Credit institutions / Institutions de crédit								82. Insurance / Assurances					
		Total	1	2	3	4	5	6	Total	I	II	III	IV	V	VI
NEDERLAND															
Noord	f/m · 100	58,0	—	.	.	.	75,5	78,7	54,5	—	—	.	.	70,8	80,6
	CV	33,4	—	.	.	.	26,9	23,4	38,6	—	—	.	.	32,3	27,1
Oost	f/m · 100	56,5	—	.	40,2°	77,9°	69,4	75,3	56,1	—	—	—	75,7°	72,8	69,2
	CV	33,2	—	.	20,6°	41,4°	28,2	24,3	46,4	—	—	—	26,4°	27,2	49,7
Zuid	f/m · 100	58,3	.	.	.	73,5	74,5	75,8	62,6	.	.	61,6	84,9	78,7	76,2
	CV	37,2	.	.	.	31,6	30,4	28,5	46,1	.	.	59,5	28,7	29,9	31,1
West	f/m · 100	51,7	—	.	.	63,0	67,7	73,0	56,3	—	—	39,1	75,0°	74,1	75,5
	CV	54,9	—	.	.	41,1	27,1	69,5	34,6	—	—	19,6	32,8°	33,4	19,2
BELGIQUE/BELGIË															
Vlaams Gebied	f/m · 100	67,9	—	.	81,5°	87,6	84,9	79,4	63,9	.	.	.	91,0	91,2	89,5
	CV	26,5	—	.	22,0°	20,2	22,5	27,2	29,5	.	.	.	16,9	21,5	20,1
Région Wallonne	f/m · 100	75,0	—	—	.	92,4	93,0	92,5°	69,7	—	—	—	92,4	89,9	74,4
	CV	26,8	—	—	.	20,2	22,5	24,9	36,1	—	—	—	23,5	21,9	24,2
Bruxelles	f/m · 100	71,9	—	.	83,8	83,6	82,5	86,8	70,2	.	87,7°	76,4	92,1	88,5	91,8
	CV	31,1	—	.	21,0	21,9	26,3	28,7	31,8	.	22,1°	30,3	17,6	23,7	22,8
UNITED KINGDOM															
South-East	f/m · 100	55,1	—	—	78,8°	77,1	76,1	69,9	53,7	—	—	.	83,5°	77,6	79,6
	CV	37,7	—	—	31,7°	27,1	27,6	36,2	36,3	—	—	.	32,9°	30,2	27,7
East Anglia	f/m · 100	32,0°	—	—	—	.	21,6°	27,2°	59,6°	—	—	.	.		33,5°
	CV	38,8	—	—	—	.			40,8°	—	—	.	.		
South-West	f/m · 100	44,5°	—	—	.	.	68,5°	78,8°	54,0°	—	—	—	.	72,1°	24,1°
	CV	38,8	—	—	.	.	33,9	22,6	24,4	—	—	—	.	16,7	
West Midlands	f/m · 100	60,3°	—	—	.	95,7°	98,7°	66,9°	41,6°	—	—	—	.	17,4	22,1
	CV	36,8	—	—	.	22,5	25,1	25,5	22,6	—	—	—	.		
East Midlands	f/m · 100	57,7°	—	—	—	.	84,0°	27,6°	34,6°	—	—	—	.	17,4	
	CV	33,2	—	—	—	.	22,5			—	—	—	.		
Yorkshire and Humberside	f/m · 100	50,4	—	—	—	.	77,2°	24,0	50,8°	—	—	—	.	25,9°	28,3°
	CV	28,5	—	—	—	.	26,1		35,2°	—	—	—	.		
North-West	f/m · 100	55,5°	—	—	—	73,9°	77,2°	80,1	30,3	—	—	—	23,1	64,2°	36,6°
	CV	28,6	—	—	—	21,4°	24,7	24,9		—	—	—		24,0	
North	f/m · 100	61,2	—	—	—	74,4°	97,5°	13,4	61,3°	—	—	—	.	37,9°	.
	CV	30,1	—	—	—	20,6°	29,2°		37,6°	—	—	—	.		.

TAB. 77
(continued)
(suite)

1974

		812/813. Credit institutions / Institutions de crédit							82. Insurance / Assurances						
		Total	1	2	3	4	5	6	Total	I	II	III	IV	V	VI
Wales	f/m · 100	49,4°	–	–	–	·	87,6	·	50,6°	–	–	–	·	·	·
	CV	25,2	–	–	–	·	23,2°	·	31,0°	–	–	–	·	32,8°	·
Scotland	f/m · 100	53,9°	–	–	·	72,2	88,2	19,6	44,9°	–	–	–	·	22,9	25,1°
	CV	24,6	–	–	·	10,3	22,2		29,6	–	–	–	·		
Northern Ireland	f/m · 100	37,8°	–	–	–	·	·	·	·	–	–	–	–	·	·
	CV		–	–	–	·	32,3	·	·	–	–	–	–	·	·
IRELAND	f/m · 100	61,7	–	·	99,5°	94,0	91,4	58,6°	58,9	–	–	·	70,4	86,0	–
	CV	35,3	–	·	37,8°	29,3	19,2	31,3°	33,5	–	–	·	25,2	27,5	–
DANMARK															
Øerne øst for Storebælt	f/m · 100	70,5	–	·	89,1	90,3	99,7	89,5	63,9	–	·	86,4	93,7	90,6	92,2
	CV	24,5	–	·	17,6	21,0	15,2	16,2	21,9	–	·	13,3	11,3	16,1	25,9
Jylland og Fyn	f/m · 100	69,7	–	·	94,0	97,2	100,4	85,6	58,0	–	·	·	·	9,3	·
	CV	21,4	–	·	13,3	14,7	11,8	14,1	14,3	–	·	·	·	·	·

Banking / **Banques**

Directors, top management	1	Personnel supérieur de direction
Senior executives	2	Cadres supérieurs
Executives (junior management)	3	Personnel de conception (cadres inférieurs)
Highly-qualified clerical staff	4	Personnel d'exécution très qualifié
Qualified clerical staff	5	Personnel d'exécution qualifié
Other employees	6	Autres agents

Insurance / **Assurances**

Managers and senior management executives	I	Dirigeants et cadres supérieurs de direction
Middle management executives	II	Cadres intermédiaires
Junior executives and personnel with equivalent qualification	III	Agents d'encadrement et assimilés
Highly-skilled employees	IV	Travailleurs très qualifiés
Skilled employees	V	Travailleurs qualifiés
Other employees	VI	Autres travailleurs

TAB. 78

Persons employed during the reference week by continuity of employment and hours of work (1 000)

Travailleurs occupés pendant la semaine de référence, selon la continuité de l'emploi et l'horaire de travail (1 000)

	BR Deutschland		France		Italia		Nederland		Belgique België	
	F	M	F	M	F	M	F	M	F	M
1973										
Persons with a main occupation	9 106	16 478	7 554	12 640	4 328	12 691	981	3 325	1 073	2 443
full time	7 284	16 321	6 705	12 464	3 960	12 396	829	3 289	986	2 432
part time	1 822	157	849	176	368	295	152	36	88	11
Persons with an occasional occupation	586	145	411	234	568	589	255	60	25	14
full time	41	11	93	79	252	395	82	17	.	.
part time	545	135	318	155	316	193	173	44	24	13
Total persons who worked during the reference week	9 692	16 623	7 965	12 874	4 896	13 280	1 236	3 385	1 099	2 456
full time	7 325	16 332	6 798	12 543	4 213	12 791	911	3 305	987	2 432
part time	2 367	292	1 168	332	683	489	324	80	112	24
1975										
Persons with a main occupation	8 997	15 703	7 807	13 056	4 761	13 139	1 076	3 350	1 132	2 428
full time	6 944	15 525	6 713	12 778	4 289	12 791	875	3 300	1 001	2 414
part time	2 053	179	1 094	278	471	348	200	49	131	14
Persons with an occasional occupation	501	121	313	164	407	410	169	37	20	12
full time	18	(6)	67	63	223	297	12	4	.	.
part time	483	115	246	102	184	112	158	33	18	11
Total persons who worked during the reference week	9 498	15 824	8 120	13 220	5 168	13 549	1 245	3 386	1 152	2 440
full time	6 962	15 530	6 781	12 841	4 512	13 088	887	3 304	1 002	2 415
part time	2 536	294	1 340	379	655	461	358	82	149	25
1977										
Persons with a main occupation	9 012	15 738	8 078	12 917	5 266	13 010	1 155	3 405	1 120	2 437
full time	6 813	15 571	6 846	12 621	4 955	12 860	936	3 354	939	2 413
part time	2 199	167	1 232	296	311	150	219	51	181	24
Persons with an occasional occupation	516	123	352	178	852	952	163	39	8	(4)
full time	17	8	81	70	438	642	9	(3)	.	.
part time	499	115	271	108	414	310	154	36	7	(4)
Total persons who worked during the reference week	9 528	15 862	8 431	13 095	6 117	13 963	1 318	3 444	1 128	2 441
full time	6 830	15 580	6 929	12 691	5 391	13 503	945	3 356	940	2 413
part time	2 698	282	1 502	404	726	460	373	88	188	28

TAB. 78

Persons employed during the reference week by continuity of employment and hours of work (1 000)

Travailleurs occupés pendant la semaine de référence, selon la continuité de l'emploi et l'horaire de travail (1 000)

Luxembourg		United Kingdom		Ireland		Danmark		EUR 9		
F	M	F	M	F	M	F	M	F	M	
					1973						
36	98	8 711	14 972	:	:	:	:	:	:	Personnes ayant un emploi principal
31	97	5 352	14 656	:	:	:	:	:	:	à temps complet
5	(1)	3 326	276	:	:	:	:	:	:	à temps partiel
2	.	230	187	:	:	:	:	:	:	Personnes ayant une activité occasionnelle
.	.	59	113	:	:	:	:	:	:	à temps complet
2	.	171	74	:	:	:	:	:	:	à temps partiel
										Total des personnes ayant travaillé au cours de la semaine de référence
38	99	8 907	15 199	:	:	:	:	:	:	
31	98	5 411	14 769	:	:	:	:	:	:	à temps complet
7	(1)	3 496	350	:	:	:	:	:	:	à temps partiel
					1975						
40	101	9 078	14 804	268	739	838	1 292	33 996	64 612	Personnes ayant un emploi principal
34	100	5 369	14 482	241	726	500	1 268	25 967	63 383	à temps complet
6	(1)	3 709	322	26	14	338	24	8 029	1 229	à temps partiel
(1)	(1)	44	45	29	9	79	41	1 563	839	Personnes ayant une activité occasionnelle
.	.	10	20	5	(3)	(3)	(2)	339	396	à temps complet
(1)	.	34	25	24	6	76	39	1 223	443	à temps partiel
										Total des personnes ayant travaillé au cours de la semaine de référence
41	101	9 122	14 849	297	748	917	1 333	35 558	65 451	
34	100	5 379	14 502	247	729	502	1 270	26 306	63 780	à temps complet
7	(1)	3 743	347	50	20	414	63	9 252	1 672	à temps partiel
					1977						
40	98	9 373	14 847	265	741	879	1 346	35 189	64 540	Personnes ayant un emploi principal
35	97	5 586	14 540	240	729	506	1 309	26 857	63 495	à temps complet
5	(1)	3 787	307	25	12	373	37	8 332	1 045	à temps partiel
2	(1)	122	89	33	11	66	40	2 113	1 437	Personnes ayant une activité occasionnelle
(1)	(1)	35	56	(2)	(2)		(2)	585	784	à temps complet
(1)	.	87	33	31	9	65	38	1 528	653	à temps partiel
										Total des personnes ayant travaillé au cours de la semaine de référence
42	99	9 495	14 936	298	752	945	1 386	37 302	65 977	
36	98	5 621	14 596	242	732	507	1 311	27 441	64 279	à temps complet
6	(1)	3 874	340	56	20	438	75	9 861	1 698	à temps partiel

TAB. 79

Average number of hours worked by females employed during the reference week (average number of hours worked by male workers = 100)

Nombre moyen d'heures de travail effectuées par les travailleuses occupées au cours de la semaine de référence (nombre moyen d'heures effectuées par les travailleurs = 100)

	BR Deutschland $\frac{f}{m}\cdot100$	France $\frac{f}{m}\cdot100$	Italia $\frac{f}{m}\cdot100$	Nederland $\frac{f}{m}\cdot100$	Belgique/België $\frac{f}{m}\cdot100$	Luxembourg $\frac{f}{m}\cdot100$	United Kingdom $\frac{f}{m}\cdot100$	Ireland $\frac{f}{m}\cdot100$	Danmark $\frac{f}{m}\cdot100$	EUR 9 $\frac{f}{m}\cdot100$
1973										
Persons with a main occupation / Personnes ayant un emploi principal	85,9	86,6	92,1	81,0	91,1	92,7	71,6	:	:	:
full time / à temps complet	94,1	91,2	94,0	86,5	94,7	99,1	88,2	:	:	:
part time / à temps partiel	95,1	77,8	90,3	87,6	101,4	97,6	93,8	:	:	:
Persons with an occasional occupation / Personnes ayant une activité occas.	90,4	75,0	77,6	124,0	94,7	:	62,3	:	:	:
full time / à temps complet	99,0	93,7	81,1	121,7	.	:	85,7	:	:	:
part time / à temps partiel	89,7	76,9	90,0	118,2	95,7	:	89,2	:	:	:
Total persons who worked during the reference week / Total des personnes ayant travaillé au cours de la semaine de référence	83,8	85,0	89,5	74,4	90,0	89,8	71,2	:	:	:
full time / à temps complet	94,1	91,0	93,1	84,7	94,7	99,1	88,0	:	:	:
part time / à temps partiel	97,0	83,3	88,7	98,4	110,2	96,9	96,5	:	:	:
1975										
Persons with a main occupation / Personnes ayant un emploi principal	86,9	86,3	91,5	80,8	89,7	93,5	70,6	80,0	75,7	82,9
full time / à temps complet	96,6	91,9	93,2	86,2	94,8	100,2	88,2	82,3	90,0	92,8
part time / à temps partiel	92,7	83,9	95,3	83,0	98,6	94,2	97,5	75,5	100,0	85,0
Persons with an occasional occupation / Personnes ayant une activité occas.	87,6	72,5	72,6	89,7	83,2	:	70,2	75,4	84,6	69,2
full time / à temps complet	89,3	93,2	73,5	94,3	84,4	:	87,6	84,9	79,9	79,0
part time / à temps partiel	87,8	83,6	87,1	101,4	86,7	:	110,9	87,6	88,2	88,0
Total persons who worked during the reference week / Total des personnes ayant travaillé au cours de la semaine de référence	84,8	85,3	89,1	75,0	88,8	91,6	70,6	73,6	73,6	81,7
full time / à temps complet	96,6	91,9	92,1	86,5	94,8	100,0	88,2	82,3	90,0	92,3
part time / à temps partiel	95,2	86,3	92,6	86,0	106,8	102,5	100,0	73,5	128,3	88,2
1977										
Persons with a main occupation / Personnes ayant un emploi principal	85,6	87,2	91,1	77,9	88,8	92,5	68,8	79,9	76,4	82,2
full time / à temps complet	96,4	93,2	92,5	84,6	95,1	98,1	86,0	82,9	91,8	92,3
part time / à temps partiel	97,4	87,0	89,3	79,2	95,5	93,6	97,9	87,7	105,5	88,1
Persons with an occasional occupation / Personnes ayant une activité occas.	87,1	72,5	80,9	98,1	101,2	76,0	63,8	91,1	91,1	71,0
full time / à temps complet	78,4	93,3	83,3	99,6	(135,0)	76,3	79,7	91,0	118,1	85,0
part time / à temps partiel	89,6	79,8	92,6	104,8	91,6	91,1	113,2	108,4	93,0	84,0
Total persons who worked during the reference week / Total des personnes ayant travaillé au cours de la semaine de référence	83,7	86,0	88,6	73,8	88,7	90,8	68,7	76,0	74,5	80,9
full time / à temps complet	96,1	93,0	91,6	84,8	95,1	97,4	85,8	82,9	91,8	92,1
part time / à temps partiel	100,0	87,9	92,1	84,7	98,7	99,0	102,2	92,5	131,1	89,9

TAB. 80

Average number of hours worked by female workers with a principal occupation by situation and sector of activity (average number of hours worked by male workers = 100)

Nombre moyen d'heures effectuées par les travailleuses ayant un emploi principal, selon le statut professionnel et le secteur d'activité (nombre moyen d'heures effectuées par les travailleurs = 100)

	BR Deutschland $\frac{f}{m}$ 100	France $\frac{f}{m}$ 100	Italia $\frac{f}{m}$ 100	Nederland $\frac{f}{m}$ 100	Belgique Belgïe $\frac{f}{m}$ 100
1973					
Employers and self-employed	85,4	88,7	92,6	72,8	88,9
Agriculture	78,7	71,1	83,6	(71,8)	74,5
Industry	80,5	85,8	91,8	(61,5)	78,7
Services	88,1	93,6	96,6	76,2	92,6
Employees	85,0	87,2	92,3	83,5	91,1
Agriculture	87,4	79,4	87,1	(82,2)	(83,5)
Industry	86,2	91,1	97,1	88,0	95,9
Services	83,2	86,1	88,3	82,3	88,8
Family workers	91,6	82,3	89,9	81,0	86,0
Agriculture	92,2	75,5	84,8	69,9	75,9
Industry	102,5	120,5	95,5	(85,8)	91,8
Services	88,2	91,6	94,9	95,5	93,0
Total	85,9	86,6	92,1	81,0	91,1
Agriculture	83,0	75,0	86,5	71,1	74,2
Industry	85,5	91,0	96,2	87,0	93,9
Services	83,0	86,6	90,6	81,1	90,3
1975					
Employers and self-employed	87,2	87,9	92,4	73,3	85,8
Agriculture	83,4	77,4	86,2	62,6	66,0
Industry	79,9	89,6	88,9	72,2	77,0
Services	89,4	92,0	96,3	77,5	89,3
Employees	85,9	87,1	91,2	81,9	90,1
Agriculture	89,7	79,4	89,8	80,2	84,5
Industry	87,8	90,5	95,1	85,5	95,6
Services	84,0	85,7	88,5	80,4	87,7
Family workers	90,5	86,1	89,7	78,6	83,5
Agriculture	90,6	80,7	84,8	65,8	69,9
Industry	89,2	105,1	94,6	95,5	87,8
Services	94,6	95,5	92,8	91,3	93,8
Total	87,0	86,3	91,3	80,0	89,7
Agriculture	83,8	77,2	87,8	69,8	69,1
Industry	86,8	90,4	94,0	85,5	93,3
Services	83,4	83,5	89,9	79,4	88,7
1977					
Employers and self-employed	84,9	88,1	91,9	72,3	90,0
Agriculture	77,3	78,0	84,8	66,5	76,1
Industry	80,0	88,0	88,9	76,9	79,3
Services	87,6	91,9	95,9	75,9	92,9
Employees	85,7	88,1	91,0	79,8	88,8
Agriculture	89,4	83,3	91,4	76,0	73,8
Industry	88,2	92,9	96,4	85,9	95,0
Services	83,3	86,1	87,7	78,4	86,7
Family workers	93,0	84,8	88,9	74,9	86,2
Agriculture	94,8	81,2	88,9	60,0	78,9
Industry	81,2	105,6	89,5	83,9	100,5
Services	96,0	93,7	87,6	91,8	94,4
Total	85,6	87,2	91,1	77,9	88,8
Agriculture	84,2	92,3	88,7	66,6	76,8
Industry	87,1	92,3	95,0	85,4	93,9
Services	82,3	86,0	88,9	77,4	88,0

TAB. 80

Average number of hours worked by female workers with a principal occupation by situation and sector of activity (average number of hours worked by male workers = 100)

Nombre moyen d'heures effectuées par les travailleuses ayant un emploi principal, selon le statut professionnel et le secteur d'activité (nombre moyen d'heures effectuées par les travailleurs = 100)

Luxembourg $\frac{f}{m}100$	United Kingdom $\frac{f}{m}100$	Ireland $\frac{f}{m}100$	Danmark $\frac{f}{m}100$	EUR 9 $\frac{f}{m}100$	
		1973			
93,9	78,7	:	:	:	Employeurs et indépendants
.	79,2	:	:	:	Agriculture
.	62,0	:	:	:	Industrie
100,0	80,4	:	:	:	Services
92,2	72,2	:	:	:	Salariés
.	62,3	:	:	:	Agriculture
91,6	78,6	:	:	:	Industrie
94,2	69,9	:	:	:	Services
76,0	.	:	:	:	Aides familiaux
68,9	.	:	:	:	Agriculture
.	.	:	:	:	Industrie
.	.	:	:	:	Services
92,7	71,6	:	:	:	Total
67,9	63,9	:	:	:	Agriculture
92,9	78,0	:	:	:	Industrie
96,4	69,4	:	:	:	Services
		1975			
96,3	77,5	83,1	79,2	87,2	Employeurs et indépendants
(66,0)	80,0	80,5	65,5	80,6	Agriculture
.	74,4	75,6	93,7	84,6	Industrie
105,1	77,2	95,2	81,7	90,1	Services
92,6	71,4	88,3	79,0	82,9	Salariés
.	60,2	76,0	72,2	82,1	Agriculture
93,8	78,1	90,8	83,4	83,3	Industrie
91,9	69,1	88,4	77,5	80,6	Services
77,8	.	72,0	(77,1)	89,6	Aides familiaux
69,6	.	68,8	.	85,0	Agriculture
.	.	.	.	95,9	Industrie
.	.	90,6	.	97,1	Services
93,5	70,4	79,8	75,7	83,1	Total
67,2	63,1	75,6	61,0	82,2	Agriculture
95,1	77,4	89,9	83,0	86,9	Industrie
94,6	68,0	87,8	75,2	80,7	Services
		1977			
95,7	74,6	80,1	84,5	85,6	Employeurs et indépendants
66,3	72,5	75,4	94,2	77,5	Agriculture
94,9	67,7	84,3	88,3	82,3	Industrie
103,0	75,9	87,6	88,5	89,2	Services
92,3	69,6	88,2	78,5	82,1	Salariés
.	57,3	85,5	69,3	81,7	Agriculture
94,8	78,0	91,7	85,1	88,0	Industrie
91,8	67,5	88,1	77,1	79,5	Services
76,2	:	70,4	.	89,1	Aides familiaux
68,8	:	67,8	.	87,6	Agriculture
.	:	.	.	92,6	Industrie
88,4	:	84,7	.	91,6	Services
92,5	68,8	80,1	76,4	82,2	Total
69,6	61,5	73,2	69,7	82,0	Agriculture
95,6	77,7	90,9	84,4	87,5	Industrie
92,9	66,7	85,6	75,5	79,6	Services

TAB. 81

Average number of hours worked by female employees by branch of economic activity (average number of hours worked by male employees = 100)

Nombre moyen d'heures effectuées par les salariées par branche d'activité économique (nombre moyen d'heures prestées par les travailleurs = 100)

	BR Deutschland	France	Italia	Nederland	Belgique Belgïe
	$\frac{f}{m}$ 100	$\frac{f}{m}$ 100	$\frac{f}{m}$ 100	$\frac{f}{m}$ 100	$\frac{f}{m}$ 100
1973					
Agriculture, foresty, fishing, hunting	87,4	79,4	87,1	(82,2)	83,5
Energy and water	89,3	95,0	98,3	92,1	92,4
Extraction and processing of non-energy-producing minerals and derived products, chemical industry	87,9	93,7	96,9	85,9	95,2
Metal manufacture; mechanical, electrical and instrument engineering	88,9	93,9	98,0	87,7	96,8
Other manufacturing industries	83,6	90,1	96,9	89,2	95,5
Building and civil engineering	80,9	84,0	99,6	81,3	93,2
Distributive trades, hotels, restaurants and cafés, repairs	82,9	86,6	95,1	90,0	92,3
Transport and communications	79,9	85,4	93,4	81,1	92,0
Financing, insurance, etc.	83,4	90,0	97,3	85,8	92,6
Public administration	85,6	88,4	88,2	90,0	92,6
Other services	81,6	87,8	88,0	82,1	91,6
Total	85,0	87,2	92,3	83,5	91,1
1975					
Agriculture, foresty, fishing, hunting	89,7	79,2	89,8	80,2	84,5
Energy and water	90,0	89,6	95,9	90,6	92,6
Extraction and processing of non-energy-producing minerals and derived products, chemical industry	90,3	89,9	95,3	82,4	95,4
Metal manufacture; mechanical, electrical and instrument engineering	89,4	93,6	95,0	86,3	97,3
Other manufacturing industries	86,1	90,1	95,4	86,3	94,8
Building and civil engineering	80,8	85,2	96,9	80,8	92,6
Distributive trades, hotels, restaurants and cafés, repairs	84,1	85,7	93,3	81,3	88,5
Transport and communications	81,0	86,9	95,0	79,2	92,0
Financing, insurance, etc.	82,4	88,7	96,3	83,5	90,0
Public administration	85,2	85,3	95,0	88,4	86,9
Other services	82,3	89,2	89,3	80,6	92,9
Total	85,9	87,1	91,2	82,1	90,1
1977					
Agriculture, foresty, fishing, hunting	89,4	83,3	91,4	76,0	73,8
Energy and water	89,5	92,3	96,8	86,4	90,8
Extraction and processing of non-energy-producing minerals and derived products, chemical industry	88,2	95,9	96,8	82,8	94,6
Metal manufacture; mechanical, electrical and instrument engineering	90,5	95,0	98,3	87,8	96,8
Other manufacturing industries	86,2	92,1	96,6	86,7	95,0
Building and civil engineering	79,5	85,3	95,7	80,6	94,5
Distributive trades, hotels, restaurants and cafés, repairs	83,6	85,7	94,2	79,4	87,1
Transport and communications	80,6	86,5	96,2	79,6	91,2
Financing, insurance, etc.	82,4	89,5	97,0	84,1	89,2
Public administration	85,8	85,5	91,7	86,1	89,7
Other services	81,1	89,1	89,8	79,0	91,8
Total	85,7	88,1	91,0	79,8	88,8

TAB. 81

Average number of hours worked by female employees by branch of economic activity (average number of hours worked by male employees = 100)

Nombre moyen d'heures effectuées par les salariées par branche d'activité économique (nombre moyen d'heures prestées par les travailleurs = 100)

Luxembourg	United Kingdom	Ireland	Danmark	EUR 9	
$\frac{f}{m}$ 100	$\frac{f}{m}$ 100	$\frac{f}{m}$ 100	$\frac{f}{m}$ 100	$\frac{f}{m}$ 100	
		1973			
.	62,3	:	:	:	Agriculture, sylvicult., pêche, chasse
.	83,2	:	:	:	Énergie et eau
(96,6)	77,7	:	:	:	Extraction et transformation de minéraux non énergétiques et produits dérivés; industrie chimique
	80,9	:	:	:	Industries transformatrices des métaux, mécanique de précision
90,8	78,0	:	:	:	Autres industries manufacturières
.	68,6	:	:	:	Bâtiment et génie civil
69,2	67,6	:	:	:	Commerce, restauration et hébergement, réparations
.	77,9	:	:	:	Transports et communications
95,3	79,6	:	:	:	Crédits, assurances
90,3	74,3	:	:	:	Administrations générales
95,8	67,4	:	:	:	Autres services
92,2	79,2	:	:	:	Total
		1975			
.	60,2	76,0	72,2	81,9	Agriculture, sylvicult., pêche, chasse
.	81,6	91,1	84,5	86,6	Énergie et eau
(92,3)	79,6	87,0	84,3	87,5	Extraction et transformation de minéraux non énergétiques et produits dérivés; industrie chimique
.	80,2	92,3	85,6	88,5	Industries transformatrices des métaux, mécanique de précision
95,1	77,8	91,2	82,1	87,8	Autres industries manufacturières
(92,3)	66,8	87,5	78,6	79,3	Bâtiment et génie civil
92,7	67,6	91,4	76,1	79,5	Commerce, restauration et hébergement, réparations
(89,6)	75,8	92,8	77,6	82,8	Transports et communications
96,0	80,2	92,1	83,5	84,6	Crédits, assurances
90,5	84,0	88,7	80,5	86,1	Administrations générales
91,2	66,7	85,8	79,2	80,6	Autres services
92,6	71,5	88,3	79,0	82,9	Total
		1977			
.	57,3	85,5	69,3	81,7	Agriculture, sylvicult., pêche, chasse
.	81,7	89,2	74,7	86,8	Énergie et eau
100,0	78,7	91,7	81,3	88,2	Extraction et transformation de minéraux non énergétiques et produits dérivés; industrie chimique
95,3	80,1	92,5	86,8	89,4	Industries transformatrices des métaux, mécanique de précision
93,3	77,8	91,7	84,9	88,3	Autres industries manufacturières
91,4	64,7	87,9	82,8	79,4	Bâtiment et génie civil
94,0	65,8	89,8	76,5	78,4	Commerce, restauration et hébergement, réparations
90,0	74,3	94,8	77,4	82,6	Transports et communications
94,2	78,2	92,5	79,1	84,6	Crédits, assurances
89,5	82,1	87,2	79,4	86,1	Administrations générales
90,6	66,7	85,5	78,4	80,4	Autres services
92,3	69,6	88,2	78,5	82,1	Total

TAB. 82

Employees who worked fewer than 40 hours during the reference week (1 000)

Salariés ayant travaillé moins de 40 heures pendant la semaine de référence (1 000)

	BR Deutschland		France		Italia		Nederland		Belgique Belgïe	
	F	M	F	M	F	M	F	M	F	M
1973										
Total employees who worked during the reference week	7 594	14 369	6 069	10 176	3 101	9 190	866	2 794	831	1 990
of which: total employees who worked less than 40 hours	2 424	768	1 568	963	854	1 290	386	530	221	187
of which: employees who usually work less than 40 hours per week	2 041	215	955	300	563	558	266	153	104	90
other employees who worked less than 40 hours	383	553	613	663	291	732	118	377	117	97
1975										
Total employees who worked during the reference week	7 620	13 688	6 410	10 649	3 450	9 608	969	2 897	887	1 989
of which: total employees who worked less than 40 hours	2 559	1 123	2 480	2 215	1 052	1 282	482	694	267	206
of which: employees who usually work less than 40 hours per week	2 020	246	1 211	495	693	715	305	166	113	100
other employees who worked less than 40 hours	539	877	1 269	1 720	359	567	177	528	154	106
1977										
Total employees who worked during the reference week	7 778	13 794	6 659	10 573	3 857	9 407	1 048	2 986	928	2 042
of which: total employees who worked less than 40 hours	2 542	864	1 967	1 309	1 216	1 257	502	590	348	281
of which: employees who usually work less than 40 hours per week	2 092	215	1 350	487	1 034	989	338	156	284	198
other employees who worked less than 40 hours	451	649	617	822	183	268	164	434	64	83

TAB. 82

Employees who worked fewer than 40 hours during the reference week (1 000)

Salariés ayant travaillé moins de 40 heures pendant la semaine de référence (1 000)

Luxembourg		United Kingdom		Ireland		Danmark		EUR 9		
F	M	F	M	F	M	F	M	F	M	
				1973						
27	82	8 082	12 924	:	:	:	:	:	:	Salariés ayant travaillé au cours de la semaine de référence
										dont:
6	7	4 941	2 458	:	:	:	:	:	:	salariés ayant travaillé moins de 40 heures
										dont:
4	2	4 371	1 477	:	:	:	:	:	:	salariés qui normalement travaillent moins de 40 heures p. semaine
2	5	570	981	:	:	:	:	:	:	autres salariés qui ont travaillé moins de 40 heures
				1975						
31	86	8 011	12 296	227	489	737	1 014	28 341	52 716	Salariés ayant travaillé au cours de la semaine de référence
										dont:
8	8	5 272	2 416	82	74	395	136	12 594	8 154	salariés ayant travaillé moins de 40 heures
										dont:
6	(1)	4 756	1 646	66	45	316	62	9 482	3 477	salariés qui normalement travaillent moins de 40 heures p. semaine
2	7	516	770	16	29	79	74	3 112	4 677	autres salariés qui ont travaillé moins de 40 heures
				1977						
33	85	8 913	13 157	228	496	777	1 083	30 221	53 624	Salariés ayant travaillé au cours de la semaine de référence
										dont:
8	8	6 560	3 606	94	94	413	155	13 650	8 164	salariés ayant travaillé moins de 40 heures
										dont:
6	2	5 744	2 578	82	65	280	54	11 208	4 744	salariés qui normalement travaillent moins de 40 heures p. semaine
2	6	816	1 028	12	29	133	101	2 442	3 420	autres salariés qui ont travaillé moins de 40 heures

TAB. 83

Employees who as an exception worked fewer than 40 hours during the reference week, by reasons (1 000)

Salariés ayant travaillé exceptionnellement moins de 40 heures pendant la semaine de référence, selon les motifs (1 000)

	BR Deutschland		France		Italia		Nederland		Belgique Belgïe	
	F	M	F	M	F	M	F	M	F	M
1973										
Employees who worked less than 40 hours	383	553	613	663	291	732	118	377	117	97
of which:										
technical or economic reasons	12	(6)	36	39	82	224	.	(5)	(4)	(4)
strike	.	.	(4)	8	58	275	.	(4)	.	6
sickness, accident	162	273	361	417	115	190	26	98	23	39
holiday	122	219	85	148	5	26	86	263	13	35
start or finish of a job	.	(3)	18	14	6	12	.	(2)	.	.
other reasons	85	52	110	37	23	(6)	(4)	5	76	12
1975										
Employees who worked less than 40 hours	539	877	1 269	1 720	359	567	177	528	154	106
of which:										
technical or economic reasons	109	206	104	147	111	206	5	26	17	32
strike	.	.	8	34	52	105	–	–	.	.
sickness, accident	136	249	330	371	132	181	40	117	21	30
holiday	187	325	558	759	12	33	118	360	12	29
start or finish of a job	(3)	(5)	19	17	9	23	(3)	(4)	.	.
other reasons	105	90	251	392	43	19	12	21	104	13
1977										
Employees who worked less than 40 hours	451	649	617	822	183	268	164	434	64	83
of which:										
technical or economic reasons	20	5	34	85	27	51	(4)	13	14	22
strike	.	.	(4)	21	7	39	.	.	.	(3)
sickness, accident	181	274	383	397	111	110	50	145	17	25
holiday	127	250	119	198	16	46	86	245	7	17
start or finish of a job	.	(6)	21	28	.	(5)	(3)	5	.	.
other reasons	121	68	57	92	20	17	22	26	25	15

TAB. 83

Employees who as an exception worked fewer than 40 hours during the reference week, by reasons (1 000)
Salariés ayant travaillé exceptionnellement moins de 40 heures pendant la semaine de référence, selon les motifs (1 000)

Luxembourg		United Kingdom		Ireland		Danmark		EUR 9		
F	M	F	M	F	M	F	M	F	M	
				1973						
2	5	570	981							Salariés ayant travaillé moins de 40 heures
										dont:
.	.	28	61							raisons techniques ou économiq.
–	–	18	94							conflit de travail
.	2	148	277							maladie, accident
.	3	283	459							congé
.	.	10	10							début ou cessation d'une activité
.	.	84	80							autres raisons
				1975						
2	7	516	770	16	29	79	74	3 112	4 677	Salariés ayant travaillé moins de 40 heures
										dont:
:	(1)	69	122	(3)	5	8	16	425	762	raisons techniques ou économiq.
–	–	21	23	.	.	.	.	63	164	conflit de travail
.	2	166	304	(3)	8	28	22	855	1 282	maladie, accident
(1)	(4)	132	198	5	9	26	24	1 050	1 743	congé
.	.	8	11	.	.	(2)	(3)	45	63	début ou cessation d'une activité
(1)	.	139	113	5	5	16	9	674	662	autres raisons
				1977						
2	6	816	1 028	12	29	133	101	2 442	3 420	Salariés ayant travaillé moins de 40 heures
										dont:
.	.	22	42	.	(2)	7	14	128	280	raisons techniques ou économiq.
.	.	(4)	25	.	(2)	.	(3)	163	95	conflit de travail
(1)	2	247	401	(4)	10	34	25	1 026	1 388	maladie, accident
(1)	3	215	312	(3)	5	31	28	605	1 106	congé
.	.	11	11	.	.	.	.	41	58	début ou cessation d'une activité
(1)	.	316	236	(4)	9	61	30	626	494	autres raisons

TAB. 84

Persons working at night or on Sundays or public holidays (as % of all persons with a main occupation)

Personnes travaillant de nuit ou le dimanche, ou pendant les jours fériés (en % de toutes les personnes ayant un emploi principal)

1975

	BR Deutschland		France		Italia		Nederland		Belgique Belgïe	
	F	M	F	M	F	M	F	M	F	M
Persons working at night	6,7	17,1	7,3	19,3	6,3	16,8	9,4	17,3	8,5	19,3
of which:										
regularly	2,6	7,3	2,8	9,2	2,1	5,1	6,0	9,3	4,1	10,1
Employees:	4,3	14,5	4,2	14,5	4,2	12,9	8,3	13,8	4,0	14,6
in industry	0,7	7,7	0,3	6,6	0,7	5,7	(0,2)	6,0	(0,3)	7,3
in services	3,5	6,7	3,9	7,5	3,4	6,5	8,0	7,4	3,7	7,1
Self employed	0,9	2,4	1,0	4,3	1,0	3,5	(0,4)	3,2	2,2	4,2
Family workers	1,5	0,2	2,0	0,4	1,1	0,4	(0,7)	(0,2)	2,3	0,5
Persons working on Sundays	17,4	23,2	24,6	29,8	19,3	31,2	18,7	23,3	20,1	24,6
of which:										
regularly	10,4	9,3	17,9	17,3	5,9	5,2	12,5	13,1	15,1	14,1
Employees:	8,9	17,0	12,5	18,0	8,9	19,7	15,7	17,0	9,4	16,3
in industry	0,7	7,3	0,8	5,7	1,2	8,1	0,4	5,5	0,5	6,2
in services	7,9	9,2	11,6	11,4	6,6	9,3	15,1	10,7	3,8	9,9
Self employed	2,2	5,6	3,8	10,7	4,6	10,3	1,0	5,8	5,0	7,5
Family workers	6,3	0,6	8,3	1,1	5,8	1,2	2,0	0,3		0,8

TAB. 84

Persons working at night or on Sundays or public holidays (as % of all persons with a main occupation)

Personnes travaillant de nuit ou le dimanche, ou pendant les jours fériés (en % de toutes les personnes ayant emploi principal)

1975

Luxembourg		United Kingdom		Ireland		Danmark		EUR 9		
F	M	F	M	F	M	F	M	F	M	
8,1		6,3	22,2	14,1	23,5	12,1	23,9	7,0	19,0	Personnes travaillant de nuit
										dont:
2,6	13,7	3,9	12,4	6,9	9,1	5,9	9,8	3,2	8,7	régulièrement
(2,5)	23,8	5,3	18,5	10,4	13,6	11,2	19,0	4,9	15,2	Emploi salarié:
0,0	18,8	0,6	10,5	(1,2)	5,4	(0,8)	7,1	0,6	7,6	dans l'industrie
(2,5)	(5,0)	4,7	7,6	9,3	7,5	10,2	11,2	4,2	7,1	dans les services
(2,5)	(3,0)	0,5	2,3	(1,9)	8,9	(0,4)	4,9	0,9	3,3	Indépendants
(2,5)	(1,0)	:	:	(1,6)	(1,1)	(0,7)	:	1,1	0,3	Aides familiaux
23,2	34,4	18,9	43,4	28,0	45,4	32,6	42,4	20,4	31,8	Personnes travaill. les diman.
										dont:
14,9	16,0	10,1	18,4	15,7	28,8	20,1	18,5	12,0	13,7	régulièrement
10,0	26,7	15,5	33,9	17,5	17,6	26,6	30,0	12,3	21,1	Emploi salarié:
0,0	17,8	1,6	17,3	0,8	6,8	1,7	9,7	1,0	9,5	dans l'industrie
10,0	7,9	13,6	15,1	16,3	10,7	25,1	17,8	10,9	1,1	dans les services
5,0	6,9	1,9		6,2	22,8	1,5	13,4	2,9	8,4	Indépendants
7,5	1,0	:	:	4,3	2,9	4,6	0,0	4,6	0,7	Aides familiaux

TAB. 85

Average number of hours worked by female workers (average number of hours worked by male workers = 100) according to sector of activity by region

Nombre moyen d'heures effectuées par les travailleuses (nombre moyen d'heures effectuées par les travailleurs = 100) selon le secteur d'activité par région

1975

	Total $\frac{f}{m}$ 100	Agriculture $\frac{f}{m}$ 100	Industry/Industrie $\frac{f}{m}$ 100	Services $\frac{f}{m}$ 100
BR DEUTSCHLAND	87,0	83,8	86,8	83,4
Schleswig-Holstein	80,5	83,9	82,0	78,9
Hamburg	79,6	.	82,0	78,0
Niedersachsen	84,5	79,7	87,2	80,9
Bremen	81,2	.	85,0	79,6
Nordrhein-Westfalen	85,6	80,8	87,6	83,9
Hessen	86,8	81,7	88,7	84,0
Rheinland-Pfalz	88,8	76,6	88,1	87,9
Baden-Württemberg	86,2	85,2	86,0	82,4
Bayern	89,9	86,6	86,7	85,8
Saarland	90,4	57,1	94,2	87,8
Berlin (West)	87,4	.	92,2	84,7
FRANCE	86,3	77,2	90,4	86,1
Région parisienne	89,8	82,8	91,5	88,6
Bassin parisien	86,2	77,4	91,1	85,6
Nord	88,2	71,3	91,7	86,5
Est	85,9	71,3	91,2	83,9
Ouest	84,7	77,3	90,4	85,7
Sud-Ouest	85,2	79,2	89,8	85,5
Centre-Est	84,5	68,9	89,2	84,8
Méditerranée	85,7	80,0	89,1	85,5
ITALIA	91,3	87,8	94,0	89,9
Nord-Ovest	93,6	83,8	95,1	92,8
Lombardia	94,0	80,4	95,3	93,6
Nord-Est	91,6	82,2	95,8	89,8
Emilia-Romagna	90,1	85,5	94,6	88,3
Centro	90,8	87,4	95,4	88,7
Lazio	91,5	85,1	94,2	91,2
Campania	91,4	91,8	97,0	87,5
Abruzzi e Molise	89,1	85,3	89,4	90,6
Sud	87,9	89,2	95,2	85,0
Sicilia	89,7	96,0	92,0	87,8
Sardegna	88,3	86,8	95,7	88,8
NEDERLAND	80,0	69,8	85,5	79,4
Noord	78,1	67,4	88,7	78,8
Oost	81,2	69,0	88,1	81,5
West	78,3	69,4	81,9	77,9
Zuid	84,0	74,5	88,6	82,4
Zuidwest	79,2	64,5	80,1	79,4
BELGIQUE/BELGIË	89,7	69,1	93,3	88,7
Région de langue néerlandaise	90,0	69,5	93,7	89,4
Région de langue française	89,1	68,0	92,1	88,5
Bruxelles capitale	89,6	88,6	92,2	88,4
LUXEMBOURG	93,5	67,2	95,1	94,6
UNITED KINGDOM	79,6	63,1	77,4	68,0
North	71,0	92,1	78,5	67,9
Yorkshire and Humberside	69,8	66,9	74,8	67,1
North-West	71,9	60,9	80,8	67,1
East Midlands	69,3	62,4	75,9	65,8
West Midlands	71,3	54,5	78,2	66,1
East Anglia	64,7	59,0	76,1	61,7
South-East	71,3	55,7	76,4	69,8
South-West	66,1	74,4	76,0	64,0
Wales	71,8	79,0	78,8	68,3
Scotland	71,9	60,1	79,6	70,8
Northern Ireland	72,6	80,6	81,8	73,6
IRELAND	80,0	75,6	89,9	87,8
DANMARK	75,7	61,0	83,3	75,2
EUR 9	82,9	82,2	86,9	80,7

TAB. 85
(continued)
(suite)

	1977			
	Total	Agriculture	Industry/Industrie	Services
	$\frac{f}{m}100$	$\frac{f}{m}100$	$\frac{f}{m}100$	$\frac{f}{m}100$
BR DEUTSCHLAND	85,6	84,2	87,1	82,2
Schleswig-Holstein	79,8	77,6	84,1	77,9
Hamburg	80,8	94,2	86,8	77,9
Niedersachsen	83,9	82,7	86,3	80,0
Bremen	81,8	92,8	89,3	78,5
Nordrhein-Westfalen	85,5	87,5	87,6	82,1
Hessen	86,4	79,2	87,5	84,6
Rheinland-Pfalz	85,8	78,8	85,3	84,7
Baden-Württemberg	84,7	85,3	85,1	81,4
Bayern	89,2	85,1	88,8	84,7
Saarland	90,7	77,0	92,7	88,1
Berlin (West)	85,3	91,2	88,9	83,0
FRANCE	87,2	78,9	92,3	86,0
Région parisienne	90,0	89,0	92,0	89,1
Bassin parisien	86,3	78,7	92,8	84,4
Nord	89,9	77,9	95,5	85,9
Est	86,6	67,4	93,2	85,3
Ouest	84,9	78,8	91,2	83,7
Sud-Ouest	86,1	80,6	93,3	86,7
Centre-Est	86,7	73,0	91,6	85,5
Méditerranée	85,2	80,7	90,9	83,6
ITALIA	91,1	88,7	95,0	88,9
Nord-Ovest	92,5	83,6	96,3	90,6
Lombardia	93,3	87,9	95,9	90,5
Nord-Est	90,4	83,5	94,7	89,4
Emilia-Romagna	90,2	86,6	95,1	88,5
Centro	89,5	85,2	95,0	87,1
Lazio	91,8	94,6	96,2	90,4
Campania	91,8	92,0	95,9	88,3
Abruzzi e Molise	89,1	86,6	95,1	89,5
Sud	89,0	91,2	94,0	86,1
Sicilia	88,4	90,5	99,3	86,6
Sardegna	85,4	85,0	96,4	85,9
NEDERLAND	77,9	66,6	85,4	77,4
Noord	75,9	67,9	86,9	75,6
Oost	79,7	67,7	88,0	79,5
West	76,4	61,8	81,5	76,1
Zuid	77,5	60,5	96,3	76,2
Zuidwest	82,2	69,9	88,0	80,9
BELGIQUE/BELGIË	88,8	76,8	93,9	87,8
Région de langue néerlandaise	89,0	74,5	94,1	88,2
Région de langue française	88,3	79,4	93,4	87,3
Bruxelles capitale	89,6	96,7	92,3	88,6
LUXEMBOURG	92,5	69,6	95,6	92,7
UNITED KINGDOM	68,8	61,5	77,7	66,7
North	67,9	67,4	78,2	64,7
Yorkshire and Humberside	66,7	56,1	76,9	63,0
North-West	70,2	56,7	78,8	66,2
East Midlands	66,6	59,5	74,0	64,5
West Midlands	70,4	53,7	79,9	65,1
East Anglia	65,8	58,6	73,4	64,5
South-East	70,3	61,2	76,2	68,8
South-West	64,3	52,5	74,4	63,5
Wales	67,0	63,5	80,2	67,0
Scotland	70,9	98,7	81,3	69,3
Northern Ireland	69,4	52,1	84,8	68,2
IRELAND	79,9	73,4	90,7	85,6
DANMARK	76,4	69,7	84,4	75,5
EUR 9	82,2	82,0	87,5	79,6

TAB. 86

Time taken and distance travelled by employees to get to work (%)

Temps nécessaire et distance parcourue par les salariés pour se rendre à leur travail (%)

1975

	BR Deutschland		France		Italia		Nederland		Belgique Belgïe	
	F	M	F	M	F	M	F	M	F	M
Time										
Agriculture	100,0	100,0	100,0	100,0	100,0	100,0	100,0	100,0	100,0	100,0
< 30 minutes	83,1	80,3	88,3	90,4	81,0	74,5	88,8	89,5	89,1	83,1
30–59 minutes	16,2	17,6	10,9	8,2	17,7	23,9	11,2	9,4	5,2	12,0
60–119 minutes	0,7	1,5	0,9	1,3	1,3	1,2	0,0	0,8	5,7	4,8
> 120 minutes	0,0	0,6	0,0	0,1	0,0	0,4	0,0	0,3	0,0	0,0
Industry	100,0	100,0	100,0	100,0	100,0	100,0	100,0	100,0	100,0	100,0
< 30 minutes	76,2	65,5	73,9	73,9	81,1	72,9	85,2	80,0	77,3	72,3
30–59 minutes	22,4	29,1	18,8	18,7	17,1	22,8	12,9	16,1	18,4	20,4
60–119 minutes	1,4	4,5	7,3	7,0	1,7	3,8	1,7	3,4	3,9	6,5
> 120 minutes	0,0	0,8	0,1	0,3	0,1	0,4	0,1	0,5	0,4	0,8
Services	100,0	100,0	100,0	100,0	100,0	100,0	100,0	100,0	100,0	100,0
< 30 minutes	73,5	70,5	73,3	72,6	79,8	75,1	82,4	78,3	73,4	68,4
30–59 minutes	24,7	26,2	18,7	19,0	17,7	21,1	15,2	17,1	20,5	21,5
60–119 minutes	1,7	2,8	7,7	7,7	2,1	3,1	2,2	3,9	5,5	8,4
> 120 minutes	0,1	0,4	0,4	0,7	0,3	0,6	0,3	0,7	0,7	1,7
Distance										
Agriculture	100,0	100,0	100,0	100,0	100,0	100,0	100,0	100,0	100,0	100,0
< 10 km	83,2	73,2	81,6	83,2	80,8	75,2	84,4	81,3	83,9	71,1
10–24 km	14,0	21,8	14,2	13,5	17,2	21,2	13,6	14,1	10,4	18,3
25–49 km	2,2	4,0	4,2	2,6	1,6	2,9	2,0	4,0	0,0	8,9
> 50 km	7,0	1,0	0,0	0,7	0,4	0,7	0,0	0,7	5,7	1,7
Industry	100,0	100,0	100,0	100,0	100,0	100,0	100,0	100,0	100,0	100,0
< 10 km	76,0	64,8	77,8	70,7	81,9	68,8	76,7	65,6	72,3	61,4
10–24 km	20,5	26,3	17,8	21,8	13,7	22,6	19,8	24,0	20,4	25,0
25–49 km	3,0	7,2	3,7	6,2	4,0	6,7	3,3	6,9	5,3	9,1
> 50 km	0,4	1,8	0,6	1,3	0,4	2,0	0,1	3,5	2,7	4,6
Services	100,0	100,0	100,0	100,0	100,0	100,0	100,0	100,0	100,0	100,0
< 10 km	74,1	61,6	80,5	71,3	79,6	74,1	76,2	64,0	70,9	60,1
10–24 km	21,8	28,1	14,8	20,5	15,6	18,5	19,1	24,7	19,1	22,0
25–49 km	3,6	7,8	3,6	6,1	4,0	5,7	3,9	7,8	6,5	10,9
> 50 km	0,6	2,5	1,1	2,0	0,8	1,7	0,8	3,6	3,5	6,9

TAB. 86

Time taken and distance travelled by employees to get to work (%)
Temps nécessaire et distance parcourue par les salariés pour se rendre à leur travail (%)
1975

Luxembourg		United Kingdom		Ireland		Danmark		EUR 9		
F	M	F	M	F	M	F	M	F	M	
Temps										
100,0	100,0	100,0	100,0	100,0	100,0	100,0	100,0	100,0	100,0	**Agriculture**
75,0	90,4	81,2	91,4	80,9	82,3	96,5	89,3	82,6	82,1	< 30 minutes
25,0	9,6	14,1	7,9	19,1	16,3	3,5	8,9	15,8	16,4	30–59 minutes
0,0	0,0	4,7	0,4	0,0	1,4	0,0	0,7	1,7	1,1	60–119 minutes
0,0	0,0	0,0	0,3	0,0	0,0	0,0	1,1	0,0	0,4	> 120 minutes
100,0	100,0	100,0	100,0	100,0	100,0	100,0	100,0	100,0	100,0	**Industrie**
81,4	79,6	78,4	72,4	69,6	67,4	84,0	82,6	77,7	73,3	< 30 minutes
17,3	16,7	19,1	22,6	27,4	27,0	14,2	15,6	19,1	22,0	30–59 minutes
1,3	3,5	2,4	4,6	3,0	5,6	1,7	1,6	3,1	4,2	60–119 minutes
0,0	0,2	0,0	0,4	0,0	0,0	0,1	0,2	0,1	0,4	> 120 minutes
100,0	100,0	100,0	100,0	100,0	100,0	100,0	100,0	100,0	100,0	**Services**
77,0	83,0	78,4	68,2	67,1	68,1	82,1	78,2	76,3	71,7	< 30 minutes
19,6	15,6	18,4	24,3	28,5	17,2	16,1	18,8	19,9	22,5	30–59 minutes
2,9	1,2	3,1	6,9	4,4	4,7	1,8	2,6	3,6	5,2	60–119 minutes
0,4	0,3	0,1	0,7	0,0	0,0	0,1	0,5	0,2	0,6	> 120 minutes
Distance										
100,0	100,0	100,0	100,0	100,0	100,0	100,0	100,0	100,0	100,0	**Agriculture**
100,0	86,5	79,5	86,1	74,3	83,2	93,3	74,5	81,2	78,7	< 10 km
0,0	5,8	15,9	12,2	22,9	14,0	6,7	19,7	16,0	17,8	10–24 km
0,0	7,7	4,1	1,3	2,8	2,1	0,0	3,8	2,4	2,8	25–49 km
0,0	0,0	0,6	0,4	0,0	0,6	0,0	2,1	0,4	0,7	> 50 km
100,0	100,0	100,0	100,0	100,0	100,0	100,0	100,0	100,0	100,0	**Industrie**
73,7	71,2	79,6	61,6	83,3	68,9	74,0	64,9	78,1	65,8	< 10 km
19,1	20,5	18,7	30,4	14,1	23,6	28,5	26,1	18,3	25,6	10–24 km
6,7	7,3	1,9	6,1	2,4	6,4	4,0	7,2	3,1	6,7	25–49 km
0,5	1,1	0,3	1,9	0,2	1,1	0,4	1,7	0,5	1,9	> 50 km
100,0	100,0	100,0	100,0	100,0	100,0	100,0	100,0	100,0	100,0	**Services**
69,2	69,8	76,7	57,1	80,5	75,1	76,0	63,8	76,9	64,7	< 10 km
20,3	22,2	20,4	32,1	15,3	19,5	18,6	24,8	18,8	25,4	10–24 km
6,5	7,4	2,3	7,6	3,7	4,7	4,9	8,8	3,4	7,2	25–49 km
1,3	0,6	0,6	3,2	0,4	0,6	0,5	2,6	0,8	2,7	> 50 km

TAB. 87

Means of transport used by persons with a principal occupation who travel a fixed distance to get to work (%)

Moyens de transport utilisés par les personnes ayant un emploi principal parcourant une distance fixe pour se rendre à leur travail (%)

1975

	BR Deutschland		France		Italia		Nederland		Belgique België	
	F	M	F	M	F	M	F	M	F	M
Only one mode of transport:										
On foot only	23,3	11,9	25,8	13,0	30,7	18,4	10,4	6,4	16,0	8,2
Bicycle/moped/motorcycle	8,5	10,1	11,8	18,8	17,2	20,6	41,6	33,2	16,4	15,9
Private car	30,0	58,2	34,5	48,5	24,4	41,3	26,0	46,6	36,6	55,2
Tramway/bus/underground	33,0	15,2	19,4	11,5	23,6	14,6	16,8	7,9	20,7	10,3
Train	2,9	2,4	2,1	1,9	1,6	1,9	1,8	1,8	7,8	8,0
Other	0,1	0,1	0,3	0,7	0,6	0,6	0,3	1,1	0,0	0,0

TAB. 87

Means of transport used by persons with a principal occupation who travel a fixed distance to get to work (%)

Moyens de transport utilisés par les personnes ayant un emploi principal parcourant une distance fixe pour se rendre à leur travail (%)

1975

Luxembourg		United Kingdom		Ireland		Danmark		EUR 9		
F	M	F	M	F	M	F	M	F	M	
										Un seul moyen de transport:
25,4	16,4	28,1	12,8	34,5	17,9	14,2	7,0	25,5	13,3	Marche à pied uniquement
1,9	10,3	3,7	7,5	5,4	12,0	25,5	24,7	10,7	14,8	Vélo/Cyclomoteur/Motocyclette
30,7	49,4	30,6	56,0	28,0	51,1	36,9	56,5	30,5	51,6	Voiture
28,1	16,1	33,7	18,5	27,9	14,4	18,9	8,0	27,8	14,5	Tramway/Métro/Bus/Car
7,6	3,2	2,5	3,6	1,5	1,0	0,8	0,8	2,5	2,6	Train/Tramway extra-urbain
0,1	0,0	0,1	0,1	0,4	2,0	0,0	0,0	0,2	0,4	Autres

TAB. 88

Subjective assessment of working conditions by sector of activity (%)
Évaluation personnelle des conditions de travail selon le secteur d'activité (%)
1972

	BR Deutschland		Nederland		Belgique Belgïe		United Kingdom		Ireland		
	F	M	F	M	F	M	F	M	F	M	
Agriculture	100,0	100,0	100,0	100,0	100,0	100,0	100,0	100,0	100,0	100,0	**Agriculture**
Very quiet	13,7	14,2	8,9	10,8	43,3	40,1	41,1	51,1	56,2	49,0	Très calme
Normal	77,4	69,5	80,7	77,6	48,4	48,2	34,2	38,6	41,3	48,0	Normal
Noisy	8,9	16,4	10,4	11,6	7,3	11,8	19,7	10,3	2,5	3,6	Bruyant
Very hygienic	2,6	2,6	6,0	7,2	15,5	15,5	78,4	18,6	18,6	16,3	Très hygiénique
Normal hygienic	68,8	61,5	82,5	79,3	73,2	74,6	17,6	50,8	76,8	79,9	Normal
Unhygienic	28,6	35,8	11,4	13,6	11,4	10,4	4,6	30,4	4,5	3,8	Mauvais
Risks of accident or illness											Risque d'accident ou de maladie
No	11,2	10,0	72,6	55,4	42,3	32,5	65,0	10,4	45,1	28,5	Sans
Some	75,4	71,0	28,0	42,8	55,9	61,2	32,9	74,6	51,7	64,8	Avec quelque
Serious	13,4	19,0	0,0	1,8	1,7	6,3	2,1	14,5	3,2	6,8	Avec beaucoup
Industry	100,0	100,0	100,0	100,0	100,0	100,0	100,0	100,0	100,0	100,0	**Industrie**
Very quiet	14,0	6,4	6,3	2,9	13,9	7,4	31,4	17,4	12,8	11,0	Très calme
Normal	55,6	46,5	63,1	50,1	43,5	37,0	35,3	38,9	46,2	44,5	Normal
Noisy	30,4	47,2	30,6	46,9	42,6	55,6	33,3	43,6	41,0	44,5	Bruyant
Very hygienic	27,7	12,8	18,0	9,2	23,4	14,8	65,0	33,0	37,6	22,5	Très hygiénique
Normal hygienic	59,7	52,7	73,8	71,1	68,6	66,1	25,7	34,4	57,5	59,4	Normal
Unhygienic	12,6	34,6	8,3	19,7	7,9	19,0	9,3	32,5	5,1	18,,2	Mauvais
Risks of accident or illness											Risque d'accident ou de maladie
No	41,2	17,7	86,0	50,7	66,0	31,8	59,5	21,7	60,6	25,8	Sans
Some	38,9	51,7	13,3	44,3	31,9	55,7	38,1	61,0	35,4	58,0	Avec quelque
Serious	19,9	30,6	0,7	5,6	2,1	12,5	2,4	17,3	4,6	16,1	Avec beaucoup
Services	100,0	100,0	100,0	100,0	100,0	100,0	100,0	100,0	100,0	100,0	**Services**
Very quiet	23,1	16,0	10,9	8,3	27,8	19,6	44,4	32,3	24,6	21,6	Très calme
Normal	59,8	56,6	72,1	66,0	52,9	49,7	40,9	46,0	60,9	58,7	Normal
Noisy	17,2	27,5	16,9	25,6	19,2	30,7	14,7	21,6	14,6	19,7	Bruyant
Very hygienic	47,7	32,3	31,4	21,6	40,7	29,5	84,6	63,6	50,5	36,1	Très hygiénique
Normal hygienic	48,7	54,8	65,2	71,2	56,2	62,7	14,2	25,3	46,6	55,2	Normal
Unhygienic	3,6	12,8	3,5	7,8	3,1	7,7	1,8	11,0	3,5	8,7	Mauvais
Risks of accident or illness											Risque d'accident ou de maladie
No	51,7	36,4	90,6	70,9	83,5	58,0	67,4	39,2	75,2	48,0	Sans
Some	29,4	38,4	9,0	25,0	15,6	34,9	30,7	49,7	22,3	42,8	Avec quelque
Serious	18,4	25,2	0,4	3,6	1,0	7,1	1,4	11,0	2,5	9,1	Avec beaucoup

TAB. 89

Female employees by number of children and type of work (%)
Salariées selon le nombre d'enfants et le régime de travail (%)
1972

	BR Deutschland	France	Italia	Nederland	Belgique België	Luxembourg	
1 child							**1 enfant**
full time	67,8	91,3	84,9	28,1	87,9	83,3	à temps complet
part time	30,0	7,9	6,4	52,8	10,6	11,1	à temps partiel
occasionally	2,2	0,8	8,7	19,1	1,5	5,6	occasionnellement
total	100,0	100,0	100,0	100,0	100,0	100,0	total
2 children							**2 enfants**
full time	53,8	84,1	91,6	15,3	82,6	81,0	à temps complet
part time	43,6	14,0	2,1	51,8	12,3	19,0	à temps partiel
occasionally	2,6	1,9	6,3	32,9	5,1	–	occasionnellement
total	100,0	100,0	100,0	100,0	100,0	100,0	total
3 children							**3 enfants**
full time	65,8	82,5	88,5	32,5	83,7	75,0	à temps complet
part time	31,6	15,8	1,9	50,0	16,3	25,0	à temps partiel
occasionally	2,6	1,7	9,6	17,5	–	–	occasionnellement
total	100,0	100,0	100,0	100,0	100,0	100,0	total
4 children							**4 enfants**
full time	54,5	83,3	77,8	22,7	58,3	60,0	à temps complet
part time	36,4	12,5	11,1	68,2	33,3	20,0	à temps partiel
occasionally	9,1	4,2	11,1	9,1	8,4	20,0	occasionnellement
total	100,0	100,0	100,0	100,0	100,0	100,0	total
5 children and more							**5 enfants et plus**
full time	50,0	44,4	78,6	100,0	89,5	–	à temps complet
part time	50,0	55,6	–	–	10,5	–	à temps partiel
occasionally	–	–	21,4	–	–	–	occasionnellement
total	100,0	100,0	100,0	100,0	100,0	–	total
Total							**Total**
full time	62,4	87,0	87,1	25,0	85,3	80,7	à temps complet
part time	35,1	11,6	4,4	52,5	12,2	14,8	à temps partiel
occasionally	2,5	1,4	8,5	22,5	2,5	4,5	occasionnellement
total	100,0	100,0	100,0	100,0	100,0	100,0	total

TAB. 90

Female employees by number of children and days of special leave enjoyed (%)

Salariées selon le nombre d'enfants et le bénéfice de jours de congé extraordinaire (%)

1972

	BR Deutschland	France	Italia	Nederland	Belgique België	Luxembourg	
1 child							**1 enfant**
have enjoyed	14,2	5,6	13,1	33,0	8,9	1,8	ont bénéficié
have not enjoyed	85,8	94,4	86,9	67,0	91,1	98,2	n'ont pas bénéficié
total	100,0	100,0	100,0	100,0	100,0	100,0	total
2 children							**2 enfants**
have enjoyed	13,7	9,0	14,2	31,0	13,7	4,8	ont bénéficié
have not enjoyed	86,3	91,0	85,8	69,0	86,3	95,2	n'ont pas bénéficié
total	100,0	100,0	100,0	100,0	100,0	100,0	total
3 children							**3 enfants**
have enjoyed	10,9	14,6	8,2	22,7	14,0	–	ont bénéficié
have not enjoyed	89,1	85,4	91,8	72,3	86,0	100,0	n'ont pas bénéficié
total	100,0	100,0	100,0	100,0	100,0	100,0	total
4 children							**4 enfants**
have enjoyed	6,7	12,5	12,5	21,7	33,3	–	ont bénéficié
have not enjoyed	93,3	87,5	87,5	78,3	66,7	100,0	n'ont pas bénéficié
total	100,0	100,0	100,0	100,0	100,0	100,0	total
5 children and more							**5 enfants et plus**
have enjoyed	15,4	–	–	40,0	5,6	–	ont bénéficié
have not enjoyed	84,6	100,0	100,0	60,0	94,4	–	n'ont pas bénéficié
total	100,0	100,0	100,0	100,0	100,0	–	total
Total							**Total**
have enjoyed	13,6	7,9	12,5	29,9	11,0	2,2	ont bénéficié
have not enjoyed	86,4	92,1	87,5	70,4	89,0	97,8	n'ont pas bénéficié
total	100,0	100,0	100,0	100,0	100,0	100,0	total

TAB. 91

Female employees by reasons for working, age and marital status (%)
Salariées selon la motivation au travail, l'âge et l'état civil (%)
1972

	BR Deutschland		France		Italia		Nederland		Belgique België		
	A	B	A	B	A	B	A	B	A	B	
< 21	100,0	100,0	100,0	100,0	100,0	100,0	100,0	100,0	100,0	100,0	**< 21**
Necessity	22,2	55,6	44,4	29,9	–	20,6	–	13,5	21,4	18,5	Par nécessité
Insuffic. salary of the spouse	33,4	0,5	5,6	4,8	75,0	30,9	60,0	14,9	21,4	12,3	Salaire du conjoint insuffisant
Specific economic reasons	33,3	10,2	11,1	4,0	–	1,7	–	1,0	14,3	3,1	Raisons économiques
To improve standard of living	–	4,3	33,3	11,3	12,5	16,9	–	1,0	21,4	20,0	Amélioration du niveau de vie
Reasons other than economic	–	23,0	5,6	45,2	12,5	23,7	20,0	44,7	7,2	26,1	Motifs non économiques
To save	11,1	6,4	–	4,8	–	6,2	20,0	24,9	14,3	20,0	Épargne
21 – 35	100,0	100,0	100,0	100,0	100,0	100,0	100,0	100,0	100,0	100,0	**21 – 35**
Necessity	13,6	79,8	9,8	63,6	8,3	27,9	5,0	42,1	4,5	46,0	Par nécessité
Insuffic. salary of the spouse	9,7	1,1	31,6	4,3	52,8	22,8	32,9	8,9	20,7	6,5	Salaire du conjoint insuffisant
Specific economic reasons	43,0	5,3	17,2	1,1	5,6	2,6	2,9	1,3	19,8	4,3	Raisons économiques
To improve standard of living	7,2	2,1	30,7	8,5	16,2	10,7	5,8	0,4	37,9	15,8	Amélioration du niveau de vie
Reasons other than economic	22,2	11,7	10,7	22,5	16,2	30,5	49,2	29,8	9,7	17,3	Motifs non économiques
To save	4,3	–	–	–	0,9	5,5	4,2	17,5	7,4	10,1	Épargne
35 – 55	100,0	100,0	100,0	100,0	100,0	100,0	100,0	100,0	100,0	100,0	**35 – 55**
Necessity	12,3	91,6	14,9	98,3	16,3	73,3	5,2	67,2	6,4	86,3	Par nécessité
Insuffic. salary of the spouse	16,4	0,6	34,3	0,5	49,8	7,8	34,9	4,2	27,4	1,8	Salaire du conjoint insuffisant
Specific economic reasons	37,4	4,2	10,0	–	5,9	2,6	7,3	1,7	16,4	1,8	Raisons économiques
To improve standard of living	10,6	0,6	32,7	0,6	11,7	1,7	1,1	0,8	40,9	5,5	Amélioration du niveau de vie
Reasons other than economic	22,3	3,0	7,4	0,6	16,3	13,8	51,0	24,4	7,1	4,6	Motifs non économiques
To save	1,0	–	0,7	–	–	0,8	0,5	1,7	1,8	–	Épargne
≥ 55	100,0	100,0	100,0	100,0	100,0	100,0	100,0	100,0	100,0	100,0	**≥ 55**
Necessity	15,6	79,4	15,4	100,0	20,0	84,6	12,5	72,7	11,5	95,8	Par nécessité
Insuffic. salary of the spouse	22,2	1,5	38,5	–	40,0	7,7	31,2	6,1	26,9	–	Salaire du conjoint insuffisant
Specific economic reasons	31,1	2,9	5,1	–	6,7	–	6,3	3,0	7,7	4,2	Raisons économiques
To improve standard of living	11,1	1,5	25,6	–	13,3	–	–	–	38,5	–	Amélioration du niveau de vie
Reasons other than economic	20,0	14,7	15,4	–	20,0	7,7	50,0	18,2	3,9	–	Motifs non économiques
To save	–	–	–	–	–	–	–	–	11,5	–	Épargne
Total	100,0		100,0		100,0		100,0		100,0		**Total**
Necessity	43,5		40,0		25,8		23,4		23,9		Par nécessité
Insuffic. salary ot the spouse	7,7		18,8		34,3		20,3		17,6		Salaire du conjoint insuffisant
Specific economic reasons	23,2		7,4		3,5		2,7		12,6		Raisons économiques
To improve standard of living	5,8		19,6		12,4		1,8		29,6		Amélioration du niveau de vie
Reasons other than economic	17,6		13,6		21,0		40,5		10,1		Motifs non économiques
To save	2,2		0,7		3,1		11,3		6,2		Épargne

A: married – mariées.
B: not married – non mariées.

TAB. 92

Female employees by number of children and help with housework (%)

Salariées selon le nombre d'enfants et l'aide dans le travail ménager (%)

1972

Number of children	BR Deutschland	France	Italia	Nederland	Belgique België	Luxembourg	Nombre d'enfants
1							**1**
Helped by:							Avec l'aide de:
nobody	71,7	59,2	52,7	69,8	43,4	38,2	aucune aide
husband	14,7	21,0	8,9	18,8	39,8	30,9	du mari
salaried help	1,3	5,6	8,8	6,2	4,6	5,4	personne rémunérée
member of the family	10,0	10,5	20,7	4,2	10,4	16,4	membre de la famille
housework done by a member of the family	2,3	3,7	8,9	1,0	1,8	9,1	travail ménager exécuté par un membre de la famille
Total	100,0	100,0	100,0	100,0	100,0	100,0	Total
2							**2**
Helped by:							Avec l'aide de:
nobody	69,7	53,3	43,5	77,5	54,3	18,2	aucune aide
husband	12,0	17,8	5,1	12,5	31,2	31,8	du mari
salaried help	3,4	12,5	15,9	10,0	9,4	18,2	personne rémunérée
member of the family	14,3	15,1	33,3	–	2,9	9,1	membre de la famille
housework done by a member of the family	0,6	1,3	2,2	–	2,2	22,7	travail ménager exécuté par un membre de la famille
Total	100,0	100,0	100,0	100,0	100,0	100,0	Total
3							**3**
Helped by:							Avec l'aide de:
nobody	67,3	52,8	36,0	70,6	48,0	75,0	aucune aide
husband	9,6	21,8	4,0	23,5	24,0	12,5	du mari
salaried help	5,8	10,9	32,0	2,9	12,0	–	personne rémunérée
member of the family	17,3	12,7	22,0	3,0	14,0	–	membre de la famille
housework done by a member of the family	–	1,8	6,0	–	2,0	12,5	travail ménager exécuté par un membre de la famille
Total	100,0	100,0	100,0	100,0	100,0	100,0	Total
4 and more							**4 et plus**
Helped by:							Avec l'aide de:
nobody	67,9	43,3	26,7	41,2	39,3	33,3	aucune aide
husband	17,8	6,7	–	41,2	3,6	16,7	du mari
salaried help	–	6,7	23,3	11,7	7,1	16,7	personne rémunérée
member of the family	14,3	33,3	36,7	5,9	39,3	33,3	membre de la famille
housework done by a member of the family	–	10,0	13,3	–	10,7	–	travail ménager exécuté par un membre de la famille
Total	100,0	100,0	100,0	100,0	100,0	100,0	Total
Total							**Total**
Helped by:							Avec l'aide de:
nobody	70,5	55,8	45,8	70,5	46,7	36,2	aucune aide
husband	13,5	19,2	6,4	19,0	33,7	28,6	du mari
salaried help	2,3	8,3	15,0	7,5	6,9	8,8	personne rémunérée
member of the family	12,3	13,5	26,1	2,6	10,3	14,3	membre de la famille
housework done by a member of the family	1,4	3,2	6,7	0,4	2,4	12,1	travail ménager exécuté par un membre de la famille
Total	100,0	100,0	100,0	100,0	100,0	100,0	Total

TAB. 93

Absences from work of female employees, by reasons (%)
Absences du travail des salariées selon les motifs (%)
1972

	BR Deutschland	France	Italia	Nederland	Belgique België	Luxembourg	
Short absence permitted	10,3	15,1	12,1	10,7	6,9	–	Courte absence autorisée
Sickness	74,2	57,5	51,3	67,4	63,6	91,3	Maladie
Sickness and short absence permitted	–	0,6	1,3	1,2	–	–	Maladie et courte absence autorisée
Sickness of child	2,1	6,2	3,9	3,7	6,9	–	Maladie d'un enfant
Sickness of a member of the family	5,2	3,3	6,9	4,6	2,9	1,5	Maladie d'un membre de la famille
Own sickness concurrent with sickness of a member of the family	1,5	–	1,0	–	–	–	Maladie survenue en même temps que pour un membre de la famille
Domestic matters to settle	1,5	1,1	10,4	1,3	1,2	–	Occupations domestiques
Visit to administrative bodies	–	3,3	3,6	0,8	2,3	2,9	Démarches administratives
Other reasons	5,2	12,9	9,5	10,3	16,2	4,3	Autres motifs
Total	100,0	100,0		100,0	100,0	100,0	Total

TAB. 94
Unemployed persons (1 000)

Personnes en chômage (1 000)

	BR Deutschland		France		Italia		Nederland		Belgique België	
	F	M	F	M	F	M	F	M	F	M
1968	62	128	149	186	179	443	(8)	52	32	59
1970	22	35	146	167	180	337	:	:	15	18
1973	69	64	190	185	282	435	17	65	29	30
1975	295	455	355	350	248	370	32	116	65	54
1977	353	386	524	434	394	442	40	115	138	77

Unemployment rates (%)

Taux de chômage (%)

	BR Deutschland		France		Italia		Nederland		Belgique België	
	F	M	F	M	F	M	F	M	F	M
1968	0,7	0,8	1,9	1,4	3,4	3,1	(0,8)	1,5	3,2	2,3
1970	0,3	0,9	1,9	1,3	3,6	2,4	:	:	1,4	0,7
1973	0,8	0,4	2,6	1,5	6,1	3,3	1,7	1,9	2,6	1,2
1975	3,2	2,8	4,3	2,6	4,9	2,7	2,9	3,4	5,5	2,2
1977	3,8	2,4	6,1	3,3	7,0	3,3	3,3	3,3	10,9	3,1

TAB. 94
Unemployed persons (1·000)
Personnes en chômage (1 000)

Luxembourg		United Kingdom		Ireland		Danmark		EUR 9		
F	M	F	M	F	M	F	M	F	M	
.	.	:	:	:	:	:	:	:	:	1968
.	.	:	:	:	:	:	:	:	:	1970
.	.	154	361	:	:	:	:	:	:	1973
.	.	501	646	26	82	59	98	1 577	2 176	1975
(1)	(1)	427	754	21	80	86	81	1 983	2 371	1977

Unemployment rates (%)
Taux de chômage (%)

Luxembourg		United Kingdom		Ireland		Danmark		EUR 9		
F	M	F	M	F	M	F	M	F	M	
.	.	:	:	:	:	:	:	:	:	1968
.	.	:	:	:	:	:	:	:	:	1970
.	.	1,7	2,4	:	:	:	:	:	:	1973
.	.	5,2	4,2	8,7	10,0	6,5	7,0	4,4	3,3	1975
(1,5)	(1,0)	4,4	4,8	7,4	9,8	8,9	5,7	5,3	3,5	1977

TAB. 95

Unemployment rates by age groups (%)

Taux de chômage par groupe d'âge (%)

	BR Deutschland		France		Italia		Nederland		Belgique België	
	F	M	F	M	F	M	F	M	F	M
1960										
14–19	0,8	0,5	8,3	6,3	9,3	9,1	1,6	1,7	5,9	2,9
20–24	0,4	0,2	5,1	2,3	6,7	6,6	1,7	0,7	2,5	3,7
25–29	0,7	0,2	2,8	0,4	3,5	2,8	1,0	0,6	1,5	1,1
30–34	0,6	0,2	2,3	0,3	2,0	2,0	2,0	0,4	2,0	1,4
35-39										
40–44	0,7	0,3	1,8	0,5	1,2	1,5	2,1	0,6	2,0	1,3
45–49										
50–54	0,6	0,5	1,5	1,0	1,0	2,0	0,9	1,0	4,7	3,7
55-59										
60–64	0,9	0,4	0,4	1,6	:	0,8	:	0,5	:	6,8
65+	:	0,4	2,1	1,3	:	:	:	2,6	:	2,6
1968										
14–19	1,1	1,2	5,2	3,8	9,6	11,6	:	2,2	:	3,9
20–24	0,8	0,9	2,7	2,3	7,2	8,8	1,5	2,8	4,7	3,4
25–29	0,7	0,6	1,7	1,1	3,4	3,3	0,3	1,5	3,4	2,4
30–34	0,7	0,5	1,6	1,0	1,8	2,1	0,6	1,2	3,8	1,6
35–39	0,7	0,7	1,3	1,0	1,7	1,6	:	:	:	1,2
40–44	0,6	0,7	1,2	0,9	1,1	1,7	:	:	:	1,6
45–49	0,8	0,7	1,7	0,9	1,3	1,5	:	1,4	:	:
50–54	0,9	0,9	1,7	1,3	:	1,8	:	:	:	2,3
55–59	1,0	1,2	1,3	1,6	:	1,6	:	2,4	:	2,9
60–64	1,1	1,7	1,5	1,9	:	0,9	:	:	:	6,2
65+	:	0,8	:	:	:	:	:	:	:	:
1975										
14–19	6,7	6,3	16,7	8,8	17,0	15,2	5,9	8,1	13,0	7,3
20–24	3,7	5,1	6,4	5,9	12,2	10,7	2,7	7,2	8,6	5,5
25–29	3,3	3,8	3,9	2,3	5,5	4,2	3,0	4,1	5,7	2,5
30–34	3,3	2,6	3,5	2,0	2,2	1,4	(2,9)	3,1	3,7	(1,4)
35–39	2,9	2,3	2,8	1,6	1,5	0,9	:	2,4	4,1	(1,2)
40–44	2,6	2,4	3,2	1,8	1,5	1,0	:	2,3	(3,3)	(1,1)
45–49	2,5	1,9	2,4	1,9	1,2	0,9	:	1,9	(2,7)	(1,3)
50–54	2,2	1,6	2,8	1,6	(1,1)	0,8	:	1,8	(3,4)	(0,9)
55–59	2,7	1,7	3,2	2,3	:	1,0	:	1,8	:	(1,4)
60–64	(1,2)	2,7	(2,2)	2,7	:	(0,8)	:	3,2	:	3,1
65+	:	:	:	:	:	:	:	:	:	:
Total	3,2	2,8	4,3	2,6	4,9	2,7	2,9	3,4	5,5	2,2
1977										
14–19	7,1	5,2	24,5	13,5	25,0	18,8	8,7	7,1	16,7	8,4
20–24	5,1	4,4	11,6	6,9	17,8	14,6	3,6	6,1	16,1	6,4
25–29	4,5	3,4	5,7	2,9	8,3	4,9	3,0	4,1	12,5	2,7
30–34	3,9	2,3	4,0	2,0	2,9	1,3	(2,0)	2,7	9,4	1,8
35–39	2,8	1,7	3,2	1,8	2,2	0,9	.	2,1	7,5	2,1
40–44	2,9	1,6	2,9	2,0	1,6	1,0	(2,3)	2,8	7,9	1,8
45–49	2,6	1,7	3,2	2,3	(1,2)	1,0	.	2,0	7,2	2,3
50–54	3,1	1,6	3,5	2,4	(1,0)	1,2	.	1,8	9,3	2,6
55–59	2,7	2,1	4,0	2,6	.	0,9	.	2,4	(7,9)	3,5
60–64	2,4	2,2	5,1	5,0	.	.	.	4,8	.	4,6
65+	.	.	.	.	.	.	.	.	.	.
Total	3,8	2,4	6,1	3,3	7,0	3,3	3,3	3,3	10,9	3,1

TAB. 95

Unemployment rates by age groups (%)

Taux de chômage par groupe d'âge (%)

Luxembourg		United Kingdom		Ireland		Danmark		EUR 9		
F	M	F	M	F	M	F	M	F	M	

1960

:	:	:	:	:	:	:	:	:	:	14–19
:	:	:	:	:	:	:	:	:	:	20–24
:	:	:	:	:	:	:	:	:	:	25–29
:	:	:	:	:	:	:	:	:	:	30–34
:	:	:	:	:	:	:	:	:	:	35–39
:	:	:	:	:	:	:	:	:	:	40–44
:	:	:	:	:	:	:	:	:	:	45–49
:	:	:	:	:	:	:	:	:	:	50–54
:	:	:	:	:	:	:	:	:	:	55–59
:	:	:	:	:	:	:	:	:	:	60–64
:	:	:	:	:	:	:	:	:	:	65+

1968

:	:	:	:	:	:	:	:	:	:	14–19
:	:	:	:	:	:	:	:	:	:	20–24
:	:	:	:	:	:	:	:	:	:	25–29
:	:	:	:	:	:	:	:	:	:	30–34
:	:	:	:	:	:	:	:	:	:	35–39
:	:	:	:	:	:	:	:	:	:	40–44
:	:	:	:	:	:	:	:	:	:	45–49
:	:	:	:	:	:	:	:	:	:	50–54
:	:	:	:	:	:	:	:	:	:	55–59
:	:	:	:	:	:	:	:	:	:	60–64
:	:	:	:	:	:	:	:	:	:	65+

1975

:	:	9,3	8,8	20,6	22,3	14,8	11,2	11,0	9,4	14–19
:	:	6,9	7,1	8,0	12,9	12,0	16,0	6,7	7,3	20–24
:	:	8,1	4,1	(6,7)	9,8	7,3	7,7	5,1	3,7	25–29
:	:	7,1	3,5	:	7,8	5,8	5,5	4,1	2,5	30–34
:	:	4,9	3,2	:	8,7	5,8	4,9	3,3	2,1	35–39
:	:	3,6	3,0	:	7,4	(4,3)	5,5	2,9	2,1	40–44
:	:	3,7	3,0	:	7,8	4,9	4,0	2,7	2,0	45–49
:	:	3,2	2,8	:	8,2	(3,7)	5,9	2,6	1,9	50–54
:	:	3,7	3,0	:	8,9	(4,0)	4,6	3,0	2,3	55–59
:	:	2,7	5,2	:	9,2	:	8,0	2,0	3,5	60–64
:	:	2,4	4,9	:	:	:	6,3	1,0	2,1	65+
:	:	5,2	4,2	8,7	10,0	6,5	7,0	4,4	3,3	Total

1977

.	.	10,7	10,4	18,3	21,8	18,4	9,1	14,4	10,9	14–19
.	.	7,0	8,0	7,8	13,6	18,1	9,5	9,8	8,0	20–24
.	.	5,4	5,9	(5,5)	10,5	10,9	7,7	6,1	4,3	25–29
.	.	4,4	4,1	.	8,9	6,7	4,5	4,2	2,6	30–34
.	.	3,4	3,6	.	7,5	6,0	2,8	3,1	2,0	35–39
.	.	2,8	3,7	.	8,3	5,4	2,9	2,9	2,1	40–44
.	.	2,7	3,4	.	7,2	5,5	4,9	2,7	2,2	45–49
.	.	2,9	3,4	.	7,0	5,6	4,2	3,0	2,2	50–54
.	.	3,1	3,6	.	8,3	(4,4)	5,2	3,1	2,6	55–59
.	.	(1,6)	5,1	.	8,5	.	6,5	2,6	3,9	60–64
.	.	.	2,0	.	.	.	8,7	1,1	1,5	65+
(1,5)	(1,0)	4,4	4,8	7,4	9,8	8,9	5,7	5,3	3,5	Total

TAB. 96

Main categories of persons seeking employment (1 000)

Principaux groupes de personnes à la recherche d'un emploi (1 000)

	BR Deutschland		France		Italia		Nederland		Belgique België	
	F	M	F	M	F	M	F	M	F	M
1973										
1. Unemployed persons	69	64	190	185	282	435	17	65	29	30
after a voluntary spell away from work	17	13	25	16	.	.	.	(2)	.	.
looking for their first job	14	13	38	26	202	249	(4)	6	7	5
2. Non-active persons looking for a job	:	:	304	64	567	274	48	17	12	5
after a voluntary spell away from work	:	:	91	(7)	85	4	14	.	(2)	.
looking for their first job	:	:	78	19	316	74	16	11	8	(4)
3. Active persons looking for another job	.	.	225	314	184	634	34	103	10	22
Total	:	:	719	563	1 033	1 345	98	184	50	61
1975										
1. Unemployed persons	295	455	351	354	248	370	32	116	65	54
after a voluntary spell away from work	49	59	67	21	.	.	.	(3)	.	.
looking for their first job	48	49	58	42	175	207	6	10	17	9
2. Non-active persons looking for a job	62	77	344	122	392	206	84	27	7	4
after a voluntary spell away from work	.	.	151	8	42	.	55	10	(2)	:
looking for their first job	.	.	104	76	(3)	.	25	15	(4)	(4)
3. Active persons looking for another job	60	100	277	416	192	594	46	115	14	25
Total	418	632	982	878	832	1 171	162	258	86	84
1977										
1. Unemployed persons	353	386	524	434	394	442	40	115	138	77
after a voluntary spell away from work	103	113	81	27	(5)	(4)	.	(3)	.	.
looking for their first job	52	53	102	69	297	284	8	13	20	10
2. Non-active persons looking for a job	83	88	387	103	492	320	94	57	36	16
after a voluntary spell away from work	.	.	182	(6)	47	.	63	30	8	.
looking for their first job	.	.	98	56	322	145	26	20	24	13
3. Active persons looking for another job	90	153	350	469	120	299	54	148	26	48
Total	526	627	1 261	1 006	1 006	1 061	188	320	200	141

TAB. 96

Main categories of persons seeking employment (1 000)

Principaux groupes de personnes à la recherche d'un emploi (1 000)

Luxembourg		United Kingdom		Ireland		Danmark		EUR 9		
F	M	F	M	F	M	F	M	F	M	
						1973				
.	.	154	361	:	:	:	:	:	:	1. Personnes en chômage
.	.	42	43	:	:	:	:	:	:	après interruption volontaire
.	.	11	15	:	:	:	:	:	:	à la recherche d'un 1er emploi
.	.	278	116	:	:	:	:	:	:	2. Personnes non actives à la recherche d'un emploi
.	.	141	14	:	:	:	:	:	:	après interruption volontaire
.	.	45	41	:	:	:	:	:	:	à la recherche d'un premier emploi
.	.	256	534	:	:	:	:	:	:	3. Personnes actives recherchant un autre emploi
(1)	(1)	686	1 011	:	:	:	:	:	:	Total
						1975				
.	.	501	646	26	82	59	98	1 577	2 176	1. Personnes en chômage
.	.	158	61	.	.	8	(3)	286	148	après interruption volontaire
.	.	24	35	10	12	4	5	342	369	à la recherche d'un 1er emploi
(1)	:	85	64	18	9	21	11	1 014	519	2. Personnes non actives à la recherche d'un emploi
.	.	9	.	6	.	9	4	274	25	après interruption volontaire
.	.	.	.	.	.	4	(4)	144	104	à la recherche d'un premier emploi
.	.	279	487	6	24	26	29	900	1 791	3. Personnes actives recherchant un autre emploi
(1)	(1)	865	1 197	49	115	105	138	3 491	4 486	Total
						1977				
(1)	(1)	427	754	21	80	86	81	1 983	2 371	1. Personnes en chômage
.	.	72	66	.	.	9	.	273	215	après interruption volontaire
.	.	45	48	6	10	6	5	535	492	à la recherche d'un 1er emploi
(1)	.	493	208	26	13	32	26	1 644	831	2. Personnes non actives à la recherche d'un emploi
.	.	214	15	7	.	8	4	529	57	après interruption volontaire
.	.	133	118	9	8	19	19	632	380	à la recherche d'un premier emploi
.	(1)	405	627	7	25	22	18	1 074	1 288	3. Personnes actives recherchant un autre emploi
2	2	1 325	1 589	55	118	139	126	4 200	4 990	Total

TAB. 96.1
Main categories of persons seeking employment (%)
Principaux groupes de personnes à la recherche d'un emploi (%)

	BR Deutschland		France		Italia		Nederland		Belgique België	
	$\frac{f}{F}100$	$\frac{f}{f+m}100$	$\frac{f}{F}100$	$\frac{f}{f+m}100$	$\frac{f}{F}100$	$\frac{f}{f+m}100$	$\frac{f}{F}100$	$\frac{f}{f+m}100$	$\frac{f}{F}100$	$\frac{f}{f+m}100$
1973										
1. Unemployed persons	:	51,9	26,4	50,7	27,3	39,3	17,3	20,7	58,0	49,2
after a voluntary spell away from work	24,6	56,7	13,2	61,0	.	.	.	.	.	.
looking for their first job	20,3	51,9	20,0	59,4	71,6	44,8	(23,5)	(40,0)	24,1	58,3
2. Non-active persons looking for a job	:	:	42,3	82,6	54,9	67,4	49,0	73,8	24,0	70,6
after a voluntary spell away from work	:	:	29,9	(92,9)	15,0	95,5	29,2	93,3	(16,7)	(100,0)
looking for their first job	:	:	25,7	80,4	55,7	81,0	33,3	59,3	66,7	(66,7)
3. Active persons looking for another job	:	:	31,3	41,7	17,8	22,5	34,7	24,8	20,0	31,3
Total	100,0	:	100,0	56,1	100,0	43,4	100,0	34,8	100,0	45,0
1975										
1. Unemployed persons	70,6	39,3	36,1	49,7	29,8	40,1	19,7	21,6	75,6	54,6
after a voluntary spell away from work	16,6	45,4	19,1	76,1	.	.	.	.	.	.
looking for their first job	16,3	49,5	16,5	58,0	70,6	45,8	18,7	37,5	26,1	63,4
2. Non-active persons looking for a job	14,8	44,6	35,3	73,8	47,1	65,6	51,8	75,7	8,1	63,6
after a voluntary spell away from work	.	.	43,9	95,0	10,7	.	65,5	84,6	(28,6)	:
looking for their first job	.	.	30,2	57,8	(0,8)	(100,0)	29,8	62,5	(57,1)	:
3. Active persons looking for another job	14,4	37,5	28,5	40,0	23,1	24,4	28,4	28,6	16,3	35,9
Total	100,0	39,8	100,0	52,2	100,0	41,5	100,0	38,6	100,0	50,6
1977										
1. Unemployed persons	67,1	47,8	41,6	54,7	39,2	47,1	21,3	25,8	69,0	64,2
after a voluntary spell away from work	29,2	47,7	15,5	75,0	(1,3)	(55,6)	.	.	.	.
looking for their first job	14,7	49,5	19,5	59,6	75,4	51,1	20,0	38,1	14,5	66,7
2. Non-active persons looking fo a job	15,8	48,5	30,7	79,0	48,9	60,6	50,0	62,3	18,0	69,2
after a voluntary spell away from work	.	.	47,0	96,8	9,6	96,9	67,0	67,7	22,2	93,3
looking for their first job	.	.	25,3	63,6	65,4	69,0	27,7	56,5	66,7	64,9
3. Active persons looking for another job	17,1	37,0	27,8	42,7	11,9	28,6	28,7	26,7	13,0	35,1
Total	100,0	45,6	100,0	55,6	100,0	48,7	100,0	37,0	100,0	58,7

TAB. 96.1
Main categories of persons seeking employment (%)
Principaux groupes de personnes à la recherche d'un emploi (%)

Luxembourg		United Kingdom		Ireland		Danmark		EUR 9		
$\frac{f}{F}100$	$\frac{f}{f+m}100$	$\frac{f}{F}100$	$\frac{f}{f+m}100$	$\frac{f}{F}100$	$\frac{f}{f+m}100$	$\frac{f}{F}100$	$\frac{f}{f+m}100$	$\frac{f}{F}100$	$\frac{f}{f+m}100$	
1973										
.	.	22,4	29,9	:	:	:	:	:	:	1. Personnes en chômage
.	.	27,3	49,4	:	:	:	:	:	:	après interruption volontaire
.	.	7,1	42,3	:	:	:	:	:	:	à la recherche d'un 1er emploi
.	.	40,5	70,6	:	:	:	:	:	:	2. Personnes non actives à la recherche d'un emploi
.	.	50,7	91,0	:	:	:	:	:	:	après interruption volontaire
.	.	16,2	52,3	:	:	:	:	:	:	à la recherche d'un premier emploi
.	.	37,3	32,4	:	:	:	:	:	:	3. Personnes actives recherchant un autre emploi
(100,0)	(50,0)	100,0	40,4	:	:	:	:	:	:	Total
1975										
.	.	57,9	43,7	53,1	24,1	56,2	37,6	45,2	42,0	1. Personnes en chômage
.	.	31,5	72,1	.	.	13,5	(72,7)	18,1	65,9	après interruption volontaire
.	.	4,8	40,7	38,5	45,5	6,8	44,4	21,7	48,1	à la recherche d'un 1er emploi
(100,0)	:	9,8	57,0	36,7	48,6	20,0	65,6	29,0	66,1	2. Personnes non actives à la recherche d'un emploi
.	.	10,6	.	33,3	.	42,8	69,2	27,0	91,6	après interruption volontaire
.	.	.	.	.	.	19,0	(50,0)	14,2	58,1	à la recherche d'un premier emploi
.	.	32,2	36,4	12,2	20,0	24,8	47,3	25,8	33,4	3. Personnes actives recherchant un autre emploi
(100,0)	(50,0)	100,0	41,9	100,0	30,0	100,0	43,2	100,0	43,8	Total
1977										
(38,3)	(37,7)	32,2	36,2	38,9	20,8	61,4	51,5	42,2	45,5	1. Personnes en chômage
.	.	16,9	52,2	.	.	10,5	91,1	13,8	55,9	après interruption volontaire
.	.	10,5	48,4	28,6	37,5	7,0	54,5	27,0	52,1	à la recherche d'un 1er emploi
50,8	(74,7)	37,2	70,3	48,1	66,7	22,9	55,2	35,0	66,4	2. Personnes non actives à la recherche d'un emploi
.	.	43,4	93,4	26,9	97,5	25,0	66,7	32,2	90,3	après interruption volontaire
.	.	27,0	53,0	34,6	52,9	59,4	50,0	38,4	62,5	à la recherche d'un premier emploi
.	.	30,6	39,2	13,0	21,9	15,7	55,0	22,8	37,5	3. Personnes actives recherchant un autre emploi
100,0	44,0	100,0	45,5	100,0	31,8	100,0	52,5	100,0	48,5	Total

TAB. 97
Unemployed persons by age groups (%)
Personnes en chômage par groupe d'âge (%)

	BR Deutschland		France		Italia		Nederland		Belgique België	
	$\frac{f}{F}100$	$\frac{f}{f+m}100$	$\frac{f}{F}100$	$\frac{f}{f+m}100$	$\frac{f}{F}100$	$\frac{f}{f+m}100$	$\frac{f}{F}100$	$\frac{f}{f+m}100$	$\frac{f}{F}100$	$\frac{f}{f+m}100$
1973										
Unemployed persons	100,0	51,9	100,0	50,7	100,0	39,3	100,0	20,7	100,0	49,2
14–19	19,4	51,1	18,6	58,2	31,8	43,8	33,4	52,5	16,5	(63,2)
20–24	12,9	53,3	26,0	55,2	34,1	42,2	31,3	28,8	25,6	59,0
25–34	21,3	53,8	19,5	54,8	22,3	40,4	(15,1)	(11,6)	22,5	57,8
35–44	18,3	51,9	11,0	43,5	7,0	33,0	.	.	15,4	49,3
45–54	18,9	56,2	14,9	48,6	4,1	22,6	.	.	(12,9)	(45,4)
55–59	(5,6)	.	4,3	45,5	.	.	.	.	(6,3)	(37,6)
60–64	.	.	4,6	33,4	.	.	.	.	.	.
65+	.	.	.	.	.	.	.	.	.	.
1975										
Unemployed persons	100,0	39,3	100,0	49,7	100,0	40,1	100,0	21,6	100,0	54,6
14–19	20,0	47,4	20,5	59,5	29,0	45,1	27,4	46,5	16,1	60,6
20–24	16,2	41,7	24,0	49,9	37,2	43,9	25,5	23,6	29,6	57,5
25–34	22,6	36,5	22,9	49,9	21,9	37,9	25,0	17,6	26,6	57,7
35–44	19,1	35,0	13,9	48,7	6,7	32,8	8,4	12,7	14,5	57,3
45–54	15,4	43,1	12,1	44,4	4,8	30,2	10,2	20,5	9,5	49,6
55–59	5,2	48,4	3,9	43,5	.	.	.	.	.	.
60–64	1,3	13,7	2,2	32,1	.	.	.	.	.	.
65+	.	.	.	.	.	.	.	.	.	.
1977										
Unemployed persons	100,0	47,8	100,0	54,7	100,0	47,1	100,0	25,8	100,0	64,2
14–19	16,4	53,7	18,9	59,6	29,4	50,9	25,0	58,8	8,7	63,2
20–24	19,3	53,1	30,0	62,1	37,6	49,2	30,0	34,3	29,0	69,0
25–34	24,6	46,0	23,1	56,3	23,1	48,4	15,0	17,8	34,1	75,8
35–44	17,6	44,6	9,4	46,7	6,3	43,9	(5,0)	(8,7)	13,8	65,5
45–54	14,7	46,8	10,9	44,9	3,0	25,5	.	.	11,6	51,6
55–59	5,7	44,4	4,6	47,1	.	.	.	.	(2,9)	(36,4)
60–64	(1,4)	(26,3)	2,7	40,0	.	.	.	.	.	.
65+	.	.	.	.	.	.	.	.	.	.

TAB. 97

Unemployed persons by age groups (%)
Personnes en chômage par groupe d'âge (%)

Luxembourg		United Kingdom		Ireland		Danmark		EUR 9		
$\frac{f}{F}100$	$\frac{f}{f+m}100$	$\frac{f}{F}100$	$\frac{f}{f+m}100$	$\frac{f}{F}100$	$\frac{f}{f+m}100$	$\frac{f}{F}100$	$\frac{f}{f+m}100$	$\frac{f}{F}100$	$\frac{f}{f+m}100$	
					1973					
100,0	.	100,0	29,9	:	:	:	:	:	:	Personnes en chômage
.	.	14,4	36,3	:	:	:	:	:	:	14–19
.	.	17,4	34,5	:	:	:	:	:	:	20–24
.	.	25,4	33,7	:	:	:	:	:	:	25–34
.	.	14,9	27,7	:	:	:	:	:	:	35–44
.	.	15,7	29,9	:	:	:	:	:	:	45–54
.	.	7,5	30,5	:	:	:	:	:	:	55–59
.	.	(4,0)	12,9	:	:	:	:	:	:	60–64
.	.	.	.	:	:	:	:	:	:	65+
					1975					
100,0	.	100,0	43,7	100,0	24,1	100,0	37,8	100,0	42,0	Personnes en chômage
.	.	12,7	47,5	43,5	43,0	11,3	50,0	19,3	49,4	14–19
.	.	16,3	41,4	24,7	31,0	24,6	39,8	22,5	43,5	20–24
.	.	28,6	50,5	15,6	19,8	29,4	41,7	24,9	43,2	25–34
.	.	17,0	46,9	.	.	15,5	38,7	14,5	40,3	35–44
.	.	15,3	45,2	.	.	12,0	35,4	12,4	41,4	45–54
.	.	6,1	42,9	.	.	(4,7)	(33,2)	4,2	39,3	55–59
.	.	2,8	18,0	.	.	.	.	1,8	17,6	60–64
.	.	(1,1)	(17,2)	.	.	.	.	(0,4)	(14,6)	65+
					1977					
100,0	(37,7)	100,0	36,2	100,0	20,8	100,0	51,5	100,0	45,6	Personnes en chômage
.	.	18,7	46,8	38,1	40,0	10,5	60,0	19,8	52,6	14–19
.	.	20,4	39,2	28,6	28,6	27,9	61,5	27,4	51,4	20–24
.	.	23,2	34,0	(14,3)	12,5	29,1	53,2	24,3	45,3	25–34
.	.	12,2	35,2	.	.	12,8	55,0	11,7	41,5	35–44
.	.	14,3	36,7	.	.	10,5	42,9	10,1	40,0	45–54
.	.	(6,8)	36,3	.	.	(3,5)	33,3	4,2	38,0	55–59
.	.	1,6	11,1	.	.	.	.	1,5	19,9	60–64
.	.	.	.	.	.	.	.	0,4	25,0	65+

TAB. 98

Non-active persons seeking employment and persons with a main occupation seeking another job (%)

Personnes non actives à la recherche d'un emploi et personnes ayant un emploi principal à la recherche d'un autre emploi (%)

	BR Deutschland		France		Italia		Nederland		Belgique België	
	F	M	F	M	F	M	F	M	F	M
1973										
Non-active persons looking for a job	100,0	100,0	100,0	100,0	100,0	100,0	100,0	100,0	100,0	100,0
14–19	31,0	24,4	12,2	24,1	20,9	16,6	22,0	49,5	26,4	38,3
20–24	13,1	13,5	17,4	17,0	22,4	20,1	17,0	24,6	28,0	28,0
25–34	17,2	15,8	25,0	14,1	26,5	19,7	30,2	13,4	20,9	15,5
35–44	14,3	10,9	20,5	4,4	18,3	18,7	16,9	.	14,3	.
45–54	11,5	15,4	16,5	9,4	9,2	15,6	9,9	3,5	7,1	.
55–59	5,7	2,5	2,8	7,3	1,7	4,7	2,4	.	.	.
60–64	5,5	14,5	3,0	10,5	0,6	2,9	.	3,4	.	.
65+	1,7	3,1	2,6	13,1	0,4	1,6	.	1,4	.	.
Persons with a main occupation looking for another job	100,0	100,0	100,0	100,0	100,0	100,0	100,0	100,0	100,0	100,0
14–19	13,0	4,5	10,1	4,5	22,9	11,2	17,4	6,8	13,4	6,5
20–24	21,6	16,1	33,4	21,8	28,1	17,9	32,8	17,7	31,8	25,1
25–34	30,9	40,5	25,2	37,1	24,7	31,6	27,1	37,5	32,1	33,4
35–44	12,0	23,7	13,8	20,0	13,6	22,7	12,6	21,3	13,8	19,3
45–54	15,7	9,0	12,4	12,5	9,3	13,5	6,5	11,5	8,5	11,4
55–59	3,0	3,6	3,6	2,5	0,9	2,3	2,5	3,1	.	2,9
60–64	2,0	1,9	1,3	1,4	0,4	0,8	.	1,8	.	.
65+	1,8	0,7	0,3	0,2	.	.	.	.	.	.
1975										
Non-active persons looking for a job	100,0	100,0	100,0	100,0	100,0	100,0	100,0	100,0	100,0	100,0
14–19	12,5	7,3	22,1	42,0	24,3	20,9	19,0	30,0	31,1	38,3
20–24	14,8	20,4	20,0	23,5	22,7	22,2	16,8	24,8	32,6	38,5
25–34	30,3	26,7	24,8	11,7	26,5	21,0	32,4	21,9	12,3	12,6
35–44	18,6	20,0	17,5	3,4	15,4	15,4	18,8	10,5	14,0	.
45–54	17,4	17,0	11,4	6,1	8,5	13,3	8,1	4,7	9,0	.
55–59	3,7	2,7	1,6	3,9	1,2	3,4	2,7	3,0	.	.
60–64	2,7	5,6	1,6	4,3	1,0	2,3	1,5	2,5	.	.
65+	.	.	0,9	5,1	0,4	1,4	0,6	2,6	.	.
Persons with a main occupation looking for another job	100,0	100,0	100,0	100,0	100,0	100,0	100,0	100,0	100,0	100,0
14–19	15,0	7,5	10,2	6,2	18,8	11,4	17,3	5,2	12,4	9,1
20–24	20,5	11,6	29,9	24,5	29,7	19,4	40,4	19,4	31,7	19,1
25–34	25,5	34,6	28,1	36,5	27,1	30,9	26,0	48,1	33,6	40,2
35–44	21,4	28,5	16,2	17,9	14,9	23,4	10,7	17,5	13,0	16,5
45–54	13,9	12,7	12,5	10,7	8,6	12,7	4,4	8,0	9,2	11,8
55–59	1,8	2,1	1,9	2,4	0,4	1,5	0,4	1,3	.	.
60–64	1,5	3,1	0,8	1,5	.	0,5	0,8	0,4	.	.
65+	.	.	0,3	0,3	.	0,2	.	.	.	.
1977										
Non-active persons looking for a job	100,0	100,0	100,0	100,0	100,0	100,0	100,0	100,0	100,0	100,0
14–19	10,3	8,7	17,3	39,4	19,3	24,3	19,0	21,6	28,4	41,9
20–24	17,8	14,4	19,1	19,8	21,3	19,8	16,3	15,7	32,8	40,1
25–34	24,5	26,6	27,4	12,4	27,3	21,5	29,7	19,0	21,8	.
35–44	16,9	20,3	19,5	(5,0)	15,7	12,6	18,3	9,6	11,2	.
45–54	18,7	18,1	12,4	7,9	8,8	10,8	10,0	10,9	.	.
55–59	8,6	(7,0)	2,9	(7,2)	2,2	3,9	(2,3)	7,2	.	.
60–64	.	(4,4)	(1,1)	(5,0)	1,6	2,9	(3,7)	12,9	.	.
65+	.	.	.	(3,7)	3,7	4,2	.	.	.	.
Persons with a main occupation looking for another job	100,0	100,0	100,0	100,0	100,0	100,0	100,0	100,0	100,0	100,0
14–19	13,3	5,9	11,4	5,1	21,2	12,0	13,5	3,8	8,4	(5,4)
20–24	26,7	15,4	31,3	24,7	29,1	18,8	39,7	18,6	46,7	26,2
25–34	30,8	40,0	29,6	38,4	21,5	33,1	33,3	50,9	29,0	39,6
35–44	16,2	25,6	13,5	17,5	18,2	21,2	8,1	17,6	9,9	15,4
45–54	9,6	10,0	10,8	10,5	7,6	12,8	(4,9)	7,0	5,1	10,8
55–59	.	(2,4)	2,7	3,1	.	(1,3)	.	(1,7)	0,9	.
60–64	.	.	.	.	.	.	.	.	.	.
65+	.	.	.	.	.	.	.	.	.	.

TAB. 98

Non-active persons seeking employment and persons with a main occupation seeking another job (%)
Personnes non actives à la recherche d'un emploi et personnes ayant un emploi principal à la recherche d'un autre emploi (%)

Luxembourg		United Kingdom		Ireland		Danmark		EUR 9		
F	M	F	M	F	M	F	M	F	M	
					1973						
100,0	100,0	100,0	100,0	100,0	100,0	100,0	100,0	100,0	100,0	Personnes non actives à la recherche d'un emploi
.	.	69,5	88,7	:	:	:	:	:	:	14–19
.	.	4,8	2,5	:	:	:	:	:	:	20–24
.	.	8,5	1,4	:	:	:	:	:	:	25–34
.	.	5,6	0,9	:	:	:	:	:	:	35–44
.	.	4,5	1,4	:	:	:	:	:	:	45–54
.	.	1,6	0,5	:	:	:	:	:	:	55–59
.	.	1,6	1,5	:	:	:	:	:	:	60–64
.	.	4,0	3,0	:	:	:	:	:	:	65+
										Personnes ayant un emploi principal à la recherche d'un autre emploi
100,0	100,0	100,0	100,0	100,0	100,0	100,0	100,0	100,0	100,0	
.	.	10,6	6,1	:	:	:	:	:	:	14–19
.	.	14,4	12,4	:	:	:	:	:	:	20–24
.	.	17,5	26,4	:	:	:	:	:	:	25–34
.	.	20,2	19,5	:	:	:	:	:	:	35–44
.	.	22,6	19,2	:	:	:	:	:	:	45–54
.	.	7,0	6,7	:	:	:	:	:	:	55–59
.	.	5,3	6,8	:	:	:	:	:	:	60–64
.	.	2,2	2,8	:	:	:	:	:	:	65+
					1975						
100,0	100,0	100,0	100,0	100,0	100,0	100,0	100,0	100,,0	100,0	Personnes non actives à la recherche d'un emploi
.	.	42,0	56,7	29,6	67,2	21,0	29,0	24,0	29,8	14–19
.	.	16,4	23,4	13,2	15,6	18,9	33,5	20,1	22,8	20–24
.	.	16,5	8,2	21,0	.	25,8	22,8	25,6	17,8	25–34
.	.	10,5	1,7	11,3	.	17,7	.	16,1	10,7	35–44
.	.	5,9	2,2	13,7	.	9,7	6,1	9,9	9,9	45–54
.	.	3,5	.	5,6	.	4,1	.	1,9	3,0	55–59
.	.	2,3	2,2	3,7	.	2,4	.	1,5	3,3	60–64
.	.	2,9	4,9	2,0	6,2	.	.	0,8	2,7	65+
										Personnes ayant un emploi principal à la recherche d'un autre emploi
100,0	100,0	100,0	100,0	100,0	100,0	100,0	100,0	100,0	100,0	
.	.	9,2	5,8	26,1	9,9	25,7	11,0	13,0	8,0	14–19
.	.	19,5	17,5	30,0	18,2	25,5	24,1	26,5	19,7	20–24
.	.	28,9	38,1	24,6	25,6	26,3	32,1	27,8	35,5	25–34
.	.	20,2	20,7	.	17,1	10,9	14,4	17,0	21,0	35–44
.	.	17,4	11,8	.	15,3	6,1	11,2	12,7	11,7	45–54
.	.	3,1	3,3	.	8,2	3,0	2,7	1,9	2,3	55–59
.	.	1,6	2,0	.	4,8	2,2	2,1	1,0	1,4	60–64
.	.	0,1	0,7	.	.	.	2,5	0,2	0,4	65+
					1977						
100,0	100,0	100,0	100,0	100,0	100,0	100,0	100,0	100,0	100,0	Personnes non actives à la recherche d'un emploi
.	.	27,4	60,0	38,5	72,6	46,7	55,9	21,9	35,4	14–19
.	.	11,3	10,2	(14,4)	(17,2)	28,0	24,0	17,6	17,0	20–24
.	.	29,7	3,9	21,7	.	15,5	17,6	27,6	15,7	25–34
.	.	15,7	3,4	(13,3)	.	(6,8)	.	16,5	9,2	35–44
.	.	9,2	4,5	.	.	.	.	10,0	9,0	45–54
.	.	3,5	(3,0)	.	.	.	.	3,0	4,5	55–59
.	.	2,2	7,4	.	.	.	.	1,7	5,0	60–64
.	.	(1,1)	7,6	.	.	.	.	1,7	4,2	65+
										Personnes ayant un emploi principal à la recherche d'un autre emploi
100,0	100,0	100,0	100,0	100,0	100,0	100,0	100,0	100,0	100,0	
.	.	13,8	9,0	.	(15,8)	19,5	(19,5)	13,8	7,9	14–19
.	.	19,4	18,7	(36,8)	21,7	25,1	(18,6)	26,9	20,2	20–24
.	.	28,7	39,5	(28,9)	25,7	36,6	38,8	28,8	38,9	25–34
.	.	21,4	17,4	.	16,9	(13,7)	(12,2)	16,8	18,7	35–44
.	.	12,4	10,4	.	12,2	.	.	10,3	10,5	45–54
.	.	3,6	3,1	.	.	.	.	2,7	2,6	55–59
.	.	.	1,3	.	.	.	.	(0,4)	0,9	60–64
.	.	.	(0,6)	.	.	.	.	(0,3)	(0,3)	65+

TAB. 99

Main categories of persons seeking employment, by method adopted (%)

Principaux groupes de personnes à la recherche d'un emploi selon le mode de la recherche (%)

	BR Deutschland		France		Italia		Nederland		Belgique België	
	$\frac{f}{F}$ 100	$\frac{f}{f+m}$ 100	$\frac{f}{F}$ 100	$\frac{f}{f+m}$ 100	$\frac{f}{F}$ 100	$\frac{f}{f+m}$ 100	$\frac{f}{F}$ 100	$\frac{f}{f+m}$ 100	$\frac{f}{F}$ 100	$\frac{f}{f+m}$ 100
1973										
Unemployed persons	100,0	51,9	100,0	50,7	100,0	39,3	100,0	20,7	100,0	49,2
Registration at an official employment exchange	63,6	51,0	56,8	47,6	54,0	36,3	77,0	17,5	79,1	47,9
Registration at a private employment office	(9,3)	58,9	(2,3)	35,5	.	.	.	.	.	.
Advertisement in a newspaper/journal	(8,2)	54,4	(3,5)	.	.	.	.	.	.	.
Investigating offers of employment	11,7	57,3	11,4	53,4	20,6	49,2	19,1	57,5	(8,4)	.
Investigating by personal contacts	(7,2)	42,7	26,0	57,7	23,9	40,8	.	.	(6,5)	.
Non-active persons	:	:	100,0	82,6	100,0	67,4	100,0	73,9	100,0	70,6
Registration at an official employment exchange	:	:	20,3	79,7	36,1	60,2	27,1	75,1	.	.
Registration at a private employment office	:	:	(2,2)	.	(0,8)	54,2	(6,2)	.	.	.
Advertisement in a newspaper/journal	:	:	4,9	.	(0,9)	.	.	.	(27,5)	.
Investigating offers of employment	:	:	17,9	85,2	17,3	71,7	47,1	73,3	(24,9)	.
Investigating by personal contacts	:	:	54,7	84,1	44,9	73,0	16,1	71,1	35,8	61,9
Persons with an occupation seeking another	:	:	100,0	41,7	100,0	22,5	100,0	24,8	100,0	31,3
Registration at an official employment exchange	:	:	18,5	44,0	29,7	18,3	23,9	19,3	21,5	38,7
Registration at a private employment office	:	:	(3,1)	.	.	.	.	.	.	.
Advertisement in a newspaper/journal	:	:	5,1	37,5	.	.	.	.	23,0	32,3
Investigating offers of employment	:	:	17,5	34,3	23,4	32,7	60,9	27,2	.	.
Investigating by personal contacts	:	:	55,8	43,6	45,5	22,3	(10,1)	(24,1)	(34,2)	30,3
1975										
Unemployed persons	100,0	39,3	100,0	49,7	100,0	40,1	100,0	21,6	100,0	54,6
Registration at an official employment exchange	83,7	37,2	76,3	43,4	48,3	35,5	77,9	18,8	83,4	53,1
Registration at a private employment office	3,7	47,0	(1,8)	(48,4)	.	.	.	.	.	.
Advertisement in a newspaper/journal	4,1	63,9	(1,5)	(46,6)	(1,3)	.	.	.	(5,0)	.
Investigating offers of employment	4,2	57,7	5,3	47,9	5,0	51,2	14,8	48,9	(4,3)	(55,8)
Investigating by personal contacts	2,8	51,6	12,8	59,5	12,1	46,9	.	.	6,6	.
Other methods	(1,6)	.	(2,3)	58,7	33,1	44,6	.	.	.	.
Non-active persons	100,0	44,6	100,0	73,8	100,0	65,6	100,0	75,7	100,0	63,6
Registration at an official employment exchange	80,0	43,6	30,2	74,5	33,4	57,1	25,6	66,6	.	.
Registration at a private employment office	.	.	(3,3)	65,1	.	.	(4,5)	.	.	.
Advertisement in a newspaper/journal	.	.	(2,4)	71,5	(1,0)	.	.	.	.	.
Investigating offers of employment	(5,3)	.	13,2	76,7	6,9	69,0	50,0	79,7	.	.
Investigating by personal contacts	.	.	41,7	76,6	26,7	75,9	9,3	.	(44,2)	.
Other methods	.	.	9,2	61,9	31,5	66,9	9,3	73,2	.	.
Persons with an occupation seeking another	100,0	37,5	100,0	40,0	100,0	24,4	100,0	28,6	100,0	35,9
Registration at an official employment exchange	43,8	38,7	29,5	46,9	30,7	19,8	16,8	22,7	(21,1)	(46,1)
Registration at a private employment office	13,9	35,0	(2,7)	31,6	.	.	.	.	.	.
Advertisement in a newspaper/journal	16,9	39,9	5,5	46,6	.	.	.	.	(21,0)	(36,3)
Investigating offers of employment	(10,5)	(32,2)	15,2	31,8	8,3	24,4	58,9	28,6	(27,3)	(37,3)
Investigating by personal contacts	(8,8)	(33,0)	38,2	39,0	22,7	25,2	10,7	35,4	(24,2)	(29,4)
Other methods	(6,2)	(50,8)	8,8	41,7	37,1	29,3	8,5	26,8	.	.

TAB. 99

Main categories of persons seeking employment, by method adopted (%)
Principaux groupes de personnes à la recherche d'un emploi selon le mode de la recherche (%)

Luxembourg		United Kingdom		Ireland		Danmark		EUR 9		
$\frac{f}{F}100$	$\frac{f}{f+m}100$	$\frac{f}{F}100$	$\frac{f}{f+m}100$	$\frac{f}{F}100$	$\frac{f}{f+m}100$	$\frac{f}{F}100$	$\frac{f}{f+m}100$	$\frac{f}{F}100$	$\frac{f}{f+m}100$	
				1973						
.	.	100,0	29,9	:	:	:	:	:	:	**Personnes en chômage**
.	.	39,1	17,5	:	:	:	:	:	:	Inscription à un office public de placement
.	.	(5,1)	(70,7)	:	:	:	:	:	:	Inscription à un office privé de placement
.	.	(3,1)	.	:	:	:	:	:	:	Annonce faite dans un journal
.	.	47,4	56,3	:	:	:	:	:	:	Recherche parmi les offres d'emploi
.	.	(5,3)	(34,5)	:	:	:	:	:	:	Recherche par relations personnelles
.	.	100,0	70,6	:	:	:	:	:	:	**Personnes non actives**
.	.	9,2	38,7	:	:	:	:	:	:	Inscription à un office public de placement
.	.	4,5	.	:	:	:	:	:	:	Inscription à un office privé de placement
.	.	5,0	.	:	:	:	:	:	:	Annonce faite dans un journal
.	.	74,0	77,8	:	:	:	:	:	:	Recherche parmi les offres d'emploi
.	.	7,3	62,7	:	:	:	:	:	:	Recherche par relations personnelles
.	.	100,0	32,4	:	:	:	:	:	:	**Personnes ayant un emploi cherchant un autre**
.	.	7,1	30,7	:	:	:	:	:	:	Inscription à un office public de placement
.	.	10,0	57,1	:	:	:	:	:	:	Inscription à un office privé de placement
.	.	(3,5)	(27,6)	:	:	:	:	:	:	Annonce faite dans un journal
.	.	72,0	31,9	:	:	:	:	:	:	Recherche parmi les offres d'emploi
.	.	7,4	25,1	:	:	:	:	:	:	Recherche par relations personnelles
				1975						
100,0	.	100,0	43,7	100,0	.	100,0	.	100,0	.	**Personnes en chômage**
.	.	24,2	20,8	.	.	.	.	.	.	Inscription à un office public de placement
.	.	6,1	79,8	.	.	.	.	.	.	Inscription à un office privé de placement
.	.	4,1	76,1	.	.	.	.	.	.	Annonce faite dans un journal
.	.	54,6	68,4	.	.	.	.	.	.	Recherche parmi les offres d'emploi
.	.	4,0	62,0	.	.	.	.	.	.	Recherche par relations personnelles
.	.	7,0	54,1	.	.	.	.	.	.	Autres modes
100,0	.	100,0	57,1	100,0	.	100,0	.	100,0	.	**Personnes non actives**
.	.	(6,6)	43,9	.	.	.	.	.	.	Inscription à un office public de placement
.	.	(5,4)	56,6	.	.	.	.	.	.	Inscription à un office privé de placement
.	.	.	.	.	.	.	.	.	.	Annonce faite dans un journal
.	.	55,9	65,6	.	.	.	.	.	.	Recherche parmi les offres d'emploi
.	.	(5,6)	45,0	.	.	.	.	.	.	Recherche par relations personnelles
.	.	22,6	47,5	.	.	.	.	.	.	Autres modes
100,0	.	100,0	36,4	100,0	.	100,0	.	100,0	.	**Personnes ayant un emploi cherchant un autre**
.	.	4,8	32,9	.	.	.	.	.	.	Inscription à un office public de placement
.	.	6,4	49,8	.	.	.	.	.	.	Inscription à un office privé de placement
.	.	5,1	40,5	.	.	.	.	.	.	Annonce faite dans un journal
.	.	68,4	36,4	.	.	.	.	.	.	Recherche parmi les offres d'emploi
.	.	4,5	23,3	.	.	.	.	.	.	Recherche par relations personnelles
.	.	10,8	39,7	.	.	.	.	.	.	Autres modes

TAB. 99
(continued)
(suite)

	BR Deutschland		France		Italia		Nederland		Belgique België	
	$\frac{f}{F}$ 100	$\frac{f}{f+m}$ 100	$\frac{f}{F}$ 100	$\frac{f}{f+m}$ 100	$\frac{f}{F}$ 100	$\frac{f}{f+m}$ 100	$\frac{f}{F}$ 100	$\frac{f}{f+m}$ 100	$\frac{f}{F}$ 100	$\frac{f}{f+m}$ 100
1977										
Unemployed persons	100,0	47,8	100,0	55,7	100,0	47,1	100,0	25,6	100,0	64,1
Registration at an official employment exchange	84,1	46,2	82,1	51,7	55,8	41,8	86,8	23,8	90,3	63,7
Registration at a private employment office	5,7	31,4	(1,6)	55,8	(1,5)	46,4	.	.	.	.
Advertisement in a newspaper/journal	4,9	60,5	(1,1)	58,7	3,4	52,4	.	.	(2,5)	55,7
Investigating offers of employment	2,8	63,8	5,1	56,1	3,5	55,4	(7,4)	48,2	4,2	70,2
Investigating by personal contacts	(1,7)	(51,6)	8,5	55,9	10,5	44,8	.	.	(1,9)	49,8
Other methods	.	.	1,7	67,1	25,3	62,4	.	.	.	.
Non-active persons	100,0	48,6	100,0	79,1	100,0	60,6	100,0	62,4	100,0	69,0
Registration at an official employment exchange	80,4	46,6	30,7	76,4	41,6	55,6	42,2	51,9	.	.
Registration at a private employment office	(7,1)	(55,6)	(2,2)	66,6	(1,9)	65,2	4,6	88,5	.	.
Advertisement in a newspaper/journal	(5,3)	58,7	4,9	86,0	3,2	65,1	.	.	(21,4)	(77,1)
Investigating offers of employment	.	.	14,0	82,8	3,9	68,0	33,6	75,7	32,8	71,6
Investigating by personal contacts	.	.	38,3	79,6	22,3	61,6	7,6	66,0	32,6	82,8
Other methods	.	.	10,0	73,6	27,1	62,8	11,2	62,4	.	.
Persons with an occupation seeking another	100,0	37,0	100,0	42,7	100,0	28,6	100,0	26,9	100,0	35,1
Registration at an official employment exchange	37,4	39,5	28,3	51,2	33,4	27,9	13,0	24,1	(17,0)	44,1
Registration at a private employment office	16,2	33,1	3,6	42,3	.	.	.	.	.	.
Advertisement in a newspaper/journal	23,8	40,4	(3,0)	32,6	.	.	.	.	(16,5)	25,2
Investigating offers of employment	9,5	30,2	18,2	35,5	7,5	38,6	59,6	26,2	31,3	35,7
Investigating by personal contacts	(5,9)	(21,3)	37,9	40,3	20,8	23,7	(7,3)	26,2	28,4	39,6
Other methods	7,2	56,5	9,0	48,3	33,7	28,1	15,9	28,3	.	.

TAB. 99
(continued)
(suite)

Luxembourg		United Kingdom		Ireland		Danmark		EUR 9		
$\frac{f}{F}$ 100	$\frac{f}{f+m}$ 100	$\frac{f}{F}$ 100	$\frac{f}{f+m}$ 100	$\frac{f}{F}$ 100	$\frac{f}{f+m}$ 100	$\frac{f}{F}$ 100	$\frac{f}{f+m}$ 100	$\frac{f}{F}$ 100	$\frac{f}{f+m}$ 100	
				1977						
100,0	(37,7)	100,0	36,2	100,0	21,0	100,0	51,3	100,0	45,5	**Personnes en chômage**
.	.	60,7	26,9	47,1	13,1	80,2	48,4	72,9	41,2	Inscription à un office public de placement
.	.	3,2	85,4	.	.	.	.	2,5	62,7	Inscription à un office privé de placement
.	.	(1,3)	(70,0)	.	.	.	.	2,3	58,9	Annonce faite dans un journal
.	.	28,7	72,5	29,7	42,3	13,1	73,6	10,1	65,2	Recherche parmi les offres d'emploi
.	.	(1,4)	(23,3)	(14,8)	(33,9)	5,9	62,2	5,4	50,0	Recherche par relations personnelles
.	.	4,6	63,6	.	.	.	.	6,7	62,3	Autres modes
100,0	(74,7)	100,0	70,3	100,0	66,2	100,0	54,6	100,0	66,4	**Personnes non actives**
.	.	23,3	53,6	(13,6)	(55,7)	(8,3)	(63,9)	34,0	56,1	Inscription à un office public de placement
.	.	2,0	93,1	.	.	.	.	2,5	70,5	Inscription à un office privé de placement
.	.	2,9	92,7	.	.	.	.	3,6	76,3	Annonce faite dans un journal
.	.	57,7	80,4	49,3	79,3	48,5	64,5	28,3	78,4	Recherche parmi les offres d'emploi
.	.	3,4	56,3	24,1	67,6	39,4	46,1	17,5	67,3	Recherche par relations personnelles
.	.	10,7	60,8	.	.	.	.	14,1	63,6	Autres modes
100,0	.	100,0	39,2	100,0	22,5	100,0	54,6	100,0	37,5	**Personnes ayant un emploi cherchant un autre**
.	.	14,5	39,2	.	.	33,2	63,4	22,4	38,9	Inscription à un office public de placement
.	.	3,8	59,1	.	.	.	.	4,5	42,7	Inscription à un office privé de placement
.	.	1,8	35,4	.	.	.	.	4,4	34,8	Annonce faite dans un journal
.	.	65,1	39,3	44,7	29,4	47,2	51,4	40,7	37,1	Recherche parmi les offres d'emploi
.	.	3,8	30,0	.	.	(17,8)	(48,6)	15,6	33,9	Recherche par relations personnelles
.	.	11,0	39,0	.	.	.	.	12,4	35,6	Autres modes

TAB. 100

Main categories of persons seeking employment, by duration of search (%)
Principaux groupes de personnes à la recherche d'un emploi selon la durée de la recherche (%)

	BR Deutschland		France		Italia		Nederland		Belgique België	
	$\frac{f}{F}$100	$\frac{m}{M}$100	$\frac{f}{F}$100	$\frac{m}{M}$100	$\frac{f}{F}$100	$\frac{m}{M}$100	$\frac{f}{F}$100	$\frac{m}{M}$100	$\frac{f}{F}$100	$\frac{m}{M}$100
1973										
1. Unemployed persons	100,0	100,0	100,0	100,0	100,0	100,0	100,0	100,0	100,0	100,0
<1 month	25,8	27,6	11,8	17,6	4,6	6,0	(20,5)	11,1	(9,2)	(9,7)
1−2 months	35,9	22,8	26,1	25,3	5,9	8,7	28,7	19,0	19,3	14,1
3−5 months	19,3	20,1	18,8	18,6	19,1	20,1	(22,4)	23,9	15,1	17,5
6−11 months	(8,9)	13,8	23,0	15,4	33,0	28,8	(13,0)	22,5	20,6	18,8
12+ months	(10,1)	15,8	20,4	23,0	37,4	36,4	(15,4)	23,5	35,8	39,9
2. Non-active persons seeking employment	:	:	100,0	100,0	100,0	100,0	100,0	100,0	100,0	100,0
<1 month	:	:	15,1	18,3	1,4	(1,8)	22,4	40,5	34,9	(44,2)
1−2 months	:	:	24,8	28,5	2,7	(1,3)	35,3	37,4	(27,0)	.
3−5 months	:	:	15,8	15,4	8,2	6,5	17,9	.	.	.
6−11 months	:	:	17,0	13,1	36,7	37,9	15,1	.	.	.
12+ months	:	:	27,4	24,6	51,0	52,5	9,4	.	(17,3)	.
3. Persons with a job and seeking another	:	:	100,0	100,0	100,0	100,0	100,0	100,0	100,0	100,0
<1 month	:	:	18,2	17,6	.	1,4	33,5	20,2	(23,6)	23,9
1−2 months	:	:	23,6	27,3	(3,6)	3,5	30,1	26,6	(25,9)	26,3
3−5 months	:	:	15,8	14,3	12,6	10,9	16,9	21,3	.	(16,7)
6−11 months	:	:	19,7	16,1	32,2	35,8	10,4	16,4	.	(11,9)
12+ months	:	:	22,6	24,7	50,3	48,4	(9,0)	15,4	(18,5)	21,2
1975										
1. Unemployed persons	100,0	100,0	100,0	100,0	100,0	100,0	100,0	100,0	100,0	100,0
Not yet started	(2,1)	0,8	5,4	4,0	.	.	.	.	.	.
<1 month	10,7	9,6	9,2	15,0	7,3	6,7	23,3	13,5	6,3	9,0
1−2 months	24,6	25,4	18,6	23,1	6,0	9,0	10,4	10,9	14,9	21,8
3−5 months	27,1	28,2	19,6	23,2	16,2	20,5	25,3	31,3	19,8	20,7
6−11 months	24,7	23,4	28,4	20,7	36,1	30,6	25,1	24,9	25,3	21,4
12+ months	10,8	12,5	18,8	13,9	34,5	33,3	15,9	19,4	32,3	26,7
2. Non-active persons seeking employment	100,0	100,0	100,0	100,0	100,0	100,0	100,0	100,0	100,0	100,0
Not yet started	.	.	21,9	25,8	.	0,2	.	.	.	.
<1 month	11,9	10,6	11,9	16,3	3,9	4,1	26,0	35,4	.	.
1−2 months	27,7	22,6	17,8	24,5	6,6	7,3	16,9	(14,6)	(37,3)	.
3−5 months	27,2	23,4	15,0	12,5	17,2	17,9	24,8	25,0	.	.
6−11 months	19,8	16,5	15,0	10,7	30,5	33,5	16,8	(11,5)	.	.
12+ months	(9,4)	23,4	18,4	10,2	41,4	37,1	15,5	(13,6)	.	.
3. Persons with a job and seeking another	100,0	100,0	100,0	100,0	100,0	100,0	100,0	100,0	100,0	100,0
Not yet started	(10,1)	8,3	22,4	19,7	.	.	.	.	.	.
<1 month	30,9	23,8	12,3	13,9	(3,8)	3,1	35,0	21,8	(18,3)	16,7
1−2 months	26,9	26,6	17,9	19,2	8,9	6,4	21,5	16,0	(20,7)	23,8
3−5 months	15,3	18,4	11,5	16,2	26,7	18,5	22,0	21,1	(17,8)	19,8
6−11 months	(8,8)	9,6	19,2	15,0	30,4	31,6	13,3	19,6	.	(12,4)
12+ months	(8,0)	13,3	16,7	16,1	30,2	40,3	(8,1)	21,6	(22,6)	20,4
1977										
1. Unemployed persons	100,0	100,0	100,0	100,0	100,0	100,0	100,0	100,0	100,0	100,0
Not yet started	(1,1)	(0,9)	3,5	1,9	2,9	(1,5)	.	.	4,0	.
<1 month	9,5	9,6	6,5	10,1	3,2	5,8	(10,8)	9,3	8,2	10,2
1−2 months	20,2	19,2	16,4	20,5	5,0	6,4	(9,8)	7,3	10,6	15,7
3−5 months	21,9	20,3	17,5	21,1	12,8	14,2	23,3	19,6	11,6	16,5
6−11 months	24,5	19,7	27,3	22,4	26,9	24,2	26,2	21,1	17,1	18,0
12+ months	22,8	30,2	28,7	24,0	49,3	47,9	28,5	41,0	48,5	38,3
2. Non-active persons seeking employment	100,0	100,0	100,0	100,0	100,0	100,0	100,0	100,0	100,0	100,0
Not yet started	4,9	.	19,2	19,3	7,2	5,2	(5,1)	(10,5)	55,1	65,0
<1 month	10,2	(9,1)	9,5	13,7	6,7	8,7	21,4	28,1	14,5	.
1−2 months	18,2	17,7	18,6	20,7	5,2	6,2	15,5	15,3	(9,3)	.
3−5 months	19,4	18,0	14,7	13,4	14,0	13,5	20,1	15,7	(6,4)	.
6−11 months	20,3	17,8	14,5	14,1	24,1	22,7	17,0	(9,0)	.	.
12+ months	26,9	36,1	23,5	18,8	42,9	43,7	20,9	21,4	(9,7)	.
3. Persons with a job and seeking another	100,0	100,0	100,0	100,0	100,0	100,0	100,0	100,0	100,0	100,0
Not yet started	10,3	8,5	15,2	16,9	7,9	5,1	.	(2,5)	18,8	.
<1 month	21,3	16,6	9,5	10,9	(5,4)	3,8	33,0	22,1	19,4	.
1−2 months	25,2	20,0	16,0	17,8	(6,4)	7,1	20,5	15,2	16,2	.
3−5 months	14,4	16,7	13,8	14,5	17,1	14,6	19,9	20,5	(15,8)	.
6−11 months	15,5	17,3	17,2	15,3	24,4	22,5	13,9	18,2	(8,8)	.
12+ months	13,3	21,0	28,4	24,5	38,9	46,8	9,9	21,5	21,0	.

TAB. 100

Main categories of persons seeking employment, by duration of search (%)
Principaux groupes de personnes à la recherche d'un emploi selon la durée de la recherche (%)

Luxembourg		United Kingdom		Ireland		Danmark		EUR 9		
$\frac{f}{F}$100	$\frac{m}{M}$100	$\frac{f}{F}$100	$\frac{m}{M}$100	$\frac{f}{F}$100	$\frac{m}{M}$100	$\frac{f}{F}$100	$\frac{m}{M}$100	$\frac{f}{F}$100	$\frac{m}{M}$100	
						1973				
100,0	100,0	100,0	100,0	:	:	:	:	:	:	1. Personnes en chômage
.	.	30,8	17,2	:	:	:	:	:	:	<1 mois
.	.	21,6	14,7	:	:	:	:	:	:	1–2 mois
.	.	17,4	15,5	:	:	:	:	:	:	3–5 mois
.	.	14,3	16,2	:	:	:	:	:	:	6–11 mois
.	.	15,9	36,3	:	:	:	:	:	:	12+ mois
100,0	100,0	100,0	100,0	:	:	:	:	:	:	2. Personnes non actives à la recherche d'un emploi
.	.	35,4	29,3	:	:	:	:	:	:	<1 mois
.	.	24,1	22,3	:	:	:	:	:	:	1–2 mois
.	.	15,8	16,7	:	:	:	:	:	:	3–5 mois
.	.	11,1	10,1	:	:	:	:	:	:	6–11 mois
.	.	13,7	21,6	:	:	:	:	:	:	12+ mois
100,0	100,0	100,0	100,0	:	:	:	:	:	:	3. Personnes ayant un emploi et en recherchant un autre
.	.	34,4	22,8	:	:	:	:	:	:	<1 mois
.	.	23,7	18,4	:	:	:	:	:	:	1–2 mois
.	.	17,4	17,8	:	:	:	:	:	:	3–5 mois
.	.	12,2	13,4	:	:	:	:	:	:	6–11 mois
.	.	12,2	27,6	:	:	:	:	:	:	12+ mois
						1975				
100,0	100,0	100,0	100,0	100,0	100,0	100,0	100,0	100,0	100,0	1. Personnes en chômage
.	.	2,1	(0,6)	(15,8)	7,5	(7,1)	(3,7)	2,8	1,5	Recherche pas encore commencée
.	.	29,9	19,7	(17,8)	10,6	13,2	11,5	15,4	13,0	<1 mois
.	.	27,0	25,6	32,7	25,7	14,8	17,5	19,8	20,9	1–2 mois
.	.	16,8	16,7	(14,6)	17,7	29,3	34,7	20,1	22,7	3–5 mois
.	.	15,0	18,0	(10,2)	16,1	24,7	24,2	24,6	22,6	6–11 mois
.	.	9,0	19,3	.	22,4	10,9	8,4	17,2	19,3	12+ mois
100,0	100,0	100,0	100,0	100,0	100,0	100,0	100,0	100,0	100,0	2. Personnes non actives à la recherche d'un emploi
.	.	22,1	10,0	25,8	(32,8)	27,5	.	11,5	9,3	Recherche pas encore commencée
.	.	31,4	29,3	(17,9)	(27,4)	22,7	(31,8)	12,1	14,0	<1 mois
.	.	30,7	34,2	31,0	(27,4)	(19,4)	(20,5)	15,9	18,5	1–2 mois
.	.	(8,4)	17,8	.	.	(12,6)	.	16,6	17,4	3–5 mois
.	.	(4,5)	(7,1)	.	.	(9,8)	.	19,8	19,5	6–11 mois
.	.	.	.	(11,6)	.	(7,9)	.	24,1	21,4	12+ mois
100,0	100,0	100,0	100,0	100,0	100,0	100,0	100,0	100,0	100,0	3. Personnes ayant un emploi et en recherchant un autre
.	.	7,4	5,3	.	21,4	25,2	19,8	11,5	7,8	Recherche pas encore commencée
.	.	33,4	24,3	.	(10,5)	24,3	22,0	20,4	14,9	1 mois
.	.	24,1	22,0	.	19,9	(16,1)	15,9	19,1	16,5	1–2 mois
.	.	12,5	13,1	.	(10,4)	(12,2)	16,3	15,4	16,3	3–5 mois
.	.	13,2	17,1	.	(9,9)	(9,6)	(12,4)	17,9	20,3	6–11 mois
.	.	9,3	18,2	.	28,0	(12,5)	(13,7)	15,7	24,2	12+ mois
						1977				
100,0	100,0	100,0	100,0	100,0	100,0	100,0	100,0	100,0	100,0	1. Personnes en chômage
.	.	3,9	1,3	.	.	5,1	3,6	(3,1)	(1,5)	Recherche pas encore commencée
.	.	16,2	12,8	.	(5,4)	7,5	12,6	8,8	10,0	<1 mois
.	.	20,2	18,3	(22,2)	14,9	13,7	12,5	15,1	15,8	1–2 mois
.	.	18,8	17,5	(17,9)	14,0	18,6	25,6	17,4	18,3	3–5 mois
.	.	21,0	18,2	(22,6)	19,4	26,1	21,0	24,5	20,6	6–11 mois
.	.	19,9	31,8	23,0	43,4	29,0	24,7	31,1	33,8	12+ mois
100,0	100,0	100,0	100,0	100,0	100,0	100,0	100,0	100,0	100,0	2. Personnes non actives à la recherche d'un emploi
.	.	12,1	7,0	26,8	35,3	26,2	22,7	13,5	10,1	Recherche pas encore commencée
.	.	22,4	21,8	(10,4)	.	27,0	35,4	14,1	15,0	<1 mois
.	.	21,8	26,6	26,2	(27,3)	17,5	19,0	16,0	16,5	1–2 mois
.	.	17,7	19,0	(13,1)	.	18,4	(11,3)	15,8	15,3	3–5 mois
.	.	12,2	11,9	(9,8)	.	.	.	16,1	16,0	6–11 mois
.	.	13,9	13,8	(13,7)	.	.	.	24,4	27,1	12+ mois
100,0	100,0	100,0	100,0	100,0	100,0	100,0	100,0	100,0	100,0	3. Personnes ayant un emploi et en recherchant un autre
.	.	.	.	.	(12,7)	(17,0)	(12,6)	7,7	7,1	Recherche pas encore commencée
.	.	27,1	21,5	.	.	(19,5)	(21,1)	18,4	15,2	1 mois
.	.	25,0	21,0	.	17,0	(16,4)	(17,6)	19,5	17,3	1–2 mois
.	.	16,9	18,2	.	(11,3)	(12,4)	(13,4)	15,7	16,3	3–5 mois
.	.	14,0	16,2	.	(15,9)	(17,7)	(13,3)	16,2	17,0	6–11 mois
.	.	17,0	23,4	.	35,7	(17,0)	(22,1)	22,5	27,1	12+ mois

TAB. 101

Unemployed persons, by cause (%)
Personnes en chômage selon les motifs (%)

	BR Deutschland		France		Italia		Nederland		Belgique Belgïe	
	$\frac{f}{F}100$	$\frac{m}{M}100$	$\frac{f}{F}100$	$\frac{m}{M}100$	$\frac{f}{F}100$	$\frac{m}{M}100$	$\frac{f}{F}100$	$\frac{m}{M}100$	$\frac{f}{F}100$	$\frac{m}{M}100$
1973										
Unemployed persons	100,0	100,0	100,0	100,0	100,0	100,0	100,0	100,0	100,0	100,0
After losing main occupation	55,5	59,4	55,9	68,4	21,9	33,5	56,0	80,1	72,3	78,9
Dismissal	23,1	34,0	31,9	44,8	13,9	22,1	40,0	66,3	61,0	65,0
Resignation	29,7	22,5	21,2	20,1	(1,8)	3,1	(15,2)	8,6	(10,7)	(12,3)
Retirement	.	.	.	.	–	–	.	.	.	.
Previously self-employed	.	.	(2,8)	(3,3)	6,2	8,2	.	5,1	.	.
After losing occasional occupation	–	–	–	–	6,0	8,7	.	.		
Voluntary spell away from work	24,5	20,8	15,9	10,1	.	.	.	(3,5)	.	.
Seeking a 1st job	20,0	12,7	24,2	15,9	71,7	57,1	(23,7)	10,6	22,7	17,7
Other reasons	–	–	(4,0)	5,6	.	.	.	4,6	.	.
1975										
Unemployed persons	100,0	100,0	100,0	100,0	100,0	100,0	100,0	100,0	100,0	100,0
After losing main occupation	67,0	76,3	55,2	73,1	21,9	34,9	75,2	88,7	72,9	81,5
Dismissal	53,9	67,7	34,4	51,9	17,4	26,8	44,9	71,3	66,1	73,4
Resignation	12,3	6,8	19,4	18,8	3,5	5,2	28,1	12,7	6,0	7,5
Retirement	.	(0,7)	.	.	.	.	.	.	.	.
Previously self-employed	.	(1,1)	(1,5)	2,3	.	2,5	.	4,7	.	.
After losing occasional occupation	.	.	9,1	9,1	7,4	9,3	.	.	.	.
Voluntary spell away from work	16,7	12,9	19,1	5,9	.	.	.	(2,5)	.	.
Seeking a 1st job	16,3	10,8	16,6	11,9	70,7	55,8	19,1	8,8	26,0	16,8
Other reasons	.	.	.	.	.	.	.	.	.	.
1977										
Unemployed persons	100,0	100,0	100,0	100,0	100,0	100,0	100,0	100,0	100,0	100,0
After losing main occupation	56,1	56,9	64,9	77,8	18,4	27,9	73,2	86,1	85,5	86,9
Dismissal	37,6	46,5	34,2	49,5	8,3	16,8	46,9	65,4	81,8	83,3
Resignation	17,0	8,2	18,6	15,1	(1,4)	2,4	23,9	16,0	3,3	(2,8)
Retirement	.	.	.	.	.	.	.	.	.	.
Previously self-employed	(1,4)	(1,8)	(1,2)	2,2	.	(1,0)	.	4,6	.	.
After losing occasional occupation	.	.	10,9	10,9	8,1	7,5	.	.	.	.
Voluntary spell away from work	29,2	29,3	15,6	6,3	(1,4)	(1,1)	.	(2,4)	.	.
Seeking a 1st job	14,6	13,8	19,5	15,9	80,0	70,8	22,3	11,5	14,5	13,1
Other reasons	.	.	.	.	.	.	.	.	.	.

[1] Including resignation.

TAB. 101
Unemployed persons, by cause (%)
Personnes en chômage selon les motifs (%)

Luxembourg		United Kingdom		Ireland		Danmark		EUR 9		
$\frac{f}{F}100$	$\frac{m}{M}100$	$\frac{f}{F}100$	$\frac{m}{M}100$	$\frac{f}{F}100$	$\frac{m}{M}100$	$\frac{f}{F}100$	$\frac{m}{M}100$	$\frac{f}{F}100$	$\frac{m}{M}100$	
						1973				
100,0	100,0	100,0	100,0							**Personnes en chômage**
.	.	56,0	75,6							Après perte d'un emploi principal
.	.	19,8	53,3							Licenciement
.	.	33,7	18,5							Démission
–	–	.	(1,7)							Retraite
.	.	.	2,1							Ancien indépendant
–	–	6,4	7,8							Après perte d'une activité occasionnelle
.	.	29,1	12,2							Après interruption volontaire
.	.	8,0	4,2							Recherchant un 1er emploi
.	.	.	.							Autres raisons
						1975				
100,0	100,0	100,0	100,0	100,0	100,0	100,0	100,0	100,0	100,0	**Personnes en chômage**
.	.	46,5	73,4	46,7	72,0	62,6	72,0	51,0	68,0	Après perte d'un emploi principal
.	.	20,4	45,7	33,0	61,8	62,4	71,1	34,4	52,2	Licenciement
.	.	24,1	20,7	(13,6)	8,9	.	.	15,3	12,3	Démission
.	.	(1,3)	4,2	.	.	.	.	(0,4)	1,3	Retraite
.	.	.	2,8	.	.	.	.	0,9	2,2	Ancien indépendant
.	.	6,8	8,1	.	7,2	16,0	19,6	5,9	6,5	Après perte d'une activité occasionnelle
.	.	40,1	11,5	.	.	14,2	(2,9)	19,5	7,3	Après interruption volontaire
.	.	6,0	6,7	44,8	18,0	7,2	5,4	23,4	18,1	Recherchant un 1er emploi
.	.	.	.	.	.	.	.	.	.	Autres raisons
						1977				
100,0	100,0	100,0	100,0	100,0	100,0	100,0	100,0	100,0	100,0	**Personnes en chômage**
.	.	52,5	67,1	69,3	86,5	82,2	92,1	54,3	63,3	Après perte d'un emploi principal
.	.	18,4	40,3	40,3	60,2	81,9[1]	90,6[1]	33,0	44,5	Licenciement
.	.	27,7	20,7	22,4	13,4	:	:	14,6	11,7	Démission
.	.	.	1,1	.	.	.	.	0,1	0,5	Retraite
.	.	.	2,0	.	.	.	.	0,9	1,9	Ancien indépendant
.	.	5,6	3,1	.	9,4	.	.	5,7	4,8	Après perte d'une activité occasionnelle
.	.	22,8	12,8	.	.	10,3	.	14,8	10,3	Après interruption volontaire
.	.	14,0	9,3	27,0	12,9	7,5	6,9	29,0	23,7	Recherchant un 1er emploi
.	.	10,7	10,8	.	.	.	.	1,9	2,7	Autres raisons

[1] Y compris démission.

TAB. 102
Unemployment rates by region (%)
Taux de chômage par région (%)

	T			M			F		
	1973	1975	1977	1973	1975	1977	1973	1975	1977
BR DEUTSCHLAND	0,5	2,9	2,9	0,4	2,8	2,4	0,8	3,2	3,8
Schleswig-Holstein	(0,7)	4,3	4,0	(0,6)	4,4	3,4	(0,9)	4,1	5,0
Hamburg	(0,5)	2,7	3,0	.	2,8	2,9	.	2,5	3,2
Niedersachsen	0,8	3,3	3,2	(0,6)	3,1	2,6	1,1	3,7	4,4
Bremen	.	(1,6)	3,6	.	(1,9)	(3,3)	.	.	(4,0)
Nordrhein-Westfalen	0,4	2,9	3,4	0,3	2,5	2,8	0,6	3,7	4,6
Hessen	0,3	3,1	1,8	(0,3)	3,0	1,7	(0,5)	3,2	2,2
Rheinland-Pfalz	0,5	3,1	3,2	(0,4)	3,0	2,7	(0,6)	3,3	4,1
Baden-Württemberg	0,4	2,1	2,0	0,2	2,2	1,4	(0,6)	2,1	2,9
Bayern	0,6	3,2	2,7	0,4	3,1	2,1	0,9	3,2	3,5
Saarland	(0,8)	3,1	3,5	.	2,6	(2,2)	.	(4,3)	6,2
West Berlin	0,8	2,7	4,1	0,8	2,7	4,5	(0,8)	2,8	3,5
FRANCE	1,9	3,3	4,4	1,5	2,6	3,3	2,6	4,3	6,1
Région parisienne	2,2	3,1	4,3	2,1	3,1	4,2	2,3	3,1	4,5
Bassin parisien	1,3	3,0	3,9	1,0	2,3	2,7	1,7	4,1	5,8
Nord	1,9	3,3	5,0	1,7	2,6	3,7	2,3	4,5	7,4
Est	0,9	2,3	2,7	(0,6)	1,7	2,0	1,3	3,2	3,9
Ouest	1,4	3,2	4,2	1,1	2,7	2,8	2,0	4,1	6,4
Sud-Ouest	2,4	3,5	4,9	1,6	2,6	3,1	3,7	5,1	7,9
Centre-Est	1,7	3,0	4,3	1,1	2,0	2,7	2,8	4,5	6,9
Méditerranée	3,7	5,5	6,0	2,7	3,9	4,5	5,6	8,6	8,8
ITALIA	4,0	3,3	4,4	3,3	2,7	3,3	6,1	4,9	7,0
Nord-Ovest	2,5	2,1	3,3	1,9	1,6	2,4	4,0	3,3	5,3
Lombardia	2,0	1,3	2,0	1,5	1,0	1,5	3,1	2,0	3,1
Nord-Est	2,4	2,0	2,2	1,9	1,7	1,4	3,7	2,6	3,8
Emilia-Romagna	3,5	3,5	2,4	1,8	1,8	1,3	7,1	6,9	4,4
Centro	3,0	2,4	3,5	2,2	1,8	2,7	5,1	3,8	5,2
Lazio	5,4	5,1	7,8	4,5	4,2	5,6	8,6	8,0	13,3
Campania	7,6	5,6	6,4	6,6	4,8	5,7	10,7	8,1	8,2
Abruzzi e Molise	6,2	4,3	5,7	5,2	3,9	4,1	8,6	5,3	9,4
Sud	7,5	5,9	7,6	6,6	5,3	5,3	10,0	7,8	14,0
Sicilia	5,7	4,9	7,2	4,7	3,9	5,1	11,0	10,1	15,5
Sardegna	5,7	6,0	8,6	4,6	4,9	6,1	10,3	10,1	16,9
NEDERLAND	1,9	3,2	3,3	1,9	3,4	3,3	1,7	2,9	3,3
Noord	1,9	4,5	4,1	1,8	4,8	4,3	.	(3,1)	(3,5)
Oost	1,8	3,4	3,4	1,8	3,5	3,4	(1,6)	3,1	3,4
West	1,7	2,3	2,5	1,7	2,3	2,5	1,6	2,4	2,6
Zuid	2,2	4,7	4,6	2,4	4,9	4,5	(1,7)	3,9	4,9
Zuidwest	(2,5)	(2,5)	(3,3)	(2,6)	.	3,1	.	.	.
BELGIQUE/BELGIË	1,6	3,2	5,7	1,2	2,2	3,1	2,6	5,5	10,9
Région de langue néerlandaise	1,4	2,7	5,3	1,1	1,9	2,6	2,2	4,6	11,1
Région de langue française	2,2	4,1	6,5	1,4	2,6	3,6	3,8	7,3	12,3
Bruxelles capitale	1,4	3,6	5,3	(1,4)	2,7	4,2	(1,6)	5,0	7,1
LUXEMBOURG	(0,6)	(0,6)	1,1	.	.	(1,0)	.	.	(1,5)
UNITED KINGDOM	2,1	4,6	4,7	2,4	4,2	4,8	1,7	5,2	4,4
North	3,6	6,3	6,2	4,7	6,4	6,2	1,6	6,0	6,3
Yorkshire and Humberside	2,2	4,5	4,2	2,4	3,8	4,5	1,7	5,6	3,9
North-West	2,8	5,1	5,4	3,3	5,2	5,8	1,8	4,8	4,8
East Midlands	1,7	4,4	3,8	1,9	3,9	3,9	1,4	5,4	3,6
West Midlands	1,7	4,0	4,5	1,8	3,5	4,6	1,6	5,0	4,2
East Anglia	1,1	4,0	4,5	(1,0)	3,4	4,3	1,1	5,1	4,8
South-East	1,3	3,7	3,8	1,3	3,2	3,8	1,3	4,4	3,7
South-West	1,9	5,4	4,0	2,1	4,9	4,2	1,5	6,2	3,6
Wales	2,1	5,1	4,8	2,5	4,6	5,2	(1,3)	6,0	4,1
Scotland	3,7	5,5	6,5	3,8	5,2	7,1	3,6	6,0	5,7
Northern Ireland	4,6	7,1	8,5	4,9	6,2	8,8	3,9	8,8	7,9
IRELAND	:	9,6	9,2	:	10,0	9,8	:	8,7	7,4
DANMARK	:	6,8	7,0	:	7,0	5,7	:	6,5	8,9
EUR 9	:	3,7	4,2	:	3,3	3,5	:	4,4	5,3

TAB. 103

Unemployed persons registered at employment offices, annual averages (1 000)
Personnes en chômage inscrites dans les bureaux de placement, moyennes annuelles (1 000)

		1971	1972	1973	1974	1975	1976	1977	1978
BR Deutschland	F	84,3	105,8	123,6	257,8	451,6	493,8	512,5	504,1
	M	100,8	140,6	149,9	324,7	622,6	566,5	517,5	488,8
	f/f+m.100	45,5	42,9	45,2	44,3	42,0	46,6	49,8	50,8
France	F	150,1	175,9	200,5	263,1	412,2	490,0	572,7	615,5
	M	188,1	207,6	193,4	234,6	427,5	443,5	499,1	551,4
	f/f+m.100	44,4	45,9	50,9	52,9	49,1	52,5	53,4	52,7
Italia	F	332,6	342,2	341,8	358,6	406,6	440,7	540,9	634,0
	M	705,5	705,6	663,0	638,6	700,3	741,0	838,7	894,6
	f/f+m.100	32,0	32,7	34,0	36,0	36,7	37,3	39,2	41,5
Nederland	F	11,5	17,4	21,5	28,2	42,3	51,0	61,0	69,2
	M	50,5	90,7	88,4	106,7	153,0	159,8	145,9	136,4
	f/f+m.100	18,5	16,1	19,6	20,9	21,7	24,2	29,5	33,7
Belgique/België	F	35,1	43,7	53,3	66,1	108,7	151,8	183,0	201,0
	M	49,4	61,5	57,9	58,0	99,1	114,7	124,6	132,4
	f/f+m.100	41,5	41,5	47,9	53,3	52,3	57,0	59,5	60,3
Luxembourg	F	0,018	0,033	0,032	0,035	0,093	0,177	0,327	0,507
	M	0,002	0,009	0,014	0,023	0,172	0,280	0,494	0,659
	f/f+m.100	90,0	78,6	69,6	61,4	35,2	38,7	39,8	43,5
United Kingdom	F	126,2	146,9	103,6	101,3	200,5	335,3	414,4	434,8
	M	665,9	728,7	515,2	513,8	777,1	1 022,3	1 069,2	1 040,2
	f/f+m.100	15,9	16,8	16,7	16,5	20,5	24,7	27,9	29,5
Ireland	F	11,9	13,1	12,0	13,2	19,3	21,1	21,8	20,8
	M	49,9	58,6	54,5	57,2	79,4	89,4	87,2	80,0
	f/f+m.100	19,4	18,3	18,0	18,8	19,6	19,1	20,0	20,6
Danmark	F	5,6	5,4	4,1	12,3	33,2	44,0	62,1	76,7
	M	23,1	23,4	13,7	35,6	80,3	74,2	84,9	93,1
	f/f+m.100	19,5	18,8	23,0	25,7	29,3	37,2	42,2	45,2
EUR 9	F	757,3	850,2	860,4	1 100,4	1 674,5	2 030,4	2 368,7	2 553,1
	M	1 833,2	2 016,7	1 736,0	1 969,2	2 939,5	3 211,7	3 367,6	3 415,8
	f/f+m.100	29,2	29,7	33,1	35,8	36,3	38,7	41,3	42,8

TAB. 104

Unemployed persons registered at employment offices at the end of each month (1 000)

Personnes en chômage inscrites dans les bureaux de placement à la fin de chaque mois (1 000)

	BR Deutschland		France		Italia		Nederland		Belgique Belgïe	
	F	M	F	M	F	M	F	M	F	M
1977										
01/77	549.4	699.5	570.5	497.9	505.2	837.2	57.9	171.4	171.2	121.3
02/77	537.4	676.3	560.3	494.7	490.9	808.0	55.6	166.9	168.5	116.7
03/77	514.6	569.6	540.5	480.1	502.9	802.8	53.3	151.6	167.5	112.4
04/77	516.4	522.8	526.8	473.1	489.5	771.3	51.3	139.8	165.9	110.4
05/77	482.4	464.1	514.7	461.4	477.5	787.4	50.5	132.6	165.3	109.1
06/77	479.8	451.2	512.6	455.1	507.4	808.6	56.4	133.3	165.4	107.5
07/77	507.6	465.0	533.0	471.3	534.3	847.3	62.4	142.1	194.3	131.0
08/77	510.2	453.3	565.5	498.4	557.5	878.2	69.1	142.8	199.8	135.5
09/77	487.0	424.2	640.0	535.1	601.2	899.8	70.5	138.1	201.1	136.4
10/77	511.6	442.8	657.8	548.0	612.8	878.4	70.1	136.7	200.5	137.7
11/77	522.7	481.6	639.1	540.3	612.1	876.2	68.2	142.3	200.2	139.8
12/77	531.4	559.3	611.7	533.2	599.8	869.3	66.3	153.0	197.0	137.2
1978										
01/78	556.4	657.1	597.5	528.6	629.5	953.1	66.4	158.4	196.2	138.4
02/78	536.3	688.0	579.8	528.4	621.9	945.5	62.7	156.3	191.3	133.4
03/78	514.3	584.7	567.4	521.0	615.9	920.9	60.5	142.5	188.9	127.1
04/78	505.4	495.0	553.9	511.3	606.7	873.9	58.8	131.4	187.2	124.4
05/78	473.8	439.2	539.3	497.8	605.6	865.6	57.7	122.3	186.4	121.4
06/78	467.8	409.5	543.6	495.7	601.9	853.3	63.7	122.6	183.8	115.7
07/78	493.3	428.9	573.1	521.1	604.2	850.7	71.0	132.0	208.4	135.6
08/78	500.6	423.4	607.7	549.0	610.5	847.2	79.0	134.9	215.4	139.8
09/78	475.6	388.7	691.2	593.4	656.9	881.9	79.7	130.6	215.8	138.7
10/78	498.8	402.8	722.9	621.2	673.4	897.1	79.0	129.2	215.0	138.2
11/78	505.4	421.6	711.3	618.7	688.3	903.5	77.1	131.6	213.4	138.6
12/78	511.7	495.0	697.2	631.1	693.2	942.3	74.5	145.2	210.3	137.3

	$\frac{f}{f+m}$ 100	$\frac{f}{f+m}$ 100	$\frac{f}{f+m}$ 100	$\frac{f}{f+m}$ 100	$\frac{f}{f+m}$ 100
1977					
01/77	44.0	53.4	37.6	25.3	58.5
02/77	44.3	53.1	37.8	25.0	59.1
03/77	47.5	53.0	38.5	26.0	59.8
04/77	49.7	52.7	38.8	26.8	60.0
05/77	51.0	52.7	37.8	27.6	60.2
06/77	51.5	53.0	38.6	29.7	60.6
07/77	52.2	53.1	38.7	30.5	59.7
08/77	53.0	53.2	38.8	32.6	59.6
09/77	53.4	54.5	40.1	33.8	59.6
10/77	53.6	54.6	41.1	33.9	59.3
11/77	52.0	54.2	41.1	32.4	58.9
12/77	48.7	53.4	40.8	30.2	58.9
1978					
01/78	45.9	53.1	39.8	29.5	58.6
02/78	43.8	52.3	39.7	28.6	58.9
03/78	46.8	52.1	40.1	29.8	59.8
04/78	50.5	52.0	41.0	30.9	60.1
05/78	51.9	52.0	41.2	32.1	60.6
06/78	53.3	52.3	41.4	34.2	61.4
07/78	53.5	52.4	41.5	35.0	60.6
08/78	54.2	52.5	41.9	36.9	60.6
09/78	55.0	53.8	42.7	37.9	60.9
10/78	55.3	53.8	42.9	37.9	60.9
11/78	54.5	53.5	43.2	36.9	60.6
12/78	50.8	52.5	42.4	33.9	60.5

TAB. 104

Unemployed persons registered at employment offices at the end of each month (1 000)

Personnes en chômage inscrites dans les bureaux de placement à la fin de chaque mois (1 000)

Luxembourg		United Kingdom		Ireland		Danmark		EUR 9		
F	M	F	M	F	M	F	M	F	M	
1977										
0.277	0.460	374.1	1074.1	22.8	93.3	55.3	104.1	2306.7	3599.3	01/77
0.279	0.398	366.3	1055.5	22.8	92.6	56.4	104.9	2258.5	3516.0	02/77
0.261	0.413	355.3	1028.5	22.5	91.5	56.2	91.8	2213.1	3328.7	03/77
0.284	0.390	359.9	1032.4	21.9	89.8	59.2	88.1	2191.2	3228.1	04/77
0.246	0.363	347.4	994.3	21.4	87.4	58.0	76.5	2117.4	3113.2	05/77
0.202	0.391	399.3	1050.8	20.9	85.5	57.6	70.8	2199.6	3163.2	06/77
0.275	0.428	489.7	1132.7	21.8	84.9	58.1	73.7	2401.5	3348.4	07/77
0.334	0.491	492.3	1143.5	21.8	85.5	64.1	74.1	2480.6	3411.8	08/77
0.370	0.511	484.8	1124.3	20.8	82.8	66.0	74.5	2571.8	3415.7	09/77
0.414	0.587	447.5	1070.8	21.4	82.3	70.3	79.8	2592.4	3377.1	10/77
0.479	0.703	435.9	1063.2	21.6	83.4	72.0	85.3	2572.3	3412.8	11/77
0.495	0.796	420.1	1060.7	22.7	87.1	72.0	95.6	2521.5	3496.2	12/77
1978										
0.528	0.869	433.8	1114.7	22.4	88.7	74.7	116.3	2577.4	3756.2	01/78
0.475	0.853	419.1	1089.6	22.0	88.5	76.2	116.8	2509.8	3747.4	02/78
0.458	0.813	402.6	1058.4	22.2	87.3	73.2	114.3	2445.5	3557.0	03/78
0.444	0.696	406.4	1045.4	21.2	83.6	74.9	91.3	2414.9	3357.0	04/78
0.419	0.627	385.7	1001.1	20.5	80.4	73.3	83.3	2342.7	3211.7	05/78
0.431	0.571	423.1	1023.0	19.8	76.8	71.7	77.5	2375.8	3174.7	06/78
0.482	0.617	498.5	1087.3	20.2	76.5	71.6	79.4	2540.8	3312.1	07/78
0.515	0.650	509.3	1099.0	20.2	77.3	76.5	81.9	2619.7	3353.1	08/78
0.582	0.585	476.6	1041.1	18.6	73.0	78.2	81.2	2693.2	3329.2	09/78
0.573	0.482	439.8	989.7	20.7	73.0	82.6	85.3	2732.8	3337.0	10/78
0.600	0.532	421.6	970.4	21.1	75.8	83.0	88.6	2721.8	3349.3	11/78
0.579	0.608	401.8	962.5	21.2	78.6	83.9	101.5	2694.4	3494.1	12/78

$\frac{f}{f+m}$ 100	$\frac{f}{f+m}$ 100	$\frac{f}{f+m}$ 100	$\frac{f}{f+m}$ 100	$\frac{f}{f+m}$ 100	
1977					
37.6	25.8	19.6	34.7	39.1	01/77
41.2	25.8	19.8	35.0	39.1	02/77
38.7	25.7	19.7	38.0	39.9	03/77
42.1	25.8	19.6	40.2	40.4	04/77
40.4	25.9	19.7	43.1	40.5	05/77
34.1	27.5	19.6	44.9	41.0	06/77
39.1	30.2	20.4	44.1	41.8	07/77
40.5	30.1	20.3	46.4	42.1	08/77
42.0	30.1	20.1	47.0	43.0	09/77
41.4	29.5	20.6	46.8	43.4	10/77
40.5	29.1	20.6	45.8	43.0	11/77
38.3	28.4	20.7	43.0	41.9	12/77
1978					
37.8	28.0	20.2	39.1	40.7	01/78
35.8	27.8	19.9	39.5	40.1	02/78
36.0	27.6	20.3	39.0	40.7	03/78
38.9	28.0	20.2	45.1	41.8	04/78
40.1	27.8	20.3	46.8	42.2	05/78
43.0	29.3	20.5	48.1	42.8	06/78
43.9	31.4	20.9	47.4	43.4	07/78
44.2	31.7	20.7	48.3	43.9	08/78
49.9	31.4	20.3	49.1	44.7	09/78
54.3	30.8	22.1	49.2	45.0	10/78
53.0	30.3	21.8	48.4	44.8	11/78
48.8	29.5	21.2	45.3	43.5	12/78

TAB. 105

Unemployed persons registered at employment offices, situation at the end of June (1 000)

Personnes en chômage inscrites dans les bureaux de placement, situation à la fin juin (1 000)

	1973			1974			1975		
	F	M	$\frac{f}{f+m}$ 100	F	M	$\frac{f}{f+m}$ 100	F	M	$\frac{f}{f+m}$ 100
BR DEUTSCHLAND									
Registered unemployed	100,5	100,4	50,0	217,8	232,9	48,3	427,8	574,4	42,7
of which:									
organizers, administrative and clerical staff	19,5	10,6	64,8	40,2	17,2	70,0	90,9	33,4	73,1
producers of metal and metal goods, locksmiths, mechanics and the like	8,3	16,3	33,7	21,4	41,5	34,0	63,5	144,5	30,5
goods and services sales personnel and allied occupations	13,1	5,8	69,3	28,2	13,2	68,1	56,2	29,9	65,3
building trade, fittings and furnishings, upholstery, painting, varnishing and allied trades	0,3	7,4	3,9	1,1	43,2	2,5	1,9	100,1	1,9
warehouse managers, storage and transport workers	1,5	10,9	12,1	3,7	23,0	13,9	6,5	51,3	11,2
FRANCE									
Registered unemployed	161,6	167,9	49,0	200,9	177,8	53,0	351,6	386,7	47,6
of which:									
clerical work and the like	48,1	19,2	71,6	61,7	20,6	75,0	115,4	37,1	75,7
handling and storage	21,3	36,6	36,8	25,9	35,5	42,3	39,1	69,5	36,0
commerce and the like	21,2	11,1	65,8	27,5	12,3	69,1	46,0	20,4	69,2
conversion of common metals	4,2	15,7	21,0	5,8	15,9	26,9	16,3	50,6	24,4
construction and maintenance of buildings	0,1	15,7	0,6	0,1	15,4	0,6	0,3	54,8	0,5
ITALIA									
Registered unemployed	331,7	626,0	34,6	345,8	599,4	36,6	398,0	685,7	36,7
of which:									
unskilled labourers				58,5	119,9	32,8			
farmwork, hunting and fishing				97,7	99,8	49,5			
managers, employees and junior staff				62,8	54,6	53,5			
construction work				0,0	113,6	0,0			
production of metals and metal and mechanical work				6,1	66,1	8,5			
NEDERLAND									
Registered unemployed	18,6	74,1	20,0	23,4	87,1	21,2	38,7	137,8	21,9
of which:									
clerical work, teachers	5,5	8,5	39,3	6,3	8,8	41,4	10,4	13,4	43,9
persons in general service	2,0	9,1	18,0	2,6	10,3	20,2	5,2	20,6	20,2
metal workers	0,1	10,6	0,9	0,1	11,0	0,9	0,2	20,7	1,0
construction workers	0,1	12,9	0,8	0,1	22,1	0,5	0,1	32,6	0,3
commerce	1,8	5,1	26,1	2,6	5,5	32,1	4,6	7,5	38,0
BELGIQUE/BELGIË									
Registered unemployed	45,0	49,7	47,6	53,5	46,8	53,3	93,6	85,1	52,4
of which:									
employed persons	14,8	6,8	68,2	19,4	8,1	70,5	32,9	14,8	69,0
unskilled labourers	5,0	17,5	22,2	5,3	15,7	25,1	7,7	21,8	26,1
mechanics, tool makers, electricians	2,6	5,7	31,7	3,0	4,8	38,5	5,7	13,0	30,3
tailors, cutters, furriers	4,7	0,6	90,4	5,8	0,5	92,1	12,6	0,8	94,0
other specialist service workers	5,2	0,6	89,7	6,0	0,7	89,6	9,2	1,1	89,3

TAB. 105

Unemployed persons registered at employment offices, situation at the end of June (1 000)

Personnes en chômage inscrites dans les bureaux de placement, situation à la fin juin (1 000)

1976			1977			1978			
F	M	$\frac{f}{f+m}$ 100	F	M	$\frac{f}{f+m}$ 100	F	M	$\frac{f}{f+m}$ 100	
									BR DEUTSCHLAND
448,3	472,7	48,7	479,8	451,2	51,5	467,8	409,5	53,3	**chômeurs inscrits**
									dont:
117,5	39,2	75,0	119,4	35,9	76,9	107,5	31,0	77,6	professions administratives et de bureau
41,1	109,0	27,4	37,3	96,4	27,9	38,8	92,4	29,6	fabrication et travail des métaux, mécaniques etc.
65,8	31,2	67,8	73,0	29,4	71,3	69,6	25,5	73,1	commerce, vente de services et professions analogues
1,4	48,7	2,8	1,1	48,2	2.2	1,2	37,2	3,1	bâtiment, tapissiers, peintres, etc.
6,9	47,1	12,8	7,1	45,8	13,4	7,1	45,5	13,5	gestion des stocks, magasiniers et transporteurs
									FRANCE
424,5	388,5	52,2	512,6	455,1	53,0	543,6	495,7	52,3	**chômeurs inscrits**
									dont:
143,5	42,0	77,4	173,3	48,9	78,0	177,3	49,5	78,2	emplois de bureau et assimilés
31,6	57,2	35,6	33,6	65,9	33,6	34,4	65,1	34,5	manutention et stockage
57,4	22,1	72,1	71,3	25,4	73,7	78,4	28,0	73,8	emplois de commerce et assimilés
21,8	52,8	29,2	31,8	68,3	31,8	40,6	76,7	34,6	transformation des métaux ordinaires
0,4	49,3	0,8	0,6	56,7	1,0	0,7	69,1	1,0	construction et entretien des bâtiments
									ITALIA
423,4	717,8	37,1	507,4	808,6	38,6	606,3	866,6	41,2	**chômeurs incrits**
									dont:
									main d'œuvre non qualifiée
									agriculture, pêche, sylviculture, chasse
									dirigeants, employées et subalternes
									travaux de contruction
									production de métaux et travaux techniques de tous genres
									NEDERLAND
46,4	147,7	23,9	56,4	133,3	29,7	63,7	122,6	34,2	**chômeurs inscrits**
									dont:
12,5	15,3	45,0	15,6	16,7	48,3	18,0	16,7	51,9	employés, enseignants
4,9	20,9	19,0	5,9	18,5	24,3	6,2	16,7	27,1	personnel en service général
0,2	23,6	0,8	0,2	19,0	1,0	0,2	16,2	1,2	travail des métaux
0,2	22,0	0,9	0,2	15,3	1,3	0,3	10,9	2,7	ouvriers du bâtiment
5,4	7,7	40,9	7,6	7,7	49,7	9,2	7,0	56,8	commerçants
									BELGIQUE/BELGIË
136,9	101,1	57,5	165,5	107,4	60,6	183,8	115,7	61,4	**chômeurs inscrits**
									dont:
49,9	20,6	70,8	57,7	20,8	73,4	65,5	21,2	75,5	employés
9,3	21,4	30,3	10,0	22,2	31,1	10,0	21,5	31,7	main d'œuvre ordinaire
8,5	17,4	32,8	10,6	18,6	36,3	11,2	20,9	34,9	mécaniciens, outilleurs, électriciens
19,0	0,9	95,5	26,1	1,0	96,7	29,1	1,0	96,7	tailleurs, coupeurs, fourreurs
13,9	1,4	90,8	17,6	1,5	91,7	20,5	1,7	92,3	autres travailleurs specialisés dans les services

TAB. 105
(continued)
(suite)

	1973			1974			1975		
	F	M	$\frac{f}{f+m}$ 100	F	M	$\frac{f}{f+m}$ 100	F	M	$\frac{f}{f+m}$ 100
LUXEMBOURG									
Registered unemployed	–	–	–	–	–	–	0,031	0,070	30,7
of which:									
unskilled workers	–	–	–	–	–	–	0,004	0,039	9,3
organizers, administrative and clerical staff	–	–	–	–	–	–	0,022	0,011	66,7
commerce and the like	–	–	–	–	–	–	0,002	0,003	40,0
UNITED KINGDOM									
Registered unemployed [1]	91,6	483,0	15,9	81,7	459,8	15,1	159,4	706,6	18,4
of which:									
unskilled labourers	18,7	237,1	7,3	18,1	216,0	7,7	35,7	304,5	10,5
clerical and related	23,0	52,8	30,3	22,2	50,3	30,6	44,7	64,2	41,0
processing making, repairing (metal and electrical)	0,9	44,1	2,0	0,6	39,0	1,5	1,8	71,2	2,5
transport operating, materials moving and storing and related	0,8	33,8	2,3	0,7	34,2	2,0	1,4	64,6	2,1
construction, mining and related	0,0	23,1	0,0	0,0	30,2	0,0	0,0	53,5	0,0
catering, cleaning, hairdressing and other personal service	14,2	10,6	57,3	12,3	9,7	55,9	19,5	15,5	55,9
IRELAND									
Registered unemployed [2]	11,4	50,7	18,3	12,2	52,6	18,8	18,6	77,5	19,4
of which:									
agricultural occupations and fishermen	0,0	18,1	0,0	0,0	18,0	0,0	0,0	21,0	0,0
general labourers	–	9,1	–	–	9,8	–	–	13,8	–
other and undefined workers	1,4	3,2	30,4	1,5	3,7	28,8	3,0	8,8	25,4
unskilled building workers	–	3,5	–	–	3,7	–	–	7,1	–
skilled workers not elsewhere classified	0,9	2,1	29,0	1,2	2,6	31,6	2,4	5,1	32,0
clerks, typists, book-keepers	2,3	0,6	76,7	2,4	0,6	80,0	3,3	1,2	73,3
DANMARK									
Registered unemployed [3]	:	:	:	:	:	:	:	:	:
of which:									
unskilled workers	:	:	:	:	:	:	:	:	:
commercial and clerical employees	:	:	:	:	:	:	:	:	:
Metal workers	:	:	:	:	:	:	:	:	:

[1] Unemployed persons registered at careers offices are not included.
[2] Short-time workers are included.
[3] The analysis relates to unemployment among full-time insured members of the trade unions unemployment insurance funds (situation from 28.4.76 to 13.4.77).

TAB. 105
(continued)
(suite)

1976			1977			1978			
F	M	$\frac{f}{f+m}$ 100	F	M	$\frac{f}{f+m}$ 100	F	M	$\frac{f}{f+m}$ 100	
									LUXEMBOURG
0,121	0,210	36,6	0,202	0,391	34,1	0,431	0,571	43,0	**Chômeurs inscrits**
									dont:
0,033	0,108	23,4	0,058	0,218	21,0	0,151	0,240	38,6	ouvriers non qualifiés
0,055	0,034	61,8	0,090	0,070	56,3	0,173	0,079	68,7	agents administratifs et employés de bureau
0,017	0,005	77,3	0,021	0,009	70,0	0,038	0,029	56,7	agents commerciaux, représentants vendeurs
									UNITED KINGDOM
322,4	1009,4	24,2	399,3	1050,8	27,5	423,1	1023,0	29,3	**Chômeurs inscrits** (1)
									dont:
57,6	383,8	13,0	65,6	384,9	14,6	72,7	389,6	15,7	main d'œuvre ordinaire et divers
81,7	77,2	51,4	102,3	80,0	56,1	103,9	78,8	56,9	employés de bureau et assimilés
2,6	103,9	2,4	2,4	99,4	2,4	2,3	93,8	2,4	traitem., fabric., rép. et assim. (métaux, et électr.)
2,5	93,0	2,6	3,1	95,0	3,2	3,5	92,0	3,7	transport, déménagement de matériaux, emmag. et assimilés
0,0	74,6	0,0	0,0	77,3	0,0	0,1	68,2	0,1	construction, mines et assimilés
34,2	24,8	58,0	44,2	28,6	60,8	48,5	27,0	64,3	hôtellerie, café, restaurant, nettoyage, coiffure et autres
									IRELAND
19,9	87,2	18,6	20,9	85,5	19,6	19,8	76,8	20,5	**Chômeurs inscrits** (2)
									dont:
0,0	22,0	0,0	0,0	21,6	0,0	0,1	20,0	0,5	agriculteurs, pêcheurs
–	15,2	–	–	15,4	–	–	13,9	–	main d'œuvre non specialisée
3,3	8,3	28,4	3,4	8,8	27,9	2,9	8,7	25,0	main d'œuvre de profession non déterminée
–	8,3	–	–	8,0	–	–	7,1	–	travailleurs non spécialisés du bâtiment
2,1	5,3	28,4	2,4	5,1	32,0	2,2	4,7	31,9	personnes spécialisées non classées ailleurs
4,1	1,4	74,5	4,5	1,4	76,3	4,2	1,2	77,8	clercs, dactylos, comptables
									DANMARK
39,9	71,1	35,9	59,2	88,1	40,2	74,9	91,3	50,2	**Chômeurs inscrits** (3)
									dont:
8,9	31,7	21,9	12,7	43,8	22,5	14,8	42,3	29,8	ouvriers non spécialisés
8,4	3,0	73,7	11,7	3,5	77,0	15,6	4,2	78,8	employés de commerce et employés de bureau
0,1	8,3	1,2	0,1	9,8	1,0	0,1	10,2	1,0	métallurgistes

(1) Les chômeurs inscrits auprés des «Carreers offices» ne sont pas compris.
(2) Y compris les chômeurs partiels.
(3) L'analyse porte sur les chômeurs membres assurés complets des caisses d'assurance-chômage des syndicats (situation du 28.4.1976 au 13.4.1977).

TAB. 106
Women registered at employment offices as a proportion of the total number of registered unemployed, by region

Femmes inscrites dans les bureaux de placement par rapport au total des inscrits, par région

	1971	1972	1973	1974	1975	1976	1977	1978
BR DEUTSCHLAND	45,5	42,9	45,2	44,3	42,0	46,6	49,8	50,8
Schleswig-Holstein	46,7	46,8	47,2	41,7	41,5	48,7	51,0	51,9
Hamburg	46,9	44,4	47,3	40,5	37,1	45,7	47,6	47,4
Niedersachsen	47,7	46,5	49,3	45,8	42,6	46,8	50,2	52,2
Hannover	41,2	41,7	43,3	42,4	39,4	44,6	50,3	51,8
Hildesheim	54,2	53,3	55,6	47,5	46,2	48,7	51,3	53,9
Lüneburg	50,0	46,3	48,9	42,7	41,2	49,1	53,1	54,4
Stack	43,8	42,9	45,0	44,4	39,3	44,7	50,6	53,3
Osnabrück	33,3	30,4	41,7	48,2	44,3	48,5	51,0	53,1
Awich	34,7	32,4	33,8	32,0	34,6	33,8	35,3	36,4
Braunschweig	62,5	63,8	65,6	60,4	48,8	52,8	55,6	57,5
Oldenburg	44,7	45,8	48,3	43,4	43,0	48,9	50,0	52,4
Bremen	50,0	45,8	50,0	51,7	45,9	44,6	48,1	44,9
Nordrhein-Westfalen	42,7	37,9	43,0	44,7	42,5	45,9	47,7	47,9
Düsseldorf	41,6	37,2	42,3	43,9	42,0	45,4	46,2	46,2
Köln	41,1	40,5	43,4	41,5	39,2	43,4	46,7	48,7
Münster	47,3	42,5	48,7	48,0	45,0	47,9	49,8	48,7
Detmold	51,3	45,5	51,7	50,8	45,5	50,5	53,5	54,7
Arnsberg	37,9	31,9	36,6	42,9	43,5	46,0	47,7	47,3
Hessen	47,9	45,4	48,3	45,4	41,3	47,6	52,0	52,4
Darmstadt	51,1	49,2	49,3	45,1	41,5	48,4	52,6	53,1
Kassel	42,0	39,2	46,7	46,2	40,7	45,9	50,0	51,0
Rheinland-Pfalz	39,3	40,0	42,1	38,5	35,9	42,2	48,8	51,2
Koblenz	28,6	28,6	31,8	32,8	33,1	39,9	47,6	49,0
Trier	23,8	26,1	27,3	27,5	27,7	32,5	39,5	43,4
Rheinhessen-Pfalz	54,9	52,3	54,1	44,9	40,0	46,2	52,2	54,2
Baden-Württemberg	56,5	53,2	48,1	47,8	44,4	49,4	53,9	56,3
Stuttgart	59,5	53,8	48,4	48,4	45,9	50,8	57,0	59,7
Karlsruhe	71,1	34,5	59,2	52,7	44,1	49,1	53,7	55,5
Freiburg	56,7	51,4	42,9	46,1	43,3	47,5	50,4	52,7
Tübingen	28,6	34,8	38,7	40,5	43,1	49,1	52,9	56,3
Bayern	44,9	44,0	42,6	43,5	42,8	47,5	52,2	54,7
Oberbayern	56,2	55,6	52,3	46,4	44,1	51,1	56,7	58,4
Niederbayern	27,8	27,8	26,1	30,5	33,7	36,3	40,7	42,3
Oberpfalz	36,4	33,7	31,8	45,8	37,2	39,4	44,3	48,8
Oberfranken	52,3	47,7	46,0	40,8	46,7	49,5	51,5	53,9
Mittelfranken	57,5	54,5	52,5	48,0	46,2	51,3	55,1	57,7
Unterfranken	50,0	43,8	50,0	47,3	41,8	49,2	55,2	58,0
Schwaben	54,3	56,8	54,0	49,6	45,8	51,4	56,5	59,8
Saarland	40,9	36,8	45,1	39,9	37,4	39,7	43,5	43,8
Berlin (West)	43,2	39,8	44,0	41,2	42,0	45,0	43,6	43,6
FRANCE	44,4	45,8	50,9	52,9	49,1	52,5	53,4	52,7
Île-de-France	:	:	:	:	:	:	45,4	45,2
Bassin parisien	:	:	:	:	:	:	57,9	56,9
Champagne-Ardenne	:	:	:	:	:	:	58,4	57,1
Picardie	:	:	:	:	:	:	56,3	55,9
Haute-Normandie	:	:	:	:	:	:	56,1	55,2
Centre	:	:	:	:	:	:	59,7	58,5
Basse-Normandie	:	:	:	:	:	:	56,2	54,9
Bourgogne	:	:	:	:	:	:	61,6	60,9
Nord-Pas-de-Calais	:	:	:	:	:	:	52,2	49,6

TAB. 106
(continued)
(suite)

	1971	1972	1973	1974	1975	1976	1977	1978
Est	:	:	:	:	:	:	55,4	55,3
Lorraine	:	:	:	:	:	:	54,9	53,6
Alsace	:	:	:	:	:	:	52,5	54,1
Franche-Comté	:	:	:	:	:	:	61,8	61,6
Ouest	:	:	:	:	:	:	58,0	57,3
Pays-de-la-Loire	:	:	:	:	:	:	56,4	54,6
Bretagne	:	:	:	:	:	:	57,6	58,1
Poitou-Charentes	:	:	:	:	:	:	61,8	60,8
Sud-Ouest	:	:	:	:	:	:	58,6	58,4
Aquitaine	:	:	:	:	:	:	59,4	58,8
Midi-Pyrénées	:	:	:	:	:	:	56,8	57,1
Limousin	:	:	:	:	:	:	62,0	61,5
Centre-Est	:	:	:	:	:	:	56,8	55,8
Rhône-Alpes	:	:	:	:	:	:	55,1	53,8
Auvergne	:	:	:	:	:	:	62,8	62,9
Méditerranée	:	:	:	:	:	:	50,1	48,6
Languedoc-Roussillon	:	:	:	:	:	:	55,0	53,8
Provence-Alpes-Côte d'Azur	:	:	:	:	:	:	47,7	46,1
Corse	:	:	:	:	:	:	51,0	50,0
ITALIA	32,0	32,7	34,0	36,0	36,7	37,4	39,0	41,4
Nord-Ovest	42,5	43,9	47,0	50,1	51,1	51,4	53,8	55,5
Piemonte	47,9	49,0	51,9	54,6	54,6	55,0	58,1	59,9
Valle d'Aosta	30,0	41,7	40,0	40,0	41,7	38,5	43,7	47,1
Liguria	32,2	32,5	34,9	39,1	41,0	41,4	42,8	45,6
Lombardia	40,3	41,8	44,4	49,1	52,2	51,7	54,4	57,4
Nord-Est	33,8	35,6	38,2	42,2	44,1	45,5	48,1	52,2
Trentino-Alto-Adige	33,9	37,4	41,5	46,0	46,4	47,5	48,5	52,4
Veneto	33,5	34,7	37,0	41,1	43,1	44,6	47,6	51,8
Friuli-Venezia-Giulia	34,7	38,3	40,2	43,7	45,8	46,2	49,4	54,0
Emilia-Romagna	53,5	54,3	57,2	59,0	58,4	59,5	63,0	65,1
Centro	31,3	32,5	35,0	38,8	41,3	42,6	44,9	48,4
Toscana	31,1	32,3	34,9	38,8	42,5	43,6	45,6	49,7
Umbria	28,5	30,6	33,3	36,4	37,9	38,4	41,5	44,6
Marche	33,6	34,1	37,1	40,7	42,2	42,2	47,0	49,0
Lazio	29,4	31,1	33,2	35,2	33,7	35,5	37,2	41,5
Campania	30,1	29,2	29,5	30,8	31,6	32,3	33,6	34,6
Abruzzi-Molise	20,7	22,6	26,2	29,8	31,2	32,2	34,9	37,0
Abruzzi	20,8	23,1	27,1	30,4	31,5	32,3	35,0	36,8
Molise	20,5	20,9	24,4	27,6	30,4	30,9	34,4	37,4
Sud	32,7	31,8	31,9	32,9	33,2	32,4	32,7	33,0
Puglia	41,5	40,6	40,1	40,1	40,1	37,3	35,2	34,6
Basilicata	25,3	27,6	28,7	30,7	31,8	32,8	35,5	38,4
Calabria	16,6	17,4	18,0	21,1	22,7	24,6	27,5	28,0
Sicilia	19,1	20,3	22,0	23,4	23,3	24,4	27,0	26,8
Sardegna	30,5	28,7	30,6	32,2	34,1	34,0	36,6	37,4

TAB. 106

(continued)

(suite)

	1971	1972	1973	1974	1975	1976	1977	1978
NEDERLAND	18,5	16,0	19,6	20,9	21,7	24,2	28,7	33,7
Noord-Nederland	12,9	11,3	15,6	17,0	18,3	20,9	25,5	31,4
Groningen	15,8	12,7	16,7	17,7	19,8	21,0	26,3	31,4
Friesland	11,8	10,9	14,0	16,4	17,4	20,4	26,4	31,7
Drenthe								
Oost-Nederland	10,7	9,8	13,5	15,3	17,3	19,8	24,7	31,1
Overijssel	17,1	15,5	20,4	20,5	20,3	24,6	29,8	36,2
Gelderland	16,3	15,7	20,2	20,0	20,0	24,4	29,3	35,0
West-Nederland	17,9	15,5	20,6	21,1	20,5	25,2	30,5	36,6
Utrecht	21,7	17,1	19,8	22,9	23,8	24,6	28,4	32,6
Noord-Holland	20,0	20,0	22,7	25,5	24,6	27,0	31,9	37,7
Zuid-Holland	23,8	18,2	20,2	23,3	24,4	26,8	31,8	36,2
Zuidwest-Nederland	20,2	16,1	18,9	22,5	23,2	22,9	25,4	29,5
Zeeland	20,0	13,8	20,0	22,2	27,3	25,6	28,2	33,3
Zuid-Nederland	17,4	17,0	20,4	20,7	21,6	24,8	29,7	34,2
Nord Brabant	13,9	13,7	16,9	17,4	19,5	23,4	27,8	32,4
Limburg	24,1	22,3	27,0	26,1	25,3	27,5	32,6	36,7
BELGIQUE/BELGIË	41,5	41,5	47,9	53,3	52,3	56,9	59,5	60,3
Vlaams Gewest/Région flamande	:	:	:	:	52,1	59,2	62,2	63,2
Région wallonne/Waals Gewest	:	:	:	:	53,7	56,0	57,8	58,6
Région bruxelloise/Brussels Gewest	:	:	:	:	47,8	49,8	51,7	50,6
Antwerpen/Anvers	34,6	37,7	44,6	50,0	51,3	59,5	62,8	63,5
Brabant	43,1	44,2	49,5	54,3	51,3	54,5	56,9	56,9
Hainaut/Henegouwen	51,7	48,5	53,2	59,5	55,4	56,8	58,2	58,7
Liège/Luik	44,6	43,6	48,0	52,0	51,7	55,2	57,5	58,8
Limburg/Limbourg	37,5	38,6	48,5	55,6	58,7	66,5	69,2	71,7
Luxembourg/Luxemburg	36,4	42,9	46,7	52,9	53,8	59,4	53,8	50,0
Namur/Namen	52,0	50,0	55,9	60,5	55,4	55,4	57,5	58,8
O. -Vlaand/Fland. or.	36,5	37,8	45,9	51,4	51,1	56,7	58,5	59,3
W. -Vlaand/Fland. oc.	30,3	30,4	39,3	43,0	45,5	52,5	57,3	58,9
LUXEMBOURG (Gr. Duché)	:	:	:	61,4	35,2	38,7	39,8	43,5

TAB. 106
(continued)
(suite)

	1971	1972	1973	1974	1975	1976	1977	1978
UNITED KINGDOM	16,0	16,9	17,0	16,5	20,5	24,8	27,9	29,5
North	15,6	17,0	17,2	16,9	20,6	26,5	29,8	30,3
Yorkshire and Humberside	14,7	15,2	15,4	14,4	19,0	24,0	27,7	29,2
East Midlands	14,7	14,9	14,8	14,2	20,2	24,2	27,2	28,5
East Anglia	14,6	15,6	15,2	14,7	19,3	22,8	25,2	27,3
South East	13,3	13,8	13,7	14,3	18,6	22,3	25,2	26,5
South West	17,4	17,4	16,8	15,5	20,2	23,7	26,7	28,9
West Midlands	14,9	15,7	17,1	17,6	22,7	25,0	29,2	30,7
North West	14,7	15,4	14,6	14,8	18,7	23,4	27,6	29,6
Wales	19,1	18,6	18,4	17,8	20,7	24,7	29,2	31,0
Scotland	23,1	26,3	27,5	19,4	23,5	27,5	31,2	33,0
Northern Ireland	19,5	21,2	21,2	25,8	29,1	31,6	31,5	31,2
IRELAND	19,4	18,3	18,4	18,8	19,6	19,1	20,0	20,6
DANMARK	19,5	18,8	23,0	25,7	29,3	27,2	42,2	45,2
EUR 9	29,2	29,7	33,1	35,9	36,3	38,7	41,3	42,8

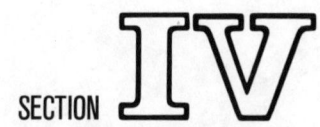

SECTION IV

Geographical and occupational mobility
Mobilité territoriale et professionnelle

TAB. 107

Population by changes compared with the situation one year before the survey (%)

Population d'après les changements intervenus par rapport à la situation un an avant l'enquête (%)

	BR Deutschland		France		Italia		Nederland		Belgique België	
	$\frac{f}{F}100$	$\frac{f}{f+m}100$	$\frac{f}{F}100$	$\frac{f}{f+m}100$	$\frac{f}{F}100$	$\frac{f}{f+m}100$	$\frac{f}{F}100$	$\frac{f}{f+m}100$	$\frac{f}{F}100$	$\frac{f}{f+m}100$
1975										
Persons with a main occupation	100,0	36,4	100,0	37,4	100,0	27,6	100,0	24,3	100,0	31,8
without change	71,9	35,3	75,9	36,6	84,0	26,8	82,8	22,5	89,2	33,2
change of country or region only	0,7	34,2	0,7	25,1	0,9	16,9	1,2	24,5	0,7	24,2
change in situation (^{1})	11,5	59,1	11,2	53,7	9,2	49,7	10,6	48,7	7,1	47,3
change of activity (^{2})	15,8	32,1	12,2	33,5	5,9	24,1	5,3	30,4	3,0	28,8
Unemployed persons	100,0	39,4	100,0	49,7	100,0	40,1	100,0	21,6	100,0	54,6
without change	18,4	36,2	20,1	56,3	47,1	39,7	(12,3)	(14,3)	31,3	58,8
change of country or region only	.	.	.	.	(1,7)	(57,1)	.	.	.	.
change in situation (^{1})	81,0	40,0	79,0	48,3	51,3	40,2	86,6	23,5	67,9	52,4
Non-active persons	100,0	71,9	100,0	69,3	100,0	71,9	100,0	71,6	100,0	69,5
without change	83,9	71,4	82,1	69,1	94,3	72,5	92,1	71,7	97,0	70,1
change of country or region only	0,8	70,7	1,6	74,7	1,3	66,8	1,2	73,5	0,7	73,1
change in situation (^{1})	15,4	74,6	16,3	69,8	4,4	63,7	6,7	69,7	2,3	52,5
Total population	100,0	53,5	100,0	52,1	100,0	52,1	100,0	50,3	100,0	51,6
without change	79,0	54,0	78,7	52,1	91,4	47,5	89,7	50,3	93,6	52,1
change of country or region only	0,8	51,6	1,2	52,1	1,2	44,0	1,2	52,5	0,7	45,8
change in situation (^{1})	14,8	66,4	15,4	62,3	6,0	55,1	8,0	55,6	4,8	50,1
change of activity (^{2})	5,4	32,2	4,6	33,6	1,4	24,1	1,1	30,4	0,9	28,8

(^{1}) Change in usual situation with regard to economic activity.
(^{2}) Change in professional status and/or branch of activity.
(^{3}) For comparison with the preceding year the figures of employment include occasional occupation.

TAB. 107

Population by changes compared with the situation one year before the survey (%)

Population d'après les changements intervenus par rapport à la situation un an avant l'enquête (%)

Luxembourg		United Kingdom		Ireland		Danmark		EUR 9		
$\frac{f}{F}100$	$\frac{f}{f+m}100$	$\frac{f}{F}100$	$\frac{f}{f+m}100$	$\frac{f}{F}100$	$\frac{f}{f+m}100$	$\frac{f}{F}100$	$\frac{f}{f+m}100$	$\frac{f}{F}100$	$\frac{f}{f+m}100$	
				1975						
100,0	28,4	100,0	38,0	100,0	26,6	100,0	39,3	100,0	34,6	**Personnes ayant un emploi principal**
87,0	26,9	78,7	35,6	86,1	25,6	(77,9)	(38,9)	77,6	33,0	sans changement
.	.	0,6	27,5	.	.	.	.	0,7	24,9	changement pays ou région seulement
9,0	66,7	13,1	65,2	9,2	46,3	(8,8)	(54,8)	11,2	57,0	changement situation ([1])
(3,6)	(25,0)	7,5	35,8	4,3	22,9	(13,3)	(34,9)	10,5	32,1	changement activité ([2])
100,0	.	100,0	43,7	100,0	24,1	100,0	37,6	100,0	42,0	**Personnes en chômage**
.	.	11,0	28,1	(16,8)	12,1	(6,1)	(30,8)	21,0	37,7	sans changement
.	.	.	47,0	.	.	.	.	0,7	47,8	changement pays ou région seulement
.	.	88,9	.	82,8	28,8	(93,8)	(38,2)	78,3	43,3	changement situation ([1])
100,0	73,8	100,0	72,4	100,0	74,7	100,0	67,1	100,0	71,3	**Personnes non actives**
96,3	74,1	90,6	75,3	95,8	75,0	(76,0)	(64,1)	88,4	71,8	sans changement
(0,6)	(60,0)	1,1	76,2	0,7	.	.	.	1,1	71,7	changement pays ou région seulement
3,1	60,0	8,3	72,1	3,5	65,9	(24,0)	(78,0)	10,5	71,2	changement situation ([1])
100,0	51,7	100,0	52,2	100,0	49,7	100,0	50,9	100,0	52,3	**Population totale**
93,6	51,6	83,7	52,6	91,5	50,9	(75,0)	(49,7)	83,8	52,7	sans changement
(0,6)	(50,0)	0,9	51,7	0,6	53,8	.	.	1,0	49,3	changement pays ou région seulement
4,9	63,6	12,3	63,0	6,8	43,5	(19,5)	(65,0)	11,8	62,2	changement situation ([1])
0,9	25,0	3,0	35,8	1,1	24,5	(5,5)	(34,7)	3,5	32,1	changement activité ([2])

[1] Changement de la situation habituelle au regard de l'activité économique.
[2] Changement du statut professionnel et/ou de la branche d'activité.
[3] Pour la comparaison avec l'année précédente, les données de l'emploi incluent l'emploi occasionnel.

TAB. 107
(continued)
(suite)

	BR Deutschland		France		Italia		Nederland		Belgique België	
	$\frac{f}{F}100$	$\frac{f}{f+m}100$	$\frac{f}{F}100$	$\frac{f}{f+m}100$	$\frac{f}{F}100$	$\frac{f}{f+m}100$	$\frac{f}{F}100$	$\frac{f}{f+m}100$	$\frac{f}{F}100$	$\frac{f}{f+m}100$
1977										
Persons with a main occupation	100,0	36,4	100,0	38,5	100,0	30,5	100,0	25,3	100,0	31,5
without change	70,7	35,2	79,5	37,9	80,5	28,8	84,0	23,8	81,0	31,1
change of country or region only	0,8	37,8	0,6	26,0	0,6	18,9	1,2	28,0	1,0	29,6
change in situation ([1])	11,5	56,3	11,2	52,4	12,3	50,4	10,6	46,8	9,3	49,3
change of activity ([2])	17,0	33,3	8,7	32,9	6,6	31,1	4,1	28,0	8,7	24,1
Unemployed persons	100,0	47,8	100,0	54,7	100,0	47,1	100,0	25,8	100,0	64,2
without change	30,0	39,4	31,9	56,4	54,8	50,0	24,1	16,8	55,1	69,5
change of country or region only	.	.	(1,1)	(54,6)	(1,0)	(57,1)	.	.	.	.
change in situation ([1])	69,3	52,5	67,0	53,9	44,2	45,6	75,9	31,0	44,3	58,5
Non-active persons	100,0	70,8	100,0	68,4	100,0	69,9	100,0	71,0	100,0	68,4
without change	85,1	70,6	82,6	67,7	92,6	71,8	92,8	71,2	94,0	68,8
change of country or region only	0,7	69,4	1,5	71,6	0,6	65,6	1,0	69,1	0,8	68,6
change in situation ([1])	14,2	73,2	16,0	71,8	6,8	70,4	6,2	68,4	5,2	61,5
Total population	100,0	53,3	100,0	52,4	100,0	52,1	100,0	50,6	100,0	51,4
without change	79,5	54,0	80,1	52,0	88,7	52,3	90,4	50,7	89,1	52,7
change of country or region only	0,7	53,3	1,1	51,9	0,6	38,6	1,1	50,3	0,8	47,3
change in situation ([1])	14,0	66,0	15,4	63,0	8,9	58,9	7,6	55,7	7,7	56,2
change of activity ([2])	5,8	33,4	3,4	33,0	1,8	31,1	0,9	28,0	2,4	24,1

[1] Change in usual situation with regard to economic activity.
[2] Change in professional status and/or of branch of activity.
[3] For comparison with the preceding year the figures of employment include occasional occupation.

TAB. 107
(continued)
(suite)

Luxembourg		United Kingdom		Ireland		Danmark		EUR 9		
$\frac{f}{F}\,100$	$\frac{f}{f+m}\,100$	$\frac{f}{F}\,100$	$\frac{f}{f+m}\,100$	$\frac{f}{F}\,100$	$\frac{f}{f+m}\,100$	$\frac{f}{F}\,100$	$\frac{f}{f+m}\,100$	$\frac{f}{F}\,100$	$\frac{f}{f+m}\,100$	
				1977						
100,0	28,9	100,0	38,7	100,0	26,3	100,0	39,5	100,0	35,5	**Personnes ayant un emploi principal**
87,1	27,3	81,9	37,2	86,6	25,4	76,1	39,2	78,3	34,2	sans changement
		0,5	28,8	.	.	.	.	0,6	27,6	changement pays ou région seulement
9,4	61,6	11,3	58,2	10,2	43,9	12,7	54,1	11,4	54,0	changement situation (¹)
(2,8)	(28,7)	6,3	35,7	2,8	21,2	11,2	35,4	9,7	32,9	changement activité (²)
100,0	(37,7)	100,0	36,2	100,0	20,8	100,0	51,5	100,0	45,6	**Personnes en chômage**
.	.	21,4	24,9	33,0	13,8	35,6	53,1	35,1	42,7	sans changement
.	.	.	.	.	.	.	.	0,7	51,7	changement pays ou région seulement
.	.	78,2	41,3	66,5	28,1	64,4	54,2	64,1	47,4	changement situation (¹)
100,0	72,6	100,0	70,7	100,0	74,2	100,0	66,7	100,0	70,0	**Personnes non actives**
97,3	73,1	86,6	71,7	96,6	74,4	80,9	68,1	87,6	70,5	sans changement
		1,0	70,0	0,6	70,4	.	.	0,9	69,6	changement pays ou région seulement
2,3	56,0	12,4	64,3	2,8	70,0	19,1	65,9	11,5	69,8	changement situation (¹)
100,0	51,7	100,0	52,0	100,0	49,9	100,0	50,9	100,0	52,3	**Population totale**
94,3	51,8	83,4	51,9	92,9	50,2	77,1	51,5	83,5	52,4	sans changement
(0,5)	(54,0)	0,8	51,1	0,6	53,9	.	.	0,8	49,0	changement pays ou région seulement
4,4	57,1	13,2	58,5	5,8	44,1	18,0	60,1	12,4	61,4	changement situation (¹)
(0,7)	(28,7)	2,6	35,7	0,7	21,1	4,9	35,4	3,3	32,9	changement activité (²)

(¹) Changement de la situation habituelle au regard de l'activité économique.
(²) Changement du statut professionnel et/ou de la branche d'activité.
(³) Pour la comparaison avec l'année précédente, les données de l'emploi incluent l'emploi occasionnel.

TAB. 108

Persons who have changed their country or region of residence compared with one year before the survey (%)
Personnes ayant changé de pays ou de région par rapport à un an avant l'enquête (%)

	BR Deutschland		France		Italia		Nederland		Belgique Belgïe	
	$\frac{f}{F}100$	$\frac{f}{f+m}100$	$\frac{f}{F}100$	$\frac{f}{f+m}100$	$\frac{f}{F}100$	$\frac{f}{f+m}100$	$\frac{f}{F}100$	$\frac{f}{f+m}100$	$\frac{f}{F}100$	$\frac{f}{f+m}100$
1975										
Persons who have changed their country of residence	19,4	54,9	22,2	44,9	11,0	28,8	19,8	48,6	51,5	37,0
of which:										
persons with a main occupation	5,9	34,0	6,0	24,5	2,3	10,1	5,5	27,8	15,2	17,9
labour force	6,6	33,9	7,4	26,2	2,6	10,5	5,5	25,0	18,2	19,4
non-active persons aged 14 years and over	12,8	80,4	14,8	69,6	8,1	59,5	13,3	75,0	33,3	68,8
of which: housewives	7,3	100,0	9,7	100,0	6,5	100,0	12,1	100,0	24,2	100,0
Persons who have changed their region of residence	80,6	49,2	37,8	51,1	89,0	40,5	80,2	51,0	48,5	45,7
of which:										
persons with a main occupation	32,9	36,3	26,2	33,5	19,8	18,7	24,2	31,4	18,2	28,6
labour force	36,0	36,7	33,8	36,2	21,8	18,7	25,3	31,5	21,2	30,4
non-active persons aged 14 years and over	44,6	67,2	44,0	74,5	67,5	65,4	54,9	78,4	27,3	75,0
of which: housewives	23,5	100,0	28,5	100,0	40,3	100,0	42,9	100,0	18,2	100,0
Persons who have changed their country or region of residence	100,0	50,2	100,0	49,5	100,0	38,8	100,0	50,6	100,0	40,7
1977										
Persons who have changed their country of residence	13,2	45,7	24,4	55,2	29,3	34,9	18,3	51,7	26,8	34,4
of which:										
persons with a main occupation	3,2	23,1	4,6	26,9	10,3	20,5	(4,9)	(28,6)	(9,8)	(19,0)
labour force	3,6	23,3	6,3	30,9	12,6	22,2	(4,9)	(25,0)	(9,8)	(18,2)
non-active persons aged 14 years and over	9,6	73,0	18,0	76,3	16,7	61,7	13,4	78,6	17,1	70,0
of which: housewives	6,4	100,0	11,4	100,0	12,1	100,0	11,0	100,0	12,2	100,0
Persons who have changed their region of residence	86,8	51,5	75,6	49,3	70,7	32,8	81,7	49,6	73,2	45,5
of which:										
persons with a main occupation	36,1	39,0	26,9	32,7	23,6	18,1	26,8	31,9	29,3	30,8
labour force	40,7	41,0	34,8	36,8	24,7	16,8	29,3	33,3	34,1	33,3
non-active persons aged 14 years and over	46,1	66,5	40,9	69,4	46,0	67,2	52,4	69,4	39,0	64,0
of which: housewives	23,9	100,0	26,1	100,0	22,4	100,0	40,2	100,0	24,4	100,0
Persons who have changed their country or region of residence	100,0	50,7	100,0	50,6	100,0	33,4	100,0	50,0	100,0	41,8

TAB. 108

Persons who have changed their country or region of residence compared with one year before the survey (%)
Personnes ayant changé de pays ou de région par rapport à un an avant l'enquête (%)

Luxembourg		United Kingdom		Ireland		Danmark		EUR 9		
$\frac{f}{F}100$	$\frac{f}{f+m}100$	$\frac{f}{F}100$	$\frac{f}{f+m}100$	$\frac{f}{F}100$	$\frac{f}{f+m}100$	$\frac{f}{F}100$	$\frac{f}{f+m}100$	$\frac{f}{F}100$	$\frac{f}{f+m}100$	
				1975						
(100,0)	(50,0)	31,3	46,9	100,0	50,0	100,0	50,0	22,7	44,2	Personnes ayant changé de pays
										dont:
.	.	11,5	32,5	(27,3)	(30,0)	.	.	6,8	25,3	personnes ayant un emploi principal
.	.	14,5	34,5	(36,4)	(28,6)	(40,0)	(40,0)	8,3	27,0	forces de travail
(100,0)	.	16,8	67,9	63,6	77,8	(60,0)	(75,0)	14,4	70,0	personnes non actives de 14 ans et plus
.	.	11,8	100,0	54,5.	100,0	.	.	10,1	100,0	dont: ménagères
–	–	68,7	49,9	–	–	–	–	77,3	47,5	Personnes ayant changé de région
										dont:
–	–	29,8	35,8	–	–	–	–	27,0	30,7	personnes ayant un emploi principal
–	–	36,0	37,9	–	–	–	–	31,1	32,1	forces de travail
–	–	32,7	76,6	–	–	–	–	46,2	70,3	personnes non actives de 14 ans et plus
–	–	22,7	100,0	–	–	–	–	29,0	100,0	dont: ménagères
(100,0)	(50,0)	100,0	48,9	100,0	50,0	100,0	50,0	100,0	46,7	Personnes ayant changé de pays ou région
				1977						
100,0	55,0	31,3	49,3	45,0	45,0	55,6	55,6	25,1	46,7	Personnes ayant changé de pays
										dont:
.	.	10,8	36,2	(10,0)	25,0	22,2	36,4	7,1	27,2	personnes ayant un emploi principal
.	.	13,3	37,8	(15,0)	27,3	33,3	46,2	8,9	29,3	forces de travail
.	.	18,0	63,3	30,0	66,7	(22,2)	(80,0)	16,2	69,3	personnes non actives de 14 ans et plus
.	.	11,4	100,0	25,0	100,0	(11,1)	100,0	10,9	100,0	dont: ménagères
–	–	68,7	50,1	–	–	–	–	74,9	47,0	Personnes ayant changé de région
										dont:
–	–	27,2	36,6	–	–	–	–	28,2	32,0	personnes ayant un emploi principal
–	–	31,6	37,7	–	–	–	–	33,1	33,7	forces de travail
–	–	37,3	70,2	–	–	–	–	41,8	68,5	personnes non actives de 14 ans et plus
–	–	24,4	100,0	–	–	–	–	25,1	100,0	dont: ménagères
100,0	55,0	100,0	49,8	100,0	45,0	100,0	55,6	100,0	46,9	Personnes ayant changé de pays ou région

General and vocational training
Formation générale et professionnelle

TAB. 109
Student population by level of studies (%)

Population étudiante selon le degré d'études (%)

	1970 – 1971		1971 – 1972		1972 – 1973		1973 – 1974	
	$\frac{f}{F}$ 100	$\frac{m}{M}$ 100	$\frac{f}{F}$ 100	$\frac{m}{M}$ 100	$\frac{f}{F}$ 100	$\frac{m}{M}$ 100	$\frac{f}{F}$ 100	$\frac{m}{M}$ 100
First level								
BR Deutschland	42,5	40,4	42,5	40,2	41,1	39,0	39,2	37,7
France	49,8	51,2	47,9	49,4	46,5	47,9	46,0	47,4
Italia	54,8	49,9	53,6	48,9	52,3	47,8	50,8	46,8
Nederland	59,6	53,4	58,0	52,2	56,6	51,5	55,1	50,3
Belgique/België	55,7	54,2	55,2	52,8	53,0	51,1	51,8	50,1
Luxembourg	59,3	57,7	58,9	58,9	57,6	56,1	57,3	55,8
United Kingdom	56,3	55,0	55,8	54,6	54,9	53,9	52,7	51,9
Ireland	62,9	63,1	61,6	61,9	60,5	61,1	59,6	60,5
Danmark	45,4	44,4	46,0	45,5	45,6	45,5	45,5	45,5
Second level								
BR Deutschland	52,6	51,1	52,1	50,5	53,3	51,2	54,3	52,3
France	43,6	40,4	45,0	42,2	46,0	43,4	46,5	43,8
Italia	39,3	41,7	40,0	42,1	41,1	43,0	42,3	43,9
Nederland	36,6	37,7	37,9	38,5	39,0	39,5	40,4	40,6
Belgique/België	39,3	37,9	39,5	39,1	41,0	40,4	41,8	41,1
Luxembourg	38,5	37,4	38,6	36,2	39,6	38,7	40,0	38,8
United Kingdom	40,1	40,0	40,6	40,3	41,4	41,0	43,6	43,1
Ireland	34,2	31,6	35,4	32,7	36,3	33,5	37,1	34,1
Danmark	47,8	44,9	46,8	42,9	46,2	42,6	46,0	42,3
of which: 1st stage								
BR Deutschland	46,7	44,9	45,9	43,9	46,6	44,3	47,1	45,2
France	28,2	26,3	28,9	27,4	29,8	28,7	30,3	29,2
Italia	23,3	22,6	23,8	23,0	24,4	23,6	24,9	24,1
Nederland	29,4	29,7	30,0	29,7	30,3	30,2	30,9	30,7
Belgique/België	26,4	27,1	26,0	28,1	27,1	28,8	27,5	29,0
Luxembourg	28,0	26,7	27,8	25,5	28,1	26,1	27,9	25,9
United Kingdom	23,9	23,3	23,8	23,5	24,2	23,8	23,9	23,7
Ireland	23,9	24,0	24,5	24,6	25,0	25,2	25,5	25,5
Danmark	40,2	37,7	38,8	35,6	37,9	35,0	37,2	34,4
Third level								
BR Deutschland	4,9	8,5	5,4	9,3	5,6	9,8	6,5	10,0
France	6,6	8,4	7,2	8,4	7,5	8,7	7,5	8,8
Italia	6,0	8,4	6,4	9,0	6,6	9,2	6,9	9,3
Nederland	3,8	8,9	4,1	9,3	4,4	9,0	4,5	9,1
Belgique/België	5,1	7,9	5,3	8,1	6,0	8,5	6,4	8,8
Luxembourg	2,2	4,9	2,5	4,9	2,8	5,2	2,7	5,4
United Kingdom	3,6	5,0	3,6	5,1	3,7	5,1	3,7	5,0
Ireland	2,9	5,3	3,0	5,4	3,2	5,4	3,3	5,4
Danmark	6,8	10,7	7,2	11,6	8,2	11,9	8,5	12,2

TAB. 109
Student population by level of studies (%)
Population étudiante selon le degré d'études (%)

1974 – 1975		1975 – 1976		1976 – 1977		1977 – 1978		
$\frac{f}{F}100$	$\frac{m}{M}100$	$\frac{f}{F}100$	$\frac{m}{M}100$	$\frac{f}{F}100$	$\frac{m}{M}100$	$\frac{f}{F}100$	$\frac{m}{M}100$	
								Premier degré
37,7	36,5	35,6	34,6	33,8	33,2	32,0	31,6	BR Deutschland
45,2	46,7	44,0	45,6	42,9	45,2	43,2	45,1	France
49,5	45,9	47,4	43,9	45,5	42,7	44,3	41,7	Italia
53,9	49,5	52,1	48,2	50,9	47,1	50,1	42,1	Nederland
51,0	49,7	50,2	49,0	48,8	47,9	47,6	47,2	Belgique/België
56,5	55,3	55,8	54,1	54,7	53,4	53,0	52,4	Luxembourg
51,6	51,0	50,4	49,8	49,3	48,9	48,5	48,0	United Kingdom
58,4	59,3	57,1	58,3	56,1	57,5	55,5	57,2	Ireland
44,9	45,6	42,6	43,1	41,5	42,0			Danmark
								Deuxième degré
55,2	53,2	57,2	54,8	58,9	56,1	60,4	57,5	BR Deutschland
47,2	44,2	47,8	45,1	48,7	45,5	48,3	45,5	France
43,2	44,5	45,2	46,1	46,8	47,1	47,7	48,1	Italia
41,5	41,4	42,7	42,2	43,5	42,9	43,9	42,8	Nederland
42,3	41,4	42,7	41,8	43,8	42,6	44,4	42,8	Belgique/België
40,6	39,2	41,0	40,0	42,3	40,6	43,1	42,6	Luxembourg
44,7	44,1	45,8	45,1	46,8	45,9	47,8	46,7	United Kingdom
38,3	35,2	39,3	36,2	40,0	36,8	40,4	37,0	Ireland
46,2	42,5	48,4	44,7	49,0	45,8			Danmark
								dont: 1er cycle
47,6	46,0	48,9	47,3	50,7	48,8	51,4	49,7	BR Deutschland
30,7	29,5	31,0	30,0	31,5	30,3	30,9	30,0	France
25,4	24,6	26,4	25,5	27,0	25,9	27,6	26,6	Italia
31,4	31,1	33,3	31,7	33,5	31,9	33,2	31,5	Nederland
27,2	28,6	27,1	28,3	27,2	28,5	27,2	28,6	Belgique/België
27,7	25,0	27,5	25,5	28,6	25,4	28,7	26,8	Luxembourg
24,4	24,2	24,6	24,4	24,9	24,7	25,2	25,1	United Kingdom
25,6	26,2	25,8	26,3	25,8	26,3	25,8	26,3	Ireland
37,3	34,6	38,9	36,6	39,1	37,9			Danmark
								Troisième degré
7,1	10,3	7,2	10,6	7,3	10,7	7,6	10,9	BR Deutschland
7,6	9,1	8,2	9,3	8,2	9,3	8,5	9,4	France
7,3	9,6	7,4	10,0	7,7	10,2	8,0	10,2	Italia
4,6	9,1	5,2	9,6	5,6	10,0	6,0	10,3	Nederland
6,7	8,9	7,1	9,2	7,4	9,5	8,0	10,0	Belgique/België
2,9	5,5	3,2	5,9	3,0	6,0	4,0	5,0	Luxembourg
3,7	4,9	3,8	5,1	3,9	5,2	3,7	5,3	United Kingdom
3,3	5,5	3,6	5,5	3,9	5,7	4,1	5,8	Ireland
8,9	11,9	9,0	12,2	9,5	12,2			Danmark

TAB. 110

Growth of the student population at each level (index 1970/1971 = 100)

Évolution de la population étudiante à chaque degré (indice 1970/1971 = 100)

	1971 – 1972		1972 – 1973		1973 – 1974		1974 – 1975	
	F	M	F	M	F	M	F	M
First level								
BR Deutschland	104,5	104,5	104,8	105,0	103,7	104,2	102,2	102,8
France	98,1	97,8	96,9	96,0	96,3	96,2	94,9	95,4
Italia	101,5	101,2	102,4	101,9	102,3	101,7	101,8	100,7
Nederland	100,2	100,3	100,1	100,0	99,6	99,7	99,0	99,3
Belgique/België	100,5	99,2	98,0	94,8	96,2	93,1	94,9	92,0
Luxembourg	100,3	111,1	99,1	101,0	101,5	100,7	101,4	100,5
United Kingdom	101,5	101,6	101,6	101,7	101,4	101,6	100,3	100,4
Ireland	99,7	99,8	100,8	101,1	101,7	102,4	102,6	103,4
Danmark	104,3	106,0	107,7	109,7	111,3	113,6	111,3	114,5
Second level								
BR Deutschland	103,7	103,5	109,9	108,7	116,1	113,9	121,2	118,3
France	105,4	106,1	109,6	111,2	111,5	113,1	113,3	114,4
Italia	105,6	104,6	112,5	109,8	119,1	114,2	123,8	116,9
Nederland	106,5	105,0	112,5	108,9	119,0	114,1	124,0	117,9
Belgique/België	101,8	105,1	107,5	106,9	109,9	109,2	111,6	109,5
Luxembourg	101,2	105,4	105,1	107,6	109,3	108,4	112,4	110,1
United Kingdom	103,5	103,3	107,4	106,7	117,5	115,9	121,6	119,5
Ireland	105,4	105,4	111,2	110,4	116,4	115,3	123,8	122,3
Danmark	100,5	98,6	103,6	101,3	107,0	104,5	108,5	105,3
of which: 1st stage								
BR Deutschland	102,9	102,5	108,3	107,2	113,4	112,1	117,8	116,3
France	104,7	105,7	109,8	112,9	112,1	115,9	113,7	117,3
Italia	105,8	105,2	112,6	111,0	118,1	115,5	122,7	118,8
Nederland	105,3	102,7	109,0	105,7	113,5	109,5	117,0	112,3
Belgique/België	99,8	105,3	106,0	106,5	107,6	107,7	107,0	105,8
Luxembourg	100,5	103,7	102,7	101,7	105,0	101,1	105,5	98,1
United Kingdom	102,1	103,2	106,2	106,5	109,2	109,5	112,2	113,4
Ireland	104,0	104,0	109,2	109,3	114,2	113,6	118,3	119,6
Danmark	99,2	97,5	101,0	99,3	102,8	101,4	104,2	102,2
Third level								
BR Deutschland	115,9	113,5	124,3	125,0	148,6	130,8	166,3	137,3
France	111,5	100,5	118,1	106,0	119,8	108,1	121,1	112,2
Italia	111,2	111,6	119,6	116,6	128,3	120,3	137,5	125,7
Nederland	112,3	107,6	123,5	105,3	128,0	108,7	132,7	109,8
Belgique/België	106,9	104,4	121,1	108,3	131,4	112,0	137,8	112,8
Luxembourg	114,6	107,7	129,9	110,0	127,8	114,4	141,8	118,7
United Kingdom	103,3	103,3	107,1	104,4	111,5	106,2	113,1	105,5
Ireland	105,5	102,5	116,8	104,6	122,8	108,0	128,9	113,0
Danmark	108,3	112,0	129,8	118,7	139,5	126,1	146,2	123,8
Total (excluding pre-school level)								
BR Deutschland	104,6	104,8	108,5	108,6	112,4	111,4	115,3	113,6
France	102,2	101,4	103,8	103,5	104,5	104,0	104,6	104,5
Italia	103,7	103,5	107,4	106,4	110,4	108,5	112,5	109,5
Nederland	103,0	102,7	105,5	103,8	107,8	105,9	109,4	107,2
Belgique/België	101,3	101,8	102,9	100,4	103,4	100,7	103,6	100,3
Luxembourg	101,0	108,8	102,1	103,9	105,1	104,3	106,5	105,0
United Kingdom	102,4	102,4	104,1	103,8	108,2	107,5	109,3	108,3
Ireland	101,9	101,7	104,8	104,3	107,4	106,8	110,6	109,6
Danmark	102,8	103,3	107,5	106,9	111,4	110,9	112,6	111,4

TAB. 110

Growth of the student population at each level (index 1970/1971 = 100)
Évolution de la population étudiante à chaque degré (indice 1070/1971 = 100)

1975 – 1976		1976 – 1977		1977 – 1978		
F	M	F	M	F	M	
						Premier degré
98,3	98,8	94,2	95,1	88,7	89,7	BR Deutschland
93,4	93,5	91,4	93,7	92,5	92,5	France
99,5	98,5	97,5	96,6	95,4	93,9	Italia
99,5	99,7	99,3	99,4	99,1	89,6	Nederland
93,3	90,5	91,1	88,4	89,3	87,0	Belgique/België
101,0	100,0	99,6	97,7	97,9	96,3	Luxembourg
98,8	98,9	97,3	97,5	94,8	95,0	United Kingdom
103,0	104,1	103,3	104,7	104,4	105,7	Ireland
107,2	108,2	104,5	104,8			Danmark
						Deuxième degré
128,1	123,6	132,7	126,7	135,5	128,5	BR Deutschland
116,1	117,2	118,4	119,9	118,3	118,6	France
132,4	123,8	140,1	127,6	143,3	129,9	Italia
132,8	124,0	137,9	128,4	141,1	129,4	Nederland
112,5	110,6	116,0	112,2	117,9	112,7	Belgique/België
114,5	114,2	118,3	114,8	122,6	120,9	Luxembourg
126,1	123,4	129,1	126,3	130,9	127,5	United Kingdom
130,5	129,3	135,8	133,8	139,6	136,7	Ireland
115,7	110,7	117,1	113,0			Danmark
						dont: 1er cycle
123,3	121,6	128,8	125,7	129,9	126,7	BR Deutschland
116,2	120,0	118,3	122,6	116,7	120,0	France
130,5	126,2	135,8	129,4	139,7	132,6	Italia
129,0	118,3	132,6	121,3	132,9	120,7	Nederland
106,4	104,7	107,2	104,9	107,7	105,0	Belgique/België
105,5	101,9	110,0	100,4	112,4	106,4	Luxembourg
114,6	114,8	115,4	116,6	115,9	117,4	United Kingdom
122,2	123,4	125,0	125,8	127,4	127,8	Ireland
110,6	108,1	111,2	111,4			Danmark
						Troisième degré
173,2	143,9	175,7	145,3	183,2	145,7	BR Deutschland
132,5	115,7	134,6	116,6	138,1	117,7	France
143,6	133,7	151,4	137,5	157,2	137,6	Italia
157,5	120,4	173,0	127,2	187,2	132,6	Nederland
145,0	116,3	153,1	119,6	165,5	125,7	Belgique/België
154,1	128,1	148,6	128,5	196,2	108,8	Luxembourg
116,9	110,2	119,1	112,4	113,7	114,6	United Kingdom
142,4	116,6	155,6	122,4	168,1	126,0	Ireland
151,6	127,3	159,3	126,8			Danmark
						Total
						(sans préprimaire)
117,6	115,3	118,4	115,5	118,0	114,3	BR Deutschland
105,9	105,0	106,0	106,2	106,7	105,2	France
115,1	112,0	117,4	112,9	117,9	112,6	Italia
113,9	110,7	116,2	112,8	117,8	113,8	Nederland
103,5	100,2	104,0	99,9	104,4	99,8	Belgique/België
107,4	106,7	107,8	105,6	109,6	106,1	Luxembourg
110,4	109,3	110,8	109,7	110,0	109,0	United Kingdom
113,5	112,7	115,9	114,8	118,3	116,6	Ireland
114,6	111,3	114,6	110,8			Danmark

TAB. 111

Overall degrees of scholarization (%)
Taux globaux de scolarisation (%)

	1962–1963		1965–1966		1970–1971		1974–1975		1975–1976		1976–1977	
	F	M	F	M	F	M	F	M	F	M	F	M
School population as a percentage of the total population												
Effectifs scolaires en pourcentage de la population totale												
BR Deutschland	11,9	14,3	12,4	14,7	14,7	17,8	16,7	19,9	17,1	20,4	17,2	20,5
France	18,9	18,6	18,8	19,5	19,2	20,8	19,5	21,2	19,7	21,0	19,6	21,2
Italia	12,8	15,6	13,7	16,7	15,8	19,4	17,2	20,5	17,5	20,9	17,7	20,9
Nederland	18,7	20,9	18,6	21,0	18,9	22,6	19,9	23,5	20,5	23,9	20,8	24,3
Belgique/België	16,2	18,8	17,0	19,0	18,2	21,3	18,6	21,1	18,5	21,0	18,6	20,9
Luxembourg	13,0	14,7	13,7	15,6	15,2	16,0	15,5	17,0	15,6	17,3	15,8	17,1
United Kingdom	:	:	15,9	18,1	17,8	20,1	19,3	21,6	19,5	21,8	19,5	21,9
Ireland	:	:	20,0	20,4	21,0	21,7	22,1	22,7	22,4	23,1	22,7	23,4
Danmark	:	:	:	:	16,5	17,8	18,1	19,5	18,4	19,5	18,3	19,3
School population as a percentage of the population aged from 5 to 24 years												
Effectifs scolaires en pourcentage de la population âgée de 5 à 24 ans												
BR Deutschland	:	:	48,9	49,7	54,8	58,2	59,0	61,6	60,5	63,0	61,1	63,2
France	:	:	62,3	58,2	60,3	60,0	63,0	62,5	63,9	62,8	63,9	63,6
Italia	:	:	46,3	53,8	53,1	60,0	58,5	64,0	59,7	65,3	60,5	65,4
Nederland	:	:	54,1	57,6	54,8	61,6	58,9	65,7	60,7	67,2	61,8	68,3
Belgique/België	:	:	60,5	62,2	60,7	65,4	62,4	64,9	62,2	64,6	62,5	64,5
Luxembourg	:	:	50,3	53,3	54,1	56,8	53,8	55,6	54,8	57,1	55,5	56,8
United Kingdom	:	:	57,8	59,1	61,1	63,0	66,3	67,2	66,8	67,4	66,9	67,6
Ireland	:	:	57,0	56,8	57,8	57,7	60,1	59,4	60,7	60,2	61,3	60,6
Danmark	:	:	:	:	54,6	55,2	61,9	62,2	63,4	62,6	63,3	62,2

TAB. 112
Student population by level and type of studies (unit)
Population étudiante selon le type et le degré d'études (unité)

	1970 – 1971		1972 – 1973		1973 – 1974	
	F	M	F	M	F	M
BR Deutschland						
Elementarstufe	594 851	599 307	670 557	714 910	707 096	756 885
Kindergarten	580 368	580 368	641 700	678 154	673 400	714 681
Schulkindergärten und Vorklassen ⎫ Sonderschulkindergärten und V. ⎭	14 483	18 939	28 857	36 756	33 696	42 204
Primarstufe	1 990 751	2 092 431	2 086 893	2 197 530	2 063 829	2 179 587
Grundschulen	1 946 414	2 026 090	2 030 776	2 115 515	2 008 076	2 098 102
Grundstufe der Gesamtschulen	–	–	6 191	6 384	6 288	6 665
Sonderschulen (an Grundschulen)	44 337	66 341	49 926	75 631	49 465	74 820
Sekundarstufe	2 459 285	2 651 065	2 703 375	2 882 422	2 854 148	3 020 670
Sonderschulen (an Haupt- und Realschulen)	85 402	125 957	96 256	142 875	102 153	151 328
Unterstufe	2 097 988	2 202 505	2 267 550	2 352 465	2 373 027	2 458 146
Hauptschulen	1 166 543	1 208 404	1 149 440	1 213 555	1 154 217	1 239 362
Realschulen	456 784	406 666	527 148	454 054	562 665	480 905
Gesamtschulen	–	–	31 710	34 277	43 248	46 230
Gymnasien	474 661	587 435	556 872	648 252	607 606	684 276
Berufsgrundschuljahr	–	–	2 380	2 327	5 291	7 373
Oberstufe	275 895	322 603	339 569	387 082	378 968	411 195
Gymnasien	131 536	185 823	159 252	202 898	178 710	216 028
Gesamtschulen			2148	2 543	2 115	2 419
Berufsaufbauschulen	4 375	9 050	3 416	11 694	6 283	17 516
Fachgymnasien	11 955	47 018	26 669	78 997	30 965	84 059
Berufsfachschulen	128 029	80 712	148 084	90 950	160 895	91 173
Tertiarstufe	230 255	442 227	286 339	552 700	342 242	578 399
Wiss. Hochschulen, Universitäten	87 348	260 957	117 380	346 764	149 935	362 130
Fachschulen	35 930	52 462	43 988	71 508	48 900	70 212
Schulen des Gesundheitswesens	54 248	7 185	58 575	9 315	61 875	11 176
Fachhochschulen	11 561	93 692	15 080	88 406	25 563	96 820
Pädagogische Hochschulen	37 054	21 748	46 031	28 753	49929	29 175
Kunsthochschulen	4 114	6 289	5 285	7 954	6 040	8 886
Insgesamt (ohne Elementarstufe)	4 680 291	5 185 723	5 076 607	5 632 652	5 260 219	5 778 656
Insgesamt (inkl. Elementarstufe)	5 275 142	5 785 030	5 747 164	6 347 562	5 967 315	6 535 541
France						
Enseignement préprimaire	1 083 050	1 130 296	1 130 000*	1 240 614*	1 204 000*	1 253 700*
Ens. préscolaire	1 083 050	1 130 296	:	:	:	:
Ens. spécial	–	–	–	–	:	:
Enseignement du 1er degré	2 496 834	2 650 448	2 418 800*	2 568 339	2 404 000*	2 550 000*
Ens. élémentaire	2 348 845	2 450 166	:	:	:	:
Cl. de fin d'etudes	63 554	77 118	:	:	:	:
Ens. spécial	84 435	123 164	:	:	:	:
Enseignement spécial (niveau scolaire indéterminé)	:	:	:	:	:	:
Enseignement du 2e degré	2 192 518	2 101 245	2 391 436	2 322 137	2 432 787	2 360 938
Ens. spécial	10 533	13 568	22 400	28 507	26 902	35 856
1er cycle	1 413 228	1 358 327	1 528 667	1 505 300	1 557 398	1 538 326
Premier cycle	1 413 228	1 358 327	1 507 163	1 469 559	1 516 678	1 468 074
Classes nouvelles	–	–	21 504	35 741	40 720	70 252
2e cycle	768 757	729 350	840 369	788 330	848 487	786 756
Ens. professionnel court	325 655	332 620	331 054	355 948	332 810	361 271
Deuxième cycle long	443 102	396 730	509 315	432 382	515 677	425 485
– Ens. général	370 576	318 174	414 916	285 274	410 436	278 385
– Ens. technologique	72 526	78 556	94 399	147 108	105 241	147 100
Enseignement du 3e degré						
Universités	329 568	436 319	389 121	465 539	394 779	471 863
dont:	294 000	367 156	345 474	389 577	346 480	394 957
– IUT	5 795	18 400	10 284	25 138	11 933	27 347
– ENSI – INP	271	4 486	405	4 783		
Non universitaire	35 568	69 163	43 647	75 962	48 299	76 906
dont:	21 279	38 162	25 100	36 695	29 496	38 279
– CPGE – STS	12 864	10 297	16 280	11 518	16 424	11 399
– Ecoles normales et CRF	1 425	20 704	2 267	27 749	2 379	27 228
– Grandes écoles (école ing. non un.)	5 018 920	5 118 849	5 199 357	5 356 015	5 231 566	5 382 801
Total (sans préprimaire)	6 101 970	6 249 145	6 329 357	6 596 629	6 435 566	6 636 501
Total (préprimaire inclus)						

TAB. 112

Student population by level and type of studies (unit)
Population étudiante selon le type et le degré d'études (unité)

1974 – 1975		1975 – 1976		1976 – 1977		1977 – 1978		
F	M	F	M	F	M	F	M	
BR Deutschland								
800 209	853 374	795 440	849 985	854 436	910 775	780 522	852 275	**Elementarstufe**
762 200	805 200	756 000	801 000	817 300	864 600	745 968	808 132	Kindergarten
								{ Schulkindergärten und Vorklassen
38 009	48 174	39 440	48 985	37 136	46 175	34 554	44 143	{ Sonderschulkindergärten und V.
2 034 005	2 150 690	1 956 300	2 067 899	1 875 035	1 989 517	1 766 507	1 876 629	**Primarstufe**
1 978 267	2 068 321	1 901 243	1 987 184	1 822 268	1 910 081	1 714 777	1 797 694	Grundschulen
6 619	6 957	7 330	7 439	7 594	7 728	5 678	5 660	Grundstufe der Gesamtschulen
49 119	75 412	47 727	73 276	45 173	71 708	46 052	73 275	Sonderschulen (an Grundschulen)
2 981 260	3 135 138	3 149 873	3 276 750	3 263 462	3 358 871	3 332 980	3 407 403	**Sekundarstufe**
105 102	155 255	109 576	163 221	113 511	167 784	111 994	166 694	Sonderschulen (an Haupt- und Realschulen)
2 467 772	2 552 990	2 583 093	2 667 663	2 699 017	2 758 568	2 754 771	2 808 101	Unterstufe
1 163 020	1 272 201	1 205 812	1 330 877	1 206 001	1 339 214	1 181 714	1 324 943	Hauptschulen
594 781	505 530	620 001	527 216	676 378	572 274	712 088	604 581	Realschulen
56 175	60 389	69 313	74 534	78 714	84 208	85 223	90 912	Gesamtschulen
646 190	705 368	675 453	719 064	715 492	740 993	746 040	759 570	Gymnasien
7 606	9 502	12 514	15 972	22 432	21 879	29 706	28 095	Berufsgrundschuljahr
408 386	426 893	457 204	445 866	450 934	432 519	466 215	432 608	Oberstufe
196 697	231 386	217 690	251 272	211 632	245 837	218 347	247 751	Gymnasien
2 537	2 771	3 428	3 768	3 993	4 645	4 989	5 773	Gesamtschulen
3 863	10 815	4 017	10 095	3 439	8 641	2 961	6 881	Berufsaufbauschulen
32 860	84 657	34 118	80 109	38 285	83 549	37 624	78 069	Fachgymnasien
172 429	97 264	197 951	100 622	193 585	89 847	202 294	94 134	Berufsfachschulen
383 125	607 215	398 850	636 248	404 647	642 494	421 726	644 174	**Tertiarstufe**
175 951	386 447	191 286	404 858	202 314	423 489	219 193	436 641	Wiss. Hochschulen, Universitäten
53 193	69 441	42 938	67 638	35 899	48 941	34 443	36 539	Fachschulen
68 046	12 949	73 799	14 721	75 710	14 682	75 505	13 768	Schulen des Gesundheitswesens
29 145	101 163	33 347	112 055	36 551	121 102	40 503	125 584	Fachhochschulen
50 554	28 291	51 044	28 069	47 649	25 500	45 261	23 107	Pädagogische Hochschulen
6 236	8 924	6 436	8 907	6 524	8 780	6 821	8 535	Kunsthochschulen
5 398 390	5 893 043	5 505 023	5 980 897	5 543 144	5 990 882	5 521 213	5 928 206	**Insgesamt** (ohne Elementarstufe)
6 198 599	6 746 417	6 300 463	6 830 882	6 397 580	6 901 657	6 301 735	6 780 481	**Insgesamt** (inkl. Elementarstufe)
France								
1 217 000*	1 326 300*	1 275 000*	1 333 400*	1 270 000*	1 346 900*	1 264 000*	1 334 000*	**Enseignement préprimaire**
		1 270 042	1 321 100	1 264 883	1 333 786	1 257 000	1 319 000	Ens. préscolaire
:	:	:	:	:	:	:	:	Ens. spécial
2 369 838	2 529 236	2 333 000*	2 478 400	2 281 000*	2 483 600*	2 330 000*	2 479 000*	**Enseignement du 1er degré**
:	:	2 253 200	2 357 284	2 203 211	2 364 923	2 249 000	2 369 400	Ens. élémentaire
		1 280	1 793	–	–	–	–	Cl. de fin d'études
:	:	:	:	:	:	:	:	Ens. spécial
		10 000*	17 000*	15 000*	22 000*	13 000*	24 000*	**Enseignement spécial** (niveau scolaire indéterminé)
2 471 295	2 387 636	2 532 942	2 447 532	2 584 413	2 503 257	2 537 063	2 504 900	**Enseignement du 2e degré**
31 456	42 228	45 000*	64 095	60 000	81 900	63 000	94 000	Ens. spécial
1 575 381	1 550 357	1 596 740	1 565 793	1 611 386	1 583 959	1 604 700	1 565 100	1er cycle
1 516 961	1 451 217	1 531 128	1 458 224	1 541 934	1 472 689	1 532 100	1 451 300	Premier cycle
58 420	99 140	65 612	107 569	69 452	111 270	72 600	113 800	Classes nouvelles
864 458	795 051	891 202	818 644	913 027	837 353	932 300	845 800	2e cycle
342 120	371 082	354 372	391 968	354 318	397 919	355 200	400 800	Ens. professionnel court
522 338	423 969	536 830	426 679	558 709	439 434	577 100	445 000	Deuxième cycle long
408 041	272 802	428 781	328 119	443 300	336 423	456 700	340 000	– Ens. général
114 297	151 167	108 049	98 557	115 409	103 011	120 400	105 000	– Ens. technologique
399 344	489 657	436 650	504 904	443 656	508 789	455 100	513 600	**Enseignement du 3e degré**
357 900	402 690	383 800	422 468	390 181	426 100	399 200	432 900	Universités
								dont:
12 650	29 299	13 543	29 983	14 148	30 095	15 700	31 700	– IUT
		700	5 196	:	:	900	6 335	– ENSI – INP
41 444	86 967	52 850	82 436	53 075	82 689	55 900	80 700	Non universitaire
								dont:
22 863	49 372	35 162	46 366	37 236	47 885	41 900	49 100	– CPGE – STS
15 803	10 714	14 577	10 028	12 811	8 510	10 600	7 300	– Écoles normales et CRF
2 778	26 881	3 111	26 042	3 428	26 294	3 400	24 300	– Grandes écoles (école ing. non un.)
5 240 477	5 406 529	5 312 592	5 447 836	5 324 069	5 517 646	5 335 163	5 521 500	**Total** (sans préprimaire)
6 457 477	6 732 829	6 587 592	6 781 236	6 594 069	6 864 546	6 599 163	6 855 500	**Total** (préprimaire inclus)

TAB. 112
(continued)
(suite)

	1970 – 1971		1972 – 1973		1973 – 1974	
	F	M	F	M	F	M

Italia

	F	M	F	M	F	M
Educazione prescolastica	777 874	808 911	823 128	863 254	850 313	884 397
Scuole del grado preparatorio	777 874	808 911	823 128	863 250	850 313	884 397
Educazione primaria	2 378 259	2 550 445	2 435 633	2 599 163	2 432 710	2 594 252
Scuole elementari e sussidiate	2 351 309	2 505 644	2 412 119	2 561 762	2 410 594	2 563 287
Scuole speciali	26 950	44 801	23 514	33 966	22 116	38 800
Educazione secondaria	1 705 114	2 127 890	1 919 041	2 335 765	2 031 018	2 429 138
Ciclo inferiore	1 012 464	1 155 075	1 140 117	1 281 682	1 196 050	1 334 411
Scuola media inferiore	1 012 464	1 155 075	1 140 117	1 281 682	1 196 050	1 334 411
Ciclo superiore	692 650	972 815	778 924	1 054 083	834 968	1 094 727
Istr. professionale	107 787	152 682	127 660	169 348	138 567	178 558
Istr. tecnica	161 840	514 827	204 807	558 710	229 079	579 618
Istr. magistrale	197 380	23 977	180 946	19 472	181 382	19 037
– Scuole magistrali	24 814	–	22 741	–	23 956	–
– Istituti magistrali	172 566	23 977	158 205	19 473	157 426	17 963
Istr. scientifica e classica	198 207	260 185	231 160	279 155	249 543	289 387
– Licei scientifici	92 813	160 684	124 157	186 312	141 753	198 519
– Ginnasi e licei classici	105 394	99 501	107 003	92 843	107 790	90 868
Istr. artistica	27 436	18 144	34 351	27 397	36 397	29 201
– Scuole e istituti d'arte	11 675	9 173	13 999	11 310	14 972	11 941
– Licei artistici	11 886	6 498	15 168	8 722	15 739	9 108
– Conservatori ed ist. di musica	3 875	5 473	5 184	7 365	5 686	8 152
Educazione superiore	258 995	428 153	309 800	499 081	332 181	515 140
Università	256 489	425 242	306 940	495 663	329 042	511 455
Studenti iscritti	210 833	349 772	254 055	403 561	266 373	408 803
Studenti fuori corso	45 656	75 470	52 885	92 102	62 669	102 652
Accademia di belle arti	2 506	2 911	2 860	3 418	3 139	3 685
Totale (Senza ed. prescolastica)	4 342 368	5 106 488	4 664 474	5 434 010	4 695 909	5 538 530
Totale (Con ed. prescolastica)	5 120 242	5 915 399	5 487 602	6 297 264	5 646 222	6 422 927

Nederland

	F	M	F	M	F	M
Kleuteronderwijs	240 408	253 039	242 006	255 070	248 145	260 134
Kleuteronderwijs	239 680	252 052	241 218	253 843	247 295	258 694
Buitengewoon onderwijs	728	987	788	1 277	850	1 440
Eerste niveau	739 974	789 761	740 830	789 936	736 689	787 540
Gewoon lager onderwijs	717 218	745 158	717 913	743 631	714 094	740 877
Buitengewoon onderwijs	22 756	44 603	22 917	46 305	22 595	46 663
Tweede niveau	454 610	556 601	511 482	606 293	541 157	634 840
Buitengewoon onderwijs	1 864	3 123	2 423	4 472	2 973	5 773
Lagerecyclus	362 774	435 428	395 018	459 223	410 865	474 331
Algemeen woortgezet ond.	230 707	239 454	254 970	255 490	270 934	266 973
Lager beroepsonderwijs	132 067	195 974	140 048	203 733	139 931	207 358
Daaronder:						
Lager tech. ondernw.	860	155 682	2 269	167 852	3 079	170 400
Lager huishoud. N.	113 840	137	117 576	496	116 122	1 022
Hogere cyclus	89 972	118 050	114 041	142 598	127 319	154 836
Algemeen voortgezet onder.	50 575	70 575	64 136	87 549	73 494	95 178
Middelbaar bereopsond.	39 397	47 475	49 095	55 049	53 825	59 658
Daaronder:						
Middelbaar tech.	963	31 272	1 219	36 599	1 445	3 273
Middelbaar huis. ennij.	27 057	9	32 460	95	34 990	153
Opleidm kleuterdeist	7 429	–	10 685	–	10 831	–
Derde niveau	46 715	131 090	57 672	138 040	59 806	142 452
Hoger beroepsonderwijs	26 377	48 046	31 672	51 540	33 806	55 952
Daaronder:						
Hoger tech. onderw.	2 263	16 810	2 957	19 588	2 930	20 921
Oplei dincssh. voorondeɪ	7 640	10 359	10 720	10 971	11 701	12 150
Wetenshappelijk onderwijs	20 338	83 044	26 000*	86 500*	26 000*	86 500*
Total (zonder kleuteronder.)	1 241 299	1 477 452	1 309 984	1 534 269	1 337 652	1 564 832
Total (met kleuteronder.)	1 481 707	1 730 491	1 551 990	1 789 339	1 585 797	1 824 966

TAB. 112
(continued)
(suite)

1974 – 1975		1975 – 1976		1976 – 1977		1977 – 1978		
F	M	F	M	F	M	F	M	
			Italia					
866 077	901 535	892 143	930 384	915 865	950 239	928 822	965 416	**Educazione prescolastica**
866 077	901 525	892 143	930 384	915 865	950 239	928 822	965 416	Scuole del grado preparatorio
2 420 725	2 567 181	2 366 495	2 513 028	2 314 439	2 456 481	2 268 890	2 406 610	**Educazione primaria**
2 401 527	2 536 662	2 349 490	2 485 996	2 300 970	2 435 070	2 258 465	2 390 039	Scuole elementari e sussidiate
19 198	30 519	17 005	27 032	13 469	21 411	10 425	16 571	Scuole speciali
2 110 497	2 487 398	2 258 340	2 633 301	2 364 299	2 722 144	2 455 865	2 774 090	**Educazione secondaria**
1 242 586	1 372 607	1 321 447	1 457 150	1 367 255	1 502 338	1 405 196	1 533 595	Ciclo inferiore
1 242 586	1 372 607	1 321 447	1 457 150	1 367 255	1 502 338	1 405 196	1 533 595	Scuola media inferiore
867 911	1 114 791	936 893	1 176 151	997 044	1 219 806	1 050 669	1 240 495	Ciclo superiore
143 714	181 427	157 203	190 390	168 595	201 929	181 742	217 603	Istr. professionale
252 195	595 522	290 361	641 642	324 276	670 419	351 641	678 565	Istr. tecnica
178 934	16 883	183 161	15 265	187 412	14 053	193 034	13 265	Istr. magistrale
25 458	–	27 330	–	28 876	–	30 229	–	– Scuole magistrali
153 476	16 883	155 831	15 265	158 536	14 053	162 805	13 265	– Istituti magistrali
255 605	291 533	266 518	297 970	275 042	300 469	280 025	297 034	Istr. scientifica e classica
150 002	203 531	161 720	211 894	171 535	215 310	176 756	213 021	– Licei scientifici
105 603	88 002	104 798	86 076	103 507	85 159	103 269	84 013	– Ginnasi e licei classici
37 463	29 326	39 650	30 884	41 719	32 936	44 227	34 028	Istr. artistica
		16 406	12 583	17 860	13 053	19 785	13 249	– Scuole e istituti d'arte
31 081	20 593	16 164	8 919	15 807	8 835	15 477	8 514	– Licei artistici
6 382	7 456	7 080	9 382	8 052	11 048	8 965	12 265	– Conservatori ed ist. di musica
356 021	538 284	371 865	572 523	396 957	593 436	411 562	592 567	**Educazione superiore**
352 428	534 466	367 780	568 015	392 549	588 799	407 254	588 908	Universita
284 897	423 860	291 363	444 940	306 048	456 020	314 925	447 900	Studenti iscritti
67 531	110 606	76 417	123 075	86 501	132 779	92 329	141 008	Studenti fuor corso
3 593	3 818	4 085	4 508	4 408	4 637	4 308	3 659	Accademia di belle arti
4 887 243	5 592 863	4 996 700	5 718 852	5 075 695	5 772 061	5 136 317	5 773 267	**Totale** (Senza ed. prescolastica)
5 753 320	6 494 398	5 888 843	6 649 236	5 991 560	6 722 300	6 065 139	6 738 683	**Totale** (Con ed. prescolastica)
			Nederland					
251 773	264 178	253 706	267 634	244 150	257 181	228 634	239 958	**Kleuteronderwijs**
250 905	262 701	252 806	266 084	243 250	255 581	227 684	238 308	Kleuteronderwijs
868	1 477	900*	1 550*	900*	1 600*	950*	1 650*	Buitengewoon onderwijs
732 886	783 946	736 453	787 414	734 633	784 951	728 748	778 457	**Eerste niveau**
710 545	736 805	714 053	739 414	711 833	736 251	705 748	728 957	Gewoon lager onderwijs
22 341	47 141	22 400*	48 000*	22 800*	48 700*	23 000*	49 500*	Buitengewoon onderwijs
563 465	656 245	603 723	690 362	626 999	714 882	644 657	727 876	**Tweede niveau**
3 166	6 359	3 400*	7 100*	3 500*	7400*	3 400*	7 800*	Buitengewoon onderwijs
423 438	486 043	466 947	511 814	479 823	524 712	484 702	529 314	Lagerecyclus
284 242	275 397	293 643	282 211	303 970	288 366	310 047	291 226	Algemeen woortgezet ond.
139 196	210 606	173 304	229 603	175 853	236 346	174 655	238 088	Lager beroepsonderwijs
								Daaronder:
3 920	171 122	5 869	185 203	7 024	188 522	7 705	188 091	Lager tech. ondernw.
112 865	1 378	141 920	1 718	141 069	2 296	137 328	2 681	Lager huishoud. N.
136 861	163 843	133 376	171 448	143 676	182 770	156 555	190 762	Hogere cyclus
80 231	100 370	86 471	104 066	93 293	109 116	98 202	112 523	Algemeen voortgezet onder.
56 630	63 473	46 905	67 382	50 383	73 654	58 353	78 239	Middelbaar bereopsond.
								Daaronder:
1 659	41 386	2 011	42 990	2 305	45 283	2 616	46 718	Middelbaar tech.
36 577	294	25 534	499	26 487	853	32 715	1 068	Middelbaar huis. ennij.
10 820	–	10 789	–	10 643	57	10 031	66	Opleidm kleuterdeist
62 000*	143 900*	73 570	157 809	80 799	166 752	87 430	173 758	**Derde niveau**
36 000*	57 400*	43 575*	67 674*	46 997	71 384	49 908	73 854	Hoger beroepsonderwijs
								Daaronder:
2 957	20 675	2 919	21 451	2 990	22 502	3 157	23 417	Hoger tech. onderw.
12 359	12 404	12 908	12 317	14 051	12 069	14 317	11 090	Oplei dincssh. vooronder
26 000*	86 500*	29 995	90 135	33 802	95 368	37 522	99 904	Wetenshappelijk onderwijs
1 358 351	1 584 091	1 413 746	1 635 585	1 442 431	1 666 581	1 460 835	1 680 091	**Total** (zonder kleuteronder.)
1 610 124	1 848 269	1 667 452	1 903 219	1 686 581	1 923 762	1 689 469	1 920 071	**Total** (met kleuteronder.)

TAB. 112
(continued)
(suite)

	1970 – 1971		1972 – 1973		1973 – 1974	
	F	M	F	M	F	M
Belgique/België						
Enseignement préprimaire	223 990	235 096	217 125	226 743	216 925	225 741
Ens. préscolaire	222 734	232 584	215 697	224 643	215 632	223 872
Ens. spécial	1 256	2 512	1 428	2 340	1 293	1 869
Enseignement du 1er degré	498 294	545 378	488 184	516 798	479 613	507 573
Ens. du 1er niveau	485 407	510 827	468 907	487 013	464 035	477 885
Ens. spécial	12 887	34 551	19 277	29 785	15 578	29 688
Enseignement du 2e degré	351 630	381 406	377 844	407 778	386 371	416 580
Ens. spécial	2 071	8 839	5 126	10 631	6 309	11 988
1er cycle	233 923	264 269	245 064	280 281	247 636	282 195
4e degré primaire	4 603	3 315	3 128	2 399	3 222	2 064
Ens. moyen inf.	104 573	115 547	87 106	98 320	84 178	93 333
Ens. tech. et prof.	124 747	145 407	114 550	132 594	108 555	126 118
Ens. rénové	–	–	40 280	46 968	51 681	60 680
2e cycle	115 636	108 298	127 654	116 866	132 426	122 397
Ens. moyen sup.	47 082	59 771	59 763	67 588	60 163	67 118
Ens. tech. et prof.	57 210	43 857	64 240	48 182	64 485	47 389
Formation de maîtres	11 344	4 670	2 218	–	1 281	–
– Ens. normal gardien	4 087	4 087	2 218	–	1 281	–
– Ens. normal primaire	7 257	4 670	–	–	–	–
Ens. rénové	–	–	1 433	1 096	6 497	7 890
Enseignement du 3e degré	45 231	79 626	54 774	86 228	59 418	89 210
Formation universitaire	21 483	53 623	23 858	54 474	25 206	54 271
Form. tech. supérieure	19 156	24 042	21 270	26 965	22 400	29 007
Form. de maîtres	4 592	1 961	9 646	4 789	11 812	5 932
– Ens. normal gardien	–	–	–	–	–	–
– Ens. normal primaire	–	–	2 809	1 106	3 760	1 526
– Ens. normal moyen	2 914	1 660	5 272	3 200	6 600	3 837
– Ens. normal tech. moyen	1 678	301	1 565	483	1 452	569
Total (sans préprimaire)	895 155	1 006 410	920 802	1 010 804	925 402	1 013 363
Total (préprimaire inclus)	1 119 145	1 241 506	1 137 927	1 237 547	1 142 327	1 239 104
Luxembourg						
Enseignement préprimaire	3 981	4 011	4 268	4 485	4 307	4 540
Ens. précolaire	3 981	4 011	4 247	4 465	4 296	4 523
Ens. spécial	–	–	21	20	11	17
Enseignement du 1er degré	15 600	16 560	15 464	16 724	15 837	16 680
Ens. primaire	15 052	15 747	14 784	15 734	15 092	15 658
Ens. spécial	548	813	680	999	745	1 022
Enseignement du 2e degré	10 133	10 723	10 649	11 542	11 073	11 621
Ens. spécial	–	–	–	–	–	–
1e cycle	7 366	7 668	7 563	7 796	7 733	7 752
Ens. secondaire	2 715	3 153	2 447	2 610	2 561	2 482
Ens. moyen	597	620	1 091	1 226	1 104	1 256
Clas. complémentaires	2 075	1 982	2 008	2 162	1 904	2 107
Ens. tech. et prof.	1 979	1 913	2 017	1 798	2 164	1 907
2e cycle	2 767	3 055	3 086	3 746	3 340	3 869
Ens. secondaire	1 569	2 139	1 793	2 332	1 828	2 199
Ens. moyen	141	218	278	365	312	391
Ec. de commerce et de gestion	2	14	16	17	40	41
Ec. tech.	–	72	3	188	–	215
Ens. tech. et prof.	1 055	612	996	844	1 160	1 023
Enseignement du 3e degré	582	1 403	756	1 543	744	1 605
Inst. pédagogique	73	84	113	74	119	74
Cours universitaires	63	77	64	106	44	104
Étudiants univ. à l'étranger	430	1 031	561	1 223	563	1 277
École technique	–	175	–	98	1	109
Miami University	16	36	18	42	17	41
Total (sans préprimaire)	26 315	28 686	26 869	29 809	27 654	29 906
Total (préprimaire inclus)	30 296	32 697	31 137	34 294	31 961	34 446

TAB. 112
(continued)
(suite)

1974 – 1975		1975 – 1976		1976 – 1977		1977 – 1978		
F	M	F	M	F	M	F	M	
Belgique/België								
216 143	225 889	214 631	224 333	209 242	219 178	198 307	208 659	**Enseignement préprimaire**
214 843	223 489	213 355	222 541	208 085	217 395	197 227	207 002	Ens. préscolaire
1 300	1 800	1 276	1 792	1 157	1 783	1 080	1 657	Ens. spécial
472 755	501 897	465 032	493 621	453 897	481 903	445 138	474 313	**Enseignement du 1er degré**
456 255	473 077	449 474	468 083	438 455	456 496	429 694	448 820	Ens. du 1er niveau
16 500	28 820	15 558	25 538	15 442	25 407	15 444	25 493	Ens. spécial
392 294	417 679	395 654	422 020	407 942	428 120	414 391	429 904	**Enseignement du 2e degré**
7 844	13 356	7 856	14 615	8 432	16 022	8 914	16 438	Ens. spécial
244 507	275 586	243 290	271 198	244 580	270 358	245 495	270 440	1er cycle
2 695	1 737	404	70	–	–	–	–	4e degré primaire
82 749	90 734	81 139	88 194	79 665	85 704	77 592	82 247	Ens. moyen inf.
99 101	111 991	94 541	104 593	91 790	100 816	87 699	97 999	Ens. tech. et prof.
59 972	71 114	67 206	78 341	73 125	83 838	80 204	90 194	Ens. rénové
139 943	128 737	144 508	136 207	154 930	141 740	159 982	143 026	2e cycle
58 291	64 453	55 003	60 914	52 772	57 541	51 912	56 123	Ens. moyen sup.
64 710	43 878	60 530	40 855	63 217	38 763	63 918	37 699	Ens. tech. et prof.
–	–	–	–	–	–	–	–	Formation de maîtres
–	–	–	–	–	–	–	–	– Ens. normal gardien
–	–	–	–	–	–	–	–	– Ens. normal primaire
16 942	20 406	28 975	34 438	38 941	45 436	44 152	49 204	Ens. rénové
62 329	89 800	65 603	92 570	69 210	95 225	74 501	98 657	**Enseignement du 3e degré**
26 404	54 576	27 773	55 587	29 608	57 299	31 209	58 140	Formation universitaire
22 743	29 035	25 115	31 262	27 390	32 414	29 601	34 699	Form. tech. supérieure
13 182	6 189	12 715	5 721	12 212	5 512	13 691	5 818	Form. de maîtres
839	–	973	4	1 104	80	1 413	9	– Ens. normal gardien
4 028	1 625	3 774	1 499	3 779	1 465	4 128	1 629	– Ens. normal primaire
6 709	3 873	6 303	3 757	5 491	3 440	6 111	3 619	– Ens. normal moyen
1 606	691	1 665	461	1 838	527	2 039	561	– Ens. normal tech. moyen
927 378	1 009 376	926 289	1 008 211	931 049	1 005 248	934 030	1 002 874	**Total** (sans préprimaire)
1 143 521	1 235 265	1 140 920	1 232 544	1 140 291	1 224 426	1 132 337	1 211 533	**Total** (préprimaire inclus)
Luxembourg								
4 321	4 465	4 364	4 545	4 141	4 472	3 508	3 800	**Enseignement préprimaire**
4 309	4 446	4 354	4 533	4 141	4 472	3 508	3 800	Ens. précolaire
12	19	10	12	:	:	:	:	Ens. spécial
15 780	16 674	15 759	16 567	15 532	16 178	15 267	15 945	**Enseignement du 1er degré**
15 064	15 680	14 959	15 510	14 821	15 176	14 590	14 988	Ens. primaire
716	994	800	1 057	711	1 002	677	957	Ens. spécial
11 391	11 804	11 601	12 251	11 983	12 305	12 421	12 960	**Enseignement du 2e degré**
–	–	–	–	–	–	–	–	Ens. spécial
7 770	7 520	7 773	7 814	8 105	7 698	8 279	8 162	1e cycle
2 562	2 130	2 534	2 335	2 587	2 354	2 727	2 483	Ens. secondaire
1 084	1 210	1 492	1 366	1 641	1 604	1 739	1 755	Ens. moyen
1 940	1 990	1 735	1 958	1 901	1 939	1 825	1 908	Clas. complémentaires
2 181	1 990	2 012	2 155	1 976	1 801	1 988	2 016	Ens. tech. et prof.
3 621	4 284	3 827	4 438	3 878	4 607	4 142	4 798	2e cycle
1 905	2 234	2 024	2 211	2 114	2 180	2 166	2 169	Ens. secondaire
372	515	428	551	527	538	605	544	Ens. moyen
84	82	120	139	163	179	221	204	Ec. de commerce et de gestion
3	271	2	313	2	289	8	355	Ec. tech.
1 257	1 182	1 253	1 224	1 072	1 421	1 142	1 526	Ens. tech. et prof.
825	1 666	897	1 797	865	1 803	871	1 824	**Enseignement du 3e degré**
144	125	122	110	81	51	65	35	Inst. pédagogique
56	107	68	127	83	159	55	109	Cours universitaires
597	1 284	673	1 405	688	1 375	739	1 450	Étudiants univ. à l'étranger
1	124	–	130	1	161	2	173	École technique
27	26	34	25	12	57	10	57	Miami University
28 025	30 116	28 257	30 615	28 380	30 286	28 559	30 729	**Total** (sans préprimaire)
32 346	34 581	32 621	35 160	32 521	34 758	32 067	34 529	**Total** (préprimaire inclus)

TAB. 112
(continued)
(suite)

	1970 – 1971		1972 – 1973		1973 – 1974	
	F	M	F	M	F	M
United Kingdom						
Pre-school level	148 000	156 000	177 000	185 000	182 000	19 000
Nursery	11 000	12 000	11 000	12 000	11 000	12 000
Primary schools	136 000	143 000	164 000	171 000	169 000	176 000
Special schools	1 000	1 000	2 000	2 000	2 000	2 000
First level	2 850 000	2 997 000	2 897 000	3 049 000	2 890 000	3 044 000
Primary schools	2 834 000	2 972 000	2 874 000	3 014 000	2 868 000	3 009 000
Special schools	16 000	25 000	23 000	35 000	22 000	35 000
Second level	2 034 000	2 177 000	2 184 000	2 322 000	2 390 000	2 523 000
Special schools	24 000	37 000	32 000	49 000	33 000	52 000
First stage	1 178 000	1 231 000	1 245 000	1 301 000	1 279 000	1 336 000
Secondary schools	1 178 000	1 231 000	1 245 000	1 301 000	1 279 000	1 336 000
Second stage	832 000	909 000	907 000	972 000	1 078 000	1 135 000
Secondary schools	737 000	792 000	796 000	849 000	966 000	1 020 000
Further education	95 000	117 000	111 000	123 000	112 000	115 000
Third level	183 000	274 000	196 000	286 000	204 000	291 000
Universities	69 000	167 000	76 000	171 000	80 000	171 000
Colleges of education	89 000	34 000	90 000	37 000	91 000	39 000
Further education-other	25 000	73 000	30 000	78 000	33 000	81 000
Total (Excluding pre-school level)	5 067 000	5 748 000	5 277 000	5 657 000	5 484 000	5 858 000
Total (Including pre-school level)	5 215 000	5 904 000	5 454 000	5 842 000	5 666 000	6 048 000
Ireland						
Pre-school level	64 028	67 464	65 888	69 273	66 591	69 844
Pre-primary education	63 850	67 250	65 643	69 028	66 363	69 603
Special education	178	214	245	245	233	251
First level	195 672	204 057	197 320	206 353	199 067	208 937
Primary education	192 700	200 600	193 975	202 077	195 412	204 358
Special education	2 972	3 383	7 540	4 195	3 655	4 578
Others	–	–	–	–	–	–
Second level	106 365	102 180	118 236	112 857	123 850	117 928
First stage	74 463	77 669	81 322	84 860	85 019	88 230
Secondary schools and s. tops	60 382	47 973	64 527	49 393	66 460	50 386
Comprehensive s. and comm. s.	583	588	1 765	2 275	3 387	4 089
Vocational educ. (2–3 year)	13 498	29 108	15 030	33 192	15 172	33 755
Second stage	31 902	24 511	36 914	27 997	38 831	29 599
Secondary schools and s. tops	24 300	20 222	27 710	22 251	28 943	23 062
Residential s. of domestic ec.	254	–	174	–	163	–
Vocational educ. (4–5 year)	4 975	2 764	6 054	3 640	6 190	3 930
Establishment off. tech. c.	82	196	245	291	242	271
Comprehensive and comm. s.	257	191	629	567	1 224	1 106
Others	2 034	1 138	2 102	1 248	2 064	1 230
Third level	8 930	17 288	10 434	18 180	10 963	18 677
Universities (inc. St Patrick C.)	6 664	12 988	7 468	13 050	7 685	12 675
Royal College of Surgeons	145	551	154	561	155	556
Teacher training	1 416	684	1 629	706	1 778	911
Establishment off. tech. c.	545	1 777	1 038	3 589	1 103	3 404
School of art	79	51	75	39	75	39
Others	81	1 237	70	941	167	1 092
Total (Excluding pre-school level)	310 967	323 525	325 990	337 390	333 880	345 443
Total (Including pre-school level)	374 995	390 989	391 878	406 663	400 471	415 341

TAB. 112
(continued)
(suite)

1974 – 1975		1975 – 1976		1976 – 1977		1977 – 1978		
F	M	F	M	F	M	F	M	
United Kingdom								
183 000	191 000	192 000	200 000	173 000	181 000	160 000	169 000	**Pre-school level**
10 000	11 000	10 000	11 000	10 000	11 000	10 000	11 000	Nursery
171 0000	178 000	180 000	187 000	161 000	168 000	148 000	155 000	Primary schools
2 000	2 000	2 000	2 000	2 000	2 000	2 000	2 000	Special schools
2 858 000	3 009 000	2 815 000	2 965 000	2 772 000	2 922 000	2 701 000	2 848 000	**First level**
2 836 000	2 976 000	2 794 000	2 932 000	2 751 000	2 889 000	2 681 000	2 815 000	Primary schools
22 000	33 000	21 000	33 000	21 000	33 000	21 000	33 000	Special schools
2 474 000	2 602 000	2 564 000	2 686 000	2 626 000	2 749 000	2 663 000	2 775 000	**Second level**
34 000	53 000	35 000	55 000	36 000	57 000	36 000	58 000	Special schools
1 314 000	1 372 000	1 342 000	1 400 000	1 362 000	1 422 000	1 369 000	1 431 000	First stage
1 314 000	1 372 000	1 342 000	1 400 000	1 362 000	1 422 000	1 369 000	1 431 000	Secondary schools
1 126 000	1 177 000	1 187 000	1 231 000	1 228 000	1 270 000	1 258 000	1 286 000	Second stage
998 000	1 051 000	1 028 000	1 083 000	1 064 000	1 117 000	1 085 000	1 135 000	Secondary schools
128 000	126 000	159 000	148 000	164 000	153 000	173 000	151 000	Further education
207 000	289 000	214 000	302 000	218 000	308 000	208 000	314 000	**Third level**
85 000	172 000	91 000	178 000	95 000	184 000	100 000	188 000	Universities
85 000	33 000	123 000	124 000	123 000	124 000	108 000	126 000	Colleges of education / Further education-other
37 000	84 000							
5 539 000	5 900 000	5 593 000	5 953 000	5 616 000	5 979 000	5 572 000	5 937 000	**Total** (Excluding pre-school level)
5 722 000	6 091 000	5 785 000	6 153 000	5 789 000	6 160 000	5 732 000	6 106 000	**Total** (Including pre-school level)
Ireland								
64 464	67 599	66 352	69 839	69 069	72 738	69 136	72 807	**Pre-school level**
64 320	67 411	66 179	69 604	68 878	72 514	68 919	72 535	Pre-primary education
144	188	173	235	191	224	217	272	Special education
200 751	210 199	201 474	212 413	202 114	213 627	204 275	215 713	**First level**
196 744	205 475	197 491	207 327	197 984	208 448	200 066	210 336	Primary education
4 007	4 724	3 983	5 086	4 130	5 179	4 209	5 377	Special education
–	–	–	–	–	–	–	–	Others
131 704	124 968	138 851	132 105	144 393	136 728	148 486	139 624	**Second level**
88 087	92 871	90 983	95 873	93 111	97 709	94 883	99 284	First stage
68 152	52 055	70 772	53 970	71 935	55 496	73 374	56 809	Secondary schools and s. tops
4 455	5 719	4 866	6 690	5 925	7 145	6 545	8 138	Comprehensive s. and comm. s.
15 480	35 097	15 345	35 213	15 251	35 068	14 964	34 337	Vocational educ. (2–3 year)
43 617	32 097	47 868	36 232	51 282	39 019	53 603	40 340	Second stage
31 345	24 085	33 817	25 906	35 420	27 643	36 324	27 887	Secondary schools and s. tops
150	–	161	–	229	–	174	–	Residential s. of domestic ec.
8 083	5 213	9 524	6 868	10 579	7 455	10 930	8 197	Vocational educ. (4–5 year)
182	277	376	389	430	624	497	445	Establishment off. tech. c.
1 793	1 476	2 180	1 955	2 615	2 141	3 135	2 481	Comprehensive and comm. s.
2 064	1 046	1 810	1 114	2 012	1 156	2 543	1 330	Others
11 508	19 541	12 712	20 163	13 893	21 154	15 009	21 789	**Third level**
8 623	12 148	8 921	12 396	9 198	12 723	9 792	12 984	Universities (inc. St Patrick C.)
159	595	182	582	214	592	170	598	Royal College of Surgeons
1 767	906	1 709	875	2 260	914	2 513	841	Teacher training
613	4 642	1 421	4 910	1 657	5 179	1 833	5 354	Establishment off. tech. c.
103	68	139	106	164	136	185	153	School of art
243	1 182	340	1 294	400	1 610	516	1 859	Others
343 963	354 708	353 037	364 681	360 400	371 509	367 770	377 126	**Total** (Excluding pre-school level)
408 427	422 247	419 389	434 520	429 469	444 247	436 906	449 933	**Total** (Including pre-school level)

TAB. 112
(continued)
(suite)

	1970 – 1971		1972 – 1973		1973 – 1974	
	F	M	F	M	F	M
Danmark						
Forskoleniveau	10 109	10 765	18 261	19 377	20 076	21 280
Børnehavekl.	10 109	10 765	18 261	19 377	20 076	21 280
Første niveau	189 450	199 863	200 856	202 373	207 705	220 859
Folkeskolen (1-5 K)	183 576	188 594	194 379	163 780	201 356	208 676
Special kl.	5 874	11 269	6 477	12 381	6 349	12 183
Andet niveau	193 768	191 485	203 893	199 336	210 462	205 740
Nedre trin	162 466	159 620	167 131	163 780	170 069	167 259
Folkeskolen (6-10 K.)	106 647	112 492	105 341	112 237	106 280	114 107
Realkl. (1-3 Real)	50 815	41 539	56 294	45 757	58 078	47 275
Realkurser	2 113*	2 155*	2 297	2 103	2 246	1 970
Efterskoler	2 840	3 360	3 140	3 591	3 381	3 813
Ungdomskostskoler	51	74	59	92	84	94
Øvre trin	31 302	31 865	36 762	35 556	40 393	38 481
Gymnasier (1–3 G)	16 336	17 306	18 542	18 790	19 965	20 076
Studenterkurser	2 125	2 646	2 314	2 603	2 301	2 349
HF-Kurser	2 593	2 564	4 661	4 242	5 923	5 251
Folke-og ungdom.	2 614	1 527	2 500	1 575	2 556	1 501
Husholdningss.	830*	9*	968	12	901	13
Tekniske s.	6 774*	6 504*	7 713*	6 840	8 665	7 728
Landbrugss.	30*	1 309*	64	1 494	82	1 563
Tredje niveau	27 997	46 895	36 354	55 681	39 048	59 144
Universiteter	12 666	22 747	15 664	26 689	16 799	28 133
Læreruddannelse	6 342	4 889	7 769	6 146	8 440	6 861
Tekniske sk.	950*	12 250	1 230*	13 950	1 198	16 630
Læreanstalterne	3 861 =	6 436	4 641	7 844	5 283	8 460
Andre videregående udd.	4 178*	573	7 050*	1 052	7 328	2 060
I alt (Uden forskoleniveau)	411 215	438 243	441 103	468 308	457 215	485 743
I alt (med forskoleniveau)	421 324	449 008	459 364	487 685	477 291	507 023

TAB. 112
(continued)
(suite)

1974 – 1975		1975 – 1976		1976 – 1977		1977 – 1978		
F	M	F	M	F	M	F	M	
Danmark								
20 823	22 109	21 800*	23 084*	23 500*	25 300*	26 400*	28 581*	**Forskoleniveau**
20 823	22 109	21 800*	23 084*	23 500*	25 300*	26 400*	28 581*	Børnehavekl.
207 628	222 665	200 000*	210 000*	195 000*	203 700*	192 000*	200 000*	**Første niveau**
201 662	211 081	:	:	:	:	:	:	Folkeskolen (1–5 K)
5 966	11 584	:	:	:	:	:	:	Special kl.
213 496	207 343	227 597	217 849	230 411	222 325	239 598	222 617	**Andet niveau**
172 330	168 564	183 000	178 575	183 845	183 804	191 080	184 936	Nedre trin
106 191	114 012	115 000*	123 000*	138 000*	146 000	:	:	Folkeskolen (6-10 K.)
60 429	48 786	62 114	49 565	40 099	31 925	:	:	Realkl. (1–3 Real)
2 250	1 584	2 275	1 507	1 985	1 324	:	:	Realkurser
3 379	4 084	3 528	4 409	3 683	4 457	:	:	Efterskoler
81	98	83	94	78	98	:	:	Ungdomskostskoler
41 166	38 779	44 597	39 274	44 566	38 521	48 518	37 681	Øvre trin
20 596	20 172	20 997	20 240	21 661	20 247	:	:	Gymnasier (1–3 G)
1 725	1 961	1 691	1 825	1 624	1 528	:	:	Studenterkurser
6 602	5 478	7 252	5 387	7 724	4 958	:	:	HF-Kurser
2 500	1 755	2 440	1 899	2 413	1 749	:	:	Folke-og ungdom.
972	10	1 056	12	1 048	11	:	:	Husholdningss.
9 392	7 146	11 061	8 213	11 990	8 229	:	:	Tekniske s.
79	1 557	100	1 698	106	1 799	:	:	Landbrugss.
40 928	58 055	42 440	59 704	44 610	59 454	55 483	63 233	**Tredje niveau**
18 333	30 195	19 466	31 395	20 782	32 140	:	:	Universiteter
8 574	7 136	8 526	7 408	7 673	6 725	:	:	Læreruddannelse
516	10 237	518	9 927	541	9 930	:	:	Tekniske sk.
5 815	8 242	6 512	8 700	8 207	8 641	:	:	Læreanstalterne
7 690	2 245	7 418	2 274	7 407	2 018	:	:	Andre videregående udd.
462 052	488 063	470 037	487 553	470 021	485 479	487 081	485 850	**I alt** (Uden forskoleniveau)
482 875	510 159	491 837	510 637	493 521	510 779	513 481	514 431	**I alt** (med forskoleniveau)

TAB. 112.1

Student population by level and type of studies (%)
Population étudiante selon le degré et le type d'études (%)

	1970 – 1971		1972 – 1973		1973 – 1974	
	$\frac{f}{F}100$	$\frac{f}{f+m}100$	$\frac{f}{F}100$	$\frac{f}{f+m}100$	$\frac{f}{F}100$	$\frac{f}{f+m}100$
BR Deutschland						
Elementarstufe	100,0*	49,8	100,0*	48,4	100,0*	48,3
Kindergarten	97,6	50,0	95,7	48,6	95,2	48,5
Schulkindergärten und Vorklassen ⎫	2,4	43,3	4,3	44,0	4,8	44,4
Sonderschulkindergärten und V. ⎭						
Primarstufe	100,0	48,8	100,0	48,7	100,0	48,6
Grundschulen	97,8	49,0	97,3	49,0	97,3	48,9
Grundstufe der Gesamtschulen	–	–	0,3	49,2	0,3	48,5
Sonderschulen (an Grundschulen)	2,2	40,1	2,4	39,8	2,4	39,8
Sekundarstufe	100,0	48,1	100,0	48,4	100,0	48,6
Sonderschulen (an Haupt- und Realschulen)	3,5	40,4	3,6	40,3	3,6	40,3
Unterstufe	85,3	48,8	83,9	49,1	83,1	49,1
Hauptschulen	47,4	49,1	42,5	48,6	40,4	48,2
Realschulen	18,6	52,9	19,5	53,7	19,7	53,9
Gesamtschulen	–	–	1,2	48,1	1,5	48,3
Gymnasien	19,3	44,7	20,6	46,2	21,3	47,0
Berufsgrundschuljahr	–	–	0,1	50,1	0,2	41,8
Oberstufe	11,2	46,1	12,6	46,7	13,3	48,0
Gymnasien	5,6	41,4	5,9	44,0	6,3	45,3
Gesamtschulen	–	–	0,1	45,8	0,1	46,6
Berufsaufbauschulen	0,2	32,6	0,1	22,6	0,2	26,4
Fachgymnasien	0,5	20,3	1,0	25,2	1,1	26,9
Berufsfachschulen	5,2	61,3	5,5	62,0	5,6	63,8
Tertiarstufe	100,0	34,2	100,0	34,1	100,0	37,2
Wiss. Hochschulen, Universitäten	37,9	25,1	41,0	25,3	43,8	29,3
Fachschulen	15,6	40,6	15,4	38,1	14,3	41,1
Schulen des Gesundheitswesens	23,6	88,3	20,5	86,3	18,1	84,7
Fachhochschulen	5,0	11,0	5,3	14,6	7,5	20,9
Pädagogische Hochschulen	16,1	63,0	16,9	61,6	14,6	63,1
Kunsthochschulen	1,8	39,6	1,9	39,9	1,8	40,5
Insgesamt (ohne Elementarstufe)	88,7	47,4	88,3	47,4	88,2	47,6
Insgesamt (inkl. Elementarstufe)	100,0	47,7	100,0	47,5	100,0	47,7
France						
Enseignement préprimaire	100,0	48,9	100,0	47,7	100,0	49,0*
Ens. préscolaire	100,0	48,9	:	:	:	:
Ens. spécial	–	–	–	–	:	:
Enseignement du 1ᵉʳ degré	100,0	48,5	100,0	48,5	100,0	48,5*
Ens. élémentaire	94,1	48,9	:	:	:	:
Cl. de fin d'études	2,5	45,2	:	:	:	:
Ens. spécial	3,4	40,7	:	:	:	:
Enseignement du 2ᵉ degré	100,0	51,1	100,0	50,7	100,0	50,7
Ens. spécial	0,5	43,7	0,9	44,0	1,1	42,9
1ᵉʳ cycle	64,4	51,0	64,0	50,4	64,0	50,3
Premier cycle	64,4	51,0	62,9	50,6	62,3	50,8
Classes nouvelles	–	–	0,9	37,6	1,7	36,7
2ᵉ cycle	35,1	51,3	35,1	51,6	34,9	51,9
Ens. professionnel court	14,9	49,5	13,8	48,2	13,7	47,9
Deuxième cycle long	20,2	52,8	21,3	54,1	21,2	54,8
– Ens. général	16,9	53,8	17,3	59,3	16,9	59,6
– Ens. technologique	3,3	48,0	3,9	39,1	43,2	41,7
Enseignement du 3ᵉ degré	100,0	43,0	100,0	45,5	100,0	45,6
Universités	89,2	44,5	88,8	47,0	87,8	46,7
dont:						
– IUT	1,8	24,0	2,6	29,0	3,0	30,4
– ENSI – INP	0,1	5,7	0,1	7,8	:	:
Non universitaire	10,8	34,0	11,2	36,5	12,2	38,6
dont:						
– CPGE – STS	6,5	35,8	6,5	40,6	7,5	43,5
– Écoles normales et CRF	3,9	55,5	4,2	58,6	4,1	59,0
– Grandes écoles (école ing. non un.)	0,4	6,4	0,6	7,6	0,6	8,0
Total (sans préprimaire)	82,3	49,5	82,1	49,3	81,3	49,3
Total (préprimaire inclus)	100,0	49,4	100,0	49,0	100,0	49,2

TAB. 112.1
Student population by level and type of studies (%)
Population étudiante selon le degré et le type d'études (%)

1974 – 1975		1975 – 1976		1976 – 1977		1977 – 1978		
$\frac{f}{F}100$	$\frac{f}{f+m}100$	$\frac{f}{F}100$	$\frac{f}{f+m}100$	$\frac{f}{F}100$	$\frac{f}{f+m}100$	$\frac{f}{F}100$	$\frac{f}{f+m}100$	
BR Deutschland								
100,0	48,4	100,0*	48,3	100,0	48,4	100,0	47,8	**Elementarstufe**
95,3	48,6	95,0	48,6	95,7	48,6	95,6	48,0	Kindergarten
4,7	44,1	5,0	44,6	4,3	44,6	4,4	43,9	{ Schulkindergärten und Vorklassen
								{ Sonderschulkindergärten und V.
100,0	48,6	100,0	48,6	100,0	48,5	100,0	48,5	**Primarstufe**
97,3	48,9	97,2	48,9	97,2	48,8	97,1	48,8	Grundschulen
0,3	48,8	0,4	49,6	0,4	49,6	0,3	50,1	Grundstufe der Gesamtschulen
2,4	39,4	2,4	39,4	2,4	38,7	2,6	38,6	Sonderschulen (an Grundschulen)
100,0	48,7	100,0	49,0	100,0	49,3	100,0	49,5	**Sekundarstufe**
3,5	40,4	3,5	40,2	3,5	40,4	3,4	40,2	Sonderschulen (an Haupt- und Realschulen)
82,8	49,2	82,1	49,2	82,7	49,5	82,7	49,5	Unterstufe
39,0	47,8	38,3	47,5	37,0	47,4	35,5	47,1	Hauptschulen
20,0	54,1	19,7	54,0	20,7	54,2	21,4	54,1	Realschulen
1,9	48,2	2,2	48,2	2,4	48,3	2,6	48,4	Gesamtschulen
21,7	47,8	21,4	48,4	21,9	49,1	22,4	49,6	Gymnasien
0,3	44,5	0,4	43,9	0,7	50,6	0,9	51,8	Berufsgrundschuljahr
13,7	48,9	14,5	50,6	13,8	51,0	14,0	46,9	Oberstufe
6,6	45,9	6,9	46,2	6,5	46,3	6,6	46,4	Gymnasien
0,1	47,8	0,1	47,6	0,1	46,2	0,2	30,1	Gesamtschulen
0,1	26,3	0,1	28,5	0,1	28,5	0,1	32,5	Berufsaufbauschulen
1,1	28,0	1,1	29,9	1,2	31,4	1,1	51,4	Fachgymnasien
5,6	63,9	6,3	66,3	5,9	68,3	6,1	68,2	Berufsfachschulen
100,0	38,7	100,0	38,5	100,0	38,6	100,0	39,6	**Tertiarstufe**
45,9	31,3	48,0	32,1	50,0	32,3	52,0	33,4	Wiss. Hochschulen, Universitäten
13,9	43,4	10,8	38,8	8,9	42,3	8,2	48,5	Fachschulen
17,8	84,0	18,5	83,4	18,7	83,8	17,9	84,6	Schulen des Gesundheitswesens
7,6	22,4	8,4	22,9	9,0	23,2	9,6	24,4	Fachhochschulen
13,2	64,1	12,8	64,5	11,8	65,1	10,7	66,2	Pädagogische Hochschulen
1,6	41,1	1,6	42,0	1,6	42,6	1,6	44,4	Kunsthochschulen
87,1	47,8	87,4	47,9	86,6	48,1	87,6	48,2	**Insgesamt** (ohne Elementarstufe)
100,0	47,9	100,0	48,0	100,0	48,1	100,0	48,2	**Insgesamt** (inkl. Elementarstufe)
France								
100,0	47,9*	100,0	48,9*	100,0	48,5	100,0	48,7	**Enseignement préprimaire**
:	:	99,6*	49,0	99,6*	48,7	99,5*	48,8	Ens. préscolaire
:	:	:	:	:	.	:	:	Ens. spécial
100,0	48,4*	100,0	48,5*	100,0	47,9	100,0	48,5	**Enseignement du 1er degré**
:	:	96,6*	48,9	96,6	48,2	96,5	48,7	Ens. élémentaire
:	:	0,1*	41,7	–	–	–	–	Cl. de fin d'études
:	:	:	:	:	:	:	:	Ens. spécial
100,0	50,9	100,0	50,9	100,0	50,8	100,0	50,3	**Enseignement du 2e degré**
1,3	42,7	1,8	41,3	2,3	42,3	2,5	40,1	Ens. spécial
63,7	50,4	63,0	50,5	62,4	50,4	63,3	50,6	1er cycle
61,4	51,1	60,4	51,2	59,7	51,2	60,4	51,4	Premier cycle
2,4	37,1	2,6	37,9	2,7	38,4	2,9	39,0	Classes nouvelles
35,0	52,1	35,2	52,1	35,3	52,2	36,8	52,4	2e cycle
13,8	48,0	14,0	47,5	13,7	47,1	14,0	47,0	Ens. professionnel court
21,1	55,2	21,1	55,7	21,6	56,0	22,8	56,5	Deuxième cycle long
16,5	59,9	16,9	56,6	17,2	56,9	18,0	57,3	– Ens. général
4,5	43,1	4,2	52,3	4,5	52,8	4,8	53,4	– Ens. technologique
100,0	44,9	100,0	46,4	100,0	46,6	100,0	47,0	**Enseignement du 3e degré**
87,8	47,1	87,9	47,6	88,0	47,8	87,7	48,0	Universités
								dont:
3,0	30,2	3,1	31,1	3,2	32,0	3,5	33,1	– IUT
		0,2	11,9	:	:	0,2	12,4	– ENSI – INP
12,2	32,3	12,1	39,1	12,0	39,1	12,3	40,9	Non universitaire
								dont:
7,5	31,7	8,1	43,1	8,4	43,7	9,2	46,0	– CPGE – STS
4,1	59,6	3,3	59,2	2,9	60,1	2,3	59,2	– Écoles normales et CRF
0,6	9,4	0,7	10,7	0,8	11,5	0,8	12,3	– Grandes écoles (école ing. non un.)
81,2	49,2	80,6	49,4	83,3	49,1	80,9	49,1	**Total** (sans préprimaire)
100,0	49,0	100,0	49,3	100,0	49,0	100,0	49,1	**Total** (préprimaire inclus)

TAB. 112.1
(continued)
(suite)

	1970 – 1971		1972 – 1973		1973 – 1974	
	$\frac{f}{F}100$	$\frac{f}{f+m}100$	$\frac{f}{F}100$	$\frac{f}{f+m}100$	$\frac{f}{F}100$	$\frac{f}{f+m}100$
Italia						
Educazione prescolastica	100,0	49,0	100,0	48,8	100,0	49,0
Scuole del grado preparatorio	100,0	49,0	100,0	48,8	100,0	49,0
Educazione primaria	100,0	48,2	100,0	48,4	100,0	48,4
Scuole elementari e sussidiate	98,9	48,4	99,0	48,5	99,1	48,5
Scuole speciali	1,1	37,6	1,0	44,2	0,9	36,3
Educazione secondaria	100,0	44,5	100,0	45,1	100,0	45,5
Ciclo inferiore	59,4	46,7	59,4	47,1	58,9	47,3
Scuola media inferiore	59,4	46,7	59,4	47,1	58,9	47,3
Ciclo superiore	40,6	41,6	40,6	42,5	41,1	43,3
Istr. professionale	6,3	41,4	6,7	43,0	6,8	43,7
Istr. tecnica	9,5	23,9	10,7	26,8	11,3	33,0
Istr. magistrale	11,6	89,2	9,4	90,3	8,9	90,5
– Scuole magistrali	1,5	100,0	1,2	100,0	1,2	100,0
– Istituti magistrali	10,2	87,8	8,2	89,0	7,8	89,8
Istr. scientifica e classica	11,6	43,2	12,1	45,3	12,3	46,3
– Licei scientifici	5,4	36,6	6,5	40,0	7,0	41,6
– Ginnasi e licei classici	6,2	51,4	5,6	53,5	5,3	54,3
Istr. artistica	1,6	56,5	1,8	55,6	1,8	55,5
– Scuole e istituti d'arte	0,7	56,0	0,7	55,3	0,7	55,6
– Licei artistici	0,7	64,7	0,8	63,5	0,8	63,3
– Conservatori ed ist. di musica	0,2	41,5	0,3	41,3	0,3	41,1
Educazione superiore	100,0	37,6	100,0	38,2	100,0	39,2
Università	99,0	37,6	99,1	38,6	99,1	39,1
Studenti iscritti	81,4	37,7	82,0	36,5	80,2	39,5
Studenti fuori corso	17,6	46,3	17,1	45,6	18,9	37,9
Accademia di belle arti	1,0		0,9		0,9	46,0
Totale (Senza ed. prescolastica)	84,8	46,0	85,0	46,2	83,2	46,4
Totale (Con ed. prescolastica)	100,0	46,4	100,0	46,6	100,0	46,8
Nederland						
Kleuteronderwijs	100,0	48,7	100,0	48,7	100,0	48,8
Kleuteronderwijs	99,7	48,7	99,7	48,7	99,7	48,9
Buitengewoon onderwijs	0,3	42,4	0,3	39,1	0,3	37,1
Eerste niveau	100,0	48,4	100,0	48,4	100,0	48,3
Gewoon lager onderwijs	96,9	49,0	96,9	49,1	96,9	49,1
Buitengewoon onderwijs	3,1	33,8	3,1	33,1	3,1	32,6
Tweede niveau	100,0	45,0	100,0	45,8	100,0	46,1
Buitengewoon onderwijs	0,4	37,4	0,5	35,1	0,5	33,2
Lagerecyclus	79,8	45,4	77,2	46,2	76,0	46,4
Algemeen woortgezet ond.	50,8	49,1	49,8	49,9	50,1	50,4
Lager beroepsonderwijs	29,0	40,3	27,4	40,7	25,9	40,3
Daaronder:						
Lager tech. ondernw.	0,2	0,5	0,4	1,3	0,6	1,8
Lager huishoud. N.	25,0	99,9	23,0	99,6	21,5	99,1
Hogere cyclus	19,8	43,3	22,3	44,4	23,5	45,1
Algemeen voortgezet onder.	11,1	41,7	12,5	42,3	13,6	43,6
Middelbaar bereopsond.	8,7	45,3	9,8	47,5	9,9	47,4
Daaronder:						
Middelbaar tech.	0,2	3,0	0,2	3,2	0,3	3,1
Middelbaar huis. ennij.	6,0	100,0	6,3	99,7	6,5	99,6
Opleidm kleuterdeist	1,6	100,0	2,1	100,0	2,0	100,0
Derde niveau	100,0	26,3	100,0	29,5	100,0	29,6
Hoger beroepsonderwijs	56,5	35,4	54,9	38,1	56,5	37,7
Daaronder:						
Hoger tech. onderw.	4,8	11,9	5,1	13,1	4,9	12,6
Oplei dincssh. vooronder	16,4	42,4	18,6	49,4	19,6	49,1
Wetenshappelijk onderwijs	43,5	19,7	45,1*	23,1*	43,5*	23,1*
Total (zonder kleuteronder.)	83,8	45,7	84,4	46,1	84,4	46,1
Total (met kleuteronder.)	100,0	46,1	100,0	46,5	100,0	46,5

TAB. 112.1
(continued)
(suite)

$\frac{f}{F}100$	$\frac{f}{f+m}100$	$\frac{f}{F}100$	$\frac{f}{f+m}100$	$\frac{f}{F}100$	$\frac{f}{f+m}100$	$\frac{f}{F}100$	$\frac{f}{f+m}100$	
1974 – 1975		1975 – 1976		1976 – 1977		1977 – 1978		
				Italia				
100,0	49,0	100,0	49,0	100,0	49,1	100,0	49,0	**Educazione prescolastica**
100,0	49,0	100,0	49,0	100,0	49,1	100,0	49,0	Scuole del grado preparatorio
100,0	48,5	100,0	48,5	100,0	48,5	100,0	48,5	**Educazione primaria**
99,2	48,6	99,3	48,6	99,3	48,6	99,5	48,6	Scuole elementari e sussidiate
0,8	38,6	0,7	38,6	0,7	38,6	0,5	38,6	Scuole speciali
100,0	45,9	100,0	46,2	100,0	46,5	100,0	47,0	**Educazione secondaria**
58,9	47,5	58,5	47,6	57,8	47,7	57,2	47,8	Ciclo inferiore
58,9	47,5	58,5	47,6	57,8	47,7	57,2	47,8	Scuola media inferiore
41,1	43,8	41,5	44,3	42,2	45,0	42,8	45,9	Ciclo superiore
6,8	44,2	7,0	45,2	7,1	45,5	7,4	45,5	Istr. professionale
12,0	29,7	12,9	31,2	13,7	32,6	14,3	34,1	Istr. tecnica
8,5	91,4	8,1	92,3	7,9	93,0	7,9	93,6	Istr. magistrale
1,2	100,0	1,2	100,0	1,2	100,0	1,2	100,0	– Scuole magistrali
7,3	90,1	6,9	91,1	6,7	91,9	6,6	92,5	– Istituti magistrali
12,1	46,7	11,8	47,2	11,6	47,8	11,4	48,5	Istr. scientifica e classica
7,1	42,4	7,2	43,3	7,3	44,3	7,2	45,3	– Licei scientifici
5,0	54,5	4,6	54,9	4,4	54,9	4,2	55,1	– Ginnasi e licei classici
1,8	56,1	1,8	56,2	1,8	55,9	1,8	56,5	Istr. artistica
1,5	60,1	0,7	56,6	0,8	57,8	0,8	59,9	– Scuole e istituti d'arte
		0,7	64,4	0,7	64,2	0,6	64,5	– Licei artistici
0,3	46,1	0,3	43,0	0,3	42,2	0,4	42,2	– Conservatori ed ist. di musica
100,0	39,8	100,0	39,4	100,0	40,1	100,0	41,0	**Educazione superiore**
99,0	39,7	98,9	39,3	98,9	40,0	99,0	40,9	Università
80,0	40,2	78,4	39,6	77,1	40,2	76,6	41,3	Studenti iscritti
19,0	37,9	20,5	38,3	21,8	39,5	22,4	39,6	Studenti fuori corso
1,0	45,9	1,1	47,5	1,1	48,7	1,0	54,1	Accademia di belle arti
85,0	46,6	84,9	46,6	84,7	46,8	84,7	47,1	**Totale** (Senza ed. prescolastica)
100,0	47,0	100,0	47,0	100,0	47,1	100,0	47,4	**Totale** (Con ed. prescolastica)
				Nederland				
100,0	48,8	100,0	48,7	100,0	48,7	100,0	48,8	**Kleuteronderwijs**
99,7	48,9	99,7	48,7	99,6	48,8	99,6	48,9	Kleuteronderwijs
0,3	37,0	0,3	36,7	0,4	36,0	0,4	36,5	Buitengewoon onderwijs
100,0	48,3	100,0	48,3	100,0	48,3	100,0	48,4	**Eerste niveau**
97,0	49,1	97,0	49,1	96,9	49,2	96,8	49,2	Gewoon lager onderwijs
3,0	32,2	3,0	31,8	3,1	31,9	3,2	31,7	Buitengewoon onderwijs
100,0	46,2	100,0	46,7	100,0	46,7	100,0	47,0	**Tweede niveau**
0,6	33,2	0,6	32,4	0,6	32,1	0,5	30,4	Buitengewoon onderwijs
75,1	46,6	77,3	47,7	76,5	47,8	75,2	47,8	Lagerecyclus
50,4	50,8	48,6	51,0	48,5	51,3	48,1	51,6	Algemeen woortgezet ond.
24,7	39,8	28,7	43,0	28,1	42,7	27,1	42,3	Lager beroepsonderwijs
								Daaronder:
0,7	2,2	1,0	3,1	1,1	3,6	1,2	3,9	Lager tech. ondernw.
20,0	98,8	23,5	98,8	22,5	98,4	21,3	98,1	Lager huishoud. N.
24,3	45,5	22,1	43,8	22,9	44,0	24,3	45,1	Hogere cyclus
14,2	44,4	14,3	45,4	14,9	46,1	15,2	46,6	Algemeen voortgezet onder.
10,0	47,2	7,8	41,0	8.0	40,6	9,1	42,7	Middelbaar bereopsond.
								Daaronder:
0,3	3,9	0,3	4,5	0,4	4,8	0,4	5,3	Middelbaar tech.
6,5	99,2	4,2	98,1	4,2	96,9	5,1	98,6	Middelbaar huis. ennij.
1,9	100,0	1,8	100,0	1,7	99,5	1,6	99,3	Opleidm kleuterdeist
100,0	30,1	100,0	31,8	100,0	32,6	100,0	33,5	**Derde niveau**
58,1	38,5	59,2	39,2	58,2	39,7	57,1	40,3	Hoger beroepsonderwijs
								Daaronder:
4,8	12,5	4,0	12,0	3,7	11,7	3,6	11,9	Hoger tech. onderw.
19,9	49,9	17,6	51,2	17,4	53,8	16,4	56,4	Oplei dincssh. vooronder
41,9*	23,1*	40,8*	25,0	41,8	26,2	42,9	27,3	Wetenshappelijk onderwijs
84,4	46,2	84,8	46,4	85,5	46,4	86,5	46,4	**Total** (zonder kleuteronder.)
100,0	46,6	100,0	46,7	100,0	46,7	100,0	46,8	**Total** (met kleuteronder.)

TAB. 112.1
(continued)
(suite)

	1970 – 1971		1972 – 1973		1973 – 1974	
	$\frac{f}{F}100$	$\frac{f}{f+m}100$	$\frac{f}{F}100$	$\frac{f}{f+m}100$	$\frac{f}{F}100$	$\frac{f}{f+m}100$
Belgique/België						
Enseignement préprimaire	100,0	48,8	100,0	48,9	100,0	49,0
Ens. préscolaire	99,4	48,9	99,3	49,0	99,4	49,1
Ens. spécial	0,6	33,3	0,7	40,5	0,6	40,9
Enseignement du 1er degré	100,0	47,7	100,0	48,6	100,0	48,6
Ens. du 1er niveau	97,4	48,7	96,0	49,1	96,8	49,3
Ens. spécial	2,6	27,2	4,0	39,3	3,2	34,4
Enseignement du 2e degré	100,0	48,0	100,0	48,1	100,0	48,1
Ens. spécial	0,6	19,0	1,4	32,5	1,6	34,5
1er cycle	66,5	47,0	64,9	46,6	64,1	46,7
4e degré primaire	1,3	58,1	0,8	56,6	0,8	61,0
Ens. moyen inf.	29,7	47,5	23,0	47,0	21,8	47,4
Ens. tech. et prof.	35,5	46,2	30,3	46,3	28,1	46,3
Ens. rénové	–	–	10,7	46,2	13,4	46,0
2e cycle	32,9	51,6	33,8	52,2	34,3	52,0
Ens. moyen sup.	13,4	44,1	15,8	46,9	15,6	47,3
Ens. tech. et prof.	16,3	56,6	17,0	57,1	16,7	57,6
Formation de maîtres	3,2	70,8	0,6	100,0	0,3	100,0
– Ens. normal gardien	1,2	100,0	0,6	100,0	0,3	100,0
– Ens. normal primaire	2,1	60,8	–	–	–	–
Ens. rénové	–	–	0,4	56,7	1,7	45,2
Enseignement du 3e degré	100,0	36,2	100,0	38,8	100,0	40,0
Formation universitaire	47,5	28,6	43,6	30,5	42,4	31,7
Form. tech. supérieure	42,4	44,3	38,8	44,1	37,7	43,6
Form. de maîtres	10,1	70,1	17,6	66,8	19,9	66,6
– Ens. normal gardien	–	–	–	–	–	–
– Ens. normal primaire	–	–	5,1	71,7	6,4	71,1
– Ens. normal moyen	6,4	63,7	9,6	62,2	11,1	63,2
– Ens. normal tech. moyen	3,7	84,8	2,9	76,4	2,4	71,8
Total (sans préprimaire)	80,0	47,1	80,9	47,7	81,0	47,7
Total (préprimaire inclus)	100,0	47,4	100,0	47,9	100,0	48,0
Luxembourg						
Enseignement préprimaire	100,0	49,8	100,0	48,8	100,0	48,7
Ens. précolaire	100,0	49,8	99,5	48,7	99,7	48,7
Ens. spécial	–	–	0,5	51,2	0,3	39,3
Enseignement du 1er degré	100,0	48,5	100,0	48,0	100,0	48,7
Ens. primaire	96,5	48,9	95,6	48,4	95,3	49,1
Ens. spécial	3,5	40,2	4,4	40,5	4,7	42,2
Enseignement du 2e degré	100,0	48,6	100,0	48,0	100,0	48,8
Ens. spécial	–	–	–	–	–	–
1e cycle	72,7	49,0	71,0	49,2	69,8	49,9
Ens. secondaire	26,8	46,3	23,0	48,4	23,1	50,8
Ens. moyen	5,9	49,1	10,2	47,1	10,0	46,8
Clas. complémentaires	20,5	51,1	18,9	48,2	17,2	47,5
Ens. tech. et prof.	19,5	50,8	18,9	52,9	19,5	53,2
2e cycle	27,3	47,5	29,0	45,2	30,2	46,3
Ens. secondaire	15,5	42,3	16,8	43,5	16,5	45,4
Ens. moyen	1,4	39,3	2,6	43,2	2,8	44,4
Ec. de commerce et de gestion	0,0	12,5	0,2	48,5	0,4	49,4
Ec. tech.	–	–	0,0	1,6	–	–
Ens. tech. et prof.	10,4	63,3	9,4	54,1	10,5	53,1
Enseignement du 3e degré	100,0	29,3	100,0	32,9	100,0	31,7
Inst. pédagogique	12,5	46,5	14,9	60,4	16,0	61,7
Cours universitaires	10,8	45,0	8,5	37,6	5,9	29,7
Étudiants univ. à l'étranger	73,9	29,4	74,2	31,4	75,7	30,6
École technique	–	–	–	–	0,1	0,9
Miami University	2,7	30,8	2,4	30,0	2,3	29,3
Total (sans préprimaire)	86,9	47,8	86,3	47,4	86,5	48,0
Total (préprimaire inclus)	100,0	48,1	100,0	47,6	100,0	48,1

TAB. 112.1
(continued)
(suite)

1974 – 1975		1975 – 1976		1976 – 1977		1977 – 1978		
$\frac{f}{F}$ 100	$\frac{f}{f+m}$ 100	$\frac{f}{F}$ 100	$\frac{f}{f+m}$ 100	$\frac{f}{F}$ 100	$\frac{f}{f+m}$ 100	$\frac{f}{F}$ 100	$\frac{f}{f+m}$ 100	
				Belgique/België				
100,0	48,9	100,0	48,9	100,0	48,8	100,0	48,7	**Enseignement préprimaire**
99,4	48,9	99,4	48,9	99,5	48,9	99,5	48,8	Ens. préscolaire
0,6	41,9	0,6	41,6	0,5	39,4	0,5	39,5	Ens. spécial
100,0	48,5	100,0	48,5	100,0	48,5	100,0	48,4	**Enseignement du 1er degré**
96,5	49,1	96,7	49,0	96,6	49,0	96,5	48,9	Ens. du 1er niveau
3,5	36,4	3,3	37,9	3,4	37,8	3,5	37,7	Ens. spécial
100,0	48,4	100,0	48,4	100,0	48,8	100,0	49,1	**Enseignement du 2e degré**
2,0	37,0	2,0	35,0	2,1	34,5	2,2	35,2	Ens. spécial
62,3	47,0	61,5	47,3	60,0	47,5	59,0	47,6	1er cycle
0,7	60,8	0,1	85,2	–	–	–	–	4e degré primaire
21,1	47,7	20,5	47,9	19,5	48,2	18,7	48,5	Ens. moyen inf.
25,3	46,9	23,9	47,5	22,5	47,7	21,2	47,2	Ens. tech. et prof.
15,3	45,8	17,0	46,2	17,9	46,6	19,4	47,1	Ens. rénové
35,7	52,1	36,5	51,5	38,0	52,2	38,6	52,8	2e cycle
14,9	47,5	13,9	47,5	12,9	47,8	12,5	48,1	Ens. moyen sup.
16,5	59,6	15,3	59,7	15,5	62,0	15,4	62,9	Ens. tech. et prof.
–	–	–	–	–	–	–	–	Formation de maîtres
–	–	–	–	–	–	–	–	– Ens. normal gardien
–	–	–	–	–	–	–	–	– Ens. normal primaire
4,3	45,4	7,3	45,7	9,6	46,2	10,7	47,3	Ens. rénové
100,0	41,0	100,0	41,5	100,0	42,1	100,0	43,0	**Enseignement du 3e degré**
42,4	32,6	42,3	41,5	42,8	34,1	41,9	34,9	Formation universitaire
36,5	43,9	38,3	44,5	39,6	45,8	39,7	46,0	Form. tech. supérieure
21,1	68,1	19,4	69,0	17,6	68,9	18,4	70,2	Form. de maîtres
1,3	100,0	1,5	99,6	1,6	99,5	1,9	99,4	– Ens. normal gardien
6,5	71,3	5,8	71,6	5,5	71,1	5,5	71,7	– Ens. normal primaire
10,9	63,4	9,6	62,7	7,9	61,5	8,2	62,8	– Ens. normal moyen
2,6	69,9	2,5	78,3	2,7	77,7	2,7	78,4	– Ens. normal tech. moyen
81,1	47,9	81,2	47,9	81,7	48,1	82,5	48,2	**Total** (sans préprimaire)
100,0	48,1	100,0	48,1	100,0	48,2	100,0	48,3	**Total** (préprimaire inclus)
				Luxembourg				
100,0	49,2	100,0	49,0	100,0	40,1	100,0	48,0	**Enseignement préprimaire**
99,7	49,2	99,8	49,0	100,0	40,1	100,0	48,0	Ens. précolaire
0,3	38,7	0,2	45,5	:	:	:	:	Ens. spécial
100,0	48,6	100,0	48,8	100,0	49,0	100,0	48,9	**Enseignement du 1er degré**
95,5	49,0	94,9	49,1	95,4	49,4	95,6	49,3	Ens. primaire
4,5	41,9	5,1	43,1	4,6	41,5	4,4	41,4	Ens. spécial
100,0	49,1	100,0	48,6	100,0	49,3	100,0	48,9	**Enseignement du 2e degré**
–	–	–	–	–	–	–	–	Ens. spécial
68,2	50,8	67,0	49,9	67,6	51,3	66,7	50,4	1e cycle
22,5	52,4	21,8	52,0	21,6	52,4	22,0	52,3	Ens. secondaire
9,5	47,3	12,9	52,2	13,7	50,6	14,0	49,8	Ens. moyen
17,0	49,4	15,0	64,4	15,9	49,5	14,7	48,9	Clas. complémentaires
19,2	52,3	17,3	48,3	16,5	52,3	16,0	49,7	Ens. tech. et prof.
31,8	45,8	33,0	46,3	32,4	45,7	33,4	46,3	2e cycle
16,7	46,0	17,5	47,8	17,6	49,2	17,4	50,0	Ens. secondaire
3,3	41,9	3,7	43,7	4,4	49,5	4,9	52,7	Ens. moyen
0,7	50,6	1,0	46,3	1,4	47,7	1,8	52,0	Ec. de commerce et de gestion
0,0	1,1	0,0	0,6	0,0	0,7	0,1	2,2	Ec. tech.
11,0	51,5	10,8	50,6	9,0	43,0	9,2	42,8	Ens. tech. et prof.
100,0	33,1	100,0	33,3	100,0	32,4	100,0	32,3	**Enseignement du 3e degré**
17,4	53,5	13,6	52,6	9,4	61,4	7,5	65,0	Inst. pédagogique
6,8	34,4	7,6	34,9	9,6	34,3	6,3	33,5	Cours universitaires
72,4	31,7	75,0	32,4	79,5	33,4	84,9	33,8	Étudiants univ. à l'étranger
0,1	0,8	–	–	0,1	0,6	0,2	1,1	École technique
3,3	50,9	3,8	57,6	1,4	17,4	1,2	14,9	Miami University
86,6	48,2	86,6	48,0	87,3	48,4	89,1	48,2	**Total** (sans préprimaire)
100,0	48,3	100,0	48,1	100,0	48,3	100,0	48,2	**Total** (préprimaire inclus)

TAB. 112.1
(continued)
(suite)

	1970 – 1971		1972 – 1973		1973 – 1974	
	$\frac{f}{F}100$	$\frac{f}{f+m}100$	$\frac{f}{F}100$	$\frac{f}{f+m}100$	$\frac{f}{F}100$	$\frac{f}{f+m}100$
United Kingdom						
Pre-school level	100,0	48,7	100,0	48,9	100,0	48,9
Nursery	7,4	47,8	6,2	47,8	6,0	47,8
Primary schools	91,9	48,8	92,7	49,0	92,9	49,0
Special schools	0,7	50,0	1,1	50,0	1,1	50,0
First level	100,0	48,7	100,0	48,7	100,0	48,7
Primary schools	99,4	48,8	99,2	48,8	99,2	48,8
Special schools	0,6	39,0	0,8	39,7	0,8	38,6
Second level	100,0	48,3	100,0	48,5	100,0	48,7
Special schools	1,2	39,3	1,5	39,5	1,4	38,8
First stage	57,9	48,9	57,0	48,9	53,5	48,9
Secondary schools	57,9	48,9	57,0	48,9	53,5	48,9
Second stage	40,9	47,8	41,5	48,3	45,1	48,7
Secondary schools	36,2	48,2	36,5	48,4	40,4	48,6
Further education	4,7	44,8	5,1	47,4	4,7	49,3
Third level	100,0	40,0	100,0	40,7	100,0	41,2
Universities	37,7	29,2	38,8	30,8	39,2	31,9
Colleges of education	48,6	72,4	45,9	70,9	44,6	70,0
Further education-other	13,7	25,5	15,3	27,8	16,2	29,0
Total (Excluding pre-school level)	97,2	46,9	96,8	48,3	96,8	48,4
Total (Including pre-school level)	100,0	46,9	100,0	48,3	100,0	48,4
Ireland						
Pre-school level	100,0	48,7	100,0	48,7	100,0	48,8
Pre-primary education	99,7	48,7	99,6	48,7	99,7	48,8
Special education	0,3	45,4	0,4	55,7	0,3	48,1
First level	100,0	49,8	100,0	48,9	100,0	48,8
Primary education	95,8	49,0	98,3	49,0	98,2	48,9
Special education	1,5	45,5	1,7	44,4	1,8	44,4
Others	–	–	–	–	–	–
Second level	100,0	51,0	100,0	51,2	100,0	51,2
First stage	70,0	48,9	70,0	48,9	68,6	49,1
Secondary schools and s. tops	56,8	55,7	56,8	56,6	53,7	56,9
Comprehensive s. and comm. s.	0,5	49,8	0,5	43,7	2,7	45,3
Vocational educ. (2–3 year)	12,7	31,7	12,7	31,2	12,2	31,0
Second stage	30,0	56,5	30,0	56,9	31,4	56,7
Secondary schools and s. tops	22,8	54,6	22,8	55,5	23,4	55,7
Residential s. of domestic ec.	0,2	100,0	0,2	100,0	0,1	100,0
Vocational educ. (4–5 year)	4,7	64,3	4,7	62,5	5,0	61,2
Establishment off. tech. c.	0,1	29,5	0,1	45,7	0,2	47,2
Comprehensive and comm. s.	0,2	57,4	0,2	52,6	1,0	52,5
Others	1,9	64,1	1,9	62,7	1,7	62,7
Third level	100,0	34,1	100,0	36,5	100,0	37,0
Universities (inc. St Patrick C.)	74,6	33,9	71,6	36,4	70,1	37,7
Royal College of Surgeons	1,6	20,8	1,5	21,5	1,4	21,8
Teacher training	15,9	67,4	15,6	69,8	16,2	66,1
Establishment off. tech. c.	6,1	23,5	9,9	26,5	10,1	24,5
School of art	0,9	60,8	0,7	65,8	0,7	65,8
Others	0,9	6,1	0,7	6,9	1,5	13,3
Total (Excluding pre-school level)	82,9	49,0	83,2	49,1	83,4	49,1
Total (Including pre-school level)	100,0	49,0	100,0	49,1	100,0	49,1

TAB. 112.1
(continued)
(suite)

1974 – 1975		1975 – 1976		1976 – 1977		1977 – 1978		
$\frac{f}{F}100$	$\frac{f}{f+m}100$	$\frac{f}{F}100$	$\frac{f}{f+m}100$	$\frac{f}{F}100$	$\frac{f}{f+m}100$	$\frac{f}{F}100$	$\frac{f}{f+m}100$	
				United Kingdom				
100,0	48,9	100,0	49,0	100,0	48,9	100,0	48,6	**Pre-school level**
5,5	47,6	5,2	47,6	5,8	47,6	6,3	47,6	Nursery
93,4	49,0	93,8	49,1	93,1	48,9	92,5	48,8	Primary schools
1,1	50,0	1,0	50,0	1,1	50,0	1,2	50,0	Special schools
100,0	48,7	100,0	48,7	100,0	48,7	100,0	48,7	**First level**
99,2	48,8	99,2	48,8	99,2	48,8	99,2	48,8	Primary schools
0,8	40,0	0,8	38,9	0,8	38,9	0,8	38,9	Special schools
100,0	48,7	100,0	48,8	100,0	48,9	100,0	49,0	**Second level**
1,4	39,1	1,4	38,9	1,4	38,7	1,4	38,3	Special schools
53,1	48,9	52,3	48,9	51,9	48,9	51,4	48,9	First stage
53,1	48,9	52,3	48,9	51,9	48,9	51,4	48,9	Secondary schools
45,5	48,9	46,3	49,1	46,8	49,2	47,2	49,5	Second stage
40,3	48,7	40,1	48,7	40,5	48,8	40,7	48,9	Secondary schools
5,2	50,4	6,2	51,8	6,3	51,7	6,5	53,4	Further education
100,0	41,7	100,0	41,5	100,0	41,4	100,0	39,9	**Third level**
41,1	33,1	42,5	33,8	43,6	34,1	48,1	34,7	Universities
41,1	72,0	57,5	49,8	56,4	49,8	51,9	46,2	Colleges of education
17,8	30,6							Further education-other
96,8	48,4	96,7	48,4	97,0	48,4	97,2	48,4	**Total** (Excluding pre-school level)
100,0	48,4	100,0	48,5	100,0	48,5	100,0	48,4	**Total** (Including pre-school level)
				Ireland				
100,0	48,8	100,0	48,7	100,0	48,7	100,0	48,7	**Pre-school level**
99,8	48,8	99,7	48,7	99,7	48,7	99,7	48,7	Pre-primary education
0,2	43,4	0,3	42,4	0,3	46,0	0,3	44,4	Special education
100,0	48,9	100,0	48,7	100,0	48,6	100,0	48,6	**First level**
98,0	48,9	98,0	48,8	98,0	48,7	97,9	48,8	Primary education
2,0	45,9	2,0	43,9	2,0	44,4	2,1	43,9	Special education
–	–	–	–	–	–	–	–	Others
100,0	51,3	100,0	51,2	100,0	51,4	100,0	51,5	**Second level**
66,9	48,7	65,5	48,7	64,5	48,8	63,9	48,9	First stage
51,7	56,7	51,0	56,7	49,8	56,5	49,4	56,4	Secondary schools and s. tops
3,4	43,8	3,5	42,1	4,1	45,3	4,4	44,6	Comprehensive s. and comm. s.
11,8	30,6	11,0	30,4	10,6	30,3	10,1	30,4	Vocational educ. (2–3 year)
33,1	57,6	34,5	56,9	35,5	56,8	36,1	57,1	Second stage
23,8	56,5	24,3	56,6	24,5	56,2	24,5	56,6	Secondary schools and s. tops
0,1	100,0	0,1	100,0	0,2	100,0	0,1	100,0	Residential s. of domestic ec.
6,1	60,8	6,9	58,1	7,3	58,7	7,4	57,1	Vocational educ. (4–5 year)
0,1	39,7	0,3	49,2	0,3	40,8	0,3	52,8	Establishment off. tech. c.
1,4	54,8	1,6	52,7	1,8	55,0	2,1	55,8	Comprehensive and comm. s.
1,6	66,4	1,3	61,9	1,4	63,5	1,7	65,7	Others
100,0	37,1	100,0	38,7	100,0	39,6	100,0	40,8	**Third level**
74,9	41,5	70,2	41,8	66,2	42,0	65,2	43,0	Universities (inc. St Patrick C.)
1,4	21,1	1,4	23,8	1,5	26,6	1,1	22,1	Royal College of Surgeons
15,4	66,1	13,4	66,1	16,3	71,2	16,7	74,9	Teacher training
5,3	11,7	11,2	22,4	11,9	24,2	12,2	25,5	Establishment off. tech. c.
0,9	60,2	1,1	56,7	1,2	54,7	1,2	54,7	School of art
2,1	17,1	2,7	20,8	2,9	19,9	3,4	21,7	Others
84,2	49,2	84,2	49,2	83,9	49,2	84,2	49,4	**Total** (Excluding pre-school level)
100,0	49,2	100,0	49,1	100,0	49,2	100,0	49,3	**Total** (Including pre-school level)

TAB. 112.1
(continued)
(suite)

	1970 – 1971		1972 – 1973		1973 – 1974	
	$\frac{f}{F}100$	$\frac{f}{f+m}100$	$\frac{f}{F}100$	$\frac{f}{f+m}100$	$\frac{f}{F}100$	$\frac{f}{f+m}100$
Danmark						
Forskoleniveau	100,0	48,4	100,0	48,5	100,0	48,5
Børnehavekl.	100,0	48,4	100,0	48,5	100,0	48,5
Første niveau	100,0	48,6	100,0	48,5	100,0	48,5
Folkeskolen (1-5 K)	96,9	49,3	96,8	49,2	96,9	49,1
Special kl.	3,1	34,2	3,2	34,3	3,1	34,3
Andet niveau	100,0	50,3	100,0	50,6	100,0	50,6
Nedre trin	83,8	50,4	82,0	50,5	80,8	50,4
Folkeskolen (6-10 K.)	55,0	48,7	51,8	48,4	50,5	48,2
Realkl. (1-3 Real)	26,2	55,0	27,6	55,2	27,6	55,1
Realkurser	1,1	49,5	1,1	52,2	1,1	53,3
Efterskoler	1,5	45,8	1,5	46,6	1,6	47,0
Ungdomskostskoler	0,0	40,8	0,0	39,1	0,0	47,2
Øvre trin	16,2	49,6	18,0	50,8	19,2	51,2
Gymnasier (1-3 G)	8,5	48,6	9,1	49,7	9,6	49,9
Studenterkurser	1,1	44,5	1,1	47,1	1,1	49,5
HF-Kurser	1,3	50,3	2,3	52,4	2,8	53,0
Folke-og ungdom.	1,3	63,1	1,2	61,3	1,2	63,0
Husholdningss.	0,4	98,9	0,5	98,8	0,4	98,6
Tekniske s.	3,6	51,0	3,8	53,0	4,1	52,9
Landbrugss.	0,0	2,2	0,0	4,1	0,0	5,0
Tredje niveau	100,0	37,4	100,0	39,5	100,0	39,8
Universiteter	45,2	35,8	43,0	37,0	43,0	37,4
Læreruddannelse	22,7	56,5	21,4	55,8	21,6	55,2
Tekniske sk.	3,4	7,2	3,4	8,1	3,1	8,1
Læreanstalterne	13,8	37,5	12,8	37,2	13,5	38,4
Andre videregående udd.	14,9	87,9	19,4	87,0	18,8	78,1
I alt (Uden forskoleiveau)	97,6	48,4	96,0	48,5	95,8	48,5
I alt (med forskoleniveau)	100,0	48,4	100,0	48,5	100,0	48,5

TAB. 112.1
(continued)
(suite)

1974 – 1975		1975 – 1976		1976 – 1977		1977 – 1978		
$\frac{f}{F}\,100$	$\frac{f}{f+m}\,100$	$\frac{f}{F}\,100$	$\frac{f}{f+m}\,100$	$\frac{f}{F}\,100$	$\frac{f}{f+m}\,100$	$\frac{f}{F}\,100$	$\frac{f}{f+m}\,100$	
			Danmark					
100,0	48,5 #	100,0	48,6*	100,0	48,2*	100,0	48,0*	**Forskoleniveau**
100,0	48,5 #	100,0	48,6*	100,0	48,2*	100,0	48,0	Børnehavekl.
100,0	48,3	100,0	48,8*	100,0	48,9*	100,0	49,0*	**Første niveau**
97,1	48,9	:	:	:	:	:	:	Folkeskolen (1–5 K)
2,9	34,0	:	:	:	:	:	:	Special kl.
100,0	50,7	100,0	51,1	100,0	50,9	100,0	51,8	**Andet niveau**
80,7	50,6	80,4	50,6	79,8	50,0	79,8	50,8	Nedre trin
49,7	48,2 #	50,5	48,3*	59,9	48,6	:	:	Folkeskolen (6–10 K.)
28,3	55,3	27,3	55,6	17,4	55,7	:	:	Realkl. (1–3 Real)
1,1	58,7	1,0	60,2	0,9	60,0			Realkurser
1,6	45,3	1,6	44,5	1,6	45,3			Efterskoler
0,0	45,3	0,0	46,9	0,0	44,3			Ungdomskostskoler
19,3	51,5	19,6	53,2	19,3	53,6	20,2	56,3	Øvre trin
9,6	50,5	9,2	50,9	9,4	51,7	:	:	Gymnasier (1–3 G)
0,8	46,8	0,7	48,1	0,7	51,5	:	:	Studenterkurser
3,1	54,7	3,2	57,4	3,4	60,9	:	:	HF-Kurser
1,2	58,8	1,1	56,2	1,1	58,0	:	:	Folke-og ungdom.
0,5	99,0	0,5	98,9	0,5	99,0	:	:	Husholdningss.
4,4	56,8	4,9	57,4	5,2	59,3	:	:	Tekniske s.
0,9	4,8	0,0	5,6	0,1	5,6	:	:	Landbrugss.
100,0	41,3	100,0	41,5	100,0	42,9	100,0	46,7	**Tredje niveau**
44,8	37,8	45,9	38,3	46,6	39,3	:	:	Univeristeter
20,9	54,6	20,1	53,5	17,2	53,3	:	:	Læreruddannelse
1,3	4,8	1,2	5,0	1,2	5,2	:	:	Tekniske sk.
14,2	41,4 #	15,3	42,8	18,4	48,7	:	:	Læreanstalterne
18,8	77,4 #	17,5	76,5	16,6	78,6	:	:	Andre videregående udd.
95,7	48,6	95,6	49,1	95,2	49,2	94,9	50,1	**I alt** (Uden forskoleniveau)
100,0	48,6	100,0	49,1	100,0	49,1	100,0	50,0	**I alt** (med forskoleniveau)

TAB. 113
Female students of the third level by field of study (%)
Étudiantes du troisième degré selon le domaine d'études (%)

	Arts Lettres		Teaching Pédagogie		Fine arts Beaux-arts		Law Droit		Social Sciences Sciences sociales	
	$\frac{f}{F}100$	$\frac{f}{f+m}100$	$\frac{f}{F}100$	$\frac{f}{f+m}100$	$\frac{f}{F}100$	$\frac{f}{f+m}100$	$\frac{f}{F}100$	$\frac{f}{f+m}100$	$\frac{f}{F}100$	$\frac{f}{f+m}100$
BR DEUTSCHLAND [1]										
1965/66 [2]	28,2	39,3	36,2	62,2	3,8	42,4	2,9	11,2	5,8	12,5
1970/71 [2]	28,8	44,2	39,0	61,1	2,9	40,5	3,4	13,2	4,6	13,3
1974/75 [3]	8,4	44,2	55,2	52,8	5,8	34,2	4,2	23,5	12,0	26,3
FRANCE										
1974/75	44,2	66,1	–	–	–	–	15,0	43,7	4,7	34,0
ITALIA										
1965/66	54,5	74,5	11,9	64,9	2,8	29,3	4,5	15,0	10,6	15,9
1970/71	47,5	73,9	16,5	73,8	2,6	24,5	4,6	20,3	9,6	21,8
1974/75	35,8	72,9	12,5	76,3	4,1	28,6	9,6	32,7	8,7	26,1
NEDERLAND										
1965/66	20,8	40,1	28,6	40,2	8,8	40,1	4,1	25,1	14,4	25,1
1970/71	20,9	41,2	26,1	43,1	7,1	39,8	4,0	20,4	17,4	28,7
1974/75	19,1	42,4	27,2	49,8	7,1	41,8	3,9	22,2	16,8	30,6
BELGIQUE/BELGIË [4]										
1970/71	20,5	50,7	8,2	50,2	–	–	10,4	26,3	21,2	25,3
1974/75	21,9	54,4	8,6	55,0	–	–	12,3	32,2	12,2	24,5
LUXEMBOURG										
1965/66	9,4	38,8	62,4	49,4	–	–	4,5	20,5	–	–
1970/71	15,1	54,8	48,0	52,1	–	–	3,3	22,7	2,0	60,0
1973/74	9,2	59,4	57,5	61,3	–	–	5,3	27,5	0,5	20,0
UNITED KINGDOM [5]										
1974/75	14,4	54,4	41,2	68,7	7,3	39,6	.l.	.l.	17,9	25,5
IRELAND										
1965/66	46,4	36,1	19,5	70,5	1,5	31,9	1,0	18,0	6,6	22,7
DANMARK										
1965/66	33,1	58,1	34,1	56,1	2,0	29,0	5,7	30,3	3,3	10,6
1970/71	36,2	55,1	32,4	58,7	2,6	27,3	4,7	30,6	4,3	11,7
1973/74	29,2	55,7	32,7	60,5	2,2	26,1	3,2	31,8	6,5	18,0

[1] Figures for FR of Germany include West Berlin.
[2] The data under the heading 'Engineering science' include 'Architecture'.
[3] The criteria used for the allocation between fields of study are different from those employed in the preceding years. In particular the heading 'Teaching' now includes in its entirety the training of teaching personnel.
[4] Only universities and equivalent institutions.
[5] Law is included with Social sciences.

TAB. 113

Female students of the third level by field of study (%)
Étudiantes du troisième degré selon le domaine d'études (%)

Natural Sciences Sciences naturelles		Engineering Sciences ingénieur		Medical Sciences Sciences médicales		Agricultural Sciences Sciences agraires		Not stated Non indiqué		Total		
$\frac{f}{F}100$	$\frac{f}{f+m}100$	$\frac{f}{F}100$	$\frac{f}{f+m}100$	$\frac{f}{F}100$	$\frac{f}{f+m}100$	$\frac{f}{F}100$	$\frac{f}{f+m}100$	$\frac{f}{F}100$	$\frac{f}{f+m}100$	$\frac{f}{F}100$	$\frac{f}{f+m}100$	
												BR DEUTSCHLAND [1]
5,7	13,3	2,0	1,8	14,7	29,8	0,7	12,5	0,0	10,5	100,0	23,6	1965/66 [2]
9,2	18,7	2,0	2,3	8,5	25,6	1,5	24,5	0,1	19,9	100,0	26,9	1970/71 [2]
4,5	17,8	1,5	3,6	6,1	29,1	2,1	34,2	0,2	17,8	100,0	33,3	1974/75 [3]
												FRANCE
11,6	29,9	–	–	20,3	41,2	–	–	4,2	32,3	100,0	46,9	1974/75
												ITALIA
10,6	31,7	0,2	0,5	4,7	17,0	0,1	2,2	0,1	6,7	100,0	33,7	1965/66
11,5	36,2	0,3	1,1	7,0	20,4	0,3	4,5	0,1	15,0	100,0	37,7	1970/71
13,8	50,6	0,5	2,0	14,5	27,1	0,5	9,4	1,4	15,2	100,0	39,2	1974/75
												NEDERLAND
3,5	12,6	2,1	2,0	5,0	19,2	1,0	9,0	11,7	59,8	100,0	25,2	1965/66
3,3	13,9	5,1	6,3	4,8	20,9	1,3	13,1	10,0	71,8	100,0	27,7	1970/71
3,9	17,1	4,9	7,3	4,3	23,5	1,7	18,6	11,1	68,6	100,0	31,0	1974/75
												BELGIQUE/BELGIË [4]
11,5	33,5	0,7	2,3	25,9	28,9	1,3	8,4	0,3	13,9	100,0	28,6	1970/71
12,2	38,0	1,0	4,4	29,4	32,5	2,1	14,2	0,3	19,2	100,0	32,6	1974/75
												LUXEMBOURG
2,5	26,3	–	–	3,9	20,5	–	–	17,3	17,9	100,0	32,8	1965/66
7,9	42,9	–	–	13,2	33,9	–	–	10,5	24,2	100,0	41,9	1970/71
2,4	22,7	–	–	3,9	18,2	–	–	21,2	37,6	100,0	45,2	1973/74
												UNITED KINGDOM [5]
9,6	24,7	1,1	2,5	7,9	41,7	0,6	21,4	–	–	100,0	35,7	1974/75
												IRELAND
9,9	27,4	3,9	11,1	10,9	24,1	0,3	2,3	–	–	100,0	30,5	1965/66
												DANMARK
3,9	22,3	0,8	2,1	14,1	34,1	0,7	9,1	2,3	58,3	100,0	35,1	1965/66
3,8	22,0	1,0	3,1	12,8	37,7	0,6	12,7	1,6	53,4	100,0	36,7	1970/71
3,2	21,8	0,7	4,3	21,4	61,5	0,8	25,1	0,1	42,4	100,0	43,4	1973/74

[1] Les données pour la RF d'Allemagne incluent la ville de Berlin.
[2] Les données relatives à la rubrique «Sciences ingénieur» comprennent l'architecture.
[3] Les critères utilisés pour la répartition entre les domaines d'études sont différents de ceux utilisés les années précédentes. En particulier la rubrique «Pédagogie» comprend maintenant la formation du personnel enseignant dans son ensemble.
[4] Seulement universités et institutions équivalentes.
[5] Le droit est classé avec les «Sciences sociales».

TAB. 114
Female graduates by field of study (%)
Diplômées du troisième degré selon le domaine d'études (%)

	Arts Lettres		Teaching Pédagogie		Fine Arts Beaux-arts		Law Droit		Social Sciences Sciences sociales	
	$\frac{f}{F}100$	$\frac{f}{f+m}100$	$\frac{f}{F}100$	$\frac{f}{f+m}100$	$\frac{f}{F}100$	$\frac{f}{f+m}100$	$\frac{f}{F}100$	$\frac{f}{f+m}100$	$\frac{f}{F}100$	$\frac{f}{f+m}100$
BR DEUTSCHLAND										
1964/65 [1]	2,5	22,5	74,0	59,0	.l.	.l.	1,5	9,7	2,4	11,0
1972/73 [2]	9,6	37,2	70,0	55,6	0,3	10,1	2,4	10,8	2,4	11,1
FRANCE [3]										
1966/67	58,0	63,7	–	–	–	–	7,5	23,0	.l.	.l.
1972/73	52,5	64,3	–	–	–	–	10,1	34,0	3,0	24,2
ITALIA										
1965/66	49,0	78,5	10,7	63,9	2,4	33,4	7,5	17,6	8,2	18,6
1970/71	55,1	74,8	12,3	70,3	2,8	32,6	3,9	17,2	8,4	24,3
1973/74	47,1	76,7	17,2	72,3	3,7	33,2	3,7	22,6	7,5	29,0
NEDERLAND										
1965/66	6,1	29,3	55,8	42,3	2,7	38,5	1,2	20,4	15,5	51,3
1971/72	8,1	32,6	45,3	44,4	4,3	34,3	2,3	20,4	16,1	35,0
1973/74 [4]	3,9	33,8	39,8	50,0	4,2	34,7	2,2	18,9	25,4	42,1
BELGIQUE/BELGIË										
1965/66	8,9	41,1	43,7	70,0	2,2	26,5	1,3	13,8	15,1	32,8
1970/71 [2]	33,5	50,1	7,2	45,7	–	–	7,4	21,4	13,2	21,3
1973/74 [2]	29,5	54,6	7,9	52,1	–	–	7,8	26,0	15,7	27,3
LUXEMBOURG										
1966/67	–	–	100,0	48,3	–	–	–	–	–	–
1971/72	–	–	100,0	56,2	–	–	–	–	–	–
1973/74	–	–	100,0	70,1	–	–	–	–	–	–
UNITED KINGDOM [5]										
1966/67	30,6	48,0	17,3	45,0	2,9	29,1	1,6	12,9	20,4	34,8
1970/71	29,3	50,0	21,3	50,0	2,9	27,4	1,8	17,0	19,5	32,2
1973/74	28,8	53,0	15,9	46,6	3,4	32,2	2,4	21,9	20,9	35,0
IRELAND [2]										
1965/66	56,3	41,6	22,1	72,1	0,6	41,7	0,9	22,2	7,5	28,0
1973/74 [6]	80,3	53,8	.l.	.l.	0,5	37,8	1,4	26,3	5,2	21,6
DANMARK										
1965/66	21,2	77,9	58,6	57,5	1,0	21,9	1,6	18,7	2,3	11,9
1970/71	21,7	72,3	55,4	59,0	1,2	23,7	2,7	25,2	3,8	13,9
1973/74	9,1	59,2	47,1	68,0	1,3	22,8	2,2	28,3	4,7	14,2

[1] Agriculture is grouped with 'Engineering science'.
[2] Universities and equivalent institutions only.
[3] Diplomas obtained from universities and schools of engineering only. 'Arts' includes social science but not economics.
[4] Teacher training diplomas for second level schools are not included.
[5] Universities only.
[6] Teaching is grouped with 'Arts'.

TAB. 114
Female graduates by field of study (%)
Diplômées du troisième degré selon le domaine d'études (%)

Natural Sciences Sciences naturelles		Engineering Sciences ingénieur		Medical Sciences Sciences Médicales		Agricultural Sciences Sciences agraires		Not stated Non indiqué		Total		
$\frac{f}{F}100$	$\frac{f}{f+m}100$	$\frac{f}{F}100$	$\frac{f}{f+m}100$	$\frac{f}{F}100$	$\frac{f}{f+m}100$	$\frac{f}{F}100$	$\frac{f}{f+m}100$	$\frac{f}{F}100$	$\frac{f}{f+m}100$	$\frac{f}{F}100$	$\frac{f}{f+m}100$	
												BR DEUTSCHLAND
1,2	5,3	1,8	1,4	15,9	34,3	0,7	9,6	–	–	100,0	26,0	1964/65 [1]
1,7	7,3	0,2	1,3	12,2	26,1	1,2	18,5	–	–	100,0	34,0	1972/73 [2]
												FRANCE [3]
22,8	31,4	1,5	4,3	10,0	38,5	0,2	3,2	–	–	100,0	38,2	1966/67
16,2	30,3	1,2	5,3	8,9	38,7	–	–	8,1	26,3	100,0	39,3	1972/73
												ITALIA
14,8	42,5	0,2	0,6	7,1	21,1	0,1	2,3	–	–	100,0	36,5	1965/66
12,6	43,9	0,1	0,6	4,7	20,7	0,1	3,4	–	–	100,0	43,2	1970/71
12,3	46,1	2,0	0,9	8,0	18,2	0,3	6,5	0,1	23,1	100,0	42,7	1973/74
												NEDERLAND
1,2	11,2	3,2	2,8	1,8	20,3	0,3	4,0	12,2	59,1	100,0	27,7	1965/66
1,7	11,3	6,5	9,3	2,0	16,7	0,6	7,2	13,1	98,0	100,0	31,6	1971/72
1,3	10,9	6,8	8,7	2,6	17,8	0,7	8,5	13,1	99,0	100,0	33,2	1973/74 [4]
												BELGIQUE/BELGIË
7,3	32,8	1,1	3,0	20,2	51,0	0,1	1,4	0,1	3,0	100,0	39,2	1965/66
20,1	36,7	0,3	1,0	17,4	30,5	0,5	4,6	0,4	12,5	100,0	29,8	1970/71 [2]
17,3	38,9	0,5	2,3	20,4	34,4	6,0	5,9	3,0	14,0	100,0	33,9	1973/74 [2]
												LUXEMBOURG
–	–	–	–	–	–	–	–	–	–	100,0	48,3	1966/67
–	–	–	–	–	–	–	–	–	–	100,0	56,2	1971/72
–	–	–	–	–	–	–	–	–	–	100,0	70,1	1973/74
												UNITED KINGDOM [5]
18,2	20,7	0,4	0,7	7,8	21,9	0,8	11,1	–	–	100,0	27,0	1966/67
16,8	22,2	0,9	1,8	6,6	24,7	0,9	15,7	–	–	100,0	29,3	1970/71
17,7	25,1	1,4	3,2	8,3	32,1	1,1	19,6	0,1	17,2	100,0	31,7	1973/74
												IRELAND [2]
6,1	25,1	–	–	6,3	22,5	0,2	1,4	–	–	100,0	36,1	1965/66
6,3	32,0	0,8	4,5	5,3	31,3	0,2	2,4	–	–	100,0	41,2	1973/74 [6]
												DANMARK
1,4	24,2	0,7	1,5	12,5	46,5	0,6	7,0	0,1	7,1	100,0	39,3	1965/66
1,5	19,4	0,7	1,8	12,3	45,8	0,6	8,8	0,1	6,6	100,0	40,0	1970/71
1,0	20,6	1,0	4,2	33,1	71,8	0,5	12,5	–	–	100,0	47,8	1973/74

[1] L'agriculture est classée avec les «Sciences ingénieur».
[2] Seulement universités et institutions équivalentes.
[3] Seulement les diplômes obtenus auprès d'universités et d'écoles d'ingénieurs. Les «Lettres» comprennent les sciences sociales mais pas les sciences économiques.
[4] Les diplômes de l'école pour la formation des enseignants des écoles secondaires sont exclus.
[5] Universités seulement.
[6] La pédagogie est classée avec les «Lettres».

TAB. 115

Women aged between 14 and 65 undergoing out-of-school vocational training by type of training, age and type of activity (%)

Femmes âgées de 14 à 65 ans en cours de formation professionnelle extra-scolaire, selon le type de formation, l'âge et les critères d'activité (%)

1975

	BR Deutschland		France		Italia		Nederland		Belgique/ België	
	$\frac{f}{F}$ 100	$\frac{f}{f+m}$ 100	$\frac{f}{F}$ 100	$\frac{f}{f+m}$ 100	$\frac{f}{F}$ 100	$\frac{f}{f+m}$ 100	$\frac{f}{F}$ 100	$\frac{f}{f+m}$ 100	$\frac{f}{F}$ 100	$\frac{f}{f+m}$ 100
Type of training:										
Basic training	74,3	38,5	18,0	28,3	49,3	41,6	35,4	31,0	32,4	29,7
Further training	25,6	29,4	82,0	34,0	50,6	33,3	64,5	27,8	67,5	23,7
Total	100,0	35,7	100,0	32,8	100,0	36,9	100,0	28,8	100,0	25,3
Age groups:										
14–17 years old	37,1	41,6	6,4	23,8	24,0	44,2	6,0	44,7	10,3	30,7
18–24 years old	46,1	37,4	34,1	41,1	36,5	41,4	43,7	36,5	34,2	29,3
25–34 years old	10,3	24,2	32,9	29,6	21,4	30,3	30,6	21,7	29,6	23,6
35–49 years old	5,4	25,1	20,5	30,6	12,9	28,5	16,4	26,4	19,8	20,9
50–65 years old	1,1	35,3	6,1	36,5	5,2	42,7	3,3	31,9	6,1	25,6
Total	100,0	35,7	100,0	32,8	100,0	36,9	100,0	28,9	100,0	25,4
Type of activity:										
Persons with an occupation	85,6	35,3	84,8	30,7	45,4	26,8	71,5	22,9	76,8	21,6
Unemployed persons	1,5	35,5	3,1	56,5	10,9	54,4	2,6	29,6	4,2	48,5
Non-active persons	13,0	39,7	12,1	52,9	43,5	53,6	26,0	92,7	19,0	63,7
of which: students	9,4	37,7	5,7	43,5	22,8	41,7	–	–	8,2	44,9
Total	100,0	35,7	100,0	32,8	100,0	36,9	100,0	28,9	100,0	25,4

TAB. 116

Participation in out-of-school vocational training courses by certain categories of persons of working age (%)

Participation à des cours de formation professionnelle extra-scolaire de certaines catégories de personnes en âge de travailler (%)

	BR Deutschland		France		Italia		Nederland		Belgique/ België	
	$\frac{f}{F}$ 100	$\frac{m}{M}$ 100	$\frac{f}{F}$ 100	$\frac{m}{M}$ 100	$\frac{f}{F}$ 100	$\frac{m}{M}$ 100	$\frac{f}{F}$ 100	$\frac{m}{M}$ 100	$\frac{f}{F}$ 100	$\frac{m}{M}$ 100
Persons aged between 14 and 65 undergoing training (%):										
1973										
persons aged between 14 and 65	3,1	5,8	2,8	5,5	0,5	0,9	3,0	5,9	0,1	1,1
persons with an occupation	6,2	6,1	4,1	5,8	1,1	0,8	8,0	7,0	0,6	1,2
unemployed persons	0,9	4,1	3,4	3,3	3,4	2,3	8,2	3,9	0,4	2,0
1975										
persons aged between 14 and 65	2,9	5,7	3,0	6,2	1,1	2,0	3,0	7,3	1,2	3,5
persons with an occupation	6,0	6,3	5,4	7,4	2,1	2,1	8,9	9,5	2,6	4,4
unemployed persons	3,0	3,6	4,4	3,4	9,7	5,3	10,6	6,8	2,5	3,1

TAB. 115

Women aged between 14 and 65 undergoing out-of-school vocational training by type of training, age and type of activity (%)
Femmes âgées de 14 à 65 ans en cours de formation professionnelle extra-scolaire, selon le type de formation, l'âge et les critères d'activité (%)

1975

Luxembourg		United Kingdom		Ireland		Danmark		EUR 9		
$\frac{f}{F}100$	$\frac{f}{f+m}100$	$\frac{f}{F}100$	$\frac{f}{f+m}100$	$\frac{f}{F}100$	$\frac{f}{f+m}100$	$\frac{f}{F}100$	$\frac{f}{f+m}100$	$\frac{f}{F}100$	$\frac{f}{f+m}100$	
										Type de formation:
44,2	26,6	44,3	22,6	56,8	28,4	87,0	32,8	47,8	32,2	Formation de base
55,7	27,0	55,6	40,3	43,1	30,0	12,9	52,2	52,2	33,4	Formation complémentaire
100,0	26,8	100,0	29,9	100,0	29,1	100,0	34,4	100,0	32,8	Total
										Groupes d'âge:
26,8	31,3	7,4	29,2	20,0	35,0	2,8	20,8	18,1	37,6	14–17 ans
39,0	30,8	38,8	26,0	55,0	2,9	84,2	34,9	40,9	34,6	18–24 ans
17,7	17,6	24,5	27,8	11,9	24,0	8,2	31,9	21,9	27,2	25–34 ans
13,4	25,0	23,4	40,5	8,5	26,3	4,2	50,0	15,0	31,8	35–49 ans
3,1	33,3	5,9	44,2	4,6	34,1	0,6	66,7	4,1	38,5	50–65 ans
100,0	27,0	100,0	30,0	100,0	29,1	100,0	34,5	100,0	32,8	Total
										Critères d'activité:
87,3	24,6	76,6	26,0	73,2	25,3	84,2	32,1	77,7	29,6	Personnes ayant un emploi
0,6	80,0	3,2	48,1	4,9	38,5	1,4	45,5	3,5	47,9	Personnes en chômage
12,1	59,2	20,3	62,1	21,9	55,4	14,4	61,0	18,8	53,7	Personnes non actives
6,7	33,5	9,8	46,6	13,4	43,6	13,5	60,8	9,5	42,2	dont: étudiants
100,0	27,0	100,0	30,0	100,0	29,1	100,0	34,5	100,0	32,8	Total

TAB. 116

Participation in out-of-school vocational training courses by certain categories of persons of working age (%)
Participation à des cours de formation professionnelle extra-scolaire de certaines catégories de personnes en âge de travailler (%)

Luxembourg		United Kingdom		Ireland		Danmark		EUR 9		
$\frac{f}{F}100$	$\frac{m}{M}100$	$\frac{f}{F}100$	$\frac{m}{M}100$	$\frac{f}{F}100$	$\frac{m}{M}100$	$\frac{f}{F}100$	$\frac{m}{M}100$	$\frac{f}{F}100$	$\frac{m}{M}100$	
										Personnes âgées de 14 à 65 ans en cours de formation en %:
										1973
1,7	3,5	:	:	:	:	:	:	:	:	des personnes de 14 à 65 ans
3,4	3,9	:	:	:	:	:	:	:	:	des personnes ayant un emploi
–	2,9	:	:	:	:	:	:	:	:	des personnes en chômage
										1975
1,6	4,4	2,5	5,9	2,8	6,6	2,1	4,0	2,4	5,0	des personnes de 14 à 65 ans
4,4	5,2	3,8	6,7	7,1	8,0	3,6	5,1	4,7	5,8	des personnes ayant un emploi
2,5	–	2,8	2,4	5,5	2,7	0,9	0,6	4,4	3,5	des personnes en chômage

TAB. 117

Population by type of training completed (1 000)
Population selon le type de formation acquise (1 000)

1973

	BR Deutschland F	BR Deutschland M	France F	France M	Italia F	Italia M	Nederland F	Nederland M	Belgique/België F	Belgique/België M	Luxembourg F	Luxembourg M	
General training at school	18 935	17 356	11 660	10 970	13 600	13 344	4 190	4 219	2 848	2 873	114	113	Formation scolaire générale
Vocational training at school	2 248	2 951	1 865	2 483	1 628	2 185	1 247	1 610	636	796	7	21	Formation scolaire professionnelle
Basic vocational training	6 791	10 445	1 954	1 733	419	805	88	191	67	171	16	20	Formation professionnelle de base
Further vocational training	549	1 899	759	1 537	81	235	112	381	33	119	4	10	Formation professionnelle complémentaire

TAB. 117.1

Population by type of training completed (%)
Population selon le type de formation acquise (%)

1973

As a percentage of the population aged from 14 to 65 years / **En pourcentage de la population âgée de 14 à 65 ans**

	BR Deutschland f/F·100	BR Deutschland f/(f+m)·100	France f/F·100	France f/(f+m)·100	Italia f/F·100	Italia f/(f+m)·100	Nederland f/F·100	Nederland f/(f+m)·100	Belgique/België f/F·100	Belgique/België f/(f+m)·100	Luxembourg f/F·100	Luxembourg f/(f+m)·100	
General training at school	91,2	52,2	70,9	51,5	74,1	50,5	98,1	49,8	88,6	49,8	95,8	50,2	Formation scolaire générale
Vocational training at school	10,8	42,2	11,3	42,9	8,9	42,7	29,2	43,6	19,8	44,4	5,9	25,0	Formation scolaire professionnelle
Basic vocational training	32,7	39,4	11,9	53,0	2,3	34,2	2,1	31,5	2,1	28,1	13,4	44,4	Formation professionnelle de base
Further vocational training	2,6	22,4	4,6	33,1	0,4	25,6	1,9	22,7	1,0	21,7	3,4	28,6	Formation professionnelle complémentaire

TAB. 118

Indices of non-completion of general and vocational training
Indices d'abandon de la formation générale et professionnelle

1973

	BR Deutschland F	BR Deutschland M	France F	France M	Italia F	Italia M	Nederland F	Nederland M	Belgique/België F	Belgique/België M	Luxembourg F	Luxembourg M	
Training at school (total)	0,3	0,3	28,1	28,5	:	:	0,7	1,0	7,2	6,1	4,2	5,0	Formation scolaire (total)
– General training	0,3	0,3	27,5	28,0	:	:	0,7	0,9	6,5	5,4	4,2	4,2	– Formation scolaire générale
– Vocational training	6,1	6,6	31,0	26,5	:	:	22,6	20,1	24,0	19,4	22,2	12,5	– Formation scolaire professionnelle
Basic vocational training	10,8	6,7	31,9	52,9	–	–	11,1	2,1	30,2	31,9	11,1	9,1	Formation professionnelle de base
Further vocational training	9,9	5,9	18,2	13,8	–	–	9,7	2,6	17,5	13,1	0,0	0,0	Formation professionnelle complémentaire

Indices of non-completion = the number of drop-outs as a percentage of those who followed a particular type of training.

The number of drop-outs was calculated by subtracting the number of persons who completed a certain type of training from the number who began it.

Indice d'abandon: rapport entre le nombre de personnes ayant abandonné et le nombre de personnes ayant suivi la formation considérée.

Nombre de personnes ayant abandonné: différence entre le nombre de personnes ayant suivi et le nombre de personnes ayant terminé la formation considérée.

TAB. 119

Population by highest level of study attained as part of general schooling and vocational training (%)
Population selon le niveau d'études le plus élevé atteint dans le cadre de la formation scolaire générale et professionnelle (%)

1973

	BR Deutschland		France		Italia		Nederland		Belgique/ België		Luxembourg		
	$\frac{f}{F}100$	$\frac{m}{M}100$	$\frac{f}{F}100$	$\frac{m}{M}100$	$\frac{f}{F}100$	$\frac{m}{M}100$	$\frac{f}{F}100$	$\frac{m}{M}100$	$\frac{f}{F}100$	$\frac{m}{M}100$	$\frac{f}{F}100$	$\frac{m}{M}100$	
Within the general education system													**Dans le cadre scolaire**
compulsory school	84,6	78,0	61,0	59,1	72,7	74,9	86,0	79,6	72,7	69,2	89,1	83,1	scolarité obligatoire
2nd level 2nd stage	2,9	3,7	5,7	6,0	4,3	9,1	7,6	11,3	10,4	14,1	3,4	7,6	2e niveau supérieur
teacher training	1,3	0,5	0,5	0,4	3,3	0,8	2,6	1,4	2,5	1,4	1,7	0,8	formation des maîtres
3rd level	2,4	7,8	4,1	5,5	1,3	3,0	2,0	5,5	3,0	5,5	1,7	3,4	3e niveau
Total	100,0	100,0	100,0	100,0	100,0	100,0	100,0	100,0	100,0	100,0	100,0	100,0	Total
Within the general system of school education													**Dans le cadre de la formation scolaire générale**
compulsory school	95,6	92,2	88,2	87,1	98,1	97,2	93,9	90,0	88,8	84,1	94,7	89,4	scolarité obligatoire
2nd level 2nd stage	4,4	7,8	11,8	12,9	1,9	2,8	6,1	10,0	11,2	15,9	5,3	10,6	2e niveau supérieur
Total	100,0	100,0	100,0	100,0	100,0	100,0	100,0	100,0	100,0	100,0	100,0	100,0	Total
Within the system of school vocational training													**Dans le cadre de la formation scolaire professionnelle**
2nd level 1st stage	58,4	41,1	49,2	49,1	15,8	15,3	72,1	66,4	49,4	49,5	57,1	61,9	2e niveau inférieur
2nd level 2nd stage	6,8	4,7	10,0	13,6	32,1	54,7	12,2	15,1	22,8	22,9	–	9,5	2e niveau supérieur
teacher training	12,0	3,4	4,8	2,4	37,4	6,4	9,0	3,9	12,7	5,8	28,6	4,8	formation des maîtres
3rd level	22,8	50,8	36,0	34,9	14,7	23,6	6,7	14,6	15,1	21,8	14,3	23,8	3e niveau
Total	100,0	100,0	100,0	100,0	100,0	100,0	100,0	100,0	100,0	100,0	100,0	100,0	Total

TAB. 120

Further general and vocational training (%)
Compléments à la formation générale et professionnelle (%)

1973

	BR Deutschland		France		Italia		Nederland		Belgique/ België		Luxembourg		
	$\frac{f}{F}100$	$\frac{m}{M}100$	$\frac{f}{F}100$	$\frac{m}{M}100$	$\frac{f}{F}100$	$\frac{m}{M}100$	$\frac{f}{F}100$	$\frac{m}{M}100$	$\frac{f}{F}100$	$\frac{m}{M}100$	$\frac{f}{F}100$	$\frac{m}{M}100$	
General training at school supplemented by:													**Formation scolaire générale complétée par:**
Vocational training at school	11,9	17,0	15,4	21,4	1,9	2,5	29,7	38,1	22,3	27,7	6,1	19,4	formation scolaire professionnelle
Basic training	35,8	60,1	14,8	13,2	2,5	5,0	2,1	4,5	2,2	5,8	14,4	17,7	formation de base
Further training	2,9	10,9	5,9	12,0	0,5	2,8	2,6	9,0	1,1	4,1	3,2	8,5	formation complément.
Vocational training at school supplemented by:													**Formation scolaire profession. complétée par:**
Basic training	46,0	68,4	1,2	1,3	5,9	7,5	2,3	8,7	2,6	5,1	8,8	12,7	formation de base
Further training	7,1	16,5	6,9	13,8	1,4	2,7	3,3	12,4	1,7	4,6	6,1	13,7	formation compément.
Basic training after previously completed:													**Formation de base aprés avoir terminé:**
Vocational training at school	15,2	19,3	1,1	1,9	22,9	20,2	32,8	73,3	24,2	23,8	3,8	13,2	formation scolaire professionnelle
Further training after previously completed:													**Formation complément. après avoir terminé:**
Vocational training at school	29,3	25,7	17,0	22,3	28,5	24,8	37,0	52,2	33,3	30,9	11,8	29,7	formation scolaire professionnelle
Basic training	64,6	85,3	12,3	12,5	10,9	12,9	3,5	14,8	10,0	13,8	35,1	42,1	formation de base

TAB. 121

Population by age and type of training completed (%)
Population selon l'âge et le type de formation acquise (%)

1973

	BR Deutschland		France		Italia		Nederland		Belgique/Belgïe		Luxembourg	
	f/F 100	m/M 100	f/F 100	m/M 100	f/F 100	m/M 100	f/F 100	m/M 100	f/F 100	m/M 100	f/F 100	m/M 100
18–24 years / **18–24 ans**												
General training at school / Formation scolaire générale	90,8	89,6	83,6	79,3	81,7	83,9	98,9	98,8	92,1	93,4	95,3	97,3
Vocational training at school / Formation scolaire professionnelle	11,3	7,7	18,3	19,2	17,2	15,8	40,1	42,2	32,7	35,1	8,4	15,7
Basic vocational training / Formation professionnelle de base	43,9	46,0	16,0	14,6	5,9	7,0	3,7	7,0	3,1	4,3	18,7	14,2
Further vocational training / Formation professionnelle complémentaire	2,7	2,9	3,9	6,1	0,6	0,7	2,3	3,8	1,2	1,7	3,2	3,9
25–34 years / **25–34 ans**												
General training at school / Formation scolaire générale	91,0	89,0	77,2	76,0	79,8	78,1	98,5	97,8	92,0	93,2	93,2	93,9
Vocational training at school / Formation scolaire professionnelle	16,2	20,4	22,6	28,3	13,8	19,6	44,1	49,5	31,9	39,3	9,4	26,4
Basic vocational training / Formation professionnelle de base	47,5	64,4	17,7	17,3	3,9	8,0	3,7	8,1	3,5	7,7	17,9	20,6
Further vocational training / Formation professionnelle complémentaire	3,7	11,5	7,6	14,7	0,7	2,1	3,8	12,1	1,6	4,9	4,1	9,3
35–49 years / **35–49 ans**												
General training at school / Formation scolaire générale	92,0	90,2	66,8	64,1	73,8	76,9	98,1	97,7	88,4	89,0	95,5	94,6
Vocational training at school / Formation scolaire professionnelle	11,4	18,0	9,6	16,0	8,0	12,7	29,2	42,6	18,2	23,8	6,3	18,1
Basic vocational training / Formation professionnelle de base	33,7	62,1	12,9	11,4	1,5	4,5	1,7	3,8	2,1	6,7	14,4	19,6
Further vocational training / Formation professionnelle complémentaire	2,8	13,2	5,6	13,0	0,5	1,9	3,2	13,0	1,3	5,1	3,4	10,4
50 years and over / **50 ans et plus**												
General training at school / Formation scolaire générale	91,2	91,0	56,8	61,7	59,1	66,0	97,3	97,5	83,6	86,6	97,3	96,5
Vocational training at school / Formation scolaire professionnelle	9,4	17,4	4,4	9,4	4,4	9,5	16,8	30,0	9,0	14,7	2,8	15,0
Basic vocational training / Formation professionnelle de base	26,3	60,4	6,4	6,6	0,6	2,4	0,8	1,5	1,1	4,5	10,6	18,2
Further vocational training / Formation professionnelle complémentaire	2,4	11,6	3,2	8,0	0,2	0,9	2,2	8,7	0,6	3,9	2,8	9,8

TAB. 122

Population by age and highest level of study attained within the school system (%)
Population selon l'âge et le niveau le plus élevé atteint dans le cadre scolaire (%)
1973

	BR Deutschland		France		Italia		Nederland		Belgique België		Luxembourg		
	$\frac{f}{F}100$	$\frac{m}{M}100$	$\frac{f}{F}100$	$\frac{m}{M}100$	$\frac{f}{F}100$	$\frac{m}{M}100$	$\frac{f}{F}100$	$\frac{m}{M}100$	$\frac{f}{F}100$	$\frac{m}{M}100$	$\frac{f}{F}100$	$\frac{m}{M}100$	
18–24 years old													**18 à 24 ans**
compulsory school	81,2	79,5	67,3	66,2	76,3	76,6	78,9	79,6	61,7	64,6	87,2	85,2	scolarité obligatoire
2nd level 2nd stage	6,8	8,7	12,3	10,8	13,3	19,6	16,3	17,2	24,5	25,8	7,0	11,3	2e niveau supérieur
teacher training	10,4	–	0,3	0,2	6,8	1,1	2,6	1,0	2,6	0,8	1,2	0,4	formation des maîtres
3rd level	1,8	1,4	4,6	3,5	0,4	0,1	1,1	1,0	3,3	1,9	0,5	0,6	3e niveau
25–34 years old													**25 à 34 ans**
compulsory school	81,2	72,4	60,1	58,9	78,3	75,2	80,9	72,5	65,5	61,2	84,6	75,7	scolarité obligatoire
2nd level 2nd stage	3,2	4,6	7,5	7,7	6,2	15,3	9,7	15,4	14,9	18,5	4,8	10,0	2e niveau supérieur
teacher training	2,3	0,8	1,0	0,6	4,5	0,8	4,5	1,5	5,0	2,9	2,2	2,3	formation des maîtres
3rd level	4,3	11,2	9,4	10,3	2,7	3,8	3,5	7,5	6,5	10,6	2,0	5,8	3e niveau
35–49 years old													**35 à 49 ans**
compulsory school	85,4	77,5	58,6	53,7	72,9	75,7	86,9	76,7	74,8	67,9	88,3	81,7	scolarité obligatoire
2nd level 2nd stage	2,3	2,3	4,5	5,1	2,8	7,1	6,3	10,6	8,3	13,0	3,8	6,7	2e niveau supérieur
teacher training	1,3	0,6	0,5	0,3	3,2	0,8	2,6	1,6	2,4	1,4	1,6	0,8	formation des maîtres
3rd level	2,8	9,7	3,5	5,9	1,6	4,1	2,4	8,9	2,9	6,6	1,6	5,0	3e niveau
50 years old and over													**50 ans et plus**
compulsory school	85,8	78,4	50,9	51,9	58,7	65,2	89,1	82,4	75,8	71,5	93,7	84,9	scolarité obligatoire
2nd level 2nd stage	2,4	3,4	3,4	5,0	1,3	4,5	4,4	8,7	4,7	9,4	2,4	6,0	2e niveau supérieur
teacher training	1,1	0,6	0,6	0,5	1,9	0,9	1,2	1,1	1,7	1,3	1,1	1,2	formation des maîtres
3rd level	3,3	8,8	1,8	4,6	0,8	3,5	1,6	5,6	1,4	4,4	0,5	4,0	3e niveau

TAB. 123

Population gaving completed third-level studies by duration of studies (%)
Population ayant achevé des études du troisième niveau, selon la durée des études (%)
1973

	BR Deutschland		France		Italia		Belgique België		Luxembourg		
	$\frac{f}{F}100$	$\frac{m}{M}100$	$\frac{f}{F}100$	$\frac{m}{M}100$	$\frac{f}{F}100$	$\frac{m}{M}100$	$\frac{f}{F}100$	$\frac{m}{M}100$	$\frac{f}{F}100$	$\frac{m}{M}100$	
< 2 years	19,4	17,8	3,6	1,4	–	–	:	:	–	0,8	< 2 années
2 – 4 years	51,2	48,3	45,8	30,4	1,0	1,0	:	:	42,0	18,6	2 – 4 années
4 – 6 years	18,8	20,0	32,8	39,2	89,1	72,6	:	:	49,2	63,1	4 – 6 années
> 6 years	10,6	14,0	17,4	28,7	9,8	26,4	:	:	8,9	17,5	> 6 années

TAB. 124

Population having completed vocational training by main occupational criteria (%)

Population ayant achevé une formation professionnelle, selon les principaux critères d'activité (%)

1973

	BR Deutschland		France		Italia		Nederland		Belgique België		Luxembourg		
	$\frac{f}{F}100$	$\frac{m}{M}100$	$\frac{f}{F}100$	$\frac{m}{M}100$	$\frac{f}{F}100$	$\frac{m}{M}100$	$\frac{f}{F}100$	$\frac{m}{M}100$	$\frac{f}{F}100$	$\frac{m}{M}100$	$\frac{f}{F}100$	$\frac{m}{M}100$	
As % of the corresponding population													**En % de la population correspondante**
Persons with an occupation	48,0	67,2	36,5	38,4	24,6	19,6	47,8	50,6	35,7	36,1	33,3	40,9	Personnes ayant un emploi
Employers and self-employed	47,1	71,2	27,4	30,5	8,3	14,0	39,9	51,1	28,3	33,4	31,7	52,5	Employeurs et indépendants
Employees	50,5	66,9	40,4	40,3	31,8	21,8	48,9	50,6	39,0	36,7	46,3	34,1	Salariés
Unemployed persons	38,2	42,2	36,5	30,3	42,4	26,5	47,5	33,7	30,6	22,8	11,4	16,7	Chômeurs
Non-active persons	32,5	23,9	17,7	11,7	6,0	9,5	27,5	12,6	15,0	13,2	15,7	11,0	Non actifs

TAB. 125

Vocational training of employers and self-employed persons by sector of activity (%)

Formation professionnelle des employeurs et des indépendants selon le secteur d'activité (%)

1973

	BR Deutschland		France		Italia		Nederland		Belgique België		Luxembourg		
	$\frac{f}{F}100$	$\frac{m}{M}100$	$\frac{f}{F}100$	$\frac{m}{M}100$	$\frac{f}{F}100$	$\frac{m}{M}100$	$\frac{f}{F}100$	$\frac{m}{M}100$	$\frac{f}{F}100$	$\frac{m}{M}100$	$\frac{f}{F}100$	$\frac{m}{M}100$	
Total													**Total**
2nd level 1st stage	8,4	13,2	4,5	5,9	1,2	1,7	19,1	33,0	11,6	10,9	4,5	20,3	2e niveau scolaire infér.
2nd level 2nd stage	1,1	1,2	0,6	1,8	1,3	3,7	3,3	8,1	6,6	5,7	0,3	0,9	2e niveau scolaire supér.
3rd level	9,7	13,2	7,7	6,2	0,9	4,6	9,5	5,0	4,7	7,7	2,6	5,5	3e niveau scolaire
Basic vocational training	43,8	60,9	11,2	12,3	3,5	4,5	4,3	3,4	5,0	7,9	23,0	26,1	Formation prof. de base
Further training	6,1	13,4	5,4	6,8	0,8	0,9	8,3	9,6	1,8	4,1	7,1	22,1	Formation complément.
Agriculture													**Agriculture**
2nd level 1st stage	3,9	15,2	1,2	3,6	0,1	0,3	42,4	44,0	8,8	6,8	−	19,6	2e niveau scolaire infér.
2nd level 2nd stage	0,3	0,4	−	0,8	−	0,5	3,4	11,8	0,5	1,7	−	0,5	2e niveau scolaire supér.
3rd level	0,2	3,5	−	0,6	−	0,3	−	0,4	−	0,2	−	0,2	3e niveau scolaire
Basic vocational training	6,6	29,4	2,5	4,3	−	0,6	−	0,2	1,3	3,1	18,2	3,1	Formation prof. de base
Further training	1,2	5,5	1,6	3,8	−	0,2	−	0,3	0,6	2,9	3,0	5,5	Formation complément.
Industry													**Industrie**
2nd level 1st stage	6,5	14,7	8,8	10,6	1,3	2,2	11,7	44,9	14,9	17,6	5,0	29,1	2e niveau scolaire infér.
2nd level 2nd stage	5,2	1,7	0,0	2,0	0,9	4,5	0,0	8,7	13,9	8,4	0,0	0,9	2e niveau scolaire supér.
3rd level	3,8	12,0	3,4	1,3	0,0	1,0	8,5	2,9	7,1	2,7	0,0	4,7	3e niveau scolaire
Basic vocational training	60,9	83,9	19,1	23,4	7,5	7,9	0,0	7,8	6,3	12,2	60,0	55,9	Formation prof. de base
Further training	9,8	23,6	6,0	8,9	1,6	1,4	9,5	26,0	2,6	5,9	30,0	45,5	Formation complément.
Services													**Services**
2nd level 1st stage	8,4	11,3	4,9	5,8	1,8	2,6	18,3	20,8	11,5	9,7	5,1	16,7	2e niveau scolaire infér.
2nd level 2nd stage	1,1	1,5	0,9	2,8	2,0	5,7	3,5	5,3	6,9	6,3	0,4	1,4	2e niveau scolaire supér.
3rd level	9,7	19,3	10,4	15,8	1,6	10,8	10,2	8,9	5,2	13,7	3,1	10,9	3e niveau scolaire
Basic vocational training	43,8	66,8	12,9	14,8	3,7	5,3	4,8	4,1	5,4	8,2	20,7	33,5	Formation prof. de base
Further training	6,1	12,7	6,4	9,0	0,9	1,2	8,9	10,1	1,9	3,8	5,9	26,5	Formation complément.

TAB. 126

Vocational training of employees by sector of activity (%)
Formation professionnelle des salariés selon le secteur d'activité (%)
1973

	BR Deutschland		France		Italia		Nederland		Belgique Belgïe		Luxembourg		
	$\frac{f}{F}100$	$\frac{m}{M}100$	$\frac{f}{F}100$	$\frac{m}{M}100$	$\frac{f}{F}100$	$\frac{m}{M}100$	$\frac{f}{F}100$	$\frac{m}{M}100$	$\frac{f}{F}100$	$\frac{m}{M}100$	$\frac{f}{F}100$	$\frac{m}{M}100$	
Total													**Total**
2nd level 1st stage	8,5	6,3	9,4	10,2	2,6	2,3	25,0	88,4	12,2	13,8	6,5	11,2	2ᵉ niveau scolaire infér.
2nd level 2nd stage	1,0	0,7	2,1	2,7	6,7	8,1	6,6	6,3	8,9	6,8	0,5	1,9	2ᵉ niveau scolaire supér.
3rd level	3,4	8,4	6,7	6,2	4,9	3,6	4,9	7,2	7,3	6,6	3,1	4,5	3ᵉ niveau scolaire
Basic vocational training	41,3	60,7	15,5	12,8	8,7	6,5	4,3	5,9	3,7	6,4	17,3	18,8	Formation prof. de base
Further training	4,4	10,9	8,5	12,7	1,9	2,1	5,2	11,5	2,1	4,7	5,8	7,7	Formation complémentaire
Agriculture													**Agriculture**
2nd level 1st stage	5,7	8,4	6,6	3,3	0,2	0,3	33,3	31,7	10,3	12,9	–	4,8	2ᵉ niveau scolaire infér.
2nd level 2nd stage	–	1,0	1,1	1,5	0,5	1,3	2,7	7,5	15,2	2,4	–	–	2ᵉ niveau scolaire supér.
3rd level	1,9	4,8	0,5	0,9	–	0,3	–	1,4	–	3,5	–	–	3ᵉ niveau scolaire
Basic vocational training	24,1	38,7	11,4	3,6	0,2	1,1	–	1,1	–	4,9	33,3	3,2	Formation prof. de base
Further training	2,5	7,0	1,6	3,4	0,2	0,4	–	2,1	–	3,6	–	3,2	Formation complément.
Industry													**Industrie**
2nd level 1st stage	5,9	5,0	10,1	11,5	2,2	2,0	28,6	34,3	16,2	16,1	6,6	11,1	2ᵉ niveau scolaire infér.
2nd level 2nd stage	0,7	0,4	1,5	2,5	4,7	5,5	2,9	5,6	5,2	6,6	0,3	1,8	2ᵉ niveau scolaire supér.
3rd level	1,4	6,1	1,4	3,7	0,3	1,2	1,4	4,0	1,2	3,6	1,1	2,1	3ᵉ niveau scolaire
Basic vocational training	33,5	60,4	15,0	13,7	8,3	7,3	2,3	6,9	3,5	6,2	20,2	19,8	Formation prof. de base
Further training	3,4	9,2	4,9	11,4	1,1	1,9	1,9	10,3	1,7	4,1	5,5	6,1	Formation complément.
Services													**Services**
2nd level 1st stage	10,0	8,3	9,1	9,0	3,3	3,2	24,1	21,6	10,1	10,9	6,5	11,5	2ᵉ niveau scolaire infér.
2nd level 2nd stage	1,2	1,1	2,3	2,9	9,0	13,6	7,6	7,1	10,8	7,1	0,6	2,2	2ᵉ niveau scolaire supér.
3rd level	4,7	12,0	9,2	9,8	9,4	8,1	5,9	11,0	10,6	10,5	3,5	8,3	3ᵉ niveau scolaire
Basic vocational training	46,3	61,8	15,8	12,4	10,1	6,4	4,9	5,0	3,9	6,6	16,7	17,7	Formation prof. de base
Further training	5,1	13,6	10,2	15,1	2,7	2,8	6,1	13,4	2,6	5,5	5,8	10,3	Formation complément.

GLOSSARY AND TECHNICAL NOTES

PART 1 – DEMOGRAPHY (Tables 1–17)

The differences which are to be found in the structural characteristics of the demography of the two distinct population groups, men and women, constitute essential items of information for gaining a composite picture of our times.

The purpose of this section is to provide some useful basic demographic data for a study of women's status in the countries of the European Community. Tables 1–13 illustrate the structural and vital aspects of the female population of the Community countries. More specifically, Tables 1–4 give data on numbers and structure by age group. Tables 5–12 present the vital aspects, i.e. fertility, mortality, and marriage and divorce rates. Finally, Table 13 gives results of population forecasts.

Tables 14–17 give data on mortality by cause. These data refer either to the incidence of the main causes of death for each sex or to a number of causes of female mortality only.

Tables 1 and 2

For some countries the figures for the period 1971–1975 are averages of the figures for the beginning and end of the year, while for others they are mid-year estimates. The figures for 1976 and 1977 are estimates as at 1 January.

Tables 5–8

The definitions relating to births correspond to those contained in the United Nations publication *Principles and recommendations for a system of demographic statistics,* Series M, No 19, Rev. 1.

In particular, live-born infants who die before their birth is registered are included in the total of live births. The various countries were asked to provide a classification of all live births (legitimate and illegitimate) occurring each year, according to the total number of children (live births) already borne by the mother (including children from previous marriages or illegitimate children). Where countries were unable to provide the information on this basis, the definition used is given in a footnote.

Table 6

This table covers all legitimate and illegitimate live births. The rates are obtained by dividing the number of births to women in each age group by the total number of women in that age group. The United Kingdom was able to provide the information only for Great Britain.

Table 9

The figures given in this table were taken from the United Nations **Demographic Yearbook,** to which reference should be made for problems of definitions.

Table 10

Since the majority of the countries do not calculate life tables each year but at intervals depending on the dates of the population censuses, they were asked to give the figures from the national life tables for the years nearest to 1950, 1960 and 1970, as well as for the most recent year available. The Community figures on life expectancy at each age were obtained by: (1) adjusting the national figures where necessary to mid-1951, mid-1961 and mid-1971; (2) calculating the weighted averages of the national figures thus obtained, using as the weighting factor, for mid-1951, the total male and female population in 1951 in the ten-year age group centred about the age in question. For the ages 0 and 1, the total number of births in each country in 1951 and 1950 respectively were used as weights for the 1951 caculation. The averages for the other years were calculated by the same method.

Table 11

The information requested was the average age at the time of the first marriage for both men and women: departures from this definition are shown in the footnotes. The figures for this table were not available for the whole of the United Kingdom but for Great Britain only.

Table 12

The divorce rates represent the number of divorces each year per 1000 of the average population. Country-to-country comparisons have little significance in view of the differences in the relevant legislation. However, these figures are highly indicative of trends within each country.

Table 13

This table shows most recent population projection for each country available from official sources. Where several forecasts based on different assumptions were available, the one based on the assumption which corresponded most closely to current trends was chosen. The frequency at which the population projections are updated varies considerably from one country to another: in some cases the figures are revised annually, while in others they are updated at longer intervals and the projections are no longer a true reflection of the latest population trends.

Table 14

This table is compiled on the basis of the International Classification of Diseases (ICD), 8th revision. This is a World Health Organization classification of diseases, injuries and causes of death, based on the Recommendations of the Eighth Revision Conference, 1965, and adopted by the Nineteenth World Health Assembly.

WHO classification of diseases

	8th revision	7th revision
Infective and parasitic diseases	000–136	000–138
Neoplasms	140–239	140–239
including:		
malignant neoplasm of digestive organs	150–159	150–159
malignant neoplasm of trachea, bronchus and lung	162	162, 163
malignant neoplasm of breast	174	170
malignant neoplasm of cervix uteri	180	171
Leukaemia	204–207	204
Ischaemic heart disease	410–414	420
including:		
acute myocardial infarction	410	not shown separately
Cerebrovascular disease	430–438	330–334
Other diseases of the circulatory system	390–458	400–416, 421–468
Diseases of the respiratory system	460–519	470–527
including:		
pneumonia (adult)	480–486	490–493
bronchitis	490–493	500–502
Diseases of the digestive system	520–577	530–587
including:		
cirrhosis of the liver	571	581
other diseases of the liver	570, 572–576	580, 582–586
Other diseases	remainder of 000–796	remainder of 000–795
including:		
diabetes mellitus	250	260
Accidents and other external causes of injury		
including:	E800–E999	E800–E999
motor vehicle traffic accidents		
other accidents	E810–E823	E810–E835
	E800–E807	E800–E802
	E825–E949	E840–E965
Suicide	E950–E959	E970–E979

The table shows deaths by cause per 100 000 inhabitants for each sex.

In the majority of the countries the 8th revision was not used until the end of the 1960s; in the table it is used for the years 1970–1974. The data for 1960 and 1965 are based on the 7th revision and those for 1950 on the 6th revision. These two versions were more or less the same, whereas there are considerable differences between the 7th and 8th revisions. The corresponding ICD code numbers in the two versions are shown on the next page. In general, the amendments do not have a significant effect on the data; in two cases, however, (ischaemic heart disease and cerebrovascular disease) there is a break in the series, with the result that the data for previous years are not strictly comparable with those for 1970 and 1974. Data on 'acute myocardial infarction' are not available for the years prior to 1970.

Luxembourg

The ICD three-digit classification has been in use since 1967 only. For the data prior to 1970 a much shorter classification, consisting of list B (list of 50 causes of death), was used. Consequently, many of the data, especially some of the more detailed ones, are not available.

PART 2: WOMEN AND WORK

The purpose of the tables in this part is to show the most important aspects of women's participation in or exclusion from the world of productive work.

The mass of information contained in these tables does not give a complete picture of women's actual working life, since it is affected by the approach adopted in the sources of information used, which tends to give preference to the roles regarded as economically productive over those of housework and family care. This approach leads to a marked imbalance between the abundance of information on 'active' work (sector of the economy, occupational status, hours of work, remuneration, working conditions, etc.) and the paucity of information on housework.

It should also be borne in mind that women who carry on an activity outside the home cannot give up their traditional roles for this reason and thus have to take on two or even three jobs (occupation, housework and care of the family); information on the latter is either non-existent – which is the case when housework is the only activity (housewives) – or scanty and never taken from systematic surveys – which is the case when housework is combined with a gainful occupation.

This part is subdivided into sections so as to provide a general reference framework for the detailed information given. The tables are designed to bring out the comparison between the situations in the various countries of the Community at different times, although temporal comparison is not always valid, especially in the case of the information taken from the labour force sample survey. Although the annual surveys for the period 1968–1971 constitute a relatively uniform series, the complete revision of the Community definitions, in particular that of persons with a principal or occasional occupation, and of the nomenclature of activities in 1973 changed the content and scope of the survey entirely. Since the last revision these have remained unchanged and the surveys carried out in 1973, 1975 and 1977 may therefore be deemed to be rela-

tively comparable. It should be stressed, however, that it is difficult to obtain fully comparable series of absolute figures since the data are taken from a sample survey.

It should be noted finally that, as the most recent Italian survey introduced new definitions for the categories of persons forming part of the labour force, the figures for 1977 are not comparable with those for previous surveys. Subject to the availability of the necessary basic data, the absolute figures are accompanied by breakdowns which show both the distribution of the number of women in each of the groups shown in the table (percentages $\frac{f}{F} \times 100$) and the proportion of women in the total number of individuals classified in each group (percentages $\frac{f}{f+m} \times 100$). The sum of the percentages $\frac{f}{F} \times 100$ may be less than 100 since in some cases it was not possible to exclude the 'non-returns' and/or the data on all the variables considered were not available (either because the sampling fraction did not allow subdivision or because the figure was less than half of the unit used).

Main definitions

The definitions used in the Community Labour Force Survey are generally based on those drawn up by the ILO and OECD.

Certain discrepancies may however be noted, not only because the international definitions recommended by the ILO and OECD cannot always be rigorously applied for technical reasons, but also because certain types of employment developed in the Community countries have required specific modifications.

Persons having a principal occupation

Persons having a principal occupation are all persons 14 years old and over who:

(a) declared that they normally had a paid job which they were performing during the reference week, or not performing as a result of illness, accident, holiday, strike or other circumstances.
Persons not working for technical or climatic reasons are also included in this group;

(b) have a normal unpaid activity as family workers provided that this acitivity exceeds 14 hours per week.

The following are not included in this category:

(a) persons declaring themselves unemployed;

(b) persons declaring themselves to be non-active (housewives, students, retired persons, pensioners, others);

(c) persons without paid employment and persons having neither an agricultural nor any other enterprise but having made arrangements to commence work in a new job or to launch an agricultural holding or an enterprise at a date following the reference period;

(d) unpaid family workers working less than 14 hours in the family concern during the reference week;

(e) National Servicemen.[1]

The above groups may include persons having occasional paid employment during the reference week.

Unemployed persons

Unemployed persons are all persons declaring themselves to be unemployed and seeking a paid job. The following categories are included in this definition:

(a) persons having worked as employees and no longer having a contract of employment;

(b) persons having worked as self-employed or family workers and seeking a paid job;

(c) persons never having worked and seeking their first paid job;

(d) persons having interrupted their career for a period of over one year and seeking a paid job;

(e) persons laid off either temporarily or for an indefinite period without pay.

The following are not included in this category:

(a) persons who declare themselves unemployed but are not seeking employment or proposing to work as self-employed;

(b) persons normally having a job but not working during the reference week for economic, technical or climatic reasons (partially unemployed);

(c) non-active persons (housewives, students, etc.) who declare themselves as seeking a job;

(d) persons having a principal occupation an d seeking another job.

Labour force

The labour force is composed of persons having a principal occupation and unemployed persons.

Non-active persons

This category comprises all persons who:

(a) were less than 14 years of age on 1 January of the survey year, or

(b) although more than 14 years of age did not belong to the labour force as defined above.

This group generally comprises persons declaring themselves to be housewives, students, pensioners, etc. Persons declaring themselves unemployed but seeking a self-employed activity are also regarded as belonging to the non-active population.

Family workers declaring that they have a principal occupation, but who have in fact worked no more than between one and fourteen hours during the reference week, are also included in the non-active population.

---

[1] Professional Servicemen are included in persons in employment.

Non-active persons with an occasional occupation

This category comprises all non-active persons declaring that they have a non-permanent occupation (full or part time). Family workers not paid during the reference week who have worked from one to fourteen hours during the reference week are included in this category.

Seasonal workers are included in this category.

Persons seeking employment

Persons seeking employment are all those who at the time of the Survey declared themselves to be seeking paid employment, whether they already had a job, were unemployed or were in the non-active population. This category comprises:

(a) unemployed persons:

– who, having lost their job, are now seeking a paid job,

– seeking a first job or seeking a job after a voluntary break in their career;

(b) non-active persons seeking employment;

(c) persons having a principal occupation but seeking a different one.

Occupational status

All persons declaring a principal or occasional occupation during the reference week are asked to give their occupational status. In this publication a distinction is made only between self-employed, employees and family workers.

'Self-employed' means those persons declaring themselves to be following an activity on their own account, with or without employees. 'Employed persons' comprise salaried employees and manual workers, i.e. all persons working on a contractual basis for a public or private employer and receiving payment in cash or in kind. 'Family workers' means unpaid members of a family usually contributing to the operation of an agricultural holding or other enterprise, provided that they have worked more than 14 hours during the reference week. Those persons in the group who did not work during the reference week have nevertheless been retained in this category.

Hours of work

The number of hours worked during the reference week was recorded from the principal occupation, the occasional occupation and the secondary occupation.

The average weekly duration of work was calculated for all persons having worked for at least one hour during the reference week. For the purposes of this calculation persons not having worked during this same period by reason of illness, holiday or other cause, have not been taken into account.

Branches of activity

The results of the 1977 Survey were processed making systematic use of the following breakdown into NACE branches of activity (General Industrial Classification of Economic Activities within the European Communities):

Branches of activity	NACE code
1. Agriculture, forestry, fishing, hunting	0
2. Energy and water	1
3. Extraction and processing of non-energy-producing minerals and derived products; chemical industry	2
4. Metal manufacture; mechanical, electrical and instrument engineering	3
5. Other manufacturing industries	4
6. Building and civil engineering	5
7. Distributive trades, hotel, catering, repairs	6
8. Transport and communication	7
9. Banking and finance, insurance, business services, renting	8
10. Public administration, national defence and compulsory social security	91
11. Other services	9 (excluding 91)

These were re-grouped into sectors of activity as follows:

Sectors	NACE
Agriculture	0
Industry	1 to 5
Services	6 to 8, 91 and 9

The same nomenclature was used for the 1973 and 1975 Surveys. In earlier Surveys, however, since no uniform nomenclature covering all branches of activity and approved by each of the Member States was available, use was made of the NICE (Nomenclature of Industries in the European Communities) for industry, the preliminary version of the NACE for services and the ISIC (International Standard Industrial Classification of all Economic Activities) for agriculture.

Occupational qualifications of industrial employees

Manual workers

1 – skilled workers
2 – semi-skilled workers
3 – unskilled workers

Salaried non-manual employees

1 – top management personnel
  1A – Higher management of which: earnings more than DM 4500, FF 10000, LIT 1000000, HFL 6000, BFR 65000, LFR 65000 monthly
  1B – Higher management of which: earnings not more than DM 4500, LIT 1000000, HFL 6000, BFR 65000, LFR 65000 monthly
2 – highly qualified personnel
3 – personnel with average qualifications
4 – clerical staff
5 – supervisory staff
  5A – supervisory staff with a high level of powers and responsibilities
  5B – supervisory staff with an average level of powers and responsibilities

Occupational qualifications of agricultural workers

● **Skilled worker:** a person with the training or experience to perform certain specialized types of work and who would, for example, be able to operate, drive, repair or service certain types of agricultural machinery.

● **Unskilled worker:** a person employed on any type of work does not require special training (e.g. farm labourer).

Occupational qualifications of employees in wholesale and retail distribution, banking and insurance

As classifications of employees according to qualifications differ considerably between economic activities and between countries, it was left to the national statistical institutes to classify employees in broad groups on the basis of qualifications which were defined by common agreement for the separate sectors of wholesale and retail distribution, banking and insurance.

Every employee in these sectors was assigned to one of the following qualification groups, depending on the nature of the tasks performed, the degree of difficulty involved, the inherent reponsibilities, and the level of training or experience required for doing the job.

Occupational qualification groups in the sectors of wholesale and retail distribution

For ease of classification, separate qualification sub-groups were defined for shop staff (retail distribution) and warehouse and dispatching personnel (wholesale distribution).

1. Management personnel

  1A: Top management personnel with powers of decision and responsibilities with regard to the general running of the whole undertaking.
  1B: Management personnel and senior executives directly responsible to the persons described under 1A, with powers and responsibilities in respect of large subdivisions of the undertaking, e.g. the principal establishments, and their closest collaborators.

2. Executives and managerial staff

This category covers employees who are directly responsible to or are given their instructions by the persons described under 1B.

In general, within the limits of their instructions, employees in this category possess wide scope for initiative and responsibility.

3. Highly-qualified junior personnel

This qualification group classifies separately personnel with duties specific to the wholesale and retail trades (sub-group 3A) and other highly-qualified junior personnel (sub-group 3B).

4. Qualified junior personnel

This qualification group classifies separately personnel with duties specific to the wholesale and retail trades (sub-group 4A) and other qualified junior personnel (sub-group 4B).

5. Unqualified junior personnel

This group covers all workers performing work of a simple nature, which is normally repetitive and as a rule requires only knowledge of an elementary educational level.

Occupational qualification groups in the banking sector

1. Top management personnel

Senior management personnel with powers of decision and responsibilities in respect of the general running of the whole undertaking.

2. Senior executives

Managers and senior executives with powers and responsibilities for subdivisions of the undertaking, e.g. departments and main establishments. This category also includes managers of local or regional units having a considerable degree of autonomy in their management duties. It also covers personnel with study, research and advisory functions having a certain degree of independence and authority to take decisions.

In general, the knowledge required for such functions will be of university, college or at least higher vocational training level, although it may, of course, have been acquired by experience or private study.

3. Executives (junior management)

This group comprises personnel working directly with the senior executives (group 2) and who may exercise authority over the personnel of specific departments.

4. Highly-qualified clerical staff

This group covers highly-qualified clerical staff who are required to have knowledge of secondary school standard, who work with members of the next higher category (group 3) and are directly responsible to them and carry out their instructions. Their duties may require – within the limits of the instructions received – a certain amount of initiative and responsibility. In some cases such staff may coordinate the work of lower categories.

5. Qualified clerical staff

This group covers qualified clerical staff working to precise instructions from their immediate superiors and whose duties as a rule call for only a small amount of initiative and responsibility.

6. Other employees

This group comprises all employees not included in the five categories above (unqualified personnel).

Occupational qualification groups in the insurance sector

I. Managers and senior management executives

This group comprises employees who, as a result of extensive delegation of authority, are able to make decisions affecting either the undertaking as a whole or one or more of its main departments.

II. Middle management executives

This group comprises employees with wide decision-making powers and a high level of responsibility:

– either at the level of the undertaking, department or section which they organize or supervise,

– or in the planning, research or advisory duties assigned to them.

III. Junior executives and personnel with equivalent qualifications

This group comprises employees who by virtue of working directly or indirectly with one or more of the executives in groups 1 or 2 above:

– either supervise, explain or check the work of a group, section or team of employees,

– or are entrusted, by virtue of their ability and high occupational qualifications, with planning tasks involving special responsibilities.

IV. Highly qualified employees[1]

This group covers employees who perform work requiring proven knowledge of one or more branches of insurance or an equivalent qualification in a field outside insurance and who are able to exercise some initiative in carrying out these duties, within the limits of instructions received. In some cases these duties may include coordination and checking of the work of other employees.

V. Qualified employees[1]

This group covers employees performing work requiring only good professional knowledge of insurance or another field. In some cases these duties may include coordination and checking of the work of other employees.

VI. Other employees[1]

This group comprises employees performing tasks requiring only elementary professional knowledge and a short period of initial training.

Size of establishment or enterprise: expressed in terms of the number of employees.

Length of service in the undertaking: the number of years for which the employee had been working for the undertaking; where an employee had worked in several returning

---

[1] Non-management employees are classified in groups 4, 5 or 6, depending on their qualifications.

units of the same undertaking, the total number of years spent in the various units was shown.

Benefits in kind for agricultural workers: in view of the difficulties and uncertainties that would have been encountered in defining a Community method of assessing the value of benefits in kind, it was agreed that the survey should simply record whether the worker was provided with accommodation and/or meals, without attempting to estimate the value of these benefits.

A worker is said to receive free accommodation if he is employed on a holding and if accommodation is provided by the employer; this accommodation may be on the premises of the holding or elsewhere.

A worker is said to receive free meals if he works on the holding and is provided with at least one main meal per day.

When the results were processed, all workers were classified in one of the following four groups, depending on whether they received these benefits or not:

— free accommodation and meals

— free accommodation only

— free meals only

— no free accommodation or meals.

Notes on the tables

Section I – Population and occupation (Tables 18–27)

The tables in this section are intended to provide information on the integration of women into – or their exclusion from – productive activity, both in general terms and in respect of certain characteristics such as age and marital status. The ratio of activity is the ratio of the labour force to the population over 14 years of age.

Section II – Employment (Tables 28–93)

This section describes the part played by women in productive activity and is designed to show the structure of female employment by sector, branch of economic activity and occupational status in relation to age, marital status and the occasional nature or otherwise of the employment. It was possible subsequently to specify for each of the three sectors of economic activity the nature of employment in relation to variables such as the size of the establishment or enterprise, length of service, occupational qualifications, and the payment of benefits in kind (for female agricultural workers).

Remuneration is described by means of indices expressing average female earnings in relation to the corresponding male earnings, together with the coefficients of variation of female earnings which express the relative variability within each homogeneous group in respect of the characteristics under consideration.

----

[1] $\sigma = \sqrt{\dfrac{\sum_{i}^{n} (x_i - M)^2}{n}}$ where x_i is the value of the variable i, M the arithmetic mean of the variables, and n the total number of variables.

As the coefficient of variation ($CV = \frac{\sigma}{M} 100$)[1] is a composite measurement of the spread of the individual values around the mean value (calculated by measuring the differences between the individual values and the mean value and expressing them as a percentage of the mean), the significance of the mean value increases in inverse proportion to the numerical value of the CV.

Again for female employees only, information is available on working conditions, both as regards the actual job (full-time, part-time, hours of work, etc.) and in respect of transport facilities to the place of work. The last table in this group presents female workers' subjective assessments of conditions at the workplace.
The final group of tables (Tables 89–93) gives a brief account of the difficulties encountered by female employees in combining a job with domestic and family commitments.

Section III – Unemployment (Tables 94–106)

This section comprises two groups of tables.

The first group describes unemployment trends and the structure of the population seeking employment, based on the results of the Labour Force Sample Survey (Tables 94–102). The unemployment rate is expressed as a percentage of the labour force of the corresponding sex and age. The second group of tables covers the registered unemployed who, it should be noted, do not generally include the partially unemployed, unemployed persons following a course of vocational training and persons employed on schemes designed specifically to combat unemployment.

The following data are used for the various countries:

— FR of Germany (Arbeitslose): workers aged 14 and over without a job and seeking permanent work for at least 20 hours a week.

— France (Demandeurs d'emploi): persons without work available to start work immediately and seeking permanent employment for at least 30 hours a week.

— Italy (Iscritti nelle liste di collocamento): classes I and II: unemployed persons seeking work.

— Netherlands (Werklozen) unemployed persons under 65 years of age, fit for work and seeking permanent employment for at least 30 hours a week.

— Belgium: unemployed persons receiving unemployment benefit, other persons seeking work who are obliged to register and persons seeking work registered voluntarily.

— Luxembourg (Demandeurs d'emploi): persons aged between 16 and 65 without a job, seeking full-time work (40 hours a week) and available for employment.

— United Kingdom (Unemployed): unemployed persons capable of and available for work for more than 30 hours a week.

— Ireland (Unemployed on the Live Register): unemployed persons aged between 16 and 67, capable of and available for work (claimants to unemployment benefit, applicants for unemployment assistance and other registered unemployed persons).

– Denmark (Arbejdsløsheden): unemployed persons available for and seeking work, whether or not they are members of the trade unions' unemployment insurance funds.

The data on registered unemployed were adapted as far as possible to the definitions listed above.

Section IV – Geographical and occupational mobility (Tables 107–108)

Certain data on the geographical mobility of persons of working age can be taken from the Labour Force Sample Survey.

As regards occupational mobility, it should be pointed out that the data refer only to changes of situation (unemployed persons becoming employed and vice-versa, and to a great extent, in the case of women, interchanges between reserve labour and marginal employment), transfers between sectors and changes of occupational status; there is thus no information available on female workers' vertical mobility.

PART 3 – GENERAL AND VOCATIONAL TRAINING (Tables 109–126)

This part of the study is designed to shed light on the differences existing between the two sexes with regard to general and, in particular, vocational training. These differences combine and will continue to do so – together with a set of social and cultural factors on which they are dependent – to produce the different conditions under which the two sexes confront working life. Analysis of these differences is not only of intrinsic interest but also of use in showing one of the reasons for women's fringe position in the working world. The study of general and vocational training is divided into three sections, viz.:

1. general and vocational training under way in the Community in various years both within and outside the school system (Tables 109–116);

2. the training completed by the Community population of working age (Tables 117–123);

3. the relationships between training and occupation (Tables 124–126).

1. Ongoing training

1.1 *Training within the school system (Tables 109–114)*

The data on ongoing training within the school and university system are taken almost entirely from the volume 'Education Statistics, 1970–1975' published by Eurostat in 1976. Only the overall degrees of scholarization (Table 111) were taken from another Eurostat publication, namely 'Social Indicators for the European Community, 1960–1975' published in 1977, while for third-level studies use was made of the 1976 UNESCO Yearbook, from which information on the numbers enrolled and graduates by sex and field of study was taken (Tables 113 and 114).

As a general rule the data given refer to the student population engaged in full-time study at public or private schools or universities situated within the territory of the various countries. Students enrolled at educational establishments situated outside the national territory are therefore excluded (except in the case of Luxembourg which supplies data including such students), whereas foreign students studying in the country are included.

The data for France refer only to metropolitan France and thus do not include Overseas Departments and Territories (DOM – TOM).

The total school and university population was broken down according to the levels defined in the ISCED and currently used by all the Member States of the Community:

– Pre-school: education prior to the beginning of compulsory schooling. As a rule it begins around the age of three or four and in most cases finishes around the age of six.

– First level: corresponds to elementary education, is compulsory in all cases and usually lasts five years.

– Second level, first stage: lasts three years in most cases and is also part of compulsory schooling.

– Second level, second stage: begins around the age of 14 or 15, lasts for three years in most cases and leads to the standard required for admission to university or any other type of higher education. Depending on the country, it may begin at the end of compulsory schooling or still be a part thereof.

– Third level: comprises universities and all other types of higher education.

Notes on the tables

Table 109: Student population by level of studies

This table gives a percentage breakdown – on the basis of the three levels mentioned in the above classification – of the female and male school and university population. In addition, the school population of the first stage of the second level only is shown separately as a percentage of the total student population.

Table 110: Growth of the student population at each level

This table presents an index of trends over the period 1970–1976 in the number of pupils and students of each sex enrolled at the various levels of education, based on the number of pupils and students enrolled in the 1970–71 academic year.

The index of trends in the total number of pupils and students covers the whole of the first, second and third levels and excludes, therefore, pupils enrolled in pre-school classes.

Table 111: Overall degrees of scholarization

In this table the female and male school population in various school years, irrespective of age and level of study, is shown as a proportion of the total population and of the population aged between 5 and 24.

Tables 112 and 112.1: Student population by level and type of studies

The individual national tables give a breakdown of the total number of pupils and students on the basis of the types of studies as defined in the national system and a classification of these pupils and students based on the ISCED levels. In Table 112 the breakdown is in absolute terms for both female and male students, whereas Table 112.1 gives an percentage breakdown of female students and an index of the numbers of female students in each level and type of education.

The nomenclatures of the various types of education are given in the language of each country. A translation of these nomenclatures can be found in the publication 'General and Vocational Training' previously mentioned, from which the tables were taken.

Within the classification of first- and second-level education there is a separate heading for special education: this is education in special classes or institutions for pupils (most of whom are handicapped) who constitute special cases.

Table 113: Female students of the third level by field of study

This table gives a percentage breakdown by field of study of the female students enrolled at various dates at higher education establishments and an index of the numbers of female students in each field.

The expression 'field of study' means the students's main field of specialization. The subjects covered by each field, in accordance with the classification adopted by UNESCO, are as follows:

● **Arts:** archaeology, history, languages, literature, librarianship, philosophy, psychology, theology, etc.

● **Teaching:** teaching theory and practice, physical education

● **Fine arts:** architecture, design, music, painting, sculpture, drama, etc.

● **Law**

● **Social sciences:** commerce, diplomacy, banking, public administration, economics, ethnology, geography, home economics, international relations, journalism, political sciences, social sciences, sociology, statistics, etc.

● **Exact and natural sciences:** astronomy, bacteriology, biochemistry, biology, botany, chemistry, entomology, geology, geophysics, mathematics, meteorology, mineralogy, physics, zoology, etc.

● **Engineering:** applied sciences, civil engineering, geodesy, metallurgy, mining, surveying, technology, textile industry, etc.

● **Medical sciences:** anatomy, medicine, obstetrics, optometry, pharmacy, physiotherapy, public health, dentistry, etc.

● **Agricultural sciences:** agronomy, ichthyology, forestry, horticulture, veterinary medicine, etc.

Table 114: Female graduates by field of study

This table gives a percentage breakdown by field of study of female students who obtained a degree or diploma during the academic years under consideration, irrespective of the grade obtained. It also gives an index of the number of women graduates in each field ((f/f+m) × 100). For the definition of 'field of study' and the subjects belonging to each field, see the note on Table 113.

1.2. *Ongoing training outside the school system (Tables 115 and 116)*

The training given outside the school system is solely vocational and is divided into 'basic vocational training' and 'further training'. Basic vocational training is training which follows immediately upon general or vocational education within the school system. It may be obtained in the enterprise – with or without a contract of employment – or in specialized institutions.

Further training, too, is vocational training, given under the same conditions, although it may be followed at any time. It includes post-school training after taking up employment, adult vocational training, retraining, etc.

The information given in this part of the study is taken from the 1975 Labour Force Sample Survey, during which information was collected on ongoing out-of-school vocational training during the reference week. The reference population comprises persons aged between 14 and 65 at the time of the survey.

Notes on the tables

Table 115: Persons undergoing out-of-school vocational training by type of training, age and occupational status
This table consists of three parts showing the percentage breakdown of women aged between 14 and 65 undergoing out-of-school vocational training, by type of training, age and occupational status respectively. In addition, it gives an index of the number of women falling under each of the headings into which the characteristics shown are divided.

Table 116: Participation in out-of-school vocational training courses by certain categories of persons of working age
Participation in out-of-school vocational training courses by certain categories of persons (persons of working age, employed persons, unemployed persons) was expressed as the ratio of the number of persons of each category undergoing training to the total number of persons belonging to that category, thus calculating what might be termed a 'training' rate.

2. Completed training

The information given in this section is taken from the Eurostat publication 'General and Vocational Training, 1973', Social Statistics series, No 4–1975. This volume sets out the results of the specific survey on general and vocational training, carried out in conjunction with the 1973 Community Labour Force Sample Survey and covering, amongst other things, the training completed by the Community population aged between 14 and 65 (born between 1908 and 1959).

This specific survey was not repeated as such in 1975. Labour Force Sample Survey. The data for 1973 are the most recent available on completed training. They may be brought up to date when the results of the supplementary survey on the relationship between employment and education and training are known.

Completed training, i.e. generally attested by a certificate, may be of both the academic and the out-of-school type (basic vocational training, further training). Academic training can be further divided into two types:

– general education, comprising the first and second levels of general school studies;

– vocational education, comprising the second level of vocational academic studies,

third-level education and teacher training. The various types of training are not mutually exclusive: the same person may have completed two or more different types of training.

The definitions used for the various types and levels of completed training are the same as those indicated above for ongoing training. It should be borne in mind, however, that the systems of education in each country have changed over the years. The correct classification of types of instruction given fifty years ago according to a nomenclature drawn up essentially for analysis of present-day systems presents considerable difficulties. Moreover, the presence in some countries of a considerable number of foreigners who have received their training in their country of origin and not in the country where they were interviewed makes the difficulties even greater.

Furthermore, technical difficulties arose regarding the actual definition of 'completed training' (applied particularly strictly in France) and the distinction, within the school system, between general education and vocational education (particularly in Italy).

Nevertheless, the information provided by the data presented in this section of the study constitutes a valid measure of the levels of training completed by the population of the Community.

Notes on the tables

Tables 117 and 117.1: Population by type of training completed

Table 117 shows the number of persons aged between 14 and 65 who in 1973 had completed the various types of training. For better interpretation of the table, it should be borne in mind that the same person may have completed more than one type of training.

Table 117.1, on the other hand, gives the proportion of the population aged between 14 and 65 which had completed each type of training.

Table 118: Indices of non-completion of general and vocational training

The non-completion of training the number of drop-outs as a percentage of those who followed a particular type of training.

The number of drop-outs was calculated by subtracting the number of persons who completed a certain type of training from the number of persons who began it.

Table 119: Population by highest level of study attained as part of general schooling and vocational training

This table refers to the highest level of studies attained: it does not show, therefore, whether more than one type of training was followed.

The percentage breakdown according to the highest level of studies attained was calculated both overall for the female and male population who received training within the school system and separately for those who received general academic training and those who received a vocational education as well.

Table 120: Further general and vocational training

This table shows the percentage of cases in which general or vocational education is supplemented by other types of training and the extent to which out-of-school vocational training is preceded by the various types of training.

Table 121: Population by age type of training completed

This table shows the percentage of the female and male population in each age group having completed the various types of training.
The age groups were chosen so as to enable a distinction to be made between persons undergoing vocational training or beginning working life (aged between 18 and 24), persons in the prime of their working life (aged from 25 to 34 and 35 to 49) and persons who are more or less over working age and have thus definitely completed their training (aged 50 and over).

Table 122: Population by age and highest level of study attained within the school system

This table gives a breakdown of the female and male population in the same age groups as in the previous table, by the highest level of study attained within the school system.

The total population of each age group includes persons who did not complete compulsory schooling; this means that the sum of the percentages is generally less than 100.

Table 123: Population having completed third level studies by duration of studies

This table gives the percentage distribution of persons having completed third level studies by sex and the duration (in years) of these studies.

3. Training and occupation

The information given in this section also refers to the population aged between 14 and 65 in 1973.

Notes on the tables

Table 124: Population having completed vocational training, by main occupational criteria

The figures given in this table constitute, so to speak, vocational training rates for certain categories of persons differentiated according to the main occupational criteria, irrespective of the type of vocational training completed.

Table 125: Vocational training of employers and self-employed persons

In this table the breakdown given in the previous table is presented in greater detail in respect of employers and self-employed persons, on the basis of the various levels and types of vocational training.

Table 126: Vocational training of employees

This table is constructed in similar fashion to the previous one and refers to employees.

SOURCES

A) EUROSTAT PUBLICATIONS

Social statistics
– *Censuses of population 1968–1972, 1977*
– *Demographic statistics 1960–1976, 1977*
– *Demographic statistics 1977, 1978*
– *Demographic statistics 1978, 1980*
– *Population and employment 1968–1972, 1973*
– *Population and employment 1950–1976, 1977*
– *Employees in Industry in the Community 1973–1976*
– *Employment and Unemployment 1972–1978, 1979*
– *Statistical Telegrams 'Unemployment' since January 1977*
– *Labour Force Sample Survey 1973, 1975*
– *Labour Force Sample Survey 1975, 1976*
– *Labour Force Sample Survey 1977, 1978*
– *Labour Force Sample Survey 1973–1975–1977, 1980*
– *Labour Force Sample Survey-Methods and definitions, 1977*
– *Working conditions in the EC 1975, 1977*
– *Social indicators for the European Community 1960–1975, 1977*
– *Social indicators for the European Community 1960–1978, 1980*
– *Structure of earnings in industry, 1972*
– *Earnings in agriculture, 1975*
– *Earnings in agriculture, 1976, 1977*
– *Structure of earnings in wholesale and retail distribution, banking and insurance, 1974*
– *Hourly earnings – Hours of work 2, 1976*
– *Hourly earnings – Hours of work IV–1977, 1978*
– *Hourly earnings – Hours of work X–1977, 1978*
– *Hourly earnings – Hours of work IV–1978, 1979*
– *General and vocational training, 1973, 1975*
– *Education statistics 1970/71–1976/77, 1978*

Regional statistics

– *Population, Employment, Living standards 1973–1974, 1975*
– *Population, Employment, Living standards 1975, 1976*
– *Population, Employment, Living standards 1977, 1978*

B) OTHER SOURCES

– UN: *Demographic Yearbook* 1962, 1972, 1976
– WHO: *World Health Statistics Report*, 1975
– WHO: *World Health Statistics Report 1973–1976*, 1976
– CEE: *Les conditions de travail des femmes salariées*, 1972

NOTES EXPLICATIVES ET TECHNIQUES

PARTIE 1 – DÉMOGRAPHIE (tableaux 1 à 17)

Les différences observees dans les caractéristiques structurelles de la dynamique démographique des deux ensembles distincts que forment les femmes et les hommes dans la population, constituent certains éléments de connaissance indispensables pour établir une synthèse de la période historique actuelle.

Ce chapitre a précisément pour but de fournir quelques données démographiques de base, utiles à l'étude de la condition de la femme dans les pays de la Communauté européenne.

Les tableaux 1 à 13 comportent une description des aspects structurels et dynamiques de la population féminine des pays de la Communauté. Plus précisément, les tableaux 1 à 4 contiennent les données relatives aux effectifs et à la structure par âge. Les tableaux 5 à 12 contiennent les données relatives aux aspects dynamiques, c'est-à-dire à la fécondité, à la mortalité ainsi qu'aux taux de mariages et de divorces.

Enfin, sont mentionnés dans le tableau 13 certains résultats des projections de la population.

Les tableaux 14 à 17 contiennent des données relatives à la mortalité par causes. Ces tableaux indiquent la ventilation de la mortalité des femmes et des hommes selon les principales causes communes aux deux sexes ainsi que les chiffres concernant les causes de décès spécifiques à la femme.

Tableaux 1 et 2

Les données relatives à la période 1971–1975 constituent, pour certains pays, des moyennes entre le début et la fin de l'année, et pour d'autres, des estimations à mi-année. Les données relatives aux années 1976 et 1977 sont des estimations au 1er janvier.

Tableaux 5 à 8

Les définitions concernant les naissances sont celles décrites dans *Principes et recommandations pour un système de statistiques démographiques,* série M n° 19, Rév. 1, de l'ONU.

En particulier, les enfants nés vivants qui meurent avant l'enregistrement de leur naissance doivent être inclus dans le total des naissances vivantes. Il a été demandé aux différents pays de fournir chaque année une classification du total des naissances vivantes (légitimes et illégitimes), selon le nombre total des enfants déjà nés (vivants) de la même mère, que ces naissances soient survenues pendant le mariage actuel ou durant un mariage précédent ou encore soient illégitimes. Lorsque les pays n'étaient pas en mesure de fournir les données sur cette base, les définitions utilisées sont indiquées dans des notes.

Tableau 6

Ce tableau comprend toutes les naissances vivantes légitimes et illégitimes. Les taux ont été obtenus en divisant les naissances survenues aux femmes de chaque groupe d'âge par le total des femmes dans ces groupes. Le Royaume-Uni n'a pu fournir les données que pour la Grande-Bretagne.

Tableau 9

Les données figurant dans ce tableau ont été empruntées au «Demographic Yearbook», de l'ONU, auquel on se réfèrera pour tout problème de définition.

Tableau 10

Comme la plupart des pays ne préparent pas de tableaux de mortalité chaque année, mais plutôt à des intervalles dépendant des dates de recensement de la population, il leur a été demandé de communiquer les chiffres des tableaux de mortalité pour les années les plus proches de 1950, 1960, 1970, ainsi que les derniers chiffres disponibles. Les chiffres communautaires pour l'espérance de vie à certains âges ont été calculés de la manière suivante: 1) les chiffres nationaux ont été ajustés, si nécessaire, à la mi-1951, mi-1961 et mi-1971; 2) les moyennes pondérées des chiffres nationaux ont été calculées en utilisant comme coefficient de pondération, pour la mi-1951, la population totale, hommes et femmes de 1951 dans les groupes d'âge de 10 ans centrés sur les âges en question. Pour les âges 0 et 1 an, on a utilisé comme coefficient de pondération pour le calcul relatif à 1951 le total des naissances enregistrées respectivement en 1951 et 1950 dans chaque pays.

Les moyennes relatives aux autres années ont été calculées selon la même méthode.

Tableau 11

L'âge moyen à la date du premier mariage a été demandé pour les hommes et les femmes, les écarts par rapport à cette définition sont indiqués dans des notes. Les chiffres relatifs à ce tableau n'étaient pas disponibles pour l'ensemble du Royaume-Uni mais uniquement pour la Grande-Bretagne.

Tableau 12

Les taux de divorces correspondent au rapport entre le nombre de divorces par an et la population moyenne en milliers. Les comparaisons entre pays n'ont pas grande signification, étant donné les différences d'ordre juridique concernant le divorce. Toutefois, les chiffres sont d'une haute importance comme indicateurs des tendances à l'intérieur des pays.

Classification internationale des maladies de l'OMS

	8e révision	7e revision
Maladies infectieuses et parasitaires	000–136	000–138
Néoplasmes	140–239	140–239
dont:		
tumeur maligne de l'appareil digestif et du péritoire	150–159	150–159
tumeur maligne de la trachée, des bronches et du poumon	162	162, 163
tumeur maligne du sein	174	170
tumeur maligne du col de l'utérus	180	171
leucémie	204–207	204
Maladies ischémiques du cœur	410–414	420
dont:		
infarctus aigu du myocarde	410	donnée non disponible séparément
Maladies cérébro-vasculaires	430–438	330–334
Autres maladies de l'appareil circulatoire	390–458	400–416, 421–468
Maladies de l'appareil respiratoire	460–519	470–527
dont:		
pneumonies (adultes)	480–486	490–493
bronchites	490–493	500–502
Maladies de l'appareil digestif	520–577	530–587
dont:		
cirrhose du foie	571	581
autres maladies du foie	570, 572–576	580, 582–586
Autres maladies	000–796 reste	000–795 reste
dont:		
diabète sucré	250	260
Accidents et autres causes extérieures	E800–E999	E888–E999
dont:		
accidents de la circulation intéressant des véhicules à moteur	E810–E823	E810–E835
autres accidents	E825–E949	E840–E965
Suicide	E950–E959	E970–E979

Le tableau exprime les décès, ventilés par cause, pour 100 000 habitants de chaque sexe.

Tableau 13

Ce tableau présente pour chaque pays la projection de la population la plus récente provenant des sources officielles. Dans le cas où il existe plusieurs projections, basées sur des hypothèses différentes, celle qui est la plus proche des tendances démographiques actuelles a été choisie. La pratique en ce qui concerne la mise à jour des projections de la population diffère beaucoup d'un pays à l'autre. Dans quelques pays, les chiffres sont révisés chaque année; dans d'autres, ceci n'a lieu qu'à intervalles irréguliers, de sorte que les projections ne représentent pas, de manière complète, les tendances les plus récentes de la population.

Tableau 14

Ce tableau est établi sur la base de la classification internationale des maladies (CIM), 8ᵉ révision. Il s'agit d'une classification de l'Organisation mondiale de la santé, relative aux maladies, traumatismes et causes de décès, basée sur les recommandations de la conférence pour la 8ᵉ révision tenue en 1965, et adoptée par la 19ᵉ assemblée de l'Organisation mondiale de la santé.

Dans la plupart des pays, la 8ᵉ révision n'a été appliquée qu'à la fin des années 60; dans le tableau, elle est appliquée aux années 1970–1974. Les données relatives à 1960 et 1965 se basent sur la 7ᵉ révision et celles relatives à 1950, sur la 6ᵉ révision. Alors que ces deux versions sont assez semblables, des différences considérables existent entre la 7ᵉ et la 8ᵉ révision. Les correspondances entre les numéros de code CIM des deux versions sont présentées ci-après. En général, les modifications n'influencent pas sensiblement les séries; toutefois, dans deux cas (maladies-ischémiques du cœur et maladies cérébro-vasculaires), on observe une rupture de série, de sorte que les données relatives aux années précédentes ne sont pas rigoureusement comparables à celles de 1970 et de 1974. Quant à l'infarctus aigu du myocarde, on ne dispose pas de données pour les années antérieures à 1970.

Luxembourg

La classification CIM à trois chiffres n'est appliquée que depuis 1967. Les données antérieures à 1970 ont été présentées selon une classification fort abrégée, constituée par la liste B (liste de 50 causes de décès). Par conséquent, de nombreuses données, et surtout les plus détaillées, ne sont pas disponibles.

PARTIE 2: LA FEMME ET LE TRAVAIL

Les tableaux qui composent cette partie tendent à mettre en évidence les aspects les plus importants de la participation de la femme au monde du travail productif, ou de son exclusion.

Les sources disponibles tendant à privilégier les tâches considérées comme économiquement productives au détriment du travail domestique et familial, la masse d'informations contenue dans ces tableaux ne permet pas de décrire complètement le travail réel de la femme. On observe en effet un fort déséquilibre entre l'abondance des informations relatives au travail «actif» (secteur d'activité économique, statut professionnel, durée du travail, salaire,

conditions de travail, etc.) et la pauvreté de celles ayant trait au travail domestique.

Par ailleurs, il ne faut pas perdre de vue que les femmes qui exercent une activité extra-domestique ne peuvent pas pour autant abandonner les rôles qui leur sont traditionnellement assignés, et assument ainsi un double, voire même un triple travail (activité professionnelle, travaux domestiques et soins à la famille).

Or dans le cas où le travail domestique est exercé à titre exclusif (ménagère), les données de ce genre sont inexistantes, elles sont peu fréquentes et ne font jamais l'objet de relevés systématiques lorsque ce travail s'ajoute à une activité professionnelle.

La subdivision en chapitres adoptée ici vise à fournir un cadre général de référence qui, au fil de l'ouvrage sera progressivement précisé.

Les tableaux sont conçus de manière à favoriser la comparaison entre les situations existantes dans les différents pays de la Communauté à différentes dates, au détriment de la comparaison dans le temps, dans la mesure où cette dernière n'est pas toujours rigoureuse surtout lorsqu'il s'agit d'informations empruntées à l'enquête par sondage sur les forces de travail. En effet, si les enquêtes annuelles menées de 1968 à 1971 représentent une série relativement uniforme, la révision complète des définitions communautaires, en particulier celle des personnes exerçant une activité principale ou occasionnelle, et l'introduction en 1973 de la nomenclature des activités en ont modifié complètement le contenu et la portée.

Depuis la dernière révision, le contenu et la portée de l'enquête sont restés inchangés, et l'on peut donc affirmer que les enquêtes effectuées en 1973, 1975 et 1977 sont relativement comparables. Il convient cependant de souligner qu'il est difficile d'obtenir des séries en valeur absolue parfaitement cohérentes, vu que les informations sont tirées d'une enquête par sondage.

Enfin, rappelons que, dans le cas de l'Italie, le dernier relevé a introduit de nouvelles définitions pour les catégories faisant partie des forces de travail, de sorte que les chiffres relatifs à 1977 ne sont pas comparables avec ceux des enquêtes précédentes.

Dans tous les cas où les données de base nécessaires étaient disponibles, on trouvera, en plus des valeurs absolues, certaines données élaborées qui indiquent d'une part la distribution des femmes entre les différents postes constituant le tableau (pourcentages $\frac{f}{F}$ 100) et la proportion de ces dernières dans l'ensemble des individus classés dans chacun des postes d'autre part (pourcentages $\frac{f}{f+m} \times 100$). La somme des pourcentages $\frac{f}{F} \times 100$ peut être inférieure à 100 car, dans certains cas, il n'a pas été possible d'exclure les «non déclarés» où les données relatives à tous les postes considérés n'étaient pas disponibles (soit parce que le taux d'échantillonnage ne permettait pas la subdivision, soit parce que le chiffre était inférieur à la moitié de l'unité indiquée).

Principales définitions

Les définitions utilisées dans l'enquête communautaire sur les forces de travail sont, en principe, basées sur celles élaborées dans le cadre du BIT et de l'OCDE.

Certaines divergences peuvent toutefois être constatées, non seulement parce que les définitions internationales recommandées par le BIT et l'OCDE ne peuvent pas toujours être rigoureusement appliquées pour des raison d'ordre technique, mais aussi parce que certains développements particuliers de l'emploi dans les pays de la Communauté ont exigé des adaptations spécifiques.

Personnes ayant un emploi principal

Les personnes ayant un emploi principal sont toutes les personnes âgées de 14 ans et plus qui:

(a) ont déclaré qu'elles avaient normalement un travail rémunéré, qu'elles exerçaient au cours de la semaine de référence ou qu'elles n'exerçaient pas par suite de maladie, accident, congé, grève ou autres circonstances. Font également partie de ce groupe, les personnes n'ayant pas travaillé pour des raisons techniques ou météorologiques;

(b) ont une activité normale non rémunérée comme aides familiaux, pour autant que cette activité dépasse 14 heures par semaine.

Ne sont pas comprises dans cette catégorie:

(a) les personnes ayant déclaré être en chômage;

(b) les personnes ayant déclaré être non actives (ménagères, étudiants, retraités, pensionnés, autres);

(c) les personnes sans emploi salarié et les personnes n'ayant ni exploitation agricole, ni autre entreprise, mais ayant pris leurs dispositions en vue de commencer à travailler dans un nouvel emploi ou d'ouvrir une exploitation agricole ou une entreprise à une date postérieure à la période de référence;

(d) les aides familiaux non rémunérés ayant travaillé moins de 15 heures dans l'exploitation familiale au cours de la semaine de référence;

(e) les militaires du contingent(¹),

Les groupes ci-dessus comprennent éventuellement des personnes ayant une activité occasionnelle rémunérée au cours de la semaine de référence.

Personnes en chômage

Les personnes en chômage sont toutes les personnes ayant déclaré être en chômage et être à la recherche d'un emploi salarié. Sont comprises dans cette définition les catégories suivantes:

(a) les personnes ayant travaillé en tant que salarié et n'ayant plus de contrat de travail;

(b) les personnes ayant travaillé en tant qu'indépendants ou aides familiaux et recherchant un emploi salarié;

(c) les personnes n'ayant jamais travaillé et à la recherche d'un premier emploi salarié;

(d) les personnes ayant interrompu leur vie active pour une période supérieure à un an et à la recherche d'un emploi salarié;

(e) les personnes mises à pied temporairement ou pour une durée indéfinie, sans rémunération.

Ne sont pas comprises dans cette catégorie:

(a) les personnes qui, tout en se déclarant en chômage ne cherchent pas d'emploi ou recherchent un emploi d'indépendant;

(b) les personnes ayant normalement un emploi, mais n'étant pas au travail au cours de la semaine de référence pour des raisons économiques, techniques ou météorologiques (chômage partiel);

(c) les personnes non actives (ménagères, étudiants, etc.) qui se déclarent à la recherche d'un emploi salarié;

(d) les personnes ayant un emploi principal à la recherche d'un autre emploi.

Forces de travail

Les forces de travail se composent des personnes ayant un emploi principal et des personnes en chômage.

Personnes non actives

Sont considérées comme non actives toutes les personnes qui:

(a) étaient âgées de moins de 14 ans au 1er janvier de l'année de l'enquête;

(b) quoique âgées de plus de 14 ans, ne faisaient par partie des forces de travail selon la définition indiquée.

Sont comprises généralement dans ce groupe les personnes s'étant déclarées ménagères, étudiants, pensionnés, etc.

Font également partie de la population non active les personnes ayant déclaré être en chômage mais recherchant une activité indépendante.

Les aides familiaux ayant déclaré avoir une occupation principale, mais qui, en fait, n'avaient travaillé que 1 à 14 heures pendant la semaine de référence, font également partie de la population non active.

Personnes non actives avec emploi occasionnel

Sont considérées comme personnes non actives avec un emploi occasionnel toutes les personnes non actives ayant déclaré avoir un emploi non permanent (à temps complet ou à temps partiel). Les aides familiaux non rémunérés au cours de la semaine de référence ayant travaillé de 1 à 14 heures pendant la semaine de référence sont classés dans ce groupe.

Sont compris dans cette catégories les travailleurs saisonniers.

(¹) Les militaires de carrière sont inclus dans les personnes ayant un emploi.

Personnes recherchant un emploi

Sont considérées comme recherchant un emploi toutes les personnes qui, au moment de l'enquête, ont déclaré rechercher un emploi salarié qu'elles aient déjà un emploi, qu'elles soient en chômage ou sans activité.

Sont comprises dans cette catégorie:

a) les personnes en chômage:

- ayant perdu l'emploi antérieur,
- recherchant un premier emploi ou recherchant un emploi après une période d'interruption volontaire de la vie active,

b) Les personnes non actives à la recherche d'un emploi,

c) les personnes ayant un emploi principal, mais en recherchant un autre.

Statut professionnel

Le statut professionnel est demandé à toutes les personnes ayant déclaré avoir un emploi principal ou occasionnel au cours de la semaine de référence. Dans cette publication on fait uniquement la distinction entre: indépendants, salariés et aides familiaux.

Sont considérées comme «indépendants» toutes les personnes ayant déclaré exercer une activité pour leur propre compte, avec ou sans employés. Les salariés comprennent les employés et les ouvriers, c'est-à-dire toutes les personnes qui travaillent sur base d'un contrat pour un employeur public ou privé et reçoivent une rémunération en espèces ou en nature.

Sont considérés comme «aides familiaux» les membres de la famille non rémunérés collaborant de façon habituelle au fonctionnement d'une exploitation agricole ou d'une entreprise, pour autant qu'ils aient travaillé plus de 14 heures pendant la semaine de référence. Les personnes de ce groupe n'ayant aucune heure de travail pendant la semaine de référence ont néanmoins été maintenues dans cette catégorie.

Heures de travail

Le nombre d'heures travaillées pendant la semaine de référence a été relevé tant pour l'activité principale que pour l'activité occasionnelle et pour la deuxième activité.

La durée hebdomadaire moyenne du travail a été calculée pour toutes les personnes ayant travaillé au moins une heure pendant la semaine de référence. N'ont pas été prises en considération pour ce calcul les personnes n'ayant pas travaillé pendant cette même période, que ce soit pour raison de maladie, de congé ou pour d'autres motifs.

Branches d'activité

Les résultats de l'enquête 1977 ont été exploités en utilisant d'une façon systématique la ventilation suivante en branches d'activités NACE (Nomenclature générale des activités économiques dans les Communautés européennes):

Branches d'activité	Code NACE
1. Agriculture, sylviculture, pêche, chasse	0
2. Énergie et eau	1
3. Extraction et transformation des minéraux non énergétiques et produits dérivés: industrie chimique	2
4. Industries transformatrices des métaux, mécanique de précision	3
5. Autres industries manufacturières	4
6. Bâtiment et génie civil	5
7. Commerce, restauration et hébergement, réparations	6
8. Transports et communications	7
9. Institutions de crédit, assurances, services fournis aux entreprises, location	8
10. Administration générale, défense nationale et sécurité sociale obligatoire	91
11. Autres services	9 (sauf 91)

Le regroupement en secteurs d'activité a été effectué comme suit:

Secteurs	NACE
Agriculture	0
Industrie	1 à 5
Services	6 à 8, 91 et 9

Cette même nomenclature a été utilisée pour les enquêtes de 1973 et 1975. Par contre, en ce qui concerne les enquêtes antérieures, faute de disponibilité d'une nomenclature uniforme de toutes les branches d'activité approuvée par chacun des États membres, on a eu recours à la NICE (Nomenclature des industries établies dans les Communautés européennes) pour l'industrie, à la version préliminaire de la NACE pour les services, et à la CITI (Classification internationale type par industrie de toutes les branches d'activité économique) pour l'agriculture.

Qualifications professionnelles des travailleurs salariés de l'industrie

Ouvriers

1 – ouvriers qualifiés
2 – ouvriers semi-qualifiés
3 – ouvriers non qualifiés

Employés

1 – cadres supérieurs
    1A – cadres dont la rémunération mensuelle dépasse 4500 DM, 10 000 FF, 1 000 000 LIT, 6000 HFL, 65 000 BFR, 65 000 LFR
    1B – cadres dont la rémunération mensuelle est inférieure ou égale à 4500 DM, 10 000 FF, 1 000 000 LIT, 6000 HFL, 65 000 BFR. 65 000 LFR
2 – personnel hautement qualifié
3 – personnel moyennement qualifié
4 – personnel d'exécution
5 – personnel intermédiaire
    5A – ayant des compétences et des responsabilités étendues
    5B – ayant des compétences et des responsabilités de niveau moyen.

Qualifications professionnelles des salariés agricoles

● **salarié qualifié:** personne ayant acquis une formation ou une expérience lui permettant d'exécuter certains travaux spécialisés et qui, par exemple, serait en mesure de faire fonctionner, de conduire ou de réparer certaines machines agricoles ou de s'occuper de leur entretien;

● **salarié non qualifié:** travailleur affecté à des travaux n'exigeant pas une formation particulière (par exemple, ouvriers agricoles).

Qualifications professionnelles des travailleurs salariés du commerce, du crédit et des assurances

Les modes de classification des salariés selon la qualification professionnelle différant sensiblement suivant les activités économiques et les pays, il a été décidé de laisser le soin aux instituts nationaux de statistique de classer les salariés dans de grands groupes de qualification professionnelle définis d'un commun accord pour chacun des secteurs: commerce de gros et de détail, banques et assurances.

Tout le personnel salarié de ces secteurs a été réparti dans les groupes de qualification ci-caprès. La répartition a été effectuée sur la base de la nature des tâches accomplies en tenant compte du degré de difficulté de celles-ci, de l'étendue de la responsabilité afférente et de la formation ou des connaissances nécessaires pour s'en acquitter.

Groupes de qualifications professionnelles dans les secteurs du commerce de gros et du commerce de détail

Afin de faciliter la répartition des salariés, on a défini, à titre explicatif, des sous-groupes de qualification spéciaux pour le personnel de rayon (commerce de détail) et le personnel de magasin/expédition (commerce de gros).

1. Personnel de direction

1A. Personnel supérieur de direction avec capacité de décision et responsabilités relatives à la marche générale des affaires pour l'ensemble de l'entreprise.

1B. Personnel de direction et cadres supérieurs dont l'activité se situe immédiatement sous les personnes décrites au point 1A, avec compétences et responsabilités relatives aux subdivisions importantes, telles que, par exemple, les établissements principaux de l'entreprise, et leurs plus proches collaborateurs.

2. Personnel d'exécution et d'encadrement

Ce groupe comprend le personnel travaillant sous la responsabilité immédiate et suivant les directives émanant des personnes décrites au point 1B.
Le personnel de cette catégorie possède en général un champ étendu d'initiative et de responsabilité.

3. Personnel subalterne très qualifié

À l'intérieur de ce groupe de qualification on trouve le personnel ayant des tâches propres au commerce de gros et de détail, d'une part (sous-groupe 3A), et le reste du personnel subalterne très qualifié, d'autre part (sous-groupe 3B).

4. Personnel subalterne qualifié

À l'intérieur de ce groupe de qualification on classe distinctement le personnel ayant des tâches spécifiques du commerce de gros et de détail, d'une part (sous groupe 4A) et le reste du personnel subalterne qualifié, d'autre part (sous groupe 4B).

5. Personnel subalterne non qualifié

Ce groupe comprend tous les salariés remplissant des fonctions de nature simple, qui normalement se répètent constamment et pour lesquelles on n'exige, en général, que des connaissances du niveau de l'enseignement élémentaire.

Groupes de qualification professionnelle dans le secteur des banques

1. Direction, top management

Personnel supérieur de direction avec capacité de décision et responsabilités relatives à la marche générale des affaires pour l'ensemble de l'entreprise.

2. Cadres supérieurs

Personnel de direction et cadres supérieurs avec compétences et responsabilités relatives aux subdivisions telles que, par exemple, les départements et les établissements principaux de l'entreprise. Les directeurs des unités locales ou régionales jouissant d'une large autonomie dans leurs fonctions de direction appartiennent à cette catégorie.

Il faut également y ajouter les personnes employées à des fonctions d'étude, de recherche et de conseil qui possèdent un certain degré d'indépendance et de pouvoir de décision.

En général, des connaissances d'un niveau universitaire, de grande école ou pour le moins d'enseignement professionnel supérieur sont exigées pour des fonctions de ce genre. Ce niveau de connaissance peut, de par sa nature, également être acquis par l'expérience ou l'étude personnelle.

3. Personnel de conception (cadres inférieurs)

Ce groupe comprend les collaborateurs directs des cadres supérieurs (groupe 2 ci-dessus) qui peuvent exercer une fonction de commandement sur le personnel dans des secteurs déterminés.

4. Personnel d'exécution très qualifié

Ce groupe comprend le personnel d'exécution très qualifié dont on exige des connaissances de niveau moyen, qui collabore avec les personnes de la catégorie supérieure (groupe 3) et travaille sous la responsabilité et les directives de celles-ci. Sa tâche peut comporter – dans les limites des directives reçues – une certaine part d'initiative et de responsabilité. Dans certains cas, ce personnel peut coordonner le travail des catégories inférieures.

5. Personnel d'exécution qualifié

Ce groupe comprend le personnel qualifié travaillant sur la base de directives précises de ses supérieurs hiérarchiques et dont les tâches ne demandent, en général, qu'une part réduite d'initiative et de responsabilité.

6. Autres agents

Ce groupe comprend tout le personnel salarié non qualifié, n'étant pas compris dans les cinq catégories ci-dessus.

Groupes de qualifications professionnelles dans le secteur des assurances

I. Dirigeants – Cadres supérieurs de direction

Ce sont les membres du personnel salarié qui, en raison d'une très large délégation de pouvoir, disposent dans l'entreprise d'une capacité de décision au niveau de l'ensemble de l'entreprise ou d'un ou plusieurs des départements importants de celle-ci.

II. Cadres intermédiaires

Ce sont les membres du personnel salarié qui, à un niveau de responsabilité élevé, jouissent d'une large autonomie de décision:

– soit au niveau de l'établissement, département ou service dont ils assument l'animation et le contrôle

– soit dans les fonctions de conception, d'étude ou de conseil qui leur sont confiées.

III. Agents d'encadrement et assimilés

Ce sont les membres du personnel salarié qui, en tant que collaborateurs directs ou indirects d'un ou plusieurs cadres répondant à la définition du groupe I ou du groupe II ci-dessus:

– soit assument des fonctions de contrôle, de mise au courant ou de vérification du travail d'un groupe, d'une section ou d'une équipe d'employés,

– soit se voient confier, en raison de leur compétence et qualification professionnelle élevées, des tâches de conception comportant des responsabilités particulières.

IV. Travailleurs très qualifiés ([1])

Ce sont les membres du personnel salarié qui exécutent des travaux requérant une connaissance confirmée d'une ou plusieurs techniques de l'assurance ou bien une qualification équivalente dans un domaine hors assurance et qui disposent à cet effet, dans les limites des directives reçues, d'une part d'initiative dans lesdites fonctions. Dans

certains cas, ces fonctions peuvent comporter la coordination et la vérification du travail d'autres employés.

V. Travailleurs qualifiés ([1])

Ce sont les membres du personnel salarié qui exécutent des travaux requérant seulement de bonnes connaissances professionnelles assurance ou hors assurance. Dans certains cas, ces fonctions peuvent comporter la coordination et la vérification du travail d'autres employés.

VI. Autres travailleurs salariés ([1])

Ce sont les membres du personnel salarié qui exécutent des travaux ne requérant que des connaissances professionnelles simples et ne demandant qu'une initiation de courte durée.

Taille de l'entreprise ou de l'exploitation: elle est exprimée en nombre de travailleurs salariés occupés.

Ancienneté de service dans l'entreprise: nombre d'années de service du salarié dans l'entreprise; lorsque le salarié a fréquenté plusieurs unités d'une même entreprise, c'est le total des années passées dans les diverses unités qui a été indiqué.

Avantages en nature pour les salariés ágricoles: en raison des difficultés et des incertitudes qu'aurait rencontrées la définition d'une méthode communautaire de valorisation des avantages en nature, il a été convenu de retenir uniquement le fait de savoir si l'ouvrier bénéficiait ou non d'avantages en matière de logement ou de nourriture, sans tenter d'en évaluer la valeur.

L'ouvrier logé est celui qui travaille sur l'exploitation et dont le logement est assuré par l'employeur; ce logement peut se trouver en dehors ou sur le lieu même de l'exploitation.

L'ouvrier nourri est celui qui travaille sur l'exploitation et qui reçoit au moins un repas principal par jour.

Lors de l'exploitation des résultats, tous les ouvriers ont été classés, en fonction du fait qu'ils bénéficiaient ou non de ces avantages, dans l'un des quatre groupes suivants:

– ouvriers logés et nourris,

– ouvriers logés seulement,

– ouvriers nourris seulement,

– ouvriers ni logés, ni nourris.

Notes sur les tableaux

Section I – Population et activité (tableaux 18 à 27)

Les tableaux de cette section ont pour but de fournir des informations sur l'insertion ou sur l'exclusion de la femme

---

([1]) Le personnel ouvrier est classé dans l'un des niveaux IV, V ou VI suivant son degré de qualification.

dans l'activité productive, soit d'une manière générale, soit par rapport à certains critères tels que l'âge ou l'état civil.

Le taux d'activité désigne le rapport entre les forces de travail et la population âgée de 14 ans et plus.

Section II – Emploi (tableaux 28 à 93)

La seconde section décrit les caractéristiques et les modes de participation de la femme à l'activité productive, et vise à mettre en évidence la structure par secteur, la branche d'activité économique et le statut professionnel de l'emploi féminin compte tenu de l'âge, de l'état civil et du caractère occasionnel du travail.

Il a été possible de préciser ensuite séparément pour les trois secteurs de l'activité économique, les caractéristiques de l'emploi salarié en fonction de certains critères tels que la taille de l'établissement ou de l'exploitation, l'ancienneté et la qualification professionnelles, ou l'octroi ou non d'avantages en nature (pour les salariées dans l'agriculture).

L'aspect salarial est décrit au moyen d'indices qui expriment en pourcentage le rapport entre la rémunération féminine moyenne et la rémunération masculine moyenne correspondante. Ils sont accompagnés de coefficients de variation de la rémunération féminine qui expriment la dispersion à l'intérieur de chaque groupe homogène par rapport aux critères considérés.

Le coefficient de variation ($CV = \frac{\sigma}{M} 100$) [1] étant une mesure synthétique du degré de dispersion des valeurs individuelles autour de la valeur moyenne (calculée en mesurant les écarts entre les valeurs individuelles et la valeur moyenne et en les exprimant en % de cette valeur moyenne), il permet d'attribuer à la valeur moyenne une signification d'autant plus importante qu'il est numériquement petit.

Toujours en ce qui concerne les travailleuses salariées, on dispose d'informations sur leurs conditions de travail, tant sous l'angle de la durée effective du travail (temps complet, temps partiel, horaire de travail etc.) que sur celui des plus ou moins grandes facilités que présente le trajet domicile–travail que sous celui de la facilité plus ou moins grande avec laquelle elles peuvent gagner le lieu de travail.

Enfin les conditions de travail font l'objet d'une évaluation personnelle notamment sur les aspects, du bruit, de l'hygiène et du risque d'accident.

Le dernier groupe de tableaux (tableaux 89 à 93) exprime succinctement la difficulté que rencontrent les travailleuses salariées pour concilier leurs obligations professionnelles avec leurs tâches domestiques et familiales.

Section III – Chômage (tableaux 94 à 106)

Cette section comprend deux groupes de tableaux.

Le premier groupe décrit l'évolution du chômage dans le temps, ainsi que la structure de la population à la recher-

che d'un emploi, telle qu'elle se dégage de l'enquête par sondage sur les forces de travail (tableaux 94 à 102).

Le taux de chômage est exprimé en % des forces de travail de sexe et d'âge correspondants.

Le second groupe de tableaux se rapporte aux chômeurs inscrits sur les listes des bureaux de placement. Rappelons que ces listes excluent généralement les personnes en chômage partiel, ainsi que les chômeurs qui suivent un cours de formation professionnelle, et les personnes employées à des travaux ou dans des chantiers expressément organisés pour lutter contre le chômage.

Il s'agit, pour les différents pays, des séries suivantes:

— République fédérale d'Allemagne (Arbeitslose): travailleurs de 14 ans et plus, sans contrat de travail, à la recherche d'un emploi durable de plus de 20 heures par semaine.

— France (demandeurs d'emploi): chômeurs, immédiatement disponibles, à la recherche d'un emploi durable à temps complet (30 heures par semaine ou davantage).

— Italie (Iscritti nelle liste di collocamento): classes I et II: chômeurs à la recherche d'un emploi.

— Pays-Bas (Werklozen): personnes âgées de moins de 65 ans, sans emploi, aptes au travail, à la recherche d'un travail salarié à temps complet (30 heures par semaine ou davantage).

— Belgique: travailleurs en chômage complet qui perçoivent une indemnité de chômage, autres travailleurs à la recherche d'un emploi inscrits obligatoirement et chômeurs inscrits volontairement.

— Luxembourg (Demandeurs d'emploi): chômeurs âgés de 16 à 65 ans, à la recherche d'un emploi à temps complet (40 heures par semaine) et disponibles pour le marché du travail.

— Royaume-Uni (Unemployed): chômeurs aptes au travail et disponibles pour un emploi de plus de 30 heures par semaine.

— Irlande (Unemployed on the Live Register): chômeurs âgés de 16 à 67 ans, aptes au travail et disponibles pour un emploi (demandeurs d'une indemnité de chômage, demandeurs d'une assistance de chômage et autres chômeurs inscrits).

— Danemark (Arbejsløsheden): chômeurs disponibles, à la recherche d'un emploi, inscrits ou non inscrits auprès des caisses d'assurance chômage des syndicats.

Les séries relatives aux chômeurs inscrits ont été adaptées, autant que possible, aux définitions énoncées.

Section IV – Mobilité territoriale et professionnelle (tableaux 107 à 108)

Certaines informations relatives à la mobilité territoriale des personnes en âge de travailler sont issues de l'enquête sur les forces de travail.

---

[1]
$$\sigma = \sqrt{\frac{\sum_{i}^{n}(x_i - M)}{n}}$$ où x_1 est la valeur d'indice i, M la moyenne arithmétique des observations, et n le nombre total des observations.

En ce qui concerne la mobilité professionnelle, il convient de rappeler que les données se rapportant uniquement à des changements de conditions (personnes non actives devenant actives et vice versa, le plus souvent pour les femmes, précisément; transferts dans les deux sens entre la main-d'oeuvre de réserve et l'emploi marginal), à des mouvements intersectoriels et à des changements de statut professionnel, aucune information n'étant disponible au sujet de la mobilité verticale des travailleuses.

PARTIE 3 – FORMATION GÉNÉRALE ET PROFESSIONNELLE (tableaux 109 à 126)

Cette partie de l'étude a pour but de mettre en lumière les différences qui subsistent entre les sexes au plan de la formation générale et, surtout, professionnelle. Conjuguées à un ensemble de facteurs socioculturels dont elles dépendent à leur tour, ces différences ont été et sont encore en partie responsables des conditions particulières dans lesquelles les deux sexes abordent la vie professionnelle. L'analyse de ces différences est non seulement intéressante en elle-même, mais contribue également à dégager une des causes de la position marginale de la femme dans le monde du travail.

L'étude de la formation générale et professionnelle s'articule en 3 sections, consacrées respectivement:

1. à la formation générale ou professionnelle dispensée dans la Communauté à différentes dates, dans le cadre scolaire ou en dehors de celui-ci (tableaux 109 à 116);

2. à la formation acquise par la population de la Communauté en âge de travailler (tableaux 117 à 123);

3. aux rapports entre la formation et l'activité (tableaux 124 à 126).

1. Formation en cours

1.1. *Formation dans le cadre scolaire (tableaux 109 à 114)*

Les données relatives à la formation en cours dans le cadre scolaire et universitaire sont presques toutes empruntées au volume «Statistiques de l'enseignement, 1970–1975», publié par l'EUROSTAT en 1976. Seuls les taux globaux de scolarisation (tableau 111) sont extraits d'un autre volume de l'Eurostat («Indicateurs sociaux pour la Communauté, 1960–1975», publié en 1977). En ce qui concerne les études du **3e degré,** les informations relatives aux inscrits et aux diplômés, par sexe et par domaine d'études (tableaux 113 à 114) ont été tirées de l'annuaire 1976 de l'Unesco.

En général, les informations fournies ont trait à la population étudiante fréquentant à plein temps des écoles ou des universités publiques ou privées installées sur le territoire des différents pays.

Elles ne portent donc pas sur les étudiants inscrits dans les établissements scolaires situés en dehors du territoire national (à l'exception du Luxembourg qui, au contraire, fournit des données incluant ces étudiants), mais portent en revanche sur les étudiants étrangers qui effectuent leurs études dans le pays.

Les données relatives à la France concernent uniquement la métropole, à l'exclusion donc des départements et territoires d'outre-mer (DOM-TOM).

L'ensemble des effectifs scolaires et universitaires a été réparti selon les degrés définis dans la CITE et actuellement en usage dans tous les États membres de la Communauté.

– Enseignement préprimaire. C'est celui qui précède le début de la scolarité obligatoire. Il débute généralement vers 3 ou 4 ans et se termine le plus souvent vers 6 ans.

– Enseignement du premier degré. Il correspond à un enseignement de base (primaire ou élémentaire), toujours obligatoire, qui dure généralement 5 ans.

– Enseignement du deuxième degré, premier cycle. Généralement d'une durée de 3 ans, il rentre également, le plus souvent, dans le cadre de la scolarité obligatoire.

– Enseignement du deuxième degré, second cycle. Il commence vers l'âge de 14 ou 15 ans, dure le plus souvent 3 ans et conduit au niveau d'instruction requis pour accéder à l'université ou à toute autre forme d'enseignement supérieur. Selon les pays, son début peut coïncider avec la fin de la scolarité obligatoire, ou s'inscrire encore dans le cadre de celle-ci.

– Enseignement du troisième degré. Il englobe les universités et tous les autres types d'enseignement supérieur.

Notes relatives aux tableaux

Tableau 109: Population étudiante selon le degré d'études

Ce tableau présente la répartition (en %) de la population scolaire et universitaire féminine et masculine entre les 3 degrés de la classification proposée ci-dessus.

En outre, la part des effectifs ressortant du seul 1er cycle du deuxième degré a été isolée.

Tableau 110: Évolution de la population étudiante à chaque degré

Le tableau présente un indice de l'évolution du nombre des élèves et étudiants de chaque sexe inscrits aux différents degrés d'enseignement pendant la période allant de 1970 à 1976, en prenant comme base le nombre d'inscrits de l'année scolaire 1970–1971.

L'indice d'évolution du total porte sur l'ensemble des premier, deuxième et troisième degrés et exclut donc les enfants inscrits dans les classes préprimaires.

Tableau 111: Taux globaux de scolarisation

Dans ce tableau, la population scolaire féminine et masculine, indépendamment de l'âge et du degré d'études, est rapportée à la population totale et à la population âgée de 5 à 24 ans, dans diverses années scolaires.

Tableaux 112 et 112.1: Population étudiante par degré et type d'enseignement

Chacun des tableaux nationaux répartit l'ensemble des élèves et étudiants selon les types d'enseignements définis dans le cadre national, et les regroupe selon les degrés d'enseignement de la CITE.

Dans les tableaux 112, la répartition est donnée en valeurs absolues pour les étudiantes et les étudiants, tandis que les tableaux 112.1 présentent une répartition en % des étudiantes ainsi qu'un indice de la présence féminine à chaque degré et type d'école.

Les nomenclatures de types d'enseignement sont présentées dans la langue de chaque pays. On trouvera une traduction de ces nomenclatures dans les autres langues dans le volume «Formation générale et professionnelle» déjà cité, dont les tableaux ont été extraits.

Dans le cadre de l'enseignement du premier et du deuxième degré figure une rubrique particulière pour l'enseignement spécial. Celle-ci correspond à l'enseignement qui s'adresse, au sein de classes ou d'institution spécialisées, à des élèves qui représentent des cas exceptionnels, handicapés pour l'essentiel.

Tableau 113: Étudiantes du 3ᵉ degré selon le domaine d'études.

Le tableau présente une répartition par domaines d'études (en %) des étudiantes inscrites à différentes dates dans des établissements du 3ᵉ degré, ainsi qu'un indice de la présence féminine dans chaque domaine.

L'expression «domaine d'études» désigne le principal domaine de spécialisation de l'étudiant.

Conformément à la classification adoptée par l'Unesco, les différents domaines comprennent les disciplines suivantes:

● **Lettres:** archéologie, histoire, langues, littérature, bibliothéconomie, philosophie, psychologie, théologie, etc.

● **Pédagogie:** théorie et pratique de la pédagogie, éducation physique.

● **Beaux-arts:** architecture, dessin, musique, peinture, sculpture, etc.

● **Droit**

● **Sciences sociales:** formation pour le commerce, la diplomatie, les banques, les administrations publiques, les sciences économiques, l'ethnologie, la géographie, l'économie domestique, l'étude des relations internationales, le journalisme, les sciences politiques, les sciences sociales, la sociologie, la statistique, etc.

● **Sciences exactes et naturelles:** astronomie, bactériologie, biochimie, biologie, botanique, chimie, entomologie, géologie, géophysique, mathématiques, météorologie, minéralogie, physique, zoologie, etc.

● **Sciences de l'ingénieur:** sciences appliquées, constructions, géodésie, métallurgie, industries extractives, prospections, technologie, industrie textile etc.

● **Sciences médicales:** anatomie, médecine, obstétrique, optométrie, pharmacie, physiothérapie, hygiène publique, odontologie.

● **Sciences agraires:** agronomie, ichtyologie, sylviculture, horticulture, médecine vétérinaire, etc.

Tableau 114: Diplômées du 3ᵉ degré selon le domaine d'études

Ce tableau présente la répartition (en %) des étudiantes ayant obtenu un diplôme durant les années académiques considérées, selon le domaine d'études et indépendamment du niveau du diplôme obtenu. On y trouvera en outre un indice de la présence féminine parmi les diplômés de chaque domaine ((f/f+m) x 100).

1.2. *Formation en cours, en dehors du cadre scolaire (tableaux 115 et 116)*

La formation que l'on peut acquérir en dehors du cadre scolaire est exclusivement professionnelle et se répartit en «formation professionnelle de base» et «formation complémentaire».

La formation professionnelle de base est celle qui suit immédiatement la formation scolaire, qu'elle ait été générale ou professionnelle. Elle peut être dispensée dans le cadre de l'entreprise, avec ou sans contrat, ou dans des institutions spécialisées.

La formation complémentaire est également une formation professionnelle, dispensée dans les mêmes conditions mais qui peut être suivie à tout moment. Elle comprend la formation post-scolaire après l'entrée dans la vie active, la formation professionnelle des adultes, la reconversion, etc.

Les informations présentées dans cette partie de l'étude sont tirées de l'enquête par sondage sur les forces de travail de 1975 qui a permis de recueillir des informations relatives à la formation professionnelle extra-scolaire en cours pendant la semaine de référence.

La population de référence est constituée par les personnes âgées de 14 à 65 ans au moment de l'enquête.

Notes relatives aux tableaux

Tableau 115: Femmes en cours de formation professionnelle extra-scolaire selon le type de formation, l'âge et la condition professionnelle ou non professionnelle

Ce tableau comporte 3 parties présentant la répartition (en %) des femmes âgées de 14 à 65 ans en cours de formation professionnelle extra-scolaire, selon respectivement le type de formation, l'âge et les critères d'activité.

Il contient en outre un indice de la présence féminine pour chacun des postes figurant dans le tableau.

Tableau 116: Participation à des cours de formation professionnelle extra-scolaire de certaines catégories de personnes en âge de travailler

La participation à des cours de formation professionnelle extra-scolaire de certaines catégories de personnes (personnes en âge de travailler, actives, en chômage) a été exprimée en rapportant le nombre des personnes en formation de chacune des catégorie, au total des personnes appartenant à la catégorie en cause, c'est-à-dire en calculant ce que l'on pourrait appeler un «taux de formation».

2. Formation acquise

Les informations fournies dans cette section sont empruntées au volume de l'Eurostat «Formation générale et professionnelle», 1973 série «Statistiques sociales» 4, 1975. Ce volume contient les résultats de l'enquête spécifique sur la formation générale et professionnelle, qui s'est déroulée en même temps que l'enquête sur les forces de travail de la Communauté en 1973, et qui portait notamment sur la formation acquise par la population de la Communauté âgée de 14 à 65 ans (née entre 1908 et 1959).

L'enquête spécifique sur la formation générale et professionnelle n'ayant pas été répétée selon les mêmes modalités en 1975, les données relatives à l'année 1973 sont les plus récentes dont on dispose pour étudier la formation acquise. Elles pourront être actualisées quand les résultats de l'enquête complémentaire sur les forces de travail concernant les liens entre emploi et formation seront connus.

La formation acquise, c'est-à-dire celle qui, en général, est sanctionnée par un diplôme, peut être soit du type scolaire, soit du type extra-scolaire (formation professionnelle de base, formation complémentaire). La formation scolaire recouvre en outre en deux types de formation:

- la formation scolaire générale, qui comprend le 1er niveau et le 2e niveau d'études scolaires générales,

- la formation scolaire professionnelle, qui comprend le deuxième niveau d'études scolaires professionnelles, le troisième niveau, ainsi que la formation des maîtres.

Les différents types de formation ne s'excluent pas mutuellement: une même personne peut avoir terminé deux ou plusieurs types de formation différents.

Les définitions adoptées pour les différents types et niveaux de formation acquise sont les mêmes que celles indiquées ci-avant pour la formation en cours. Il convient cependant de ne pas oublier que les systèmes d'enseignement se sont modifiés avec le temps à l'intérieur de chaque pays. Classer correctement dans une nomenclature essentiellement prévue pour l'analyse des systèmes actuels d'enseignement les types d'enseignement dispensés il y a 50 ans est une tâche extrêmement ardue. De plus, la présence dans certains pays d'un grand nombre d'étrangers ayant acquis leur formation dans leur pays d'origine et non pas dans le pays où ils ont été interrogés ajoute encore à la difficulté.

En outre, des problèmes d'ordre technique ont surgi du fait même de la définition de «formation acquise» (appliquée d'une façon particulièrement stricte en France), et de la distinction dans le cadre scolaire, entre enseignement général et enseignement professionnel (tout particulièrement en Italie).

Néanmoins, les informations fournies par les données présentées dans cette section de l'étude représentent un ordre de grandeur valable des niveaux de formation de la population de la Communauté.

Notes relatives aux tableaux

Tableaux 117 et 117.1: Population selon le type de formation acquise

Le tableau 117 présente le nombre des personnes âgées de 14 à 65 ans qui, en 1973, avaient achevé les différents types de formation. Pour une meilleure lecture des tableaux, rappelons qu'une même personne peut avoir suivi un ou plusieurs types de formation.

Le tableau 117.1 exprime les pourcentages de la population âgée de 14 à 65 ans ayant terminé les différents types de formation.

Tableau 118: Indices d'abandon de la formation générale et professionnelle

L'abandon de la formation s'exprime par le rapport, en %, entre le nombre des personnes ayant abandonné et le nombre de personnes ayant suivi un type de formation déterminé.

Le nombre des abandons correspond à la différence entre le nombre de personnes ayant suivi un type de formation et le nombre de personnes ayant achevé cette même formation.

Tableau 119: Population selon le niveau d'études atteint, le plus élevé, dans le cadre de la formation scolaire générale et professionnelle

Ce tableau se rapporte au niveau d'études atteint le plus élevé: il ne tient donc pas compte des formations multiples.

La répartition en % de la population selon le degré d'études atteint le plus élevé a été déterminée, soit globalement pour la population féminine et masculine ayant reçu une formation dans le cadre des structures scolaires, soit pour ceux qui ont reçu une formation scolaire générale et pour ceux qui ont aussi reçu une formation scolaire professionnelle.

Tableau 120: Compléments à la formation générale et professionnelle

Le contenu de ce tableau exprime en pourcentage le nombre de cas où une formation scolaire générale ou professionnelle est complétée par d'autres types de formation, ainsi que la mesure dans laquelle les formations professionnelles extra-scolaires sont précédées des différents types de formation.

Tableau 121: Population selon l'âge et le type de formation acquise

Ce tableau exprime en pourcentage la ventilation de la population féminine et masculine de chaque classe d'âge suivant les différents types de formation achevés.

Les classes d'âge ont été choisies de façon à pouvoir distinguer les personnes en cours de formation professionnelle ou qui abordent la vie active (18 à 24 ans) de celles qui se trouvent pleinement en âge de travailler (25 à 34 et 35 à 49 ans), ainsi que de celles qui ont largement dépassé l'âge de travailler et qui ont donc définitivement clos leur formation (50 ans et plus).

Tableau 122: Population selon l'âge et le niveau atteint le plus élevé dans le cadre scolaire

Ce tableau présente la répartition de population féminine et masculine comprise dans les mêmes classes d'âge qu'au tableau précédent, en fonction du niveau atteint le plus élevé dans le cadre scolaire.

La population totale de chaque classe d'âge englobant également les personnes qui ont échappé à la scolarité obligatoire, la somme des pourcentages est généralement inférieure à 100.

Tableau 123: Population ayant achevé des études du troisième niveau, selon la durée des études

Le tableau présente la répartition en % des personnes ayant achevé des études du troisième niveau, selon le sexe et la durée de ces études en années.

3. Formation et activités

Les informations publiées dans cette section portent également sur la population âgée de 14 à 65 ans en 1973.

Notes relatives aux tableaux

Tableau 124: Population ayant terminé une formation professionnelle selon les principaux critères d'activité

Les valeurs figurant dans ce tableau représentent en quelque sorte des taux de formation professionnelle de quelques catégories de personnes définies selon les principaux critères d'activité, indépendamment du type de la formation achevée.

Tableau 125: Formation professionnelle des indépendants et employeurs

Dans ce tableau, l'analyse effectuée dans le tableau précédent est étendue à la catégorie des employeurs et des travailleurs indépendants, en prenant en considération les différents niveaux et types de formation professionnelle.

Tableau 127: Formation professionnelle des salariés

Ce tableau est construit de la même façon que le précédent et concerne les travailleurs salariés.

SOURCES

A) PUBLICATIONS DE L'EUROSTAT

Statistiques sociales

– *Recensement de la population 1968–1972, 1977*
– *Statistiques démographiques 1960–1976, 1977*
– *Statistiques démographiques 1977, 1978*
– *Statistiques démographiques 1978, 1980*
– *Population et emploi 1968–1972, 1973*
– *Population et emploi 1950–1976, 1977*
– *Emploi salarié dans l'industrie de la Communauté 1973–1976,*
– *Emploi et chômage 1972–1978, 1979*
– Télégrammes statistiques «Chômage» à partir de janvier 1977
– *Enquête par sondage sur les forces de travail 1973, 1975*
– *Enquête par sondage sur les forces de travail 1975, 1976*
– *Enquête par sondage sur les forces de travail 1977, 1978*
– *Enquête par sondage sur les forces de travail 1973–1975–1977, 1980*
– *Enquête par sondage sur les forces de travail – Méthodes et définitions, 1977*
– *Conditions de travail dans la CEE – 1975, 1977*
– *Indicateurs sociaux pour la Communauté européenne, 1960–1975, 1977 et 1960–1978, 1980*
– *Structures des salaires dans l'industrie, 1972*

– *Gains dans l'agriculture, 1975*
– *Gains dans l'agriculture, 1976, 1977*
– *Structure des salaires dans le commerce, les banques et les assurances, 1974*
– *Gains horaires – durée du travail 2, 1976*
– *Gains horaires – durée du travail IV-1977, 1978*
– *Gains horaires – durée du travail X-1977, 1978*
– *Gains horaires – durée du travail IV-1978, 1979*
– *Formation générale et professionnelle, 1973, 1975*
– *Statistiques de l'enseignement 1970/71–1976/77, 1978*

Statistiques régionales

– *Population, emploi, conditions de vie – 1973/1974, 1975*
– *Population, emploi, conditions de vie – 1975, 1976*
– *Population, emploi, conditions de vie – 1977, 1978*

B) AUTRES SOURCES

– ONU: *Demographic Yearbook* 1962, 1972, 1976
– OMS: *World Health Statistics Report,* 1975
– OMS: *World Health Statistics Report, 1973–76,* 1976
– CEE: *Les conditions de travail des femmes salariées,* 1972

EUROSTAT-PUBLIKATIONER

De europæiske Fællesskabers statistiske Kontors program vedrørende de publikationer, der udgives i løbet af året, offentliggøres, inddelt efter emner, i årets første nummer af brochuren »Eurostat News« (»Informations de l'Eurostat«), der udkommer hvert kvartal.

De publikationer, der netop er udkommet, eller som er under forberedelse, er nævnt i en meddelelse, der er indhæftet i »Eurostat News« under overskrifterne »Published« (»Vient de Paraître«) og »To be published« (»Va paraître«).

EUROSTAT-VERÖFFENTLICHUNGEN

Das Veröffentlichungsprogramm des Statistischen Amtes der Europäischen Gemeinschaften für das jeweilige Kalenderjahr ist, nach Themenkreisen gegliedert, im ersten Heft jedes Jahrgangs der vierteljährlich erscheinenden Broschüre „Eurostat-Mitteilungen" enthalten.

Auf die neuerschienenen oder in Vorbereitung befindlichen Veröffentlichungen wird in den „Eurostat-Mitteilungen" unter den Rubriken „Erschienen" und „In Vorbereitung" hingewiesen.

EUROSTAT PUBLICATIONS

The programme of publications by the Statistical Office of the European Communities to appear during the year is published, using the classification based on themes, in the first number each year of the quarterly booklet 'Eurostat News'.

'Eurostat News' also lists the latest publications and publications being prepared under the headings 'Published' and 'To be published'.

PUBLICATIONS DE L'EUROSTAT

Le programme de l'Office statistique des Communautés européennes relatif aux publications qui seront éditées en cours d'année est publié, selon le classement par thèmes traités, dans le premier numéro de l'année de la brochure trimestrielle intitulée « Informations de l'Eurostat ».

Les publications nouvellement sorties de presse ou celles qui sont en préparation font l'objet d'une annonce insérée dans ces mêmes « Informations de l'Eurostat » sous les rubriques « Vient de paraître » ou « Va paraître ».

PUBBLICAZIONI DELL'EUROSTAT

L'Istituto statistico delle Comunità europee pubblica ogni anno, nel primo numero del fascicolo trimestrale «Informations de l'Eurostat» («Eurostat News»), il programma delle pubblicazioni previste nel corso dell'anno, classificate per argomenti.

Inoltre, in ogni numero delle «Informations de l'Eurostat» le rubriche «Vient de paraître» («Published») e «Va paraître» («To be published») annunciano rispettivamente le ultime pubblicazioni uscite e quelle in preparazione.

PUBLIKATIES VAN EUROSTAT

Het programma van het Bureau voor de Statistiek van de Europese Gemeenschappen met de publikaties die in de loop van het jaar worden uitgegeven, is, ingedeeld naar onderwerp, opgenomen in het eerste nummer van de dreimaandelijkse brochure „Eurostat News" („Eurostat Mitteilungen").

De zojuist verschenen publikaties en de in voorbereiding zijnde publikaties worden in deze brochure aangekondigd in de rubrieken „Published" („Erschienen") of „To be published" („In Vorbereitung").

European Communities — Commission
Communautés européennes — Commission

Economic and social position of women in the Community
Condition économique et sociale des femmes dans la Communauté

Luxembourg: Office des publications officielles des Communautés européennes

1981 — 347 p. — 21,0 × 29,7 cm

Population and social conditions (yellow cover)
Population et conditions sociales (couverture jaune)

EN/FR

ISBN 92-825-1444-7

Cat.: CA-30-80-172-2A-C

Price (excluding VAT) in Luxembourg
Prix publics au Luxembourg, TVA exclue

ECU 14,40   BFR 600   UKL 8.70   USD 21   IRL 10

The Statistical Office has always attached great importance to collecting data on the social and economic position of women in Member States. Virtually all social statistics drawn up for the Community make a systematic distinction between men and women.

However, a large amount of the information available is spread over several different publications and is not always presented in a suitable form.

That is why the Statistical Office has undertaken this study, which provides an overall picture of the position of women in Member States through a series of statistical tables.

The study is divided into three parts. The first is concerned with demographic aspects. The second covers the problems of employment and unemployment, earnings and working conditions. The third deals with education and vocational training.

The statistical tables are accompanied by a technical note giving the sources and definitions of the data.

L'Office statistique a toujours attaché une grande importance à la collecte de données concernant la condition économique et sociale des femmes dans les États membres. Pratiquement toutes les statistiques sociales sont établies au niveau communautaire distinctement pour les hommes et pour les femmes d'une façon systématique.

Mais un grand nombre d'informations disponibles apparaissent dans plusieurs publications sans être toujours rassemblées dans une optique appropriée.

C'est pour cela, que l'Office a lancé cette étude qui, à travers une série de tableaux statistiques, fournit la «radiographie» de la condition féminine dans les États membres.

L'étude comporte trois parties. La première est consacrée aux aspects démographiques. La deuxième porte sur les problèmes d'emploi et de chômage, de salaires et de conditions de travail. La troisième concerne l'éducation et la formation professionnelle.

Les tableaux statistiques sont accompagnés d'une note technique expliquant les sources et les définitions des données présentées.